¡MALDITO CORONAVIRUS!

¡Maldito Coronavirus!
Mapping Latin American Musical Responses to the Pandemic Moment

Daniel S. Margolies and J.A. Strub

SHEFFIELD UK   BRISTOL CT

Published by Equinox Publishing Ltd

UK: Office 415, The Workstation, 15 Paternoster Row, Sheffield, South Yorkshire, S1 2BX
USA: ISD, 70 Enterprise Drive, Bristol, CT 06010

www.equinoxpub.com

First published 2024

© Daniel S. Margolies and J.A. Strub 2024

All rights reserved. No part of this publication may be reproduced or transmitted in any form or by any means, electronic or mechanical, including photocopying, recording or any information storage or retrieval system, without prior permission in writing from the publishers.

British Library Cataloguing-in-Publication Data

A catalogue record for this book is available from the British Library.

ISBN-13 978 1 80050 396 0 (hardback)
978 1 80050 397 7 (paperback)
978 1 80050 398 4 (ePDF)
978 1 80050 471 4 (ePub)

Library of Congress Cataloging-in-Publication Data

Names: Margolies, Daniel S., 1969- author. | Strub, J. A. (John Adam), author.
Title: Maldito coronavirus! : mapping Latin American musical responses to the pandemic moment / Daniel S. Margolies and J.A. Strub
Description: Sheffield, South Yorkshire : Equinox Publishing Ltd, 2024. | Includes bibliographical references and index. | Summary: "This book offers an expansive survey and analysis of local and regional musical responses to the global coronavirus moment"-- Provided by publisher.
Identifiers: LCCN 2023032376 (print) | LCCN 2023032377 (ebook) | ISBN 9781800503960 (hardback) | ISBN 9781800503977 (paperback) | ISBN 9781800503984 (pdf) | ISBN 9781800504714 (epub)
Subjects: LCSH: Popular music--Latin America--2011-2020--History and criticism. | Popular music--Latin America--2021-2030--History and criticism. | Popular music--Social aspects--Latin America. | COVID-19 Pandemic, 2020---Songs and music--History and criticism. | COVID-19 Pandemic, 2020---Latin America.
Classification: LCC ML3487.A1 M35 2024 (print) | LCC ML3487.A1 (ebook) | DDC 782.42164--dc23/eng/20230719
LC record available at https://lccn.loc.gov/2023032376
LC ebook record available at https://lccn.loc.gov/2023032377

Typeset by S.J.I. Services, New Delhi, India

Contents

	Acknowledgements	vii
	Introduction: Music and Sound in the Pandemic Moment	1
1	*Viru Viru Viru Viru*	33
2	Las Cumbias del Coronavirus	78
3	*Un Huapango para esta Cuarentena*	108
4	Los Corridos del Coronavirus	143
5	Llorando, Tomando, Bailando, Rezando	173
6	Maldita Pandemia	219
	References	268
	Index	299

Acknowledgements

Finishing this book came, happily, at the end of the era we defined as the pandemic moment, but in significant and welcome ways the experiences and connections we had writing it will be with us forever.

We were fortunate to present our ongoing research during the pandemic at several excellent conferences and symposia dedicated to music making during COVID, all of which helped us to sharpen our thinking and inspired us to continue our work. Some of these events yielded important special journal issues and edited volumes in which we were honored to be included, such as *Frontiers in Psychology*'s 'Social Convergence in Times of Spatial Distancing: The Role of Music During the COVID-19 Pandemic', the *Journal of Music, Health, and Wellbeing*'s 'Musicking through COVID-19: Challenges, Adaptations, and New Practices' issue, and the superb edited volume *Sounds of the Pandemic: Accounts, Experiences, Perspectives in Times of COVID-19* (Routledge, 2023). We are especially grateful for the efforts and inspiration of Niels Chr. Hansen, Melanie Wald-Fuhrmann, Jane Whitfield Davidson, Giulia Sarno, Daniele Palma, Maurizio Agamennone, Nisha Gupta, Kim Anne Carter Muñoz, and Ruthie Meadows. We would also like to thank Esther Morgan-Ellis, Lee Bidgood, Mark Thorley, Michaël Spanu, Remi Chiu, Austin Okigbo, Mike Levine, Debbie Sharnak, Seran Schug, Jessica Hajek, and Jennifer Ronyak, as well as the anonymous peer reviewers of our published work on música del coronavirus for their insight.

We extend deep gratitude to the individuals whose voices appear in this volume by way of interviews: Francisca 'Pachita' Castro of El Charco, Nariño, Colombia; Arsenio Hinostroza of Los Atuq del Perú; Iván Montemayor, the one and only Mister Cumbia; Omar Quiñones of El Maguireño; Maria del Carmen Camarera Torres of QuerrequeFilms; Gabino Vera Benito of GaVbroadcast; Gilberto Salvador Perez Baeza of Son Michoacán; and Cesar Castro 'El Jarochelo'.

Translating and interpreting various texts of coronavirus music from the Andes would not have been possible without the counsel of Quechua scholar Jermani Ojeda-Ludena. We appreciate the help of musicians Francisco 'Chico' Gabriel and Juan Soto Uruni for helping to translate their COVID-related lyrics from Náhuatl and Aymara, respectively, into Spanish.

We would like to recognize the scholarly guidance of Raquel Paraíso and Robin Moore, two experts on Latin American ethnomusicology who were exceedingly generous with their feedback, support, and constructive critique. Other colleagues on whom we relied for insight and critique throughout the pandemic moment include Patrick Sparks, Rogelio Núñez, Santiago Jimenez, Jr., Bradley Tatar, Greg Reish, John Tolojuanito Fabke, Belen Escobedo, Ramon Gutierrez, Felipe Perez, Gilbert Reyes, Derek Larimer, Arnu Pless Farm, Mark Rubin, Brian Marshall, Cullen Strawn, Todd Cambio, Ramiro Paz, Osíris Caballero, Luís Jesusito Lopez Bravo, and Ukulele George Pendergast. Dirk Bonker at Duke University and Glenn Martinez at the University of Texas-San Antonio provided essential access to research databases, which was tremendously helpful. Frank Motley made excellent musical suggestions and told some good stories, as always. Lance Ledbetter of Dust to Digital brought very welcome attention to our project, and Bruce Triggs cheerily helped to spread word about our study of música del coronavirus to his enthusiastic Accordion Noir following. We are extremely grateful to our friend Alec Dempster for his inspired cover art.

It has been a pleasure working with Equinox Publishing, Ltd, especially with Alyn Shipton, Christopher Partridge, Sarah Lee, Janet Joyce, and Val Hall. Richard Bartholomew was a great help with the copyediting.

J.A. would like to extend special thanks to his family, particularly to his parents John and Glenda, to his sister Emma, and to his grandmother Carol, for their constant love and support throughout the pandemic moment and the production process of this book alike. He would also like to recognize the contributions of Israel Navarro, a friend and fellow avid listener with whom he spent the first weeks of quarantine. Navarro's insights on many of the musical expressions represented in this book helped to inform perspectives that shaped several of the major themes contained herein. Finally, J.A. would like to extend warm thanks to certain friends, colleagues, and loved ones who have left their mark on this project through discursive conversations, creative collaboration, and pure affection, particularly Juan Pablo Jaúregui Magriñá, Jerónimo Sexton, Marina Saldaña, Mario Luna, Elisa Alfonso, Kyrie Bouressa, Catherine Heemann, Mercedes Alejandra Ramirez Payán, Francisco Lopez, Abraham Ávila Quintero, Dunia Salas Ríos, Arturo Castillo Tristán, Guillermo Escaño, Jeannelle Ramirez, Helana Reyad, Joseph Borrello, Anastasio Utrera Luna and Maria Claudia Cao Romero Alcalá, Sirani Guevara, James Kogan, and Liliana Toledo Guzmán.

Dan would like to thank his loving family, his parents Sylvia and Larry, and especially his children Lark, Aura, and Birch for not only encouraging this project throughout but for actively engaging in the effort of gathering and helping to listen to the enormous body of música del coronavirus in all forms – and often at great, repetitive length. A key component of our shared family pandemic experience during the early lockdown came at the end of each virtual school day as the kids came into Dan's office to listen to the new music emerging in a constant stream and to discuss it. His lovely wife Skye Ochsner Margolies is, as always, filled with good ideas, love, and encouragement and this book could not have been completed without her support.

This book is dedicated to musicians who tragically did not survive the pandemic, especially Emilio 'El Querreque' Valentin, beloved jaranero and trovador from Santiago Tuxtla, Veracruz; Santos Antonio Salvador Cruz, violinist for Trio Los Microsónicos and an irreplaceable figure in contemporary Tenek culture; vallenato accordionist and trovador Miguel Durán Jr.; Colombian-born and New York-based currulao marimba master Diego Obregon; and Conjunto Hall of Fame accordionist Lorenzo Martinez of San Antonio, Texas. All of the above musicians, with the exception of Lorenzo, lost their lives due to complications associated with COVID-19. While Lorenzo did not die of COVID specifically, the enforced isolation of the pandemic and his inability to teach his beloved students hastened his tragic death in October 2020. To the unknowable number of other musicians throughout the Americas, professional and amateur alike, who lost their lives during the COVID pandemic moment – we hear you and we remember you.

Introduction: Music and Sound in the Pandemic Moment

The COVID-19 pandemic was a profoundly sonic experience. As the coronavirus's spread disrupted the rhythms of daily life, existence itself became newly framed and defined by sound. In once-noisy urban spaces across the globe, ambient sounds of nature and of the built environment replaced the hum of human activity.[1] These new soundscapes, and the novel musical productions that emerged alongside them, shaped the experiences and perceptions of what this book calls the *pandemic moment* – the intensely experienced, emotionally wrought period from early 2020 to the summer of 2022.

The pandemic moment triggered an unprecedented explosion of diverse and often profound musical responses, ranging from hastily penned dance songs on coronavirus-related themes to complex musical meditations expressing the feelings of fear, boredom, and social isolation that characterized the pandemic shutdowns. New sonic experiences and spaces of musical production and consumption helped make the pandemic moment's possible meanings legible, and its experiences endurable, for millions of people.

Possibly the greatest diversity and number of musical responses to the pandemic emerged from Latin America, where amateur and professional musicians alike responded to the shared global crisis in locally contingent ways.[2] Varied and highly localized forms of pandemic-era Latin American musical production and consumption – what this book shorthands as 'música del coronavirus' – connect to shared transnational modes of expressive culture and virtual interaction in a moment of global crisis. This book explores the spectrum and reach of Latin American musical responses across an array of regional styles, lyrical approaches, rhythmic interpretations, and cultural attitudes.

Música del coronavirus presents us with powerful and captivating regional assertions of space and place, emotion, and ideology, communitarianism and commercialism. This book describes and contextualizes this emergent musical phenomenon of the pandemic moment through a variety of interdisciplinary social, historical, technological, and aesthetic lenses. *¡Maldito Coronavirus!* uses examples drawn from analysis of more than 3500 original musical pieces to map broader extramusical questions about social attitudes and transnational cultural production in the context of this moment. Alejandra Bronfman and Andrew Grant Wood argue that 'soundscapes, music, noise, and silence all reveal to us something about prevailing worldviews, technologies, epistemologies, and aspirations past and present.'[3] The inspired musical responses to the coronavirus by Latin American artists, and the textures of the virtual spaces where they were distributed and circulated, address similar themes through distinct cultural lenses informed by local histories, affects, and artistic conventions.

There is no single style that unifies the diverse range of Latin American musical responses to the pandemic moment. Eric F. Clarke writes that 'musical sounds take place in a wider context of other sounds' and 'the perception of musical meaning is therefore the awareness of meaning in music while listening to it.'[4] Musicians and listeners ascribe meaning to the musical responses as well as to the global crisis itself: 'SARS-CoV-2 does not have a crown', writes Joseph Osmundson, explaining that '[t]he only crown it has is one we give it. And we're under no such obligation. The meaning we give it is up to us.'[5]

Overall, música del coronavirus reflects the full range of Latin America's magnificently diverse and innovative musical patrimony, with dozens of folk, vernacular, popular, and newly created digital styles represented within a still-growing body of work.[6] There are, for example, several hundred different DJ remixes and cumbias from across the region and hundreds of unique corridos from the Mexico–US borderlands and beyond, together the most represented genres. There are also numerous cuecas and chacareras from Chile and western Argentina recounting narratives of the pandemic.[7] Huaynos and jaranas from the Andes are an especially rich vein of coronavirus songs, displaying unabashedly emotive responses to the fear and social devastation produced by the pandemic in remote Indigenous communities and urban *vecindarios* alike. Música del coronavirus appeared in all of the popular genres of commercial regional Mexican music, including banda, duranguense, sierreño, and norteño. There are rich examples of COVID-oriented verses throughout regional styles of Mexican son, mariachi, and música grupera, music from Tierra Caliente and the Costa Chica, and urban sonidero mixes. There are also hundreds of música del coronavirus examples from the Hispanic Caribbean, ranging from merengue and son Cubano to bachata and reggaetón. Dembow, an urban dance music from the Dominican Republic, proved to be a particularly fruitful style for COVID-inspired songs. New works appeared with astonishing regularity during the pandemic moment from artists like Yofrangel, who wrote a full series of songs reflecting on it starting with his 'CORONA VIRUS' released on 9 February 2020.[8] Colombia's Caribbean and Pacific coastal regions also were remarkably productive sites of regional and popular manifestations of música del coronavirus. Bawdy vallenatos about the frustration of being trapped in the house sit alongside mournful acoustic ballads from the Pacific region bemoaning coronavirus as an act of an angry God. Christian messaging appears across all genres, as does skepticism toward the nation-state and modern medicine. Musicians also deployed international-facing idioms such as rock en Español, pop ballads, hip hop, punk, and metal. Parodies and reworkings of old songs were also very common. Dozens of Coronavirus-inspired compositions encompassing forró, samba, bossa nova, MPB, marakatú, sertanejo, axé, and other popular Brazilian styles can be found on YouTube as well.[9]

Even as this introduction is being completed, new música del coronavirus continues to be released. For example, Duo Guayabamba from Peru released their song 'Homenaje a Nuestros Hermanos caídos en Pandemia por el Covid-19', memorializing those killed by the virus, on 22 August 2022. Conjunto accordionist Felipe Perez wrote and recorded his 'Coronavirus Polka' at the age of 82, for his new album released in March 2023. Other new songs continue to emerge often more than two and half years into the pandemic – but nowhere near the flood of new music that appeared online every day in 2020–2021, during the height of the pandemic moment.[10]

Alongside the many different genres, regional styles, and instrumentations, música del coronavirus also emerged at a variety of scales. While many major professional recording artists released market-oriented coronavirus music in slickly produced music videos, a majority of the material was produced and released by amateur or community musicians using smartphones and webcams. Música del coronavirus is performed by individuals in indigenous languages such as Nahuatl, Quechua, Guarani, Nasa Yuwe, and many others. Original coronavirus songs are performed by individuals singing acapella into their phone cameras, in their living rooms or cars, by solitary buskers playing beat-up guitars on street corners and by very talented but underrecognized bands from small towns singing to virtual audiences of widely varying sizes.

Despite the authors' personal tastes, this book does not reify individual musical expressions. The aesthetic values and social meanings of música del coronavirus are not tied to view counts, numbers of streams or downloads, commercial earnings, or any other market-driven valuations, although metrics are critically important gauges of popularity and reach. Indeed, the wide reception of many of the songs discussed in this book underscores the broad cultural resonance of the musical pandemic moment. For many artists, external validation, view counts, and memetic power are important personally as well as professionally, which was a critical aspect of the pandemic-era musi-cultural ecosystem. This book accordingly focuses on many impactful and widely imitated artists, such as Cardi B, Anuel AA, Chimbala, and Residente. However, it also considers the undercurrents of meaning created by solitary performers whose little-viewed and sometimes peculiar musical uploads seem to defy the logic of artistic self-promotion. On YouTube, high-budget productions with millions of views and home videos with almost none appear side-by-side, all accessible to the same potential global audiences. Despite YouTube's scale-privileging algorithms and increasingly pay-to-play model for content promotion, many of the most widely viewed videos of música del coronavirus were uploaded by small, independent content producers. The fact that some uploads might garner a handful of views does not change the innate significance of their creation, intent, and performance. Rather than shying away from these examples as insignificant or unworthy of study, the authors take an inclusive approach. Honing in on obscure uploads clarifies the full range of popular expressive culture during the pandemic moment. It provides a glimpse into perspectives not expressed in works oriented towards mass audiences.

Some COVID-inspired music videos gained millions of views within hours of release; others have had zero views other than those of the authors. This means, incredibly, that some creators did not even view their own uploaded songs, but merely released them into the world with no context or expectations. YouTube can feel like quicksand, with many videos being uploaded only to disappear – difficult to find, swallowed by the algorithm, or deleted by their users. In many instances, coronavirus music videos were uploaded but subsequently removed within hours or days. Approximately 15% of the database created for this book, representing hundreds of musical uploads the authors categorized since 2020, is no longer available online. If they were heard by any others at all, it was only for in a fleeting, now-vanished moment.[11]

This book considers the statistics of view counts, but it is more concerned with what is said, played, and acted out, and how viewers react to said production. It seems challenging, if not unwise and unnecessary, to formally enumerate the comparative heft or impact of a music video uploaded during a pandemic moment, in which the impact of the pandemic was itself, ultimately, singular. The meaning of these videos was likewise singular. The virus was a global menace that at its most meaningful point of impact attacked a single individual with unpredictable results. Meaning was derived at that point of contact; it was individually experienced even as the context was global. Each individual exhibited distinct symptoms, found themselves in contingent life situations, and lived out their contagion in unique ways that challenge the assumptions of aggregation. Likewise, the musicultural products of individuals matter intrinsically in their creation, without any need to reference the external accounting measures constructed by corporate commercial entities like YouTube or Spotify, signs of wider cultural popularity or assessed network connections. 'Music, in its finest incarnations, whether in a popular song with mass appeal or in an arcane work of instrumental music cherished by a few, may have qualities hidden from others, but essential to oneself', writes Leon Botstein, one of the first music scholars to consider the COVID-19 musical moment in 2020: 'Like sacred texts, music operates on more than one level and is a sacred possession of personhood.'[12]

This book explores how música del coronavirus opened new framings of performativity. The quality, intensity, and expressive empathy of these uploaded performances rarely correlates to a measure such as view count. For example, Gabriel y Esneider Restrepo's guitar duo setting for 'canción del coronavirus dueto restrepo' uploaded on 10 September 2020 and heard by a mere 40 people in two years, is a moving and well-executed performance.[13] Toña León, a well-known female cuatrista from Venezuela, uploaded her piece 'Toña León combate el Coronavirus' because she was 'motivated by love for the Homeland' ('*motivada por el Amor a la Patria*') and wanted an end to sanctions. Uploaded on 22 April 2020, this piece was viewed only 29 times in over two years. This was only one of many rarely viewed solo cuatro performances of coronavirus compositions uploaded in the same month. As of writing, José Hinojosa's thoughtful 'combate el Coronavirus' on solo cuatro has been viewed only five times since 2020, at least three of which can be attributed to the authors of this book.[14] Andrés Leobardo Contreras Orduño was moved to play a lively 'Canción Del Coronavirus' on solo guitar on 6 May 2020, for which the authors were the first viewers.[15] Hector Zayas posted his 'Canción anti Covid -19', which encourages handwashing and other precautions, on 11 May 2021. In a year and half, the song was heard seven times.[16] Antonio Marin Granada of Colombia posted his song 'Coronavirus' on YouTube the same month as a personal warning to other Colombians to take care and 'abide by our leaders' recommendations to deal with this pandemic' ('*Acatar todas recomendaciones de nuestros mandatarios para hacer frente a esta pandemia*'). Granada disabled the feature which allowed his song to be added to playlists, and gained a mere 41 views in a year.[17] An anonymous solo huayno violinist who taught himself to play by watching videos during the pandemic posted his own improvised 'beautiful Peruvian huayno' ('*se improvisó este bello huayno peruano*'), but then shortly thereafter deleted his entire account. 'In pandemic time I learned with the help of YouTube to play the violin and others [...] and thanks to the harp master I put it into practice. It is important to keep busy', he wrote as a form of self-validation before extinguishing his own YouTube channel entirely.[18] There are hundreds of other similar, compelling examples of música del coronavirus which were essentially released into the void as part of a historic outpouring of musical engagement with the pandemic moment. Some responses endured, others were ephemeral. Some uploaded pieces, no less heartfelt, exhibit rougher executions on out-of-tune and out-of-time instruments. Instead of writing off these performances as shabby, ridiculous, or unsuccessful, this book considers all of this musical production in terms of the stories it tells individually and collectively.[19]

The themes expressed across the body of música del coronavirus range as widely as the genres and audiences. They reflect the regional and cultural origins of the artists, and occasional claims of authenticity, although they also sometimes project an alternative global sensibility which challenges provincialism. Michael Gibson argues that 'artists mobilize competing conceptions of authenticity strategically and ideologically to frame themselves and their music in relation to the history, conventions, or prospects of their field. They do so not to legitimize the genre as a whole, but to vindicate and distinguish their own work within it.'[20] Many songs are genre-constrained in form even as they address an entirely new threat. Música del coronavirus variously deploys sonic signifiers, humor, didacticism, and poetry to address themes such as the alleviation of fear, anxiety, and grief. There is sometimes an emphasis on celebrating and partying in the face of disease, danger, and death. Another common thematic current underscores the collective need of humanity to unite in the face of crisis, often accompanied by a celebration of first responders. Other compositions deploy ghastly anti-Chinese stereotypes or other forms of xenophobic language alongside pronouncements of regional pride. These tendencies and themes are not entirely separate, and many songs integrate several of them. Conversely, many songs place emphasis on the rhythmic qualities of the word 'co-ro-na-vi-rus' or 'co-vid di-eci-nu-eve' to build irresistible hooks while commenting little on the pandemic. The title of this book, ¡Maldito Coronavirus!, reflects a commonly sampled shout originally released online by dembow star Anuel AA and sampled widely by DJs for dance remixes, as discussed in Chapter One. It is a signifying shout that resonated across musical and virtual spaces, and in many ways helped to define the sound of the pandemic moment.

Situating Música del Coronavirus in the Pandemic Moment

The pandemic moment was a uniquely textured period. As an individualized experience, it can and must be understood on numerous scales and in different modalities – in terms of global disparities, evolving health policy debates, issues of state development, and questions of space, community, and wellbeing, as well as in terms of individual psychological responses and dimensions of consciousness.

The pandemic moment must also be understood as a musical moment, which is the central emphasis explored throughout this book. Música del coronavirus presents a distinctive glimpse into how that moment was experienced, interpreted, and confronted in locally contingent, idiosyncratic, and highly personalized ways. The pandemic moment had been marked by radical changes in our collective relationship to communications technologies. It is essential to recognize the inherent fraughtness of the massive move online during the pandemic moment, and the exposure of a true 'digital divide' which underscores global inequities and systems of cultural subordination and social control. This book, focused on virtual communities dedicated to subgenres of music and on Latin American musical styles uploaded to user-generated media platforms, is only one component of a much larger endeavor to capture the complex roles of these technologies on communitarian development and individual psychology during the pandemic.[21] What are the implications of music making and listening during this historical inflection point, in an era of unprecedented internet access, media saturation, and opportunities for user-generated content to reach global audiences?

Because of globalization and technological changes, the musical productions inspired by the pandemic moment are different in scale and expression from any other previous global event. Popular and vernacular music styles around the world have long been an essential expressive route for artistic response to disaster and disease.[22] Earlier viral outbreaks of diseases such as avian flu, HIV/AIDS, Ebola, zika, dengue, and chikungunya also fostered important localized Latin American musical responses, with the release of dozens of cumbias, merengues, canciones, corridos, vallenatos, and other popular styles.[23] Songs about monkeypox (*la viruela del mono*) began to emerge in the summer of 2022, as the disease was becoming a point of international concern.[24] YouTube and other social media sites became important sites for the distribution of narratives about these diseases, including via original music.[25] The experience of illness has also been innately connected to sonic perception. For example, 'harmonic convergence', the way in which mosquitos perceive and assess each other's buzzing, is an important component of their mating ritual, and at least one piece of electronic music was judged to prevent the spread of disease by interfering with dengue's primary vector, *Aedes aegypti*.[26]

Compared to the flurried musical responses to earlier viral outbreaks, música del coronavirus spans a far more totalizing and complex range of regional and local musical styles. Coronavirus-inspired compositions fit neatly into this history, but exist on an entirely different scale because of the size, speed, and range of their production, and their dominance of the sonic spaces of the pandemic moment. Since January 2020, música del coronavirus has been released continuously and relentlessly via online platforms. The earliest compositions started to emerge in early 2020, and by March the trickle had become a torrent. Hundreds of new songs appeared during the first half of the year, undergirded by an explosion of online engagement on the part of musicians, Do-It-Yourself (DIY) organizers, promoters, cultural advocates, enthusiasts, and listeners. This research project began in February 2020 as a somewhat whimsical endeavor to capture a few new musical expressions; it rapidly evolved into a full exploration of a profound and explosive cultural response – a musical moment unlike anything that came before.

The interdisciplinary literature on COVID-era music making has developed rapidly since the start of the pandemic.[27] Many scholars have focused on clarifying and investigating the impact of COVID-19 on musicians, touring, festivals, community music making, digital listening and various forms of musicking.[28] Music is a well-established intervention for fostering wellbeing.[29]

As Remi Chiu observes in comparing the 'trans-historical' musical responses to pandemics over more than a century to COVID times:

> Looking across pandemics – and reconciling necessarily different kinds of documentary evidence, from chronicles and medical treatises in the past to news reports, interviews, and empirical experiments in the present – there are two functions of music that appear particularly valuable in times of medical disaster and isolation: 'mood or affect regulation' and 'social cohesion.'[30]

A recent series of more than 53 articles focuses on various connections between community music making and issues of wellbeing during the pandemic.[31] As this book demonstrates, a central function of música del coronavirus is to link these affective and communitarian imperatives in the context of the pandemic moment.

Interestingly, despite innovative explorations of a wide range of music-related issues during the pandemic moment, very few scholars researching the intersection of COVID-19 and music making have principally focused on the body of original music created during this uniquely interconnected and digitally facilitated moment, and none have examined the overall output of Latin American music. Scholars have already given attention to processes of disruption and resilience in music making during the pandemic, but few have considered the music of the pandemic as a cultural object in itself.

While scholars have largely ignored *música del coronavirus*, some individuals on social media sites have responded to the notion that the pandemic moment was uniquely musical by curating collections and playlists, a handful of which have engaged some aspect of the Latin American output. These playlists indicate an urge to shape the pandemic moment experience and to assert a kind of spatial self-sovereignty, or what Anja Nylund Hagen calls a 'mastery over the self' via the curation of personal playlists.[32] Writing with Marika Lüders she also observes that

> the act of sharing music with friends and peers in music-streaming services instigates theoretical reflections of music as personal, and how streaming users consider their own experiences of social interaction in music-streaming services, from the perspective of self performances as reflexive and social practices. [...] Music listening and discovery practices are distinctively social.[33]

This understanding of the utility of playlist creation directly connects with Chiu's emphasis on mood regulation as a key aspect of pandemic-era musical involvement. He builds on a variety of earlier ethnographic research to conclude that the 'pleasure of collecting in playlist making' was one 'kind of musical activity that provided mood regulation and social cohesion during COVID lockdowns'.[34] Most of these public playlist efforts have sidestepped music specifically responding to the pandemic, though all deal with pandemic-engendered feelings. For example, a huge number of YouTube users created playlists of songs for listening to during the pandemic, although the songs themselves are not necessarily reflective of the coronavirus. Many of these lists focused on US-centric pop songs whose lyrics took on a new meaning in light of social distancing, washing hands, or falling ill. Spinditty made a jocular 'Pandemic Playlist: 58 Songs for Quarantine', comprising common inclusions on these kind of lists, such as REM's 'It's the End of the World as We Know It', the Police's 'Don't Stand So Close to Me', and Paul McCartney and Wings' 'Live and Let Die', among other obvious choices.[35] Other playlists offered listeners respite during the slow accretion of pandemic time in shutdown, such as the now-defunct YouTube 'Quarantine | It's Corona time' playlist,[36] the 'Tik Tok Songs That Will Get You Through Coronavirus During Quarantine | Top 10 Best Songs' playlist,[37] the 'Positive songs during coronavirus pandemic' playlist,[38] and the 'MÚSICA PARA ANIMAR LA CUARENTENA' playlist, which focused on pop hits.[39]

Other playlists provided important exceptions by focusing on the body of coronavirus music itself. *Billboard* continually updated its playlist 'Latin Songs Born During Coronavirus Quarantine' during 2021.[40] The YouTube playlist 'MÚSICA para la CUARENTENA 2020 🎶 | Las MEJORES CANCIONES sobre el CORONAVIRUS COVID-19, el CONFINAMIENTO y la DESESCALADA 😷 [Quédate En Casa] 🏠' collected 284 songs, largely, although not entirely, reflective of pandemic-era music composition.[41] This book project itself originated from a curated playlist. Beginning in February 2020, co-author Daniel Margolies began compiling a YouTube playlist titled 'Música del Coronavirus' on his 'Puro Conjunto' channel, a collecting effort which in turn evolved into a comprehensive research initiative. This project came to involve digital ethnography on YouTube, direct interviews with the creators of coronavirus music and a deeper investigative dive into the musical meanings of the pandemic moment and the tsunami of cultural output it inspired.[42] The original process of sifting and winnowing through videos to construct this playlist indeed served a wellbeing function as Chiu described: a fun diversion that both auto-organized and consumed time during the pandemic shutdown. The effort ultimately yielded a productive if highly unanticipated result: the book you are reading right now.

A broader collecting effort built on streaming metadata serves as a symbol of the temporal warp of both music and lived time in the pandemic moment. Glenn McDonald, a Spotify data analyst, created an English-language music playlist with some global music inclusions called 'The Sound of the Virus', which he built as a 'daily chart of songs about the coronavirus pandemic, selected by title-matching and ranked by popularity'. Although this methodology led to some questionably relevant inclusions (e.g. a great many versions of something called '#hot16challenge2' that were not COVID-themed), the Spotify list did usefully aggregate a very large amount of virus-associated music. By the time McDonald stopped compiling his music list on 27 July 2020, it included 8314 songs and could run for an eye-popping 429 hours and 32 minutes of continuous music at least algorithmically related to the pandemic.[43]

These hundreds of hours highlight a defining characteristic of the pandemic moment, especially early on: a fracturing of the experience of time itself, with music playing a critical role at the heart of this timelessness, or suspension of time. The texture of such temporal warps differed across individual experience, but the sentiment of off-kilter time was widely shared. Alister Wedderburn bemoaned the 'unbounded shapelessness of my life at the moment,' which he referred to as 'inhabiting the temporality of a dog.'[44] Disorientation and transformation of the experience of time could be closely tied to hours of musical engagement, whether by playing, making, or consuming it on virtual platforms. The monotony of self-isolation and the erosion of social routines during the early stages of the pandemic augmented and distorted the ways individuals experienced time and conceptualized their experience of it. This dislocative experience was especially pronounced when it came to social life and work.[45] Arsenio Hinostroza, a Huayno harpist, recalled that 'we thought this would last two weeks, but now we are in the same situation nearly two years later.'[46]

This interpretation of the fluid temporal dimensions of life during the pandemic has recently begun to be explored by scholars in a variety of fields. 'Pandemic time' altered the perception and experience of time's passage.[47] As Paricia Arés-Muzio describes it:

> The coronavirus, with its peculiar capacity to disrupt all points of reference, makes time appear to go by swiftly and slowly at once. We live through a distorted sort of time that seems slow if taken day-by-day...paused, stalled. But if we look back, then we see time has vanished as if in an instant.

Time each day, she writes, 'goes by in a perpetual present tense, accompanied by a sensation of strangeness and even at times, surreality'.[48] Cressida J. Heyes builds on Françoise Dastur's concept of the temporality of 'the event' to argue that 'in the context of the COVID-19 pandemic, Dastur's characterization of the event could hardly be more apt: it seized us, wrongfooted us, changed our understanding of the future, and put "the flow of time out of joint." Whole worlds were abruptly transformed.' Among other efforts Heyes explores are the 'existential attempts to eradicate a peculiarly extended event and restore ordinary temporality, in order that our experience can again become our own.'[49]

The experience of pandemic time can be framed by Timothy Morton's concept of the 'hyperobject',[50] frequently described as 'a real event or phenomenon so vast that it is beyond human comprehension'.[51] The concept has been variously applied to COVID-19, and Morton himself wrote on Twitter on 3 March 2020 'duh [sic] the coronavirus is a hyperobject'.[52] In Morton's conceptualization, hyperobjects are marked by five qualities: viscosity, non-locality, temporal undulation, phasing, and interobjectivity. The coronavirus can be seen as viscous because we are 'stuck to it', and nonlocal in that 'it is not here, even though humans can feel its presence'.[53] Morton's concept of temporal undulation is that hyperobjects are 'time-stretched to such a vast extent' that it becomes 'almost impossible to hold in mind'.[54] This idea ties well into the concept of pandemic time used here; the overall experience of time has been thoroughly warped and reshaped, sometimes to the point of surreality.[55] Research has only begun to explore the full dimensions of the pandemic's cultural, social, economic, and psychological ramifications. Like all hyperobjects, the pandemic moment is 'interobjective', in that it constitutes a mesh that interlinks other objects.[56] COVID-19 provided the matrix for an unprecedented set of sonic expressions, undergirded by new social technologies and supported by a rich history of regional cultural expression.

This book observes this exact, often successful, effort to capitalize on this fluid and expanding sense of time as a space itself through music making and consumption. One common form was the experience of watching or listening to new music video uploads or livestreams on YouTube or Facebook for hours during pandemic lockdowns. Another, even more immersive, modality was to engage with multi-hour livestreamed performances on a phone or computer screen, whether stationary or while engaged in some other task. Some livestreams lasted for eight to twelve hours, easily consuming the better part of a day. This musical involvement produced feelings of simultaneous and autonomous experience alike. 'With space disappearing as a coordination device for many people' as a result of the pandemic-era shutdowns and social isolation, 'time is often the most salient coordination mechanism that structures days and weeks' write Sven Kunisch and co-authors.[57] Researchers observe the connections between 'the situated enactment of time' and 'the dynamics that underpin the emergence, change, continuity, and persistence of socio-temporal orders'.[58] The present authors, both musicians, collectively spent hundreds of hours during the pandemic in these musical spaces as participant-observers. Both additionally planned and ran virtual music festivals on YouTube which ran for between four- and twelve-hour stretches, with transnational audiences in the thousands.[59] The timelessness of varied and prolonged musical immersion also shaped their own personal experiences of the pandemic moment.

Music was one mode of experiential and perceptual traction in this suspension of time. As Robert Owen Gardner notes:

> Viewing music as a process of human communication rather than a static product of culture sheds light on the dynamic role of music in social life and its potential for meaningful social action. It also

draws our attention to the situated spaces where individuals come together to share music experiences.[60]

The spatial aspect of music interaction is essential, as the absence of physical gathering was keenly felt in music scenes throughout Latin America, especially subcultural ones.[61] Many Latin American music styles circulate in diasporic communities whose participants' mobility is constrained, leading to an even more impactful respatialization of shared musical expression during the pandemic moment. COVID-19 reduced the aperture of life experiences that could be explored safely in the flesh; music and social technologies are the essential portal in this new reality.

Situating Sound and Soundscape in the Pandemic Moment

These 'situated enactments of time', which shaped and gave texture to the pandemic moment for many musicians and listeners, were mediated by technology. For many, the principal window on the world during the pandemic moment was the screen of a smartphone. Embracing powerful new opportunities opened up by the use of cell phones and webcams both to capture and to share embodied audiovisual expressions, online musical content creators helped to underscore the pandemic's erosion of linear perceptions of place and time. Such experimentations began long before the emergence of the coronavirus, but the pandemic moment centered them and afforded them new significance.

Media produced on mobile devices link online producers and consumers.[62] In addition to allowing recordings of localized significance to find a global stage, cellphone-captured media also facilitate a raw emotional perception and feelings both of 'being there' and of 'in-betweenness' on the part of many viewers.[63] Corporate advertisers took early notice of the power of cellphones to act as a portal into the minds of potential customers. For example, the Peruvian consumer goods brand San Fernando used cellphone-generated advertising content for their #FamiliasEnCuarentena advertising campaign rather than 'professional cameras', to lend 'communication an air of "truth", or honesty that encourages a sense of trust'.[64] Music and sound experiences captured on phones 'break through the sound barrier between humans and machines; their mobility allows for a relational engagement with the technological'.[65] Cellphone-produced recordings uploaded to global virtual spaces in the COVID era elicited a sense of embodied authenticity and emotional connection.[66]

Recordings made with smartphones to capture COVID-19 soundscapes, sometimes called sound maps, enabled new uses of the technology while building transnational connections in spaces of embodiment. These projects clarified the roles social media and new recording technologies played in capturing and sharing sonic experiences, especially with attention to the emotional and affective responses that soundscape recording evoked in listeners alongside música del coronavirus. This truly global soundscape recording project, which consisted of many different but congruent efforts, produced unique and highly evocative samples of pandemic-era sonic media through participatory efforts and analysis of contingent responses.[67] Projects ranged from scientific monitoring initiatives to global crowdsourced collection efforts.[68] Scientists determined that the pandemic moment quieted global high-frequency seismic noise for a time by up to an astonishing 50%.[69] Researchers have even listened to the sounds of the coronavirus itself, using a variety of 'sonification' techniques to transpose the 'SARS-CoV-2 genomic RNA sequence results in a complex auditory stream composed of up to 12 individual audio tracks'.[70]

The coronavirus has a measurable effect on individual 'relational' or emotional states and even on planetary scales of sound. Theorists have termed the pandemic experience of these sonic changes the 'anthropause', an extraordinarily complex moment of cession and reconnection with nonhuman soundscapes. It presents a break from the cacophonous onrush of the 'Anthropocene'.[71] Adam Searle and co-authors, who coined the term, note that 'the multiplicity of anthropause events [during the pandemic] means they are experienced differently across various sociocultural, economic, and environmental striations'. They argue that 'the vernacular offers a reading of the COVID-19 anthropause in a minor key'.[72]

Soundscape collection projects in this anthropause formed a key aspect of the tapestry of investigations into the pandemic moment. Soundscape-capturing projects happened all over the world, with ambient sounds collected from a variety of rural and urban spaces alike.[73] Researchers sensitive to the sounds of tragic silence produced hundreds of recordings in Fukushima, Japan. WindowSwap created a virtual system where individual isolation could be punctured by opening an unusual and oddly enticing portal into other spaces which were, in turn, proxied from other users' devices. This system allowed users to 'open a window somewhere in the world' for ten minutes and listen directly to the sound outside as well as the sounds inside homes with closed windows.[74]

The 'COVID-19 Sound Map' created by Pete Stollery in 2020 used Google Earth as a platform for individuals to upload their own sounds, the vast majority of which were in the UK.[75] Explaining the project, he wrote that

> it took a pandemic to give many of us the time and space to listen to the sounds around us. Let's hope this is one of the things we can take from this immensely difficult time to help enrich our lives in a post lockdown world – by seeking out these sounds which brought us comfort and by keeping our ears open to experience fully the soundscapes we live in.[76]

Another organization, Soundesign, created a pandemic-era participatory campaign called 'The Sound Outside – Listening to the World at Covid-19 Time', with the intent 'to gather and make public a collective sound archive dedicated to soundscapes of as many places in the world as we can, in this strange time when cities and whole countries [are] in lockdown due to Covid-19. New sounds emerge, others are recovered, others have been lost.'[77] The sounds were presented as unedited captured recordings – some musical and others urban or natural – with most in Europe and North America but several in Latin America. The emotional content of these clips was left up to listeners to interpret. A link beneath the songs led not to commentary, but back to the original webpage announcing the project.

Some of the sound collection efforts produce especially powerful and immediate emotions, such as Edifício JK Bloco B's 26-minute recording of 'Banging Pans Protest against Bolsonaro during COVID-19 Crisis' (or '*panelaço*') on the second day of protests, which featured a steady, foregrounded beat accompanied by plaintive cries from several individuals that ran the gamut from soaring glissandos to raspy grunts. R. Paulo Orozimbo uploaded a recording in Cambuci, São Paulo which captured a similar protest but without the raw emotion of the other recordings.[78] In the database collection, these rhythmic political protest sounds sat alongside a 'Covid Sunrise' with natural sounds recorded in Bogotá on 26 May 2020, or 'The Awakening Song of the Melodious Blackbird' in Xalapa, Veracruz, Mexico.[79] Political agitation and natural sounds were placed into the same listening frame without comment or context. Soundesign promises on its main page that 'participation is free. It will allow us to feel closer. It's time to be united!'[80] However, it does not detail precisely how that process of closeness was to be produced through sound. This was left to the interpretation of the listeners.

Cities and Memory's 'Sounds from the Global Covid-19 Lockdown #StayHomeSounds' is a world-spanning repository of ambient sounds recorded on cell phones during the onset of the pandemic.[81] As of December 2021, only six of the recordings in this collection were submitted from Latin America. Among them are an eerie recording of an echoing loudspeaker encouraging residents of a Bogota neighborhood to stay home ('Cuarentena en santafe', by Ricker Silva), residents applauding first responders from a distance in Lima ('Cheering the Police from Afar', by César Callirgos), and the sounds of crickets and a passing train in Córdoba, Argentina ('Mas calmo [sic] que lo normal – quieter than usual', by Mariano Morcos). Many recordings capture the reemergent sounds of the natural world: birdsong, rain, or the rustle of wind. Others contain the sounds of mechanized civilization: bells and chimes, loudspeakers, passing vehicles. Notably absent are the types of sounds made by crowds of human bodies, except for examples of public cheering. A handful of musical recordings, including a lively Persian New Year (Nowruz) performance from Tehran, recorded by Negarzojaji, and the haunting 'Corona Song', recorded by Luca Piparo in Saint-Louis, Senegal, pepper the user-generated collection. Only one of the recordings from Latin America – a reverberating performance of the pandemic-era standard 'Resistiré' (a piece discussed more in Chapter Six) – is explicitly musical.

The soundscape recordings captured a critical aspect of the sonic and emotional experiences of the pandemic moment. Because of their episodic emphasis on distinct environments, the emotional range of the responses they produced was necessarily fractured and even, perhaps, uncertain and dissolute. Researchers have observed the highly changeable preferences for, and experiences of, soundscapes during the pandemic.[82]

Sound takes many forms, and even seemingly unorganized or random sound clips can deliver emotional solace. In Argentina, for example, researchers identified 'the types of sounds that showed significant differences before and during the lockdown' as 'mechanical, biological, environmental, and human'.[83] Perception of 'pleasantness' was a function of the pre-pandemic noise levels. As the many non-musical sounds were captured with wildly disparate methods, in different locales and representing enormously diverse subject matter, their evocative character necessarily remains or becomes even more elusive. The meaning of the sound is not inherent to its existence during the pandemic; it is entirely external to it and produced by the listener in interaction with the place, as a recent study by Luis Hermida and co-authors of soundscape in Lisbon and Bogotá has argued.[84] Yet achieving a feeling of 'pleasantness' because of noise reduction is not equivalent to the experience of emotionally evocative music making. Música del coronavirus links the pre-existing affective power of sound with communitarian and creative needs.

Social Technologies as Community Site and Archive in the Pandemic Moment

The massive musical response to the pandemic moment was facilitated by the recent exponential growth in, and easy accessibility of, online social media platforms as essential sources of global musical consumption.[85] This book focuses particularly on the use of YouTube, a digital space for the production, distribution, and consumption of musical videos, livestreams, and chatrooms that took on new significance when billions of people globally were quarantined inside their homes starting in early 2020. YouTube was a key tool for communication and community connection during the pandemic moment, and provided a fertile space for human relationships and expressive culture in transformative ways not entirely anticipated before the crisis.

Other social media transmissions were also essential aspects of musical life during the pandemic moment, especially Facebook livestreams in the first half of 2020, Instagram shorts, and TikTok dance videos. It is crucial to note how fluid this period of time, these platforms, and the understanding of the role of these technologies in music consumption remain at this writing. YouTube usage dominated music consumption during the pandemic moment, but over two years the tenor of its dominance and usage has shifted in response to the challenge presented by other platforms, especially TikTok. This has led to a pronounced fracturing of music video content, changes to streamed video queues and chatroom use on YouTube, and the emergence and success of the vertical-framed 'shorts' format. Ironically, at the same time, TikTok has become more competitive through its rollout of longer video uploads.[86] These YouTube shorts are 'harder-to-monetize,'[87] and harder to organize. These new formats also change the ways musicians create and share content. Aparajita Bhandari and Sara Bimo have observed that while YouTube is 'predicated primarily on the sharing of visual media', TikTok has revolutionized the form through the 'the forefronted algorithm'. This marks a difference with the YouTube model and a critical shift in usage observable during the pandemic moment. Bhandari and Bimo argue that

> while algorithms are becoming increasingly prevalent across the social media landscape, on other platforms, they are still ostensibly only an 'element' (or enhancement) of an otherwise user-driven experience. Of the major social media platforms on the market, TikTok is the only one to position its algorithm at the center of the social experience it engenders.[88]

These critical transformations are ongoing as this book is being written, and will certainly transform the contextual meaning and overall understanding of the música del coronavirus moment itself over time.

Nevertheless, YouTube's outsized significance as a *de facto* digital repository of música del coronavirus during the pandemic moment was immense and unmatched. As a wide array of interdisciplinary scholarship has demonstrated, YouTube is a highly influential digital space for participatory DIY cultural production and music consumption, with 405 million unique monthly viewers in Latin America before the pandemic.[89] YouTube usage increased exponentially during the pandemic moment; in some locales, usage increased by an astonishing 500%.[90] As a platform designed to host user-generated content, YouTube's consumers are often simultaneously its producers, with up to 500 hours of original content being uploaded per minute at times.[91]

Music is a vast content category on YouTube and an excellent case study for experiencing firsthand the complexities of transnational cultural production in the twenty-first century. YouTube is a principal music streaming service across the globe. Users and scholars alike have approached it as a critical repository of culturally significant music; as music consumption has increasingly shifted online, attention has focused on platforms, multinodal sites that facilitate the circulation of content and services. YouTube 'is now a global repository for popular music and the entry point for a vast number of listeners-consumers searching for new music'.[92] Regional music genres have notably wide reach on YouTube, and researchers have found especially meaningful linkages between social media platforms and regional expressive cultures in the Spanish-speaking world.[93] Research has shown that a surprisingly small amount of user-uploaded music is actually original on YouTube, in the range of 3% to 4%.[94] This highlights the significance of the surge of original compositions addressing coronavirus uploaded to YouTube. Música del coronavirus demonstrates the continued centrality of user-generated musical content on the platform, even in the face of an evident shift toward commercial content.

Other music-sharing platforms have broad reach, but for various reasons are unable to recapitulate YouTube's combination of DIY ethos, ease of use, and open sensibility. These aspects are not readily apparent to musicians, consumers, and producers on the other platforms. David Hesmondhalgh, Ellis Jones, and Andreas Rauhon have examined the strictures and externalized values that are laid bare in the 'platformization of cultural production' in music platforms other than YouTube. They argue that 'consumer-oriented' and 'producer-oriented' platforms like Soundcloud and Bandcamp, while professing to be putatively 'independent' or 'alternative' and claiming to oppose the 'mainstream', actually serve to reify central corporate sensibilities. YouTube shares similarities to these convergences, but these authors argue correctly that 'its extraordinary multiplicity' has placed it into a separate category.[95]

The pandemic moment witnessed a rise in DIY music uploads and the expansion of YouTube channels as key types of user-generated content on YouTube. This marked an acceleration of the evolving dynamic between the global, local, and individual in streamed music and virtual spaces. This book focuses a great deal on the music+video upload, a uniquely consequential form during the pandemic moment. These videos sometimes take the established form of a music video, showing performers playing (or lip-syncing) in real-time, while others are fully realized musical dramas, live recordings of performances, or slideshows overlaid onto sound recordings. While music videos themselves have a long history as commercial products for the music industry, YouTube's structure and ease of use combined with fast streaming rates encourages the connection between sound and image in ways which accelerated during COVID.[96]

YouTube is a space with its own inherent logic demanding interaction. The layout of the YouTube frame, with a video as the main feature, a comment stream below, a chat alongside (if a livestream), and a list of queued videos on the side waiting for the viewer's attention, underscores the visual and the textual as well as the sonic aspect of all music uploads. YouTube livestreams have unique characteristics, as music and chats can be frozen and restarted by viewers and viewed out of sync if the page is not refreshed. At the time of writing, YouTube also scans new videos for coronavirus content, and places a link to official (government-published) pandemic information pages below videos it targets as relevant. These suggested links vary, determined by the location of the viewer. Música del coronavirus on YouTube is consequently a visual as well as a sonic modality, and this book considers both aspects in tandem as consequential elements of the cultural response to the pandemic moment.

A combination of deep uncertainty about the future, social isolation, and a shifting sense of the 'normal' during the pandemic moment facilitated an outpouring of distinctly personal musical production. As both object and process, música del coronavirus reveals the intimacies of performers' lives as well as the communitarian needs of listeners. During the pandemic moment, YouTube channels featuring music livestreams and streamed video queues became critical spaces of social gathering, community fellowship, and musical self-expression. The communities that coalesced in these virtual spaces formed into a new and significant emergent phenomenon in the pandemic moment, which is explored more granularly in Chapter Three. The virtual musical ecosystem which arose on YouTube during the pandemic moment served as a site of artistic production and dissemination, a space of psychological sustenance on both the community and individual levels, and, for some, an engine of commercial potential.

A significant amount of COVID-related-music content was also streamed to Facebook Live. Research on Facebook is inherently difficult due to limited access issues: it is a closed platform to non-members and, more significantly, the query and filing system for the videos is not amenable to complex and multidimensional searching. Uploads, especially livestreamed events, effectively disappear on Facebook in ways less common on YouTube, where individual channels maintain content with ready access as long as the channel owner desires. YouTube's query function, an essential if contested mechanism for accessing uploaded content on the platform, can serve as an effective tool of user-driven research by offering the ability to filter content by upload date, type of video, duration, eleven different defined features, and, importantly, a robust keyword system.[97]

One key connection between all platformized music consumption is the reliance on algorithms to shape listening and to trigger and maintain viewer interest and time on the site. This serves YouTube commercial interests as well as shapes the consumption of a variety of cultural products by its viewers.[98] Researchers have observed that YouTube's algorithmic approach, and its internal development of Content ID to track copyright in songs, transforms the entire notion of the website or platform into an ongoing content- and user-generated flow. Guillaume Heuguet argues that

> YouTube's development of Content ID is at the crossroads of strategic issues and techniques related to the music industry and the Web economy, more specifically the trade-off between the circulation of cultural forms and their control as works and goods: [...] part of the system is based on anchoring the musical form in sound,

through a modeling approach to music, sound and listening that leads to the 'naturalization' of the work in computer data.[99]

Sheenagh Pietrobruno refers to 'real-time streams as dispersed narratives', drawing on the work of David Berry.[100] The streams themselves, in this analysis, are combined with user data and 'evaluated, combined, and rechanneled back to the user as well as other users in the form of patterns of data.'[101] Importantly for scholars interested in vernacular music communities, Pietrobruno argues provocatively that this endlessly rechanneled stream built off the unique flow of YouTube user-generated streams could in fact enable expanded expression of cultural heritage and 'the potential to challenge the homogenizing of culture.'[102] However, Massimo Airoldi argues that 'the recommender system used by YouTube largely relates music videos of the same genre, thus reinforcing pre-existing artistic classifications in the digital circulation of culture.'[103]

As discussed throughout this book, many of the YouTube channels offering música del coronavirus, especially ones featuring nightly streams of videos, built their own community ecosystems within the broader and ever-expanding system of algorithmically defined meaning. While new viewers consistently found their way to the uploaded videos or channels via YouTube's algorithms, the nightly queue streams were designed with a consistency and length that allowed pandemic-era participants in effect to relax into virtual spaces to which they returned nightly. YouTube became an emergent disembodied space where time grew fluid and online life and musical communities replaced the experiences abruptly arrested by the coronavirus.

The multiple ways that singular musical traditions are expressed and disseminated on YouTube have been increasingly explored, and argued over, by scholars in media studies, archives studies, ethnomusicology, critical heritage studies, and other fields. Much critical thought especially considers its function, as described by Jean Burges and Joshua Green, to be 'an unfiltered, bottom-up cultural archive',[104] although classifying such platforms as archives poses complications of its own. YouTube is of particular significance to participatory and global DIY culture in terms of the documentation of intangible cultural heritage and community archival efforts.[105] John H. McDowell argues that if indeed the site is 'an archive of expressive culture, it is [...] an unusual archive that makes special demands on those who would use it', because of its user-generated and unregulated nature, and its lack of 'signposts'.[106] Writing more generally on archives as 'spaces of memory', Eric Ketelaar observes

> nor is the archive ever finished [...]. The file may have been closed, but it will be reactivated again and again. Every interaction, intervention, interrogation, and interpretation by creator, user, and archivist is an activation of the record [...]. All these activations are acts of co-creatorship determining the record's meaning.[107]

Many DIY archiving efforts, these 'acts of co-creatorship', started as simple functions of fan culture with little regard given to structure or longevity. Nonetheless, some have transformed into culturally significant and even profitable enterprises, as the content curators developed their craft and extended their reach to communities of viewers who understand the efforts as both project and process. Perhaps the virtual community spaces themselves act as the key signposts to a broader virtual archival project for preserving and exhibiting cultural heritage. YouTube 'creates spaces for engagement and community-formation', with 'spillover into other sites of everyday culture, meaning, identity, and practice'.[108] This 'participatory turn' has consequently transformed 'the relationship between the individual and a global, culturally diverse idea of community'.[109]

Researchers have highlighted the advantages of this decentered and DIY character, which has allowed informal cultural arbiters to build distinctive spaces. These spaces in turn attract transnational communities of shared affinity in search of personal wellbeing and communal connection. Pietrobruno further argues that 'YouTube's archives of intangible heritage seem to be forging a new form of structure that absorbs both dominant and marginal perspectives and is produced by the efforts of the human and machine'.[110]

Scholars writing on the connections between virtual communities and online communities built around social media platforms have stressed connections to the textures of existing communities. 'What the Internet does not do is create a community if there are no pre-existing common interests,' writes Janice Waldron.[111] Latin American cultural entities and communities, particularly musicians, have accordingly had notable use and 'reappropriation' of rising social technologies and social media platforms like YouTube.[112] These virtual spaces seem to operate unrestrained by intrusive state interdiction, time, or physical place, although in reality they remain shaped by legal regimes of copyright and censorship and by YouTube's algorithms and fluid terms of service. The site maintains the power of full removal for copyright violation or other terms-of-service violations, although it also facilitates royalty payments in ways which permit uploading copyrighted content. Likewise, its transnational operations make YouTube subject to a patchwork of national legal agreements surrounding intellectual property, censored speech, and content access.

YouTube users uploading videos thus develop an expansive atmosphere of co-creative placemaking in virtual space. This is particularly true for channels that are dedicated to a particular geographical region, musical style or locally relevant theme. Its channels can be seen usefully in the framework developed by Doris Elena Pinos Calderón and Cristina Venegas to describe artistic and cultural projects for 'local and co-creative work'. Instead of focusing on the redevelopment or reclamation of actual physical spaces in cities, numerous channels used the platform of YouTube at the critical time-space nexus of the pandemic moment to build unique spaces of cultural and communitarian-minded connection. Pinos Calderón and Venegas argue that 'effective forms of technological appropriation require co-creative approaches that can contribute to new socio-technical and communicational processes that make local initiatives visible, strengthen cultural-identity, and re-articulate urban space as a place of social, community innovation, and political organization.'[113]

Uploaded content on YouTube during the pandemic moment allowed musicians and listeners to transcend physical space and time and reimagine and foster anew virtual spaces of music making and consumption when social gathering was impossible. These were new virtual communities oriented around music as cultural expression – communities of hopeful celebration, collective mourning, mutual aid, and creative inspiration in the face of fear, death, and pandemic.

The Plan of the Book

This book is divided into six chapters, each of which explores a different thematic aspect of música del coronavirus produced during the pandemic moment. While the chapter order provides an overall intellectual scaffolding, it is not necessary to read this book sequentially. As a work built in part on digital ethnography, this book reflects extensive participant-observation in all aspects of the virtual musicultural ecosystems it describes. Some elements of the vast cultural production it examines have not persisted past the pandemic moment, as many uploads have disappeared or been taken offline. These absences are noted throughout the book.[114]

Chapter One examines remix culture and the relationship between sampling, repetition, and virtual music platforms during the pandemic moment. Drawing on música del coronavirus in Afro-Caribbean música urbana styles like reggaetón, dembow, and Latin trap, it situates conceptual framings of virality in music and global culture flows in the context of global contagion.

Chapter Two hones in on cumbia as an explicitly transnational form repurposed in expansive, diverse, and idiosyncratic ways across the region during the pandemic moment. In both its massified and subcultural manifestations, cumbia has proven to be a highly flexible style for creative repurposing, self-expression, and marketing opportunism – topical music with an infectious beat during a time of crisis.

The third chapter turns attention to the psychological and social significance of YouTube channels, livestreams, and live chats dedicated to son huasteco and son jarocho, two regionally based musical traditions from Mexico. Building on two years of digital ethnography, this chapter provides an assessment of the new digital intimacies, spaces of musical wellbeing, and intersections of music and communitarianism which blossomed in virtual spaces during the pandemic moment.

Chapter Four explores the hundreds of compositions labeled as 'corridos' that address the COVID pandemic. The corrido, a deeply rooted regional ballad style, is one of the principal genres Latinos of the Mexico–US borderlands have used to express their experiences and interpretations of the pandemic moment. As in the case of cumbia, amateur and professional musicians adopted a malleable musical form and shared cultural space in original ways to express individual and regional responses to the collective crisis.

Chapter Five examines the affective tenor and ideological orientation of a wide range of musical responses to the pandemic moment. It explores the emotional spectrum and contingencies of assigned meaning in música del coronavirus, running the gamut from comedic pieces to melancholic songs about death, and from public service announcements on effective social distancing to party anthems encouraging people to ignore the pandemic completely.

The final chapter is in some ways a microcosm of the book at large, exploring how música del coronavirus presented identitarian and locally contingent responses to the global pandemic. This chapter considers music ranging from genre-spanning global pop to highly regional repertories and indigenous musical expressions. It contrasts and interlinks the global totality of the pandemic moment with distinctive, place-rooted modes of emotion, thought, and musical creativity.

Notes

1. Elizabeth P. Derryberry, Jennifer N. Phillips, Graham E. Derryberry, Michael J. Blum, and David Luther, 'Singing in a Silent Spring: Birds Respond to a Half-Century Soundscape Reversion during the COVID-19 Shutdown', *Science* 370.6516 (2020): 575–9.
2. Isabel Duque Franco, Catalina Ortiz, Jota Samper, and Gynna Millan, 'Mapping Repertoires of Collective Action Facing the COVID-19 Pandemic in Informal Settlements in Latin American Cities', *Environment and Urbanization* 32.2 (2020): 523–46, pp. 523–6; Diana C. Mitlin, 'Dealing with COVID-19 in the Towns and Cities of the Global South', *International Institute for Environment and Development Blog*, 27 March 2020, https://www.iied.org/dealingcovid-19-towns-cities-global-south (accessed 12 September 2021); Catalina Ortiz and María Mercedes Di Virgilio, 'Laboratorios de Vivienda (LAVs): Asentamientos precarios y vivienda social: impactos del covid-19 y respuestas', Urban Housing Practioners Hub working paper (2020), https://www.uhph.org/sites/default/files/2020-11/lav_covid-10_y_asentamientos_sisca.pdf (accessed 17 March 2021).
3. Alejandra Bronfman and Andrew Grant Wood, 'Introduction: Media, Sound, and Culture', in Alejandra Bronfman and Andrew Grant Wood, eds, *Media, Sound, and Culture in Latin America and the Caribbean* (Pittsburgh, PA: University of Pittsburgh Press, 2012), ix–xviii, p. x. We approach the subject while also reflecting Michelle Bigenho's caution of 'inevitable slippage about our mode of knowledge construction and our representations of cultural life' – Michelle Bigenho, *Sounding Indigenous: Authenticity in Bolivian Music Performance* (New York: Palgrave Macmillan, 2002), p. 23.
4. Eric F. Clarke, *An Ecological Approach to the Perception of Musical Meaning* (Oxford: Oxford University Press, 2005), pp. 4–5.

5. Joseph Osmundson, *Virology: Essays for the Living, the Dead, and the Small Things in Between* (New York: Norton, 2022), p. 31.
6. As Jennifer Lena argues, genres are cultural constructs – Jennifer C. Lena, *Banding Together: How Communities Create Genres in Popular Music* (Princeton, NJ: Princeton University Press, 2021), pp. 1–20. Accordingly, the present book uses these genre categories, which are often reproduced in música del coronavirus artists' own descriptions, with great care, reflecting on Sydney Hutchinson's admonitions in her '*Típico, Folklórico* or *Popular*? Musical Categories, Place, and Identity in a Transnational Listening Community', *Popular Music* 30.2 (2011): 245–62 (esp. pp. 245–9).
7. The many cuecas collected for this project are not analyzed due to space considerations, although many examples are included on the book's 'Música del Conoravirus' playlist at https://www.youtube.com/playlist?list=PL1U7D0mTlpEO3sRj4aMnHj92DB sD6mVAN
8. 'CORONA VIRUS ⓒ✎ – Yofrangel (Official Video)', https://www.youtube.com/watch?v=uF3dg5seGLs (accessed 2 February 2022).
9. Brazilian music is absent from this book for language and spatial reasons, and also reflecting divisions in the scholarship and popular thinking for ways that 'Brazil remained marginal to the Latin American music phenomenon' due to widespread support for 'de-Latin Americanization' – Mauricio Tenorio-Trillo, *Latin America: The Allure and Power of an Idea* (Chicago: University of Chicago Press, 2020), esp. p. 116; see also Leslie Bethell, 'Brazil and "Latin America"', *Journal of Latin American Studies* 47 (2010): 457–85; Janina Onuki, Fernando Mouron, and Francisco Urdinez, 'Latin American Perceptions of Regional Identity and Leadership in Comparative Perspective', *Contexto Internacional* 38 (2016): 433–65.
10. 'Homenaje a Nuestros Hermanos caídos en Pandemia por el Covid-19 ✓🎵✎ DUO GUAYABAMBA', https://www.youtube.com/watch?v=30aJZfJXktw (accessed 5 September 2022); Felipe Perez, 'Dulce Sueño' (Jalopy Records, 2023). A singer calling himself El Tigre del Norte, obviously hoping to cash in on the fame of Los Tigres del Norte, released 'El Tigre del Norte – Covid 19 Canción Norteña', https://www.youtube.com/watch?v=O4fyl6WiRjI (accessed 29 September 2022) on 5 July 2022; and Los Compadres del Carnaval released an atonal 'CANCIÓN - EL CORONAVIRUS GEUPO L9S COMPADRES DEL CARNAVAL', https://www.youtube.com/watch?v=ayyasSCx6WA (accessed 29 September 2022) on 28 September 2022. Both had zero views until watched by Dan Margolies.
11. Some of these were magnificent pieces of music too, from solo whistled pieces to compelling band settings like 'LA CANCION DEL CORONA VIRUS -DOMINICANA', https://www.youtube.com/watch?v=_NPN7r3KwIc (accessed 13 September 2020); 'IVANCITO _ UCHUCUTA & AGUILA DE PUQIO // CORONAVIRUS //HUAYNO SENTIMENTAL ✎✎♪', https://www.youtube.com/watch?v=aQSYDqTWvVY (accessed 13 September 2020); or 'Sonido Escorpión ~ La Cueca Del CoronaVirus (Sept.2020)', https://www.youtube.com/watch?v=AinbKsbnRlg (accessed 13 September 2020). These were all uploaded in 2020 and are no longer available.
12. Leon Botstein, 'The Future of Music in America: The Challenge of the COVID-19 Pandemic', *Musical Quarterly* 102.4 (2020): 351–60, p. 356.
13. 'canción del coronavirus dueto restrepo', https://www.youtube.com/watch?v=K6my7hf5Oik (accessed 13 September 2020).
14. 'Toña León combate el Coronavirus', https://www.youtube.com/watch?v=9kQYvuE83-I (accessed 7 September 2022); 'José Hinojosa combate el Coronavirus', https://www.youtube.com/watch?v=ztqECIw8GmU. As of September 2022 'Viover combate el Coronavirus', https://www.youtube.com/watch?v=FdT3Z3bUvv8 (accessed 18 September 2022) had gained 17 views; 'Nilson José González combate el Coronavirus', https://www.youtube.com/watch?v=UFf8wp2SDPs (accessed 18 September 2022), 16 views; 'Julio Martínez con el Coronavirus', https://www.youtube.com/

watch?v=gxBn6pzE7og (accessed 18 September 2022), 12 views; 'Manaure Cantor combate el Coronavirus', https://www.youtube.com/watch?v=CUIQ5GaXa7M (accessed 18 September 2022), 17 views.
15. 'O #Music Cantautor : Andrés Leobardo Contreras Orduño Tema : Canción Del Coronavirus', https://www.youtube.com/watch?v=DIfM8CTxgj8 (accessed 6 May 2020). By September 2022 it had a small but respectable 323 number of views.
16. 'Canción anti Covid -19', https://www.youtube.com/watch?v=OfrU36nu4Po (accessed 7 September 2022).
17. 'Coronavirus', https://www.youtube.com/watch?v=-yAACSDz1WY (accessed 7 September 2022).
18. 'En tiempo de pandemia aprendí con ayuda de YouTube a tocar el violín y otros... y gracias al maestro del arpa pongo en practica. Importante mantenerse ocupado', https://www.youtube.com/watch?v=_KN--toHquQ (accessed 26 June 2021).
19. Notable examples include 'Camerino cantando el Corrido del corona virus', https://www.youtube.com/watch?v=AwY1JZr9dxs (accessed 7 September 2022), with 59 views; 'cancion para mi amiga que vencio al covid-19', https://www.youtube.com/watch?v=hMvJaK_hXsU (accessed 7 September 2022), with 16 views; 'COVID-19 CORRIDO ECUADOR', https://www.youtube.com/watch?v=FgKItWlFQoc (accessed 7 September 2022), with 62 views; 'El corrido del corona virus', https://www.youtube.com/watch?v=jBehR9GhCqQ (accessed 7 September 2022), with 54 views; 'Coronavirus -El Músico _ Covid19 cd juarez', https://www.youtube.com/watch?v=7qYjBOA0lO8 (accessed 7 September 2022), with 240 views; 'Copla al Coronavirus', https://www.youtube.com/watch?v=ZhssdAkzFuo (accessed 7 September 2022), with 463 views.
20. Michael Gibson, '"That's Hip-Hop to Me!": Race, Space, and Temporal Logics of Authenticity in Independent Cultural Production', *Poetics* 46 (2014): 38–55, p. 39. On politics and global fusion musics, see Nadeem Karkabi, 'Electro-Dabke: Performing Cosmopolitan Nationalism and Borderless Humanity', *Public Culture* 30.1 (2018): 173–96.
21. Beth A. Buchholz, Jason DeHart, and Gary Moorman, 'Digital Citizenship during a Global Pandemic: Moving Beyond Digital Literacy', *Journal of Adolescent & Adult Literacy* 64.1 (2020): 11–17; John Lai and Nicole O. Widmar, 'Revisiting the Digital Divide in the COVID-19 Era', *Applied Economic Perspectives and Policy* 43.1 (2021): 458–64; Ian Litchfield, David Shukla, and Sheila Greenfield, 'Impact of COVID-19 on the Digital Divide: A Rapid Review', *BMJ Open* 11.10 (2021): Article e053440; Marlen M. Domínguez and Angélica Gómez, 'Usos del internet por jóvenes estudiantes durante la pandemia de la covid-19 en México', *PAAKAT: Revista De Tecnología y Sociedad* 12.22 (2022): http://dx.doi.org/10.32870/Pk.a12n22.724.
22. Robert Neustadt, 'Bone Flutes and Quechua Love Songs: Excavating Traces of Colonial Trauma in Néstor Taboada Terán's *Manchay Puytu*', *Confluencia* 23.1 (2007): 29–42; Bonnie B. McConnell and Buba Darboe, 'Music and the Ecology of Fear: Kanyeleng Women Performers and Ebola Prevention in The Gambia', *Africa Today* 63.3 (2017): 29–42; Michael Rivera, 'Music, Media, and the Ethnopoetics of Two Ebola Songs in Liberia', *Africa Today* 63.3 (2017): 63–76; Benson A. Mulemi, 'Lyrics and Artistic Improvisations in Health Promotion for the COVID-19 Pandemic Control in East Africa', *Global Health Promotion* 28.1 (2021): 23–32.
23. Interestingly, there is not yet any scholarly writing on this earlier body of disease songs, which featured a similar mix of comedic and serious themes to música del coronavirus in examples like 'Renovación Vallenata – El chikungunya', https://www.youtube.com/watch?v=RkliLPVAyR4 (accessed 5 September 2022); 'La cumbia de la chikungunya Yucatán', https://www.youtube.com/watch?v=0EiPAY5oh5A (accessed 5 September 2022); 'Esta es "La cumbia del mosquito del zika"', https://www.youtube.com/watch?v=dWCtK1UX-Y (accessed 5 September 2022); 'La Cumbia del Ebola', https://www.youtube.com/watch?v=HlGc5kr4_Wk (accessed 5 September 2022); 'Cumbia del

H1NI1', https://www.youtube.com/watch?v=dIy7Eii-ByY (accessed 5 September 2022); 'La Cumbia Del Sida', https://www.youtube.com/watch?v=8Bzx8n_Drdw (accessed 5 September 2022).

24. 'Jordi Ganchitos – La viruela del mono', https://www.youtube.com/watch?v=czax8QKTl9M (accessed 5 September 2022); '🐒LA VIRUELA DEL MONO🐒 El Niño del Ukelele', https://www.youtube.com/watch?v=mL7Zh-BoyEE (accessed 5 September 2022).

25. Anneliese Depoux, Sam Martin, Emilie Karafillakis, Raman Preet, Annelies Wilder-Smith, and Heidi Larson, 'The Pandemic of Social Media Panic Travels Faster than the COVID-19 Outbreak', *Journal of Travel Medicine* 27.3 (2020): Article taaa031; Zhang Jin, Chen Ye, Zhao Yuehua, Dietmar Wolfram, and Feicheng Ma, 'Public Health and Social Media: A Study of Zika virus-related Posts on Yahoo! Answers', *Journal of the Association for Information Science and Technology* 71.3 (2020): 282–99; Jonas Kaiser, Adrian Rauchfleisch, and Yasodara Cordova, 'Fighting Zika with Honey: An Analysis of YouTube's Video Recommendations on Brazilian YouTube', *International Journal of Communication* 15 (2021): 1244–62.

26. Lauren J. Cator, Ben J. Arthur, Laura C. Harrington, and Ronald R. Hoy, 'Harmonic Convergence in the Love Songs of the Dengue Vector Mosquito', *Science* 323.5917 (2009): 1077–9; Hamady Dieng, Ching Chuin The, Tomomitsu Satho, Fumio Miake, Erida Wydiamala, Nur Faeza A. Kassim, Nur Aida Hashim, *et al.* 'The Electronic Song "Scary Monsters and Nice Sprites" Reduces Host Attack and Mating Success in the Dengue Vector *Aedes Aegypti*', *Acta Tropica* 194 (2019): 93–9.

27. Niels C. Hansen, John M. G. Treider, Dana Swarbrick, Joshua S. Bamford, Johanna Wilson, and Jonna Katariina Vuoskoski, 'A Crowd-Sourced Database of Coronamusic: Documenting Online Making and Sharing of Music during the COVID-19 Pandemic', *Frontiers in Psychology* 12 (2021): Article 684083; Judit Váradi, 'New Possibilities in Cultural Consumption: The Effect of the Global Pandemic on Listening to Music', *Central European Journal of Educational Research* 3.1 (2021): 1–15.

28. Along with many recent articles too numerous to cite here, significant studies include June Boyce-Tillman, 'Heart's Ease: Eudaimonia, Musicking in the Pandemic, and its Implications for Music Education', *Frontiers in Psychology* 12 (2021): Article 698941; Cho Eun and Beatriz Senoi Ilari, 'Mothers as Home DJs: Recorded Music and Young Children's Well-Being during the COVID-19 Pandemic', *Frontiers in Psychology* 12 (2021): Article 637569; Alexandre Garnizé, 'Music, Pandemic, and Creative Idleness!' *Streetnotes* 28 (2022): 104–8; Moses Iten, 'Mexican Sonidero Sound System Culture Online: From Dancing on the Streets to Social Media in Times of Covid-19', *Dancecult* 13.1 (2021): https://dx.doi.org/10.12801/1947-5403.2021.13.01.12; Eric T. Lehman, '"Washing Hands, Reaching Out" – Popular Music, Digital Leisure and Touch during the COVID-19 Pandemic', *Leisure Sciences* 43.1–2 (2021): 273–9; Maruša Levstek, Rubie Mai Barnby, Katherine L. Pocock, and Robin Banerjee, '"It All Makes Us Feel Together": Young People's Experiences of Virtual Group Music-Making during the COVID-19 Pandemic', *Frontiers in Psychology* 12 (2021): Article 703892; Daniel Margolies and J. A. Strub, 'Community Music Making, Improvisation and Social Technologies in Música Huasteca', *Frontiers in Psychology* 12 (2021): Article 648010; id., '#QuédateEnCasa y Huapango! Diasporic Community and Musical Wellbeing in Streamed Live Performances of Son Huasteco music', in J. Williams, E. Ruddock, A. Mohseni, S. J. Gibson, N. Fleshner, P. Yeoh, A. Cusworth, J. Leong, S. Cohen, and D. Stringham, eds, *Musicking through COVID-19: Challenges, Adaptations, and New Practices*, special issue of *Journal of Music, Health and Wellbeing* (2021); Esther Morgan-Ellis, 'Non-Participation in Online Sacred Harp Singing during the COVID-19 Pandemic', *International Journal of Community Music* 14.2–3 (2021): 223–44; Kaila C. Putter, Amanda E. Krause, and Adrian C. North, 'Popular Music Lyrics and the COVID-19 Pandemic', *Psychology of Music* 50.4 (2021): 1280–95; James Rendell,

'Staying in, Rocking Out: Online Live Music Portal Shows during the Coronavirus Pandemic', *Convergence* 27.4 (2021): 1092–111.
29. Brynjulf Stige, 'Health Musicking: A Perspective on Music and Health as Action and Performance', in Raymond MacDonald, Gunter Kreutz, and Laura Mitchell, eds, *Music, Health, and Wellbeing* (Oxford: Oxford University Press, 2012), 183–95; Even Ruud, 'Can Music Serve as a "Cultural Immunogen"? An Explorative Study', *International Journal of Qualitative Studies on Health and Well-being* 8.1 (2013): 20597–609; Gary Ansdell, *How Music Helps in Music Therapy and Everyday Life* (Farnham, UK: Ashgate, 2014); Peregrine Horden, ed., *Music As Medicine: The History of Music Therapy Since Antiquity* (New York: Routledge, 2016); Daniella B. Victorino, Carla A. Scorza, Ana C. Fiorini, Josef Finsterer, and Fulvio A. Scorza, '"Mozart Effect" for Parkinson's Disease: Music as Medicine', *Neurological Sciences* 42.1 (2021): 319–20. Earlier health issues generated cultural productions and new popular songs such as Fito Olivares' popular cumbia 'El Colesterol', 'FITO OLIVARES. El Colesterol. PROGRAMUSIC DE LOS 90's', https://www.youtube.com/watch?v=Ihhm5HgSRv8 (accessed 18 September 2022).
30. Remi Chiu, 'Functions of Music Making Under Lockdown: A Trans-Historical Perspective Across Two Pandemics', *Frontiers in Psychology* 11 (2020): Article 616499, p. 2. On affect and 'the staging of a binaristic relation between the intimate interiority of hearing and the objective, exteriority of vision', see Marie Thompson and Ian Biddle, 'Introduction: Somewhere Between the Signifying and the Sublime', in Thompson and Biddle, eds, *Sound, Music, Affect: Theorising Sonic Experience* (New York : Bloomsbury Academic, 2013), 1–24, p. 19.
31. The full series is available in J. Williams, E. Ruddock, A. Mohseni, S. J. Gibson, N. Fleshner, P. Yeoh, A. Cusworth, J. Leong, S. Cohen, and D. Stringham, eds, *Musicking through COVID-19: Challenges, Adaptations, and New Practices*, special issue of *Journal of Music, Health and Wellbeing* (2021). See also Lauren K. Fink, Lindsay A. Warrenburg, Claire Howlin, William M. Randall, Niels C. Hansen, and Melanie Wald-Fuhrmann, 'Viral Tunes: Changes in Musical Behaviours and Interest in Coronamusic Predict Socio-Emotional Coping during COVID-19 Lockdown', *Humanities and Social Science Communications* 8 (2021): Article 180.
32. Anja Nylund Hagen, 'The Playlist Experience: Personal Playlists in Music Streaming Services', *Popular Music and Society* 38.5 (2015): 625–45, p. 642.
33. Anja Nylund Hagen and Marika Lüders, 'Social Streaming? Navigating Music as Personal and Social', *Convergence: The International Journal of Research into New Media Technologies*, 23.6 (2017): 643–59, pp. 644–5.
34. Chiu, 'Functions', p. 7.
35. https://spinditty.com/playlists/Pandemic-Playlist.
36. https://www.youtube.com/playlist?list=PL53dQXA_E4e1-I7o_Qe0780uAD4qyiX8I (accessed 12 October 2021), now gone.
37. https://www.youtube.com/watch?v=20UgD1YC6uU (accessed 22 September 2022).
38. https://www.youtube.com/playlist?list=PLF8axpz9VYG2F0uhYUn7l5f9mOn853j2C (accessed 22 September 2022).
39. https://www.youtube.com/playlist?list=PLYsDHipSFWbjEwp3HSXrljMitpl-gckF5 (accessed 22 September 2022).
40. Jessica Roiz, 'Latin Songs Born during Coronavirus Quarantine (Updating)', *Billboard*, 2 January 2021, https://www.billboard.com/music/latin/latin-songs-quarantine-coronavirus-9355057/ (accessed 1 July 2022).
41. https://www.youtube.com/playlist?list=PLIftLgpNhmOf7cxEf4e4s2ik7CZ2Luiwu (accessed 7 September 2022).
42. 'Música del Coronavirus' playlist, https://www.youtube.com/playlist?list=PL1U7D 0mTlpEO3sRj4aMnHj92DBsD6mVAN. A 'Música del Coronavirus' Spotify playlist replicates some but not all of the YouTube playlist, because not as many songs are available as streams on that platform.

43. 'The Sound of the Virus', https://open.spotify.com/playlist/5iz0GLSFdfR5sTX50JEzwn. The playlist received a lot of media attention, e.g. Ann Powers, 'A Playlist Tracking the Many New Tracks Being Written about the Coronavirus', NPR, 23 March 2020, https://www.npr.org/sections/coronavirus-live-updates/2020/03/23/820305127/a-playlist-tracking-the-many-new-tracks-being-written-about-the-coronavirus (accessed 1 July 2022).
44. Alister Wedderburn, 'Pandemic Time', *Soundings* 75 (2020): 31–5, pp. 31–2.
45. Juan Sandoval-Reyes, Sandra Idrovo-Carlier, and Edison J. Duque-Oliva, 'Remote Work, Work Stress, and Work–Life during Pandemic Times: A Latin America Situation', *International Journal of Environmental Research and Public Health* 18.13 (2021): Article 7069.
46. Interview with Arsenio Hinostroza, by J. A. Strub, 11 April 2022.
47. Luiza Bialasiewicz and Christina Eckes, '"Individual Sovereignty" in Pandemic Times – A Contradiction in Terms?' *Political Geography* 85 (2021): Article 102277; Raymundo M. Campos-Vazquez and Gerardo Esquivel, 'Consumption and Geographic Mobility in Pandemic Times. Evidence from Mexico', *Review of Economics of the Household* 19: 2 (2021): 353–71; Irene Skovgaard-Smith, 'Transnational Life and Cross-Border Immobility in Pandemic Times', *Global Networks* 23.1 (2023): 59–74.
48. Paricia Arés-Muzio, 'The Mysteries of "Pandemic Time"', *MEDICC Review* 23.2 (2021): 80.
49. Cressida J. Heyes, 'The Short and the Long of it: A Political Phenomenology of Pandemic Time', *Philosophy Today* 64.4 (2020): 859–63, pp. 859, 861.
50. Timothy Morton, *Hyperobjects: Philosophy and Ecology After the End of the World* (Minneapolis: University of Minnesota Press, 2013).
51. This phrasing is often attributed to Morton himself, although it doesn't seem to be an exact quote.
52. https://twitter.com/the_eco_thought/status/1234828156449759232; see also Stefan Bengtsson and Katrien Van Poeck, 'What Can We Learn from COVID-19 as a Form of Public Pedagogy?' *European Journal for Research on the Education and Learning of Adults* 12.3 (2021): 281–93; Morgan Meis, 'Timothy Morton's Hyper-Pandemic', *New Yorker*, 8 June 2021, https://www.newyorker.com/culture/persons-of-interest/timothy-mortons-hyper-pandemic (accessed 12 September 2021).
53. Morton, *Hyperobjects*, pp. 25, 48.
54. Morton, *Hyperobjects*, p. 58
55. On the disorientations of the moment, Carlos A. Gadea and Rafael Bayce, 'Coronavirus: una pandemia hiperreal', *Estudios Sociológicos* 39.115 (2021): 209–36.
56. Morton, *Hyperobjects*, p. 93
57. Sven Kunisch, Blagoy Blagoev, and Jean M. Bartunek, 'Complex Times, Complex Time: The Pandemic, Time-Based Theorizing and Temporal Research in Management and Organization Studies', *Journal of Management Studies* 58.5 (2021): 1411–14, pp. 1411–12.
58. On music and time, see Rose S. Gitirana Hikiji, 'Música para matar o tempo intervalo, suspensão e imersão', *Mana* 12.1 (2006): 151–78.
59. Dan Margolies served as artistic director for the online Sixth Annual Festival of Texas Fiddling, the first time it was held virtually, and as coordinator for the first virtual conjunto festival ever held, the '39th Annual Tejano Conjunto Festival en San Antonio', https://www.youtube.com/playlist?list=PLVbzsIotpDI2A_SXqTEbgB_BVb1i8lvgu (https://guadalupeculturalarts.org/tejano-conjunto-festival/). J. A. Strub created and directed 'El Primer Gran Foro de la Cultura Huapanguera en Texas', https://www.youtube.com/watch?v=AD7dQXX_htU&t=2339s (accessed 27 September 2022).
60. Robert O. Gardner, 'Introduction: Spaces of Musical Interaction: Scenes, Subcultures, and Communities', *Studies in Symbolic Interaction* 35 (2010): 71–7, p. 71.

61. For example, Bogotá – Minerva Campion Canelas and Javier A. Rodríguez-Camacho, 'Efectos del coronavirus en el circuito punk de chapinero a partir de la cartografía de la territorialidad nómada: producción, consumo y participación', *Análisis Político* 33: 100 (2020): 27–54.
62. Donya Alinejad, 'Mapping Homelands through Virtual Spaces: Transnational Embodiment and Iranian Diaspora Bloggers', *Global Networks* 11.1 (2011): 43–62.
63. Caridad Botella, 'The Mobile Aesthetics of Cell Phone Made Films: From the Pixel to The Everyday', *Revista Kepes* 9.8 (2012): 73–87, pp. 81–2.
64. Melanie S. Hammond Cisneros and Laura R. León Kanashiro, '#FamiliasDeCuarentena, radiografía de una comunicación en contexto de pandemia. Caso: San Fernando', *Repositorio Institucional – Ulima* (2021), p. 21 (translated), https://repositorio.ulima.edu.pe/bitstream/handle/20.500.12724/12675/Hammond-Leon_Caso-estudio.pdf (accessed 9 March 2022).
65. Alexander G. Weheliye, 'Rhythms of Relation: Black Popular Music and Mobile Technologies', in Sumanth Gopinath and Jason Stanyek, eds, *The Oxford Handbook of Mobile Music Studies*, vol. 2 (Oxford: Oxford University Press, 2014): 361–80, p. 365.
66. This has been explored by a variety of scholars in other contexts: e.g. Ulrike Schultze, 'Performing Embodied Identity in Virtual Worlds', *European Journal of Information Systems* 23.1 (2012): 84–95; Jean Ho Chu and Ali Mazalek, 'Embodied Engagement with Narrative: A Design Framework for Presenting Cultural Heritage Artifacts', *Multimodal Technologies and Interaction* 3.1 (2019): 1–23.
67. Andrew Mitchell, Tin Obermanc, Francesco Alettad, Magdalena Kachlickae, Matteo Lionellof, Mercede Erfaniang, and Jian Kangh, 'Investigating Urban Soundscapes of the COVID-19 Lockdown: A Predictive Soundscape Modeling Approach', *Journal of the Acoustical Society of America* 150 (2021): Article 4474; Lenzi Sara, Sádaba Juan, and Lindborg PerMagnus, 'Soundscape in Times of Change: Case Study of a City Neighbourhood during the COVID-19 Lockdown', *Frontiers in Psychology* 12 (2021): Article 570741.
68. Soundscapes of Pandemia website, https://soundscapesofpandemia.info/ (accessed 1 July 2022). See also the list curated by the World Forum for Acoustic Ecology, which includes several projects: 'COVID-19 Soundscape Resources', https://www.wfae.net/covid-19-soundscapes.html (accessed 1 July 2022); Samuel Challéat, Amandine Gasc, Nicolas Farrugia and Jérémy Froidevaux, 'Silent·Cities: A Participatory Monitoring Programme of an Exceptional Modification of Urban Soundscapes', https://renoir.hypotheses.org/files/2020/03/Silent%C2%B7Cities-Project.pdf (accessed 1 July 2022); Corona Concréte website, https://corona-concrete.lasse-marc-riek.de/index.php (accessed 6 February 2022).
69. Thomas Lecocq, Stephen P. Hicks, Koen Van Noten, Kasper Van Wijk, Paula Koelemeijer, Raphael S. M. De Plaen, Frédérick Massi, *et al.*, 'Global Quieting of High-Frequency Seismic Noise due to COVID-19 Pandemic Lockdown Measures', *Science* 369.6509 (2020): 1338–43.
70. Mark D. Temple, 'Real-Time Audio and Visual Display of the Coronavirus Genome', *BMC Bioinformatics* 21 (2020): Article 431. Others have sonified the protein coating of the virus, as in Holger Schulze, 'Scientific Sonification – The Sound of Corona', *Passive/Aggressive*, 1 May 2020, http://passiveaggressive.dk/scientific-sonification-the-sound-of-corona/ (accessed 1 July 2022).
71. The concept of the Anthropocene is usefully critiqued in Eileen Crist, 'On the Poverty of Nomenclature', in Jason W. Moore, ed., *Anthropocene or Capitalocene?: Nature, History, and the Crisis of Capitalism* (Oakland, CA: PM Press, 2016), 14–33, alongside other chapters in the same volume.
72. This pause, they argue, is 'embodied and felt differently across various types of housing tenure, health, cultural background and socio-economic status, which are themselves inflected by existing inequalities underpinned by gender, race, and class' – Adam Searle,

Jonathon Turnbull, and Jamie Lorimer, 'After the Anthropause: Lockdown Lessons for More-Than-Human Geographies', *Geographical Journal* 187.1 (2021): 69–77, p. 72.
73. Burcu Yaşin, 'The Soundscape of Covid-19 In Istanbul', *terrabayt*, 17 Nisan [=11 April] 2020, https://terrabayt.com/dusunce/english/the-soundscape-of-covid-19-in-istanbul/ (accessed 1 July 2022); Matt Mikkelsen, 'Hear the Soundscapes of Cities Transformed', *AtlasObscura*, 17 April 2020, https://www.atlasobscura.com/articles/changing-sound-of-cities (accessed 12 September 2021); Sune Anderberg, 'Lyden af 2020', *Seismograf*, April 2020, https://seismograf.org/fokus/lyden-af-2020 (accessed 6 February 2022).
74. https://www.window-swap.com/Window
75. Pete Stollery, 'COVID-19 Sound Map', Google Earth, https://tinyurl.com/covid-19soundmap (accessed 1 July 2022).
76. Pete Stollery, 'This is What lockdown Sounds Like', *The Conversation*, 29 January 2021, https://theconversation.com/this-iswhat-lockdown-sounds-like-153590 (accessed 1 July 2022).
77. Sara Lenzi, 'The Sound Outside – Listening to the world at Covid-19 Time', *Soundesign*, 28 March 2020, https://www.soundesign.info/2020/03/28/the-sound-outside/ (accessed 2 November 2021).
78. radio aporee, 'Panelaço (Pot-banging protest) - Fora Bolsonaro! - 20h30', https://aporee.org/maps/work/projects.php?project=corona (accessed 1 July 2022).
79. radio aporee, 'Cl. 44 #50, Bogotá, Colombia, Covid sunrise', https://aporee.org/maps/work/projects.php?project=corona (accessed 1 July 2022).
80. Lenzi, 'The Sound Outside'.
81. *Cities and Memory*, 'Sounds from the Global Covid-19 Lockdown', https://citiesandmemory.com/covid19-sounds/ (accessed 6 February 2022).
82. Chiara Bartalucci, Raffaella Bellomini, Sergio Luzzi, Paola Pulella, and Giulia Torelli, 'A Survey on the Soundscape Perception before and during the COVID-19 Pandemic in Italy', *Noise Mapping* 8.1 (2021): 65–88; Pamela Jordan and André Fiebig, 'COVID-19 Impacts on Historic Soundscape Perception and Site Usage', *Acoustics* 3.3 (2021): 594–610; Maria D. Redel-Macías, Pilar Aparicio-Martinez, Sara Pinzi, Pedro Arezes, and Antonio J. Cubero-Atienza, 'Monitoring Sound and Its Perception during the Lockdown and De-Escalation of COVID-19 Pandemic: A Spanish Study', *International Journal of Environmental Research and Public Health* 18.7 (2021): Article 3392; Liu Jinxuan, Xu Jian, Wu Zhicai, Cheng Yuru, Gou Yuxin, and Ridolfo Jesse, 'Soundscape Preference of Urban Residents in China in the Post-pandemic Era', *Frontiers in Psychology* 12 (2021): Article 750421.
83. Ana L. Maggi, Jimena Muratore, Sara Gaetán, Mauricio F. Zalazar-Jaime, Diego Evin, Jorge Pérez Villalobo, and María Hinalaf, 'Perception of the Acoustic Environment during COVID-19 Lockdown in Argentina', *Journal of the Acoustical Society of America* 149.6 (2021): 3902–9.
84. Luis Hermida, Ignacio Pavón, Antonio Carlos Lobo Soares, and J. Luis Bento-Coelho, 'On the Person-Place Interaction and its Relationship with the Responses/Outcomes of Listeners of Urban Soundscape (Compared Cases of Lisbon and Bogotá): Contextual and Semiotic Aspects', *International Journal of Environmental Research and Public Health* 16.4 (2019): 551–72.
85. Steven C. Brown and Amanda E. Krause, 'Freedom of Choice: Examining Music Listening as a Function of Favorite Music Format', *Psychomusicology: Music, Mind, and Brain* 30.2 (2020): 88–102; Allan B. de Guzman, John Christopher B. Mesana, Maxeen E. Manuel, Kyle Christian A. Arcega, Rupert Lance T. Yumang, and Kylie Niechols V. Miranda, 'Examining Intergenerational Family Members' Creative Activities during COVID-19 Lockdown Via Manifest Content Analysis of YouTube and TikTok Videos', *Educational Gerontology* 48.10 (2022): 458–71; Amanda E. Krause, Adrian C. North, and Brody Heritage, 'The Uses and Gratifications of Using Facebook Music Listening Applications', *Computers in Human Behavior* 39 (2014): 71–7; Raphaël Nowak,

'Understanding Everyday Uses of Music Technologies in the Digital Age', in Andy Bennett and Brady Robards eds, *Mediated Youth Cultures: The Internet, Belonging and New Cultural Configurations* (Basingstoke, UK: Palgrave Macmillan, 2014), 146–61.
86. AFP, 'TikTok Videos Get Longer in Challenge to YouTube', *TechXplore*, 28 February 2022, https://techxplore.com/news/2022-02-tiktok-videos-longer-youtube.html (accessed 31 March 2022); Drew Kirchhoff, 'More Tok on the Clock: Introducing longer videos on TikTok', TikTok, 1 July 2021, https://newsroom.tiktok.com/en-us/longer-videos (accessed 7 September 2022); Chris Lindahl, 'TikTok Is Making YouTube Change Its Game – and It's Costing Alphabet a Fortune', *IndieWire*, 18 June 2022, https://www.indiewire.com/2022/06/youtube-competes-tiktok-1234734526/ (accessed 16 September 2022).
87. Lindahl, 'TikTok'.
88. Aparajita Bhandari and Sara Bimo, 'Why's Everyone on TikTok Now? the Algorithmized Self and the Future of Self-Making on Social Media', *Social Media + Society* 8.1 (2022): https://doi.org/10.1177/20563051221086241, p 2.
89. Min Wonjung, Dal Yong Jin, and Benjamin Han, 'Transcultural Fandom of the Korean Wave in Latin America: Through the Lens of Cultural Intimacy and Affinity Space', *Media, Culture & Society* 41.5 (2019): 604–19; Yu Hui and Sary Schroeder, 'Distribution and Popularity Patterns of Chinese Music on YouTube: A Case Study of Local Music's Representation on a Global Internet Platform', *Journal of New Music Research* 47.1 (2018): 68–77.
90. Will D. Heaven, 'Why the Coronavirus Lockdown is Making the Internet Even Stronger', *MIT Technology Review* 7 April 2020, https://www.technologyreview.com/2020/04/07/998552/why-the-coronavirus-lockdown-is-making-the-internet-better-than-ever/ (accessed 2 November 2021); Dennis Romero, 'YouTube Thrives as a Window for Those Isolated by Coronavirus', *NBC News*, 1 April 2020, https://www.nbcnews.com/tech/social-media/youtube-thrives-window-thoseisolated-coronavirus-n1173651 (accessed 1 July 2022); Raquel Lozano-Blasco, Alberto Quilez-Robres, Diego Delgado-Bujedo,and M. Pilar Latorre-Martínez, 'YouTube's Growth in use among Children 0–5 during COVID19: The Occidental European Case', *Technology in Society* 66 (2021): Article 101648; Hiroko Terasawa, Masaki Matsubara, Visda Goudarzi, and Makiko Sadakata, 'Music in Quarantine: Connections Between Changes in Lifestyle, Psychological States, and Musical Behaviors during COVID-19 Pandemic', *Frontiers in Psychology* 12 (2021): Article 689505; Davide Marengo, Matteo Angelo Fabris, Claudio Longobardi, and Michele Settanni, 'Smartphone and Social Media use Contributed to Individual Tendencies Towards Social Media Addiction in Italian Adolescents during the COVID-19 Pandemic', *Addictive Behaviors* 126 (2022): Article 107204.
91. James Hale, 'YouTube Users Watch 450 Million Hours Of Content On TV Screens Each Day', *tubefilter* 25 June 2020, https://www.tubefilter.com/2020/06/25/youtube-brandcast-tvviewership-stats/ (accessed 16 January 2021).
92. Massimo Airoldi, Davide Beraldo, and Alessandro Gandini, 'Follow the Algorithm: An Exploratory Investigation of Music on YouTube', *Poetics* 57 (2016): 1–13.
93. David P. Valcarce and Charo O. Mallero, 'El uso del podcast para la difusión del patrimonio cultural en el entorno hispanoparlante: análisis de las plataformas iVoox y SoundCloud', *Naveg@mérica* 24 (2020): https://revistas.um.es/navegamerica/article/view/416541.
94. David Hesmondhalgh, Ellis Jones, and Andreas Rauh, 'SoundCloud and Bandcamp as Alternative Music Platforms', *Social Media + Society* 5.4 (2019): https://doi.org/10.1177/2056305119883429
95. Hesmondhalgh *et al.* 'SoundCloud', pp. 2, 10. See also See also Janice L. Waldron and Kari K. Veblen, 'The Medium is the Message: Cyberspace, Community, and Music Learning in the Irish Traditional Music Virtual Community', *Journal of Music, Technology and Education* 1.2 (2008): 99–111.

96. On connections between older music video uses and contemporary practices, see Thomas Thurnell-Read, '"A Couple of these Videos is all You really Needed to Get Pumped to Skate": Subcultural Media, Nostalgia and Re-Viewing 1990s Skate Media on YouTube', *Young* 30.2 (2022): 165–82.
97. Robert Gehl, 'YouTube as Archive: Who Will Curate this Digital Wunderkammer?', *International Journal of Cultural Studies* 12.1 (2009): 43–60; Taina Bucher, 'The Algorithmic Imaginary: Exploring the Ordinary Affects of Facebook Algorithms', *Information, Communication & Society* 20.1 (2017): 30–44.
98. Bernhard Rieder, Ariadna Matamoros-Fernández, and Òscar Coromina, 'From Ranking Algorithms to "Ranking Cultures": Investigating the Modulation of Visibility in YouTube Search Results', *Convergence* 24.1 (2018): 50–68; Sophie Bishop, 'Managing Visibility on YouTube through Algorithmic Gossip', *New Media & Society* 21.11–12 (2019): 2589–606; Jonas Kaiser and Adrian Rauchfleisch, 'Birds of a Feather Get Recommended Together: Algorithmic Homophily in YouTube's Channel Recommendations in the United States and Germany', *Social Media + Society* 6.4 (2020): https://doi.org/10.1177/2056305120969914
99. Guillaume Heuguet, 'Towards a Micropolitics of Formats', *Revue d'Anthropologie Des Connaissances* 13.3 (2019): https://doi.org/10.4000/rac.3263
100. Sheenagh Pietrobruno, 'YouTube Flow and the Transmission of Heritage: The Interplay of Users, Content, and Algorithms', *Convergence* 24.6 (2018): 523–37, p. 527.
101. David M. Berry, *The Philosophy of Software: Code and Mediation in the Digital Age* (Basingstoke, UK: Palgrave Macmillan, 2011), p. 144, quoted in Pietrobruno, 'YouTube Flow', p. 527.
102. Pietrobruno, 'YouTube Flow', p. 528.
103. Massimo Airoldi, 'The Techno-Social Reproduction of Taste Boundaries on Digital Platforms: The Case of Music on YouTube', *Poetics* 89 (2021): Article 101563.
104. Jean Burges and Joshua Green, *YouTube: Online Video and Participatory Culture*, 2nd edition (Cambridge: Polity, 2018), p. 137; Sheenagh Pietrobruno, 'YouTube and the Social Archiving of Intangible Heritage', *New Media & Society* 15.8 (2018): 1259–76.
105. Sarah Baker and Jez Collins, 'Popular Music Heritage, Community Archives and the Challenge of Sustainability', *International Journal of Cultural Studies* 20.5 (2017): 476–91.
106. John H. McDowell, '"Surfing the Tube" for Latin American Song: The Blessings (and Curses) of YouTube', *Journal of American Folklore* 128.509 (2015): 260–72, p. 263.
107. Eric Ketelaar, 'Archives as Spaces of Memory', *Journal of the Society of Archivists* 29.1 (2008): 9–27, p. 12.
108. Burges and Green, *YouTube*, p. 80.
109. Burges and Green, *YouTube*, pp. 125.
110. Pietrobruno, 'YouTube and the Social Archiving', p. 1263.
111. Janice L. Waldron, 'YouTube, Fanvids, Forums, Vlogs and Blogs: Informal Music Learning in a Convergent On- and Offline Music Community', *International Journal of Music Education* 31.1 (2013): 91–105, p. 91.
112. For example, in 2011 *Billboard* noted that 'Gerardo Ortiz was unknown in regional Mexican music until he was discovered on YouTube several years ago' – Gail Mitchell, 'Backbeat', *Billboard* (22 October 2011), 58. See also Cheryl Martens, Cristina Venegas, and Etsa F. S. Sharupi Tapuy, eds, *Digital Activism, Community Media, and Sustainable Communication in Latin America* (Cham, Switzerland: Palgrave Macmillan, 2020); Valcarce and Mallero, 'El uso del podcast'.
113. Doris Elena Pinos Calderón and Cristina Venegas, 'Sounds of the Neighborhood: Innovation, Hybrid Urban Space, and Sound Trajectories', in Martens *et al.*, eds, *Digital Activism*, 53–79, pp. 55–6.
114. Following the lead of participants in the virtual spaces, the authors have adopted the sometimes irregular conventions of capitalization, spelling, textual idiosyncrasies

in quotations, and extensive use of hashtags and emojis utilized by the channels and individuals on the platforms described in this book. This deliberate choice in language and presentation reflects the expressed interests of the individuals we interviewed as well as the reality that on user-upload sites individuals themselves have chosen to present their productions, writings, and personae in this precise way. The authors feel that to change the language used by individuals to conform to academic practice is to distort and dishonor the unique and ephemeral cultural milieu described here. All Spanish-to-English translations are by J. A. Strub unless otherwise noted. Names in the YouTube chat sessions described are utilized reflecting on approaches to ethical online ethnography for diasporic and other communities as discussed by in Ashley N. Patterson, 'YouTube Generated Video Clips as Qualitative Research Data: One Researcher's Reflections on the Process', *Qualitative Inquiry* 24.10 (2018): 759–67. On pandemic-era online research, see Magdalena Goralska, 'Anthropology from Home: Advice on Digital Ethnography for the Pandemic Times', *Anthropology in Action* 27.1 (2020): 46–52, p. 46.

1 *Viru Viru Viru Viru*

'Shit is Getting Real!'

On 10 March 2020, rapper and social media personality Cardi B uploaded a powerful 46-second video rant about the pandemic situation to her personal Instagram account. Wearing a see-through dress, Cardi passionately and profanely expressed her fears about the dangers posed by the virus, and berated individuals and governments for their slowness in grasping the seriousness of the crisis. 'Government!', she declared, 'Let me tell y'all motherfucking something! I don't know what the fuck this coronavirus is about. I don't understand how that shit went from Wuhan, China, now all of a sudden this shit is on motherfuckin' tour.' People might not be focusing on the problem or understand what was happening, Cardi warned. 'I ain't gonna front', she added: 'A bitch is scared. I'm a little scared. Shit got me panicking.' The threat posed by COVID-19 was not just to individual health: 'Just because you think you're immune to it, guess what? Your pocket ain't, bitch, cause a lot of shit comes from motherfucking China, bitch.' Punctuating the recursive word 'bitch' with a forced but melodious three-beat laugh, she exclaimed: 'Guess what, bitch? Coronavirus! Coronavirus! I'm telling you, the shit is real! Shit is getting real!' Cardi began gyrating rhythmically while stating this at the end of the video. Her plea over, she turned away from the camera while saying under her breath, 'Bitch, I'm scared' and storming off.[1]

In just 46 indelible seconds, Cardi B clarified the public policy crisis posed by the coronavirus, sketched out the geopolitical realities of the looming pandemic, anticipated the likely global economic fallout, and captured the bracing fear of what was to come.[2] Cardi B's 'rant', as it was immediately labeled across the media, rapidly became a perfect encapsulation of the memetic aspects of the early pandemic moment.

Within 24 hours of its release, Cardi B's Instagram post went viral and accrued over two million 'likes'. By November 2021, it had been viewed 36.6

million times on Instagram alone. The rant was also reposted on tens of thousands of Twitter, Facebook, and TikTok social media accounts, as well as on multiple individual and corporate YouTube channels, garnering millions of additional views.[3] It is impossible to trace the precise number of shares. In addition to public reposts, the video was circulated through SMS messaging, email chains, and groups on WhatsApp and Messenger. On YouTube, one viewer of the original reposted video named Jessa-xo opined in response, possibly wistfully, that the sound of Cardi B's rant was as 'if Coronavirus had a voice.'[4]

A few days later, on 17 March, Puerto Rican reggaetonero Anuel AA uploaded a similar video to Instagram. Rather than providing commentary on the coronavirus crisis, he captured the feeling of the moment in a single, emotional shout. Staring out from his balcony in Sunny Isles Beach, Florida, Anuel removed his mask and shouted '¡maldito coronavirus!'[5] Like Cardi B, Anuel AA had a wide reach and a well-established personal brand on social media channels. Within a week, the original video of his simple cry of '¡maldito coronavirus!' had garnered over a million views. Its numerous reposts on various channels augmented the total view count by tens of thousands.[6]

When watching either of these self-consciously performative social media products – Cardi B maniacally cackling that 'shit is getting real' or Anuel AA shouting his '¡maldito coronavirus!' condemnation into the cityscape below – the viewer is gripped by the sense of frustration, existential anguish, and deep uncertainty triggered by the early stage of the COVID-19 pandemic. In these videos, which became viral and were subsequently remixed and memed, artists captured the emotional and musical imaginations of millions at the beginning of the pandemic moment. Their timing was impressive, too. The day after Cardi B uploaded her original Instagram post, the World Health Organization declared the coronavirus crisis to have reached pandemic proportions, marking the official recognition of a global moment.[7]

Cardi B and Anuel AA are both musical 'A-listers', with shared personal characteristics and similar artistic and public personae. They are the same age, bilingual in Spanish and English, and known for their active and highly curated transnational personal brands on social media, which complement and often extend beyond their prolific artistic output.[8] Musically, they both specialize in varieties of música urbana, fusing different styles of hip hop and electronic dance music with sounds of the Latin Caribbean drawn from reggaetón, dembow, and bachata.[9] Cardi typically sings and raps in English, while Anuel records in Spanish. They have recorded together in a mix of English and Spanish, such as a hit song with Fat Joe called 'Yes', from 2019, which garnered over 85 million views on YouTube. Other songs by both artists have boasted even larger view counts in the billions.[10]

Cardi B has greater reach via her national and global dominance in both legacy and social media markets. She has been highly successful as a recording artist, with multiple No. 1 albums and songs, five American Music Awards and 18 million YouTube and 140 million Instagram followers as of September 2022. In 2019, Cardi B sold more than 31.5 million singles, making her the Recording Industry Association of America's highest certified female hip hop artist. She is the first female rapper to reach diamond status on multiple songs.[11] Anuel AA, meanwhile, has an especially large online presence and popularity that was sustained despite spending thirty months in prison in Puerto Rico.[12] He has 21.2 million subscribers on YouTube and 29.2 million on Instagram. He claims to have 'single-handedly spearheaded the Latin trap movement', and has had albums debuting at No. 1 on both the *Billboard* top Latin albums and Latin Rhythms charts in June 2020.[13] His popularity has continued to grow. For example, his song 'Leyenda' gained 35.3 million views within only two days of release in November 2021.[14]

These two internet-savvy stars are known for generating regular online content for millions of image- and sound-conscious fans. The start of the pandemic moment provided them with a perfect opportunity to produce explicitly viral content. Their viral Instagram posts constituted part of a larger outpouring of affective and interconnected sonic responses to the uncertainty and anxiety posed by the looming public health crisis. Their creative output repurposed fear and frustration into aural memes which further blossomed as remixes, unique musicultural products that were themselves adapted and repurposed in a seemingly endless stream of further remixes. The pandemic moment encouraged such reimaginations of sonic possibilities and proliferated musical expression in virtual spaces. Remixes, which rely on sonic markers and aural memes as much as musical composition, offered new and easily transmissible modalities for highly diversified and transnational cultural products during the pandemic moment.

Remix culture is often embedded within broader conceptualizations of global viral cultures. This virality offers a ready, even seductive, framing for an analysis of the pandemic moment. This chapter engages the concept and impact of viral remix culture gingerly, in the interest of avoiding an overly facile metaphor. Yet the widespread and influential adoption of sound and form, which can be framed in terms of cultural virality, was often the mode sought by artists, and at times the mode achieved. The immediately intensified thematic framework of the pandemic moment converged with easy access to digital culture to foster a unique explosion of musical expression. These cultural products furthermore emerged at a moment where traditional modes of musical employment and sales were radically pruned. The outpouring of musical responses to the pandemic occurred within a highly competitive push for market share through viral content and platform dominance for commercially oriented musicians.[15] Many performers, including a great many examined in this project, were not motivated by market share or viral dominance. However, for professionals who were, the struggle was real. Within the confines of remix culture, market impulses drove creators to embrace the reuse and repurposing of sounds, styles, beats, and sonic markers into musical memes.

In música del coronavirus remixes, we observe the emergence of a unique set of cultural responses at a singular moment which nevertheless draw on established genre modalities, sounds, and rhythms and on the global demand for consumable products. Viral remixes, dance videos, and related cultural products about the coronavirus reflect global remix culture's self-consciously infectious sounds and methods. Coronavirus remixes present novel and creative musical responses to the crisis while also drawing on established techniques of commodification, self-promotion, and searches for market saturation and domination.

In this chapter, we examine the impact and context of the foundational Cardi B and Anuel AA coronavirus remixes alongside many other examples of remixed songs and highly repetitive original tracks in a variety of highly rhythmic music styles – such as reggaetón and dembow – which are themselves deeply indebted to remix culture. As Jay David Bolter notes, 'remix is playful no matter how serious some of its subject matter may be'.[16] Coronavirus remixes produced a beat-driven and market-oriented music that opened reflective and affective spaces for sonic explorations of the pandemic moment.

We situate coronavirus remix culture at the moment that global viral and memetic cultural products and hybridized Latin American musical cultures crashed into the fragmenting realities of the global COVID-19 pandemic. We also consider remix culture within the context of theories of viral cultures and examinations of memesis and repetition in remixes. Música del coronavirus presents a rich cultural response, utilizing emergent tools and platforms to creatively repurpose existing sounds in ways that foster community spirit and address psychological needs. Coronavirus music created within remix culture demonstrates the powerful role of participatory musical culture online during the pandemic moment.

These remixes flourished alongside the multifaceted utilities of Do-It-Yourself (DIY) participatory cultures during the pandemic, as part of the sonic communitarian efforts that emerged as a response to the pandemic moment. As such, they demonstrate the power and utilities of local music cultures in a unique cultural moment fueled by new technology within an emergent ecosystem of pandemic-era music and sounds. Before focusing on the specific forms of remix culture circulating in música del coronavirus, we provide some context for approaching remix theoretically.

Remixing as Mode During the Pandemic Moment

Remixing is a form and mode of music making built upon, and expanding out from, a wide range of copying, sampling, and DJ practices honed particularly over the past three decades. Remixing fuses sonic innovation with reuse and repetition, and musical reimagination with replication. Remix is, at once, a technique, a musical modality, and a comprehensive approach to cultural production overall that can be thought of as a social technology.

The fragmentation wrought by the pandemic moment had a transformative impact on the cultural, social, and marketplace value placed on specific kinds of remixes. Coronavirus remixes were recapitulations or outright replications of cultural forms that had existed before the pandemic moment. The technological context of the pandemic moment, and the rise of effective, even ubiquitous, use of social media and media platforms, further overwrote or erased distinctions between professional and amateur musicians – distinctions which were already highly attenuated.[17]

The explosion of música del coronavirus also depended on self-reflection on broadly social, community, and individual levels. This reflexive psychological mode, produced by a mixture of fear, health concerns, thwarted desires and ambitions, and other pandemic moment themes, encouraged the recursive underpinnings familiar to the remix. Irina Cvijanovic writes that

> depending on the perspective of considering remix, the experience changes. Observer(s), reader(s), listener(s), dancer(s) find(s) seeds of a pre-existing history, or something new in that which they already know. They define remix[,] while the way how it is done and performed becomes significant.[18]

Numerous recent theorists of remix studies and participatory online culture are expansive and divergent in their definitions even when they do not outright disagree on concepts.[19] Michele Knobel and Colin Lankshear, building on Lawrence Lessig's well-worn argument that 'that culture as a whole can be construed as remix', argue that 'remix means to take cultural artifacts and combine and manipulate them into new kinds of creative blends', through mixing, sampling, and other electronic manipulations of recorded sound.[20] Eduardo Navas, one of the foremost remix analysts, argues that it is impossible to separate remixing from music making, as it is a 'creative cultural form' that 'from a technical and technological point of view, starts with an innovation that made it possible to record the world'.[21] This idea that remixing directly both *reflects* and *reflects upon* the soundscape of the world underscores this direct engagement. Navas argues that 'generally speaking, remix culture can be defined as a global activity consisting of the creative and efficient exchange of information made possible by digital technologies'.[22] This idea leads to some very large assertions. Knobel and Lankshear argue that

> at the broadest level, then, remix is the general condition of cultures: no remix, no culture [...]. We remix language every time we draw on it and remix meanings whenever we take an idea, artifact, or a particular stretch of language and integrate it into what we are saying and doing at the time.[23]

Remix is not merely the construction of novelty from existing cultural products; it is firmly embedded within the context of its creation and the social-technological frameworks of lived experience. Cvijanovic argues that 'whichever model it takes, contemplation of the remix depends on recognition of a pre-existing cultural code.'[24] Remix, in this approach, should not be understood only in terms of its digital character, since it also reflects cultural innovations that 'gave rise to ways of being digital, ways of demonstrating comprehension and skill with computing technology to a community.'[25]

So-called mashup culture was a precursor of remix culture, in which musicians and other creators similarly built on technologically mediated experience and reflected and incorporated social critique and fresh alternative readings of pre-existing sounds and cultural products. Ellis Jones views the mashup and remix techniques as more than

> simply a tool by which to draw an audience, to act as the sugar-coating that permits a surreptitious dose of ideology. Cultural texts can seem to be 'living out' technological promise in a way that the bare, concrete existence of the technology cannot (although software and hardware can of course carry affective dimensions and cultural meanings, too).[26]

Perhaps it is most useful to frame pandemic moment remixing as Aram Sinnreich, Mark Latonero, and Marissa Gluck have proposed, with '*configurability* and *configurable culture*' being 'more accurate and inclusive ways to describe the technological and social aspects of this new paradigm of digital culture.' Sinnreich and co-authors explode false dichotomies between artists and audiences, and between production and consumption, by arguing that they 'simply do not apply in obvious ways to the emerging forms and practices such as mash-ups, remixes, machinima, software mods, photoshopping, virtual worlds, and user-generated content in general.'[27] Erasing the distinctions – especially between producers and consumers, so critical in remix culture – creates a unique middle ground in the remixed spaces found in sonic and virtual space. The authors describe the remixes as an 'ongoing reconfiguration of culture, whether through a calibrated cultural intervention [...] or simply through the quotidian, and largely unconscious, rituals and interactions of daily life.'[28]

The pandemic moment, with its deeply emotional and traumatic dimensions, also requires considering some of the ways in which remixing could in fact reflect nascent forms of oppositional culture. Ethan R. Plaut quotes Theodor Adorno as observing that 'the fragment is that part of the totality of the work that opposes totality', and argues that in these elemental terms, 'remix can be conceived as oppositional.' He reminds us that for all of the optimism of remix theorizing, which centers community and creativity, none of the theorizing 'emphasizes the possibility that our ability to manipulate information might also be an ability to manipulate one another, ignoring the possibility [...]that technology inches us away from meaningful collaboration, musical and otherwise, and toward centralized control.'[29] Perhaps this control is in the form of what Michael B. MacDonald calls 'aesthetic governmentality'. During the pandemic, the reality of global shutdowns also seemed for a time to disrupt pre-existing notions of social positioning, and instead heightened the power and reach of new forms of self-expression, self-reflection, and individualized self-cultivation and renewed creativity, especially for some otherwise marginalized groups and individuals. MacDonald argues that

> whether it is folk, rock, punk, or hip-hop, these aesthetic movements are guerrilla incursions into urban youth sensibility. Youth are innovating upon technologies and techniques of the manipulation of sensibility for the construction of new forms of individual and collective subjectivity.[30]

Suddenly, all were on the shared playing field of digital music platforms. While not all had the same level of reach and opportunity, all could upload. Small-scale creators stood a chance at competing with major content studios for views and subscribers simply by releasing a explosively viral song, dance, remix, or beat.

The New Spaces Produced by the First Coronavirus Remixes

On 13 March, three days after Cardi B uploaded her coronavirus tirade, Brooklyn-based DJ iMarkKeyz uploaded a track titled 'Coronavirus (Remix)' to the music-sharing platform Soundcloud.[31] The following day, he uploaded the same song to YouTube, saying 'something dope for y'all. Had remixed Cardi B's Coronavirus video! lol Enjoy!'[32] His 'lol' (a well-known shorthand for 'laughing out loud') underscored the spontaneity of the remix. DJ iMarkKeyz's two-and-a-half-minute long track is constructed around a voice sample extracted from Cardi B's Instagram video released three days earlier, combined with a 'a beat he had already made on Ableton that he thought fit perfectly with the cadence of Cardi B's tone.'[33] DJ iMarkKeyz recalled hearing her video and immediately knowing how it would sound as a song: 'The line where she said Coronavirus, it was a hype type of feeling. In my mind, I wanted a crunk beat to it.'[34] This distinctive remix's release proved to be an explosive and generative moment that prompted further creativity from successive remixers. Thereafter, as Eduardo Cepeda wrote, 'the internet did what it did best and remixed her post visually and sonically.'[35]

The track itself is a fairly straightforward trap beat that repetitively reiterates the rhythmic cadence and distinctive timbre of Cardi B's spoken word phrase 'Coronavirus!... Shit is getting real'. This core clip is supplemented by other samples drawn and reprocessed from the same Instagram post, including Cardi B's near-tonal, salutary shout of 'Government' and a few nonverbal hoots and grunts that are hallmarks of her performance style. A prominent sample of heavy breathing and a cough, not sourced from Cardi B's Instagram video, placed the track squarely alongside some of the sonic memes already circulating at the start of the pandemic moment in other viral videos and posts.[36]

Before the release of 'Coronavirus (Remix)', DJ iMarkKeyz already had nearly 150,000 followers on Instagram, and was known for his inventive use of soundbites and voice samples sourced from news reports, viral meme videos, and the personal social media accounts of celebrities. Within four days of releasing 'Coronavirus (Remix)', DJ iMarkKeyz gained 'around 100,000' new followers on Instagram, and the track 'instantly took off' in popularity on online music streaming platforms. The song first emerged as a hit, unexpectedly, in Bulgaria and Brazil, but soon reached No. 1 in iTunes' download rankings in the United States.[37] It also reached No. 9 on the Billboard's Rap Digital Song Sales, No. 13 on the R&B/Hip-Hop Digital Song Sales charts, and became very widely used on TikTok videos. By April it was No. 1 on Spotify's Global 'Viral 50' chart. By the fall of 2021, the remix had had more than 4.3 million views on YouTube.[38] In interviews in the days after the release, DJ iMarkKeyz expressed surprise and excitement at the track's immediate global success: 'I knew it was going to be a hit to my followers, but I didn't know it would reach international level', he told *Variety*.[39]

One of the early boosters of 'Coronavirus (Remix)' was Cardi B herself, who shared the track on 15 March to her 61 million followers. This effort, combined with the cultural moment, 'was enough to get the song to chart' and then to explode across the public consciousness.[40] Cardi B suggested in a 16 March Tweet that she ought to be compensated for her 'feature' on the unexpectedly successful track, highlighting the common copyright problems produced by sample-based remixes. However, both artists eventually made it clear to the press that there was no standing disagreement, and that they planned on working together to donate any profits from the remix to a charitable organization.[41]

Cardi B later followed her original 'rant' with more coronavirus posts criticizing celebrity behavior. *Teen Vogue* considered the not-insignificant societal implications of all her coronavirus messaging: 'The moral of the story? Listen to Cardi B.'[42] Lindsay Zoladz echoed this sensibility in a 17 March *New York Times* profile of 'Coronavirus (Remix)', noting how the song became 'a fitting anthem for these unsettled times' and how 'it sounds like being inside a five-alarm fire of the mind.' Zoladz wrote that 'it is one of the only songs that makes any kind of sense to my brain right now. And people all over the world seem to agree.'[43] In May 2020, YouTube user JuanitoBarrasXX commented on DJ iMarkKeyz' video, saying 'I am a nurse and I work in a hospital that has been close to full capacity for almost three weeks [...]. You'd think I'd hate this song, but it helps me think straight. It reminds us that we have to keep moving forward, because Cardi is right about shit getting real.'[44]

Like an inverted inspirational poster, the repeated call of 'Coronavirus!' presented an unexpected source of resonance, motivation, and solace in a world turned upside down. Cardi B's rant and the remix catalyzed cathartic responses reflected in thousands of reaction videos, ranging from serious analyses to live-video diary reactions to humorous skits. TikTok presented an enormous number of video responses, and other social media responses flowed in innumerable quantities.[45] Even Anuel AA and his then girlfriend, the Colombian pop star Karol G, posted their own reaction video to Cardi B, in which they comedically pretended to avoid each other out of fear of contagion. This response to Cardi B's rant earned close to three million likes on Instagram and positive press in *Billboard*, which reported that 'reggaetón lovebirds Karol G and Anuel AA are following the Centers for Disease Control and Prevention's safety guidelines in the midst of the coronavirus disease: they're staying at home.'[46] This kind of recursive press attention is an added publicity bonus to viral remix video production.

Anuel AA's short Instagram post likewise found new life, extended reach, and a much larger global audience via remix culture. In this case, Dominican-American DJ Jamz Turn Me Up capitalized immediately on Anuel's initial shout to produce and release a short but catchy 'CORONA VIRUS DEMBOW' video remix less than 24 hours after the initial post's upload.[47] Jamz Turn Me Up wrote on the release, in English and Spanish, that 'I seen Anuel Instagram video and I immediately said, this a dembow right here lol', noting that he 'had fun doing this', and that he 'did this in a hour! hope you guys like it!'[48] Just like DJ iMarkKeyz, Jamz Turn Me Up heard the rhythm in the words and immediately capitalized on it, delivered with an 'lol'.

Released 18 March 2020, Jamz Turn Me Up also sampled Anuel BB's shout of '¡maldito coronavirus!' with a spare dembow beat and additional samples drawn from Anuel's other music. This track did not garner the same instantly vast global success as Cardi B and DJ DJ iMarkKeyz 'Coronavirus (Remix)', possibly because of the former's greater mainstream audience and the fact that the Anuel AA remix track was exclusively in Spanish. Yet it did receive enthusiastic reception and a very large audience from listeners and news sites across Latin America. It was available on all basic streaming platforms, with more than a million views on YouTube and on Spotify, where it was released as 'Coronaviru', reflecting a common practice in Caribbean Spanish of dropping the final 's'.[49]

DJ Jamz Turn Me Up's original remix video featured a dembow beat with altered and recapitulated images of the original Anuel AA post. In the video, Anuel delivers his shout, with the image flipping, turning upside down, repeating, slicing, and changing hues and exposures. All the video effects aligned with the remix's rhythmic pulse, which is built upon repetition of the word 'coronavirus'. Particular emphasis was placed on the word's final fragment: an attenuated and nearly tonal 'viru', which was was deployed 33 times in a rapid flow, as if reflecting the amplification of the coronavirus itself, or as if the virus' power could be neutered through repetition and increasing speed. Jamz Turn Me Up also added in new samples of Anuel's characteristic repetitious vocalizations and other sound effects.[50]

Anuel AA himself embraced the remix as his own composition, perhaps because of the extensive remixes from fans which had appeared immediately after the first release. For example, within 24 hours of Jamz Turn Me Up's remix release, Elie Dpble Filo and El Violento PM remixed the track and added extensive verses describing the global situation of the pandemic.[51] On 27 May, the sampler and the sampled collaborated on a fresh product by releasing an extended version of the track, accompanied by a new music video. The video was disjointed from the music, because the footage and a few of the samples had been repurposed (or, arguably, remixed) from an earlier video of El Alfa, El Jefe, and Anuel AA's significant hit 'Con Silenciador' from 2018, which itself had achieved more than 67 million views.[52]

The short video for the remixed 'CoronaVirus' fused much of the standard imagery of dembow videos with the new remixed soundtrack and a sample of laughter from 'Con Silenciador'. Anuel's cry of anger, despair, and frustration was transformed into something entirely new. The remix video, which features Anuel's friend and collaborator El Alfa, becomes a poignant vehicle for articulating masculinity and presenting a distinct expressive style in what Alfredo Nieves Moreno calls the 'barriocentric macho'.[53] In this version, Anuel is no longer crying out in despair on his balcony. Instead, to the sound of Jamz Turn Me Up's coronavirus remix, he and El Alfa gleefully flash money, display their gold jewelry, throw hand signals in a dark, smoky, studio- or strip club-like atmosphere, and sit in or pose next to sports cars. They each raise their middle finger in pure male defiance, a common move in dembow videos. All these scenes were interspliced with shots of three different women posing or dancing perreo, a form of twerking. It was as if the pandemic terrors could not penetrate the *puro party* ethos of dembow. Unlike many examples of the newly emerging música del coronavirus, there were no other symbolic references to the pandemic that inspired the original shout. There were no cartoon coronaviruses, coughing sounds, references to toilet paper shortages, mask props, or any other similar early pandemic tropes.[54] Nonetheless, the remixed repetition of the word 'coronavirus', and the core, desperate timbre and internal rhythms of Anuel AA's original vocal sample combined into an intensifying rhythm. There were no questions for the listener. For Anuel AA, as for Cardi B, the shit was getting real.

Anuel AA remixed his remix again with Jhon Bredy on 21 March 2020. This version changes the initial shout '*¡maldito coronavirus!*' in significant ways from both his earliest shouted posting and the first remix. The new version retains the persistent, repetitive echoes of that original remix, but adds additional lyrics and Jhon Bredy's own interpretation of the original shouted phrase. This re-remix is decidedly more menacing in tone, reflecting the emerging realities of the pandemic. It utilizes a trap-infused rhythm layered atop a sonic bed of cries, screams, and eerie electronic noise. The song functions to express a new frustration and anger at six months of a pandemic that nobody anticipated, let alone expected to last so long. This remix was only posted on Anuel AA's official channel on 30 September 2020, half a year after the initial remix, and had gained a miniscule 862 views by November 2021, more than year after its release. On Jhon Bredy's channel it earned a more robust, but still pauce, 11,000 views.[55]

Cardi B's and Anuel AA's initial remixes captured the zeitgeist of the early pandemic moment across the Caribbean musical diaspora in the United States and beyond. They tapped into the emotionally resonant logics of the broader global remix culture that flourished as a distinctive variant of música del coronavirus. Cardi B's potent celebrity status and viral appeal alone launched a mini-genre of remixes of DJ iMarkKeyz's original. These remixes of the remix ranged from Maki La Machete's 'Cardi B Coronavirus Dark Afro House Remix' to Jersey Club Music's 'Constantine Remix' to Tech House producer Carloh's 'Cardi B – Coronavirus (Carloh Virus Remix)', among a great many others.[56] There were a raft of dembow remixes of the original remix as well, such as DJ -O-'s 'Coronavirus dembow' remix released 23 March 2020.[57] Also released were TikTok videos of women performing pole-dancing routines to Cardi B remixes, lipsyncing videos, and many thousands of other similarly random handmade short remix clips.[58] Jas Sizzles, a professional remixer specializing largely in salacious material, released a 'clean mix' and a 'dirty mix' of 'Coronavirus (Sizzles Dembow)' in early April 2020 which combined many of the elements described throughout this chapter. Over a dembow beat and a highly processed bass line, he mixed repeated fragments of both the Cardi B rant with Anuel AA's shout layered over with a vocalized imitation of the dembow beat.[59]

Many of these remixes-of-the-remix were themselves further sampled and remixed. For example, YouTube channel 'B Cardi Shorts' reposted DJ Snake's remix on 6 October 2021, in which the popular DJ demonstrated remix techniques.[60] HPB Music remixed DJ iMarkKeyz's remix three days earlier, on 3 October.[61] Another example is Black Storm's 'Coronavirus Cardi B remix. (My version)', uploaded at the surprisingly late date of 21 October 2021 and since removed from YouTube. This video was uploaded 19 months after Cardi B's original posting and the DJ iMarkkeyz remix of it, and arguably long after the remix's own putatively viral moment had passed. Black Storm's YouTube video starts with a title card stating 'I made a Cardi B Coronavirus remix (my own version)', with no further explanation. This remix, and its video, probably as a result of being fitfully rendered and not sounding as completely realized as some others, had had a miniscule 11 views by 3 November 2021. Nonetheless, the inclusion of the phrase 'my own version' reflects the poster's need to assert authorship and originality.

The same day of Black Storm's upload, Real Life uploaded its own three-plus-minute remix 'Cardi B feat HAYASA G – Corona Virus | ✸ 2021'. This one was accompanied by an enormous block of hashtag markers in English, Spanish, Russian, Georgian, and many other languages, presumably in a bid to use Cardi B's lasting coronavirus-related influence to drive traffic to the channel, as so many remixers used the hashtags #virus, #coronavirus, #pandemia, #cuaraentena, and #COVID to attract as many clicks as possible.[62] DJ SΔM, of Dharavi, India, released a fresh remix of the DJ iMarkKeyz remix on 4 January 2022 to a scant 60 views, being sure to drive viewers to his social media channel and to claim that the sampling for the remix was done under 'fair use'.[63] For every widely viewed and shared viral remix uploaded to a major music streaming platform and distributed globally to large audiences, there were ones like these, created for essentially no audiences and released at surprisingly late dates during the pandemic.

Neither DJ iMarkKeyz nor DJ Jamz Turn Me Up requested permission from Cardi B or Anuel AA in advance of sampling them. Rather, they followed the logics and style of remix culture by taking what they found appealing in the sound and repurposing it into a new media product for a distinct market. Remix culture also encourages tagging the sampled artists via social media in the posted remixes, in part to capture viewers and listeners from the existing audiences of the artists. Tagging serves as both an indexing system and an informal means of crediting or extending notice to a relevant party, with or without prior consent. This helps to explain why, within a day of each of the remix releases, the DJs and sampled artists were publicly in communication with one another. Cardi B is self-aware of the immense value and influence of her own personal brand, using this leverage not only to promote her lines of fashion and beauty products, but also to speak directly about issues of racial and gender-based discrimination to prominent figures, including presidential candidates in the United States during the contentious election of 2020.[64] Cardi B enthusiastically cultivates and participates in the emergent model of releasing free musical and social media content for views, likes, clicks, influence, and market share. Even a seemingly throwaway coronavirus rant on social media was immediately turned into a series of products, including a market-dominating hit song, a series of virally shared memes news stories, and a charitable effort which helped foster pandemic-era political influence.

As a figure who seems as scrupulous in image control and style as she is uncensored, Cardi B's position on remixes of her own voice signaled the potential to set a new precedent for artistic borrowing that underscored the creative potentialities of the pandemic moment. Cardi B's coronavirus rant clearly had lasting cultural power, since remixes continued to come out during the fall of 2021. Arguably the bigger cultural influence came in the models of self-affirmation represented by the proliferating pandemic-era remixes themselves, with creators such as Black Storm and DJ SΔM continuing to draw from this modality two years into the pandemic moment. Remixes proved to be renewable and ever-developing forms of self-expression even if the market dominance of Cardi B or Anuel AA was not easy to replicate.

The convergence of celebrity, social media saturation, and widespread self-isolation at this time helped to produce a recursive inner narrative of frustration and fear that became amplified in the remixed and reconstituted voices of Cardi B and Anuel AA. Themes of depersonalization and their recursive, emotive calls became familiar to those who lived through the early months of the COVID-19 pandemic.

Perhaps this phenomenon of highly influential remixed rants can be characterized as a pandemic-era manifestation of interpellation, a concept borrowed from philosopher Louis Althusser and regularly utilized by an array of cultural critics and scholars in different fields. Althusser describes interpellation as a commanded call framing a moment and situating the hearer within it as a means of replicating power relations and congealing identities. Musical interpellations do not simply reflect specific cultural moments: they produce, shape, and define them. Scholars at the intersections of sound studies, ethnomusicology, and psycholinguistics have built upon the concept of interpellation to frame questions of sonic stimuli, affect, and symbolic culture. Karen Avenburg has observed how interpellations in music work culturally with multiple and differential impacts. She argues 'music can be considered as a cultural expression with certain ideological chains, socially and historically shaped, that may interpellate social actors by their articulation with particular categories, also shaped in particular periods, to constitute identities.'[65]

As Cardi B and Anuel AA discovered by unleashing their defining shouts, interpellation works culturally with visceral power to define reality itself. These calls construct life-worlds. Rebecca Kukla argues that 'these hails are vocatives; they call out to a subject, second-personally, and call upon her to recognize herself as (already) the self she is being recognized as being, with the social identity and position she is recognized as having.' Further, 'interpellations surround us', often with pronounced gendered, racial, class, and ethnic components that Althusser did not illuminate. The interpellation is by definition authoritative.[66]

The musical interpellations signaled by Cardi B and Anuel AA (and soon picked up by a range of performers and remixers utilizing related styles) were deployed at the start of the pandemic moment. The coronavirus crisis required attention as well as immediate assessment of one's new positionality and pandemic-era identity in a radically decentered world; a novel form of intersubjectivity.[67] Sandrine Sorlin has emphasized the term 'positioning' because of 'its more dynamic rendering of meaning negotiation and position processing.'[68] The coronavirus pandemic almost instantly atomized society – forcing isolation, social distancing, personal fear, and radical self-support. Who were these selves, isolated (even trapped) suddenly at home? What was this thing assaulting global society with such totalizing force? What tied people together? How did the interpellations and music function in the pandemic era, and how might they help reconstitute sonic communities rapidly fraying under the contemporary strains? As Avenburg argues, 'popular music – any music, [...] is a cultural phenomenon that provides elements that social actors may use in the construction of collective identities.'[69]

Both Cardi B and Anuel AA demanded this exact and immediate self-constitution – that command for directed attention – with their interpellations. Anuel demanded that the world both hear and feel his call: '¡*Maldito Coronavirus!*' Cardi B demanded that the individual and the whole world community, from governments on down, wake up. 'Guess what, bitch?' Cardi B demanded, 'Coronavirus! The shit is real!' We all become Cardi B's *bitch* in this interpellation. Even the governments of the world are not free from becoming Cardi's interpellated subjects. These calls demanded individuals and systems of power listen and pay attention in the context of the utter lack of individual control produced by the COVID-19 pandemic. The interpellations disrupted the bubble of isolation and also of any notion of self-delusion. Fundamentally affirmative in nature, they linked, as France Winddance Twine and Charles A. Gallagher have discussed, the Gramscian '"pose" or "style" that is simultaneously "artificial" and "deeply felt and experienced"'.[70] The interpellative calls demanded that listeners grapple with the coronavirus. They also demanded that the *virus itself* listen to the cultural power of celebrity itself. These interpellations sought to regulate attitudes toward the virus that could otherwise trigger anxiety, disorientation, and depersonalization.

In the context of remixes of Cardi B and Anuel AA, the 'single characteristic fragment' of the interpellations being described – a snippet of the human voice, voluntarily offered through a social media profile that is at once both public and personal – became the kernel of a remix, a cultural product that is both intimately tied to and completely emergent from the original posting. Just like the spread of an actual virus, there is no teleology here; nobody knows who will fall ill next, but contagiousness implies that somebody definitely would be infected.

Relegated to domestic spaces, quarantined individuals immersed in a relentless flow of online media and music consumption were bombarded with sounded calls that reminded them of the inescapability of the coronavirus, even as they sought solace and sustained social connection. This was a sociocultural moment saturated with fear, boredom, isolation, and repetition. These remixed interpellations were reproduced and reflected in songs lyrically, in sonic markers and samples of bodily noises. Such expressions are found in the thousands of repeated, disembodied shouts of 'Coronavirus' that permeate countless remixes, constituting a web of aural remembrance. They re-emerge endlessly in viral memes and viral videos of música del coronavirus. They cross-resonate with external soundings of pandemic-related calls, whether the wail of an ambulance siren, the bark of a cough, or the sound of the word 'coronavirus' itself.

Remixers further settled these questions in novel ways by reimagining the interpellation as a product and also as a beat for themselves. John Mowitt looks to the beat as the 'experience of interpellation' or the 'sonoric event of interpellation-qua-event'. The beat is a command. He argues that 'the interpellative call strikes and moves the body, hailing it "into position"'. He notes that 'in addition to music's interpellative dimension, there is the matter of music's irreducibly percussive character [...]. We are, one might say, subject to its blows'.[71] The remixes demanded attention to the beat, not just to themselves but to the sounds, words, and cultural forms that were being remixed. The earliest pandemic-era remixes to go viral, built on the strength of two interpellative calls, demanded attention to the virus. They deployed the 'irreducibly percussive character' of the very sound of the word 'coronavirus' and its fragments 'virus' and 'viru' through the captivating mechanism of the remix. This directly shaped and changed the nature of the musical articulation and individual experiences of the pandemic situation.

Viral culture, remix culture, and the pandemic moment intersected. The shared, remixed productions of the pandemic era cannot be simplified in a reductive viral frame any more than the cumbias discussed in the next chapter. Remix is many things – it is political and playful, creative and derivative, brilliant and base. Bolter argues that 'remix is original in its notion of derivation; it reimagines the very notion of originality'.[72] Remixes demand attention and seek it at the same time; pandemic-era music videos made by individuals dominated social media space and music sharing. Further, Owen Gallagher observes that 'remix, sometimes deployed as a form of culture jamming, enables people to expose and critique corporate media using its own language' and their own platforms. Remix is an assertion of self-sovereignty, or a clawing back of mass power.[73] This seemed especially liberatory during the pandemic moment. Akane Kanai has emphasized this essential DIY aspect of remix culture, and encourages the use of Jean Burgess's term 'vernacular creativity' to describe remixed products. She notes that this amateur creative act is

> loaded with political significance. Rather than being produced by a technical elite as part of a system of mass production, amateur productions speak to the possibility of social connection, creativity, and authenticity, for people who have historically constituted part of the masses, the end of the cycle of cultural consumption, rather than the originators of culture.[74]

Música del coronavirus was produced in complex interconnection with emergent digital cultures that reflected local sounds and interests while remaining symbiotic in realization with global cultural modes.

Coronavirus Remixes and Global Viral Culture

Música del coronavirus remixes and related styles of pandemic-era música urbana emerged as local variants of transnational musical cultures buffeted by the pandemic. The beats and the viral memes of the pandemic era spawned, reflected, and responded to the shared global crisis in unpredictable and consequential ways. Compelling viral musical cultural productions emerged from these social networks with suddenly essential sociocultural functions.

One of the commonest metaphors applied to remixings is that of virality; for instance, Navas likens them to parasitical vectors which have 'mutated into different forms according to the needs of a particular culture'.[75] Limor Shifman argues that the concept of the viral should be understood as one end of a 'dynamic spectrum', with internet memes at the other. He defines the viral as 'a single cultural unit (formulated in words, image or video) that is spread by multiple agents and is viewed by many millions' and that 'may or may not have derivatives'. He contrasts a viral cultural product with 'a founder-based meme', which 'is sparked by a specific (often viral) text, video, or photo [...] followed by many versions, each viewed by fewer people'. Shifman suggests focusing on 'viral content in terms of ritual', emphasizing the 'cultural implications and role in the formation of social and political identities' and the essential utilities of 'memetic content in terms of transmission'.[76] This is useful for understanding coronavirus remixes; música del coronavirus reflects the logics of this memetic content as both an artistic approach and as a means of generating market share. Remixes especially emphasize the reuse and reimagination of the most successful artistic and popular (that is, marketable) musical pieces.

Virality also illuminates the global context, cultural embeddedness, and casual impact of remixes. Viral metaphors can be appealing because, like a biological virus which is manifest viscerally through its symptoms in spite of being invisible to the human eye, cultural products circulated via social network systems are both ubiquitous and difficult to identify. As noted by Jussi Parikka, they form part of a media ecology, having agency within interconnected and interdependent technological, political and cultural systems.[77] The origins of viral products or cultures can be defined even if the particulars of their genealogy are subsumed in hybridized forms. Fredric Jameson invokes the metaphor of a virus in describing the context of global hybridization of culture, describing how 'a single characteristic fragment is selected from one gene and inserted into another one – more or less the way a virus is implanted in a cell'. This results in a product 'which is neither the parent cell nor the donor, but which in its realization or embodiment [...] is indistinguishable from either of those, and detectable only later on, in its afterlife and its impact on the ecosystem'.[78] A key aspect of this analysis is observing the hybridized fusion into new viral forms – for our purposes this means products like mashups or remixes.

Remix culture manifested on global, content-sharing sites articulates hybridization by producing spaces of dialogic interaction between the sampled and the sampler. Remixes are an entirely different category from cover songs, and invoke a different standard of hybridization and legality, yet both can be seen as interactive.[79] Sampled artists might retain greater social capital and legal leverage than the remixers who use their sounds and beats, but the spaces are shared ones nevertheless. In these spaces, a key aim of the market-based objectives of viral spread is to dominate the platform and allow for exposure and dominance on other platforms.

Shifman identifies six essential aspects of virality in cultural products. Of these, packaging, prestige, positioning, and participation have a user-generated character readily found in examples of música del coronavirus, while the other two – positivity and humor, and provocation – drive the other components and are also key elements of the viral music discussed here.[80] YouTube is a key site of remix sourcing and production and, of course, of viral culture. Some proactive scholars have drawn from case studies to provide policy suggestions on how to reform intellectual property licensing on content-sharing network sites to encourage what is determined to be ethical remixing.[81]

In studying emergent remix processes, some turn to Murray Shafer's concept of 'schizophonia', or 'the split between an original sound and its electroacoustical transmission or reproduction'.[82] Scholarly appraisals of schizophonia, like the broader literature of sampling which has consumed it, range from enthused to confused. Vanessa Chang argues that much of the discourse surrounding the issue of sampling has been hamstrung by archaic conceptions of originality, authenticity, and artistic ownership. She argues that sampling and remixing should be assessed based on the generative nature of the process itself in producing new, cross-referential cultural products.[83] The pandemic moment provided a microcosm of this approach to hybridized musical forms.

At the same time as some musicians were jostling for likes, reposts, and overall market share, the pandemic itself created a cultural moment akin to a respite. For some musicians and DJs, the enforced pause seems to have produced, or even encouraged, sonic borrowing and related acts of musical and sonic transgression. Marcus Boon has described how 'folk cultures, which collectively are equivalent to Hardt and Negri's "multitude", are always feeling their way toward situations, events, times (Hakim Bey calls them "temporary autonomous zones") where such reappropriations are possible'. Boon argues that such transgressions of reappropriation, repurposing, copying, and sampling are not significant, 'since the taboo is imposed by particular sociopolitical regimes'.[84] The pandemic shutdowns were externally manufactured by state power in reaction to an ineffable virus. Musicians responded as artists and others have so often done, by resisting external strictures, constraints, and norms in pursuit of, at the very least, a sense of autonomy, if not outright freedom itself.

It is possible to see sonic repurposing not as a form of liberation from constraint or simply discrete music acts in 'temporary autonomous zones'. Possibly, remixing or repurposing is distorting. Steven Feld has described 'schizophonic memesis' and the reframing and reuse of estranged sounds in new contexts and musical products. He analyzes the ways in which ethnographic recordings of Central African Ba'Aka singers were sampled, reinterpreted, and decontextualized in the context of avant-garde American jazz and European electronic dance music. Feld's fundamental critique is that this process of sampling and redeployment is inherently lopsided; the Ba'Aka singers being imitated or sampled were not consulted on or involved in the reproduction of their musical approach. They were likely unaware of the ways in which their performances have been used to index external and often bizarre ideological claims.[85] Feld's promotion of dialogic editing and collaborative fieldwork relationships highlights how such linear, extractive practices, whether in sampling or remixing, can distort both the process and outcomes. In related contexts of erasure and non-collaboration, researchers have often ignored or mischaracterized the fact that, as Abigail De Kosnik argues, 'black men and queer women invented digital remix culture.'[86] These issues are especially critical in framing racialized remixing in the context of global popular music where core racial issues and sounds are not seen as 'exotic additions but as constitutive elements'.[87]

These types of legitimate critiques and concerns about unharmonious extraction of sounds from cultural context, erasures, and potentially abusive reuse are not necessarily widely shared in the remix world, or even overall in studies of musical borrowing across time, space, and culture. Mark Katz argues that 'as a form of musical borrowing, the roots of digital sampling reach back more than a millennium.' Nevertheless, every sampled sound 'is most fundamentally an act of *transformation*. A sample changes the moment it is relocated.'[88] Perhaps, in the stretched and distorted space-time of the pandemic, these concerns about borrowing or even cultural theft are even deliberately resisted and denied, just as the transformations are eagerly sought. And in many cases, living shrunk to the digital and virtual realms during the pandemic opened the appeal of reconstituting the pleasures of life from materials readily at hand.

Artists profiled in this book, from Mister Cumbia to Cardi B to the vast number of unknown remix Do-It-Yourselfers, eagerly allow (and even embrace) remixes of their own products across regional genres, virtual platforms, and markets. This 'sharing economy', so familiar in and integral to social media and technology studies, has in turn transformed the individualism of cultural production in music. Remixes join artist features on musical tracks as a ubiquitous tool of enhanced viral music marketing campaigns.[89] The process at once further commodifies the music but also, in the act of sharing and replication and freely dispersing sounds and new beats, undercuts the singularity of this commodification. Adam Arvidsson writes that the sharing economy represents a new re-embedding (à la [Karl] Polanyi) of the economy within a new social that, in turn, has been massively empowered by digital mediation and that [...] contains its market-oriented logic of value within a social logic oriented to virtue.[90]

Presumably this social logic of virtue is a community-oriented one. Musicians in turn encourage reposting remixes by others of their words, sounds, or songs on their own personal or branded channels, to highlight what alternatively could be framed as the product of cultural theft. It is not, therefore, a simple exchange. There is no single, ready determination of its impact, and it raises complex questions about the social utilities and cultural meanings of sharing, reuse, and repurposing in new contexts in the world of música del coronavirus. It raises even more questions about the concepts of sharing, originality, and copying, all of which also underscore the conceptual frameworks of viral cultures.

Theorizing a global system of sharing and replication developed an especially notable menacing quality during the COVID-19 pandemic, in which viruses, like viral cultural products, spread and challenged certainties of value, connection, and influence, just as they do power. As Moulay Driss El Maarouf, Taieb Belghazi, and Farouk El Maarouf put it in their provocative article early in the pandemic in April, 2020,

> viruses show extreme resilience with our capacity at moving fast. They constitute a force of newness, of modification, of transformation and demonstrate that our genetic identities are volatile. This transformative power of an invisible entity problematizes the narcissism of our societies.[91]

One of the more basic concepts to describe the transformations produced by the embrace of virtual communities is the rise of the sharing economy, which Lawrence Lessig early on placed firmly within the ambit of remix culture. Lessig differentiates sharing economies, wherein voluntary communities of sharing can be understood as 'thin' or 'thick' sharing economies. In the former, people make exchanges 'simply because it makes them better off or because it is an unavoidable by-product of something they otherwise want to do for purely me-regarding reasons.' He argues that in 'thick sharing economies' people's 'motivations are more complex.'[92] Certainly, we can see in remixing that the thinness or thickness of the cultural economy of the musical exchange depends on the direction of the sharing itself, and that it clearly varies widely even between individual cases. Lessig theorized (in ways later widely adopted) that the new hybrid economies have come to define internet sharing, and that communitarian service needs to be coded into the new exchanges for them to operate paradigmatically. Lessig observes, bluntly, that 'you have to keep those participating in the sharing economy happy.'[93] The source of this happiness, especially in a market order, is of course highly contested. Music is an especially critical aspect of this sharing economy's operations and conceptualizations, including at the organizational level of platformization. However, the sharing economy has also conversely and consistently 'contributed to transformations in regimes of music's value.'[94]

Sharing has a fundamental connection to the expansion of not just happiness, creativity, and sonic exchange, but of deeper developments of social cohesion, community development, and feelings (and social realities) of inclusion and community which arise from relations of nonreciprocal sharing. Sharing, in this sense, is an essential component of communitarianism. Russell Belk has explored various directions of sharing to find that 'sharing tends to be a communal act that links us to other people. It is not the only way in which we may connect with others, but it is a potentially powerful one that creates feelings of solidarity and bonding.'[95] Jenny Kennedy builds on Belk to explain the two directions for sharing: *sharing in* is 'a cultural process of community inclusion', whereas *sharing out* 'creates no social ties'. Kennedy adds to this understanding by observing that

> social intensification or sociability has always been a key purpose in online communities, where intellectual and affective objects are shared as well as material culture. Communities are constructed around the identities, relationships, and communicative practices of members where exchanges among members intensify social bonds.[96]

In virtual musical spaces during the pandemic era, these social connections often, in their most idealized and impactful way, produced communitarian spaces and efforts which directly met the needs of people who may not even have known how to articulate those needs. It was within this maturing hybridized system of lateral music sharing that many forms of música del coronavirus, and especially its related remix culture, flourished. Recent scholarship following and deepening Lessig's analyses has also illuminated the community-driven ethos which underscores the sharing economies, even with assertions that the new virtual community-hybridized shared spaces can be connected with longstanding, even prehistoric, communitarian efforts.[97] This book does not need to assess the *longue dureé* to observe that the pandemic moment unquestionably fostered rich and highly idiosyncratic musical and remix cultural responses to the global experience, which directly engaged the mechanisms of sharing.

Like its co-conspirator sharing, copying can be understood as fundamental to cultural life and to the complex ways people (including but not limited to musicians) organize contemporary global and interconnected societies. Marcus Boon argues that copying is pervasive in contemporary culture, yet at the same time subject to laws, restrictions, and attitudes that suggest that it is wrong [...]. The problem is that there seems to be an almost total lack of context for understanding what it means to copy, what a copy is, what the uses of copying are.

Boon equates copying with humanity: 'Copying is not just something human – it is a part of how the universe functions and manifests.'[98]

Boon's rich dissection of the lineage and meaning of copying and of participatory replication is rooted in Buddhist sensibility of the core impermanence and essencelessness of things.[99] He also details the centrality of the absence of limitation in music, arguing that 'there are an infinite number of ways of presenting, perceiving, disassembling, and reassembling objects and selves', and that 'this activity is a collective one'. The process of copying and reassembling, or remixing, within a wide connected community of users, producers, listeners, and others is itself a generative practice:

> The users of such styles know how to work with things that don't belong to them, and they realize that nothing belongs to anyone – that everything has already been done many times in the past, but that every moment is in some sense unique, and to be newly fabricated.[100]

Musicians, possibly more than most, understand the potentials and values in copying, replication, and repetition, particularly in responding to and revisiting dominant cultural forms and currently existing social realities. This is where Boon's thoughtful and provocative work helps illuminate the ways local musical responses to the pandemic moment engaged, repurposed, reimagined, and remixed global forms:

> Profoundly at home in the uncanniness of repetition, and the particular powers of digital sound manipulation, popular Afrofuturist dance musics have proliferated in the first decade of the twenty-first century, from kuduro, to dubstep, to coupé décalé, reggaetón, and cumbia – all diasporic but developed in specific locations.

These musics, he argues, 'work with industrial capitalist commodity forms, but are committed to other forms of mass production'. The productions are copies or reappropriations of existing forms, without concern that the repetition is in any sense illegitimate. This critical role of repetition as a form of remix and copying in música del coronavirus is considered below. Building on Coco Fusco's work, Boon argues for replacing the muddy or distorted concept of appropriation with that of 'depropriation', or indifference to possession. Boon describes this as 'an ethics of care that does not require ownership, that requires an ethos other than that of ownership in order for there to be caring.'[101]

Remix culture embraced depropriation as an essential modality. If anything, the pandemic moment seemed to intensify the transgressive indifference of many musicians. Along with time, health, social interaction, and the ability to plan for the future fractured and disrupted, many other certainties were suspended in the expansive and suddenly indispensable virtual spaces. The context of the pandemic also offered a readily shared reservoir of viral tropes, themes, sonic signatures, and instant memes and other iconic and potentially valuable or useful creations. The pandemic moment thus opened a dynamic moment of the true folk process for musicians, even those with an expressly commercial orientation. Faced with the utterly novel coronavirus situation, it seemed to many that the full array of sonic tools was freely available for use and reuse – rhythms, sounds, styles, and grooves.

The complex interconnection between status and reuse has been a longstanding aspect of mashup and remix cultures. Status gets conferred by positional rankings in ways both obvious and obfuscated. The power of remixes was also clearly felt in a widespread fashion by users during the pandemic who had essentially no audiences. These users/remixers attained what is seemingly an internalized status, merely claiming, via remixes, proximity to cultural power. 'Reputations in mash-up culture depend to some extent on the capacity to produce "listenable" works, but displaying taste through listening and commenting on remixes made by others is also extremely important', John Shiga argued about the mashup era of the early 2000s.[102] He observes that what has developed is

> disregard for aesthetic values and notions of originality that developed [originally] around professional remixing during the 1990s. This defection from DJ culture's mode of validating remix work [...] is highly suggestive of the extent to which professional DJ culture has become the 'subcultural Other' or 'the mainstream' against which amateur remix culture defines itself. The emergence of mash-up culture is in this sense a backlash against the cultural authority of professional DJs.[103]

Remixers freely used the viral elements of música del coronavirus to create their own versions during the pandemic, often built on established and highly realized genres like dembow and cumbia, or on DIY handcrafted styles that ranged quite widely in their realization.

A certain amount of DJ status (and streams) could be claimed merely by laying claim to the pandemic moment itself for one's remix. A great many remixes were created and released to varying audience sizes, which invoked the pandemic in name as their mode of release. Sqrwiel released its 'Pandemia Mix 2020', with a single repeating refrain about Facebook and impending death, on 7 April 2020. DJ Willex's 'Mix Cuarentena' was quite popular, with 20.4 million views following its release on 30 May 2020. In the fall, RoyBeat followed the model with his own 'Cuarentena DJ Mix', which was labeled with standard hashtags like '#YoMeQuedoEnCasa', '#TODOS_EN_CASA' and '#staywithme'. Fear & Lowe Remix released 'La Pandemia featuring Franke Elyse' on 25 February 2021. DJ Smith Casma's dembow 'Mix Cuarentena 2021' was released under the hashtag '#MixCuarentena' a few months later, on 3 June. There were a great number of other not purely música del coronavirus remixes posted, which were labeled 'Pandemia mix', 'la Pandemia Remix', 'El Coronavirus Remix', 'Remix Cuarentena' and similar, precisely to capitalize on this marketing language and the viral moment in all senses. Deejay JJ, from Lima, Peru, released his 'OMNICRO MIX 2021' in December 2021 and DJ Erick Orozco released his hour-long 'Omicron Session' mix on 12 January 2022. It is counter-intuitive to think of a deadly disease being the core marketing hook unless you recognize that the totemic labels of the pandemic bestowed cultural power to generic remixes.[104]

Some of the remixes took the form of cumbia remixes selling tracks. Soca was another genre which took advantage of the pandemic to sell beats, as in DJ Sweetman's 'COVID 19 HOT SOCA CHUTNEY MIX', the 'GRENADA SOCA 2021 COVID 19 EDITION MIX' from DC Mac11, and in Blazeituprecords246's 'Covid 19 Riddim 2020 Bashment Soca Instrumental', which directly solicited donations for the beats.[105]

A significant part of remix culture developed out of the credibility and reputation that comes from musical execution, successful sharing, and audience engagement rather than from some fungible notion of originality. That is, the cultural power of the remix comes from its realization online via posting and the reification of its creator in the digital hierarchy of the platform, on the virtual scales of assessment, reuse, and influence. This placement and pursuit status, like so many things in the digital world, was of course signaled by social media metrics: likes, views, repostings, remixes, and TikTok dance challenges. Indeed, social media consultants encourage creators to seek and reward remixes and reuses through collateral networks which amplify the original. The amplification effect is considered a key feature of using contemporary media platforms.[106] The exchanges of 'transnational connectivity and transcultural fabric' are so profound, argues Carla J. Maier, that in some music (like reggaetón) 'the discontinuities and multiple sites of musical production, performance, and dissemination are not the result of a former continuity of time and space, but rather constitute the very precondition of these productions.'[107]

At times, the base virality of música del coronavirus remix culture on social media bled over into the broader ecosystem of related content and other viral forms. One of the strongest examples of this tendency came in the dembow hit song 'Se Acabó la Cuarentena' ('The Quarantine's Over'), which was released by Jowell y Randy and Kiko El Crazy in the fall of 2020, to near-instant global success across social media platforms.[108] In now common fashion, the dembow song was constructed as a feature of all three artists, in order to further the viral reach of each individual. The song inspired the production of millions of short dance videos. These found particular success on the rapidly growing platform TikTok, but also were popular on YouTube, which has competitively changed some features to become more like the former.[109] Many of these dance videos, most of which are no longer than a few seconds long, originated on TikTok and Instagram Reels, but were reposted to YouTube, often as compilations. In November 2020, a channel ironically named 'no tengo canal' ('I don't have a channel') uploaded a compilation of 'Se Acabó la Cuarentena' choreographed dance videos from TikTok that received just shy of a million views within a year of its original upload.[110] Such re-posts of TikTok content proliferating on YouTube are another recursive form of viral viewseeking by remixing the subsidiary products of remixes.

This topical, catchy song seemed created for instant TikTok success. It achieved explosive growth on a platform that itself characterized the viral enthusiasms of the pandemic moment heralded by the interpellations of Cardi B and Anuel AA. In 'Se Acabó la Cuarentena', the first part of the title functioned as the core interpellative hook. This kind of introductory declaration is a common feature of dembow songs, a cry or shout preceding an intensification of sound and increase in tempo. Often, the feeling produced builds to a full release as the song hits its full velocity. The drawn-out expression of the title phrase gained the fluency of rhythm in a way highly reflective of Cardi's B's rant and Anuel AA's remixed cries.

Immediately after the song's dance challenge debuted on the site, the TikTok dance videos formed their own abbreviated physical remix of the song, recapitulating its virality in new permutations which were then themselves remixed on videos, in memes, in remix songs, and in other forms. 'Se Acabó la Cuarentena' perfectly captured the logics, pulls, commodifications, and participatory energies of the pandemic moment across Latin America and the globe, fueled by remix culture and social media like TikTok. By midway through the pandemic, TikTok had gained more than 689 million monthly users and over a billion video views daily.[111] TikTok's popularity expanded massively during the coronavirus shutdowns, particularly among a younger demographic: 69% of TikTok users at this time were under 25 years old. Many of these users actively consumed coronavirus-themed content on the platform.[112]

At least 13.3 million different video responses to 'Se Acabó la Cuarentena' were posted from a huge range of people around the globe performing the same fairly complex and fast dance routine. While many, if not most, were young women or girls, there were also many couples, young men and boys, and an indescribable array of seemingly random videos (of tools, barbequed pigs, modeling clay, and many other inanimate substances) set to the song. It is worth noting that this seemingly massive response rate was not even considered one of the top 'dance challenges' on TikTok in 2020. TikTok had become a true viral sensation during the pandemic moment, and the number of viral dance videos counted in the tens or hundreds of millions, with multiples of that in terms of views.[113] However, it does appear that 'Se Acabó la Cuarentena' was the top pandemic-related video theme on TikTok,.

The official video for 'Se Acabó la Cuarentena' was a whimsical cartoon which had 29.8 million views by the end of 2021.[114] The song also lives on in viral completeness in the ecosystem of millions of streams on other platforms, in handmade viral videos, video responses, and remixes. A version showing the lyrics has been viewed more than 16 million times; various other videos of the song many millions more. It is in the core dembow style, built around what is often (even before the pandemic) considered to be an 'infectious' beat with a viral popularity. The song starts by announcing the artists – 'Jowell! Randy! Kiko El Crazy!' – and then its title as an interpellation, accompanied by the sudden eruption of the beat. This is the *riddim*, the vernacular term for a song's defining beat and signaling a complex musical nexus of history, culture, and inspiration. Larisa Kingston Mann defines riddims as 'musical elements' that 'sonically tie together many, something hundreds, of songs in a symbolic relationship'. Development, use, and distribution of riddims is even credited for inspiring the use of sampling.[115] The dembow riddim is a fundamental 'boom-ch-boom-chick' beat which, as Wayne Marshall has described it, is inherently 'infectious'.[116] The style has gone global; Marshall writes that 'in the decade since reggaetón galloped into the mainstream, the Dembow has been Cubanized, Colombified, Peruvinated, watered-down, dressed-up and recomposed to fit a thousand new contexts.'[117] It is a beat seemingly ripe for viral utilities and remixing.

With this riddim, 'Se Acabó la Cuarentena' presents insistent and irresistible repetition about the need for the singers to get back to the street tomorrow. The chorus is repeated more than 11 times in each iteration, with an elongated delivery at a variety of pitches, which gives the song sonic depth alongside the relentless beat. The quarantine is over, the singers insist in the cloying and repeated refrain; it is time to forget about COVID. At least this was one way that wishful thinking went in the fall of 2020, and the sentiment clearly captured the imagination. A year later, in August 2021, the artists were still living on the success of the song, for example appearing at the two-day 'Se Acabo La Cuarentena Fest' [sic] at the House of Blues in Boston. And even as late as 24 December 2021, El Electroniko released a new track, unrelated to the viral hit but named (perhaps wishfully at this point during another viral surge) 'Se Acabó La Cuarentena'.[118]

The first section of the song seems constructed perfectly for the brief 15-second TikTok videos, which themselves formed a kind of viral currency during the pandemic.[119] Viral dance crazes for songs, especially on TikTok, are now often essential for artists and consumers alike 'to remain culturally relevant and in the know' and to gain market share rapidly.[120] One of the key aspects of a successful TikTok dance is that, like any good meme or viral product, it is accessible and endlessly reproducible. TikTok is also built to be participatory. As an accomplished dancer found in creating her own viral videos for the app, 'a perfect balance for TikTok dance virality' is 'something eye-catching and rhythmically satisfying but still accessible, not outside the reach of amateur dancers'.[121]

Another issue essential to consider in relation to pandemic-era TikTok dance videos is the evident sexualization of the content in these viral dances. Female sexuality is a central feature of the social media channel, an element which was enhanced and deepened during the pandemic explosion in popularity. As Melanie Kennedy observes:

> The phenomenal rise in TikTok's cultural visibility during the coronavirus crisis can be seen to contribute to the transformation of girls' 'bedroom culture' from a space previously conceptualised as private and safe from judgement, to one of public visibility, surveillance and evaluation. TikTok facilitates – indeed invites and rewards, via the logic of its metrics – the viral spectacle of girls' bedroom culture.

Further, 'so-called silly, unashamed and unfiltered girlhood on TikTok […] is highly constructed, and its characteristics restricted to a narrow set of gendered, racialised, classed and sexualized ideals'.[122] The 'Se Acabó la Cuarentena' dance borrowed heavily from existing tropes of sexually charged dembow videos, with body popping, twerking, body caresses, and other sexualized moves, but was also rendered innocent enough to be performed by a diverse array of users. At all times, though, as numerous videos revealed, it could easily be sexualized in the contradictory ways characteristic of many TikTok dance videos.[123]

The 'Se Acabó la Cuarentena' dance was inseparable from the ways TikTok is constructed as a platform. The matching, easily learnable, viral dance moves created for the song were tailormade for TikTok use and for viral explosion. However, the dance itself was not in the original video. One of the principal popularizers of the dance was viral dance and internet celebrity Alexity, owner of the YouTube channel 'Alexia's World', which had over a 1.1 billion views as of fall 2021, as well as additional channels on Instagram and other sites. Alexity released a version of the dance in November 2020 which garnered 10.5 million views. She later created an instructional video on how to dance '*la canción del momento de TIK TOK*'.[124] This also set the stage for using the song in numerous other dance videos, many of which were marketed as dance hall or Zumba exercises. There were innumerable TikTok versions by women, teens, and children from across the entire globe, and new versions were added throughout fall 2021.[125]

'Se Acabó la Cuarentena' is also the focus of a large number of remixes posted without elaborate videos beyond a simple slide show or a static image.[126] The song was already so powerful and widespread as a meme that many remixes consisted of setting the song to new footage or in mixing in other dembow songs to create essentially long dance mixes rather than proper remixes, such as one by Christian Crisóstomo.[127] Others creatively made it into house, EDM, guaracha, tribal, house, and other styles.[128]

The meaning and impact of this massive explosion in use and ubiquity of social media during the pandemic moment continues to be explored. TikTok in particular has been recognized as a tool used by young people for 'self-document[ing]' during the pandemic. However, while according to one recent study social media use could improve 'subjective well-being by improving social capital and feelings of connectedness', it was also found that 'actively and passively using TikTok was not associated with well-being, and [...] social support and upward social comparison did not appear to play a meditational role between TikTok use and well-being.'[129] The study, though, was not concerned with coronavirus-themed dance videos specifically. Research remains to be done on the social value of these during the pandemic moment, and whether the experience of viral dance videos or remixes in the pandemic uploaded to the sites had a wellbeing effect such as we have observed in other genres of music during the pandemic moment, as described elsewhere in this book.

Corona-Rona-Rona-Rona-Rona-Rona-Rona – Coronavirus!

The vast ecosystem of producers and consumers of música del coronavirus relied heavily on repetition as one of its most dominant modes. This repetition reflected pre-existing elements of certain music styles, but also was employed intentionally in new, pandemic-specific ways. Repetition in music takes a variety of forms, ranging from copying via sampling to the more plastic ways in which themes are re-explored and motifs expressed. In speech as well as in music, repetition is one of the most common characteristics found across cultures and timespans, used variably as a technique for building tension, for inducing trance states, or for ensuing that a central theme is firmly established in the mind of the listener.[130]

Remix culture must be understood in this context of repetition, itself a highly constitutive, recursive, and contingent concept. Remixing has been widely written about in terms of flow, flux, reuse, appropriation, and reappropriation, all of which reflect the core attribute of repetition. Bolter argues that 'remix culture is therefore flow culture. Remix is repetitive and iterative. The repetition occurs either within a single remix [...] or within a genre [...]. Successful videos are generative; they become memes.'[131] Repetition underlies virality as well, as it allows for 'successful replication.'[132] It is what allows the listener to get the music, and in the context of COVID-19 to grab ahold of a source of meaning in a pandemic which has challenged all manner of certainties.

The repetition of the unavoidable words 'coronavirus', 'virus', 'COVID-19', and 'cuarentena' reflect and echo the relentless repetition of daily experience of the early pandemic lockdowns. Luis Zara's 'El coronavirus dembow' sings directly about the early lockdowns, and repeats the name of the virus in a laconic, flat delivery six or eight times as a chorus throughout the song, to underscore the repetitive experience.[133] The menacing and slightly disorienting 'El Dembow del Corona Virus' of Kevin B. 'El negrote' starts with a cough and immediately launches into 15 repetitions of the word 'coronavirus' punctuated by two beats. The song presents the sound of the virus's name as a bludgeon on the listener and her life.[134] DJ Dance Nicaragua (Cristopher Alexander Muñoz Gutiérrez) starts his 'Coronavirus' dembow with a cough and then a blistering fast-paced expression of the title in bursts of 13 repetitions, followed by a slightly slower burst of another 13 iterations. In a song of just under two minutes the word 'coronavirus' is delivered over 80 times.[135]

The words 'coronavirus' or 'COVID-19' also function significantly as an interpellative call which directs all subsequent listening, and its repetition underscored the pandemic moment and the liberation from it signaled in the music. The power of the invocation was aided rhythmically by the dropping of the 's' at the end of the word 'virus', allowing for a punchy and quick repeated sound in songs that even without autotuning readily blend into a flow.

A good example of this is in one of the earliest and more repetitive dembows, released on a small YouTube channel called Ayendy90, which posted 'El coronavirus' on 6 February 2020. Kicking along at 120 beats per minute, the song has an initial chorus with the fragment of the title word 'viru' repeated a thrilling 60 times, first in of between one and six beat groupings and then articulated in a single flow 34 times, allowing for other words to be repeated over the base. The initial repetition gives way to an unstoppable flood of sound, mimicking an ever-replicating viral fragment.[136] The repetition of this song stood out in contrast to less-repetitive, more generic dembow songs like Danniloox's 'Corona virus 2020' or 'Coronavirus Dembow' from El Dubi, Tito Tijuana, Lucky Luciano, El Feka, Fido Dido, and Pikolin. These songs had repetitive choruses in ways similar to other dembow songs. Danniloox sings most verses three times, and in the chorus sings the full word 'coronavirus' four times, followed by bursts of just the first half of the word ('corona') in groups of three.[137] El Dubi and his collaborators use the fragment at the end of word 'coronavirus' in groups of six times during the chorus.[138]

Repetition is not simply a common characteristic found throughout coronavirus remixes; it is a defining component of the form that affords it much of its rhetorical, musical, and psychological power. In his 2 min 35 sec-long remix, DJ iMarkKeyz's sampled Cardi B saying 'coronavirus' 69 times, averaging slightly over one utterance per every two seconds.[139] The official video of Jamz Turn Me Up's 'CoronaVirus' remix likewise contains 97 instances of Anuel AA saying all or part of the word 'coronavirus'.[140] Similar very repetitive patterns followed in subsequent dembow songs, which began to be released in a torrent in February and especially March 2020.[141] Monkey White's 'Corona Virus', recorded in Cali, Colombia and released 20 March 2020, is a track built on heavy repetition of every syllable of the title word and especially the end of the word. The song builds through repetition to draw the sound of 'viru' into an abstracted flow rhythm of 20 repetitions punctuated with cries, spoken word, rapped verses invoking anti-Chinese sentiment, and typical early-pandemic tropes, along with bodily sounds and monkey noises.[142]

Repetition helps to drive listeners deeper into the songs, to become enveloped by them in a total experience. On a dance floor, the style works to propel motion. In the isolated pandemic context, the highly repetitive songs underscore the experience of the listener and create a tension between the pleasure and pleasurable memories produced by the music and the realities of quarantine and social isolation, the endless present so often invoked in coronavirus songs. Jerrold Levinson describes this kind of repetition and absorption in his defense of concatenationism.[143]

It might seem odd to apply this concept, more usually associated with art and experimental music, to the relentless tempos and street-level cultures of dembow. However, to dembow listeners it is arguably this critical, internally focused and self-contained rhythm that matters. Levinson writes that 'a comprehending listener is conscious of motion, direction, force, tension [...]. But his attention is not necessarily drawn to anything remote from the sounding present.'[144] The listener is absorbed by repetition, ensnared by the dembow rhythm. She gets it, just as Levinson described in other contexts. Pete Kivy observes, not supportively, that Levinson's argument is 'emotive properties are local properties not global ones'.[145] Repetition is strikingly common internally within genres of música del coronavirus with a regional focus. It is one of the aspects of this body of music that allowed it to capture and characterize the individualized experiences of the global pandemic in systemic ways reflected in the response of listeners.

Elizabeth Hellmuth Margulis has illuminated a wide range of distinct styles of repetition across music styles (although without reference to Latin America), with a keen insight into the impact of music individually internalized through its use. She argues that repetition 'can provide the scaffolding for a participatory experience' in listeners. This 'extended subjectivity of the thinking-along-with' allows music to 'seem to emerge both out of the world and out of your own imagination', which she ties in with the distinctive pleasures of repetition.'[146] The most indelible música del coronavirus drove this erasure of self and music, just as it reflected the congruent liquification of space and time of the pandemic moment. It resonated emotionally because these artists understood how to demand and hold listeners' attention. In this sense, repetition operated separately from the frameworks of virality discussed above.

Simonelmono's popular 'CORONA VIRUS', released 2 March 2020 and with over 6.4 million views by the end of 2021, was built around a repeated chanted intoning and echoing of the words 'COVID-19' contrasted with trap-style rapping in between. He utilized exactly the same model for his song on the Russian coronavirus vaccine, 'SPUTNIK V', and in the several other remixes he made of his own songs and released throughout 2020. His song 'MAÑANA NO HAY CLASES' is his most repetitive, simply repeating the title phrase over and over while text in the video urges listeners to wash their hands and take other precautions.[147] Simonelmono's approach is to make viral-style YouTube- and Instagram-ready videos. As with the remixers, repetition was utilized as the core component of the market success of the music, which is rendered more legible (fluent) to the listeners through consistent repetition.[148]

Other examples of música del coronavirus that do not explicitly draw on external sampling still reflect a similar eagerness to utilize repetition. Teenaged Mexican YouTuber Lapizin Bunny's comical dembow-style track 'Coronavirus' features 77 repetitions of the words 'corona', 'virus', and 'coronavirus' at 116 beats per minute, and has grabbed more than 15 million views since it premiered on 20 March 2020.[149] A popular dembow track by the Dominican artist Yofrangel likewise was built around 56 repetitions of the words 'corona', 'coronavirus', and the rhythmic fragment '-rona-', with a repetitive moaning cry underscoring the repetition of this last syllable. The music video, which features Yofrangel as a respirator-bound character singing from a hospital bed, earned more than 13 million views by the end of 2021. In fact, Yofrangel used repetition so powerfully that he played with the expectations for continuous repetitions in the final chorus of the song, which he choose to not complete with a repeated phrase, instead ending on a clip of spoken conversation that surprises the listener with its abruptness. Yofrangel often ends his songs in this way, but in the 'CORONA VIRUS' video the end of the song, and thus the end of the repetition, was represented by the 'death' of the singer. The end of repetition signaled death, just as the end of repetition in a typical Yofrangel track signaled the end of the party, the end of the drug supply, the end of sex, or a similar common dembow theme.[150]

A hallmark of heavily repetitious dembow tracks from the pandemic moment is their use of the core aspects of the style. Dembow riddim projects authority as a kind of Dominican musical sovereignty, and builds propulsive energy while also underscoring humor and a sense of comic musical dominance over the threatening virus. Yofrangel, who identifies as an 'artista urbano', releases popular music at a steady and productive clip, but he is not a quick-hit writer who generally reflects on current events to get viral hits. Yofrangel draws on market-dominating dembow tropes like twerking women, partying, and sports cars, while retaining an idiosyncratic and firmly rooted performance approach. He delivers often-zany lyrics in a very rapid, high-pitched, exaggerated style which might seem to preclude a wider audience, a defiant challenge to wide market appeal. As Dara E. Goldman notes:

> A singing style, register, or affectation that is somehow 'out of tune' disrupts the dominant flow of the music; in doing so, moreover, it interrogates the packaging that is generally consumed uncritically in established listening practices – especially those associated with mass cultural forms.[151]

Dembow, as a function of its distinctiveness and influence, has eschewed many of the norming elements of sonic virality even as it seeks market dominance and has influenced music all over the world. Of course, dembow performers also utilize other aspects which drive virality, especially explicitly sexual themes in lyrics and videos.[152] Undoubtedly part of dembow's singularity is a strident sound that pulls in a transnational audience drawn to its largely unvarnished style compared with reggaetón.[153] What Jenzia Burogs wrote about dembow pioneer Pablo Piddy can apply to Yofrangel: 'It's borderline assaultive, but that's the point [...]. There's nothing more real than a beat that won't let up.'[154] The insistence and undeniable propulsiveness of this style signal a lack of interest in seeking accommodation with less distinct but more widespread sounds of global popular music coming from Latin America, even as the dembow style has spread globally. Marshall observes that 'the evolution of dembow into a unique and somewhat inaccessible music' was due to 'its intensity and weirdness: the density of samples, the rapid tempos, the rough, repetitive refrains'. He argues that 'Dominican producers seemed content to pitch their music to Dominican tastes, raised on breakneck merengue, and [...] this made the music, by some measures, quite strange to outside ears and perhaps so esoteric as to resist further popularization, never mind appropriation.'[155] Yet the rhythm became widely imitated around the globe. Marshall has tracked how 'dembow has spread its distinctive boom-ch-boom-chick to glossy Latin pop, raw electro-chaabi in Egypt, transnational moombahton and Indonesian dangdut seksi, to name a few.'[156] It is an interesting crossroads – dembow is deeply local and highly realized, but also globally influential due to viral media platforms; this was especially so during a pandemic moment where the riddim was so effectively utilized to capture the moment.

Unlike many dembow stars, Yofrangel utilized his popularity and his unique musical approach to make unapologetically powerful statements about the coronavirus. He committed seriously, both as a professional and as an individual, to getting the coronavirus message out with his irresistible music. Yofrangel released a series of five coronavirus songs starting with his largest hit 'CORONA VIRUS', which was released quite early in the pandemic moment on 9 February 2020. This initial video release came with a written plea (in English and Spanish) to '😷🏠 Please stay safe at home / Por favor mantengase a salvo en casa #Cuarentena. I Love You All ♥'.[157] The bilingualism of his announcements reflected Yofrangel's transnational fan base, although he sings exclusively in Spanish. In his third video, he even put in the comments a plea to 'comenta Con Tu Bandera / Put your flag on the comments!!', to gauge the international audience of the videos.[158] He followed up his initial hit with 'CORONA VIRUS 2 #LaCuarentena' a few weeks later, on 27 March. This song was released with another explicit explanation of his purpose in encouraging people to be safe during the pandemic. Yofrangel declared that 'the Purpose of this song is to recommend everyone to stay home in quarantine in a funny way. This Corona Virus Situation is completely serious. Please pay attention to all tips-recommendations from your local authorities and health organizations'.[159]

There was a large topical difference between the two songs, even though the style was based on the same dembow beat and extreme lyrical and syllabic repetition. In the second song, Yofrangel switched from focusing on the biological danger of the virus to the social challenge of quarantine. The chorus of 'CORONA VIRUS 2 #LaCuarentena' was a repeated refrain of the first syllable of the Spanish cuarentena, in which this round syllable was repeated 24 times over a repeated moaning cry, similar to the first song. In 'El Antidoto', released two weeks later on 10 April, Yofrangel repeated the chorus rapidly 32 times alongside the constant repetition of the title as a refrain. The same approach was applied to his two dembows about the coronavirus vaccine. In 'La Vacuna', which premiered on 24 February 2021, the chorus merged into a constantly repeated, minimally vocalized stream of sound (a technique often utilized in dembow), and again stuck to a pattern of 32 repetitions of the phrase, coupled with other grouped and repeated phrases.[160] This style of dembow repetition is related to flow in terms of pulse, speed, and texture. Ben Duinker notes 'the way rhyme, syntax, narrativity, rhythm, and breathing generate segmentation markers that influence listeners' perceptual organization of flow into phrases: passages that contain beginning and end points as well as a sense of directed motion throughout.'[161] Yofrangel used exactly the same pattern again in his song celebrating the freedom provided by vaccination cards, called 'Yofrangel – Y Tu Tarjeta De Vacunacion'.[162] This song presents Yofrangel rapping his signature repetitive verses and choruses by blending interpellative shouts into the beats. Each section is built around a single phrase repeated four times, followed by 12 repetitions of a portion of the verses as a chorus. The effectiveness of this approach is easy to grasp when the song's featured artist, named Negro 12, presents a different, slightly more lagging style of repetition in a lower pitch.

Compared to other dembow music videos of the same time period, Yofrangel downplayed sexual themes in most of his distinctive series of coronavirus songs. One viewer named Lean Miño noted (to 278 likes) in the comments attached to the first 'CORONA VIRUS' song, '0% Mujeres/0% sexo/ 0% droga/ 100% coronavirus 🌎'.[163] Where the repetitive beat and sounds of dembow often have sonically driven and recapitulated sexualized dancing like perrero (twerking) or even represented the sex act itself, in these songs the repetition drove an alternative method or grappling with the pandemic moment.

Dembow musician and comedian Kaseeno grappled with sex in his highly repetitive dembow remix of Mister Cumbia's 'Pandemia', released 19 April 2020. He sang about the dangers of the of the virus and the worldwide quarantine and the pandemic. He repeated the slow-to-pronounce three-syllable title name 24 times as a chorus, and then treated viewers of his video to a one-minute view of him smoking marijuana through a gasmask.[164] His own 'Coronavirus' song, released on 15 March 2020, featured a video of him eating bat soup, being vaccinated by scantily clad, twerking nurses, and other putatively comical scenes, based around dozens of repetitions of the title word and repeated expressions of danger.[165]

In 'El Corona Virus', a powerfully voiced older woman named Negra Flow and a teenaged singer named Kevin Vin created one of the more memorable and repetitious dembow coronavirus songs.[166] The song has a skeletal but insistent dembow beat with two drums, and is entirely driven by hoarsely rapped, repetitive verses built around four- and eight-beat repeated phrases. Released 25 March 2020, the song and video presented the singers urging people repetitively to wash their hands and prepare for the pandemic. It rapidly gained 1.3 million views on YouTube. Like Yofrangel, Negra Flow and Kevin Vin used an idiosyncratic style of dembow to address the pandemic, although they have an even smaller platform and audience via Brilla Records of the Dominican Republic. One essential aspect of Negra Flow's power is her positionality in the music, not just as a woman, but as a self-evidently strong, older mature woman who fills a commanding role of at once band leader, mother figure, singer, and matriarch. She also inhabits humorous musical videos and shorts.[167] In the video of 'El Corona Virus' she wears a shirt with a drawing of herself, and she uses her own name as the interpellation to frame the song and the pandemic moment. She is the matriarch of a group of young male dembow musicians – including her grandson – who started out singing highly repetitious songs on quotidian subjects that garnered millions of views, such as their viral hits 'Fornite' and 'Pan y Leche'. As the boys have aged, their music has begun to include typical tropes like twerking girls on Dominican street corners and vehicles.[168] Most consistent in all the music is hundreds of repetitions in each song. Another group of highly productive child dembow singers from the Dominican Republic is called the Miradita Family. They specialize in repetitive pieces, and atypically released a maudlin, autotuned slow dembow called 'Mensaje A La Sociedad' to mark the COVID pandemic.[169]

The types of musical repetition found throughout coronavirus remixes are not incidental – they are in direct dialogue with the experiences of totalizing monotony, lusted-over escapism, and deep anxiety that characterized the pandemic moment. In his study of the concept of repetition, Gilles Deleuze comments on how although recurring experiences 'repeat an "unrepeatable"', they 'do not add a second and a third time to the first, but carry the first time to the "nth" power.'[170] Living through the global quarantine of the early pandemic moment involved reenactment of the day before, with mornings blurring into evenings and moments blurring into perpetuities. It produced a hyperawareness as the recurrence of daily ritual subsumed space and time once occupied by variation and novelty. One listener to Yofrangel's 'CORONA VIRUS' commented: 'Hahaha this music makes me remember the first days of the quarantine haha' (*'Jajaja esta música me hace recordar alos primeros días de la cuarentena jaja'*). Another commented a year after its release that 'I get some many early quarantine memories from this' [sic], while another mused, to some amusement from other commentators, 'Rest of the world: We are currently in a pandemic that will drastically change our way of living. Dominicans:____' – the blank space implying that the Dominican answer to the quarantine and all the fear was creativity, exuberance, and a determined continuation of the *gozadera* lifestyle.[171]

In the context of the pandemic moment, repetition did more than reflect and reaffirm the tedium of life in lockdown or the draw of a party. DJ Jamz Turn Me Up, creator of the original Anuel AA remix, repurposed audio from rapper Tory Lanez's Instagram Live 'quarantine radio show' into a dembow remix that repeated the name of the show and cut into other phrases with a relentless and intrusive sample of Lanez saying 'quarantine', as if the reality of the shutdowns necessarily had to intrude on all the sonic and psychological space of the remix.[172] This was one of the paradoxes of the pandemic moment, which for many was a time of musical creativity and excitement and for others a time of profound sameness in the private sphere accompanied by a sense of danger in the wider world. To speak of monotony as the defining characteristic of one's pandemic experience signals a certain privilege of having remained relatively insulated from the effects of the virus itself. For those who worked in the healthcare sector, lost loved ones to the disease, or came down with a grave case themselves, repetitions of 'coronavirus' resonated differently. Ultimately, regardless of how they resonated, these repetitions – informed by musical style and inspired by the crisis – represented dramatic and powerful interpellations of lived experience during the pandemic moment.

Notes

1. @iamcardib, 'Ya keep playing I'm deadass FUCKIN SCARED. I'm stocking up on food', Instagram, 10 March 2020 (https://www.instagram.com/p/B9kvv79AAUw/?hl=en, accessed 24 April 2021).
2. She later mollified the Chinese so they would not be offended by her comments and, one assumes, so that the massive market there would not be closed to her music. Instagram is not available in China, but her rant was nevertheless widely shared. Cardi B said on a livefeed on Instagram, 'Ask yourself, do you really want smoke with China?

First of all, a lot of people owe money to China because they do everything' ('Cardi B Instagram Live Talking Corona Virus and Harvey Weinstein', https://www.youtube.com/watch?v=3_D-MbIcOEQ [accessed 11 November 2021]); see also Jiayun Feng, '"I Want No Smoke with the Chinese": Cardi B Wins Fans in China with Coronavirus Rants', *SupChina*, 26 March 2020, https://supchina.com/2020/03/26/i-want-no-smoke-with-the-chinese-cardi-b-wins-fans-in-china-with-coronavirus-rants/ (accessed 11 November 2021).

3. Cardi B's post was also posted on YouTube in its entirety on several different channels such as on *Entertainment Tonight*'s channel as 'Watch Cardi B FREAK OUT Over Health and Safety', https://www.youtube.com/watch?v=7M9_0pjW1GE (accessed 12 October 2021), which had 4.9 million views by October, 2021; see also 'Coronavirus remix.Cardi B', https://www.tiktok.com/music/Coronavirus-remixCardi-B-6803888652662459142 (accessed 5 November 2021).
4. Comment added to 'Cardi B Coronavirus Rant (UNEDITED!)', https://www.youtube.com/watch?v=7KIUok5PcUY (accessed 12 October 2021).
5. @anuel, 17 March 2020. No caption, https://www.instagram.com/p/B92WjGfnBUr/?utm (accessed 24 April, 2021).
6. 'Anuel AA – Maldito Coronavirus – [Official Video]', https://www.youtube.com/watch?v=nrz5KlQYkcg (accessed 12 October 2021).
7. *AJMC*, 'COVID-19 Roundup: Coronavirus Now a National Emergency, With Plans to Increase Testing', 13 March 2020, https://www.ajmc.com/view/covid19-roundup2 (accessed 6 February 2022).
8. Cardi B Official Website, 'Cardi B Bio', https://www.cardibofficial.com/bio (accessed 9 October 2021); Paul Simpson, 'Anuel AA Biography, Songs, & Albums', *AllMusic*, https://www.allmusic.com/artist/anuel-aa-mn0003551236/biography (accessed 9 October 2021).
9. On the interconnection of these styles, see Petra R. Rivera-Rideau, *Remixing Reggaetón: The Cultural Politics of Race in Puerto Rico* (Durham, NC: Duke University Press, 2015), pp. 130–58.
10. 'Fat Joe, Cardi B, Anuel AA – YES (Official Video) ft. Dre', https://www.youtube.com/watch?v=mwwvOwhNF6M (accessed 12 October 2021); see also *Vibe*, 'Watch Fat Joe's 'Yes' Video Feat. Cardi B And Anuel AA', *Vibe*, 7 October 2019, https://www.vibe.com/music/videos/fat-joes-yes-cardi-b-anuel-aa-665966/ (accessed 1 July 2022); Suzy Exposito, 'Fat Joe, Cardi B, Anuel AA Team Up on Scorching New Song "Yes"', *Rolling Stone*, 6 September 2019, https://www.rollingstone.com/music/music-latin/cardi-b-anuel-aa-fat-joe-new-song-yes-listen-880624/ (accessed 5 January 2022). 'Anuel AA, Daddy Yankee, Karol G, Ozuna & J Balvin – China (Video Oficial)', https://www.youtube.com/watch?v=0VR3dfZf9Yg (accessed 5 January 2022) has 1.8 billion views.
11. Kiko Martinez, 'Cardi B Becomes First Female Rapper With Multiple Diamond Tracks', *Remezcla*, 1 December 2021 (accessed 2 December 2021); Glennisha Morgan, 'Cardi B Becomes RIAA's Most Certified Woman Rapper, Surpassing Nicki Minaj', *V101.9*, https://v1019.com/2019/09/06/cardi-b-becomes-riaa-most-certified-woman-rapper-surpassing-nicki-minaj/ (accessed 14 March 2021).
12. Janice Llamoca, 'Meet Anuel AA, the Viral Boricua MC Building a Hip-Hop Empire From Prison', *Remezcla*, 9 August 2016, https://remezcla.com/features/music/anuel-aa-profile/ (accessed 5 January 2022).
13. Anuel AA YouTube channel, https://www.youtube.com/c/AnuelAA (accessed 15 January 2022); Anuel AA Instagram broadcast channel, https://www.instagram.com/anuel/?hl=en (accessed 15 January 2022).
14. 'Anuel AA – Leyenda (Video Oficial)', https://www.youtube.com/watch?v=A9QH16GPEdw (accessed 9 October 2021). A year later, in September 2022, this last video was at over 71 million views. See *Hispanically Yours*, 'Anuel AA's "Emmanuel" Debuts at No. 1 on Billboard's Top Latin Albums & Latin Rhythm Albums

Charts', 9 June 2020, https://www.hispanicallyyours.com/anuel-aas-emmanuel-debuts-at-no-1-on-billboards-top-latin-albums-latin-rhythm-albums-charts/ (accessed 5 January 2022); Leila Cobo, 'Rise Interrupted: Latin Trap Star Anuel AA was on the Cusp of Stardom when He Began a 30-Month Prison Sentence. in His First Post-Release Interview, He Describes How He Held On', *Billboard* 130.18 (2018): 33; Leila Cobo, 'Super Smash Bros: Anuel AA and Ozun Revitalized Reggaetón and Forged New Paths for Independent-Minded Artists with Major-Label Visions. With a New Collaborative Album, They're Aiming Even Higher', *Billboard* 133.1 (2021): 46.
15. Tim Ingham, 'The Three Biggest Myths Deluding the Modern Music Business', *Rolling Stone*, 26 January 2021, https://www.rollingstone.com/pro/features/the-three-biggest-myths-deluding-the-modern-music-business-tim-1119106/ (accessed 7 January 2022); Andrew Hutchinson, 'YouTube Underlines Its Value for Musicians as TikTok Continues to Rise', *SocialMediaToday*, 2 June 2021, https://www.socialmediatoday.com/news/youtube-underlines-its-value-for-musicians-as-tiktok-continues-to-rise/601179/ (accessed 3 June 2021).
16. Jay D. Bolter, *The Digital Plenitude: The Decline of Elite Culture and the Rise of New Media* (Cambridge, MA: MIT Press, 2019), p. 135.
17. 'Music cultures present a problem for anyone who thinks that twentieth century culture can be summed up neatly by a division between professionals and amateurs' (Margie Borschke, 'Rethinking the Rhetoric of Remix', *Media International Australia* 141.1 [2011]: 17–25, p. 23).
18. Irina Cvijanovic, 'Performing Sound of the Past: Remix in Electronic Dance Music Culture', *Muzikologija* 17 (2014): 87–104, p. 91.
19. The taxonomic jargon around remix is fraught, as Plaut made clear in his critique of the concept of 'produsage': '[Axel] Bruns's contribution of the term "produsage" is a useful provocation but is a bit misattuned to etymological and vernacular context: "Produce" originates in the idea of extending, developing, bringing forth and into being; "user," however, is often a dirty word, as users of drugs and lovers. In Silicon Valley the term is sometimes invoked diminutively, with mere "users" dismissed as the ignorant other of digerati such as hackers' – Ethan R. Plaut, 'Enlightenment, the Remix: Transparency as a DJ's Trick of Seeing Everyone from Nowhere'. *Communication, Culture & Critique* 9.2 (2016): 303–21, p. 306.
20. Michele Knobel and Colin Lankshear, 'Remix: The Art and Craft of Endless Hybridization', *Journal of Adolescent & Adult Literacy* 52.1 (2008): 22–33, p. 22; see also Lawrence Lessig, *Remix: Making Art and Commerce Thrive in the Hybrid Economy* (New York: Penguin, 2008).
21. Eduardo Navas, 'Remix', in Eduardo Navas, Owen Gallagher, and xtine burrough, *Keywords in Remix Studies* (New York: Routledge, 2018), 246–58, p. 247.
22. Eduardo Navas, 'Regressive and Reflexive Mashups in Sampling Culture', in Stefan Sonvilla-Weiss, ed., *Mashup Cultures* (New York: Springer 2010), 157–77, p. 159.
23. Knobel and Lankshear, 'Remix', p. 23.
24. Cvijanovic, 'Performing Sound', p. 91.
25. 'By putting Black, queer, and female communities at the beginning of the history of digital remix, media scholarship can contribute to a shift in the perception of these groups' relationships to new media' (Abigail De Kosnik, 'Why it Matters that Black Men and Queer Women Invented Digital Remix Culture', *JCMS: Journal of Cinema and Media Studies* 59.1 [2019]: 156–63, p. 159).
26. Ellis Jones, 'The Role of Mashup Music in Creating Web 2.0's Democratic Promise', *Convergence* 27.4 (2021): 1112–8, pp. 1123–4.
27. Aram Sinnreich, Mark Latonero, and Marissa Gluck, 'Ethics Reconfigured: How Today's Media Consumers Evaluate the Role of Creative Reappropriation', *Information, Communication & Society* 12.8 (2009): 1242–60, p. 1243.
28. Sinnreich *et al.*, 'Ethics Reconfigured', p. 1244.

29. Plaut, 'Enlightenment, the Remix', pp. 305–6. Adorno quote taken from Theodor Adorno, *Aesthetic Theory* (trans. Robert Hullot-Kentor, London: Continuum, 2002), p. 45.
30. Michael B. MacDonald, *Remix and Life Hack in Hip Hop: Towards a Critical Pedagogy of Music* (Rotterdam: Sense Publishers, 2016), pp. ix, xvi.
31. DJ iMarkKeyz, 'Stream IMarkkeyz – Coronavirus (w/ Cardi B) by IMarkkeyz #ThisIsKeezy', SoundCloud, 13 March 2020, https://soundcloud.com/imarkkeyzthisiskeezy/imarkkeyz-coronavirus-sh-is-real-w-cardi-b (accessed 12 October 2021).
32. DJ iMarkKeyz, 'IMarkkeyz – Coronavirus (Feat. Cardi B)', https://www.youtube.com/watch?v=iiYDSOQPPhY (accessed 12 October 2021).
33. Eduardo Cepeda, 'Cardi B & DJ iMarkkeyz to Donate "Coronavirus" Remix Proceeds to Those Affected by the Pandemic', *Remezcla*, 20 March 2020, https://remezcla.com/music/cardi-b-dj-imarkkeyz-donate-coronavirus-remix-proceeds-affected-pandemic/ (accessed 12 October 2021).
34. Quoted in Shirley Ju, 'Meet the DJ Who Created the Viral Cardi B Coronavirus Rant Remix', *Variety*, 26 March 2020, https://variety.com/2020/music/news/cardi-b-coronavirus-rant-remix-dj-imarkkeyz-interwew-1203545575/ (accessed 12 October 2021).
35. Cepeda, 'Cardi B & DJ iMarkkeyz'.
36. DJ iMarkKeyz, 'IMarkkeyz – Coronavirus (Feat. Cardi B)', https://www.youtube.com/watch?v=iiYDSOQPPhY (accessed 12 November 2021).
37. Lindsay Zoladz, 'How Cardi B's Off-the-Cuff Video Became a Coronavirus Anthem', *New York Times*, 17 March 2020, https://www.nytimes.com/2020/03/17/arts/music/coronavirus-cardi-b.html (accessed 12 October 2021); Jon Lewis, 'Cardi B's Coronavirus Rant Lands On Pop Charts', *NPR*, 29 March 2020, https://www.npr.org/sections/coronavirus-live-updates/2020/03/19/818524291/cardi-bs-coronavirus-rant-lands-on-pop-charts (accessed 12 November 2021).
38. Cardi B Fan Team, 8 April 2020, https://twitter.com/CardiBTeam/status/1247995879258234880; see also Heran Mamo, 'We Found 5 Very Good TikTok Videos That Use Cardi B's Coronavirus Rant', *Billboard*, 23 March 2020, https://www.billboard.com/music/rb-hip-hop/cardi-b-coronavirus-tiktoks-9340674/ (accessed 12 November 2021); Allie Gemmill, 'Cardi B's Coronavirus Speech Remix Just Became a Billboard Hit Song', *Teen Vogue*, 26 March 2020, https://www.teenvogue.com/story/cardi-b-coronavirus-speech-remix-billboard-hit-song (accessed 12 October 2021).
39. Quoted in Ju, 'Cardi B's Coronavirus Rant'; see also Samantha Hissong, 'A Coronavirus Song Featuring Cardi B's Voice is Going Viral –and May Violate Copyright Law', *Rolling Stone*, 17 March 2020, https://www.rollingstone.com/pro/news/coronavirus-viral-song-cardi-b-copyright-968695/ (accessed 12 November 2021); Zoladz, 'Cardi B's Off-the-Cuff Video'.
40. Ju, 'Cardi B's Coronavirus Rant'.
41. Cepeda, 'Cardi B & DJ iMarkkeyz'; Ju, 'Cardi B's Coronavirus Rant'.
42. Gemmill, 'Cardi B's Coronavirus Speech Remix'.
43. Zoladz, 'Cardi B's Off-the-Cuff Video'.
44. Comment by JuanitoBarrasXX added to 'IMarkkeyz – Coronavirus (Feat. Cardi B)', 2 May 2020, https://www.youtube.com/watch?v=iiYDSOQPPhY (accessed 12 October 2021).
45. For example, the compilation of responses in 'iMarkkeyz – CORONAVIRUS Feat. Cardi B (Dance Compilation) | Chop Daily', https://www.youtube.com/watch?v=I2mWBIpC96g (accessed 7 January 2021) or 'REACCIONO A LAS CANCIONES DEL CORONAVIRUS (Cardi B ,Anuel AA y mas.', https://www.youtube.com/watch?v=DAHR3nA8Sa8 (accessed 7 January 2021); 'Cardi B #CoronaVirus Remix', https://www.youtube.com/watch?v=7dH_f2gQ3jQ (accessed 7 January 2021); 'Cardi B

Coronavirus Song REACTION', https://www.youtube.com/watch?v=QbXGLqg87DI (accessed 7 January 2021).

46. Jessica Roiz, 'Karol G & Anuel AA Are Loving Cardi B's "Coronavirus Remix" & The Rapper Loves Them Right Back', *Billboard*, 20 March 2020, https://www.billboard.com/music/latin/karol-g-anuel-aa-cardi-b-coronavirus-remix-video-9339292/ (accessed 12 October 2021); Karol G later got COVID-19, but never recorded a song about it: 'Karol G Confiesa Estar Infectada de Covid-19', https://www.youtube.com/watch?v=1L70D-2nZU4 (accessed 7 January 2022).

47. 'JAMZ TURN ME UP. ANUEL AA – CORONA VIRUS DEMBOW (PROD. JAMZ), 2020', https://www.youtube.com/watch?v=QxsHYOJ00ok (accessed 15 January 2022).

48. 'Yo vi el video de Anuel en Instagram y de imediato yo me dije, eso es un dembow lol, me diverti mucho haciendo esto, hice esto en 1hora, espero que le gusten!'

49. Elideth Barrón, '"Maldito Coronavirus!" Grita Anuel AA en su balcón', *Estación 40* (blog), 18 March 2020, https://estacion40.com.py/maldito-coronavirus-grita-anuel-aa-en-su-balcon/ (accessed 12 October 2021); Daniel F. Mejia, 'Anuel AA y su ira contra el coronavirus', 18 March 2020, http://www.lafm.com.co/entretenimiento/anuel-aa-y-su-ira-contra-el-coronavirus (accessed 12 October 2021); Izabela Pecherska, '"Maldito coronavirus": Anuel AA se desahoga gritando desde el balcón', *CiberCuba*, 18 March 2020, https://www.cibercuba.com/noticias/2020-03-18-u198484-e198484-s27065-maldito-coronavirus-anuel-aa-estalla-desahoga-gritando (accessed 12 October 2021); Monica Tirado, 'Anuel AA se hace viral gracias a su remix contra el coronavirus', *HOLA!*, 19 March 2020, https://www.hola.com/us-es/celebrities/20200319flpnqkah27/anuel-aa-remix-coronavirus-viral/ (accessed 15 November 2021).

50. 'ANUEL AA – CORONA VIRUS DEMBOW (PROD. JAMZ), 2020', https://www.youtube.com/watch?v=QxsHYOJ00ok (accessed 17 December 2021).

51. 'ANUEL AA DEMBOW Maldito Coronavirus – ✖ ☺ El Violento PM (Prod. Elie Doble Filo)', https://www.youtube.com/watch?v=3qNpi9y51Os (accessed 12 October 2021).

52. 'El Alfa El Jefe Ft. Anuel AA – Con Silenciador (Video Oficial)', https://www.youtube.com/watch?v=s1r_DQzbUik (accessed 17 December 2021).

53. Alfredo Nieves Moreno, 'A Man Lives Here: Reggaetón's Hypermasculine Resident', in Raquel Z. Rivera, Wayne Marshall and Deborah Pacini Hernandez, eds, *Reggaetón* (Durham, NC: Duke University Press 2009), 252–79, p. 256.

54. 'AnuelVEVO. CoronaVirus-Anuel AA Ft El Alfa (Official Video), 2020', https://www.youtube.com/watch?v=qr3jFMvLOOE (accessed 15 November 2021).

55. 'Anuel AA – CoronaVirus Remix Feat Jhon Bredy (Official Audio)', https://www.youtube.com/watch?v=0gLBqAsdTlY (accessed 15 November 2021); 'Anuel AA X Jhon Bredy X Mpm en el Track (Maldito Corona Virus)', https://www.youtube.com/watch?v=4u_kjKm7l4o (accessed 15 November 2021).

56. 'CARDI B – CORONAVIRUS (CONSTANTINE REMIX)', https://www.youtube.com/watch?v=Kc_yHDJNvxo (accessed 15 November 2021); 'Cardi B – Coronavirus (Carloh Virus Remix)', https://www.youtube.com/watch?v=nI_gm1ut3dA (accessed 15 November 2021); 'Cardi B Coronavirus Dark Afro House Remix', https://www.youtube.com/watch?v=ChQjGfDpum0

57. DJ -O-'s 'Coronavirus dembow' remix, released 23 March 2020, https://www.youtube.com/watch?v=AabTxxAzgys (accessed 15 November 2021). Other examples are 'Cardi B – Coronavirus (Dembow Remix)', https://www.youtube.com/watch?v=oM0ywmyXZ-E (accessed 15 November 2021) and 'CoronaVirus (feat. Cardi B) Dembow Remix', https://www.youtube.com/watch?v=AHgRsQVX3tc (accessed 15 November 2021).

58. Alliekttn, 'Corona virus remix cardi b', https://www.tiktok.com/music/Corona-virus-remix-cardi-b-6805427768948574982 (accessed 20 December 2021).

59. 'Corona song (Sizzles Dembow Dirty Mix)(Official Audio)', https://www.youtube.com/watch?v=vFVKtLTb9-I (accessed 20 December 2021); 'CORONAVIRUS

(Sizzles Dembow)(Clean) (OFFICIAL AUDIO)', https://www.youtube.com/watch?v=HD3fBxkfHvU (accessed 20 December 2021).
60. 'Dj Snake ↳ Remixes Cardi B Viral Tik Tok Audio 😊 Corona Virus', https://www.youtube.com/watch?v=hfq-pIa91EM (accessed 20 December 2021).
61. For his 143 subscribers (with a bare 626 views in a month). 'Cardi B & iMarkkeyz – Coronavirus!', https://www.youtube.com/watch?v=NtYPwynPJQI (accessed 20 December 2021).
62. This indicates that further research is needed in the utilities of hashtags in viral remix culture to help explain how these function to build virality. 'Cardi B feat HAYASA G – Corona Virus | ✺ 2021', https://www.youtube.com/watch?v=iSfusppqyx8 (accessed 11 January 2022).
63. 'CORONA VIRUS REMIX | CORONA VIRUS | DJ SΔM', https://www.youtube.com/watch?v=PqLsr6e2D48 (accessed 11 January 2022).
64. Erica Gonzales, 'Cardi B Shares Her Own #MeToo Story and Stands Up for Women in Hip-Hop', *Harper's Bazaar*, 20 March 2018, https://www.harpersbazaar.com/celebrity/latest/a19486392/cardi-b-metoo-story-women-hiphop/ (accessed 11 January 2022); Evan N. Brown, 'Cardi B Interviews Biden: "I Just Want Trump Out"', *New York Times*, 17 August 2020 https://www.nytimes.com/2020/08/17/us/elections/cardi-b-interviews-biden-i-just-want-trump-out.html (accessed 11 January 2022).
65. Karen Avenburg, 'Interpellation and Performance: The Construction of Identities through Musical Experience in the Virgen Del Rosario Fiesta in Iruya, Argentina', *Latin American Perspectives* 39.2 (2012): 134–49, p. 136.
66. Rebecca Kukla, 'Slurs, Interpellation, and Ideology', *Southern Journal of Philosophy* 56 (2018): 7–32, pp. 13, 14–16.
67. David Woodruff Smith, 'Intersubjectivity: In Virtue of Noema, Horizon, and Life-World', in Frode Kjosavik, Christian Beyer, and Christel Fricke, eds, *Husserl's Phenomenology of Intersubjectivity: Historical Interpretations and Contemporary Applications* (New York: Routledge, 2019), 114–41.
68. Sandrine Sorlin, *The Stylistics of 'You': Second-Person Pronoun and its Pragmatic Effects* (Cambridge: Cambridge University Press, 2022), p. 6.
69. Avenburg, 'Interpellation and Performance', p. 135.
70. France W. Twine and Charles A. Gallagher, 'Introduction: The Future of Whiteness: A Map of the "Third Wave"', in Charles A. Gallagher and France W. Twine, eds, *Retheorizing Race and Whiteness in the 21st Century: Changes and Challenges* (New York: Routledge, 2012), 1–20.
71. John Mowitt, *Percussion: Drumming, Beating, Striking* (Durham, NC: Duke University Press, 2002), p. 58.
72. Bolter, *The Digital Plenitude*, p. 135.
73. Owen Gallagher, *Reclaiming Critical Remix Video: The Role of Sampling in Transformative Works* (New York: Routledge, 2018), pp. 151–2.
74. Akane Kanai, 'DIY Culture', in Eduardo Navas, Owen Gallagher, and xtine burrough, *Keywords in Remix Studies* (New York: Routledge, 2018), 125–34, pp. 126–7.
75. Eduardo Navas, *Remix Theory: The Aesthetics of Sampling* (Vienna: Springer 2012), p. 126.
76. Limor Shifman, *Memes in Digital Culture* (Cambridge: MIT Press, 2014), pp. 58, 62.
77. Jussi Parikka, *Digital Contagions: A Media Archaeology of Computer Viruses* (Oxford: Peter Lang, 2007), pp. 12–15.
78. Fredric Jameson, 'Globalization and Hybridization', in Nataša Durovicová and Kathleen E. Newman, eds, *World Cinemas, Transnational Perspectives*, (New York: Routledge, 2009), 315–19, pp. 317–18; on virality and hybridization as concepts, see José-Borja Arjona-Martín, Alfonso Méndiz-Noguero, and Juan-Salvador Victoria-Mas, 'Virality as a Paradigm of Digital Communication. Review of the Concept and Update of the Theoretical Framework', *El Profesional De La Información* 29.6 (2020): 1–18.

79. A distinction discussed in Larisa K. Mann, *Rude Citizenship: Jamaican Popular Music, Copyright, and the Reverberations of Colonial Power* (Chapel Hill: University of North Carolina Press, 2022), pp. 156–7.
80. Shifman, *Memes in Digital Culture*, pp. 67–8.
81. Anders Fagerjord, 'After Convergence: YouTube and Remix Culture', in Jeremy Hunsinger, Lisbeth Klastrup, and Matthew Allen, eds, *International Handbook of Internet Research* (Dordrecht: Springer Netherlands, 2010), 187–200; Oshani Seneviratne and Andres Monroy-Hernandez, 'Remix Culture on the Web: A Survey of Content Reuse on Different User-Generated Content Websites', in *Proceedings of the WebSci10: Extending the Frontiers of Society On-Line* (2010): http://dig.csail.mit.edu/2010/Papers/WebScience/paper.pdf (accessed 11 January 2022); Leslie-Jean Thornton, 'The Photo is Live at Applifam: An Instagram Community Grapples with How Images Should be Used', *Visual Communication Quarterly* 21.2 (2014): 72–82; Maria R. Redinha, Maria R. Guimarães, and Francisco L. Fernandes, eds, *The Sharing Economy: Legal Problems of a Permutations and Combinations Society* (Newcastle-upon-Tyne: Cambridge Scholars Publishing, 2019); Zalvide Rodríguez, Carmen and Luis Fernando Ramos Simón, 'Piratas y creadores: Autoría, creatividad y automatización en Youtube', *Cuadernos De Documentación Multimedia* 31 (2020): 1–8.
82. Murray R. Shafer, *The Tuning of the World* (New York: Knopf, 1977), p. 91.
83. Vanessa Chang, 'Records That Play: The Present Past in Sampling Practice', *Popular Music* 28.2 (2009): 143–59.
84. Marcus Boon, *In Praise of Copying* (Cambridge, MA: Harvard University Press, 2010), p. 231.
85. Reinterpretations of particular Ba'Aka vocal styles, whether via direct sample or imitation, have been deployed by global recording artists to sonically reference themes of pan-Africanism and Black power (in the context of Herbie Hancock's jazz fusion) and an Eden-like so-called 'primitivism' (in the context of Deep Forest's global trance) – see Steven Feld, 'Pygmy POP. A Genealogy of Schizophonic Mimesis', *Yearbook for Traditional Music* 28 (1996): 1–35.
86. De Kosnik, 'Why it Matters', p. 156.
87. Frances Negrón-Muntaner and Raquel Z. Rivera, 'Reggaeton Nation', *NACLA Report on the Americas* 40.6 (2007): 35–9, quoted in Rivera-Rideau, *Remixing Reggaetón*, p. 4.
88. Mark Katz, *Capturing Sound: How Technology Has Changed Music* (Berkeley: University of California Press, 2010), pp. 148, 174 (emphasis in original).
89. On the rise of features, which Chris Molanphy calls 'the result of decades of music science – our most refined strains of genetically hybridized pop, clearly and unambiguously labeled', see Chris Molanphy, 'Feat. Don't Fail Me Now: The Rise of the Featured Rapper in Pop Music', *Slate*, 31 July 2015, https://slate.com/culture/2015/07/the-history-of-featured-rappers-and-other-featured-artists-in-pop-songs.html (accessed 17 January 2022).
90. Adam Arvidsson, 'Value and Virtue in the Sharing Economy', *Sociological Review* 66.2 (2018): 289–301, p. 290.
91. Moulay D. El Maarouf, Taieb Belghazi, and Farouk El Maarouf, 'COVID – 19: A Critical Ontology of the Present', *Educational Philosophy and Theory* 53.1 (2021): 71–89, p. 76.
92. Lessig, *Remix*, pp. 153–4.
93. Lessig, *Remix*, p. 178.
94. Raphaël Nowak, 'The Intricate Relationship Between Music and the Sharing Economy', in Thomas Siglar and Jonathan Corcoran, eds, *A Modern Guide to the Urban Sharing Economy* (Northampton, UK: Edward Elgar, 2021), 267–80, p. 278.
95. Russell Belk, 'Sharing', *Journal of Consumer Research* 36.5 (2010): 715–34, p. 717.
96. Jenny Kennedy, 'Conceptual Boundaries of Sharing', *Information, Communication & Society* 19.4 (2016): 461–74, pp. 462, 469.
97. Nichoas A. John, *The Age of Sharing* (Cambridge: Polity, 2017), pp. 76–89.

98. Boon, *In Praise of Copying*, pp. 6–7.
99. 'This impermanence [...] we described as a network of infinite, connected, essenceless signs with the name of Copia, is always already in a state of transformation; and upon examination, no conceptual apparatus of any kind can describe it – it is utterly beyond concepts, although words like 'suchness' and 'sameness' may point to it provisionally' (Boon, *In Praise of Copying*, p. 79).
100. Boon, *In Praise of Copying*, p. 73.
101. Boon, *In Praise of Copying*, p. 224.
102. John Shiga, 'Copy-and-Persist: The Logic of Mash-Up Culture', *Critical Studies in Media Communication* 24. 2 (2007): 93–111, p. 99.
103. Shiga, 'Copy-and-Persist', p. 104.
104. 'Cuarentena DJ Mix 🔥 (Reggaetón , Salsa, Cumbia, EDM, Pop, 80´s & 90´s) – FIESTA Y DISCO EN CASA #2', https://www.youtube.com/watch?v=2dxg1H1FXxw (accessed 15 January 2022); 'Mix Cuarentena 🔥 (Hola remix, La Cama Remix, Raka Taka, Pirueta, Amarillo, Verde, Elegí, PAM, Fornai)', https://www.youtube.com/watch?v=Zx33VC9LLT4 (accessed 15 January 2022); 'OMICRON MIX 2021', https://www.youtube.com/watch?v=pS0keqK1oBw (accessed 15 January 2022); 'Omicron Session – Erick Orozco Dj', https://www.youtube.com/watch?v=5gh6hyoCF_g (accessed 15 January 2022). 'La Pandemia feat. Frankie Elyse (Fear & Lowe Remix)', https://www.youtube.com/watch?v=hH3GLcf0urU (accessed 15 January 2022); 'Pandemia Mix', https://www.youtube.com/watch?v=MwGW1YXsl8E (accessed 15 January 2022); 'Sqrwiel – Pandemia Mix 2020', https://www.youtube.com/watch?v=o100Or149O4 (accessed 15 January 2022).
105. 'COVID 19 HOT SOCA CHUTNEY MIX', https://www.youtube.com/watch?v=c8LA5DulwRg (accessed 15 January 2022) – the message says 'THIS MIX IS 100% FIRE AKA BEST MIX EVER'; 'Covid 19 Riddim 2020 Bashment Soca Instrumental', https://www.youtube.com/watch?v=4S3eZH1KoPQ (accessed 15 January 2022); 'GRENADA SOCA 2021 COVID 19 EDITION MIX |LIL JELO | LAVAMAN| SKULL DAWG| LEDNECK | MUDDY | LIL NATTY', https://www.youtube.com/watch?v=HzjEsGd_c7k (accessed 15 January 2022).
106. Nathalie Nahai, *Webs of Influence: The Psychology of Online Persuasion* (Harlow, UK: Pearson, 2012).
107. Carla J. Maier, *Transcultural Sound Practices: British Asian Dance Music as Cultural Transformation* (New York: Bloomsbury Academic, 2020), p. 43.
108. 'Jowell y Randy, Kiko El Crazy – Se Acabó La Cuarentena (Video Oficial)', https://www.youtube.com/watch?v=EwLYDWew1rk (accessed 15 January 2022); Natasha Melina, 'Kiko El Crazy Talks Viral "Se Acabó La Cuarentena" Collab Alongside Jowell y Randy, Maffio Collab "Como Eh," and Upcoming Album "Llego El Domi"', *Urban Latino*, 8 October 2021, http://urbanlatino.com/kiko-el-crazy-talks-viral-se-acabo-la-cuarentena-collab-alongside-jowell-y-randy-maffio-collab-como-eh-and-upcoming-album-llego-el-domi/ (accessed 20 October 2021).
109. Sarah Perez, 'Kids Now Spend Nearly as Much Time Watching TikTok as YouTube in US, UK and Spain', *TechCrunch*, 4 June 2020, https://techcrunch.com/2020/06/04/kids-nowspend-nearly-as-much-time-watching-tiktok-as-youtube-in-u-s-u-k-and-spain/ (accessed 2 November 2021); Sarah Perez, 'YouTube's Latest Experiment is a TikTok Rival Focused on 15-Second Videos', *TechCrunch*, 25 June 2020, https://techcrunch.com/2020/06/25/youtubes-latest-experiment-is-a-tiktok-rival-focused-on-15-second-videos/ (accessed 2 November 2021).
110. 'Se Acabo La Cuarentena (Tiktok)', https://www.youtube.com/watch?v=qzZ1Sad-Ubo (accessed 2 November 2021).
111. Salman Aslam, 'TikTok by the Numbers: Stats, Demographics & Fun Facts', *Omnicore*, 12 February 2020, https://www.omnicoreagency.com/tiktok-statistics/ (accessed 2 November 2021); Sirin Kale, 'How Coronavirus Helped TikTok Find its Voice', *The*

Guardian, 26 April 2020, https://www.theguardian.com/technology/2020/apr/26/how-coronavirus-helped-tiktok-find-its-voice (accessed 2 November 2021); Sophie Haigney, 'TikTok is the Perfect Medium for the Splintered Attention Spans of Lockdown', *The Guardian*, 16 May 2020, https://www.theguardian.com/commentisfree/2020/may/16/tiktok-perfect-medium-splintered-attention-spans-coronavirus-lockdown (accessed 2 November 2021).

112. Li Yachao, Guan Mengfei, Paige Hammond, and Lane E. Berrey, 'Communicating COVID-19 Information on TikTok: A Content Analysis of TikTok Videos from Official Accounts Featured in the COVID-19 Information Hub', *Health Education Research* 36.3 (2021): Article PMC7989330 ; Zoya Unni and Emily Weinstein, 'Shelter in Place, Connect Online: Trending TikTok Content during the Early Days of the U.S. COVID-19 Pandemic', *Journal of Adolescent Health* 68.5 (2021): 863–8. On youth culture and TikTok, see Zeng Jing and Crystal Abidin, '"#OkBoomer, Time to Meet the Zoomers": Studying the Memefication of Intergenerational Politics on TikTok', *Information, Communication & Society* 24.16 (2021): 2459–81.
113. Meredith B. Kile, 'The Best TikTok Songs and Dance Challenges that Got Us Through 2020', *ET*, 22 December 2020, https://www.etonline.com/the-best-tiktok-songs-and-dance-challenges-that-got-us-through-2020-157969 (accessed 2 November 2021).
114. 'Jowell y Randy, Kiko El Crazy – Se Acabó La Cuarentena | Viva el Perreo [Visualizer]', https://www.youtube.com/watch?v=YNR0mFufPsE (accessed 31 December 2021).
115. Larisa K. Mann, *Rude Citizenship: Jamaican Popular Music, Copyright, and the Reverberations of Colonial Power* (Chapel Hill: University of North Carolina Press, 2022), pp. 145, 155–6.
116. Wayne Marshall, 'Dembow: A Loop History', *Red Bull Music Academy Daily*, 2 July 2013, https://daily.redbullmusicacademy.com/2013/07/dembow-a-loop-history (accessed 11 November 2021).
117. Marshall, 'Dembow'; see also Wayne Marshall, 'Dem Bow, Dembow, Dembo: Translation and Transnation in Reggaetón', *Lied Und Populäre Kultur* 53 (2008): 131–51.
118. 'Se Acabó La Cuarentena', https://www.youtube.com/watch?v=nvXwwlvi_jQ (accessed 14 January 2021).
119. Kaitlyn Tiffany, 'How Quickly Can a Girl Go Viral on TikTok?', *The Atlantic*, 16 September 2020, https://www.theatlantic.com/technology/archive/2020/09/tiktok-teens-fandom-mooptopia/616371/ (accessed 14 January 2021).
120. Trevor Boffone, *Renegades: Digital Dance Cultures from Dubsmash to TikTok* (Oxford: Oxford University Press, 2021), p. 46.
121. Siobhan Burke, 'What Makes a TikTok Dance Go Viral?', *Dance Magazine*, 28 December 2020, https://www.dancemagazine.com/popular-tiktok-dances-2649519038.html (accessed 2 November 2021).
122. Melanie Kennedy, '"If the Rise of the TikTok Dance and e-Girl Aesthetic has Taught Us Anything, it's that Teenage Girls Rule the Internet Right Now": TikTok Celebrity, Girls and the Coronavirus Crisis', *European Journal of Cultural Studies* 23.6 (2020): 1069–76, p. 1072.
123. A tendency put to humorous use by dembow star Yofrangel in his 2020 song 'Pa Tik Tok', https://www.youtube.com/watch?v=52RnmFZyfhc (accessed 7 January 2022).
124. 'DANCE – SE ACABÓ LA CUARENTENA', https://www.youtube.com/watch?v=Zxoc0CpUESU (accessed 7 January 2022).
125. 'SE ACABO LA CUARENTENA (Tiktok Hit) Jowell y Randy, Kiko El Crazy | Zumba | TML Crew Rain Dela Cruz', https://www.youtube.com/watch?v=lN__S5sqV1M (accessed 7 January 2022); a compilation of dozens of the TikTok videos is 'Se Acabó la Cuarentena *NEW TREND SONG* || 🔥 TikTok Dances Compilation Remix Challenge 2021 🔥🔥', https://www.youtube.com/watch?v=EkCg6_EWsiY (accessed 7 January 2022).

126. 'SE ACABO LA CUARENTENA (REMIX) JOWELL & RANDY ✘ DJ ALEX', https://www.youtube.com/watch?v=R-J0U6raJ7E (accessed 7 January 2022).
127. 'MIX SE ACABÓ LA CUARENTENA (TocoTocoTo, Perreo Arabe, Mi Niña, Bonita, Chica Ideal, Dembow, Aleteo)', https://www.youtube.com/watch?v=CS4Y_cc2v6o (accessed 7 January 2022).
128. 'Guaracha 😎🕺 (Se acabo La Cuarentena) Aleteo, Zapateo, Tribal House ✘ Zapaleteo Master', https://www.youtube.com/watch?v=um4iXIM6Yiw (accessed 7 January 2022); 'Jowell y Randy, Kiko El Crazy – Se Acabo La Cuarentena (REDTAPE Edit)', https://www.youtube.com/watch?v=T5w3viQRyQo (accessed 7 January 2022); 'SE ACABÓ LA CUARENTENA • KEVO DJ & LUCHO DEE JAY', https://www.youtube.com/watch?v=kVPDzPjPJrg (accessed 7 January 2022); 'Se Acabó La Cuarentena vs Marikit | Tiles Hop Edm Rush', https://www.youtube.com/watch?v=4He3HKFVQn4 (accessed 7 January 2022).
129. Alexandra Masciantonio, David Bourguignon, Pierre Bouchat, Manon Balty, and Bernard Rimé, 'Don't Put all Social Network Sites in One Basket: Facebook, Instagram, Twitter, TikTok, and their Relations with Well-Being during the COVID-19 Pandemic', *PloS One* 16.3 (2021): Article e0248384, p. 8.
130. Jean-François Augoyard and Henry Torgue, *Sonic Experience: A Guide to Everyday Sounds*, (Montreal: McGill-Queens University Press, 2005), pp. 90–7; Elrini Kartsaki, *On Repetition: Writing, Performance and Art* (Chicago: Intellect, 2016).
131. Bolter, *The Digital Plenitude*, p. 136.
132. Shifman, *Memes in Digital Culture*, p. 97.
133. 'El coronavirus Dembow – LuisZara', https://www.youtube.com/watch?v=39QI4pjic-4 (accessed 18 October 2021).
134. '😎 El Dembow del Corona Virus – Kelvin B 'El negrote', https://www.youtube.com/watch?v=q_Nk2UdVaKk (accessed 5 January 2022).
135. 'Coronavirus', https://www.youtube.com/watch?v=Z_45RjW2bAk (accessed 15 January 2022).
136. 'El coronavirus (DEMBOW)', https://www.youtube.com/watch?v=Zg9eier0vnQ (accessed 14 November 2021).
137. 'Danniloox Corona virus 2020', https://www.youtube.com/watch?v=l1u4Jl0AkBk (accessed 14 November 2021).
138. 'El Dubi, Tito Tijuana, Lucky Luciano, El Feka, Fido Dido & Pikolin – Coronavirus Dembow', https://www.youtube.com/watch?v=X9TqqQnVzuQ (accessed 14 November 2021).
139. DJ iMarkKeyz, 'IMarkkeyz – Coronavirus (Feat. Cardi B)', https://www.youtube.com/watch?v=iiYDSOQPPhY (accessed 14 November 2021).
140. 'AnuelVEVO. CoronaVirus-Anuel AA Ft El Alfa (Official Video), 2020', https://www.youtube.com/watch?v=qr3jFMvLOOE (accessed 14 November 2021).
141. Only a handful of examples are given here, such as Saymuz MC's dembow from 16 March 2020: 'SaymuZ – Si Tengo El Coronavirus – DemBow' (https://www.youtube.com/watch?v=m1ZKWnuKde4, accessed 14 January 2021) or Piero Fernandez's 'Loco Coronavirus', released 20 March 2020, (https://www.youtube.com/watch?v=BqkPTPuQ2KQ, accessed 14 November 2021); see also 'CORONA VIRUS DEMBOW (PROD. HOOLY GZ) ⚠!!', https://www.youtube.com/watch?v=PLwYE0-2bgM (accessed 14 November 2021); 'Ninsitow Joker – Corona Virus DEMBOW', https://www.youtube.com/watch?v=2U26HvV-pIg (accessed 14 November 2021). A user who posted only a dembow song online, named JN alex castro [sic], put a very short dembow online which consisted of a four-part shouted chorus saying the name of the virus: '#Coronavirus #dembow', https://www.youtube.com/watch?v=S_EGB2FPKBA (accessed 14 November 2021).

142. A version without a video was released 13 March 2020 as well: 'Corona Virus Monkey White 🐵co Dembow', https://www.youtube.com/watch?v=KKegO16JV2U (accessed 11 December 2021).
143. Jerrold Levinson, *Music in the Moment* (Ithaca, NY: Cornell University Press, 1997), pp. 22–3.
144. Levinson, *Music in the Moment*, pp. 22–3.
145. Peter Kivy, *New Essays on Musical Understanding* (Oxford: Clarendon Press, 2001), p. 188.
146. Elizabeth Hellmuth Margulis, *On Repeat: How Music Plays the Mind* (Oxford: Oxford University Press, 2021), p. 144.
147. 'CORONA VIRUS || BZRP Music Sessions #23', https://www.youtube.com/watch?v=HRm-GjgTZ1M (accessed 12 January 2021); 'CORONAVIRUS || BZRP Music Sessions -REMIX- (ft Trump – Alberto)', https://www.youtube.com/watch?v=tA8WCBLLW9w (accessed 12 January 2021); 'MAÑANA NO HAY CLASES', https://www.youtube.com/watch?v=bRb7lCHcwqs (accessed 12 January 2021); 'SPUTNIK V || BZRP Music Sessions #37', https://www.youtube.com/watch?v=-wMDsTZYcvI (accessed 12 January 2021).
148. Joseph C. Nunes, Andrea Ordanini, and Francesca Valsesia, 'The Power of Repetition: Repetitive Lyrics in a Song Increase Processing Fluency and Drive Market Success', *Journal of Consumer Psychology* 25.2 (2015): 187–99, pp. 187–9.
149. 'Lapizin Bunny – Coronavirus (Video Oficial), 2020', https://www.youtube.com/watch?v=KESa7KoDz_U (accessed 7 January 2022).
150. 'CORONA VIRUS 😷✌ – Yofrangel (Official Video), 2020', https://www.youtube.com/watch?v=uF3dg5seGLs (accessed 7 January 2022).
151. Dara E. Goldman, 'Walk Like a Woman, Talk Like a Man: Ivy Queen's Troubling of Gender', *Latino Studies* 15:4 (2017): 439–57, p. 440.
152. Goldman, 'Walk Like a Woman', 442–3; Sydney Hutchinson, *Tigers of a Different Stripe: Performing Gender in Dominican Music* (Chicago: University of Chicago Press, 2016), pp. 168–9.
153. The movement of the genre boundaries from dembow to related styles is tracked in Deborah P. Hernández, *Oye Como Va! Hybridity and Identity in Latino Popular Music* (Philadelphia: Temple University Press, 2010), esp. pp. 72–5.
154. Jenzia Burgos, 'Pablo Piddy: "Si Tu Quiere Dembow" (2011)', *Pitchfork*, 9 March 2020, https://pitchfork.com/features/lists-and-guides/guide-to-urbano-music/ (accessed 11 November 2021).
155. Wayne Marshall, 'Representing Dembow Dominicano', *Wayne & Wax*, 13 February 2019, https://wayneandwax.com/?p=9262 (accessed 11 November 2021); see also Wayne Marshall, 'From Música Negra to Reggeatón Latino: The Cultural Politics of Nation, Migration, and Commercialization', in Raquel Z. Rivera, Wayne Marshall, and Deborah Pacini Hernández, eds, *Reggaetón* (Durham, NC: Duke University Press, 2008), 19–78.
156. Marshall, 'Dembow'.
157. 'CORONA VIRUS 😷✌ – Yofrangel (Official Video), 2020', https://www.youtube.com/watch?v=uF3dg5seGLs (accessed 11 November 2021).
158. Comments added to 'EL ANTIDOTO 💊✌ – Yofrangel (Official Video)', https://www.youtube.com/watch?v=_UPHfPFj3rc (accessed 7 January 2022). He unearthed viewers from all across Latin America, the United States, and even Romania.
159. 'CORONA VIRUS 2 #LaCuarentena 😷✌ – Yofrangel (Official Video)', https://www.youtube.com/watch?v=xM3-LcF-uwU (accessed 7 January 2022).
160. 'LA VACUNA ✌ – YOFRANGEL (Official Video)', https://www.youtube.com/watch?v=RSTPQX7stsc (accessed 12 December 2021).

161. Ben Duinker, 'Good Things Come in Threes: Triplet Flow in Recent Hip-Hop Music', *Popular Music* 38.3 (2019): 423–56, p. 425; Ben Duinker, 'Segmentation, Phrasing, and Meter in Hip-Hop Music', *Music Theory Spectrum* 43.2 (2021): 221–45, p. 221.
162. 'Yofrangel – Y Tu Tarjeta De Vacunacion 🎵💃 (Video Oficial) Feat. Negro 12', https://www.youtube.com/watch?v=_MTgS5XzgwA (accessed 14 January 2021).
163. Comments added to 'CORONA VIRUS 😷✔ – Yofrangel (Official Video), 2020', https://www.youtube.com/watch?v=uF3dg5seGLs (accessed 12 December 2021).
164. The description of the song notes 'El Creador del éxito global "La Cumbia del #Coronavirus" conocido como Mister Cumbia y el artista urbano Kaseeno se unen para hacer una colaboración histórica" – see 'PANDEMIA – Kaseeno x Mister Cumbia (Video Oficial) Coronavirus 😷', https://www.youtube.com/watch?v=8MZRP-Bl8MQ (accessed 11 November 2021).
165. 'CORONAVIRUS – Kaseeno (Video Oficial) 😷', https://www.youtube.com/watch?v=nn_0F9NRfhU (accessed 12 December 2021).
166. 'El Corona Virus – Negra Flow Ft. Kevin Vin (Video Oficial)', https://www.youtube.com/watch?v=9Q0F9AhFAkM (accessed 12 December 2021).
167. 'NEGRA FLOW Y LA ÑAPA – VETE A BAÑAR', https://www.youtube.com/shorts/ysJlTQ-YdHY (accessed 13 September 2022).
168. 'Fortnite – La Ñapa, Kevin Vin, Wickypedia Mc, Negra Flow (Video Oficial)', https://www.youtube.com/watch?v=QqOD6WnKTy8 (accessed 13 September 2022); 'La Ñapa – El Pan Y La Leche (Video Oficial)', https://www.youtube.com/watch?v=0vxxuMBV-yI (accessed 12 December 2021); 'La Ñapa Ft. Kevin Vin – La Pasola (Video Oficial)', https://www.youtube.com/watch?v=9ffGks4A_D4 (accessed 12 December 2021); 'La Ñapa, Negra Flow, Kevin Vin – Camine Pa' La Casa (Video Oficial)', https://www.youtube.com/watch?v=pSSogyNx9Ac (accessed 12 December 2021).
169. 'Miradita Family – Mensaje A La Sociedad (Video Oficial)', https://www.youtube.com/watch?v=-V9iM5DXGbI (accessed 12 December 2021).
170. Gilles Deleuze, *Difference and Repetition* (trans. Paul Patton, New York: Columbia University Press, 1994), p. 2.
171. Comments added to 'CORONA VIRUS 😷✔ – Yofrangel (Official Video), 2020', https://www.youtube.com/watch?v=uF3dg5seGLs (accessed 12 December 2021). Another comment along the same lines in this thread was pulled out and remixed into a video of Yofrangel, released 10 March 2020, 'Dembow del | CoronaVirus', https://www.youtube.com/watch?v=8a04nMbRhhM (accessed 10 January 2022).
172. 'TORY LANEZ – QUARANTINE RADIO SHOW DEMBOW (PROD. JAMZ)', https://www.youtube.com/watch?v=IaZs6jxrfvo (accessed 10 January 2022).

2 Las Cumbias del Coronavirus

El Éxito Mundial

Mister Cumbia, a topical cumbia writer who styles himself as 'El Rey de las Cumbias Virales', set out to record a quick hit at the very start of the coronavirus pandemic, and succeeded. His 'La Cumbia del Coronavirus' was the first widely circulated Spanish-language song to address the coronavirus pandemic directly. He released his catchy recording on YouTube on 22 January 2020 – one week before the World Health Organization declared COVID-19 a public health emergency. 'La Cumbia del Coronavirus' rapidly became a global hit ('*el éxito mundial*'). It was also dubbed a 'viral success' in the established public understanding of the concept based on its instant ubiquity, explosive popularity, and widespread sharing and repurposing. By October 2021, the cumbia had had more than 3.5 million views on Mister Cumbia's own YouTube channel and had been very widely copied, reposted, remixed, covered, and otherwise shared to millions of others.[1] His success was followed by what became a torrent of more than 150 cumbias del coronavirus.

Unlike Mister Cumbia's smash hit, not all the cumbias responding to the pandemic moment were created deliberately for commercial purposes, or even intended for a global audience. The wide appeal and international popularity of Mister Cumbia's 'La Cumbia del Coronavirus' signaled the existence of a market for a self-consciously viral sonic product responding to the pandemic moment, while the social embeddedness and spatialities of many other cumbias del coronavirus during the COVID-19 pandemic indicated a broader and more complex transnational movement. This chapter explores this very wide array of cumbias del coronavirus which emerged following the international success of Mister Cumbia's timely and endearing recording.

Cumbias constitute an ideal case study illuminating the local and regional musical responses to the global COVID-19 pandemic. Situating the international appeal and success of 'La Cumbia del Coronavirus' among the many dozens of diverse cumbias that emerged during the pandemic moment, we argue that the spread of cumbias del coronavirus in 2020–2022 represents an impressive and encapsulating cultural movement. In the cumbia idiom, professionals and amateurs alike recognize and utilize not only a captivating rhythm but also an ensnaring mode of culturally situated and locally variable expression.

Within the cumbia megagenre, as it was among other styles responding to coronavirus in the spring of 2020, the expansion of música del coronavirus was both rhizomatic and explosive. The musical response was transnational in origin and audience, unpredictable in direction and reception, and could rarely be traced to a single source or credited to a single inspiration beyond the pandemic moment itself. Cumbia's diverse but instantaneous evocations for listeners in very different contexts, coupled with its inbuilt propulsive rhythmic attraction and means of direct emotional expression, fulfilled the needs of the musicians seeking to engage with the many meanings and impacts of the coronavirus. Artists used the accessible and elastic cumbia style to react to the pandemic in ways that were conversely transnational and local, collective and individualistic. As a result, the genre generates its own momentum, provides its own cultural cache, and, not unimportantly, carves out a particular market position for musicians.

Cumbia rhythm builds on topical relevance and resonance to spread and develop on these rhizomatic circuits. While the artistic approaches, lyrical treatment, and motivations for new song releases vary widely across the cumbias del coronavirus surveyed here, they are linked by the decisions made by their creators to utilize cumbia to respond to the pandemic moment. Some groups and individuals clearly seek to dominate the market space for topical songs on the pandemic, while others produce songs to inform and warn, to entertain a subcultural community, or simply to express a particular experience of life during the global health crisis – lack of audience be damned. The full creative explosion of cumbias del coronavirus underscores cumbia itself as a cultural force at once reflecting global musical sensibilities while showcasing diverse social and cultural systems. Cumbia, in both its globalized and hyperlocal manifestations, proves to be a durable, expansive, and highly flexible format for creative repurposing during a time of fear, crisis, and market opportunity.

Este Es el Rey de las Cumbias Virales

Iván Montemayor is not your average news junkie. Born and raised in the border city of Reynosa, Tamaulipas, Mexico, he now lives in eastern North Carolina, in a town he describes as 'totally rural and in the middle of nowhere'. During the day, Montemayor works as a DJ on WZUP, a Spanish-language radio station out of La Grange. However, he is best known for releasing comedic, salient, and danceable earworms under the persona of 'Mister Cumbia'. In his whimsical compositions, virtually all of which are written in a cumbia-pop style that resounds throughout Mexico and the borderland United States, he sings about current events, breaking news, and, most frequently, sensational content circulating around Spanish-language social media. Montemayor describes Mister Cumbia as 'a gigantic meme'.[2] Through this alter ego, he has become an unexpectedly well-received voice of commentary on a wide range of events within the Mexican popular consciousness. Montemayor's musical output has proceeded deliberately and with an emphasis on relevance. 'I began to think about how I could fuse my interest in musical production with the social media trends that were gaining traction at the time', he said to us in an interview. In order 'to stay relevant and to make a scene' he checks the news constantly: 'I work at a radio station, so even though we're a music station there's still a lot of news floating around. It's part of my job to stay on top of what is going on, to know what the next big thing is going to be before it hits the mainstream.'[3] Like a modern-day town crier, Mister Cumbia is always on the hunt for the next story to flip into a quick hit, whether silly or serious.

In 2018, after six years of releasing original music, Montemayor achieved his first internet hit with 'Los 15 de Ruby', a ditty about a quinceañera that had received national coverage in Mexico after attracting over ten thousand guests. 'There is a party going on that's become super popular/ and the birthday girl's name is Ruby', sings Montemayor. 'They've put it out on the radio and also on the internet / And now everybody wants to help out at the *quinceañera*'. In what would become a replicable pattern, the instant popularity of 'Los 15 de Ruby' was rooted in the sensational nature of the subject matter, yielding an impressive but not overwhelming 278,000 views over five years.[4]

Mister Cumbia's other songs follow a similar pattern of topicality and frivolity. A Grupo Bimbo deliveryman stole a few packages of bread from an old shopkeeper, and Mister Cumbia released 'La Cumbia del Repartidor de Bimbo' ('The Cumbia about the Bimbo Delivery Man'). A poorly executed presidential debate prompted 'La Cumbia del Debate Pt. 1', in which Mister Cumbia asks: 'What happened with that debate, can we even say who won?' A raunchy video of a Mexican soccer star indecently exposing himself inspired another cumbia that poked fun both at the player's *faux pax* and the exaggerated, voyeuristic reaction of the popular media. This is how Mister Cumbia worked and rose to prominence – taking note of a viral theme, cobbling together some verses and a catchy chorus addressing it, and laying it all on top of a danceable cumbia rhythm. Never missing a beat, in July 2022 he released 'La cumbia de Ben Afleck Y Jennifer Lopez' in response to the couple's ubiquity in summer tabloids.[5]

'I mean, there are memes, but Mister Cumbia is the biggest troll there is, because I have written songs about anything you could imagine', he told us, elaborating on his persona. Immediately before the Coronavirus pandemic struck, his most shared song was about the proposed raffling off of the presidential plane by Mexico's president, Andres Manuel Lopez Obrador: 'The sheer craziness of the news story and all of the conflicting opinions on it just made the whole country go nuts', he explained, 'so out of the chaos I made a cumbia.'[6]

Montemayor described 'La Cumbia del Coronavirus' to us as 'a very special case', noting that while most of his music is purely meant for entertainment, this composition had a social purpose. 'Effectively, these cumbias are memes, they're for trolling, they're silly, for dancing, with catchy choruses', he acknowledged,

> but when I composed the 'Cumbia de Coronavirus', I kept recalling the H1N1 epidemic that hit us ten years ago. Obviously, in those times, social media wasn't as prevalent. But I wanted to 'flip the tortilla', and in place of trolling people, I wanted to write a song that would prepare people for what was coming. After seeing what happened with the swine flu in Mexico, I had a feeling that [coronavirus] would have a similar trajectory, and it would turn into something scary, so I looked for a way to explain this to the people.'[7]

Montemayor was inspired to write what would become 'La Cumbia del Coronavirus' in December 2019. 'I knew I was doing something ahead of the curve', he told us with confidence. 'I mean, nobody was seriously concerned about Coronavirus in Mexico in those days, and all of the talk was about the situation in China.' The track was released on YouTube on 21 January 2021, nearly two months before registered COVID cases began ballooning throughout the Americas. 'My rush for composing the song was this: that the song and its lesson would come first, and the pandemic later', he said.[8]

The wise timing and poignant topicality in Mister Cumbia's song is apparent. It pairs lyrical clarity and simplicity with a heavy downbeat and a catchy melody to express the still-nascent fears about the coronavirus emerging across the globe. The lyrics both captured the uncertain mood and provided some guidance for navigating the dangers of the early pandemic. 'The whole world is scared / From a disease / That's called the Coronavirus / And it's a global alarm', the song begins. 'It is said that it was born in China / There are several dead over there.' Mister Cumbia then strikes a practical and sober tone: 'We have to pay attention / We have to take care / To put in the batteries', he sings, using an idiomatic expression for dealing with a situation head-on and with vigor. 'For this I made this song [because] not everything in life is a meme', he announces in the concluding verse.[9]

The chorus of 'La Cumbia del Coronavirus' is both danceable and educational, encouraging listeners with the messages 'don't touch your face', 'wash your hands regularly', and 'use disinfectant and avoid crowded places'. The chorus set what evolved into a standard for subsequent songs in its use of the name of the virus as the primary repetitive hook, mapping the name 'coronavirus' onto the cumbia beat. Musically, the song is straightforward. The chorus features a call-and-response of synthesized horns covering the 'coronavirus' with an accordion taking the place of the response: '*coronavirus, coronavirus / lávense las manos, háganlo seguido*' ('wash your hands, do it often').[10]

The didactic element was, to Montemayor, an essential component of the song's design. 'The chorus literally prepares you to protect yourself, and it contains advice that the whole world has already taken to heart', he said to us.[11] The catchy tune serves as both entertainment and public service announcement, giving people a reason to laugh, dance, and sing along while also teaching a lesson on the ways in which the disease's spread might be slowed or stopped. Mister Cumbia thus created a viral song and video to combat a viral pandemic.

Montemayor was alert to the potential social cost of releasing a song on such a controversial topic:

> The song almost got canned [...] and indeed there were plenty of critiques, because some people thought it was in bad taste, because a lot of people were dying and they thought I was profiting from misery, but those people didn't even listen to the lyrics, they just saw the title.

Overall, Montemayor came to see the song as 'something of a service' to the community, an 'early alarm' to the tragedy and chaos to come, set to an infectious hook.

Across Latin America, the song's popularity ballooned, especially as the coronavirus became increasingly central in the daily news cycle. 'I am accustomed to my songs going viral among Mexicans and the Hispanic community in the United States, so I am used to getting some attention on social media, but "La Cumbia del Coronavirus" was different', he told us. 'It went viral in Argentina, for example, which was the country with the most plays after Mexico and the United States. It was also very popular in Spain, where we were in the top five on New Releases on Spotify for a few weeks.' He credits much of this success to the ways algorithms on content-streaming platforms such as YouTube and Spotify 'take something that is growing and make it grow even faster'. After finding its way onto a handful of popular playlists featuring new releases, 'La Cumbia del Coronavirus' continued to grow. By late February 2020, when the coronavirus had become a top news story and a means for greater speculative concern in Mexico, several news outlets made mention of the song, including national newspapers such as *La Jornada* and *El País*.

The transnational appeal beyond Latin America of 'La Cumbia del Coronavirus' surprised Montemayor somewhat, given 'the fact that it's a cumbia – not a genre like rap or EDM, but a cumbia.' He found it 'amazing how a style that is so linked to Latin America had such success in other countries.' One reason was the special pandemic circumstances, but there was also a critical sonic aspect:

> Look, one thing that made the song so popular worldwide is that the word 'coronavirus' is pronounced the same in Japan, in Russia, in Turkey, in Poland, in Arab countries, and so this thing went viral in many places where they don't even speak Spanish.[12]

The song did not merely strike a chord outside Latin America; it found itself remixed, reinterpreted, and revamped around the globe in ways Montemayor never expected. Within a month of its release, translations into Japanese and Russian were circulating around the internet, and remixes from Poland, Korea, and various African countries were uploaded to YouTube: 'I've been asked for vocal stems by DJs from Europe and Latin America' he explained to us. Montemayor has made a point of making his music easily accessible and usable for other DJs looking to remix his material. Some of his *stems* – the isolated vocal tracks from his recordings – have found their way into remixes ranging from reggaetón to Argentinian cumbia villera.

Ultimately, the power and spread of the cumbia beat as an idiom with global appeal rests in its relative simplicity and ease of production. At least, that was true for Mister Cumbia's accessible style. Montemayor notes that the cumbia is 'a product that can be made on a laptop, with a homemade video, with very modest equipment, probably not of the highest technological standard, but always with a certain level of quality.'

All of this begs the question of how Montemayor arrived at the cumbia as his vehicle for achieving internet notoriety and serving as a voice of caution and advice. After all, Mexico's cultural history is full of musical and poetic forms that are at once both popular and informative. 'I am Mexican, and for centuries we have had the corrido style to tell popular stories of everyday people', he explained to us. The corrido, a storied musical style popular in what is now the Mexico–US borderlands, is a type of narrative ballad where the singer speaks traditionally plainly of observed events, often offering a moral lesson or a warning after recounting a story rife with violence, betrayal, and crisis (corridos del coronavirus are the subject of Chapter Five).

Montemayor respects the tradition of the corrido in Mexico, but his aspirations extend beyond the style's historical reach:

> The only way to connect to Central and South America, and the whole Spanish-speaking world, was through the cumbia, because the cumbia is a more universal language; it is a language that they speak even in Patagonia, in the Latino community in the United States, almost everywhere. The cumbia is a language that connects

people from distinct countries, which isn't the case with the corrido, which doesn't have the same sway in places like Spain or the Caribbean, because it's not part of their culture.'[13]

Just like the coronavirus, the cumbia recognizes no borders, moves at unimaginable speeds around the globe, and has historically taken root in some unexpected places.

While most of the cumbias del coronavirus that this project examines do not fit the definition of 'virality' posited by scholars of viral cultures, 'La Cumbia del Coronavirus' certainly does. Unlike the examples discussed later in this chapter, which each respond to a particular local contingency within cumbia culture's tapestry, Mister Cumbia's style represents a fairly generic global cumbia style – a cumbia so massified that it found relevance beyond the Spanish-speaking world within which nearly all cumbia subcultures are contained. Montemayor rejected the corrido form as too regionally bound in favor of a cosmopolitan style that, in his words, 'can be recognized in any nightclub in any city in Latin America, or in any town festival anywhere in Mexico or Central America.' 'La Cumbia del Coronavirus' grew from an inspiration to inform. Facilitated by the chaotic multiplicity of social media algorithms and the venerable market magic of timing, it did indeed guarantee Mister Cumbias' position as 'El Rey de las Cumbia Virales'.

Success, of course, invites imitation, and other musicians followed Montemayor's innovation very rapidly in hopes of repeating his viral success. Many of them gained substantial views. This might infer popularity, but is not an accurate measure of truly viral success, which is understood broadly to be built upon sharing, cultural influence, and ubiquity.[14] The first wave of cumbias del coronavirus were largely covers or remixes of the increasingly recognizable 'La Cumbia del Coronavirus'. Mister Cumbia's composition was rapidly covered by professionals and amateurs alike, including versions featuring performances by teams of nurses, first responders, children, and even animated cartoon animals.[15] The most successful and widespread cover of Mister Cumbia was released by Los Internacionales Conejos, a full orquesta grupera that garnered more than a million views. The video features the group playing their full-band arrangement of the original cumbia, complete with dance moves and an energetic vocalist.[16] The concert's crowded live setting and the energetic, jovial performance style of the band presented a somewhat jarring contrast to the public health catastrophe being sung about, though as made clear throughout this book, such incongruities are not uncommon in música del coronavirus. At the time of its release in early March 2020, a consensus about how to respond to the pandemic had not yet been reached. In the comments section of Los Internacionales Conejos' YouTube video, some users noted the cognitive dissonance of singing about COVID-19 in a congested concert space, with one user calling the performance 'a disgrace and a disaster'. However, most comments are positive and enthusiastic responses to the energy and pathos of the performance.

Covers and other responses kept coming. One early reaction video to Mister Cumbia's 'La Cumbia del Coronavirus' garnered a respectable 2500 views.[17] Such reaction videos were themselves variants of remix culture, in which individuals record themselves watching a video or listening to a song with included (generally banal, sometimes amusing) commentary. During the COVID-19 pandemic, numerous reaction videos to different examples of música del coronavirus were uploaded to YouTube. A variety of covers, remixes, and dance videos followed rapidly, including a wonderfully staccato cover by Martio el Sarna released on 5 March 2020.[18] The next week, on 18 March, the first of many 'wepa' remixes of Mister Cumbia appeared. Wepa, an emergent style that combines the slowed-tape sonic aesthetics of Monterrey-style cumbia rebajada with musical aspects of regional Mexican styles from the northwest, was a particularly fertile idiom for coronavirus cumbias. Conversely, at the end of March, DJ Lugomix and DJ Peto released a sped-up remix of 'La Cumbia del Coronavirus' that Montemayor liked enough to repost on his own YouTube channel.[19]

Mister Cumbia's song became so ubiquitous and widely imitated that more than a year after its release, on 21 April 2021, Grupo Abril 20 released its own 'Cumbia del Coronavirus', written by Jorge A. Montoya, and made a point to note that 'no es la versión de "La Cumbia del Coronavirus" de Mister Cumbia.'[20] Mister Cumbia, clearly savoring his initial success, attempted to rekindle it with a new but not especially riveting 'La Cumbia Del Covid-19', which by September 2021 had gained only approximately 62,000 views. He also remixed the song as a huapango norteño ('EL HUAPANGO DEL #CORONAVIRUS') in March 2020, and released two more pandemic-era cumbias: the 'Cumbia de la Cuarentena' ('quarantine cumbia') and a cumbia about the lack of toilet paper ('Se Acabó el Papel').[21] But none of these efforts approached the global dominance and impact of 'La Cumbia del Coronavirus'.

Mister Cumbia's 'La Cumbia del Coronavirus' shows how an accessible and internationalized style could link disparate global experiences. In contrast, most of the other cumbias del coronavirus highlighted a related but distinct tendency of localization and reterritorialization. As Yolanda Broyles-González has written, cumbia is 'an example of how music both deterritorializes and reterritorializes, how music becomes a force in new sociocultural geographies (of race, class, gender, aesthetics, sexuality, and ecosystem)'.[22]

Viral Cumbias, Viral Cultures, and the Pandemic Moment

Perhaps inevitably, a rather blunt use of 'viral culture' was the most obvious and immediate frame to be given to música del coronavirus, as a typical headline like 'Songs about Coronavirus Pandemic Going Viral' shows, among innumerable other examples from the start of the pandemic.[23] In writing about cumbias del coronavirus, as when writing about pandemic remixes, it can be tempting to link the rapid spread of cumbias about the pandemic to the spread of the virus itself. Certainly, there are parallels between the systems of exchange that have historically facilitated the spread of disease and the spread of culture. When considering creative production in the internet era, concepts of 'viral media', 'viral cultures', and 'virality' in general were thoroughly, and perhaps exhaustingly, theorized by academics well before the coronavirus pandemic. Anastasia Denisova has noted that 'some metaphors don't age well' and that '"viral" and "virality" might be among them'. She argues that 'what initially was coined – in sociology and media studies – as an allegory of rapid distribution of information and ideas, does strike the researcher today as a limited definition'. As a conceptual category, 'virality' may end up constricting our understandings of a phenomenon even as it promises to open new interpretative frames. For one, Denisova argues, the idea of virality has a negative connotation of toxicity and poison, whereas the spread of culture, and especially its sharing among communities of people, might in fact be considered morally neutral or even 'a force for good'. Indeed, she concludes, 'sharing is highly emotional and, unlike biological viruses, does not rely on the frailty of the immune system.'[24] Sharing is human, and not all that spreads should be negatively framed as viral.

Karine Nahon and Jeff Hemsley argue that the effects of viral cultures are driven by people within local communities in ways which often remain obscure to broader cultures. Yet the very obscurity of small-scale viral manifestations unexpectedly helps to 'create a dynamic social infrastructure'.[25] More recently, Chris Hables Gray has argued that 'cultural viruses are actually the most complicated of all because the replication processes of culture are so much more involved than those of organic nano-machines or algorithms.'[26] Such 'replication processes of culture' are at once both dizzyingly complex and so ubiquitous as to be easily overlooked.

Following the critical logic of Denisova and Gray as well as others, it is clear that cumbia should not be facilely characterized as merely 'viral'. Cumbia is not a style that spread epidemiologically to contaminate the susceptible, or an insidious musical contagion subsuming weak cultural frameworks, or any other putatively 'viral' framing. In an era where the remixing, recontextualizing, and reinterpretation of cultural objects are no longer outlier phenomena but in fact represent a new global norm, the effectiveness of virality as a defining concept is challenged by way of its very banality.

Cumbia extends beyond being a rhythm that has spread transnationally. Cumbia has formed a positive and complex cultural modality – a cultural ecosystem. The idiom is grounded by a pervasive, even trance-like rhythm that works effectively at a variety of tempos and grooves, including slowed versions of popular songs.[27] Cumbia is a diasporic cultural production eagerly adopted – and adapted – by already rich musical cultures. The coronavirus too spreads via spaces of encounter, but unlike the virus, cumbia's hosts are willing agents of its spread who invite it into their lives as a means of expression and identification. Cumbia rhythm constitutes a globally recognized backbeat to urban life in Latin America, yet highly localized variants of cumbia have emerged organically within distinctive musical subcultures.

Cumbia cultures are dynamic, not static. Nick Sciullo argues that 'mechanistic views of culture hamper the complexities and exchanges of that culture, which are better understood as tapestries of interactions.'[28] Synthetic and transnational approaches to such interactions have proven valuable in numerous studies of globalized popular and vernacular musical cultures.[29] Cumbia carves unique spaces in diverse cultural tapestries, which are contingent on region and significant expressions of gendered, racial identity, and of ethnicity, class, and spatiality. Broyles-González describes the movement, exchange, and connectivity of cumbia along a 'borderlands Norteño circuitry' and she emphasizes the cross-cultural resonances of cumbia in 'cross-border musicultural geographies,'[30] while Alejandro Madrid argues that the act of dancing cumbia can even 'define a new type of transnational cultural citizenship in a rather hostile [...] environment.'[31] The expansive and highly diverse dominion of cumbia links idiosyncratic, internally coherent, and highly realized street cultures in places as disparate and diverse as the rootsy *ruedas de bullerengue* in the palenques of Colombia, the villera parties of Buenos Aires, the psychedelic chicha jams of Amazonian Peru, the rap-cumbia hybrid street culture of 'La Raza Cumbiambera' in Santa Fe Klan's Guanajuato, Mexico and the slowed-down, druggy tempos of El Kings del Wepa of Coahuila, Mexico – and everywhere in between.[32]

Expanding far beyond its origins in Colombia's Magdalena River Delta, cumbia has since spread all over the Spanish speaking world. Héctor Fernández L'Hoeste writes that 'to speak about cumbia is to speak about Colombianness.' Yet at the same time, 'to reflect on cumbia entails a focus on a narrative of idiosyncratic resistance and collective obstinacy.'[33] Historically within Colombia, cumbia has morphed into a wide array of traditional, place-based styles Israel Márquez lists as 'cumbia sampuesana, soledeña, momposina, cartagenera, banqueña, Sanjacintera', as well as what can be considered 'national forms' played by urban dance bands. Further, Cumbia has also internationalized all over the Spanish-speaking world, with further distinctive regional styles. In the internet age, the term 'digital cumbia' has been applied to substyles born and sustained in virtual spaces.[34] Márquez generally prefers to use Alejo Carpentier's conceptualization, which is that all of the cumbias which have developed variously over time retain 'a strange family resemblance' (*'un extraño aire de familia'*).[35] In many national contexts, the class distinctions once inherent in cumbia have faded and the music has grown into new manifestations. For example, in Argentina, where cumbia has become enormously popular, as it started 'to lose its status as a marker of class distinction, there were signs of greater social cohesion within the realm of popular music'. Cumbia 'was apparently undergoing a shift from an expression of social exclusion around the turn of the millennium to a space of social integration a decade later.'[36]

Cumbia is a genre which has a clear origin but a much broader contemporary resonance in many ways expanded, and in significant ways loosened away from, its regional origins and core working-class resonances. Cumbia serves as a flexible and supple mode of expression in which musicians readily adapt the core genre to unique sensibilities in many new and seemingly endless forms. Many writers on cumbia, as on other hybrid musical forms, characterize this transformation as a flow or as a stream of culture which is recapitulated and reimagined anew in each setting. This is especially true in the new virtual era, where music is shared and directed online. Joshua Tucker argues that 'the frame of techno-utopian hybridity has cleared a space for formerly deauthorized subjects to stand forth in their fullness.'[37]

This fullness of expression and spirit in hybridized forms provided an especially rich source of cumbias del coronavirus, including and extending beyond the initial success of Mister Cumbia. An appropriately expansive reading of cumbia's resonance as a musical form as well as an expressive vehicle is the most useful means of contextualizing cumbia within the pandemic moment. Cumbia challenges the certainties of cultural definition and the boundaries of acceptable self-expression as it crosses borders. In the reading of Malvina Silba, it makes complex

> certain social hierarchies [that] are orchestrated within cumbia culture in relation to meanings of 'good taste' (in music), 'good or bad music', and 'good or bad musicians' – especially in terms of who defines these, and the aesthetic and moral parameters employed for their definition.[38]

The drive of consumers and listeners to watch, to share, and both to possess and promote music and cultural content on their own social media channels builds popularity and underscores the professed objectives of virality. As Irving Goh argues, the drive to emulate and replicate viral media success is 'narcissistically driven' and even has its own form of 'viral narcissism'. Consumers and listeners 'send echoes down the rabbit hole of social media to boost and bolster one's narcissism, one's viral status.' Goh further adds that there is 'no viral without other people too.'[39]

Goh's phrase here might be read chillingly as framing contagion with human action; but the central role of *people* rather than algorithms underscores the role of human agency in the spread of cultural productions. It restores the critical elements of interpersonal connection, and the search for communities of sound, affinity, and support. Any evaluation of the success and spread of cumbias del coronavirus must take a multidimensional and interdisciplinary approach, encompassing not just wannabe viral culture mavens but all musicians, producers, DJs, listeners, content creators, and the platforms themselves. It must consider in tandem the role of technological and human factors, as well as the unique virtual spatialities and circumstances of the pandemic moment itself.

It is useful to contrast the coronavirus cumbias during the pandemic moment with other forms of cumbia that pioneered the search for virality as a core, intentional mode of production. Throughout the pandemic era, a subgenre called 'Cumbia 420' produced music and audiovisual lifestyle content functioning as both self-conscious meme and disciplined product development. Cumbia 420 is a syncretic style linking drug culture with cumbia-infused approaches to reggaetón and hip hop. *Forbes* magazine simplified it (and possibly sought to diminish it) as 'Latin rhythms and good old weed', even while equating its steady production to efficient and expansive Taylorist capitalist production models. Cumbia 420 artists' studios crank out 'one track per week'.[40] The virality of the genre, and its energy and commercial viability, derives from its confluence of fast production, consistent sonic products, deliberate marketing strategy, and a stable of artists knowingly and consistently cultivating viral personas. The name 'Cumbia 420' also indicates a lifestyle product, and according to the music's primary producers – for example, Tinty Nasty, L-Gante, Frijo, and El Mas Ladrón – this subaltern and commercial effort also promotes cumbia itself as a form of popular cultural expression. They declared on 19 April 2021 that Cumbia 420 serves to promote 'the continuity of national popular music in our country' ('*la continuidad de la música nacional popular de nuestra Patria*'). It seems to be an effective ploy, since the song announcing this goal, 'Perrito Malvado', has gained 149 million views.[41]

However, the large group of Cumbia 420 artists did not grapple with the coronavirus, despite maintaining an extremely prolific stream of music during the pandemic era. Unlike the diversity of cumbias del coronavirus musicians, it seems that social issues and fears lay outside the subgenre's typical fare of partying, drugs, and sex. Seriously confronting the implications of the pandemic moment did not fit the Cumbia 420 brand. This stands in contrast to artists who produced stylistically and thematically similar cumbia-reggaetón-hip hop mash-ups that directly grappled with the pandemic, such as Snow Tha Product's 'NoWhere To Go (QUARANTINE LOVE)' or Li$ergico, Regu, and Menakid's 'Covid 420'.[42]

Is it really possible to separate the communitarian-directed cumbia del coronavirus virality from that of the viral media forms created in service to capitalist market dominance that Cumbia 420 represents? The essential capitalist aspects of viral cultures have been well explored, including the links between information, language, culture, commerce, and consumption spreading virally – sometimes with observable damage.[43] John Armitage and Mark Featherstone cobble together a grab-bag definition of viral culture, explaining that concepts of protection and mobility, authoritarian populism, extermination, normality, operation, the city, biopolitics, language, life, the image, utopia, leisure, and even the idea of other people are just a few of the notions subject to the agent of change that is viral culture.[44]

Nothing, it would seem, is safe or isolated from viral culture!

Perhaps cumbias del coronavirus as a cultural mode of production stood less as a market variant of viral culture than as autonomous local forms of ownership or resistance to the pressures and imperatives of virality. Localized cumbia styles often build and sustain community identities and cohesiveness as much as they serve production, and, as we will see later in this chapter, even the deliberately viral productions of Mister Cumbia possess a social relevance beyond merely marketing a product or lifestyle. The pandemic moment helped to channel and stimulate the already existing search for a viral hit: a dance song which could dominate the crowded spaces of global cumbia, bestow notoriety and windfall profits to its producer, and possibly impact the outlook and behavior of a vulnerable international community on the brink of a public health catastrophe.

Cumbia itself has been theorized not only as a genre but as a 'space of freedom' and communion. 'Cumbia is 'not only played during festive gatherings' but also serves 'as an accompaniment to people's everyday lives'.[45] During the lockdowns of the early COVID era, daily experience was, for many, reduced to the confines of a personal device, with the internet consuming the empty segments of the day that, in normal times, might have been spent outside the home.

Pandemic-era online 'sonideras' – cumbia-oriented parties featuring DJs voicing over shoutouts to community members – were curated by digital cumbia bands or remix artists.[46] While not exclusively related to the phenomenon of cumbias about coronavirus, the popularity of new cumbia mix videos uploaded to YouTube with titles such as 'cumbias pandemia', 'cumbiando en cuarentena' or 'Cumbia Coronavirus (Remix)' highlighted an aspect of genre as a perpetual soundtrack to millions stuck at home and as a potential viral product.[47] Such cumbia 'pandemia mixes' (sometimes stylized 'Rmx'), appeared along with a huge array of slowed down and sometimes indistinguishable 'wepa mixes', often presented as music-only tracks.[48] Cumbia remix culture, especially the wepa style, runs congruently with the remix culture considered in Chapter One while remaining genre-specific and self-referential. Wepa mixes continue to be released in the fall of 2022, such as Kings del Wepa's version of 'Cumbia del Coronavirus'.[49]

The apparent, even relentless, sameness of these mixes has been noted in writings on cumbia culture more broadly, and is represented by '"cookie-cutter bands", musical groups that are nearly impossible to differentiate from one another.'[50] Even while citing the pandemic in their titles, these videos and mixes sometimes had no delineated or thematic connection to COVID-19. In many cases, remix videos for the pandemic on YouTube were used by DJs to advertise tracks for sale. Some were accompanied with a repetitive vocal sample (often unexpectedly in English) to 'purchase this track today'.[51] At least as often, posted videos provided a link to a free download so people could easily repurpose them, as was the case with 'La Cumbia Del Coronavirus Kumbia Wepa 2020 Dj Gogui Mix' and in the 'Coronavírus Type Rmx'.[52] While many of these videos received tens of thousands of views, the vast majority of the content surveyed shows view counts in the hundreds or less. The sheer number of different cumbia mixes indicates just how quick and easy it was to release new remixes featuring different cumbia rhythms, each ripe for sharing and potential viral spread across digital communities.

El Mosaico Cumbiambero: Cumbias del Coronavirus after Mister Cumbia

As the gravity of the pandemic began to be felt across the globe during March 2020, the number of new cumbias del coronavirus ballooned. These variants reflect the confused, fitful, and anxious nature of early reactions to the pandemic and the way attitudes evolved over time. There were at least 32 new and different cumbias del coronavirus released during March 2020, amounting to at least one per day. When added to all the other genres of música del coronavirus discussed in this book, this represented a truly massive explosion of musical response to the pandemic moment. With this sheer volume came a wide spectrum of regional styles, production levels, and thematic appraisals of the pandemic.

Following the popularity of Mister Cumbia's viral hit, professional and amateur musicians alike began to release cumbias del coronavirus at a dizzying pace. Mister Cumbia may not have been the inspiration for most of these successive releases, given their regionalized variation, but many of the performers were clearly anxious to replicate his success. In spite of his outsized influence, though, the musical and marketing approaches of successive cumbias del coronavirus diverged from Montemayor's model. While Mister Cumbia explicitly sought to make a global impact for the sake of an admixture of both virality and public service, many of the other cumbias released during the early pandemic were geared directly at specific subcultural communities. And while some were widely viewed, many garnered relatively few views, each one exhibiting a distinctive outlook, appraisal, or attitude on living through the pandemic.

The second 'La Cumbia del Coronavirus' came out on 25 February 2020, a month after Mister Cumbia's. It too has been widely remixed and reposted in different videos and configurations, possibly because of its release early in the pandemic. This cumbia was written by El Capi, a musician from San Lucas Ojitlan, Oaxaca, Mexico, who styled himself the king of the keyboards

('El Rey de los Teclados'). Unlike Mister Cumbia's novelty one-man band, El Capi utilized a five-piece band with keyboards, electric bass, guitar, and electric drums. The recording, which is decidedly more syncopated and uptempo than Mister Cumbia's, is in a style widely recognized in southern Mexico as 'cumbia tropical' to distinguish it from other subgenres from the country's center and north. February 2020 was so early in the virus's trajectory that its danger was not yet widely known, understood, or as feared as it would become. The song reflected the lighthearted approach to the pandemic in its early days, and had some of the memetic hallmarks of early pandemic parody pieces. El Capi warns about the danger of the virus, which he describes as a relative of the tropical disease chikungunya, but also finds time to drink Corona beer ostentatiously and to sneeze theatrically during the chorus.[53] Unlike Mister Cumbia, El Capi did not provide any sort of advice in his lyrics on how to slow the spread the virus. This cumbia treats the pandemic not as a looming catastrophe, but as a strange novelty to be capitalized on. It seeks not to educate, warn, or advise, but merely to entertain. The song found a sizable but not overwhelming online success, with 389,759 views by fall 2021. It also inspired numerous remixes and covers.[54]

Argentinian cumbia tackled the coronavirus extensively early in the pandemic moment. The first, heavily autotuned 'Cumbia Coronavirus' was produced by the Kumbia Klan on 14 March 2020. It promised both cumbia and physical passion for a couple trapped in quarantine with no clothes other than face masks. This sex-filled lockdown would go on until the virus killed the singer, or perhaps forced him to speak Chinese.[55] Music journalist Carlo Benito, analyzing the first tranche of cumbias del coronavirus early in the pandemic, described Kumbia Klan's piece as the catchiest of all of the cumbias, while also remarking on its highly suggestive content, which he found hard to discern through the autotuning.[56] The next day, a DIY song called 'La Cumbia Argentina del Coronavirus', put out by Joaquin Lopumo, presented a group of people dressing in costumes (including caricaturish Chinese-style pointed hats) and acting out a series of aural skits about being sick, stuck in the house during the pandemic, and other experiences common to the pandemic moment. A scantily clad and anthropomorphic coronavirus character assaulted the unwary. Throughout, the cumbia warned Argentinians to be aware and prepared. Lopumo explained that the video was not made to harm or ridicule anyone, but was 'only made to laugh and have a good time'.[57] However, it did inevitably rely on sexualized imagery and xenophobic stereotypes to garner a laugh.

Not all cumbias came from self-promoters, humorists, and DIY musicians. Professional acts rushed into the market with cumbias throughout the pandemic in a steady stream, both to cash in on and possibly to promote hygienic behavior. It remains unclear if the lyrics promoting staying home, hand washing, and social distancing were written out of a sense of public service or a lack of creativity. James Cumbia el Pollito remixed Totó la Momposina's 'Cururá' as a coronavirus cumbia, while Jhonny López's 'Cumbia covid', recorded in collaboration with Peruvian ensemble Clase Internacional, utilized slick production techniques and features a salsa-inspired break in the chorus section.[58] Grupo Punto G MX uploaded 'Cumbia Norteña del Coronavirus / 2020' on 16 March 2020 not just to cash in on the pandemic, but straightforwardly to push people toward useful information. Their video contains weblinks to the Centers for Disease Control and, surprisingly, the National Health Service in the UK. The video is nestled under the phrase '#StayHome (#QuédateEnCasa) Play Music #WithMe (Escucha Música Conmigo)'.[59]

Efrain González of Jalisco, Mexico put out the technobanda 'Cumbia Del Coronavirus' on the same day. The following week, José Torres had considerable success with his norteño-banda 'La Cumbia Del Corona Virus – Covid 19'. Underscoring the immediacy of the song, Torres read the lyrics off a cellphone attached to his accordion. He covered an already-fairly standard set of early pandemic themes in March 2020, commenting on the problems and fears of the shortages and shutdown, and recounting a list of COVID-19 symptoms. The song is popular, with an impressive 800,000 views – this is a twenty-fold increase from the view counts on his other music videos. Torres also released a live version of his composition in a small studio setting. The musicians are seen sitting on a couch, flanked by women in designer clothing as they perform the number with some altered lyrics that add comedic effect while detracting emphasis from the virus itself. For example, the line about washing one's hands is changed to be about washing one's genitals, and references to sneezes are transformed into references to bawdy bodily functions. This version, like several other cumbias del coronavirus, seems only tangentially to reference the pandemic situation, but nonetheless calls it by name as an attempt to capitalize on the moment.[60]

Many cumbias drew from the *sonidero* practice of issuing *complacencias*, or live shout-outs overlaid atop the music. For example, 'La Cumbia contra el coronavirus con sonido Famoso en le fuerte de la union 2020' is filled with shoutouts to viewers typical of the style.[61] This allows listeners to 'imagine and make present absent people and places through cumbia sonidera performances, and appropriation of technologies.'[62] Bruno Bartra calls the space cumbia opens up 'a metaphoric territory of peace, solitude, and harmony', and he describes 'the technological Latin American utopia of digital cumbia.'[63] La Wepa Star de Gonzalo Ferrer released 'La Cumbia de La Pandemia' in a cumbia rebajada style on 27 August 2021.[64]

During the pandemic moment, virtual spaces of community and connection were opened via cumbias del coronavirus. YouTube facilitated these spaces in new and diverse ways – spaces alternatively of respite, ridicule, parody, absurdity, and warning. Cumbias provided a temporary musico-spatial escape from the terrors and tedium of the pandemic lockdowns – the ubiquitous call of '*cumbia!*' announced a kind of aural liberation, all while paradoxically reaffirming the real presence of the pandemic and the urgency of its catastrophic impacts.

Cumbia musicians have historically employed humor as a means of challenging class mores and social taboos in a non-confrontational fashion,[65] often focusing on personal and intimate themes related to the body itself, both with and without euphemism.[66] This was true in the healthcare and disease cumbias mentioned in the introduction of this book, and is also found among cumbias exploring themes such as sex and drug use. Regional styles such as cumbia villera 'articulated the lower classes' sense of alienation through brash, often grating sounds and lyrical tropes of sex, drugs and crime' in addition to providing a sharp if coded social critique.[67] Similar themes appeared in many cumbias del coronavirus as a means of accessibly discussing this challenging topic.

Cumbia generated more humorous songs, comedic videos, parodies, and other amusing responses to the pandemic than other genres. While many other styles more frequently addressed tragic themes, cumbias del coronavirus deployed a satirical and even festive tone. However, some efforts at humor were more successfully executed than others. The range of maturity and crudity was similarly wide. Some cumbias del coronavirus were vehicles for jokes directed to audiences so notably small (with a dozen or fewer views) that they functionally operated as in-jokes, if at all. The genre's rhythm and comedic potential provided a ready template for artists to create songs quickly and simply.

Cumbia lyricists drew broadly from a common list of obvious and widely used, putatively humorous themes, including the virus's Chinese origin; bats and bat soup; life on Zoom, WhatsApp, and other messaging applications; shortages of toilet paper and various food items; drunkenness during quarantine; the family quarrels that erupt on account of nobody leaving the house for days; mask use; fear of illness; and, perhaps most consistently, the monotony of lockdown life and a longing to return to the outside world. Early in the pandemic, many cumbias featured tiresome references to Corona brand beer, but the theme was soon dropped. The commonality and redeployment of tropes about bat soup, toilet paper, and other subjects in the early cumbias del coronavirus in effect constituted aural memes, earning a particular power in digital cultural spaces.[68] Memes promoting stereotypes, and the process of othering associated with and further produced by them in the media, are thought to be especially damaging forms of viral media communications during pandemics.[69] On the other hand, repetitive calls in songs to observe sanitary measures and stay abreast of the news can serve a positive social function by promoting positive habits and setting beneficial norms. Students of the Universidad Autónoma de Ciudad Juárez formed Grupo Inmune and Grupo Dank to record the humorous yet socially aware 'Cumbia Coronavirus' as part of a larger recording project that responded to the experiences of pandemic life on the border.[70]

Consuming music on YouTube is a visual as well as an auditory experience. In the music video for 'CORONA CUMBIA' Eddie Cruz y MetaLWarrioR features wigs and costumes, dancing faux medical personnel, and a disclaimer that the song was just meant to make people laugh during the 'horrible situation'.[71] Cruz is also seen wearing a face mask embroidered with a design inspired by the Argentine flag. National, regional, and local imagery are a common element found throughout the music videos that accompanied cumbias del coronavirus. Omar Angulo also dressed humorously in protective gear for a quick ditty with spoof health advice.[72] *El Show de Erazno y La Chokolata*'s 'La Cumbia del Coronavirus', released on 4 March 2020, managed to combine many of the humorous tropes into one song. Erazno, a longtime radio show host based in Los Angeles, sings while boxing cartoon viruses and joking about having to wear a neighbor's pink thong over his mouth as a mask, among other indignities resulting from the virus.[73] Like Mister Cumbia's song, this 'La Cumbia del Coronavirus' was a clear bid to expand and market a personal media brand, although it was seen by a tenth of the number of people. A cartoon rendering of a personified coronavirus made an appearance in Mak King's 'Coronavirus La Cumbia', which was one of the few to reach a significant viewership, of 1.2 million views.[74]

Even the basest humor in some of the cumbias reflected on established modalities of the form, and spoke to market interests as well as the social utilities of the music. Many of the cumbias del coronavirus are express parodies of already-absurd songs that have frequently been subject to comical reimaginations. Los Ángeles Chaplines produced a parody of '17 años' – a song that praises the virtues of having a virgin, teenaged girlfriend – in the form of 'La vacunación – (La cumbia de la vacuna)'. This cumbia warns of American vaccines turning recipients into *gringos*, Chinese vaccines shrinking one's eyes, and other claims rooted in xenophobic humor.[75]

Many other cumbias pursue comic approaches. Jerry y sus Sonora's 'La Cumbia del Covid 19' references the famous funeral march melody from Frederick Chopin's Piano Sonata No. 2, but overlays its somber tone with goofy lyrics about bad-smelling buttocks on account of the lack of toilet paper.[76] El Tiburón Mayor's 'La Cumbia del Coronavirus sin papel' likewise addresses the toilet paper shortage directly and with little subtlety.[77] Adrian Estrada and Faraon de Oro's 'La Cuarentena Coronavirus CUMBIA' makes jokes about partying by oneself and is sung in a slow, heavily auto-tuned groove.[78] The instrumental backbeat was lifted directly from Shiko_Beatz x O.T. Menace's 'Electrocumbia 2020', called simply 'Coronavirus'. This song and video, which was released at the end of March 2020, contains most of the well-established tropes found in earlier cumbia del coronavirus music videos, including singers dressed in medical garb, Corona beer, toilet paper, and scenes of entrapment at home. The last minute of the video is the poster 'El Famous Juan' of Lake Elsinore, California, asking viewers to subscribe to his various channels. The appeal appeared to work, based on the many favorable comments in Spanish and English about how this was 'probably one of the best Coronavirus songs I heard', 'This shit low key slaps', and, in Mexico–US borderlands slang, 'Puro tacuache, Al 100'. One listener mocked the sound of the cumbia with a snippet of pretend dialogue: 'juan: what's auto tune? idk im going to try it out/also juan: how much let's put it 100% see how it sounds.'[79]

Many cumbias del coronavirus address the experience of frustration and boredom stoked by days of lockdown, in both their lyrics and accompanying music videos. Flor Amargo's 'La Cumbia de la Cuarantena', released 2 March 2020, slowly plods at 82 bpm, resting on a cumbia rhythm to back up her creative songwriting. In her verses, Amargo bemoans the experience of living through pandemic shutdowns alone at home. The accompanying video illustrates the loneliness of quarantining by oneself, with scenes of her dressing up as a personified coronavirus who comes to harass her in the song's chorus, conversing with a puppet in the absence of friends and manically plinking out a recurring spacey riff on a keytar.[80]

Chilean-Canadian singer-songwriter Beto Cuevas's 'Cumba del Encierro' presents a more pensive, even sad, sensibility. It opens to a scene of an elderly woman lighting candles in her home and singing about the mundane things – such as heating up water to make breakfast and bathing – that have taken centrality in life under quarantine.[81] When Cuevas himself appears in the video, he is initially positioned behind prison bars, emphasizing the sense of being literally locked down. The scenes change to show Cuevas walking down a street and dancing in his room. The elderly woman is shown in a variety of outfits and situations, but the two never appear in the same frame or sing at the same time, further accentuating the loneliness inherent in the solitary social distancing widely experienced during the pandemic moment.

On 20 March 2020, Sony recording artist and comedian Juanito El Millonzuki and DJ Mailo put out 'El Cumbion Del Corona Virus!', which was billed as explicitly designed to get people in quarantine dancing. Describing himself as 'El rey del Urban Ranch', Juanito El Millonzuki is based in the United States and mostly produces humorous music, including other satirical cumbias in collaboration with comedian and viral internet personality El Chaparro Chuachenege. The uptempo track, played in a modified cumbia style with banda sierreña instrumentation, warns listeners to stay out of the virus' reach. In place of a music video, the YouTube listing for the track features a hackneyed still image featuring rolls of toilet paper, a cartoon coronavirus, and a bat flying out of a bowl of soup.[82]

Potro Salvaje Torreón (the 'Torreón Wild Foal') is a musical comedian specializing in danceable compositions accompanied by humorous videos. His rather dormant YouTube channel Portro Salvaje TV is small, with only 330 subscribers. It contains an odd variety of videos posted over several years (mostly *ca*. 2016–2018), and like Mister Cumbia, his output ranges widely in topical focus.[83] He produces comedy sketches, songs, comic news reports on subjects ranging from school shootings in Florida and the Virgin of the

Guadalupe, to comical songs about cholo life, twerking mashups with Scooby Doo, a recurrent series of him dressing as a dog, and other generally unclassifiable videos. His compositions span several genres and styles, with cumbia well-represented among them.[84]

For these reasons, his 'Cumbia del Corona Virus', released early in the pandemic on 4 March 2020, stands out both in its appeal as a song and for the production values of the music and video. Unlike most of his older content, 'Cumbia del Corona Virus' has a slicker sound and a more driving beat, maintaining a brisk 153 bpm. Cumbias del coronavirus ranged from an upper end of 155 bpm of La Concentracion's 'Cumbia covid' to the languid 91 bpm of El Danny Boy's 'La Covid Cumbia', or the wepa-style drag of 88 bpm of 'La Wepa Star' in Gonzalo Ferrer's Argentine cumbia sonidera-style recording 'La Cumbia de la Pandemia'.[85]

Potro Salvaje Torreón's content is entirely comical, like his other music. The video portrays the apparently drunken, shirtless singer painted as a black-faced, fluorescent green, polka-dotted coronavirus. The video features Potro Salvaje Torreón running around the streets of Torreón, the capital of the Mexican border state of Coahuila, alternately scaring and amusing bystanders with his clownish behavior. Throughout the video, he extolls the virtues of Corona beer served in a *caguamon*, or a large bottle. Meanwhile, el Potro Salvaje – as the coronavirus incarnate – is chased by a nurse carrying an oversized hypodermic needle. Only upon seeing the Cristo de las Noas, a massive statue of Christ that is widely recognized as a symbol of the city of Torreón, is the coronavirus finally vanquished.[86] While el Potro Salvaje sings of a global pandemic, the imagery of his video is firmly grounded in his home city.

A fair number of cumbias del coronavirus, especially those released early in the pandemic in the spring of 2020, made putatively humorous use of racism as frame and touchstone. Goh has observed that the spread of racism during the pandemic could itself be seen as a form of systemic virus.[87] One cumbia senselessly associated the coronavirus with Chinese celebrities like Bruce Lee and Jackie Chan.[88] Café Cargado released a satirical cumbia in February 2020 which functioned largely as a profane denouncement of the 'fucking Chinese' ('pinches Chinos').[89] Billy Balsec's 'La Cumbia del Coronavirus 2.020 Pandemia Mundial' was built around what musicologists have defined as 'the oriental riff' played on a keyboard. This 'overwhelmingly stereotyping and/or overtly racist' riff has been called 'a sonic cliché'. As Paul Bowman has concluded, the riff is 'a kind of enduring cultural "meme" or discrete cultural fragment'.[90]

This common motif was accompanied with other COVID-era visual and sonic memes: sounds of whines and screaming, lyrical references to eating rats, bats, cockroaches, and dogs, and stock footage of dogs being cooked in crowded markets, bats on spits, snake meat, and other exotic animals that the song blamed for the virus. Interestingly, this approach did not generate significant viewership (only 2752 views), and received no comments.[91]

Another cumbia which indulged in anti-Chinese comedic framings came from style-defining group La Sonora Dinamita's popular 'El Coronavirus', released on 1 April 2020. In this track, the group advises its listeners to take COVID-19 seriously, as it is not a 'Chinese story ('*cuento chino*'), a Spanish idiom that refers to a myth or a tall tale. While this lyric is not explicitly anti-Chinese, it draws on a satirical double entendre rooted in deeply embedded racist conceptions of otherness.[92]

Given the hackneyed language, absurdity, racism, and flippant jokes in so many of these songs, one might be tempted to consider cumbias del coronavirus as little more than a parody genre. However, there remain many more examples which encapsulated the cultural significance of the moment and, like Mister Cumbia, that encouraged sanitary behavior as a means of community self-preservation.

On 28 February 2020, Roberto Junior y su Bandeño released one of the first cumbias about the looming crisis. In his video, Roberto Junior sings into the camera on the street with his banda norteña arranged behind him, brass band with guitar, accordion, guira, and other instruments. A popular leader of a generally flashy band with some hits in regional music categories, Roberto Junior here presents a spontaneous-feeling cumbia on the pandemic. He reads the lyrics off a cellphone in his hand, making full use of the phrase 'el coronavirus' for a call-and-response chorus. The simple but powerfully delivered and repeated refrain of the song is given a ska feel with a loping rhythm. The band, sounding lively if unrehearsed, plays with energy and aplomb, almost like a street band. The band are shown wearing masks, which was unusual this early in the pandemic. The trumpet player has a hole cut into his mask, while Roberto Junior removes his a few seconds into singing. Overall, this song is an energetic and defiant cumbia that at once announces the arrival of the coronavirus and demands united action to defeat it.[93]

Two months later, Roberto Junior released another cumbia, called 'La Cuarentena'. This cumbia he sang alone, with no band, delivered as a person describing the feeling of not working and being trapped in his house during the pandemic. It is sung, very unusually for a cumbia, or for any of the música del coronavirus songs from professional musicians, without accompaniment. In the video, Roberto Junior is reclining in a cushy leather armchair. The verse and chorus both have an insistent descending lick which drives the music forward. Junior even sings the instrumental breaks, playing air accordion on his chest. The video features his wife yelling at him at the end, as well as some B-roll footage of various errors and retakes from the recording session.[94]

Many cumbias del coronavirus highlight ways the pandemic moment was understood in local and personal (even intimate) contexts. Salvattore Zamorini's 'El Coronavirus', uploaded on 2 March 2020, looked at the spread of coronavirus through a humorous lens of serial infidelity. Zamorini warns of the emergent threat of the coronavirus and invites the listener to imagine the problems that would follow in a town filled with promiscuous people. He then presents a humorous probable list of successive contamination. In the song, infection begins with the grocer, who infects his wife, who in turn infects the milkman, who infects his woman, who in turn infects her brother-in-law, who infects his sister, who then infects a construction worker, continuing on down the line. The virus eventually comes to infect Zamorini, who implies he got it from the listener's girlfriend. The widening circle of infidelity and infection, with Zamorini's exaggerated delivery, speaks to the ways that sexual themes commonly portrayed in cumbias were magnified in gravity and danger during the pandemic.[95]

A large number of amateur performers of varying accomplishment utilized the cumbia form to express their personal pandemic experiences. It might be tempting to focus only on the songs with hundreds of thousands or millions of views. Yet the cumbias released by marginal musicians which received relatively few views highlight a different but equally significant social media phenomenon of amateur self-expression and performativity. Many songs of little impact were posted by individuals who felt moved to share their perspectives in Do-It-Yourself cumbia form. These ranged from Luis Gámez's slow 'La Cumbia de la Pandemia', released on 20 October 2020, to videos like the 'cumbia del coronavirus' from 'Villa Goalkeeper', uploaded on 21 March 2020. Villa Goalkeeper sang his composition set to a karaoke backing track in a video that had received only 53 views as of September 2021 – and only five more for a total of 58 a year later.[96] According to the channel description he posted on YouTube, Villa Goalkeeper specializes in 'goalkeeper videos, training, and other fun content'. Nonetheless, he was moved to write his own cumbia to a karaoke track about the coronavirus to remind people to stay home, stay safe, and stay healthy.[97] Rosaura Virginia Aguiar Peschiutta of Argentina produced a karaoke song with original lyrics on 30 March 2020, another video that had only 49 views on their four-subscriber channel.[98]

There were also quite a few obscure cumbias released by individuals who made similar use of pre-recorded backing tracks. Armando Sarabia sang in his living room to a backing track of a synthesized wind band through a speaker-and-microphone setup.[99] In 'La Cumbia Del Coronavirus 1', Baldo Alvarez warned that rates of infection had surged in the states of Durango, Sinaloa and Baja California in the fall of 2020. His singling out of these northwestern states likely had more to do with his own location and the location of his viewers than the actual comparative rates of Coronavirus shown in the map displayed, considering that none of them fall into the category of highest risk. His song, filled with serious observations and suggestions, has been viewed only 75 times, a count even lower than his number of subscribers.[100]

Edgar and Eric Tepo's 'La Cumbia del covid 2021' was posted by Mario Pelaez, who has two subscribers, on 10 November 2020. Pelaez included a note that the style was a 'rhythm that spreads' ('el ritmo que contagia, quién?')[101] Cándida Montiel's 'Pandemia de cumbia', a song recorded in Paraná, Entre Ríos, Argentina in July 2020, is an intentionally DIY-style recorded piece which sings about the extreme time compression and boredom of the pandemic lockdowns, as well as concerns about the uncertainty of the new normal of the pandemic moment. The song deftly combines the idea of a cumbia pandemic with the production realities under a pandemic lockdown, recognizing the spread of cumbia itself. The video for the song is filled by a group of young people dancing and acting out their frustrations, marked by a languid shout of 'cumbia' mid-song.[102]

Another decidedly DIY 'Cumbia de la Pandemia' was performed on solo guitar by Casi Patiño, who called for dancing instead of being taken away by the sickness. His YouTube channel was a small-scale but dedicated project, featuring 14 videos for its 28 subscribers. In each, Patiño sits on a stool in what appears to be a home studio; a whiteboard behind him variously lists rhythms and chords. Each video provides lyrical subtitles. In his description of his channel's purpose, Patiño presents himself as an exhibitor of unpublished songs which 'will reveal musical and composition secrets for all people who like to learn, whether they are beginners or [people] with musical knowledge.'[103] This self-directed DIY effort to present his 'Cumbia de la Pandemia', as well as another titled 'Quédate en casa' and political songs such as 'Ganar o Morir', about criminal violence, was clearly in service to his personal and artistic vision rather than a search for viral fame.[104]

While many of the more popular cumbias del coronavirus are inherently comical and composed along the lines of commercial popular music, some examples draw upon cumbia's communitarian and spatially defining qualities to present an alternative to the isolation and hopelessness caused by quarantine. Sierra y Folclor, a non-profit organization in Bogotá, initiated a YouTube channel during the COVID-19 pandemic. The organization features an all-female gaita (flute) workshop called Flores del Folclor, which posts its own renditions of traditional repertory, including cumbia covers played on traditional instruments as an intentional way of capturing the emotional feeling of Colombian folk music. For example, the group posted a cover of Totó La Momposina y sus Tambores' classic 'Cururá', styled as 'Cumbiambero en Pandemia – Cumbia' and played on traditional acoustic instrumentation of gaitas, and tambura, tambor alegre, and lamador (traditional drums). This video was coupled with the participants musing on the significance of cumbia's resonance as a sound, rhythm, and experience during the pandemic. Sierra y Folclor also presented pandemic-moment original compositions such as '¡Ayyy Cuarentena!' in chalupa rhythm, as well as a variety of other didactic and conversational videos. Uploads by Sierra y Folclor integrated clips of earnest if amateur performance with interview segments.[105]

Flores del Folclor deliberately embraced rhythms and styles like cumbia and chalupa during the pandemic, since, as they explain, they have been 'used in an ancestral way to orally transmit the situations, experiences and experiences of daily life'. Students and leaders of the workshop describe in detail how the project seeks to fuse contemporary social media and traditional musical forms to seize autonomy and maintain cultural expression during the pandemic. The overall organizational effort is directed to foster racial, ethnic, and gender equity in access and opportunity, in addition to embracing local soundscapes, or 'los sonidos de mi tierra'. Especial emphasis is directed to the Sierra Morena communities and Cazucá neighborhood. Sierra y Folclor's efforts, begun in 2019, remain locally focused while maintaining a social media presence on major international channels. Its YouTube channel remained quite small in fall 2022, with only 95 subscribers and low viewer counts on videos.[106]

Other highly regional cumbias del coronavirus include a recording called 'La cumbia del coronavirus' by Organización Luz Azul, a *banda grupera* from the Costa Chica region of Mexico, released on 15 April 2020. In the description of the cumbia, Producciones Ramiz urges listeners to support the artists and to 'play this style of music at all of your events, birthdays, weddings, birthday parties' so as 'to not forget the traditions and culture of Oaxaca and Guerrero'.[107] Little reference in the accompanying text is made to the coronavirus itself, although some comments on the video encourage fellow viewers to take care, even going so far as to critique the band for being ignorant of the growing crisis.

Cumbia urbana singer Dennis Fernando's 'Cancion del Coronavirus' was fairly unusual among the cumbias of the early pandemic. His cumbia essentially rejected any fear of the virus besides the need to be careful, while insisting on dancing and counseling mastering fear in favor of happiness. The song gained only approximately 45,000 views, but responses indicate a wide listening audience, with favorable comments from people from Venezuela, Brazil, Mexico City, Bolivia, and elsewhere.[108] David Y. Fernando's 'Pandemia Cumbia' is a also a highly produced, professional, and profit-oriented effort clearly designed to take advantage of the topical theme of the pandemic. It was released rather late in the movement on 20 March 2021, more than a year after the original cumbias del coronavirus began emerging.[109] Sub Cumbia's 'Cumbia la Pandemia', released during this same later period, is one of the rare examples that eschewed a chorus of 'coronavirus' and instead opted for one based on official six-foot social distancing advice. Sub Cumbia seems to have been created entirely for the purposes of 'Cumbia la Pandemia'.[110]

Following this dizzying survey of a selection of the full range of cumbias del coronavirus released by fall 2021, it is fair to ask what links all these disparate examples of a style whose international spread has ranged from globally palatable recordings such as those of Mister Cumbia to a plethora of reterritorialized styles and DIY efforts. These cumbias represent differing artistic sensibilities, degrees of professionalism in production, locations of origin, commercial intents, and lyrical approaches. However, all of their creators utilized, and identified with, cumbia. Indeed, many artists claimed to be irresistibly drawn to cumbia during the pandemic. Cumbias del coronavirus channeled individual musical sensibilities as they entertained and sustained communities of listeners around the world. As a transnational and expansive musical form, cumbia provided a uniquely expressive means of generating creative and highly localized responses to the global pandemic moment.

Notes

1. 'La Cumbia del Coronavirus – Mister Cumbia', https://www.youtube.com/watch?v=KqasQyatfBQ (accessed 8 October 2021). See also the Mister Cumbia Facebook page: https://www.facebook.com/profile.php?id=100044931257229 (accessed 8 October 2021).
2. Iván Montemayor, interview by J. A. Strub and Dan Margolies, 7 September 2021.
3. Montemayor, interview.
4. 'Los 15 de Ruby', https://www.youtube.com/watch?v=l6rmxNOdl0M (accessed 8 October 2021).
5. 'La cumbia de Ben Afleck Y Jennifer Lopez', https://www.youtube.com/watch?v=hiFQQeXabVU (accessed 16 September 2022).
6. Montemayor, interview.
7. Montemayor, interview.
8. Montemayor, interview.
9. 'La Cumbia del Coronavirus', https://www.youtube.com/watch?v=KqasQyatfBQ (accessed 8 October 2021).
10. 'La Cumbia del Coronavirus'.
11. Montemayor, interview.
12. Montemayor, interview.
13. Montemayor, interview.
14. Karine Nahon and Jeff Hemsley, *Going Viral* (Cambridge: Polity, 2013), esp. p. 9. Eduardo Navas writes 'a cover version is often considered a derivative work, meaning that it does not hold the same status as that of an original recording; consequently, it is considered of lower status in the creative totem pole.' See 'The Originality of Copies: Cover Versions and Versioning in Remix Practice', *Journal of Asia-Pacific Pop Culture* 3.2 (2018): 168–87, p. 169.
15. 'La Cumbia Del Coronavirus – Mister Cumbia [Letra]', https://www.youtube.com/watch?v=SN8_C3jdYIY (accessed on 29 August 2021).
16. 'La Cumbia Del Coronavirus', https://www.youtube.com/watch?v=7ZVl2pKXaEY (accessed 29 August 2021).
17. 'La CUMBIA del CORONAVIRUS (VIDEOREACCION)', https://www.youtube.com/watch?v=o8n5HqsDbj8 (accessed 29 August 2021)
18. 'LA CUMBIA DEL CORONAVIRUS – MARITO EL SARNA', https://www.youtube.com/watch?v=vnC4fXh5bLA (accessed 7 September 2021).
19. 'CORONAVIRUS 3BALL REMIX – MISTER CUMBIA X DJ LUGOMIX X DJ PETO', https://www.youtube.com/watch?v=hmGjk25wLHg (accessed 7 September 2021).
20. Grupo Abril 20, 'Cumbia del Coronavirus', https://www.youtube.com/watch?v=wFcfGxI2GPE (accessed 7 September 2021).
21. 'La Cumbia Del Covid-19', https://www.youtube.com/watch?v=E9jwI07seNo (accessed 7 September 2021); 'El Huapango del #Coronavirus', https://www.youtube.com/watch?v=aGDsVCsw9ic (accessed 7 September 2021).
22. Yolanda Broyles-González, 'Norteño Borderlands Cumbia Circuitry: Selena Quintanilla and Celso Piña', in Gaetano Prampolini and Annamaria Pinazzi, eds, *The Shade of the Saguaro / La sombra del saguaro. Essays on the Literary Cultures of the American*

Southwest / Ensayos sobre las culturas literarias del suroeste norteamericano (Florence: Firenze University Press, 2013), 173–93, p. 177.
23. Bethonie Butler, 'Songs about Coronavirus Pandemic Going Viral', *Columbus Dispatch*, 24 March 2020, https://eu.dispatch.com/story/lifestyle/health-fitness/2020/03/24/songs-about-coronavirus-pandemic-going/1472817007/ (accessed 5 September 2023). Butler's article originally appeared in the *Washington Post* on 19 March 2020 under the headline 'Millions are now Streaming Songs about Coronavirus. Are They Good? It Doesn't Matter', https://www.washingtonpost.com/arts-entertainment/2020/03/19/cardi-b-jojo-coronavirus-songs/ (accessed 5 September 2023).
24. Anastasia Denisova, 'How to Define "Viral" for Media Studies?', *Westminster Papers in Communication and Culture* 15.1 (2020): 1–4. Robert Payne also undercuts the tropes of virality: 'So while the means of transmission of harmful computer viruses and desirable viral media may be similar, and while both may be the result of deliberate and strategic production, anxieties around the danger or nuisance of the former do not seem to have transferred evenly into the latter.' See Robert Payne, 'VIRALITY 2.0: Networked Promiscuity and the Sharing Subject', *Cultural Studies* 27.4 (2013): 540–60, p. 542.
25. Nahon and Hemsley, *Going Viral*, p. 3.
26. Chris H. Gray, 'Virus is a Language: COVID-19 and the New Abnormal', *Cultural Politics* 17.1 (2021): 92–101.
27. There are many YouTube channels dedicated to slowed-down cumbias and corridos, including Mister Cumbia's 'La Cumbia del Coronavirus'. Examples include 'La Cumbia del Coronavirus Slowed X Mister Cumbia', https://www.youtube.com/watch?v=F7KK9malbxM (accessed 8 October 2021).
28. Nick J. Sciullo, *Communicating Hip-Hop: How Hip-Hop Culture Shapes Popular Culture* (Santa Barbara, CA: Praeger, 2019), p. 9.
29. For example, of many relevant works, Carolyn Cooper, *Sound Clash: Jamaican Dancehall Culture at Large* (New York: Palgrave Macmillan, 2004); Deborah P. Hernandez, *Oye Como Va! Hybridity and Identity in Latino Popular Music* (Philadelphia: Temple University Press, 2010); Jeremy Wallach, Harris M. Berger, and Paul D. Greene, *Metal Rules the Globe: Heavy Metal Music Around the World* (Durham, NC: Duke University Press, 2011); Ashley L. Cordes, *Rave Identity and Self-Reflexive Compartmentalization: An Exploration of Rituals and Beliefs of Contemporary Rave Culture* (O'ahu: Hawaii Pacific University, 2012); Sarah Thornton, *Club Cultures: Music, Media and Subcultural Capital* (Cambridge: Polity, 2013); Melissa Castillo-Garsow and Jason Nichols, eds, *La Verdad: An International Dialogue on Hip Hop Latinidades* (Columbus: Ohio State University Press, 2016); Sofia Johansson, Ann Werner, Patrik Åker, and Greg Goldenzwaig, *Streaming Music: Practices, Media, Cultures* (New York: Routledge, 2017); Jesús A. Ramos-Kittrell, ed., *Decentering the Nation: Music, Mexicanidad, and Globalization* (Lanham, MD: Lexington Books, 2019); Helena Simonett, ed., *The Accordion in the Americas: Klezmer, Polka, Tango, Zydeco, and More!* (Champaign: University of Illinois Press, 2021).
30. Broyles-González, 'Norteño Borderlands, pp. 179–81.
31. Alejandro L. Madrid, 'Rigo Tovar, Cumbia, and the Transnational *Grupero* Boom', in Héctor Fernández L'Hoeste and Pablo Vila, eds, *Cumbia! Scenes of a Migrant Latin American Music Genre* (Durham, NC: Duke University Press 2013), 105–18, p. 114.
32. Joshua Tucker, 'From The World of the Poor to the Beaches of Eisha: Chicha, Cumbia, and the Search for a Popular Subject in Peru', in Héctor Fernández L'Hoeste and Pablo Vila, eds, *Cumbia! Scenes of a Migrant Latin American Music Genre* (Durham, NC: Duke University Press 2013), 138–67; Israel Márquez, 'Bailando Con Zizek: Orígenes y Evolución De La Cumbia Digital En Buenos Aires', *América Latina, Hoy* 78 (2018): 87–104; 'Cumbiambera Santa Fe Klan ft La Cumbita', https://www.youtube.com/

watch?v=Xkr1xHoMBy4 (accessed 8 October 2021); 'Kinds del Wepa', https://www.youtube.com/channel/UC4_dFc4a41IcInTbE_ONcAw (accessed 8 October 2021).
33. Héctor Fernández L'Hoeste, 'On Music and Colombianness: Toward a Critique of the History of Cumbia', in Héctor Fernández L'Hoeste and Pablo Vila, eds, *Cumbia! Scenes of a Migrant Latin American Music Genre* (Durham, NC: Duke University Press 2013), 248–68, p. 248.
34. 'Márquez, 'bailando Con Zizek', p. 87; see also Patricio Gómez, 'Cumbia y fuera', *Clarín*, 7 July 2009, http://edant.clarin.com/ (accessed 19 September 2022); Geoffrey Baker, '"Digital Indigestion": Cumbia, Class and a Post-Digital Ethos in Buenos Aires', *Popular Music* 34.2 (2015): 175–96.
35. Márquez, 'bailando', p. 87.
36. Baker, '"Digital indigestion"', p. 179.
37. Joshua Tucker, 'Peruvian Cumbia at the Theoretical Limits of Techno-Utopian Hybridity', in Alejandro L. Madrid, Ana R. Alonso-Minutti, and Eduardo Herrera, eds, *Experimentalisms in Practice: Music Perspectives from Latin America* (Oxford: Oxford University Press, 2018), 85–106, p. 90.
38. Malvina Silba, '"Argentina is Cumbia": Sociocultural Trajectories of Young "Cumbieros" in Urban Peripheries', *Journal of World Popular Music* 4.2 (2017): 171–90, p. 173.
39. Irving Goh, 'Virus is Other People', *Cultural Politics*, 17:1 (2021): 145–9, p. 146. See also Gerard J. Tellis, Deborah J. MacInnis, Seshadri Tirunillai, and Zhang Yanwei, 'What Drives Virality (Sharing) of Online Digital Content? The Critical Role of Information, Emotion, and Brand Prominence', *Journal of Marketing* 83.4 (2019): 1–20.
40. Javier Hasse, 'Cumbia 420: The Super Viral, Weed-Infused Musical Phenomenon Bringing Ghetto Back To The Mainstream', *Forbes*, 27 May 2021, https://www.forbes.com/sites/javierhasse/2021/05/27/cumbia-420-the-super-viral-weed-infused-musical-phenomenon-bringing-ghetto-back-to-the-mainstream/ (accessed 5 September 2023).
41. 'DAMAS GRATIS – PERRITO MALVADO Ft. L-GANTE & MARITA', https://www.youtube.com/watch?v=JasYNAEgehM (accessed 5 September 2023).
42. 'Snow Tha Product – NoWhere To Go (QUARANTINE LOVE)', https://www.youtube.com/watch?v=nW5bmRfwLHE (accessed 8 October 2021); 'Covid 420', https://www.youtube.com/watch?v=3S7OAK--TMk (accessed 8 October 2021).
43. Giulia Crippa, 'Informação pandémica e capitalismo viral: a mídia, a Covid-19 e a construção dos medos', *Liinc Em Revista* 16.2 (2020): Article e5332; Jason J. Wallin and Jennifer A. Sandlin, 'Capital Immunodeficiency and the Viral Contagion of Capitalism', *Knowledge Cultures* 8.3 (2020): 20–7.
44. John Armitage and Mark Featherstone, 'Viral Culture', *Cultural Politics* 17.1 (2021): 1–10, p. 1.
45. Silba, '"Argentina is Cumbia"', p. 171.
46. '🔟🎬Una Cumbia Desde La Cuna Del CoronaVirus 'Wepa'🎬🔟Sonido MANHATTAN🎬🔟Actopan Hgo🎬🔟', https://www.youtube.com/watch?v=R9_CXK6yVw0 (accessed 15 September 2022).
47. 'COVID 19 CUMBIA INSTRUMENTAL.. MIGUEL ALARCON Y SUS SAMBUESANOS.. WEPA JE', https://www.youtube.com/watch?v=GQbj0atr9A8 (accessed 16 September 2022); 'Cumbia Coronavirus (Remix)', https://www.youtube.com/watch?v=NBI6gz7fztk (accessed 16 September 2022); 'DJ JC WEPA VS CUMBIA NORTEÑA#CoronaVirus Mix', https://www.youtube.com/watch?v=jjd1dPBtEtg (accessed 16 September 2022); 'Corona virus cumbia mix and regaton mix', https://www.youtube.com/watch?v=Ivu3XxNN4dk (accessed 16 September 2022).
48. 'Cumbia wepa Del Coronavirus Dj Arzenik beat 😂😂😂 Hecha en caustic 3', https://www.youtube.com/watch?v=bHfygwvcTUI (accessed 16 September 2022); 'LA CUMBIA DEL CORONAVIRUS (ESTILO WEPA) ANIMO PANDILLA CUMBIAS

EDITADAS 2020', https://www.youtube.com/watch?v=gcCS7HHqeoU (accessed 16 September 2022).
49. Uploaded on 6 September 2022: 'Cumbia del Coronavirus', https://www.youtube.com/watch?v=XebUh5SvDfM (accessed 16 September 2022).
50. Silba, '"Argentina is Cumbia"', p. 172.
51. Such as in 'Cumbia 420 Beat / Beat Reggaeton Perreo RKT Instrumental / L-Gante x Cazzu x BRZP Type / 2021', https://www.youtube.com/watch?v=l9YCyI8WgL8 (accessed 16 September 2022) or 'CUMBIAS SONIDERAS PANDEMIA MIX', https://www.youtube.com/watch?v=FGj2JjWVk8I (accessed 16 September 2022).
52. 'La Cumbia Del Coronavirus Kumbia Wepa 2020 Dj Gogui Mix', https://www.youtube.com/watch?v=wHIkwFzyfNI (accessed 16 September 2022); 'Coronavírus Type Rmx', https://www.youtube.com/watch?v=CLvWZaVsVz8 (accessed 16 September 2022).
53. 'La Cumbia Del El Coronavirus', https://www.youtube.com/watch?v=Trfw-3hSpjY (accessed 16 September 2022).
54. The lack of seriousness of the composition was indicated in the way a version of it was set at a quinceañera celebration posted 13 March 2020, in which a group of young women are shown dancing, skipping, and making funny faces: 'Corona virus cumbia version quinceanera :)', https://www.youtube.com/watch?v=eZCjui5HdOs (accessed 16 September 2022).
55. Kumbia Klan, 'Cumbia Coronavirus', https://www.youtube.com/watch?v=OgwxKJ-AfB4 (accessed 16 September 2022).
56. Carlo Benito, 'La pandemia musical: cuatro horas escuchando canciones sobre el coronavirus', *El Comercio*, 28 April 2020, https://www.elcomercio.es/vivir/artes/pandemia-musical-20200428100322-ntrc.html (accessed 16 September 2022).
57. Joaquin Lopumo, 'Coronavirus Cumbia', https://www.youtube.com/watch?v=mbmTKP6gzsA (accessed 16 September 2022).
58. 'corona virus James cumbia', https://www.youtube.com/watch?v=tgGy9C5l1bw (accessed 16 September 2022); 'Cumbia covid', https://www.youtube.com/watch?v=OCOwUaiu4cQ (accessed 7 October 2021).
59. 'Cumbia Norteña del Coronavirus / 2020', https://www.youtube.com/watch?v=COxsmaNnhIQ (accessed 7 October 2021).
60. 'La Cumbia Del Corona Virus – Covid 19', https://www.youtube.com/watch?v=fz2rV7samvc (accessed 7 October 2021); 'La cumbia del coronavirus de José Torres' https://www.youtube.com/watch?v=_O4tcDnC4ug (accessed 7 October 2021).
61. 'La Cumbia contra el coronavirus con sonido Famoso en le fuerte de la union 2020', https://www.youtube.com/watch?v=IFyTuiExr-8 (accessed 7 October 2021).
62. Alexandra Lippman, 'Listening Across Borders: Migration, Dedications, and Voice in Cumbia Sonidera', *Latin American Science, Technology and Society* 1:1 (2018): 201–15, p. 203.
63. Bruno Bartra, 'Digital Cumbia and the Latin American Technological Utopia', *Review* 48.1 (2015): 95–9, p. 99.
64. 'La Cumbia de La Pandemia', https://www.youtube.com/watch?v=bbB6K9IdJeo (accessed 7 October 2021).
65. Héctor Fernández L'Hoeste and Pablo Vila, 'Introduction', in Héctor Fernández L'Hoeste and Pablo Vila, eds, *Cumbia! Scenes of a Migrant Latin American Music Genre* (Durham, NC: Duke University Press 2013), 1–27, p. 7; Rosana Diaz-Zambrana, 'Gastronomia, humor y nacion: estrategias retoricas en las letras de Calle 13', *Centro Journal* 22.2 (2010): 129–49.
66. Broyles-González, 'Norteño Borderlands', pp. 177–9.
67. Baker, '"Digital indigestion"', p. 178.
68. Bradley E. Wiggins, *The Discursive Power of Memes in Digital Culture: Ideology, Semiotics, and Intertextuality* (New York: Routledge, 2019).

69. S. Harris Ali, 'Stigmatized Ethnicity, Public Health, and Globalization', *Canadian Ethnic Studies* 40 (2008): 43–64; Evie Kendal, 'Public Health Crises in Popular Media: How Viral Outbreak Films Affect the Public's Health Literacy', *Medical Humanities* 47.1 (2021): 11–19, p. 14.
70. 'Cumbia Coronavirus', https://www.youtube.com/watch?v=Mth8o4w0dts (accessed 7 October 2021).
71. 'Corona Cumbia', https://www.youtube.com/watch?v=vrR24REIZOkel (accessed 16 September 2022).
72. 'La cumbia del Coronavirus', https://www.youtube.com/watch?v=Ol6SQTaSIpQ (accessed 16 September 2022).
73. *Erazno y La Chokolata*, 'Viernes de Nacadas, las !0 de Erazno, el Chokolatazo, La final de La Casa de las Parodias, y mucho mas', El Podcast Mas Chido E1432, https://elerazno.com/?v=f24485ae434a (accessed 16 September 2022); 'La Cumbia del Coronavirus', https://www.youtube.com/watch?v=Ui_hBqsipyU (accessed 16 September 2022).
74. 'CORONAVIRUS LA CUMBIA 😂 MAK KING || #2020 || VIDEO LETRA TIK TOK', https://www.youtube.com/watch?v=-X_8B91wdJo (accessed 16 September 2022).
75. 'La vacunación – (La cumbia de la vacuna)', https://www.youtube.com/watch?v=BbglwgeMd6I (accessed 16 September 2022).
76. 'La Cumbia del Covid 19', https://www.youtube.com/watch?v=xbTk7b3MQy0 (accessed 16 September 2022). This is the only video Jerry put on his YouTube channel, with 16 subscribers and 919 views.
77. 'La Cumbia del Coronavirus sin papel', https://www.youtube.com/watch?v=hAK778S-pPg (accessed 16 September 2022).
78. 'La Cuarentena Coronavirus CUMBIA', https://www.youtube.com/watch?v=zkkkHba5TRk (accessed 16 September 2022).
79. 'Coronavirus', https://www.youtube.com/watch?v=IynOFtUB9iA (accessed 16 September 2022).
80. 'La Cumbia de la Cuarentena', https://www.youtube.com/watch?v=yXJHUUkAmqo (accessed 7 October 2021).
81. 'Cumba del Encierro', https://www.youtube.com/watch?v=hl2cCtdtVVk (accessed 7 October 2021).
82. 'El Cumbion Del Corona Virus!', https://www.youtube.com/watch?v=fkXJBtTZufM (accessed 7 September 2021).
83. Portro Salvaje TV YouTube channel: https://www.youtube.com/channel/UC1B9m5J4NsjVQk3ibdM1Npw (accessed 7 September 2021).
84. 'Scooby Doo papa bailando con Lexy Panterra 2018', https://www.youtube.com/watch?v=z3odbVPquAc (accessed 7 September 2021); 'La cumbia de Ramón', https://www.youtube.com/watch?v=n2qLa5QPfSc (accessed 7 September 2021).
85. 'Cumbia covid', https://www.youtube.com/watch?v=hyR4jBw2pQU (accessed 7 September 2021); 'La Covid Cumbia', https://www.youtube.com/watch?v=p4-ART6OFFQ (accessed 7 September 2021); 'La Cumbia de la Pandemia', https://www.youtube.com/watch?v=dUdgv_QWnkk (7 September 2021).
86. 'Cumbia del Corona Virus', https://www.youtube.com/watch?v=T4hOffOx9GE (accessed 7 September 2021).
87. Goh, 'Virus is Other People'.
88. 'La Cumbia Del Coronavirus', https://www.youtube.com/watch?v=vzep1WZ2sGQ (accessed 7 September 2021).
89. 'La cumbia del coronavirus', https://www.youtube.com/watch?v=k8SLDmIB-T8 (accessed 7 September 2021).
90. Paul Bowman, *The Invention of Martial Arts: Popular Culture Between Asia and America* (Oxford: Oxford University, 2021), p. 91.

91. 'La Cumbia del Coronavirus 2.020 Pandemia Mundial', https://www.youtube.com/watch?v=mJs_CKuXP7g (accessed 29 September 2021). This account was terminated shortly thereafter.
92. 'El Coronavirus', https://www.youtube.com/watch?v=tu6WQcMTzpY (accessed 29 September 2021).
93. 'El Corona Virus', https://www.youtube.com/watch?v=CTeajuumfaM (accessed 29 September 2021).
94. 'La Cuarentena (Cumbia) Abril 2020', https://www.youtube.com/watch?v=EqtNSjjwE6k (accessed 29 September 2021).
95. 'El Coronavirus', https://www.youtube.com/watch?v=fDPleVoZANM (accessed 16 September 2022).
96. 'La Cumbia de la Pandemia', https://www.youtube.com/watch?v=1X_3XwhN7dM (accessed 16 September 2022).
97. 'Cumbia del Coronavirus', https://www.youtube.com/watch?v=zEFnU32iqBQ (accessed 7 September 2021 and 16 September 2022).
98. 'Cumbia coronavirus Argentina', https://www.youtube.com/watch?v=oot9ke1H1zA (accessed 7 September 2021). It gained another 5 views by September 2022.
99. 'Cumbia del Coronavirus', https://www.youtube.com/watch?v=TAHY1NikujU (accessed 16 September 2022).
100. 'La Cumbia Del Coronavirus 1', https://www.youtube.com/watch?v=DTOaPX5oy_Y (accessed 16 September 2022).
101. 'La Cumbia del covid 2021', https://www.youtube.com/watch?v=Xsu6Qt7E14Y (accessed 16 September 2022).
102. 'Pandemia de cumbia', https://www.youtube.com/watch?v=Ah2iat2jj_E (accessed 16 September 2022).
103. 'Cumbia de la Pandemia', https://www.youtube.com/watch?v=Vz90G5cYcX0; https://www.youtube.com/channel/UCQj4DPbzd1ZXr9-nxOqYX0g/about (accessed 16 September 2022).
104. Patiño, 'Quédate en casa', https://www.youtube.com/watch?v=nFF0anytAis (accessed 16 September 2022); 'Ganar o Morir', https://www.youtube.com/watch?v=Hp2WlHFJUkk (accessed 16 September 2022).
105. 'Cumbiambero en Pandemia – Cumbia', https://www.youtube.com/watch?v=aqyBsg5mh0s (accessed 16 September 2022); '¡Ayyy Cuarentena! – Chalupa', https://www.youtube.com/watch?v=k7LAbwiOP14 (accessed 16 September 2022); Sierra & Folclor YouTube channel: https://www.youtube.com/channel/UCXsGLdErGGEWQSoHc3__lZA/ (all accessed 16 September 2022).
106. Sierra y Foclor, https://www.culturarecreacionydeporte.gov.co/en/node/80955 (accessed 16 September 2022); Fundación Sierra & Foclor, https://sierrayfolclor.org/ (accessed 16 September 2022).
107. 'La cumbia del coronavirus', https://www.youtube.com/watch?v=Cna6VMqjpQ0 (accessed 16 September 2022).
108. 'Cancion del Coronavirus', https://www.youtube.com/watch?v=oNF5JXzaQxE (accessed 16 September 2022).
109. 'Pandemia Cumbia', https://www.youtube.com/watch?v=GGlLYNx0F0w (accessed 16 September 2022).
110. 'Cumbia la Pandemia', https://www.youtube.com/watch?v=OQzpc91MvQA (accessed 16 September 2022).

3 Un Huapango para esta Cuarentena

#QuédateEnCasa

In August 2020, six months into the coronavirus pandemic, a viewer named Elena Huerta welcomed others to 'come and dance' ('*pasen a zapatear*') at a virtual huapango, an online gathering of huapango enthusiasts. This huapango was one of many virtual events branded with the hashtag '#QuédateEnCasa' (stay home) involving nightly queued streams of pre-recorded music videos.[1] These videos – presented in this case by a DIY (do-it-yourself) community archivist – featured a succession of tríos huastecos, a regional grouping featuring a violin and two guitarlike instruments, performing sones, huapangos, cumbias, and more. The virtual huapango presented a series of contrasts: flashy, pristine cowboy hats above sweat-soiled work shirts, street musicians contrasted with polished festival performances, schoolboys backing up wizened old violinists, and the occasional ranchera or bolero performed huasteco-style. Perhaps the most striking aspect of this event was the palpable sense of closeness among a large group of viewers who, in spite of remaining individually quarantined and sheltered-in-place, found a novel way to maintain a sense of togetherness.

As had become usual during the pandemic era, over the course of the evening several hundred people from Mexico, the United States, Costa Rica, Spain, and other locales tuned in for music, mutual support and conviviality, 'virtual hugs', and shouts of excitement (stylized as 'aaaajjuuuaaa' and 'juuupa!!!'). There were invitations to drink beer, pulque, and mezcal, and no small amount of teasing, jokes, and flirting. By midnight Mexico City time, three hours into the twelve-hour stream, 486 watchers remained subsumed in the constant flow of music, dance, and fellowship. As the songs changed every few minutes, viewers asked others to dance ('Alright Florentino, let's dance this piece, thanks!'). People joked around with 'hand washing' and 'coughing into elbow' emojis. There were colloquial 'shout outs' to people, towns of origin, and places of current habitation, and an overall easing into the communitarian familiarity of the huapango itself. People noted who was present and who 'did not arrive'.[2]

Virtual huapangos such as this served to maintain cohesion across a Mexican diaspora fractured by distance and threatened by the coronavirus. These musical and social gatherings helped render another night in self-isolation more bearable through the promise of virtual – though emotionally visceral – connection. Similar live huapango broadcasts occurred nightly on multiple channels during the pandemic, constituting a core communitarian response to the multiple economic, social, and health crises wrought by the pandemic moment.

Mexicans in diaspora were already well served before the pandemic by a robust socio-technological infrastructure of activists and amateur archivists, enthusiasts, and entrepreneurs who had instrumentalized participatory media platforms such as YouTube to build a functional and accessible space to foster communal wellbeing and human interaction based on shared affinity and cultural reaffirmation. This digital infrastructure replicated the cultural objects and gestures of 'home', whether real or imagined, in virtual spaces, and participants often spent hours every day engaged here, listening to the music, chatting, and connecting with others. These spaces serve as powerful incubators for new sets of norms that link social distancing and sanitary precautions to cultural products, all under the banner of community wellbeing.

In mid-March 2020, this digital infrastructure seemed to have been prescient as regards preparedness for the pandemic, and it was readily scaled up to meet the challenges of the coronavirus moment and the more pressing needs for connection among these wider musical communities. This chapter examines the creative ways that diasporic digital communities with roots in Mexico quickly and creatively utilized participatory broadcasting and social media to fill affective and economic exigencies during a time of isolation and slowed work. DIY activists in both the son huasteco and son jarocho communities responded to the pandemic on digital platforms like YouTube and Facebook with speed and creativity to produce novel virtual spaces for musical engagement and collective wellbeing. The explosive growth of these emergent virtual spaces had discernable impacts on the emotional, social, artistic, and financial needs of diasporic communities in a crisis moment.

This chapter charts the distinctive trajectory by which communities enhanced wellbeing through a variety of interlinked virtual musical efforts during the pandemic moment. In the case of son huasteco, the chapter analyzes livestreamed huapangos, considers their transnational audiences, and highlights innovations on YouTube channels dedicated to these styles as immediate and explicit responses to pandemic isolation. These channels developed into popular epicenters of digital huapango culture by creating expansive nightly livestreams, queued streams of videos, and structured events such as the 'Encuentro Virtual de Tríos Huastecos' (Virtual Gathering of Huasteco Trios, or EVTH). The son jarocho case study that follows examines an emergent online community of teaching and musicultural fellowship for amateur musicians and enthusiasts, and the ways the pandemic opened new opportunities for transnational learning.

Digital spaces, community-building efforts, and virtual events together played a critical role in the maintenance of emotional and social wellbeing at a time of collective duress: online music performances and gatherings via YouTube livestreams served as foundational affective spaces in these musical communities' response to the coronavirus crisis. Streams with active chat boxes mediated community gathering, cultural participation, and shared wellbeing. They served as platforms for discussion, information sharing, and norm setting during the pandemic moment. These emergent phenomena sustained Mexican regional musical cultures at a time during which traditional huapangos and fandangos – the names for events at which these styles are typically played – became untenable due to social distancing.

The virtual spaces have also opened new avenues for transnational participation for diasporic audiences. This chapter draws upon more than two years of participant-observation in online community huapangos and #QuedateEnCasa events, as well as remote interviews with pivotal content creators and community members, to demonstrate how this emergent digital infrastructure served as a mechanism for facilitating cultural connectedness and community wellbeing among transnational affinity groups.

The pandemic required people to stay at home, but a stroke of creativity was required to make staying home appealing and even rewarding, and to transform casual digital spaces into reliable nodes of cultural solidarity and mutual support. #QuedateEnCasa, as a both marketing hashtag and signifier, began to be used by digital content creators to label virtual events in the early, unnerving moments of the coronavirus pandemic. Staying at home was transformed into an enterprise that was both health preserving and culture supporting. Online events branded with #QuedateEnCasa fused social, cultural, and symbolic capital into an enactment of ritualized wellbeing, as online spaces have been shown to serve as welcome spaces of asylum for social experience.[3] #QuedateEnCasa queued streams of pre-recorded videos reveal that the social pull online is immediate and, for the content moderators, musicians, and many of the regular attendees, all-encompassing and deeply rewarding.

Virtual musical interactions on YouTube resonated with individuals in the diaspora who participated in virtual spaces replicating the cultural objects and gestures of 'home', whether real or imagined. Many participants spent hours every day engaged within these digital spaces, listening to the music, chatting, and connecting with others. These spaces serve as powerful incubators for new sets of norms that link social distancing and sanitary precautions to cultural products, all under the banner of community wellbeing.

The digital cultural infrastructure of transregional son jarocho and son huasteco were prepared for the coronavirus pandemic in many significant ways that have proved to be remarkably appealing, resilient, even near-clairvoyant, since mid-March 2020. Before the pandemic moment, these communities were already well served by a robust socio-technological infrastructure of DIY activists and archivists, enthusiasts, and entrepreneurs. By instrumentalizing participatory media platforms such as YouTube, these content creators built a functional and accessible space to foster communal wellbeing and human interaction on the basis of a shared affinity and cultural reaffirmation.

This unique digital infrastructure, initially created before the pandemic to meet the emotional wellbeing of these diasporas, readily scaled to meet the challenges of the coronavirus moment and the needs for connection among these wider musical communities.

The arrival of coronavirus in Mexico thus catalyzed a remarkable moment of musical and organizational creativity. In the case of son huasteco, newly improvised actions and compositions alike responding to the pandemic moment came from a diverse range of performers in its regional homeland (called the Huasteca, described in more detail below) and in its far-reaching diasporic ethnosphere. Likewise, the worldwide son jarocho revival saw the continuation of workshops, performances, and virtual fandangos at a time when in-person gatherings and travel were untenable. These musical, poetical, and organizational responses to coronavirus provide an opportunity to examine a rich, expansive, and emergent musicultural discourse.[4]

Música Huasteca and the Pandemic Moment

In mid-April 2020, as the coronavirus pandemic took hold globally in its initial wave, a trío huasteco called Los Yolpakis from Ixcatepec, Veracruz, Mexico released a new version of a huapango entitled 'La Muerte' (Death). Applying a strong tradition of situational improvisation to reflect on an unprecedented modern historical moment, Los Yolpakis included original verses written expressly to respond to the pandemic.[5] After introducing themselves in an enthusiastic unison – a style common among son huasteco video performances – the trío sang verses in both Spanish and Nahuatl, the most widely spoken indigenous language in Mexico, delivering a timely message of warning and concern. In both languages, they sang the huapango's standard first line: 'Death is looking for me / To take me away' ('*La muerte me anda buscando / para poderme llevar*'). One common verse personifies death as showing up at a fandango – a communal dance – where the singer knows he will be easy to find, and where death will dance to the music. The end of 'La Muerte' usually finds the singer announcing that his death should be surrounded by joy and that he wishes to have a huapango played as he is being buried. In their interpretation, however, Los Yolpakis instead cautioned listeners not even to chance such an encounter with death in the time of the Coronavirus. 'It is not time to go on vacation / Nor to party', the trío warned; 'It's time to meditate / They're going to hit us where it hurts if they end up coming around to infect us.'[6]

This approach to original versecraft, when employed in direct response to pandemic anxieties, provides an example of the singular and complex regional musical response to the global crisis in the Huasteca. This region, which comprises segments of six Mexican states without constituting a demographic or geographical majority within any, has frequently been bounded more by the extent of its cultural affinity in musical, culinary, ritualistic, and linguistic realms than by its geography or by any one specific political or social hegemon. Perhaps the most befitting, if still nebulous, definition of the Huasteca is 'a multiethnic system whose heterogeneity is its defining feature', which earns its 'seal of identity' through being 'identified as the land of the son, the huapango, and the *zacahuil* (an enormous tamale served at huapangos), by its own inhabitants'.[7]

Música huasteca is performed by a trio featuring violin, a small stringed instrument called a jarana, and a strummed acoustic bass called a guitarra quinta or huapanguera. In between expressive violin passages, the musicians exchange verses, which are frequently articulated in a soaring falsetto. In sones, stanzas are either drawn from a historical canon of couplets or, in some contexts, situationally improvised while remaining topical to the theme of the particular son being played. Huapangos feature fixed verses but share similar musical characteristics. The poetry of the Huasteca's music, whether written or improvised, is practiced in various local indigenous languages as well as in Spanish. Another core facet of music in the Huasteca is its zapateado, a type of partnered percussive dance executed atop a raised wooden platform called a *tarima* that both responds to and underlies the trio's live performance.

Son Mexicano can be a challenging concept to define. Son has been described as a 'mega-genre' that integrates components of music (typically played on string instruments), verse (typically strophic), and choreography (often danced atop a *tarima*).[8] Raquel Paraíso González defines son as 'a generic term that describes the various regional traditions, each type associated with certain instrumental ensembles, dance styles, performance practice nuances, and texts, as well as the complex [structures] they form.' Paraíso notes that the concept of the son is intimately tied to the concept of fandango or huapango, where son is enacted. These 'events [are] where all aspects of the Mexican son – dancing, singing, playing music, and poetry – are lived and experienced along with food, attire, language, verbal interactions, and a myriad of other cultural expressions.'[9] This is the case for both son huasteco and jarocho, as it is for other regional styles. Regarding son huasteco specifically, researchers have theorized the symbolic poetics of its verses as marking and reaffirming shared ethnic, regional, or transnational identities.[10]

In both the Huasteca and in the Sotavento, son jarocho's natal region farther down the Gulf Coast, the terms 'fandango' and 'huapango' are used interchangeably by some practitioners to describe the same fiesta.[11] In the Huasteca, huapangos are communal gatherings at which people gather to participate in the region's cultural touchstones. As events, huapangos vary from private gatherings to large, semi-commercial festivals with international draw. Regardless of size, they are deeply social events where people come together to dance, drink, eat regional cuisine, purchase handcrafts, and spend time with friends and family. Such events are often organized in commemoration of a particular date in the social, religious, or political calendar, such as a birthday, a wedding, a Saint's feast day, or a national holiday.

Virtual son huasteco streams attempt to recreate these axial events on a digital platform. While the chatrooms can never fully replace the *tarima*, the spaces of virtual huapango of the son huasteco community nonetheless serve community needs for closeness and mutual aid. The social value placed on such spaces is necessarily amplified in moments of isolation, crisis, and collective anxiety.

The content of Huasteca-oriented chatrooms during the pandemic moment signals this social function in particular ways through 'narratives of belonging in digital diasporic contexts' which 'are highly condensed discourse structures that encode speaker attitude toward place and the diasporic experience'. This discourse covers the diasporic orientation that arises from self-positioning and 'nostalgia for the homeland to idealizations' of the culture.[12] As hundreds of people gathered nightly for digital broadcasts, the chats became closer and more intimate, more coherently discursively framed with earlier chats, resulting in a discernible matrix of embedded community, identity, and wellbeing connections that grew richer over time.

The pandemic-era reproduction of a virtual Huasteca relied upon the existing participatory culture fundamental to in-person huapangos. The virtual huapangos of the pandemic moment recapitulate the 'cultural politics of representations of place, space and landscape' found in traditional events.[13] An extensive literature on diaspora and authenticity examines how the seemingly eternal and traditional are in fact quite fluid and fungible in practice.[14] Danielle Fosler-Lussier observes that

> in the postcolonial world people's experiences are neither 'all modern' or 'all traditional'; most lives encompass some combination of the two. [...] The many people who live in that 'in between' or mixed state use music to define and express the complexity of their situations.[15]

Virtual huapangos of the pandemic moment represented this tendency in their fostering of communal space for cultural celebration and wellbeing during a crisis of isolation. In this case, cultural practice, especially related to regional music reimagined through digital networks, has been severed from place.[16] Music making and consumption help to reinforce a sense of identity, to foster both individual and group sense of agency, to allow difficult subjects to be culturally adjudicated, and to generate feelings of pride, pleasure, and, crucially, connection during crisis.

Virtual Huapangos and Wellbeing in the Digital Diaspora

On 23 August 2020, eight hours into a Sunday evening huapango broadcast, Jose Osorio, a very frequent participant in such events, wrote in the chat: 'Keep dancing huapangos... they are an anti-covid remedy!'[17] Indeed, #QuedateEnCasa virtual huapangos were fundamentally designed in novel and highly calibrated ways to address the needs of community wellbeing, framed as emotionally liberatory spaces in which staying safe from the virus and being socially responsible also provided an emotionally resonant experience. The platform-mediated spaces of the digital Huasteca constitute social realms within the participatory culture of YouTube similar to what Sara Marino terms the 'transconnective habitus, a connective and connected transnational everyday reality' fostered by new communication technologies.[18] This focus on the social ends of digital connectivity, which has already been utilized in other cases, can readily be applied to the virtual huapango and its contingent diasporic community during the pandemic moment.[19] Music is especially important for social coherence and wellbeing in diaspora communities, where it 'can function as a sort of social "glue" connecting diasporic communities widely dispersed around the globe', particularly in the ways it 'make[s] the experience of diasporic belonging one that is deeply pleasurable in itself and socially reassuring.'[20]

However, it should be remembered that these digital and transnational connections are dependent upon access to communication technologies that, although widespread, are far from ubiquitous. The deep connections being forged in YouTube chatrooms could be contrasted on local scales with the development of feelings of marginalization or exclusion among individuals without access to such virtual connectivity. This interesting juxtaposition in access and experience could inform a new comparative study based on digital and traditional ethnographic fieldwork.

Music has a particularly strong impact on the wellbeing of diasporic communities by enhancing community connections through shared experience and 'avenues for participants to express and consolidate their own cultural identity.'[21] As the extensive literature on music and wellbeing demonstrates, both music listening and music making also correlate very highly with direct and positive physiological and psychological health benefits,[22] including feelings of happiness, mood elevation, stress reduction, strengthened interpersonal relationships and connections, and other positive outcomes reflected in individual and group wellbeing.²³ Many other wellbeing outcomes have been well documented with quantitative measures, but work remains to be done in evaluating wellbeing with qualitative measures as well. Weinberg and Joseph argue that it is the social connectivity of music that yields the most measurable positive outcome of wellbeing, since 'the communal interaction and social medium may offer people a sense of purpose and belonging.'²⁴

Virtual music spaces during the pandemic moment demonstrate the social and wellbeing values of new communication technology in diaspora. Recent work has explored migrants' use of a variety of these technologies to respond to the challenges of maintaining meaningful transnational connections.²⁵ These new 'transconnective space[s]' for diasporic communities²⁶ are precisely where the huapango becomes an embodiment and enactment of the Huasteca's regional culture.

Cultural and Commercial Spatiality of YouTube as Site and Space

As discussed in the Introduction, YouTube is the premier digital space for participatory cultural production; during the pandemic moment, it played a central role in fostering engagement among musicians, enthusiasts, and dancers. Its outsized role during the COVID era has only begun to be understood. YouTube is of immense but still-growing importance to participatory and global DIY culture. In particular, it provides fertile ground for the documentation and diffusion of content focusing on musical events, styles, and traditions. The site 'creates spaces for engagement and community-formation' with 'spillover into other sites of everyday culture, meaning, identity, and practice'. This 'participatory turn' has consequently transformed 'the relationship between the individual and a global, culturally diverse idea of community'.²⁷ Scholars of both in-person communities and online affinity groups built around social media platforms have stressed their interrelatedness.²⁸ This thrusts the locus of analysis on the connections between flourishing real and virtual communities.

The streaming of cultural productions in real time allows individuals who identify with a particular culture or region to engage with fellow participants regardless of their distance from or access to the site of production. Social media platforms also challenge the assumed power differentials between active producer and spectatorial consumer to create new, dynamic ecosystems of power and consumption. They allow expressions of cultural identity, musical participation, and mutual aid to be tethered to specific initiatives, such as information sharing and fundraising. These are standard functions of a self-supporting community in diaspora, rendered especially urgent in periods of crisis.

YouTube's role in facilitating and influencing diasporic cultural developments has been studied extensively. For example, Koen Leurs has examined how YouTube videos evoke embodied nostalgia and affective belonging in Moroccan-Dutch youth, while Lonán Ó Briain's work among Hmong musician-activists shows how they instrumentalize YouTube to facilitate offline community making in diaspora.[29] Such studies show how YouTube's ability to consolidate diasporas socially generates a recreative and relatively osmotic space. Its modes of cultural production not only self-reproduce, but also catalyze new possibilities for in-person engagement.

The already intricate connections between real and virtual participatory social media worlds within diasporic communities were rendered significantly more complex in a time of pandemic-induced isolation. The social splintering and geographical scattering of community poses a unique set of constraints and dimensions, as connections span and warp time and space. This invokes a sense of deterritorialization, which intensifies the pursuit of cultural markers and connectivity on a global scale. In considering another style of Mexican son in diaspora, Alex Chavez considers the cadences and meanings of these transnational music-making events as sites of cultural sustenance and aural resistance from within a hostile setting.[30] The pressures and challenges forced upon migrants and their culture were further complicated by the onset of COVID-19, not only as regards health but also livelihood and mobility. The pandemic moment thus exposed a need for a linked but re-theorized approach to studying transnational musicking.

The unprecedented experience of sheltering-in-place during a social-media-saturated era has both generated and ubiquitized emergent forms of community gathering. However, it also poses an existential threat to the musicians who ordinarily have sustained cultures in physical spaces. It is both the search for connection and for work in an ever-more online world that lends power to the virtual communities created during the pandemic moment. Indeed, while virtual huapangos emerged as a response to the impossibility of physical gatherings, they came to take on a character, culture, and spatialized logic of their own.

Huapangueros, Digital Infrastructure, and Mutual Aid

On 18 March 2020, 25 new cases of the coronavirus were officially confirmed to be present in Mexico, making an overall total of 118. By this time, municipal and countrywide lockdowns were already underway around much of the world.[31] However, Mexico's political response lagged behind, with President Andrés Manuel López Obrador continually downplaying the severity of the pandemic throughout the month, and encouraging residents of Mexico City to 'continue living life as usual' as late as 22 March.[32] It took another week for Mexico to implement its first nationwide restrictions, by which point the total national case count exceeded a thousand.

While the government was slow to acknowledge the need for preventative measures to stop the spread of COVID-19, artists and cultural promoters began to organize in response to the impending crisis. On the aforementioned 18 March, DIY documentarian and promoter Gabino 'Gabo' Vera put out a video announcing a virtual *encuentro* (gathering) of son huasteco music; the 'Encuentro Virtual de Tríos Huastecos' (EVTH) was streamed a few weeks later. Vera's YouTube channel, GaVBroadcast, is a constantly growing repository of videos showcasing son huasteco performances. As of early March 2020 the channel had roughly 190,000 subscribers, and a year later this had grown to 287,000.[33]

Vera, who has nearly two decades of experience working in telecommunications and network broadcasting, left his position at Televisa in January 2019 to dedicate himself fully to his YouTube channel, which generates income through ad revenue and content sponsorships. In his announcement of the virtual encuentro, Vera spoke directly to his subscribers, noting that 'various huapangos have been cancelled', that 'staying home is the right thing to do', and that an online event might serve 'to showcase new talents in Huastecan music' and 'help us so that our time spent at home might be more enjoyable'. This early adaptation to pandemic circumstances is a prime example of the improvisational flexibility of the online huapango community and its digital infrastructure. At a moment when governments still struggled to respond effectively to the Coronavirus outbreak, community content creators such as Vera put forward solutions to a problem while also establishing a new normative connection between social responsibility and artistic engagement.[34]

As a DIY repository of música huasteca, GaVBroadcast's ad hoc content strategy actively mirrors the improvisatory readiness of the musicians whom it documents and promotes. For years, Vera managed his channel as a hobby while working in Mexico City, recording performances in private homes on occasional return visits to his home region. He created it in 2007, long before YouTube attained the prominence and ubiquity it holds today. It subsequently grew over the years with the platform, and his videos improved in resolution and editing quality. Vera was a relatively early adopter of the livestream format as a means of broadcasting local performances to a global audience of huapango enthusiasts. The YouTube livestream platform includes a chat feature that allows viewers to engage with the broadcaster and the performers, encouraging a dynamic informality that mimics the social ethos of in-person community performances. These casual and personalized streams, which turn into gatherings, cater to a diaspora that extends far beyond the geographical Huasteca. However, as the pandemic took hold and people across the globe entered into self-isolation, this digital participatory infrastructure came to serve an increasingly expansive audience of huapango enthusiasts.

YouTube began experimenting with livestreaming as early as 2008, but most of these initial broadcasts exclusively featured professional producers with mass followings. In 2013, the site began to expand streaming capabilities to user-generated content creators, and within four years livestreaming had been fully integrated into YouTube's desktop and mobile platforms. GaVBroadcast's first three livestreams were transmitted in late 2017; all are shorter than 20 minutes and are raw transmissions of outdoor performances. Upon earning his 100,000th subscriber, Vera transmitted the first of what would become a series of live-in-studio performances. The two-and-a-half-hour livestream on 25 October 2018 featured Trío Los Hidalguenses from Pachuca, Hidalgo, and was shown simultaneously on YouTube and Facebook Live. The audio-visual resolution was noticeably low, but the trío, who are in high demand at events across Mexico and even in the United States, presented naturally and charismatically in front of the camera. During the livestream, the burgeoning importance of the chat function embedded in streaming platforms became clear, as Vera acknowledged viewers across the Huasteca diaspora who were actively participating in the chat after the trío performed their first selection: 'Beginning with those who write us in YouTube, to Georgina Zuniga, who is in the United States; to Javier Martinez, from Odessa, Texas', he summarized. 'On Facebook, there is a lone wolf who says "I like the Huapangos," Hever Hasan [sic], regards from Lukfin, Texas. Juan Fernandez, from Monterrey, and Manu Perez, who is also watching on YouTube'. The trío's jarana player exclaimed in response, 'Wow! Well, greetings to all of you folks, and what a pleasure to accompany you all on this beautiful afternoon.'[35]

In the year before the pandemic, regular livestreams would become a defining characteristic of both GaVBroadcast and other popular Huasteca-oriented YouTube channels. These included the husband-and-wife team of Héctor Manuel Delgado Flores and Maria del Carmen Camarena Torres behind QuerrequeFilms, which boasted over 120,000 subscribers as of September 2022, and Tharé Gonzalez's Yo Soy Coxcatlan, which later began live-streaming walkthroughs of popular markets in the Tenek-speaking Aquismon region of San Luis Potosí in the midst of the pandemic.[36] Already acutely aware of the connective potentialities of the livestream, Vera was ideally positioned to benefit from the format's newfound centrality as a site of cultural production and social connection in the coming pandemic. In 2019, he traveled extensively throughout the Huasteca to record and transmit performances by tríos and regional wind bands. He also played an important educational role by acculturating into the digital space performers who had limited prior experience with being recorded and broadcasted online:

> I only record tríos who ask me, but everybody reacts to the camera differently. Some adapt quickly and are quite natural, while others seem less comfortable at first. It helps to encourage them from behind the camera, to give them some of the feedback that they're getting in the chat.[37]

Another aspect of his involvement is as an intermediary between the tríos and the global audience he commands via YouTube, encouraging the groups to act naturally and feel at ease: 'Like, if a close friend or relative is watching, or if someone from another trío sends a supportive comment, sometimes getting that kind of [affirmative] response helps to animate the musicians.'[38]

In addition to assisting musicians in navigating the novel mechanics of digital performativity, Vera also trains them in the technical aspects of recording and promoting their own content. This ranges from showing groups how to create and manage a YouTube channel of their own to teaching tríos in geographically remote areas how to record and transmit quality content in the absence of adequate equipment or telecommunications infrastructure:

> A lot of these musicians live up in the mountains in tiny towns where there is no broadband, no wi-fi, and cellular data is 2G at best. Many want to record promotional videos on their own, but they have limited access [to equipment and the internet]. So I try to teach them how to use a cell phone camera to record a video of passable quality, which includes making sure that you have a good lighting angle, even if you're using natural light, and that you make sure that the built-in microphone is facing the trío and protected from the wind.[39]

Vera, like most content creators working in the Huasteca, frequently includes musicians' contact information, typically a phone number, so that they can be reached by viewers who may be interested in hiring a local group. Musicians will sometimes receive messages immediately after a video is uploaded, requesting a contracted performance. In this way, the network being sewn is economically as well as socially beneficial to music-makers, a key aspect of the pandemic community connection.

In January 2019, GaVBroadcast began experimenting with yet another streaming format which came to constitute part of the crucial infrastructure utilized during the pandemic, dubbed 'Tardes de Huapangos'. Rather than featuring performances in real-time, these streams simply showcase a looped reel of pre-recorded videos from the channel's history, but broadcast as a single stream with occasional interjections of speech by Vera himself. The strength of this particular format is YouTube's built-in chat feature, which allows viewers to communicate with one another and with channel administrators while the videos stream. By early 2020, these transmissions and chats had cultivated a dedicated, regular following of viewers, some of whom became involved in the functional operation of the channel. The chat is facilitated, and lightly governed by, as Vera explained in an interview, 'a particular group of people, many of whom are older women, who have been consistently tuning into these evenings of huapango since the beginning. I have come to trust in them [...] they help me out in regulating the chat.' This group of participants helps keep the chats polite and welcoming for all current and future visitors while facilitating, and even lightly policing, the space: 'If someone is posting spam or acting out, they inform me, and we figure out ways to address the issue. Aside from that, they sometimes just use it to check in on one another, talk about their problems, and share jokes.'[40]

The age range and gender balance in huapango chats is notable. Scholars studying YouTube comments have concluded that commentators in the Latin American music videos they examined were largely (72.2%) male, and generally young (medium age of 25).[41] However, these broadly observed statistics are not reflected in the GaVBroadcast chats, where women dominate the chat as both participants and moderators. YouTube comments can be, and often are, anonymous, which makes the choices of many in the GaVbroadcast to go by their real names noteworthy. This might have an impact on the gender balance apparent in the huapango chats. The auto-regulatory nature of the chats on GaVBroadcast livestreams is not only social, but technical. For example, regular attendees are quick to remind new viewers never to post more than three successive emojis in their messages and to not post links to other webpages, as these can result in YouTube's security algorithms marking their account as spam.

While son huasteco is a deeply place-based music, the regular participants in GaVBroadcast chatrooms have diverse geographical origins and current locations. The channel's most dedicated followers are not just individuals living in the Huasteca, but also Huastecan migrants in Mexico City, Monterrey, Playa del Carmen, and throughout the United States, and non-Huastecan participants from across Mexico, the United States, Latin America, and Europe who are curious about the music and the community it cultivates. 'Especially since quarantine began, I have been seeing lots of hits from locations outside of Mexico', Vera explained, 'whether they're Mexican citizens who had to leave home to work, or people born in the United States with Huasteco roots, or sometimes complete foreigners who just like the music.'[42]

GaVBroadcast's core role within the wider huapango community during this period evolved from that of content source to community catalyst. By incubating an outlet that sustains relationships among Huasteco cultural affiliates beyond the boundaries of the physical huapango, GaVBroadcast helped to reproduce the Huasteca virtually, creating a digital environment that has proven capable of weathering the most severe challenge to global human concrescence in recent memory: the COVID-19 pandemic. This virtual space perpetuates regional culture and provides opportunities for its adherents to support each other emotionally and financially in the midst of crisis.

Virtual Huapangos of the COVID Era

As noted above, one of the earliest and most ambitious expressions of a participatory Huasteco digital space at the start of the coronavirus pandemic was the 'Encuentro Virtual de Tríos Huastecos' (EVTH), announced by Vera on 18 March 2020 in a video uploaded to his GaVBroadcast YouTube channel:

> My friends, good afternoon, I hope you are well. As you already know, over the last few days, various huapango contests have been cancelled. [...] Yesterday I was asking around on Facebook to see if any tríos wanted to participate in some sort of online competition. It won't be a contest because we don't have a panel, but we figure that we'll judge by the number of likes received on social media, like YouTube and Facebook. [...] Its purpose is to showcase new talents in Huastecan music and to promote the participants, and also to help us so that our time spent at home might be more enjoyable. [...] We are all doing the right thing by staying at home, so let's enjoy some huapangos.[43]

The concept was straightforward: tríos would record their performances and submit them to Vera, who would upload and tag them with 'EVTH'. Three age classes were established, each of which was assigned a specific son of representative difficulty that would serve as the benchmark of their performance. Similarly, each age class had a specific time window during which to submit their performances. Cash prizes were promised to the winners in each age class. 'Initially, I expected maybe twenty tríos to participate', Vera explained in interview; 'by the end of the submission window, in early April, 77 tríos had submitted videos. It was a really surprising response.'[44] Vera's decision to actively pursue digital alternatives at this early stage of the pandemic demonstrates an acute foresight about coming changes to the social landscape. For comparison, Mexico's Ministry of Culture launched its digital arts initiative 'Contigo en la Distancia' on 25 March, a week after the EVTH began accepting submissions.

In the months after the EVTH, GaVBroadcast saw its greatest increase in both views and subscriptions. In February 2020, the channel gained 4000 new subscribers, and its videos were viewed 2.6 million times. Three months later, in May, the channel gained 13,000 new subscribers and its videos reached 5.9 million views. Subscriptions to the channel then ballooned, from more than 40,000 subscribers during the brief period of this study, to an eye-popping 238,000 by 31 August. Vera credits the EVTH, as well as the general conditions of quarantine, with this exponential surge in popularity: 'At the beginning of 2020, I was already satisfied with our growth. We had been steadily gaining subscribers since 2018', he explained, adding:

And as soon as the quarantine began in earnest, we had an explosion of traffic, which I say was largely due to the EVTH, but I think it also had to do with the changing habits of people in the Republic [of Mexico]. When you are at home all of the time, two things happen: you spend more time on the computer and you consume more content, but you also grow to miss the gatherings and huapangos.[45]

The numbers tell only part of the story, as obvious commitment and enthusiasm from the Huasteco diaspora rapidly pushed the channel into being an essential aspect of daily life. Given the immediate and enormous embrace of #QuedateEnCasa by a growing audience, it is clear that the event struck a deep need for connection during the pandemic.

The earliest use of the tag #QuedateEnCasa in conjunction with a trío huasteco streaming on YouTube came early in the pandemic. On 31 March, an organization called Difusión Huasteca, which is dedicated to documenting and celebrating the cultural diversity of Mexico, featured a short COVID-related son followed by a plea to stay home and remain healthy.[46] Difusión Huasteca then released another short didactic-oriented son huasteco video, labeled 'Trío Lucero Huasteco de Tantoyuca, Veracruz #QuedateEnCasa', on 5 April, which was viewed a modest 240 times.[47]

Vera also slowly began to gear his streaming to servicing the wellbeing needs of those in quarantine throughout the Huasteco diaspora. On 18 April, GaVbroadcast streamed '#QuedateEnCasa y Escucha Huapangos Huastecos' ('Stay Home and Listen to Huapangos Huastecos'), which lasted two hours and had 6383 views. Six days later, the channel streamed '#QuedateEnCasa y Escucha Huapangos Huastecos', which lasted 85 minutes and had 7066 views.[48]

Following those uploads, regular #QuedateEnCasa huapangos continued to increase in frequency and length. By the end of August, streams of queued videos were appearing nightly for 12 hours on both GaVBroadcast and Querreque Films on YouTube. It was therefore possible to be in contact with the Huasteco virtual community via music and chat for most of each day and night, forming a critical basis of community support and connection.

Also in August, QuerrequeFilms streamed 'Huapanguitos en un domingo de cuarentena' ('Little Huapangos for a Sunday in Quarantine'). By midnight, the channel had streamed videos of groups playing música huasteca for a continuous ten hours. This stream, which like that on GaVBroadcast went out as a live queue, was a compilation of selected videos from the channel stitched into a seamless whole to create a space of fellowship and connection for the listeners. Roberto Tort exclaimed, 'the huapangos are beautiful!!!'. Elena Reyes, a regular in the chats, was happy to check in late at night to hear 'another of my favorite videos, so that I go to sleep happy'. As on GaVBroadcast, this virtual performance and community space in the QuerrequeFilms chat was an important and emotionally resonant one at this moment, when people were sheltering at home and all events and gatherings had been abruptly curtailed. 'Good evening Huapango family' was a common greeting. In the QuerrequeFilms chatroom, many listeners expressed longing for the much-loved in-person gatherings where the music is played: 'The encuentros are great experiences, and soon we will return to them', promised Santiago Pérez Gómez, an organizer from the annual and deeply beloved Encuentro de Huapango in Amatlán, Veracruz, who had logged onto the stream to share updates regarding the popular festival's transition to a digital format. In the meantime, there were YouTube huapangos to fill the void.[49]

#QuedateEnCasa and other huapango events on participatory streaming sites recreated and evoked the sonic, spatial, and visceral placemaking found across the Huasteca, both in the distinctive region itself and in its expansive diaspora in the United States. A Sunday livestream on GaVBroadcast had viewers from Puebla, Veracruz, Hidalgo, Tamaulipas, San Luis Potosí, and Querétaro, as well as Louisiana, Arizona, California, and North Carolina in the United States. 'Those heels are making a great ruckus', Tacho Mendez wrote in one live chat, commenting on the dancing. Elías Rosas, a moderator and regular attendee, agreed about the 'very good zapateado rhythm'. Florencia Fèlix was in and out of the huapango during the night. 'Elías', he said, 'I was HERE a few hours ago. VERY nice atmosphere you all have HERE', followed by two clapping emojis.[50] 'HERE', indeed, was nowhere, and yet the use of such language emphasized the sentiment of locality felt among participants within a digital space.

The participatory digital community enacted and reinforced at virtual huapangos by musicians, dancers, enthusiasts, and curators firmly reasserted the Huasteca itself as a cultural space unbounded by geography. This new construction of identity opened space for togetherness, even during the quarantines of the early pandemic moment. At a Sunday night stream titled 'Huapangos para finalizar la semana!' ('Huapangos to End the Week!') Agustin Santos directly thanked Vera for his service to the community: 'Greetings my friend Gabo, thank you for the opportunity you give us to listen to our Huasteco music.' Vera interjected in the conversation numerous times, greeting friends and extending gratitude. Saul Ortega thought of this livestream as a great way to start a new week: 'There is nothing better than starting the week with some huapangazos! [sic]' Online huapangos were not a bad option; better, in fact, than some in-person events in September, since 'during the national month, some huapangazos aren't befitting' on account of the pandemic crisis. Reaffirming the sense of safety and community felt in these spaces, José Osorio commented 'huapangos, not bullets!' Catalino Santes agreed: 'Big heels and no bullets', he wrote, linking pre-COVID security concerns with the anxieties of the pandemic moment.[51]

As the hours flowed by in the huapango, people joked, chided each other, talked of the comfort foods of home, the weather, relationships, and a wide array of other concerns. Jorge Albert Garces M. told the chat 'I have a craving for pemoles.' He wondered if anyone was familiar with them. Some shared the same craving for pemoles, with coffee. Others had never heard of them, nor knew what they were. Garces M. explained that they 'are like donuts but made of corn, as if they were *polvorones* (tea biscuits). They are known in the north of Veracruz and south of Tamaulipas.' The chat flowed on, seemingly no topic too small, too intimate, or too obscure. Martin Sanchez finally signed off with a wistful, 'I was glad to greet you, raza Huasteca, but I have to go to sleep because tomorrow there is a lot to do.' Others understood such demands of life. Olga Mayorgaaa: 'Fine, but we have to consider work a blessing, friend, because there are people who don't have it.'[52]

The #QuedateEnCasa movement deftly met the forced transformations and imperatives of the COVID era by fostering a new presentational and participatory style for enthusiasts. The varied, streaming twelve-hour huapangos, created to serve a homebound audience seeking communion and emotional release, provoked a new style of involvement. Livestreaming is 'a cultural phenomenon interesting for its technological newness, but also because this technology carries with it implications for how we construct notions of participation, labor, authorship and agency'. As Lingel and Naaman put it, those controlling 'own the moment, own the documentation.'[53] In the case of #QuedateEnCasa events and virtual huapangos, this sense of ownership arose at least as much from the non-musical aspects of life (drinking, eating, working, flirting, joking) as from the music itself. The music, as it so often does, provided an impetus for gathering, sharing, and feeling connected. The online context for the music also allows individuals to present or invent new mediated, virtual versions of themselves. 'In the YouTube universe the relation of producers, objects and recipients is re-balanced', writes Christofer Jost; 'YouTube initializes the mediatized presentation of self and everyday life in everyday life, meaning that a new "stage" is established that serves as a tool to comment on what is presented on the various other "stage" (of everyday life).'[54] Virtual spaces offered a new reordering of the community of musicians, consumers, adherents, and others during the pandemic moment.

Huapango livestreams during the pandemic also opened avenues of immediacy in a community lacking any access to an alternative. In a way, the gig-less violinist, the committed aficionado, the devoted dancer, and the lonely quarantine shut-in were unable to look away. There were no alternatives in the shadow of the coronavirus. 'I've seen these people in the chats more than I have seen my closest friends in my neighborhood during the pandemic', said one regular to #QuédateEnCasa.[55] People arrived (logged in) early at the huapangos and stayed late. 'By the way… tomorrow is Monday', joked José Osorio. It was one in the morning, and Osorio was making his final rounds, though the chatter otherwise showed few signs of flagging. Soon afterwards, however, more users began to sign off regretfully, mentioning having to attend to work or family in a few hours. They promised to see each other the next day: 'See you tomorrow – if there is a transmission around 8:00 p.m. I'll watch.' 'Yes, see you tomorrow, if God wills it', concluded ever-present Elías Rosas. 'Good night to all my friends in the chat', wrote Gabo.[56]

The virtual gatherings happened night after night, month after month, representing a truly transnational online community of mutual support and cultural sustenance in a moment of mass estrangement. Diasporic cultures contain embedded enthusiast communities, to be sure, but the pandemic experience emphasized the connections with place even as it enforced distance. Participants always ask where people are from, and where they are living now. They acknowledge their origins, give shout-outs to home, and make aspirational nods to where they currently live and why. 'I'm a country boy' ('*Soy de Rancho*') Jose Pena said in one chat. When pressed where specifically, because Rosaura Reyes Perez said 'Oh, but are you in the country (of Mexico) or not?', Pena responded with 'Nuevo Leon, but living in Texas now.'[57]

A huapango on a Monday evening livestream in July 2020 provided Elías Guzman with a chance for 'dancing a huapango before going to sleep'. Elías Rosas, a channel moderator, suggested after a good four hours: 'Well, let's dance a moment, to let off some steam, okay?' Guzman agreed in turn – using an affectionate term for someone with the same first name: 'It was very good therapy, *tocayo*.' Rosas mused that 'this music serves as a salve for the spirit' ('*y sirva estea [sic] música como bálsamo para el ánimo*'). Seven hours into a Monday night huapango 200 watchers joked and flirted with each other, exhorting each other to get excited with lines like 'ala tarimaaaaaaaaa muchachas' ('get on the dance floor, girls!').[58]

The virtual huapangos and #QuedateEnCasa musical events are similar to the Italian familial gatherings over Skype that Marino has explored as an example of 'digital togetherness'.[59] The gatherings are 'used to recreate a sense of mediated co-presence among geographically separated individuals through the (re)-enactment of family rituals that were once performed in physical togetherness.' The collective and individual search for wellbeing in the COVID era has been facilitated precisely by the 'mediated co-presence' made possible by the virtual staging of established, beloved, familiar, meaningful, and accessible events like 12-hour-long huapangos interwoven with constant interpersonal communication. Marino rightly places emotion at the center of 'co-presence' in the digital forms.[60]

The DIY Huasteco Livestream as Communitarian Space

Early in the pandemic, numerous tríos huastecos also performed livestreamed concerts on Facebook. Trío Santuario Huasteco started their 24 April 2020 stream with a simple statement, '*quédate en casa con música huasteca*' (stay at home with Huasteco music), and other exhortations to 'stay home with huapanguitos… it's worth the ask'. Listeners discussed their hometowns and jokingly thanked apocryphal public officials with comments like 'Greetings to the cheesy bull ("Toro Requesón"), who from his trench, is doing an extraordinary job with the Ministry of Health and all the staff under his leadership' – amusing because 'El Toro Requesón' is also the name of a huapango.[61]

The events generally lasted around 90 minutes but sometimes continued on for hours and were variously coded with hashtags such as '#huapangos', '#QuédateEnCasa', or simply '#EnVivo'. The first two labels spoke to the pandemic moment for the Huasteco diaspora most directly, and rapidly became the descriptors of choice. Despite the diverse origins and timings of the livestreams from the start of the pandemic, a standard format in coronavirus-era online huapangos was quickly established. Musicians grew into their evolving role as agents of community cohesion. By providing entertainment in the midst of restrictions, they established a new standard of performance and audience engagement. By May 2020, longer encuentros with multiple groups had become increasingly common. In that month, the groups Eco Potosino, Tordo Huasteco, Desafío Huasteco, and Santurio Huasteco shared a 'Huapangos Huastecos' event. Each trío performed from their respective communities, and their performances were then digitally stitched together.[62]

Among the groups that engaged with this novel format, new norms of performance emerged relatively organically, although not all musicians were quick to acclimate. In general, the tríos came to adopt a relatively consistent presentational style and adhered to a widely shared mode of audience interaction which was distinct from other pandemic-era livestream performances of traditional music observed and participated in by the authors. In the virtual huapangos, musicians positioned their music making as a service to a community in crisis, explicitly framing their performances as expressions of resilience in the shadow of the coronavirus.

Two months into the pandemic, Trío Sentimiento Huasteco played a live set on Facebook for more than an hour, standing on a small stage. They listed their representative's phone number for potential future in-person gigs, but mostly responded to listener requests. This was a pioneering livestream version of the pandemic-era virtual huapangos already happening on YouTube as described above. As is common at in-person events, listeners asked for favorite sones and huapangos; Antonio Emperador requested 'La Azucena Bella', while Francisco Javier suggested 'a happy huapango for all of us to smile'. Listeners connected and commented from Coyutla in Veracruz, Riverside in California, Tamazunchale in San Luis Potosí, Mexico City, Huejutla in Hidalgo, Matamoros in Tamaulipas, and numerous other locales. In between the sones and huapangos, a masked-up narrator came out and read the comments from the live chat off his phone to the trío, along with greetings and requests. All of the comments from the chat were read, signaling the gathering's egalitarian ethos. Like other groups in the early pandemic moment, Trío Sentimiento was not immediately comfortable with this new performance model. They spent most of the set standing stone faced, barely responding to the announcer or the cameraman, although the quinta player did smile.[63]

The tríos huastecos delivered their performances in dynamic and constant interaction with viewers via their smartphones. It was not uncommon to see all three members of a trío looking at their phones at nearly every moment of the stream not spent playing an instrument. One notable example was Trío Fuerza Imperial's livestream, where the members of this huapango arribeño[64] group started the stream but then did not start playing music for a static five minutes. In the absence of music, a phone conversation and children at play could be heard in the background. Five minutes of downtime perhaps does not seem like long – unless one is sitting watching a motionless screen. In an in-person setting, performers might recognize this long gap as 'dead air', whereas in the context of the pandemic-era stream it felt like an essential moment of connection with the audience. It was, in the language of those studying music cognition, more of a pause – an opportunity for the audience to 'be with' the trío in a moment adjacent to but not part of a staged performance. Indeed, with 2300 views, the video was widely watched; the pause did not drive away the audience, who chatted among themselves as the group prepared to start playing. Livestreamed videos are archived as originally streamed. The pauses remain built into the performance, integral to the space of the pandemic performance which lives on in the internet as a node of community interaction.[65]

In between sones during pandemic livestreams, each trío interacted directly with audience members by reading names, and noting regions and states of origin (generally in Mexico) and of current residence (often in the United States). Each group responded directly to requests for songs. These requests were listed in the chats during the stream, usually accompanying a compliment, a shout of encouragement, and a mention of the origin of the requester. The tríos then would read some, or all, of the comments to the listeners, serving to reinforce the connection between audience and performer. Trío Amanecer Huasteco's 13 June 2020 livestream followed the established practice. This was a noticeably professional group equipped with wireless microphones and amplified instruments. Their listeners tuned in from Houston and Paris in Texas, from Matamoros in Tamaulipas, from Tequisquiapan and Ahuacatlán de Guadalupe in Querétaro, from Cuetzalan in Puebla, and from Puerto Rico, among other locales. Listeners were acknowledged, their comments read and discussed, and their requests sometimes fulfilled.[66]

While the regional repertory is quite extensive, there was in fact little variety observed among the set sones performed at most live-streamed huapango events. The most commonly performed numbers (El Querreque, El Gusto, La Leva, El Cielito Lindo) are some of the most widely performed standards at in-person huapangos. All feature a standard stanza format that allows improvisation. Tríos also played a wide variety of requests as they came in, so it was not uncommon to hear other sones, huapangos, and adapted popular songs such as rancheras and cumbias, depending on the group and the requests of listeners. The responsiveness of performers to their viewers constituted part of the improvisational core of the livestream space, as it does in an in-person huapango. As is typical in live, in-person events before the pandemic, there were no set lists; the performances could go in any direction within the boundaries of the style's conventions at any point in the night. This responsiveness and changeability was a key feature of the livestreams, and a draw for both viewers and performers.

Trío Los Cantores del Alba placed a live unamplified set in a living room on 31 May 2020. Like all the other groups, they spoke with fans appearing in the chat, answered a large number of song requests, and were extremely interactive with the listeners. Younger than many groups, Los Cantores del Alba were clearly relaxed in the virtual environment. They deeply engaged with the large crowd of 2600 viewers in a way that demonstrated their generational position as digital natives. This contrasts with some of the older performers in other groups, whose discomfort in the digital space was evident in early livestreams.[67] Los Cantores del Alba were highly aware of the potentialities of this new kind of performance in the pandemic moment. They expressed their nostalgia for the pre-COVID huapangos by posting a video on YouTube which presented dancing to the huapango 'China del Alma' at the 2020 Feria de las Flores in Huauchinango, Puebla with the caption 'antes del #covid'.[68]

A livestream of Trío Las Perlitas Queretanas moved at steady, even relentless place. This trío, who are at the forefront of a current explosion in all-female son huasteco groups, followed the then new, but soon solidly established mode for virtual huapango events during the pandemic moment. Their stream started without any introduction, as the camera centered on a couch where the jarana player was scrolling on her phone and the violinist was tuning up. Although only allowing approximately one minute between songs, the trío dutifully acknowledged their listeners and their requests in rapid-fire commentary. The musicians called out the names of listeners in long lists, along with where people in the chat were from. Viewers and chat participants logged in from large cities such as Monterrey and Guanajuato, communities in the Huasteca region such as Aquismón and Xilitla in San Luis Potosí, and locations in the United States including Dallas and Houston in Texas, Charlotte and Durham in North Carolina, and Salinas, Gilroy, Madera, Oakland, and Oxnard in California.[69] The jarana player was seen texting on her phone between each son, responding to viewers in real-time in the chat. This stream was presented under the auspices of a Texas-based organization called, fittingly, Huapango Sin Fronteras ('Huapangos Without Borders'). Led by huapanguero and poet Raúl Orduña, this organization puts on an annual festival of son huasteco and huapango arribeño in Austin, Texas each May. In 2020, the festival was held virtually, with a series of performances livestreamed onto YouTube from stages in Texas and Mexico.[70]

By cultivating a communitarian sensibility within the space of the virtual huapango, these events came to constitute complex assemblages of social meaning and connection. The huapango streams created a spatialized normative frame for community connection and sustenance during the quarantine. The featured tríos promoted these events themselves, as did community-based groups like Huapangos Sin Fronteras and California-based FJ-Xichu Promotions, which put on a 'Huapango Facebook Live' on 26 November with four groups: a duo led by arribeño poet Toño Jimenez' and three all-female tríos huastecos (Perlitas Queretanas, Nueva Herencia, Palomitas Serranas). These groups represented the outgrowth of a now established, concerted initiative by huapanguero musician-educators to teach and encourage young women to perform as musicians. Although the presence of all-woman groups is no longer remarkable, their visibility nonetheless challenges patriarchal narratives that point to the old man as the archetypal son huasteco musician.[71]

Virtual huapango events during COVID-19 were distinctively informal and defied assumptions about the need for extensive, diversified branding when crafting a cultural product that keeps participants engaged. The formalized, market-based approach to pandemic music holds that successful events require advance planning, novelty, and difference. For example, the CEO of a commercial streaming concert service called LoopedLive declared that 'if you do the same thing over and over again, people won't want to tune in.'[72] Yet for digital huapango events in the heat of the pandemic moment, it was exactly this combination of malleability and consistency that produced and satisfied audiences. Quarantined listeners who logged into virtual huapangos and participated in their chats were in search not of novelty, but of the familiar sounds of home and the comfort of receiving greetings from a familiar screen name.

The dominant style of the huapango livestreams was almost studiously nontheatrical. This was in sharp contrast to other virtual events and festivals and what Raquel Paraíso González calls 'cultural projects' staged in the Huasteca, which served as a 'medium for community-building, cultural transmission, and inter-generational communication' and exchange of salient 'codes and ideological symbols'.[73] At these events, standing tríos wearing traditional outfits and performing with studied gravitas enacted Huasteca identity in pronounced but decidedly rehearsed ways.

In contrast, the virtual huapangos of the pandemic moment featured tríos sitting on couches, standing loosely outside or inside garages, or in makeshift stage areas carved out of living rooms, with bay window curtains serving as the stage and lamps as lighting. Given the casual approach to the streams, sound quality was often inconsistent, with some instruments too loud and others barely audible. However, streaming quality varied across channels and generally improved over time across the board as performers and promoters alike became increasingly adept at the format. Groups often played their sets dressed not in the matching guayaberas or vaquero suits sported by tríos in conventional festival settings, but in t-shirts and jeans. This loose style was in keeping with a wider tendency among streaming musicians, where the informality of the early pandemic era – with people thrust into at-home isolation with uncertainty and loneliness – was enacted in the videos, referenced consistently, and widely accepted. Making, watching, and capturing these types of videos produced social capital that could be shared among the assembled communities of enthusiasts.[74] Such streams induce feelings of familiarity, as if arriving at friend's house for an intimate get together or for a backyard pachanga with the neighbors. '#QuédateEnCasa' meant 'stay at home', but also came to signify a new space for performance and togetherness during the pandemic. 'Home' became not only the place where one quarantines, but also the idea of the emotional *hogar* of the Huasteca and its music, culture, and people.

By allowing for a real-time interchange between performers and viewers in diverse locales, livestreamed huapangos during the COVID era addressed the articulated needs of a coherent audience. The intimate connections among this community grew as these events became increasingly standardized. Nisha Gupta has written about the deep, human pull toward fellowship in the arts and music during a time of crisis: 'The antidote of musical solidarity in a time of coronavirus provides a joyful reminder of the deep human will to always find our way back to one another.'[75] These streams differed from the nightly huapangos put on by GaVBroadcast and other channels, because of the spontaneity of the presentation and the directly interactive modality. Nonetheless, they tracked a similar trajectory in terms of the community created in the streams and the service provided to the audience. Paraíso González has explained how interaction with the audience is a central objective of live son huasteco performances. Livestream son husateco events of the COVID era recapitulated the core 'cultural politics of representations of place, space and landscape'[76] found in such traditional, in-person events. During the coronavirus pandemic, the connections created in virtual spaces were essential recreations of the longstanding participatory culture fundamentals of huapangos.

Coronavirus huapango streaming presents a true sense of intimacy as a core component of the #QuédateEnCasa videos, providing a broadly immersive experience for the audience, and pushing viewers beyond the status of passive consumers and inviting them to participate. Scholars writing about livestreaming have recognized this immersive flow. Gupta writes: 'In this time of coronavirus, examples of therapeutic music-making unceasingly flow.'[77] Tarja Rautiainen-Keskustalo and Sanna Raudaskoski likewise explain that in the 'spatial formation of the terrain' of the livestream, 'musical material, which moved over the spaces, [and] the institutions opened up to "flowing" and "moving" when live-streaming established a connection between them.' The livestreamed space can be understood as a 'mediated community' built upon a mobility paradigm.[78] It is this adaptable, flow-like mediation that afforded such power to these livestreams, which in turn morphed to fill the need for emotional wellbeing among their audiences.

Coronavirus music livestream assemblages thus produced and perpetuated a space for intimate community building, with online intimacy 'the affective encounters with others that often matter most',[79] found in musically intimate communities of diapasonic affinity. The scholarly literature on intimacy in online social media spaces is largely concerned with the personal sharing of private, and often sexual, details,[80] mostly coming out of 'queer and feminist theorists of intimate publics'.[81] In relation to the pandemic moment, Holly Thorpe, Allison Jeffery, Simone Fullager and Nida Ahmad have explored how 'digital intimacies produce a reimagining of felt community relations through entanglements of technology, virtual touch and haptic connections' between women in the 'constitution of physical-digital spaces'.[82]

However, this visceral intimacy can extend beyond the realm of sexuality. When a stream is viewed on a large screen, either of a smart TV or a desktop monitor, the facial expressions of the players are magnified and intensified. The viewer notices smiles, raised eyebrows, glances, and other expressions directed at the screen, and in turn, at the viewer. The focal point of the players' gaze is the lens of the streaming camera, which creates penetrating eye contact with the viewer. There is a palpable sense of intimacy which is not captured in other formats. Musicians are arrayed on a couch, as if playing on the other side of the viewer's own living room. The informality of the livestreamed huapango thus contributed to its appeal during a time where such simple, everyday conviviality was craved. As Alex Lambert has argued in dissecting social capital in Facebook before the pandemic, in creating intimacies online, 'the performative element of social capital is central'.[83] In the face of lockdowns, this exigency only grew in importance.

This sensibility is magnified and seen most obviously when the listener is subsumed into the livestream and the chat, which is a key component of all streams and of the digital spaces created to meet the community needs during the pandemic. Lambert argues that 'in making reference to various musicians which take on specific meanings for this group, these friends simultaneously perform their collective stock of social and cultural capital.' He adds: 'Note the light and playful tone. Social capital imbricates through this gregarious form of public intimacy.'[84] The connections created online in these digital spaces of the pandemic clearly showed people seeking friendship and intimacy. This was especially so in the ways these participants jointly imagined, longed for, described, and anticipated the post-pandemic return to in-person events like huapangos and more general family gatherings. Online relationships can be far more profound, meaningful, and sustainable than the uninitiated might think, as Gina Lai and Ka Yi Fung found in their recent study of the social ties formed in virtual spaces.[85]

In digital huapango spaces, viewers and performers are both participants with concrete agency. Participant-observation in the livestream chats demonstrated that people are quite the opposite of silent: the chats were constantly active and considered an essential component of the stream. This utility during the digital huapangos of the pandemic moment parallels what occurs at in-person huapango events. There are regular acknowledgements of individuals, mentions of birthdays and anniversaries, appeals to place names and regional identity, and shouts of '¡*puro Huasteco!*' and '¡*ajuua!*' In seeking and finding a respite from the anxieties of the pandemic moment, participants in these spaces were able to hang on just a little longer, until they could return to the people, places, and events that remind them of who they are.

Entrepreneurial Spaces of Transnational Community

The founder of the Jarochelo YouTube channel, César Castro, has been playing son jarocho for 31 years since growing up in southern Veracruz. He kept up his passion after moving to Los Angeles, where he has resided now for over a decade. When the pandemic struck, Jarochelo, as he is known, initiated a series of livestreamed music lessons, conversations, concerts, and other sessions on YouTube. His social media presence, in addition to his podcast, has garnered a global audience and has put him into contact with communities of son jarocho musicians and enthusiasts across the world. This global community, which extends from Mexico and the United States into Canada, Japan, South America, and Europe, reflects the global nature of the *movimiento fandanguero*.[86] Castro is 'always connected', he says, 'to the point that people sometimes don't know I live in LA'.[87]

Castro has been a professional musician for years, with a small but growing online presence teaching son jarocho technique, performing shows, and building instruments. He had originally started his own virtual musical spaces on new media outlets, because he did not think radio or television was the appropriate fit for son jarocho music: 'I always felt uncomfortable – that we didn't fit, that this music didn't fit in their programming. So that's where I guess I get this idea of producing as soon as I was able to', he told us. His podcast has been in production for more than ten years, and he launched the Jarochelo channel 'to produce something that had some dignity, [that] had its own space'. From the beginning he saw his role as promoting others, which incidentally would also promote his own work. 'I am always inviting people to share', he explained to us. 'I don't do it for commercial purposes [...], it is fun. It is another way to share.'

In the case of son jarocho, the transmission of musical knowledge has always been intimately connected to community. The concept of *convivencia*, or 'togetherness', exists at the core of this sensibility. In discussing son jarocho's transformation from a regionalized music relegated to rural areas into a transnational artistic movement with large appeal in urban areas, Maria Concepción Patraca Rueda has described how this togetherness was always at the core of oral transmission and learning. She has explored how an emergent class of semi-professionalized educators drew from this sensibility in their workshops, with varying degrees of effectiveness.[88] Meanwhile, María González de Castilla Gómez has highlighted the case of Colectivo Altepee, a youth-based collective in Veracruz that runs workshops that are both didactic and oralistic.[89] As one of the leading figures of this professionalized workshop generation, Cesar Castro seeks to replicate this ethos of orality and communitarianism in spite of the constraints posed by his distance from his audience.

When the pandemic hit, Castro felt like he was fairly well positioned in the community and sought new approaches to further his mission. His channels rapidly saw a sharp rise in views and subscribers, the latter reaching almost 6000 by the end of August 2021, when he released his 175th video.[90] In an interview with the authors, Castro recalled telling his wife Xochi Flores, who teaches son jarocho dance and who has also contributed videos to the channel, 'let's use this time to get better.' On the impacts of shutdown, Castro noted that 'we don't have fandangos… that's fine. Let's detox from fandangos.' He told his listeners that the forced pandemic pause could be a good opportunity to 'study, practice, change strings, fix your instruments.' Nonetheless, Castro recalled with a wry laugh in the fall of 2021, 'of course we didn't know we were going to go more than a year!'[91]

At the start of the pandemic moment, on 16 March, Castro livestreamed on his channel for the first time. He broadcast himself in front of a plain black background, playing and singing a son, and later writing the chords and rhythms on a whiteboard. This became the first in a labeled series which continued for months.[92] Flores also continued with weekly zapateado lessons, also livestreamed on the Jarochelo channel. All these videos remain archived for future viewing. Castro soon began to expand the channel's range and coverage in response to his growing audience and to unexpected new opportunities afforded by the pandemic. His offerings came to include videos with guests in Mexico, special concerts and presentations, and the launch of a 'Música y Charla' (Music and Conversation) series of conversations with musicians, poets, luthiers, and researchers. The streams soon improved in sound and video quality. Some sessions addressed highly specific concerns such as how to restring instruments. Other sessions were labeled 'cib-VerZOOM' sessions, such as one on 26 August with guests including poet-researchers Marisol Galloso and Ana Zarina Palafox, 'La Bruja Galáctica', Lalo Jaranas, and Carlos Rosario, among others.[93]

The range of the offerings grew as the pandemic moment matured, indicating a focused effort to keep the audience engaged and returning. The evidence of the lively chats on YouTube and Facebook signal this was a highly dedicated, ever-returning audience. Castro told us in 2021 he usually has 80 people for a regular live broadcast, jumping to 120 or 150 for special event broadcasts. He said that compared to some other channels, 'it's not a huge group. But come on, 80 people together in a room, at a fandango, that is already a large audience.' It is clear that creating a community space for a committed group of regulars during the pandemic was the goal, rather than simply seeking large audiences for the sake of it. Castro believes the fact that the content is freely given on Jarochelo to be part of its success: 'People keep watching and keep commenting.'[94]

Castro has an appealing baritone voice and an easy, welcoming laugh. These produce an encouraging air and a homespun connectivity in the channel's videos, which cover a diversity of approaches and topics. Jarochelo videos can be seen as metaphorical variations on a theme: many begin with a static image and the sound of a jarana tuning, establishing the sonic world into which enters the listener. Then, Castro appears, welcomes his audience, and plays a son on the jarana, the core rhythmic instrument of son jarocho music and the entry instrument for most musicians. While easy to play at a rudimentary level, the full range of the instrument's technical possibilities and sound becomes clear in Castro's hands. He delivers the music with verve and energy, and with no performative distance from the audience. Castro admitted to us that he sometimes does not feel like playing until the very moment when his video starts filming. Nonetheless, he sees himself as a professional, and remains committed to producing a useful product for the community he has helped to foster. During the pandemic, he explained, he sought 'the good in the middle of this awful time. Sometimes it was hard for me to just turn on the camera and just work, I had to prepare.' Castro nevertheless always ensured he was 'well presented' and welcoming. When he started playing, he inevitably felt his own mood as well as his educator's sensibility engage and carry him through.[95]

The videos on Jarochelo's channel share an enveloping communitarian ethos. As the pandemic slogged on, Castro improved and expanded his home-recording setup into a professional-quality streaming studio he calls Estudio Tlacuache (Opossum Studio). This improvement was entirely facilitated by direct donations from the audience he accrued during the pandemic. He equates his viewers' support with a 'community sponsorship program'. Castro does not charge for views, but he received an outpouring of support. During livestreams, 'people would be commenting [...] being part of it.' He took suggestions live during streams for camera, lighting, and other technical ideas. Castro said he 'got a lot of support', including 'emotional support, financial support, or ego [boosting] with the nice comments [...] but all of that was very surprising to receive.'

Of all the channels and streams considered in this chapter, the chat function on the Jarochelo YouTube channel is perhaps the best-developed and critical to its embracing, communitarian feel and overall success. Castro is always extremely responsive to comments in the chat: 'Reading each comment aloud I order and respond to all of them with a comment, a joke, a laugh, and an expression of gratitude which rings with sincerity.' The comments, along with the thumbnail avatars of their authors, are also presented on the main screen. While it was a common feature of Facebook and YouTube livestream performances during the COVID pandemic to read and interact with the comments, Castro's commitment to include all the viewership stands out. He also applies this principle in his *Música y Charla* videos. For example, in his 87th session, a 1 hour 27 minute video dedicated to the son jarocho harpist Salvador Peña, Castro spent the first 15 minutes of the video playing his own song and acknowledging the presence and comments of all of the gathered viewers before turning to his guest. Jarochelo makes it clear that the people gathered were not a passive audience but rather a community partnered in the experience. He used the same format for a talk with Julio César Corro Lara from Tlacotalpan, Veracruz on 5 October 2020.[96] This accords with the ethics of the wider son jarocho revival movement, which places primacy on the idea of *convivencia*, or 'togetherness', as a mechanism for social unity, even to the level of political articulation and spiritual actualization. As noted by Martha Gonzalez, 'the lessons learned in the midst of varying translocal community struggles and triumphs translate into artivista praxis' by way of the global fandango.[97]

One of Castro's core objectives was to foster a welcoming and useful virtual space for a global son jarocho community of musicians and enthusiasts. He called this 'promoting the good energy, the good vibe'. Like others, he considers the community element to be at the core of the music, 'because if you are learning son jarocho, it is important to know other people to listen to how they learn, to listen to how they look for more information, inspiration. Everything.' Castro did not think of his channel's success in egoistic terms of personal glory. People could learn and connect there, and he understood his role as a facilitator in that space, noting that 'there are all of these other people. We can learn and in the end we can all meet at the fandango, which is our main goal'. As the participatory music events at which son jarocho music is played and danced, fandangos serve as the axial musical and social events in a son jarocho musician's life. Castro intended to build an intimate virtual space for people to gather, learn, and connect as a complement to the often-raucous in-person events. After a year-and-a-half of his efforts in pandemic mode, his videos now include a description of the 'Jarochelo Fandango Club' as 'a virtual community created from the contingency caused by the pandemic in March 2020'.[98]

Castro is the most pleased that the connections made through his channel are blossoming into real-life friendships. 'Some people in the audience, they know each other because of their comments', he told us, happily. Castro has also himself made friends through his own channel:

> As soon as I could travel, I met one of the people who was commenting on the videos and now we have a real friendship. To me that proved that I actually hit a very important [element] [...]. It is hard to say because it's my work, but I think it is profound. I actually made connections [myself].

He has already met up with some of his most loyal audience members, and he looks forward to meeting others in person. Speaking about one person from Venezuela who frequents the online spaces, he told us that 'we haven't met yet, but as soon as he shows up in Mexico at a fandango, he'll be another friend.' Castro is especially pleased that people who have never played before have learned on his channel and are even starting their own son jarocho groups. One woman from Veracruz began learning to play the jarana from Jarochelo videos and has now started all all-female ensemble. It is 'very touching, amazing to witness', Castro said.[99]

Through the Jarochelo channel, Castro even connected with lapsed acquaintances from his family's home town of Tlalixcoyan, Veracruz. He is hopeful about what this connection will yield in events and cultural programming in the region of his roots: 'We started talking about actually building up a project, a cultural project in Tlalixcoyan', he explained. While the town does not have a large presence of *fandangueros* at present, Castro is hopeful that, with the support of his local friends, 'we can get fandangos back in town... we can son jarocho back in there', because 'son jarocho is pretty absent' there. 'That was to me the most valuable conversation', he added, 'because we got inspired. I believe a lot in community projects, community support, community resources.'[100]

On 13 June 2020, Castro appeared in an online gathering of son jarocho musicians and enthusiasts. However, this time, he was not the host. The event was a virtual gathering to commemorate the 13th annual Fandango Fronterizo, an event that had taken place annually at the Mexico–US border between Tijuana and San Diego. In Friendship Park, a public plaza flanked by the Pacific Ocean, *fandangueros* had gathered once a year on both sides of the border fence to sing, play, and dance. The *tarimas* on which people did zapateado were pushed up against the fence, allowing for pairs of participants to dance and trade verses with one another from opposite sides of the frontier.

Coordinated by retired a Mexican American librarian, Jorge Castillo, the Fandango Fronterizo has captured the attention of the worldwide *fandanguero* movement. Cecilia del Mar Zamudio Serrano describes this distinctive fandango as a 'unique expression of the transnationality of son jarocho in its current state', commenting on the role of 'the border as a space of transit and fluidity' in allowing for 'cultural interchange' and 'new forms of linkage and expression.'[101] Perhaps most famously, the yearly event has captured the attention of Grammy-winning Afro-Latin jazz artist Arturo O'Farrill, who along with documentary filmmaker Kabir Segal spearheaded the 'Fandango at the Wall' creative franchise.[102]

This in-person gathering, which had already been made difficult in pre-COVID years due to an increasingly hostile political climate towards border issues and migration, was rendered impossible in 2020 due to the threat posed by COVID-19. Instead, Castillo invited the community to gather on a massive Zoom call. At one point, over a hundred participants were connected.

A few shared research or updates on their work within the movement, some performed sones, and others simply took a moment to share their gratitude and to wish safety and health to their friends. Many more remained silent, but stayed connected nonetheless. Castro was present, as were many of the central figures of son jarocho on both sides of the border. For Emilio 'Querreque' Hernandez Valentin, a jovial and beloved jaranero from Santiago Tuxtla, Veracruz, this gathering of *fandangueros* proved to be one of his last. Merely a few weeks later, he fatally contracted COVID-19.[103]

For over a decade, the Fandango Fronterizo connected son jarocho musicians separated by an aggressive geopolitical barrier. In 2020, the Fandango Fronterizo took on the challenge of bridging yet another social ravine, this time caused by the global pandemic. COVID-19 rendered in-person fandangos impossible, and took the lives of some of its most respected and beloved practitioners. Nonetheless, through virtual spaces, this collectivity of musicians, promoters, activists, and researchers continued to find hope, togetherness, and creativity in a time of unimaginable challenge.

Conclusion

At the outset of the pandemic moment, DIY activists and entrepreneurs utilized emergent digital infrastructures to serve atomized transnational music communities oriented around son huasteco and son jarocho. The digital spaces they cultivated promoted emotional wellbeing, sustained cultural production, and generated revenue for artists and content creators. From the start of the COVID-19 pandemic onward, the son huasteco community embraced the virtual huapango as a unique and necessary space to find community and pursue the social cohesion and emotional support that was previously enjoyed in-person. Likewise, among son jarocho enthusiasts and learners, daily livestreams from Cesar Castro exhibited a palpable directness and welcoming intimacy that both reflected the values of a movement in transition and responded to the demands of the pandemic moment. Simultaneously ephemeral and impactful, these spaces addressed the need for community experienced by self-isolating individuals, even if they did not replace the experience of physical events. Virtual spaces served many of the emotional needs of geographically fragmented musical communities as people searched for human connectivity and cultural maintenance in the shadow of the coronavirus.

Notes

1. 'Y Siguen los huapangos!', https://www.youtube.com/watch?v=aAi-ND2yi7I (accessed 13 August 2020).
2. 'Y Siguen los huapangos!'

3. Tia DeNora, *Music Asylums: Wellbeing through Music in Everyday Life* (Farnham, UK: Ashgate, 2013).
4. The improvisational character of the response in son huasteco verses is covered in Daniel Margolies and J. A. Strub, 'Community Music Making, Improvisation and Social Technologies in Música Huasteca', *Frontiers in Psychology* 12 (2021): Article 648010.
5. Many huapangueros attribute the principal verses of 'La Muerte' to Abraham Martinez Trejo and argue that it is a huapango with fixed lyrics, while others treat it as a son and sing varied or improvised verses.
6. 'Ya es tiempo de meditar/nos van a dar en la torre/ si se llegan a infectar', 'Los Yolpakis – La Muerte (Versos Coronavirus Nahuatl y Español)', https://www.youtube.com/watch?v=7oSdF7UotQg (accessed 20 April 2020).
7. Rosa M. Bonilla Burgos and Juan C. Gómez Rojas, 'Son huasteco e identidad regional', *Investigaciones geográficas* 80 (2013): 86–97, pp. 90–1.
8. Janet Sturman, *The Course of Mexican Music*, 2nd edition (London: Routledge, 2015), pp. 105–6. Significant scholarship has addressed the links between framings of identity and community manifest in various regional son traditions and revival movements. See Daniel Sheehy, 'The "Son Jarocho": The History, Style, and Repertory of a Changing Mexican Musical Tradition', PhD thesis, University of California Los Angeles, 1979; Marina A. Bolaños, 'Sin música no hay fiesta, no hay nada': aproximaciones a las expresiones musicales indígenas en Chiapas', *Música oral del Sur: revista internacional* 9 (2012): 241–51.
9. Raquel González Paraíso, 'Re-Contextualizing Traditions: The Performance of Identity in Festivals of Huasteco, Jarocho, and Terracalenteño Sones in Mexico', PhD thesis, University of Wisconsin-Madison, 2014.
10. Víctor Hernández Vaca, 'Son huasteco, son de costumbre. Etnolaudería del son a lo humano ya lo divino en Texquitote, San Luis Potosí', *Revista de Literaturas Populares* 10.1–2 (2000): 3–17; Bonilla Burgos and Gómez Rojas, 'Son huasteco'. The literature on son huasteco in English is fairly limited. Related transnational aspects of Mexican son have received recent attention from Alejandro Miranda Nieto, *Musical Mobilities: Son Jarocho and the Circulation of Tradition Across Mexico and the United States* (New York: Routledge, 2019) and Ishtar Cardona and Christian Rinaudo, 'Son jarocho entre méxico y estados unidos: definición "afro" de una práctica transnacional', *Desacatos* 53 (2017): 20–37.
11. Kim A. C. Muñoz, 'Huapangueros Reclaiming Son Huasteco in Trans-local Festivals: Youth, Women and Nahua Musicians', PhD thesis, University of Washington, 2013, pp. 48–50.
12. Theresa Heyd, 'Narratives of Belonging in the Digital Diaspora: Corpus Approaches to a Cultural Concept', *Open Linguistics* 2 (2016): 287–99, p. 288.
13. Gillian Rose, 'Rethinking the Geographies of Cultural "Objects" through Digital Technologies: Interface, Network and Friction', *Progress in Human Geography* 40.3 (2016): 334–51, p. 336.
14. Marc Scully, 'BIFFOs, Jackeens and Dagenham Yanks: County Identity, "Authenticity" and the Irish Diaspora', *Irish Studies Review* 21.2 (2013): 143–63; Derek Bryce, Samantha Murdy, and Matthew Alexander, 'Diaspora, Authenticity and the Imagined Past', *Annals of Tourism Research* 66 (2017): 49–60; Emily T. Yeh, 'Exile Meets Homeland: Politics, Performance, and Authenticity in the Tibetan Diaspora', *Environment and Planning D: Society & Space* 25.4 (2016): 648–67.
15. Danielle Fosler-Lussier, *Music on the Move* (Ann Arbor: University of Michigan Press, 2020), p. 205.
16. Jennifer M. Brinkerhoff, *Digital Diasporas: Identity and Transnational Engagement* (Cambridge: Cambridge University Press, 2009).
17. 'Sigan.bailando huapangos....son remedio anti covid!', https://www.youtube.com/watch?v=y8GilnoYAn8 (accessed 23 August 2020).

18. Sara Marino, 'Cook It, Eat It, Skype It: Mobile Media Use in Re-Staging Intimate Culinary Practices Among Transnational Families', *International Journal of Cultural Studies* 22.6 (2019): 788–803, p. 789.
19. Dana Diminescu, 'The Connected Migrant: An Epistemological Manifesto', *Social Science Information* 47.4 (2008): 565–79; Mihaela Nedelcu, 'Migrants' New Transnational Habitus: Rethinking Migration Through a Cosmopolitan Lens in the Digital Age', *Journal of Ethnic and Migration Studies* 38.9 (2012): 1339–56.
20. Thomas Solomon, 'Theorizing Diaspora and Music', *Lidé města* 2 (2015): 201–19, pp. 205–6.
21. Gunter Kreutz, 'Does Singing Facilitate Social Bonding?' *Music and Medicine* 6.2 (2014): 51–60; Oscar Millar and Ian Warwick, 'Music and Refugees' Wellbeing in Contexts of Protracted Displacement', *Health Education Journal* 78.1 (2019): 67–80.
22. Susan Hallam, Andrea Creech, Maria Varvarigou, and Hilary McQueen, 'Perceived Benefits of Active Engagement with Making Music in Community Settings', *International Journal of Community Music* 5 (2012): 155–74; Daniel Västfjäll, Patrik N. Juslin, and Terry Hartig, 'Music, Subjective Well-Being, and Health: The Role of Everyday Emotions', in Raymond MacDonald, Gunter Kreutz, and Laura Mitchell, eds, *Music, Health, and Well-Being* (Oxford: Oxford University Press, 2012), 405–23; Amélie Morinville, Dave Miranda, and Patrick Gaudreau, 'Music Listening Motivation is Associated with Global Happiness in Canadian Late Adolescents', *Psychology of Aesthetics, Creativity, and the Arts* 7.4 (2013): 384–90.
23. Suvi Saarikallio, 'Music as Emotional Self-Regulation throughout Adulthood', *Psychology of Music* 39.3 (2010): 307–27; Raymond MacDonald, Gunter Kreutz, and Laura Mitchell, eds, *Music, Health, and Wellbeing* (Oxford: Oxford University Press, 2012); Sabine Koch, Teresa Kunz, Sissy Lykou, and Robyn Cruz, 'Effects of Dance Movement Therapy and Dance on Health-Related Psychological Outcomes: A Meta-Analysis', *The Arts in Psychotherapy* 41.1 (2014): 46–64; Jan Packer and Julie Ballantyne, 'The Impact of Music Festival Attendance on Young People's Psychological and Social Well-Being', *Psychology of Music* 39.2 (2011): 164–81.
24. Melissa K. Weinberg and Dawn Joseph, 'If You're Happy and You Know It: Music Engagement and Subjective Wellbeing', *Psychology of Music* 45.2 (2017): 257–67, p. 265.
25. Mirca Madianou and Daniel Miller, 'Polymedia: Towards a New Theory of Digital Media in Interpersonal Communication', *International Journal of Cultural Studies* 16.2 (2012): 169–87.
26. Marino, 'Cook It', p. 788.
27. Jean Burges and Joshua Green, *YouTube: Online Video and Participatory Culture*, 2nd edition (Cambridge: Polity, 2018), pp. 80, 125.
28. Janice L. Waldron, 'YouTube, Fanvids, Forums, Vlogs and Blogs: Informal Music Learning in a Convergent On- and Offline Music Community', *International Journal of Music Education* 31.1 (2013): 91–105, p. 91.
29. Koen Leurs, *Digital Passages: Migrant Youth 2.0. Diaspora, Gender & Youth Cultural Intersections* (Amsterdam: Amsterdam University Press, 2015); Lonán Ó Briain, 'Beyond the Digital Diaspora: YouTube Methodologies, Online Networking and the Hmong Music Festival', *Journal of World Popular Music* 2.2 (2015): 289–306.
30. Alex Chávez, *Sounds of Crossing: Music, Migration, and the Aural Poetics of Huapango Arribeño* (Durham, NC: Duke University Press, 2017).
31. BBC News, 'Coronavirus: The World in Lockdown in Maps and Charts', 7 April 2020, https://www.bbc.com/news/world-52103747, *BBC News* (accessed 29 December 2020); *New York Times*, 'Mexico Coronavirus Map and Case Count', 2020–, https://www.nytimes.com/interactive/2020/world/americas/mexico-coronavirus-cases.html (accessed 29 December 2020).
32. Vanda Felbab-Brown, 'AMLO's Feeble Response to COVID-19 in Mexico', Brookings Institute website, 30 March 2020, https://www.brookings.edu/blog/

order-from-chaos/2020/03/30/amlos-feeble-response-to-covid-19-in-mexico (accessed 29 December 2020).
33. Gabino Vera, interview by J. A. Strub, 18 June 2020.
34. Vera, interview, 18 June 2020.
35. 'En vivo con El Trío Los Hidalguenses desde Pachuca Hidalgo', https://www.youtube.com/watch?v=20AtIr-pxjA&t=255s (accessed 25 July, 2020).
36. Yo Soy Coxcatlán YouTube channel, https://www.youtube.com/user/yosoycoxcatlan (accessed 30 August 2020).
37. Vera, interview, 18 June 2020.
38. Gabino Vera, interview by J. A. Strub, 2 July 2020.
39. Vera, interview, 2 July 2020.
40. Gabino Vera, interview by J. A. Strub, 19 June 2020.
41. Mike Thelwall, Pardeep Sud, and Farida Vis, 'Commenting on YouTube Videos: From Guatemalan Rock to El Big Bang', *Journal of the American Society for Information Science and Technology* 63.3 (2012): 616–29, p. 626.
42. Vera, interview, 19 June 2020.
43. 'Invitación al Encuentro Virtual de Tríos Huastecos', https://www.youtube.com/watch?v=KfouaVH5a3I (accessed 19 March 2020).
44. Vera, interview, 19 June 2020.
45. Vera, interview, 19 June 2020.
46. 'Difusión Huasteca', https://www.youtube.com/watch?v=OE52sO28nN8 (accessed 18 August 2020, no longer available).
47. 'Trío Lucero Huasteco de Tantoyuca, Veracruz #QuedateEnCasa', https://www.youtube.com/watch?v=tcJwxe6DpoM (accessed 18 August 2020).
48. '#QuedateEnCasa y Escucha Huapangos Huastecos', https://www.youtube.com/watch?v=JYO-a_Bl6dk (accessed 18 August 2020); '#QuedateEnCasa y Escucha Huapangos Huastecos', https://www.youtube.com/watch?v=0nv2piW3H7E (accessed 18 August 2020).
49. 'Huapanguitos en un domingo de cuarentena', https://www.youtube.com/watch?v=v-73LJqZBqU (accessed 13 August 2020).
50. 'Huapangos para finalizar la semana!', https://www.youtube.com/watch?v=Kqs6L3Ty6Zs (accessed 6 September 2020).
51. 'Huapangos para finalizar la semana!', https://www.youtube.com/watch?v=Kqs6L3Ty6Zs (accessed 6 September 2020).
52. 'Huapangos para finalizar la semana!', https://www.youtube.com/watch?v=Kqs6L3Ty6Zs (accessed 6 September 2020).
53. Jessa Lingel and Mor Naaman, 'You Should Have Been There, Man: Live Music, DIY Content and Online Communities', *New Media & Society* 14.2 (2011): 332–349, p. 335.
54. Christofer Jost, 'Professionalism as Style: Music Amateurs on YouTube and the Transformation of Production Techniques', *Lied und Populäre Kultur* 62 (2017): 55–70, p. 59.
55. Juanito S., interview by Dan Margolies, 6 June 2020.
56. 'Y Siguen los huapangos!', https://www.youtube.com/watch?v=aAi-ND2yi7I (accessed 13 August 2020).
57. 'Ahora escuchemos Huapangos!', https://www.youtube.com/watch?v=y8GilnoYAn8 (accessed 23 August 2020).
58. 'Lunes Huapanguero!', https://www.youtube.com/watch?v=WVYTtLeZn24 (accessed 17 August 2020).
59. Sara Marino, 'Making Space, Making Place: Digital Togetherness and the Redefinition of Migrant Identities Online', *Social Media + Society* 1.2 (2015): https://doi.org/10.1177/2056305115622479
60. Marino, 'Cook It', p. 798.

61. Trio Santuario Huasteco Facebook post, 25 April 2020, https://www.facebook.com/triosantuario.huasteco.7/videos/855159068336523/ (accessed 25 April 2020).
62. Rat De Bois Facebook post, 9 May 2020, https://www.facebook.com/permalink.php?story_fbid=1177044319301548&id=100009879738811 (accessed 9 May 2020).
63. 'Trío Sentimiento Huasteco Representante Tobias de Gaona', https://www.facebook.com/watch/live/?v=2676354835945249 (accessed 6 July 2020).
64. Huapango arribeño is a related but quite different style of traditional music from a region adjacent to Huasteca. Son huasteco and huapango arribeño have a certain amount of overlapping appeal among many listeners, especially in the diaspora, despite differences in improvisational styles, instrumental technique, and dance moves.
65. 'Trio Fuerza Imperial', https://www.facebook.com/trio.acuarela.5/videos/672973366920749/ (accessed 6 December 2020).
66. https://www.facebook.com/watch/live/?v=636191986967495 (accessed 13 June 2020) (no longer available).
67. '#EnVivo Trío Cantores del Alba ¡Pidan sus huapangos!', https://www.facebook.com/watch/live/?v=2987014701385647 (accessed 31 May 2020).
68. 'China del Alma (en vivo) – Trio Cantores del Alba en Huauchinango, Puebla', https://www.youtube.com/watch?v=iT5Zdjqmtq4 (accessed 1 June 2020).
69. 'Perlitas Queretanas', https://www.facebook.com/watch/live/?v=394495201669636 (accessed 5 December 2020).
70. 'Huapango Sin Fronteras Virtual', https://www.youtube.com/watch?v=qM4HqQP3gJc, (accessed 29 December 2020).
71. Muñoz, Huapangueros Reclaiming Son Huasteco.
72. Quoted by Sam Blake in 'Livestream Concerts Boomed During Lockdown: Are They Music's Future or Just a Pandemic Fad?' *Dot.LA*, 14 October 2020, https://dot.la/livestream-concerts-boomed-during-lockdown-is-it-musics-future-or-just-a-pandemic-fad-2648201267.html (accessed 14 December 2020).
73. Paraíso, 'Re-Contextualizing Traditions', pp. 5, 150.
74. Steven Colburn, 'Filming Concerts for YouTube: Seeking Recognition in the Pursuit of Cultural Capital', *Popular Music and Society* 38 (2015): 59–72.
75. Nisha Gupta, 'Singing Away the Social Distancing Blues: Art Therapy in a Time of Coronavirus', *Journal of Humanistic Psychology* 60.5 (2020): 593–603, pp. 596–7.
76. Rose, 'Rethinking the Geographies', p. 336.
77. Gupta, 'Singing Away', p. 596.
78. Amy Shields Dobson, Brady Robards, and Nicholas Carah, eds, *Digital Intimate Publics and Social Media* (Cham, Switzerland: Springer, 2018); Tarja Rautiainen-Keskustalo and Sanna Raudaskoski, 'Inclusion by Live Streaming? Contested Meanings of Well-Being: Movement and Non-Movement of Space, Place and Body', *Mobilities* 14:4 (2019): 469–483.
79. McGlotten quoted in Amy Shields Dobson, Nicholas Carah, and Brady Robards, 'Digital Intimate Publics and Social Media: Towards Theorising Public Lives on Private Platforms', in Amy Shields Dobson, Brady Robards, and Nicholas Carah, eds, *Digital Intimate Publics and Social Media* (Cham, Switzerland: Springer, 2018), 3–27, p. 4.
80. Michael Waugh, '"My Laptop is an Extension of my Memory and Self": Post-Internet Identity, Virtual Intimacy and Digital Queering in Online Popular Music', *Popular Music* 36.2 (2017): 233–251.
81. Amy Shields Dobson, Brady Robards, and Nicholas Carah, 'Introduction', in Amy Shields Dobson, Brady Robards, and Nicholas Carah eds, *Digital Intimate Publics and Social Media* (Cham, Switzerland: Springer, 2018), xix–xxviii, p. xx.
82. Holly Thorpe, Allison Jeffery, Simone Fullager, and Nida Ahmad, '"We Seek Those Moments of Togetherness": Digital Intimacies, Virtual Touch and Becoming Community in Pandemic Times', *Feminist Media Studies* 23.7 (2023): 3419–36.

83. A. Lambert, 'Intimacy and Social Capital on Facebook: Beyond the Psychological Perspective', *New Media & Society* 18.11 (2016): 2559–75, p. 2560.
84. Lambert, 'Intimacy and Social Capital', p. 2569.
85. Gina Lai and Ka Yi Fung, 'From Online Strangers to Offline Friends: A Qualitative Study of Video Game Players in Hong Kong', *Media, Culture & Society* 42.4 (2020): 483–501.
86. Alejandro Miranda Nieto, *Musical Mobilities: Son Jarocho and the Circulation of Tradition Across Mexico and the United States* (London: Routledge, 2017); Betto Arcos, *Music Stories from the Cosmic* Barrio (No location or publisher, 2020) pp. 137, 339.
87. Interview with Cesar Castro, by J. A. Strub and Dan Margolies, 18 September 2021.
88. María C. Patraca Rueda, 'Prácticas Educativas en la Enseñanza-Aprendizaje del Zapateado en el Son Jarocho', master's thesis, Universidad Veracruzana, Xalapa, Veracruz, Mexico, 2019.
89. María González de Castilla Gómez, 'Fandango jarocho y ciudad: juventud y construcción de sentidos. El caso del colectivo Altepee', master's thesis, Universidad de Guadalajara, Guadalajara, Jalisco, Mexico, 2017.
90. 'Son Jarocho with JAROCHELO', https://www.youtube.com/channel/UC0nKNZeA9xEjEr4SWDd13xA (accessed 16 April 2022).
91. Castro, interview.
92. '1. Cómo Afinar la Jarana y Mis Primeros Rasgueos', https://www.youtube.com/watch?v=AE5aPJkhwdI (accessed 16 April 2022); 'El Balajú', https://www.youtube.com/watch?v=qy75yM9aS-4 (accessed 16 April 2022).
93. '71. Cib-Verzoom! Noche de versada con Marisol Galloso', https://www.youtube.com/watch?v=-skPtaOVPuY (accessed 16 April 2022).
94. Castro, interview.
95. Castro, interview.
96. '87. Salvador Peña | Música y Charla', https://www.youtube.com/watch?v=0vOZo2hKdtU (accessed 17 April 2022); '85. Julio César Corro Lara desde Tlacotalpan, Ver', https://www.youtube.com/watch?v=mrMPmEaJ1mQ (accessed 17 April 2022).
97. Martha Gonzalez, *Chican@ Activistas* (Austin: University of Texas Press, 2021), p. 93.
98. '174. Relación Requinto – Jarana', https://www.youtube.com/watch?v=lZ-Id4RZZSU (accessed 16 April 2022).
99. Castro, interview.
100. Castro, interview.
101. Cecilia del Mar Zamudio Serrano, 'Dos tarimas, un fandango. Dinámicas y relaciones transfronterizas entre los jaraneros de Tijuana, México-San Diego, EUA: un análisis desde el lado sur de la frontera', master's thesis, Universidad Veracruzana, Xalapa, Veracruz, Mexico, 2014.
102. Jutharat Pinyodoonyachet, 'Arturo O'Farrill's "Fandango at the Wall"', *New Yorker*, 1 July 2022, https://www.newyorker.com/magazine/2022/07/11/arturo-ofarrills-fandango-at-the-wall (accessed 20 August 2022).
103. One of the authors was present at the XIII Fandango Fronterizo. Emilio Hernández Valentin was a friend of his whom he had originally met at the previous year's Fandango Fronterizo.

4 Los Corridos del Coronavirus

Los KDTs de Linares, a band descended from norteño music icons Los Cadetes de Linares, released a narrative ballad about the pandemic called 'El Corrido del COVID-19' on 22 April 2020. Though a relatively late addition to the first wave of songs about the virus, it set the standard for a deluge of similar compositions labeled as COVID corridos, released by amateurs and professionals alike, that flooded YouTube in the spring of 2020. 'El Corrido del COVID-19' tracked very closely to Los Cadetes's well-honed and widely imitated style, being a norteño song in triple-meter delivered with raspy, high-pitched vocals. Verses are punctuated with what is considered classic norteño accompaniment: accordion runs called *pasaditas*, quick bajo sexto licks, and snare drum rimshots.[1]

Los Cadetes de Linares was a storied norteño band from the Mexican state of Nuevo León that has been very popular since the 1970s. Along with groups such as Los Relampagos and Carlos y Jose, they helped to define what is today one of the most popular and iconic forms of commercial music from the Mexico–US borderlands. In spite of the passing on of all the founding members, contemporary bands that claim the name and legacy of Los Cadetes continue to tour in several different competing iterations in Mexico and the United States, drawing their musical legitimacy from various lineages that connect them to the original lineup. Some groups style themselves 'Los Auténicos Cadetes de Linares', 'Los Internacionales Cadetes de Linares', or 'Los Originales', while others have adopted the name of the band's founders, such as 'Los Cadetes de Linares de Dinastía Guerrero', 'Los Cadetes de Linares de Lupe Tijerina', or 'Los Cadetes de Linares de los Primos Tijerina'. Some tie into alternative lineages, such as 'Los Cadetes de Linares de Rosendo Cantu' and 'Los Cadetes de Linares de Santos Lozoya'.[2] 'Los KDTs de Linares', also known as 'Los Cadetes', is led by Homero Guerrero Jr., the son of the founding bajo sexto player from the original lineup. Guerrero Jr. wrote 'El Corrido del COVID-19'.[3]

As is standard in the emergent COVID corrido form, Los KDTs' composition starts with Guerrero describing his creative process in writing the corrido, which reflects the recent changes that have swept the world. The video shows him sitting at home, working on the corrido, with a Los KDT baseball cap on his head. Fate has brought the virus into the world, he declares in song. He announces that it came from China, just as the video cuts to images of dead fruit bats with open mouths and tongues askew, lined up in a market on display. Guerrero does not dwell on or blame China, or engage in the common, putatively humorous tropes of eating bats, as was so common in música del coronavirus across the region in March and April 2020. Instead, the corrido matter-of-factly traces the virus from China to Italy, Spain, and eventually into the whole world, just as some historical corridos have charted the movement of people and goods traversing the globe in search of new markets, experiences, and opportunities.[4] The leaders are helpless, Guerrero warns, and many people are dying. The video has images of body bags, large emergency units, empty streets, and other terrors of the early pandemic, as well as a montage of stock footage of world leaders at the time, including Donald Trump, Andrés Manuel Lopez Obrador, and delegates to the United Nations. The shutdowns have arrived, the lyrics warn, and it is necessary for people to stay isolated.[5]

Not all of the video is grave and humorless, though, as Guerrero also cheekily advises his listeners to make sure that they have stockpiled enough alcohol to drink in the event of an ongoing crisis. While mask use was not as widespread in April 2020 as it would become in the following months, Guerrero shows himself wearing a Los KDT-branded cloth face covering to venture outside. He is seen variously drinking by himself in a club, or else standing alone on a stage looking out mournfully on an empty venue. He is ready to play, but he has no audience. He is alone, like so many others. Guerrero stands inside his house in front of an accolade-laden wall plastered with pictures of his father, gold records, photos, framed albums, and other honors stretching back decades. Still, his fame and renown cannot safeguard him from the loneliness and fear of the pandemic moment. His two tour buses sit idle as well, waiting to return to the road once the crisis abates.[6]

'El Corrido del COVID-19' is a characteristically well-executed but highly formulaic composition that discusses the core facts and experiences that defined the early pandemic moment. In privileging straightforward narrative storytelling over delivering a poetic or emotive intervention, it sets a standard. The structure, lyrics and presentation are very similar to many other less well-known compositions that identify themselves as corridos del coronavirus. Curiously, however, it does not follow the traditionally linear narrative structure and focus that define traditional corridos, instead opting for a verse-and-chorus form more emblematic of the canción norteña.[7] As John Donald Robb has described the difference, 'in contrast to the romance and the corrido, which are basically narrative ballads, the canción is usually introspective in mood'.[8] Nonetheless, it helped to set a trend of using the term 'corrido' to describe almost any new performance of regional Mexican music – whether a ranchera, bolero, polka, canción, redova, or even the odd true corrido – that addressed the pandemic moment. Like the numerous, seemingly interchangeable iterations of Los Cadetes de Linares that continue to draw from the original group's name and appeal, dozens of highly similar corridos del coronavirus piggybacked on one another regardless of trueness to strict form.

Regional Mexican musicians and amateurs alike adopted the term 'corrido', however loosely defined, as a means of self-expression during the pandemic moment because the form is popular, resonant, and malleable in terms of the topics it covers and the emotions it expresses. As César Burgos Dávila and Helena Simonett note: 'The current popularity of the corrido relates to how the music industry has produced a music that appeals to an audience sensitive to the fluidity of social, regional, national, and gender boundaries that they experience.'[9] While norteño music agglomerated under the corrido moniker has its origins in northern Mexico and the borderlands of South Texas, corridos del coronavirus were uploaded from all over Mexico and the United States, with other examples coming from other parts of Latin America, particularly Guatemala and El Salvador. These narrative songs linked tropes of transborder movement found in traditional borderlands corridos to the global spread of the coronavirus.

The pandemic moment triggered a massive outpouring of corridos written by both amateurs and professional musicians. In the face of the challenges posed by the pandemic, during a time when opposing official and folk narratives about the crisis were in fierce competition, these compositions also grappled with questions of clarity, truth, and certainty. *Was the initial spread of COVID-19 a product of chance, of catastrophic negligence, or of coordinated treachery?*, the songs asked. *Is the coronavirus as deadly as it seems? Are masks, hand-washing, and social distancing effective?* And perhaps, most dangerously of all: *Is the virus even real, or is it a hoax concocted by a shadowy global cabal?* The corrido form and label also served an effective dual marketing and comforting purpose, of situating the COVID pandemic among the myriad tragedies and challenges that migrants and borderland residents have faced and surmounted through the strength of cultural resistance over time, and which corridos celebrate.[10]

Los KDTs' corrido is direct and emblematic, but its straightforward language arguably did not achieve the same emotional resonance as others did with similar compositions. Jesús Cardona's direct 'Corrido del COVID 19' and José Angel Juarez's virtuosic 'El Corrido del Coronavirus', both released a month before Los Cadetes' corrido, are examples that are similar yet significantly more impressive by way of poetic claims and musical complexity alike.[11] Nevertheless, Los Cadetes's corrido was very popular, garnering 2.8 million views by the summer of 2022 and with close to one thousand comments from enthusiastic listeners.

One likely reason for this popularity is that Los Cadetes has an enduring fan base that seeks the comforting consistency of their music. People were clearly moved by the corrido, and considered it to be a memorable poetic representation of the moment from famous artists worthy of respect. To fans of Los Cadetes and their legacy, it stood out from the several hundred other corridos del coronavirus that appeared in a flood starting in the spring of 2020. As one YouTube viewer, Gumaro Leija Barbosa, commented on the site more than a year after the corrido was released: 'The legend continues, pure cadets to the grave' ('*La leyenda continua, puro cadetes hasta la tumba*'). Another, named Karen Cervantes, declared that the corrido 'will be a legend full of memories in the future' ('*Será leyenda este corrido, lleno de recuerdos en un futuro*'). Fred PN complimented Los Cadetes on their professionalism: 'This is a corrido', he wrote definitively, 'and I like their professionalism. They don't make fun of the situation, this demonstrates their quality as a musicians' ('*Esto es un corrido, y me gusta el profesionalismo que tienen, no se burlan de la situación, esto demestra su calidad de músicos*'). Caín Figueroa declared that Los Cadetes were 'masters in the corrido', providing 'pure truth in this song, how great that the Cadetes de Linares continue to triumph' ('*Maestros en el corrido, pura verdad en esta canción, que bien que sigan triunfando los Cadetes de Linares*). A more typical version of a simpler fan response comment exclaimed: 'This corrido is awesome, it came out amazing, a very good corrido, *aguaa!*' ('*Chingon este corrido les quedo a toda madre muy buen corrido aguaa* MX🙌♂️😊🙌♂️🙌').[12]

Many comments on Los KDTs referred to the accuracy of the corrido. Truth is a highly prized value among those who compose, sing, perform, and study the corrido, and truthfulness is often asserted by its composers: in the lyrics at the beginning and the end of a corrido, and in the descriptions of YouTube postings. These narrative ballads are very often presented as 'pure truth' getting to the essence of unvarnished historical and experiential honesty.

For example, uffi hernandez (sic) uploaded 'El corrido de coronavirus' on 8 April 2020 with the explicit promise that everything in it was not just true, but *extremely* true.[13] The scholars Jose Pablo Villalobos and Juan Carlos Ramirez-Pimienta argue that 'such an understanding of the corrido as a source of transparency is best explained by understanding the mythical proportions that the corrido has acquired in recent years' and that the problem lies in the idea that 'corridos must be perceived as sincere'. They add that perhaps it is better to approach corridos not as a musical style but rather as a form of testimonial narrative writing, which gets to a more resonant form of honesty.[14] The value of the corrido lies not in the expression of raw emotion, so much as in its ability to tell an engaging story with precision and tact that, through its truth and directness, elicits a sentimental response.

A month before Guerrero penned his corrido, Fito Venegas repurposed a classic bolero hit from Los Cadetes de Linares recorded in 1979 called 'No hay novedad' ('There is no News') into a spoof, 'No hay gravedad' ('There is no Heaviness'). Israel García posted this as 'El corrido del CORONAVIRUS', somewhat confusingly, as the song being covered is, in fact, a bolero. The video showed grainy footage of yet another knockoff version of the original group, this one called 'Los Mero Meros Gigantes Cadetes de L.N.L de Epifanio Ortiz'. The audio of this version was clearly lifted from another video, as they can be seen playing a different song in the video.[15] The original 'No hay novedad' is a heartbreaking song in which the narrator contrasts the lack of change in his life at home to his total internal collapse after his lover's departure.[16] Venegas delivers a credible-sounding version with lyrics that urge the subject of the song to keep their distance, given what is known about the highly contagious virus, while also assuring the listener that everything will be okay. This cover on García's channel gained many views (over 300,000), although not everyone thought it was amusing. Misterio Univeriso 26 wrote, possibly thinking this was the actual group, 'Hahahaha they sucked with this one, but the other corrido they have, yes it's well done' (*Jajajaja se mamaron con este, pero el otro corrido que tienen, si está bien hecho*').[17]

'No hay novedad' is not actually a corrido, but it is part of the same canon of música norteña that, along with corridos, constituted the stylistic groundwork for many coronavirus songs that chose to tell stories, whether of personal pandemic experience or of massive global events. The identification of the corrido idiom itself is as important as the message contained within the lyrics. Ric Alviso has argued that the music and the narrative function 'support and reflect' each other. Musicians use the musical tropes and at the same time they deploy the idea that they are writing corridos. They are inseparable – a referential loop.[18]

This tendency to refer to regional Mexican compositions about the coronavirus pandemic as 'corridos' is perhaps most clearly manifest in the comments left under the official YouTube posting of the globally acclaimed sierreño group Fuerza Regida's song 'Pandemia'. The upload does not feature a video, with the image frame simply taken up by a still shot of an empty street. The song itself addresses themes common throughout música del coronavirus with the customary blend of pensive artistry and street profanity that fans of the band have come to expect. The L.A.-based group does not title their composition as a corrido, but they do begin the song with the cry 'From the original corridos of pure Fuerza Regida'. Many commenters also use the term to describe the song. Valeria Rodriguez left a comment of surprise, saying 'fucking coronavirus, now they even made a corrido for him, what else do you want, please!!' ('*pinche coronavirus ya hasta le hicieron un corrido que mas quieres por favorrrr!!*'). Juan H. opined that 'that corrido is better than most, they are straight badasses to the core in South Central L.A.' ('*el corrido ese si quedo major que la mayoria… son los meros chingones deamadre ahi en soutcentral*'). El Cazador del Pacifico said it plain and simple: 'well, this is a corrido' ('*si pos esto es un corrido*').[19]

Considering the Corrido

The literature on the corrido of the Mexico–US borderlands is appropriately vast given the significance of the form in this region. The formal characteristics and taxonomy of corridos have been fully delineated and often repeated. As traditionally defined and understood, a corrido is a highly structured song and lyrical form with 'a rather declamatory melody in either 2/4 or 3/4 time' that grapples with all aspects of life from personal love struggles to the extremes of human criminal and political action.[20] A corrido typically has five components, as explained by Alviso:

> corrido texts typically follow a standard formula that includes (1) the singer's announcement that he will be singing a corrido; (2) the date, place, and name of the main character(s); (3) a formula introducing the action of the corrido; (4) farewell of principal; (5) the despedida, where the person singing the corrido bids farewell.

Alviso also provides a clear structural element of the borderlands norteño corrido, which typically takes an AABAAB form.[21]

And yet, so many self-defined corridos of the pandemic era do not even try to follow this structure. One way to consider the meaning of the corrido beyond its strophic and musical definitions is to frame it as 'an abstraction'. Américo Paredes argues for the existence of the corrido as a platonic form, hypothesizing that

> what exists out there in the real world is not the corrido but *corridos* – a great many of them, each with individual characteristics of its own. But why stop there? We can go a step further and assert that individual corridos are also abstractions. And what exists out there is only the individual performance of a corrido at a specific place and time.[22]

Perhaps the performers themselves are the best situated to define and describe the ontological nature of genres and styles. As Alexander Cannon argues, 'musicians generate genre as simultaneously bounded and unbounded. They draw in musical elements and improvise on them to generate closed thematic loops to bind genres.'[23] In labeling their uploaded compositions as corridos, artists acting as individuals interlink and form a collectivity, tapping into a set of meanings and affinities that extend far beyond narrow stylistic definitions. The onset of the pandemic is an epically tragic story of global proportions, and performers are willing to tell it from their own perspective. This storytelling character, more than any formal elements of composition or text, is what links COVID corridos.

Corridos are typically framed in the literature in terms of their poetic character, sociopolitical and emotional content, and the core political power of their creation and existence as they mediate historical and current events for listeners. However, the music should not be simplified into a news flash; resonance requires awareness of the events. As Helena Simonett notes: 'Although the language employed in corridos is mostly simple and direct, the meanings of the texts are difficult for outsiders to understand.'[24] Disasters are a common theme, although these are usually physical, political, or emotional rather than epidemiological. This gives the corrido cathartic power, as is evident for example in a recent study of the ways singing and listening to corridos operated as a form of 'music therapy bereavement work' for Mexican migrants who had experienced tragedy.[25]

Due to their regional context, corridos have historically challenged the racial hierarchies of the Mexico–US border. They are, after all, musical expressions of resistance that chronicle how Mexicans and Mexican Americans navigate the fraught racial politics of the borderlands. This tendency dates back at least to 1901, when a corrido about a wrongly convicted Mexican American ranch hand became a standard-setter for biopolitically charged borderlands music.[26] Modern corridos are also commonly presented as sites of critical agency and autonomy. For example, in a typical recent formulation, borderlands corridos have been called 'not just songs' but 'epistemological strongholds' against white racist framings and institutions.[27]

Corridos define and illuminate the cross-cultural spatiality of the borderlands and of the migrant experience, moving with the people who have historically lived in these contested cultural and geopolitical spaces. The borderlands are thus defined not only as the geographical space where the United States and Mexico meet, but also as movable geographies of the diaspora that are far from the border itself. Mark Noe, observing the narrative conventions and spatialities of borderlands corridos, argues as follows:

> We might imagine the difference between boundaries and borders as the difference between maps and globes. In a map one can always find an edge, a place that is far from power, geographically as well as conceptually. […] On a globe, the Rio Grande Valley can be creatively reimagined as a cultural space along that river, a space between, a space that because of its geographical and conceptual distance from any perceived 'inside' – for instance Dallas or Mexico City, almost equidistant – has the potential to reimagine itself in quite unexpected ways.[28]

Martha I. Chew Sánchez, writing specifically about migrant corridos, notes that

> the corrido is a cultural practice that can be heavily decentralized among participants. The corridos are constantly readjusted, revised, abbreviated, created, and even forgotten, depending on the immediate reality of the people who create, sing, listen to, and perform this kind of music.[29]

The fact that the corrido was so widely invoked as the mode of self-expression about the virus, even when the song was not strictly speaking a corrido, indicates the cultural power of the form for people in the region.

The standardization of the corrido form itself also opens a clear pathway for musicians to repurpose existing examples with new words. John Holmes McDowell has commented that the shared commonalities (and even shared verses and phrases) between corridos requires musicians in fact intentionally to 'anticipate schematically' what they are going to sing: 'Songs within the corrido tradition resemble one another to a considerable extent, and performers must exert themselves in calling to mind the particular nuances of text and tune that set one piece apart from another', he notes, adding that '[c]orrido melodies also present their problems, as they fall into a small set of familiar tune families, and one melody may be differentiated from another by relatively small details.'[30] If they are indeed situating themselves within the tradition, corrido writers and singers must attend to rules of structure, cadence, and rhyme, and to thematic conventions and traditional deliveries.

Singers of corridos del coronavirus, however, often did not seem troubled about these commonalities and the tendency to overlap. Instead, many simply repurposed popular existing melodies with their own lyrics or recorded atop uncredited backing tracks. This, when combined with the shared naming conventions – specifically, dozens of videos appearing with the name 'El corrido del coronavirus' – present challenges to parsing out original compositions from contrafacta. The confusion, though, might have been part of the appeal: Rafeal Acosta Morales writes that by 'appropriating discourses, corridos permit a deterritorialization of the discourse weapons of opposing narratives'.[31]

The body of corridos, by opening these freeing discursive spaces, in some ways served as a public resource. While singers in other musical genres commonly lifted popular melodies to write what might be considered cheap facsimiles, many corrido singers self-seriously made ready use of that which already existed. Corridos, including ones about the coronavirus, share a body of melodies and structures useful for expressing themes of caution, fear, and community. What these compositions may lack in originality, they make up for in emotional and temporal resonance.

Themes in Corridos del Coronavirus

When the corrido is taken out of its regional context, or entirely placed in a new global framing, common racialized meanings become muddled. Corridos about the coronavirus lean quite commonly on pandemic-era xenophobia and race-baiting tropes found throughout música del coronavirus, as well as on complex hierarchies of racial categorization and meaning that historically have swirled among the transnational communities of the borderlands.[32] Their lyrics frequently promote stereotypes about China and Chinese people, the origins of the virus in Wuhan, Chinese eating habits which supposedly spread the virus, and other xenophobic tropes found throughout música del coronavirus. For example, a musical meme collective called 'Memes de Durango' released a mariachi-infused 'Corrido del Coronavirus' (set to the melody of José Alfredo Jiménez's classic 'El Corrido de Caballo Blanco') on 29 February 2020, which blamed the virus on the Chinese consumption of bats, dog soup, and rats.[33] El Plebe de Chihuahua's corrido blames the Chinese for supposedly eating wild animals as the cause of the deaths of 'innocent people';[34] Ab Quintero's 'El Corrido del Coronavirus', as performed by Herencia del Norte de Monclova, describes the spread from China and out of Asia;[35] Los de Alta's compelling estilo sierrieño 'Corrido Al Coronavirus' points the finger at Chinese wet markets and the consumption of exotic animals.[36] Jose Castillo's anti-Chinese 'Corrido del coronavirus', released on 6 April 2020, is delivered in a bombastic vocal style to pre-recorded music, a performance-as-meme using supposedly humorous tropes to frame the pandemic crisis.[37]

Anti-Asian language gradually became less prominent in coronavirus music over time, as the virus's origins took second place to successive waves and variants associated with different parts of the world. Nonetheless, as late as September 2021, long after most songwriters had left the casual racism of the early pandemic music behind, Fugitivo de la Sierra performed 'corrido a la pandemia', written by Luis Loya Mendoza. This corrido fixates on the supposed consumption of rats, dogs, scorpions, spiders, and frogs in China as the source of the virus.[38] YouTube channel 'welldon47' uploaded a similarly themed composition on 26 April 2020; featuring two middle-aged men performing in a garage, it follows a traditional triple-meter structure. The duo play accordion and acoustic guitar, and read off a phone to a total of ninety viewers after two years of having been uploaded. Their lyrics touch themes common across coronavirus music, but they frequently return to the idea of 'filthy' Chinese eating habits as the root cause of the global pandemic.[39]

The borderland experience is both particular and general, as made clear by the resonance of a video uploaded by Los Rancheros de Terán. This multigenerational family band from General Terán, Nuevo León, Mexico, released a very traditional norteño corrido on 6 April 2020. In the video, each member of the group gives a salutation, after which two of them perform a triple-meter corrido on accordion and bajo sexto, singing in the lilting harmonic style of Los Alegres de Terán, one of the groups that has defined borderlands music since the 1940s. The corrido starts with a standard greeting and announcement of intent. The lyrics describe the terrible pandemic afflicting the world and the challenges of not being able to work. The narrator cautions people to stay at home. The comments under this video indicate a listenership across Latin America, including such disparate locales as Chile and Nicaragua, as well as across both sides of the Mexico–US border, where the music resonates powerfully. Most comments are in Spanish, but one is in English. Los Rancheros sent musical greetings of the group to the whole world, as all people are brothers.[40] Their composition resonated across national, linguistic, and generational borders.

Reworkings of the corrido idiom and the repurposing of well-known melodies were also sometimes framed as parodies. The parody corrido has often been regarded as a devolution of the style, but it has a robust tradition that also signals 'the diffusion of the basic version in the culture, since only a knowledge of the latter would allow the speaker's audience to appreciate the humor of the imitations'.[41] Some corridos del coronavirus were definitely created in search of amusement. On 7 April 2020 someone identifying as Peña Bot 2.0 uploaded an amusing parody of the very commonly used melody of José Alfredo Jiménez's 'El corrido del Caballo blanco' as 'El Corrido del Coronavirus'. The corrido is well played on acoustic guitar and sung in a fast-paced, quavering high voice. Like a great many corridos, Peña Bot 2.0's song gives as the origins of the coronavirus a Chinese man who enjoyed eating bat soup. The virus, Peña Bot 2.0 sings, likes the lungs – but it also likes tripe – a reference that is both gastronomic and scatological. The virus hides in beans, he sings, and in milk from Zacaonapan. Peña Bot 2.0 mocks questions about the virus asked hundreds of times, as a simple cartoon sings along. This song, however, gained a scant 135 views in more than two years.[42] In contrast, on 9 April 2020 Jorge Vázquez released his quite serious 'Corrido de Coronavirus y el Río Sonora', also to the melody of 'El corrido del Caballo Blanco' but in this instance played melodiously on a solo guitar. Vázquez's lyrics describe death relentlessly spreading across cities and towns in the state in a corrido expressly geared to local Sonoran themes.[43]

Many corridos del coronavirus are performed as solos or duets by amateur musicians inspired by the moment. This creative inspiration is similar to that which moved so many thousands of musicians in other styles during the pandemic moment, but it is also unique in these many instances. Dozens of corridos del coronavirus were hastily written and performed by musicians reading lyrics off notebooks and phones, as if rushing to get the words, ideas and melodies out as fast as possible with little thought to the sonic character, recording quality or visuals.[44]

On 15 April 2020, a Mexican singer living in Dallas named El Mustang De La Sierra sang his 'El Corrido Del Corona Virus' to camera while sitting in his car next to an inland body of water. It seemed as if he had just pulled over to get the song out to the world as quickly as possible. He explained that living in isolation and not working had given him the time in which to formulate his ideas. His song is an especially evocative consideration of the myriad ways the pandemic was revealing both the frailty and the arrogance of mankind. The tools of science, weapons of war and esteemed political leaders altogether were no match for a microscopic virus. At the same time, society remained locked into the misplaced idea that people, rather than God, are in control. Staring at the viewer, singing acapella in a car, El Mustang's intervention deftly captures the nexus of social media connectivity, individual isolation, and well-thought-out artistry.[45]

This tendency for casual, spontaneous expression on the part of amateur musicians finds its apotheosis in short, unaccompanied performances like one uploaded to the YouTube channel Gb Rjs on 11 April 2020. In this 27-second video, a janitor named Juanito improvises a corrido, to the amusement of the person filming. As he wipes down monitors in a school's computer lab, 'compa Juanito' sings of his uncertainty regarding the emerging situation and comments rather vulgarly that the coronavirus will grab its victims by the genitals. Posters on the wall are emblazoned with empowering words in English – 'create', 'imagine', 'improve' – indicating that the video was likely filmed in a school in the United States. Juanito confirms this in his verses by noting that they are up north, and that they have to keep working in order to afford alcohol. Even in COVID corridos, migration remains a recurrent theme. The room is empty save for the singer and his good-humored videographer, reminding the viewer of the early days of the pandemic, when once-bustling schools turned into desolate spaces. Between verses, Juanito looks toward the camera and smiles, slyly assessing the comedic effect of his verses. At one point he stops, reconsiders, and amends his line to better fit it into the stanza's rhyme scheme, making it clear that the ditty is being improvised.[46] Such videos epitomize the off-the-cuff nature of many coronavirus corridos.

Not all COVID corridos reference the accordion-centric style of the borderlands. Indeed, various regional styles of corrido exist across Mexico, particularly in the states of Morelos and Michoacán. Los Potrillos De Turicato's quick-paced 'Corrido del Coronavirus' is a true corrido in its lyrical structure, but it is performed in a local style from the Tierra Caliente (Hotlands) region of Michoacán.[47] As Alejandro Martinez de la Rosa notes, Michoacán is marked by regional specialization in musical forms, with the municipality of Turicato in particular known for its corridos, which feature local instruments such as violins, upright basses called tololoches, and sometimes even harps.[48] Ironically, this 'Corrido del Coronavirus' strays the farthest in its arrangement and sonic valence from most other examples of pandemic-inspired música norteña labeled 'corridos', even though it is actually one of the few true examples to be so labeled. The composition describes the coronavirus as famous, and alternates between grave and humorous characterizations of the pandemic situation. The flitting *vueltas* inserted between lines of sung verse, which are played on accordion in norteño-style corridos, are here delivered by a violin.

Los Potrillos received some attention from local news outlets for their composition, including a report on the news channel Red-113 Michoacán in which the group is identified as 'widely known across the Tacámbaro region'.[49] In writing about this composition, Agustín Gurza has argued that the piece can be considered a contemporary corrido since 'the truth is, contemporary corrido composers don't feel obliged to stick religiously to the classic structure', and this song retains a theme of 'the heroic and often tragic conflict against adversity'. Gurza mentions that the town of Turicato 'gets its name from a parasite, a soft-bodied tick, that plagues primarily hogs and cattle but can cause relapsing fever in people', which he argues might provide Los Potrillos with 'a grassroots feel for the zoonotic diseases that jump from animals to humans'.[50] The feelings expressed in the corrido clearly resonated. On 31 March 2020, only eleven days after the original, a YouTube channel dedicated to fishing called 'Pesca con José. Y fredy' uploaded its cover version of the same corrido, played on violin, vihuela, guitarra de golpe, and tololoche. In the description, they approvingly declared the composition a 'corrido pesado', or a heavy corrido.[51]

As a form, corridos are deeply associated with the cultures of the Mexico–US borderlands, but there are also important examples of COVID corridos from outside the region. A Guatemalan man singing 'El corrido del corona virus' on 27 April 2020 recorded his video in front of a street sign for San Francisco La Union, affirming the importance of marking his composition in space as well as in historical time. The performer sings and plays with gusto from the song's start through its final, flagrantly out-of-tune chord.[52] Juan Ramón Villalobos Ortega 'El Tallarín' (The Noodle) of Chile played a heartfelt corrido accompanied on Hohner piano accordion and sung in a wavering voice. Mondaca discussed the global effects of the virus and the ways coronavirus could spread, and the fear old people feel throughout the world.[53] Yefri Rojas uploaded his creatively spelled, if not particularly original, 'Korrido de ese Kovid' from Murcia, Spain, which he prefaced by saying 'I am Spanish by birth and citizenship, but I was raised in Mexico and have Mexican blood, yes sir'.[54] For Rojas, like many others, the corrido form situates their performance in Mexico, even as their lyrics discuss a crisis of global proportions.

Miguel A del Conjunto San Antonio recorded his 'CORONA 2020 Corrido de la tragedia mundial del coronavirus' by playing all the instruments in a traditional conjunto norteño and singing two parts.[55] His lilting vocal delivery, complete with mumbled lyrics and a mournful timbre, amplify the feelings of loneliness, despair, and isolation induced by pandemic lockdowns. Lorraine Chavez left a comment in English, stating 'Miguel, you performed every part! Great social distancing with your quarantined recording session! Love the new songs!♥♪♫🎵'. The other two commenters wrote short notes of encouragement in Spanish, highlighting the bilingualism of the borderland style's reach and appeal. Emisora Radio Victoria de Giron released a recursive 'Corrido Sobre el Coronavirus', played on a Cuban tres, on 22 June 2020 – a song which has been listened to only six times in two years. A man wearing a cap performs this number in the entranceway to his home, executing a repetitive yet precise ostinato on the tres which is accompanied by a sharp, well-tuned vocal delivery.[56]

There are a huge number of corridos from the borderlands. A YouTube channel called Moreno De Fuego El Maima, from Nuevo Leon, Mexico, has video of an earnest original corrido set to poorly played solo guitar early in the pandemic moment, uploaded on 28 February 2020. The song, 'El Llamado, llego virus mortal, Corrido contra coronavirus', likens the virus to a serial killer with global designs. Moreno de Fuego, the singer and the channel's owner, draws from the age-old corrido trope of the outlaw murderer to tell the story of the coronavirus.[57]

A month later, Moreno de Fuego uploaded a second part, as a 'corrido progresivo'. This iteration, set to a guitar being strummed vigorously with a credit card as a pick, was dedicated to those who had died of the virus and used a metaphor of the virus as conquistador, yet another storied archetype within the idiom. Moreno de Fuego assertively marketed his music with these corridos, linking through to other pieces and adding multiple pleas to subscribe to his various channels.[58] Humberto Reyes El HR also uploaded a corrido of warning about the death creeping around the world at the end of February 2020. He played his 'alerta mundial corona virus corrido 2020' on an out-of-tune guitar, warning of a nuclear-level threat to the godless nations of the earth and to millions of people, but seeing hope for the nation of the Aztecs.[59]

Sometimes the corrido recordings present a group of friends pushing against the reality of the pandemic. This was the context for an acapella corrido sung by a group standing around drinking beer, for a duet of brothers playing 'El corrido de La Corona Virus', and for a six-person jam session playing 'EL CORRIDO AL CORONAVIRUS', all of which were released in March and April 2020 as the pandemic situation in Mexico developed from a distant concern into an immediate crisis.[60] The two brothers appear to have decided to record the song during a lunch break, as the accordion player has muddy boots and knees on his jeans and a pencil tucked behind his ear. They announce they felt inspired to record it by the 'global situation', and the corrido documents the strains of the moment. They play with energy, their sloppy timing and tuning aside.

Some corrido writers took the opportunity to argue that the virus treats everyone equally, whether rich or poor, and salvation can be found only in following the Christian way. In his 'Corrido cristiano al corona virus', Rudy Ramirez cites Matthew 24:7, a biblical verse that professes the arrival of, among other catastrophes, plagues as a sign of Christ's imminent return. Between verses, Ramirez speaks directly to his listeners and encourages those who have not already to come to Christ and find salvation before it is too late.

The song, which was released on 17 March 2020, is overlaid with pictures of both Chinese and Mexican people wearing masks in public spaces, graphics depicting the return of Christ, and a map of the United States that lists the 36 US states where COVID had been reported at the time. This map situates the composition in time, showing how in March 2020 the virus was still seen as a force whose spread could be controlled.[61]

Jacobo Ortiz makes note of these temporal changes to our collective understanding of the virus in his 'CORONAVIRUS CORRIDO/CANCION', noting how the coronavirus went from being the focus of jokes to a mortal threat that commands solemn fear. Ortiz gives the virus credit for not being racist or discriminatory, commenting that it will infect anybody who it encounters regardless of who they are. He makes note of the social chaos of the early pandemic moment and introduces his audience to Jesus Christ, who he believes is the only person who can put an end to the suffering.[62] Jacobo Ortiz overlays his singing with a single still frame of a computer-generated coronavirus model superimposed with the English-language phrase 'THE CORONAVIRUS IS MAN MADE'.[63]

This underlines yet another tendency within COVID corridos: competing narratives over the nature of the coronavirus. The relationship between storytelling and ideology in the style dates back to at least the Mexican Revolution, when, as noted by Catherine Héau de Giménez, corridos 'played a fundamental role as ideological vector, archive of collective memory and sign of regional identity'.[64] COVID corridos that question power, offer alternative views of justice, and view acts of violence or chaos as arbiters of the end times are not new phenomena; indeed, they have been a part of the tradition since the birth of the Mexican Republic.[65] One of the best known styles of corridos – narrative songs about drug smuggling and banditry called narcocorridos – focuses on related transgressive and sometimes shocking tales about transnational crime, centered on antihero figures, reversals of notions of justice, and the ever-present realities of violence and death.[66]

Corridos del COVID similarly challenge authority by directly interrogating the origins of the virus and imagining the role of governments in deliberately propagating the disease. Pandemic-era conspiracy theories abound in the music, as was also seen in societies around the globe as the crisis grew, spreading and mutating like the virus itself. Some claim that the virus was deliberately created as a bioweapon, while others conversely argue that the pandemic is a hoax concocted by elites to justify a mass rollback of individual liberties. These claims have proven to be particularly resonant among Latin Americans and also within Latino communities in the United States. In a study comparing beliefs about and attitudes toward COVID-19 in five countries, scientists from the University of Cambridge found that 33% of Mexican respondents believed that the coronavirus had been deliberately engineered in a Chinese laboratory. Mexican respondents were also more likely than those from the United States, United Kingdom, and Ireland to believe that the pandemic was 'part of a plot to enforce global vaccination' (33%) and to entertain the idea that vaccines contain undisclosed biotechnological elements, such as microchips or RFID trackers (16%).[67]

In a May 2021 op-ed in the *Los Angeles Times*, Jean Guerrero described how COVID conspiracy theories prey on Latinos in the United States. She charts the causes of this susceptibility and describes various historical examples in which health policy has been employed as a racist biopolitical tool to the detriment of Latino Americans: the mass-sterilization of Puerto Rican women, and various instances of medical experimentation in Southern California. Nonetheless, she notes that '[while] our hard-earned skepticism can be an asset [...] in the pandemic [...] it has contributed to high infection and death rates in the Latino community.'[68] Jose A. Del Real meanwhile wrote in the *Washington Post* about a conspiracy theory found specifically among migrant communities: the belief that vaccines being administered to Latino patients are specifically formulated to reduce their fertility. His reporting on attitudes towards vaccination among Mexican migrant workers in Northern California notes how social media platforms were slow to crack down on viral Spanish-language videos that peddled such claims. Even when platforms caught up, 'the false claims...[continued to spread] by word of mouth through [...] agricultural fields, wineries and restaurant kitchens, where Spanish-language fact checks could not counter them.'[69]

In the United States, general discourses regarding the relationship between migrants and COVID-19 have also relied on misinformation and racist narratives. Politicians including racist ex-president Donald Trump have scapegoated and implicated migrants as drivers of the pandemic;[70] but at the same time, conspiracy theories about the virus have proved attractive and resonant among migrant communities, undermining public health efforts. Migrants often live in precarious circumstances, and constant uncertainty has been shown to be a contributing factor to misinformation susceptibility.[71] As described by Remi Jedwab, Amjad M. Khan, Jason Russ, and Esha D. Zaveri, 'during an epidemic, bonding social capital could help individuals cope with negative life satisfaction effects.' However, 'at the same time, [...] if there is mistrust between communities, bonding social capital might contribute to reinforcing intergroup conflict. If governments fail in their policy response to the epidemic, this may negatively impact trust and communities may turn inward.'[72] This tension is not trivial: conspiracy theories and misinformation campaigns regarding COVID-19, many of which have their origins in the United States, have been credited as motivating factors in a wave of threats directed toward healthcare workers in Latin America in 2020.[73]

Many COVID corridos expound upon these transnational pandemic-era conspiracy theories. El Juglar de Tampico uploaded a video of himself on the street in Altamira, Tamaulipas, playing a nylon strung guitar hard enough to force it out of tune. The bearded performer seems unfazed by the occasional passing car as he belts out his distinctive take on the pandemic's trajectory.

Released on 26 March 2020, El Juglar tells a story of how the coronavirus was deliberately released into the world as a means of destabilizing prices in the economy for the benefit of a wealthy few. He surmises that the Chinese created, released, and promptly controlled the virus in their own country, and asserts incorrectly that Italy was more affected than any Asian country. Verses describe the virus as a smokescreen that has given governments an excuse to close borders and regulate people's behavior. In spite of this bizarre conspiratorial narrative, El Juglar nonetheless encourages people to stay home if they are ill, noting that while the virus is an invention, it is nonetheless still dangerous.[74]

Wilfredo Evora posted an energetic corrido norteño entitled 'Corrido A los Creadores del Corona virus' ('Corrido to the Creators of the Coronavirus') on 11 April 2020. Evora belts out his opinions directly to the camera while accompanied by a bajo sexto and accordion played outside the frame. He offers up a spoken introduction with vulgar exhortations in both Spanish and English, heralding 'a new corrido, folks, to this guy who invented the fucking virus' ('*un nuevo corrido, parientes, a esto vato que creó el pinche virus*') and muttering in English 'son of a bitches' [sic] before launching into song. The corrido is a strident denunciation of the supposed conspirators behind the disease, taking particular aim at the government. Evora makes his position clear in the first line, noting that if he were president, he would bill China for the damage caused by COVID-19. He mentions Chinese president Xi Jinping by name, making it clear several times that his intention is not to defame the Chinese people as a whole. It is worth observing that this conspiracy video did not garner many views or have a large impact: after two years, Evora had had only 14 views of his song on his YouTube channel, which had two subscribers.[75]

A singer named El Señor de Los Corridos posted a 'corrido de el corona virus' on 16 March 2020, inspired, he noted, by the declaration of a global pandemic. His corrido encourages people to be cautious, although he notes that the virus, at the time of the recording, is not that big of a deal where he lives. He sings his corrido seated at a table, unaccompanied and with a forceful voice. It is a very different corrido from typical examples, he explains at the beginning, because this is a new coronavirus pandemic. He suggests that the virus may have been invented in the United States as a bioweapon against China, and while there is no cure, in Mexico it has been met with corridos. His song, he says with a grin, is not propaganda like that heard commonly on radio and television. A month later, El Señor de Los Corridos posted a video of himself clearing rocks away from his fields, titled 'Quédate en tu casa'. The only sound is wind until he talks about what he is doing, which he describes as building for the future. He states that he is not afraid of quarantine, asserting matter of factly that 'we are happy to stay home, because at home there is much to do' ('*estamos contentos quedandonos en casa, porque aqui en la casa hay mucho que hacer*').[76]

Many corridos implicate governments and vested interests in the invention of the pandemic. Julio Cesar Castro's short video is entitled 'Canción al Coronavirus', but in the description he identifies it as a 'corrido corona'. The mustached performer alternates between singing short melodic lines and echoing them on a harmonica. In his lyrics, Castro calls the virus a farce perpetrated by the government and urges his fellow Mexicans to rise up against the hoax. One commenter, Vicry Isabel Garcia Mercado, agrees, saying, 'bravo uncle Carlos, the virus doesn't exist' ('*bravo tio Bravo tío Carlos el virus no existe*'). Evelio Segura Carbajal released his 'corrido del coronavirus' on 6 January 2021 to a tiny audience of 54 views after 18 months. His traditional-style corrido, including introduction and farewell accompanied by simple guitar strumming in triple meter, sings of the virus coming from China. The corrido claims the coronavirus was invented as a form of population control. However, Carbajal also speculatively implicates the consumption of unclean bats and rats in its spread. He portrays the Mexican government as criminally negligent, since there is no cure in sight and elderly people are dying left and right.[77] Before starting to sing, Jim Francis Meza sends out greetings to '*toda mi gente de mi raza*' in Durango and Sinaloa, Mexico, and also to Guatemala, Panama, Italy, and Spain. He then launches into an acapella screed where he calls out traitorous journalists and refers to the coronavirus as a maniac plan, and with irony encourages people to remain locked in the cages in which they have been trapped.[78] In another acapella performance, Flaco Sanleo sings a traditional corrido with a lilting cadence, bemoaning having to stay inside his house when what he really wants to do is go out and drink with his friends. His powerful voice is presented with a shaky image of Cerro de Cebadilla, Veracruz. In a later stanza, he sings about how the Chinese invented the virus to kill off old people. Nonetheless, he still challenges those who claim the virus is a total hoax, encouraging them to listen to the experts and take note of the mounting death toll in Mexico. While Sanleo believes the virus was a bioweapon of sorts, he recognizes its danger as such and says that, regardless of its origins, it must be dealt with carefully.[79]

Alternatively, many authors of COVID corridos challenge the conspiracy theories and remind their listeners of the gravity of the situation. In a video uploaded on 28 May 2020, David Garcia Quijas charts his changing attitudes towards the pandemic, from aloof skepticism to deep personal concern. He performs solo outside a suburban home, dressed in a white-and-red striped shirt and an Adidas baseball cap.[80] This song is written in the corrido tumbado style, an emergent, hip hop flow-influenced subgenre with roots in the sierreño genre of northwestern Mexico. While the corrido tumbado found explosive global success in 2023 with the emergence of artists such as Peso Pluma, Eslabón Armado, Junio H, and Natanael Cano on US pop charts, during the pandemic moment the style still had regional connotations. In the largely acoustic style, the 12-string requinto guitar takes the place of the accordion.[81] Garcia Quijas uses the rapid-fire vocal delivery of the style as he plays a characteristic accompaniment on his requinto. He sings about how he, like many others, had been doubtful of the virus's danger at the outset of the pandemic. However, when people around him started falling gravely ill, his mindset changed. García Quijas notes how many people in his community disregarded the virus and claimed it was a hoax promoted by the government until they or someone close to them got sick, at which point they started to take the situation seriously. The second verse critiques the tendency of people to end up in conflict during times of crisis, and encourages the audience to leave their differences behind in order to mount resistance to the common pandemic threat.[82]

Some corridos, especially from later in the pandemic moment, encourage vaccination. Reyes García Covarrubias wrote an original corrido uploaded in November 2021; in the video, he uses a norteño accordion, playing only the right-hand melody notes in borderlands style. He performs the song at home in a room with a low ceiling, in front of a wall featuring a picture of Elvis Presley alongside family photographs. Covarrubias sings that over a year after the onset of the pandemic, it continues to be an uncontrollable threat. He then notes the availability of vaccines for all people, and dedicates the remaining lines to encouraging his listeners to get immunized.[83] In July 2021, Orlando Mata de Palo uploaded a similar video of an original corrido accompanied by piano accordion and played inside a dimly lit house. In his corrido, he reminds his listeners to get whatever vaccine they can, although he concedes that if you live in the United States, you may want to try to get the Pfizer one as, in his words, it is equivalent to a luxury Porsche.[84]

A YouTube user named Javiér Gomez, whose channel content is largely dedicated to farmworkers' rights and Mexican regional music, uploaded two corridos encouraging Mexican migrants to get vaccinated. The first, uploaded on 3 June 2021, showcases an original corrido written and performed by Rosa Ramos called 'El Corrido de la Vacuna'. Ramos played the corrido at the United Farm Workers Union office in Ventura, California, supported by a Ventura County Community Foundation grant as an accompaniment to a vaccination drive. The video shows a masked Ramos performing the corrido in front of a line of farmworkers waiting to be vaccinated. The corrido promises people that the vaccine will afford them new liberty and protect not only themselves, but also their wider community. Ramos offers words of encouragement for the needle-averse, assuring them that immunization is not scary and that it just involves a small pinch.[85]

The second corrido, uploaded 25 July 2021, features a studio recording of a banda arrangement with a photo slideshow in the video frame. The lyrics for 'Banda Corrido sobre La Vacuna' and the slideshow images reinforce each other, with stanzas about the importance of vaccination paired with slides showing groups of people filling the roles of familiar Mexican cultural archetypes – mariachi musicians, lucha libre wrestlers, street mimes in animal outfits, and food cart operators – holding signs with phrases such as 'I'm vaccinated: are you?' and 'Vacúnate!'.[86]

One of the better performed corridos about the virus appears in a video of an acapella singer named Larry Donas from Mexicali, who accompanies himself with a very realistic-sounding recreation of a trumpet using only his mouth. This 'mouth trumpet' technique has been used by other corrido singers as well.[87] Following a standard corrido structure punctuated with virtuosic-sounding 'trumpet' breaks, Donas accounts for the experience of the pandemic and the fear it has produced in all, before ending amusingly in a sneezing fit. The video had gained more than five thousand views by mid-2022. Donas reposted a revised corrido about the health effects of the pandemic in January 2022, stressing the song's truth value and referring to YouTube videos that provide information about the virus, encouraging his listeners to educate themselves. In keeping with the informal set and setting of the video, his last verse is interrupted by a bleep from the phone on which it was being recorded.[88]

A great many singers posted acapella corridos, some explicitly expressing greetings to people around the world and delivering personalized warnings and suggestions for surviving the pandemic. However, despite the number of these uploads, they were often viewed by only tiny audiences.[89] Angel Mendez's sprightly 'Corrido De Coronavirus', from 14 March 2020, was sung to guitar accompaniment and covered the essentials of needing to stay safe from the pandemic while making sure one has enough to drink. Ten days later, Jose Robles El Guacho barked out his own corrido, about the challenges of the early pandemic shutdowns and finding store shelves bare. Performed in a rushed tone, El Gaucho sounds as if he is trying to get his words out as fast as possible.[90] Vicente Castorena's norteño 'Corrido del Coronavirus' was uploaded on 24 May 2020. It hews very closely to the description of the pathways of the virus in a narrative typical to corridos, although its musical structure is more reminiscent of a cumbia.[91] While many sang with a comically tragic tone to express dismay over shortages of beer and toilet paper, some used the corrido format to raise serious concerns over the food security implications of the pandemic. Diego Armando Casas, of Nayarit, uploaded his original corrido on 26 April 2020, singing it acapella while a radio played a song faintly in the background. He warned of the troubles of the pandemic spreading around the world and the difficulties for working people who live day to day but who would not even have tortillas if they were forced to stay home during the pandemic.[92]

Many of the corridos del coronavirus were performed to stock or karaoke backing tracks uploaded by individuals moved to express their feelings about the pandemic by singing original lyrics over pre-recorded music. Some simply covered a pre-existing pandemic-era song. The most popular styles were mariachi, norteño, and banda, although there are many sierreño tracks as well.[93] Fredy Aguilar y Los 2 de Guamuchil's sierrieño-style 'La cuarentena del coronavirus corrido' ('The coronavirus quarantine corrido') released on 20 March 2020, features a highly produced musical accompaniment, perhaps borrowed from another artist as a backing track, with the two vocal lines haplessly overlaid on top.[94] Taking a somewhat different approach, Los Rancheros de Valle Hermoso de Casablanca released a lively polka entitled 'El corrido del corona virus' on piano accordion and acoustic guitar. It is undergirded by a backing track of bass, drum kit, and bajo sexto. The two men are dressed informally, wearing windbreakers and sombreros, as they play and sing along to the backing track.[95]

Some of these corridos sung to pre-recorded backing tracks were performed as enactments of corridos, exaggerating the style of delivery in nasal tones, interjecting with caricaturish shouts, or otherwise making a mockery of the pandemic experience as a whole.[96] On 17 March 2020, '21 Leon', a channel with a scant four subscribers, uploaded a recording entitled 'corrido del coronavirus' set to videos of customized pick-up trucks with graphics saying 'Leon'. His corrido, perhaps more accurately characterized as a fast ballad in triple meter, laments the virus, makes beer puns, and encourages people to drink as a way to pass the time.[97] The impulse of going to get a drink being thwarted by the pandemic was very common across coronavirus music in many styles, but was especially central in corridos.

Corridos appeared in a consistent stream during the pandemic moment. On 30 March 2020, Sebatitos sang a traditionally structured corrido to a pre-recorded norteño track which charted the progress of the deadly virus around the world.[98] A channel called 'chichimor' uploaded a corrido set to a Ramon Ayala melody, while a week later, on 6 April, Anthony Hernandez uploaded a serious cover of Grupo Laberinto's 'El Corrido Del Coronavirus'.[99] The next day, a man identifying only as José or 'Charro Montero' released 'EL CORRIDO DEL CORONAVIRUS', which he sang to a stock banda karaoke track while dressed in an elaborately embroidered charro outfit and standing in what appears to be the foyer of a house. A child can be heard vocalizing during most of the track, underscoring that the song seems to have been recorded in a fleeting moment of free time while staying at home.[100] In the recording of Antonio Colores's solo bajo quinto corrido, the shouts of children and the murmur of a television are also audible. It was performed live in a home studio, and serves up a timely commentary on the early pandemic experience, including concerns over running out of essentials such as food and other products.[101] Jacobo Gutierrez sang Francisco Javier Montoya's composition 'Un corrido Norteño.. "Pandemia 2020".. El Corona Virus 2020' to a MIDI-generated backing track of electronic instrument patches. While his mix is far from the norms of glossy professionalism, Gutierrez sings with passion and strongly developed vocal phrasing clearly influenced by groups such as Los Tigres del Norte.

On 5 January 2021, El Padrino Records released a video of three men standing outside and drinking cans of Tecate beer as the oldest among them sings yet another corrido about the coronavirus. The title identifies the older man as 'Compa Pirata'. He rattles off verses about bat soup, the frustrations of stay-at-home orders, and the anxieties of living as a man of years during a pandemic where the elderly are the most at risk. Inevitably, the Chinese and Americans are at the butt of nearly all his jokes. The two younger men who are standing by smile with admiration, occasionally taking out their cell phones to take pictures, record, and stream.[102]

José N. Gallegos performed two corridos in the spring of 2020. One he sang acapella into his cellphone while driving a truck on 29 March, tracking the spread of the virus around the world and warning people of the dangers of the pandemic and the need to stay home.[103] The other corrido he read off a notebook into a shaky cellphone (possibly held by a child) soon after on 8 April to a distorted stock norteño track. While seated on a couch, the frame swinging wildly around, Gallegos sings passionately of the problems of the pandemic on both sides of the border. In other videos, recorded years earlier and posted on his channel, he shows himself to be a competent guitar player, so the choice to sing to a recording or acapella is notable.[104] These corridos appear on his Tutankamon YouTube channel, which has been up since February 2016 and has two subscribers. Corrido recordings like these are deeply personal.

Many of these highly informal, amateur performances employ flagrantly out-of-tune guitars. These videos usually have had few views, such as 'El corrido del corona virus parte 2', which was recorded in the back seat of a moving car and had gained a mere 12 views after more than two years on YouTube.[105] Marecelino Patiño, seemingly not interested in increasing his subscribers from a single one, uploaded his 'El corrido de Coronavirus' on 19 May 2020, in which he played in 3/4 on an out-of-tune guitar while singing in a different key.[106]

Conversely, lots of COVID corridos were recorded with high production values and skill, highlighting the commercial resonance of the style and musicians' invocation of the pandemic as a marketing device. Major commercial bands recorded corridos similar to that of Los KDTs de Lineras, such as Grupo Laberinto's 'El Corrido Del Coronavirus', recorded with El Plebe de Chihuahua' Ober Lopez's 'CoronaVirus, Corrido', from Guatamala; and Los Hijos del Caminante's religiously intoned 'Corrido del coronavirus'.[107] A reworking of Los Tigres del Norte's 'Con la soga al cuello' into a pandemic-era narrative song and labeled as a corrido was uploaded to YouTube in November 2020 and quickly gained 1.2 million views, although it was not an official release of the group.[108] Interestingly, although known and enormously popular for their topical songs about the experiences of migrant people across the Mexican diaspora, and for other socio-political themes, Los Tigres did not record their own corrido del coronavirus.[109]

Some corridos were produced by musicians who record topical songs responding to news, like Arnulfo 'El Rebelde' González's traditional 'El

Corrido del Coronavirus', Omar Hurtado's 'El Pulpo de Los Teclados', Juan Benito Pérez's 'El Corrido Del Coronavirus', and El Tiron del Norte's 'Corrido Del Coronavirus'. These corridos are basic factual descriptions of the situation and the spread of the virus around the world, traditionally presented in 3/4 norteño style and intended to capture the listener's ears with their topicality.[110] Juan Benito Perez recorded his newsy and informative Christian-themed 'El Corrido Del Coronavirus' on 14 March 2020; similarly, Humberto Rodriguez recorded a corrido to blame China and the United States for the spread of the virus, but most of all as a proselytizing message that this is the moment for the Church and the impending arrival of salvation. The video includes a dramatic opening sequence akin to an action film, featuring cinematic music, title credits, and B-roll from the recording session.[111] From Atlanta, Georgia, Grupo Kre-A-ctivo released 'COVID 19 CORRIDO' on 3 April 2020, more of a cancion in 3/4 time than a corrido, set to fast accordion licks and a chorus calling for the virus to take its leave. The group claimed it was posting the song because of the pandemic: 'That is why we decided to do a little bit on our end regarding the recommended course of action so that this bacteria [sic] ends and we can continue with our life normally.'[112]

Many COVID corridos opt for unadulterated earnestness in place of humor. An artist named Victor El Elegido De Oaxaca (Victor The Chosen One Of Oaxaca) released 'El Corrido Del COVID 19 💉' on 21 July 2020, a traditional corrido delivered in an elaborated sierrieño style supported by tuba. After a traditional introductory passage noting the time and place, he sang about the great suffering around the world and the ways that the Bible had foretold the tragedies occurring. Money cannot save anyone, he sang; the only way is by taking care of oneself and each other. El Elegido (the chosen one) was clearly committed to his message of safety and community support, and responded to the few comments posted on his video, which had been viewed 5700 times after a year.[113]

Some professional groups writing corridos were working norteño acts playing in restaurants and plazas, with videos uploaded by people who happened to catch the performance on the street.[114] These videos tend to date to early in the pandemic, before enforced shutdown had reached all locales. They reveal a creative and spontaneous response to the pandemic's onset, with lyrics commenting on the crisis but also directly responding in time and in verse to issues of fear and the situation in the street. For example, Francisco Javier Martinez Baños, playing at Mercado Benito Juarez in Escondido, Mexico, sings a cumbia-inflected composition labeled a COVID corrido. While he talks about the broader pandemic situation, he also sings directly to the butcher in front of him, applauding his commitment to working in spite of the crisis, commending the fact that he does not sell 'zombie meat', and making other improvised topical statements about passersby in the market.[115] 'El corrido del covid 19 coronavirus' was played by three restaurant musicians on tololoche, piano accordion, and bajo sexto, and utilized a common melody in 3/4 time and improvised lyrics, to the great amusement of the dining audience.

Interestingly, there were exceedingly few corridos del coronavirus performed by women, which is an absence deserving of further inquiry.[116] In May 2020, a youth group in Los Angeles called Get Lit sponsored Xochitl Morales's 'Covid Corrido' with a message of affirmation, sung and played on guitar. The message of the video, which includes subtitles in English, is simple and straightforward, and the comments are supportive.[117] Andrea Vega released the bizarre 'corrido Coronavirus' a year into the pandemic on 26 May 2021, in which she describes how fast both panic and memes spread at the start of the crisis. It is performed out-of-time to a pre-recorded backing track, with some parts featuring her speaking in a near whisper rather than singing. The on-screen accompaniment features text that sometimes corresponds to what is being sung, while other times appearing to be unrelated. The video had had only six views over a year after its upload, at least three of which can be attributed to the authors of this book.[118] A much more expertly crafted corrido came from a writer named Cristina Escobedo. It was sung by the duo Monse y Fatima (Monse Gaytan and Fatima Reyes), from Zacatecas, and was also uploaded more than a year into the pandemic, on 28 June 2021. The two young women harmonize a series of verses that hew closely to the structure, meter, and rhyming conventions of a traditional triple-meter corrido. After introducing the year, Monse y Fatima sing of the arrival of the virus and its danger to all humanity. The two women are seen performing outside in a covered stage. Some of the onlookers wear face coverings, while others are unmasked, reflecting the varied approaches to individual COVID protection that had emerged by the summer of 2021.[119]

Everything is a Meme

It should be clear that corridos del coronavirus encompass an enormous and notably diverse body of music in terms of genre, instrumentation, approach, and affect. The many songs discussed here are only a small sampling of the COVID-era compositions that collectively were grouped under the label of 'corrido'. Divergence from the established corrido structure, occasional sloppy performances, and detuned guitars notwithstanding, the number and diverse range of corridos written about the coronavirus indicates that amateur and professional performers alike felt compelled by the sudden disruptive and terrifying emergence of a global pandemic to adopt this specific, culturally resonant narrative form to document the experience. Beyond the musical form, the COVID corrido was an idea, an approach to expression, and a mechanism for amateur creativity in light of a crisis with innumerable narratives. The shame-free approaches to amateur performance, in particular, and the release of such music on a globally accessible platform, reifies the primacy of self-expression over staged performance and the attraction and utilities of the corrido during the pandemic moment.

Corrido performance captured the pandemic moment as a self-replicating experience of isolation, boredom, and danger punctuated by fear, humor, and creativity. Corridos were a shared cultural space on which the emotions, thoughts, fears, and desires could be readily inscribed in ways useful across transnational space. Or, as YouTube user Giovanny Baltazar commented with great clarity about Los KDTs' 'El corrido del CORONAVIRUS': 'we are Mexicans, and everything is a meme...' (*'somos mexicanos, y todo es memes...'*).[120]

Notes

1. 'CORRIDO COVID 19 LOS CADETES DE LINARES', https://www.youtube.com/watch?v=BQpIBPAhRRc (accessed 1 July 2022). On the development of norteño music history and style in the borderlands context see Cathy Ragland, *Música Norteña: Mexican Americans Creating a Nation Between Nations* (Philadelphia: Temple University Press, 2009); Luis Díaz-Santana Garza, *Historia de la música norteña mexicana: desde los grupos precursores al auge del narcocorrido* (México: Plaza y Valdés S.L., 2015); Díaz-Santana Garza, *Between Norteño and Tejano Conjunto: Music, Tradition, and Culture at the U.S.-Mexico Border* (Lanham, MD: Lexington Books, 2021).
2. It is unclear exactly how many different groups exist, since some of the band names evolve each jaripeo (rodeo) season, but it is close to a dozen iterations. The source of all the names are jaripeo posters from across the United States and Mexico from throughout the 2000s, in author Margolies' possession.
3. 'CORRIDO COVID 19 LOS CADETES DE LINARES', https://www.youtube.com/watch?v=BQpIBPAhRRc (accessed 1 July 2022).
4. Daniel F. Chamberlain, 'The Mexican *Corrido* and Identity in Regional, National, and International Contexts', *Neohelicon* 30.1 (2003): 77–87.
5. 'CORRIDO COVID 19 LOS CADETES DE LINARES', https://www.youtube.com/watch?v=BQpIBPAhRRc (accessed 1 July 2022).'
6. 'CORRIDO COVID 19 LOS CADETES DE LINARES'.
7. Rose V. Sánchez García, 'Los principles géneros liricos en la música tradicional de México', in Aurelio Tello, ed., *La música en México panorama del siglo XX* (México: FCE-CONACULTA, 2010), 106–79.
8. John D. Robb, *Cancionero: Songs of Laughter and Faith in New Mexico* (Albuquerque: University of New Mexico Press, 2015), p. 10.
9. César Burgos Dávila and Helena Simonett, 'Soy gallo de Sinaloa jugado en varios palenques: Production and Consumption of Narco-Music in a Transnational World', in Jesús A. Ramos-Kittrell, ed., *Decentering the Nation: Music, Mexicanidad, and Globalization* (Lanham, MD: Lexington Books, 2020), 99–125, p. 107.
10. Américo Paredes, *'With His Pistol in His Hand': A Border Ballad and Its Hero* (Austin: University of Texas Press, 1958).
11. 'Corrido del COVID 19', https://www.youtube.com/watch?v=9J9wMzpp9Fw (accessed 1 July 2022). The titles of virtually all these corridos are very similar, with minor differences in spelling, capitalization, and emphasis. The notes consciously reflect these tiny differences and retain the exact usage of each case.

12. 'CORRIDO COVID 19 LOS CADETES DE LINARES', https://www.youtube.com/watch?v=BQpIBPAhRRc (accessed 1 July 2022).
13. 'El corrido de coronavirus', https://www.youtube.com/watch?v=LvswcZh6KrE (accessed 1 July 2022).
14. Jose P. Villalobos and Juan Carlos Ramirez-Pimienta, '*Corridos* and *La Pura Verdad*: Myths and Realities of the Mexican Ballad', *South Central Review* 21.3 (2004): 129–49.
15. 'El corrido del CORONAVIRUS| Los Cadetes De Linares', https://www.youtube.com/watch?v=DAQI6oeexco (accessed 1 July 2022).
16. 'No Hay Novedad Cadetes de Linares', https://www.youtube.com/watch?v=sgkVBLitoV0 (accessed 1 July 2022).
17. 'El corrido del CORONAVIRUS| Los Cadetes De Linares', https://www.youtube.com/watch?v=DAQI6oeexco (accessed 1 July 2022).
18. Ric Alviso, 'What is a Corrido? Musical Analysis and Narrative Function', *Studies in Latin American Popular Culture* 29.1 (2011): 58–79, p. 59.
19. 'FUERZA REGIDA – PANDEMIA', https://www.youtube.com/watch?v=mIGxJxbSk6s (accessed 1 July 2022).
20. Americo Paredes, 'The Ancestry of Mexico's *Corridos*: A Matter of Definitions', *Journal of American Folklore* 76. 301 (1963): 231–5; Helena Simonett, *Banda: Mexican Musical Life Across Borders* (Middleton, CT: Wesleyan University Press, 2001), p. 223; Aurelio Gonzalez, 'El corrido: expresión popular y tradicional de la balada hispánica', *Olivar (La Plata)* 12.15 (2011): 11–36.
21. Alviso, 'What is a Corrido?', pp. 60, 62.
22. Américo Paredes and María Herrera-Sobek, 'The *Corrido*: An Invited Lecture at the "Music in Culture" Public Lecture Series', *Journal of American Folklore* 125.495 (2012): 23–44, p. 25.
23. Alexander M. Cannon, 'From Nameless to Nomenclature: Creating Music Genre in Southern Vietnam', *Asian Music* 47.2 (2016): 138–71, p. 160.
24. Simonett, *Banda*, p. 223.
25. Melody Schwantes, Tony Wigram, Cathy McKinney, Allison Lipscomb, and Cathy Richards, 'The Mexican *Corrido* and its Use in a Music Therapy Bereavement Group', *Australian Journal of Music Therapy* 22 (2011): 2–23.
26. Paredes, *'With His Pistol in His Hand'*.
27. Daniel J. Delgado and Joe R. Feagin, 'Latinos in the United States: Understanding the Historical and Systemic Foundations of Racial Oppression', in Martin Guevera Urbina and Sofía Espinoza Álvarez, eds, *Ethnicity and Criminal Justice in the Era of Mass Incarceration: A Critical Reader on the Latino Experience* (Springfield, IL: Charles C. Thomas, 2017), 61–81, p. 73.
28. Mark Noe, 'The *Corrido*: A Border Rhetoric', *College English* 71.6 (2009): 596–605, p. 597.
29. Martha I. Chew Sánchez, *Corridos in Migrant Memory* (Albuquerque: University of New Mexico Press, 2006), pp. 42–6, esp. 43.
30. John H. McDowell, 'Coaxing the Corrido: Centering Song in Performance', *Journal of American Folklore* 123.488 (2010): 127–49, p. 131.
31. Rafael Acosta Morales, *Drug Lords, Cowboys, and Desperadoes: Violent Myths of the U.S.-Mexico Frontier* (Notre Dame, IN: University of Notre Dame Press, 2021).
32. There is a large literature, including Katherine Benton-Cohen, *Borderline Americans: Racial Division and Labor War in the Arizona Borderlands* (Cambridge, MA, Harvard University Press, 2009); Grace Delgado, *Making the Chinese Mexican: Global Migration, Localism, and Exclusion in the U.S.-Mexico Borderlands* (Stanford, CA: Stanford University Press, 2013); Jason O. Chang, *Chino: Anti-Chinese Racism in Mexico, 1880–1940* (Urbana: University of Illinois Press, 2017).
33. It was uploaded on 19 March 2020, but the descriptions say it was written in February, so the group clearly wanted it noted, possibly to indicate their speedy response to the

moment: 'Corrido del Coronavirus', https://www.youtube.com/watch?v=d_reInePS0s (accessed 1 July 2022).
34. 'El Corrido Del Coronavirus 🐎 El Plebe De Chihuahua 🕛 Laberinto 🐎💨', https://www.youtube.com/watch?v=GsUDNO7zPz4 (accessed 1 July 2022).
35. 'El Corrido del Coronavirus', https://www.youtube.com/watch?v=RxbBxV7s4yc (accessed 1 July 2022).
36. 'Corrido Al Coronavirus', https://www.youtube.com/watch?v=Lg-E7MzidDE (accessed 1 July 2022).
37. 'Corrido del coronavirus', https://www.youtube.com/watch?v=Zz727_2P87s (accessed 1 July 2022).
38. 'corrido a la pandemia. Fugitivo de la Sierra', https://www.youtube.com/watch?v=Rz796rlkA0E (accessed 1 July 2022).
39. 'Corrido del coronavirus', https://www.youtube.com/watch?v=noJvBYGDLaQ (accessed 1 July 2022).
40. 'Corrido del corona virus con Los Rancheros de Terán', https://www.youtube.com/watch?v=TSu2w12262M (accessed 1 July 2022).
41. Dan W. Dickey, *The Kennedy Corridos: A Study of the Ballads of a Mexican American Hero* (Austin: University of Texas at Austin, 1978), p. 20; Alessandra Bonamore Graves and Henry Cohen, 'Corridos from Costa Rica', in Misheal M. Caspi, ed., *Oral Tradition and Hispanic Literature: Essays in Honor of Samuel G. Armistead* (New York: Garland Publishing, 1995), 291–322, p.299.
42. 'El Corrido del Coronavirus. Peña Bot 2.0 Pentium IV', https://www.youtube.com/watch?v=7wt9sPLJwLo (accessed 1 July 2022).
43. 'Corrido de Coronavirus y el Río Sonora', https://www.youtube.com/watch?v=Dtblvm5TIQs (accessed 1 July 2022).
44. Examples include 'Corrido AL CORONAVIRUS – Ramón Cervantes', https://www.youtube.com/watch?v=e1TaGNbYnGw (accessed 1 July 2022); 'Coronavirus corrido El Necio de Zacatecas', https://www.youtube.com/watch?v=vTrX5-KbnUk (accessed 1 July 2022); 'El Corrido Del Corona Virus (Cuarentena)', https://www.youtube.com/watch?v=VIIdvEMTgQA (accessed 1 July 2022); '#coronavirus #covid19 el corrido del coronavirus 2020', https://www.youtube.com/watch?v=GtGSrzdCo3I (accessed 1 July 2022).
45. 'El Corrido Del Corona Virus – El Mustang De La Sierra', https://www.youtube.com/watch?v=sy2OOZXWTcs (accessed 1 July 2022).
46. 'El corrido de el corona virus !!. Compa Juanito!', https://www.youtube.com/watch?v=PgEkH4CJa94 (accessed 1 July 2022).
47. 'Corrido Del Coronavirus – Los Potrillos De Turicato', https://www.youtube.com/watch?v=49lIaQzKtH0 (accessed 1 July 2022).
48. Alejandro Martínez de la Rosa, 'Investigación de campo para la regionalización del patrimonio cultural inmaterial', *Diálogos de Campo* 2.4 (2017): 2–24.
49. 'Le Componen Corrido al Coronavirus En Michoacán', https://www.youtube.com/watch?v=T-OFySEVkE4 (accessed 1 July 2022).
50. Agustín Gurza, 'Coronavirus Corridos: Tales of the Pandemic', The Strachwitz Frontera Collection of Mexican and Mexican American Recordings website, https://frontera.library.ucla.edu/blog/2020/04/coronavirus-corridos-tales-pandemic (accessed 1 July 2022).
51. 'El corrido del corona virus', https://www.youtube.com/watch?v=x6LjHzdFs-o (accessed 1 July 2022). The channel has since changed its name to "Litotv fishing".
52. 'El corrido del corona virus', https://www.youtube.com/watch?v=jBehR9GhCqQ (accessed 1 July 2022).
53. 'El Solitario De Los Luceros Del Sur – El Corona Virus (Corrido Acordeón) – Juan Villalobos Mondaca', https://www.youtube.com/watch?v=5hZ3MuvfBoA (accessed 1 July 2022).

54. 'Korrido de ese Kovid. Desde España para mis Mexicano', https://www.youtube.com/watch?v=4iDiwxIn7Ke (accessed 1 July 2022).
55. 'CORONA 2020 Corrido de la tragedia mundial del coronavirus', https://www.youtube.com/watch?v=WKaflQzcfoY (accessed 1 July 2022).
56. 'Corrido Sobre el Coronavirus', https://www.youtube.com/watch?v=u-R_xuuGo4g (accessed 30 June 2022).
57. 'El Llamado, llego virus mortal, Corrido contra coronavirus. Covid 19 primera parte', https://www.youtube.com/watch?v=U8LKnoBWiTU (accessed 1 July 2022).
58. 'El Comunicado, corrido progresivo, En contra del Covid 19', https://www.youtube.com/watch?v=v-86KCJjD3g (accessed 1 July 2022).
59. 'alerta mundial corona virus corrido 2020', https://www.youtube.com/watch?v=KKfnt1GcUCc (accessed 1 July 2022).
60. 'corrido del coronavirus', https://www.youtube.com/watch?v=kp0YzlCgdzk (accessed 1 July 2022); 'EL CORRIDO AL CORONAVIRUS', https://www.youtube.com/watch?v=Fg2G9U_goKs (accessed 1 July 2022); 'El corrido de La Corona Virus', https://www.youtube.com/watch?v=trNUbG4Fcyw (accessed 1 July 2022).
61. 'Corrido cristiano al corona virus', https://www.youtube.com/watch?v=66v7q7qo0Tw (accessed 1 July 2022).
62. 'CORONAVIRUS CORRIDO/CANCION', https://www.youtube.com/watch?v=b_wuogmQCf0 (accessed 1 July 2022).
63. 'CORONAVIRUS CORRIDO/CANCION', https://www.youtube.com/watch?v=b_wuogmQCf0 (accessed 1 July 2022).
64. Catherine H. de Giménez, 'Corrido, identité, idéologie : chant populaire de tradition orale au Mexique', *Cahiers Du Monde Hispanique et Luso-Brésilien* 48 (1987): 49–58 (our translation), p. 50.
65. Daniel John Nappo, 'Looking Back to the End of Time: Millennial Imagery in Selected Novels and Corridos of the Mexican Revolution, 1890–1947', PhD thesis, Michigan State University.
66. Narcocorridos receive an enormous amount of scholarly attention. In addition to others already cited: Amanda M. Morrison, 'Musical Trafficking: Urban Youth and the Narcocorrido-Hardcore Rap Nexus', *Western Folklore* 67.4 (2008): 379–96; Mark C. Edberg, *El Narcotraficante: Narcocorridos and the Construction of a Cultural Persona on the U.S.–Mexico Border* (Austin: University of Texas Press, 2009); Elijah Wald, *Narcocorrido: A Journey Into the Music of Drugs, Guns, and Guerrillas* (New York: HarperCollins, 2012); Juan C. Ramírez-Pimienta, 'El Narcocorrido En La Frontera y La Frontera En El Narcocorrido', *Revista Iberoamericana* 265 (2018): 1101–16; José De Jesús Chávez-Martínez, 'La romantización del narcocorrido en México', *Comhumanitas* 10.3 (2019): 43–53; José De Jesús Diego Pineda, *Política y poder en el narcocorrido: fronteras difusas entre gobierno y 'narco'* (Mauritius: Editorial Académica Española, 2019).
67. Jon Roozenbeek, Claudia R. Schneider, Sarah Dryhurst, John Kerr, Alexandra L. J. Freeman, Gabriel Recchia, Anne Marthe van der Bles, and Sander van der Linden, 'Susceptibility to Misinformation about COVID-19 around the World', *Royal Society Open Science* 7.10 (2020): https://doi.org/10.1098/rsos.201199
68. Jean Guerrero, 'Op-Ed: How Conspiracy Theories about COVID-19 Prey on Latinos', *Los Angeles Times*, 2 May 2021, https://www.latimes.com/opinion/story/2021-05-02/latinos-covid-vaccines-resistance-skepticism (accessed 1 July 2022).
69. Jose A. Del Real, 'Five Days, 100 Vaccine Doses and a Wildfire of Conspiracy Theories', *Washington Post*, 28 May 2021, https://www.washingtonpost.com/nation/interactive/2021/covid-vaccine-hesitancy-california-farmworkers/ (accessed 1 July 2022). A 2014 study of health outcomes among migrants living in rural Oregon corroborates the idea that Latinos' mistrust of the medical system is both a product of perceived discrimination and a factor in negative health outcomes when compared to the locally

born white population in the area: see Daniel F. López-Cevallos, S. Marie Harvey, and Jocelyn T. Warren, 'Medical Mistrust, Perceived Discrimination, and Satisfaction with Health Care among Young-Adult Rural Latinos', *Journal of Rural Health* 30.4 (2014): 344–51. This has particularly poignant implications in the coronavirus era, when full health enfranchisement is the only way to guarantee high vaccination rates and improve immunity outcomes across the board.
70. Michele Goodwin and Erwin Chemerinsky, 'The Trump Administration: Immigration, Racism, and COVID-19', *University of Pennsylvania Law* Review 169 (2021): 313–82; Anne G. Beckett, Loune Viaud, Michele Heisler, and Joia Mukherjee, 'Misusing Public Health as a Pretext to End Asylum — Title 42', *New England Journal of Medicine* 386.16 (2022): https://www.nejm.org/doi/full/10.1056/NEJMp2200274 (accessed 1 July 2022).
71. Joanne M. Miller, 'Psychological, Political, and Situational Factors Combine to Boost COVID-19 Conspiracy Theory Beliefs', *Canadian Journal of Political Science/Revue Canadienne de Science Politique* 53.2 (2020): 327–34.
72. Remi Jedwab, Amjad M. Khan, Jason Russ, and Esha D. Zaveri, 'Epidemics, Pandemics, and Social Conflict: Lessons from the Past and Possible Scenarios for COVID-19', *World Development* 147 (2021): Article 105629.
73. Luke Taylor, 'Covid-19 Misinformation Sparks Threats and Violence against Doctors in Latin America', *BMJ* 370 (11 August 2020): Article m3088.
74. 'CORONAVIRUS EL CORRIDO', https://www.youtube.com/watch?v=1X5przfJ85Q (accessed 1 July 2022).
75. 'Corrido A los Creadores del Corona virus', https://www.youtube.com/watch?v=VDNWmkqn1dE (accessed 1 July 2022).
76. 'Corrido de el corona virus', https://www.youtube.com/watch?v=mT07QoNepHA (accessed 1 July 2022); 'Quédate en tu casa', https://www.youtube.com/watch?v=lXQZQcuwFxk (accessed 1 July 2022).
77. 'Corrido del coronavirus. Evelio Segura Carbajal', https://www.youtube.com/watch?v=rck9Y0nqJts (accessed 1 July 2022).
78. 'El Corrido De Coronavirus (COVID-19) con el sobrino de LUIS PEREZ MEZA (Jim Francis Meza)', https://www.youtube.com/watch?v=C1HNevzwiOs (accessed 1 July 2022).
79. 'Corrido del coronavirus', https://www.youtube.com/watch?v=Wl-CIaA7m7Q (accessed 1 July 2022).
80. 'Corrido Del Coronavirus (Covid-19)', https://www.youtube.com/watch?v=UJKf9iMgj-c (accessed 1 July 2022).
81. Radio UdeG Ocotlán, 'Corridos Tumbados, una evolución del corrido mexicano', *UDG TV* (blog), 11 December 2020, https://udgtv.com/noticias/ocotlan-noticias/corridos-tumbados-una-evolucion-del-corrido-mexicano/ (accessed 1 July 2022).
82. 'Corrido Del Coronavirus (Covid-19)', https://www.youtube.com/watch?v=UJKf9iMgj-c (accessed 5 July 2022).
83. 'Corrido del coronavirus', https://www.youtube.com/watch?v=6kxDu9PyqUM (accessed 5 July 2022).
84. 'Corrido del coronavirus asi lo canto', https://www.youtube.com/watch?v=roVn8kL5aQz (accessed 5 July 2022).
85. 'El Corrido de La Vacuna', https://www.youtube.com/watch?v=TkaSF5ECug8 (accessed 5 July 2022).
86. 'Banda Corrido Sobre La Vacuna', https://www.youtube.com/watch?v=wj43mZu1vcw (accessed 5 July 2022).
87. 'Corrido martinense del Coronavirus', https://www.youtube.com/watch?v=Qk_CLdsop0E (accessed 5 July 2022).This video was uploaded on 12 January 2021 and had had five views as of 5 July 2022.
88. 'Larry Donas | Corrido del Coronavirus', https://www.youtube.com/watch?v=PSeXO74pcHs/ (accessed 2 July 2022). It was reposted without attribution as

'Corrido a capela del coronavirus', https://www.youtube.com/watch?v=suASSwNUdlE (accessed 2 July 2022); 'Larry Donas | Corrido del coronavirus 🎸♪', https://www.youtube.com/watch?v=jqw3Yx7Dv0I (accessed 2 July 2022).

89. For example, of many others covering essentially the same ground, 'CORRIDO L A PANDEMIA DEL CORONAVIRUS', https://www.youtube.com/watch?v=joQi6X5WVnw (accessed 5 July 2022); 'El corrido del coronavirus', https://www.youtube.com/watch?v=e22C37UVtJM (accessed 5 July 2022); 'Corrido del coronavirus', https://www.youtube.com/watch?v=rRVknwu6nkQ (accessed 5 July 2022); Rigoberto Cantu, 'Corrido de el coronavirus', https://www.youtube.com/watch?v=q4481a4L9BI (accessed 5 July 2022).

90. 'Coronavirus Corrido Oficial – Jose Robles', https://www.youtube.com/watch?v=IvoIdpSxEDo (accessed 5 July 2022).

91. 'Corrido del Coronavirus', https://www.youtube.com/watch?v=JY0g_C-Zke8 (accessed 5 July 2022); 'Corrido del Coronavirus', https://www.youtube.com/watch?v=Fbv-P3hTYW4 (accessed 5 July 2022).

92. 'Taller Nayarit corrido del Coronavirus Covid-19', https://www.youtube.com/watch?v=Bp4N4_tt_DU (accessed 5 July 2022).

93. For example, 'El Corrido Del Corona Virus Compuesto Y Cantado Por Jacobo Rodríguez Macías', https://www.youtube.com/watch?v=CN1f9pKUui0 (accessed 1 July 2022); 'Corrido del coronavirus', https://www.youtube.com/watch?v=NTk2ds2M9c4 (accessed 1 July 2022); 'Corrido del Coronavirus', https://www.youtube.com/watch?v=axMcPQbwpGM (accessed 1 July 2022); 'Corrido del corona virus' https://www.youtube.com/watch?v=7VJsbxCAl24 (accessed 1 July 2022).

94. 'La cuarentena del coronavirus corrido', https://www.youtube.com/watch?v=_5sYScFlEqQ (accessed 1 July 2022).

95. 'El corrido del corona virus los rancheros de valle hermoso de Casablanca', https://www.youtube.com/watch?v=LnnRTjKyOgQ (accessed 5 July 2022).

96. 'Coronavirus – Corrido de Amealco – (Duuran)', https://www.youtube.com/watch?v=NQjjFEAR31s (accessed 5 July 2022).

97. 'corrido del coronavirus', https://www.youtube.com/watch?v=EFBwRzbXFCs (accessed 5 July 2022); 'Corrido del Coronavirus', https://www.youtube.com/watch?v=axMcPQbwpGM (accessed 5 July 2022).

98. 'Cancion Del CoronaVirus[corrido]', https://www.youtube.com/watch?v=EO2faBxe2Ng (accessed 5 July 2022).

99. 'Corona virus corrido', https://www.youtube.com/watch?v=s5baYsdr0pQ (accessed 5 July 2022); 'El Corrido Del Coronavirus (Cover) Anthony Hernandez', https://www.youtube.com/watch?v=aF5tDCXyKfk (accessed 5 July 2022).

100. 'CHARRO MONTERO 'EL CORRIDO DEL CORONAVIRUS', https://www.youtube.com/watch?v=ni1KZI8xDbw (accessed 5 July 2022).

101. 'el CORRIDO del Coronavirus', https://www.youtube.com/watch?v=sosCwXT5vwY (accessed 5 July 2022).

102. 'El Corrido Del Coronavirus', https://www.youtube.com/watch?v=BvL_n-j62ok (accessed 5 July 2022).

103. 'el coronavirus..corrido de la cuarentena 29 de marzo de 2020', https://www.youtube.com/watch?v=97SEljTzJVs (accessed 5 July 2022).

104. 'Rey de corazones Jesús Jr.', https://www.youtube.com/watch?v=sBLlHHbkgao (accessed 5 July 2022).

105. 'El corrido del corona virus parte 2', https://www.youtube.com/watch?v=Pqf8x3pRgKA, posted 9 May 2020 (accessed 4 July 2022) Part 1 received 82 views: 'El corrido del corona virus parte 1', https://www.youtube.com/watch?v=JANPlLPzjAc (accessed 5 July 2022).

106. 'El corrido de Coronavirus con Marcelino Patiño', https://www.youtube.com/watch?v=RHfPf3qY3nk (accessed 5 July 2022).

107. 'El Corrido Del Coronavirus 🐴 El Plebe De Chihuahua 🍃 Laberinto 🐴', https://www.youtube.com/watch?v=GsUDNO7zPz4 (accessed 5 July 2022); 'CoronaVirus, Corrido – Ober lopez (Videoclip Oficial)', https://www.youtube.com/watch?v=ehCt2X6z9AE (accessed 5 July 2022); 'Corrido del coronavirus con los hijos del caminante', https://www.youtube.com/watch?v=TYFXtVZGPHs (accessed 5 July 2022).
108. 'Los Tigres del Norte – El Corrido del COVID-19', https://www.youtube.com/watch?v=4_HST2lugLM (accessed 30 June 2022).
109. 'El Corrido Del Coronavirus 🐴 El Plebe De Chihuahua 🍃 Laberinto 🐴', https://www.youtube.com/watch?v=GsUDNO7zPz4 (accessed 5 July 2022); Los Tigres del Norte reposted a version of their song 'El Contagio' on their Facebook page on 17 March 2020, but this was a song originally recorded before the pandemic.
110. 'El Corrido del Coronavirus', https://www.youtube.com/watch?v=nOqtVTVo3lo (accessed 5 July 2022); 'OMAR HURTADO EL PULPO DE LOS TECLADOS EL CORRIDO DEL CORONA VIRUS', https://www.youtube.com/watch?v=HVS6HMzgGbg (accessed 5 July 2022); 'El Corrido Del Coronavirus', https://www.youtube.com/watch?v=lM8sGReGWts (accessed 5 July 2022); 'Corrido Del Coronavirus', https://www.youtube.com/watch?v=Bk4QjvWkyRQ (accessed 5 July 2022).
111. 'Covid 19 El Corrido videoclip Oficial', https://www.youtube.com/watch?v=3LOCjLZjdnA (accessed 5 July 2022).
112. 'COVID 19 CORRIDO', https://www.youtube.com/watch?v=Kn42EZfQ5Oo (accessed 5 July 2022).
113. 'El Corrido Del COVID 19 🐴🍃 – Victor El Elegido De Oaxaca – [Vídeo Oficial]', https://www.youtube.com/watch?v=4oThEYNsxNc (accessed 20 June 2022).
114. 'Guadalupe Victoria | Persona de la tercera edad compone corrido del Coronavirus', https://www.youtube.com/watch?v=kz7YN5nK3oQ (accessed 2 July 2022); 'Tacos el Viejon y Corrido del Coronavirus', https://www.youtube.com/watch?v=hE2VLuDP1fg (accessed 2 July 2022).
115. 'El Corrido del Coronavirus', https://www.youtube.com/watch?v=QMmiRHfxYCM (accessed 1 July 2022).
116. Also, there were none that evoked the archetypes illuminated by María Herrera-Sobek, *The Mexican Corrido: A Feminist Analysis* (Bloomington: Indiana University Press, 1990).
117. 'Coronavirus Diaries: Vol 6 – Covid Corrido', https://www.youtube.com/watch?v=ZMjzXN5K--U (accessed 5 July 2022); 'A Corrido for COVID-19', https://www.kcet.org/shows/southland-sessions/a-corrido-for-covid-19 (accessed 5 July 2022).
118. 'corrido Coronavirus', https://www.youtube.com/watch?v=GjuuhODCjNk (accessed 1 July 2022).
119. 'Corrido del Coronavirus', https://www.youtube.com/watch?v=VFc0HtQtieQ (accessed 1 July 2022).
120. 'El corrido del CORONAVIRUS| Los Cadetes De Linares', https://www.youtube.com/watch?v=DAQI6oeexco (accessed 5 July 2022).

5 Llorando, Tomando, Bailando, Rezando

Introduction

In April 2020, a serene, balding Dominican man sat on the edge of his bed to send an encouraging message to the world with his two-row Hohner accordion. As with many of the examples discussed in this book, he introduced his music personally to the world via YouTube. The video begins with a spoken dedication to 'all of my friends, so that they protect themselves from the virus that's now here', and a prayer 'that God might liberate all of us from this damned pandemic that has taken over the whole world'. The performer, who remains unidentified in the video or description, then launches into 'EL MERENGUE CORONAVIRUS', a lively merengue típico. His verses warn of the coronavirus's lethal power and reaffirm the need for both collective action and faith in God.[1]

'EL MERENGUE CORONAVIRUS' was clearly intended as a personal expression of heartfelt emotion; it was not a song created for commercial success. The video gained barely over 100 views in two years on YouTube, many of which were repeated listenings by the authors of this book. Like so many other solo musical performance videos released on the platform during the pandemic, 'EL MERENGUE CORONAVIRUS' is a musical expression of individual experience and feeling made in response to a shared global crisis. As noted in previous chapters, although YouTube is a public-facing social media platform with global reach, many examples of coronavirus music were released by amateurs with a localized audience of friends and family in mind. While many of the highly produced musical examples considered in this chapter were created to garner maximum views as commercial products, these amateur solo videos especially exude direct emotional expression and feelings of raw intimacy.

This chapter explores the emotional spectrum, contingencies of assigned meaning, and wide diversity of affective responses in Latin American music responding to the pandemic moment. Throughout the continent, COVID-19 inspired an array of emotionally resonant responses which were consequently manifest across distinct genres, spaces, and approaches to music making. Within the corpus of música del coronavirus, contradictory and competing emotions exist alongside one another and are undergirded by a great diversity of sounds and rhythms. The music continued to morph in tone after spring 2020, reflecting the evolving and profound impact on collective emotional lives as the pandemic moment dragged on. These musical responses to the shifting crisis are examples of what Stephan Palmié has framed as 'proliferating difference and unbounded continua' in 'the situated and contingent crafting of representations of a no-less-situated and contingent world'.[2]

Musicians structured their coronavirus music with an array of paradoxes, emotional ploys, and affective framings. The compositions of the pandemic moment often contrast extraordinary events, new fears, and other complex psychological states with both mundane and treasured aspects of pre-pandemic life. Emotional musical responses also fill the often yawning spaces of time, as well as the unmooring of social and emotional lives described by the concept of 'pandemic time', as explored in this book's introduction. Música del coronavirus situates pandemic experiences amid mourning and death but also evokes partying, an umbrella term encompassing celebration, imbibing, sexual freedom, and hedonistic escapism. The compositions range from earnest didactic pieces counseling pandemic-era sanitary precautions to songs exhorting drinking, dancing, and carefree living in the face of the coronavirus. Christian songs, meanwhile, variously encourage resilient faith, musing either on salvation and agency or End Times pestilence and death. Other approaches urge a range of prosaic and radical communitarian social solutions to the world crisis. While some musicians model or preach caution, others indulge in ironic trolling, elaborate parody, or farce. Many musicians combine many or all these approaches, with varying degrees of affective success.

These highly contingent musical responses coalesce into an enormous mediating force and a significant body of work reflective of the complex experience of the pandemic moment overall. Música del coronavirus operates congruently with the sonic, affective, and emotional frameworks of local and regional musical production during this shared global crisis.

Contingency, Affect, and Musical Responses to the Pandemic

The pandemic moment can be framed contingently within analyses of sound, emotion, and affect, and amid new approaches to emotional regulation and musical wellbeing. Música de coronavirus speaks to experiences of 'the body in its lived materiality'.[3] Centering music and sound in understanding mediated experiences helps to produce, as Marie Thompson and Ian Biddle argue, 'a particular ambience or atmosphere, via the induction, modulation and circulation of moods, feelings, and intensities, which were felt but at the same time, belonged to nobody in particular.'[4] The pandemic moment was a highly disruptive and evocative experience for many in which individualized time, space, and experience suddenly became mediated by a shared global crisis. Holly Watkins writes that 'musical sounds constitute a lexicon of arousal whose interpretative possibilities span physical, physiological, emotional, and conceptual realms.'[5] The pandemic moment forced together collective global and individual realms of sonic experiences.[6]

This situation demanded conscious and psychological responses from individuals and communities alike, in a complex nexus of feeling and action that not only reflected the pandemic moment but also guided its experiential qualities. Pablo Vila has observed that 'the identitarian articulations people sequentially deploy in any music event (as mediated by the atmosphere of the events and the affects that circulate on them) always mediate these affects and emotions as well.' He argues that such 'continuous back-and-forth, or continuous processes of mediation, of all the elements that belong to a musical event [can be] understood as an "assemblage"'.[7]

These musical assemblages of the pandemic moment produced diverse affective responses. Music regulates mood and promotes social harmony, and 'evoke[s] powerful emotional experiences' in listeners.[8] As argued by Varvara Pasiali, 'music's therapeutic role in human adaptation processes' encourages developmental resilience, defined as 'the ability to withstand adverse environmental stressors'.[9] New research has demonstrated that music listening has had an especially significant and measurable response during the pandemic moment.[10]

The term *affect* has been applied to such widely diverse phenomena as to have perhaps lost some of its descriptive functionality. Ruth Leys argues that given the great and obscuring diversity of approaches,

> the important point to recognize is that they all share a single belief: the belief that affect is independent of signification and meaning [...]. Action and behavior are [...] determined by affective dispositions that are independent of consciousness and the mind's control.[11]

Affect is used in reference to overlapping if distinct theoretical concepts relating to the mediation of cultural forms and their embodied, emotional, and cognitive responses. Thompson and Biddle observe that 'the term has had a certain currency with a range of disciplinary contexts' but that its focus is 'never really what affect means [so much] as what it does'.[12] Patrik Juslin and John Sloboda note that 'researchers have tended to use words such as affect, emotion, feeling, and mood in different ways, which has made communication and integration difficult'. These terms sometimes 'refer to different things' but at other times 'to the same thing'.[13] Juslin and Sloboda define affect as an 'umbrella term' that 'comprises anything from music preference, mood, and emotion to aesthetic and even spiritual experiences'.[14] Vila meanwhile adds that 'affects emerge, circulate, and evolve everywhere. Understood as a process of mediation, there is nothing that escapes affect'.[15] Danilyn Rutherford has presented affect most usefully in terms of 'felt bodily intensity, the feeling of having a feeling' that is most useful in highlighting the contingent ways it can be 'imagine[d] how the world might look, feel, or sound if experienced by an actor situated in a particular place and time'.[16]

Reflecting the changes to meaning that arise in translation, Spanish-language research on the relationship between music and affect further interrogates the imprecision of the term in the literature. Juan Fernando Anta, Luis Felipe Oliveira, and Danilo Ramos compiled a table comparing scholarly definitions of affect (*afecto*) and related terms as a way to 'show the diversity and discrepancies' of such descriptors. They contrast the typical English usage of 'affect' as 'an evaluative state or valence', with other readings that link it to 'feelings of pleasure or pain' or limit its meaning to merely 'one of the components of emotion'. As a result, in translation there can be difficulties even defining the concept of emotion, and overlapping and imprecise uses of the terms 'affect' (*afecto*, which also translates as 'affection'), 'emotion' (*emoción*, which also translates as 'joy') 'feeling' (*sentimiento* or sometimes even the English calque *fílin*), 'embodiment' (the rarely-used *encarnamiento*), 'mood' (*humor*, which also translates as 'humor') and 'state of mind' (the rather formal *estado de ánimo*, which also sometimes translates as "willingness").[17] Pandemic-era music reflected the range of embodied and symbolic manifestations of feelings and emotional states, as well as affective embodiments of individual experiences.

As an emergent approach to songwriting and performance, coronavirus music reflected this embodied experience just as it mapped shifting pandemic moods, operating in line with Palmié's idea of a 'conceptual boundary object' which is 'shared and unshared at different levels of interest and social articulation'.[18] What happens when a crisis is so permeating and inescapable that all are placed within such 'conceptual boundary objects'?

During the pandemic moment, the physical world was laden with constraints, while virtual lives were often mediated by algorithms. The individual ability to be physically proximate with loved ones and friends became weighted with mortal peril, and the body became directly controlled by policy and new norms of collective behavior. In this decoupling of the emotional, physical, and spatial frames in the context of mass isolation, the promise of finding responsive affective experiences in music and musical spaces during the pandemic provided new, unique opportunities for connection. In the era of individualized listening experiences on personal devices and via streaming platforms, Marie Strand Skånland shows how curated listening aids individuals 'to cope better with what might otherwise be perceived as stressful surroundings'.[19] In pondering those who seek consolation in song, H. M. Evans argues that 'when music works upon us therapeutically, it expresses, recalls, and even rekindles general features of our embodied experience and of our ordinary being'.[20]

The pandemic moment directly mediated time, experience, and emotional phenomena in ways that emerged immediately in music making. The crisis re-situated music production, consumption, and the sonic being-in-the-world of individuals. Emotionally evocative música del coronavirus exhibits a complex emotional palate, reflecting the simultaneous need to mourn loss, maintain hope, make sense of the world, and have fun in a time of immense collective stress. The pandemic forcibly reassembled worlds of meaning and feeling fractured by a novel and truly existential experience for everyone involved.

Cuarentena con música

Some of the most powerful and popular affective appraisals of the pandemic moment came in the immense stream of Andean music released from the beginning of the crisis. This body of música del coronavirus ranged quite widely in approach and intent but remained consistently expressive about the emotional impact of the pandemic in ways sometimes less emphasized in other styles of música del coronavirus.

For example, 'El huayno del coronavirus', released early in the pandemic on 1 April 2020, plays the early lockdowns for laughs. The piece combines singing about the all-too-familiar experiences of the pandemic with an uproarious laughter track and a video of variously ridiculous and sometimes violent images of police crackdowns, meant humorously or ironically to illustrate the song's themes. In verses sung to an upbeat and repetitive huayno rhythm played on two guitars, the unidentified singer bemoans being forced to stay housebound doing the laundry and missing out on soccer, drinking, and pursuing women. Regardless, he is happy to have traditional Peruvian food to eat at home. Listeners especially enjoyed the comic relief, with many commenting as laughter, such as Rodrigo Saul Cycho responding with 'jajajajajajajajajajaja'. Not all listeners were amused, though. Dorgel Parka teleco (sic) responded that '[i]t was a sad reality that many Peruvians did not have [anything] to eat and were forced to look for food and face covid [sic], a pity that people do not value the humiliations of the state of Vizcarrata and the corrupt police and the unbalanced army' ('*Fue una realidad triste que muchos peruanos no tuvieron que comer y se vieron obligados a buscar comida y enfrentarse al covid, una pena que la gente no valores las humillaciones del estado de vizcarrata y la corrupta policía y el desequilibrado ejercito*').[21]

Other Peruvian musicians also approached the pandemic with smiles, laughter tracks, and upbeat music. Los Mendez, a very popular family salsa band that also plays other styles, received several million views for their thirty-part series of 'CUARENTENA con música'.²² While these songs, released in the spring and summer of 2020, were not topical songs on the virus itself, the series stood as a relentlessly effervescent refusal to accept the isolation and sadness of the pandemic. Some of Los Mendez's songs were especially designated as homages to Peru or to specific styles like classic salsa, bachata or rock en Español, or dedicated to specific artists like Vilma Palma, Agua Marina, Raul Romero, or Pedro Suárez Vértiz. Session 11 was dedicated to songs about pain and heartbreak ('A Puro Dolor y Corazón Partío'). Session 15 was dedicated to gospel music. One of their more popular videos for 'cuarentena con música parte 24' was dedicated to 'OLD SCHOOL reggaetón' ('HOMENAJE al reggaetón de la VIEJA ESCUELA').²³

Viewed successively, this notable series of live sessions yields slight shifts in the enthusiastic tonality and affect of the band. The energy of the introductions and exuded feeling of the band evince small shifts in emotional mood, tracking with the daily emotional changes of people staying at home in quarantine. The videos sometimes include musicians isolated in their own internal windows, as in memetic Zoom meetings. The sonic character and quality of the recording sound also change in the series, underscoring the home studio's limitations in the pandemic. The listener/viewer is suddenly privy to intimate, previously inaccessible spaces. The overall corpus maintains an impressively consistent front of happy feelings and expressed desire for connectivity in the face of fear.

For each session, Los Mendez used the hashtag '#YoMeQuedoEnCasa' ('IStayAtHome') for the effective purpose of reaching an enormous and self-coalescing audience seeking emotional solace and novel forms of connection via YouTube-based music consumption. This hashtag serves as an immensely powerful signpost for música del coronavirus in many other styles, by early 2022 encompassing an astonishing 223,000 videos on more than 50,000 channels posting music, dance, and movement videos responding to the pandemic.²⁴ Those numbers are so large as to themselves approach 'conceptual boundary objects'. Some of these videos were repostings of TikTok videos, while others were music or exercise sessions made by individuals coping with the pandemic via Nordic walking, dancing, mountaineering, yoga, Zumba, and other activities too numerous to list. The videos include hundreds of examples of instrument and dance practice titled with nothing other than labels such as '#musicaviral #musicaencasa #yomequedoencasa', 'Saxo cubano #YoMeQuedoEnCasa', or '#músicaviral #día2 #edmusical #yomequedoencasa'.²⁵ Bene y Josep played the classic tango 'Por una Cabeza' while in 'confinement with music #músicaviral' for 326 viewers.²⁶ Alvaro Soler, a Spanish singer popular across Latin America and especially Mexico, reposted his Instagram Live videos on YouTube under the hashtag '#YoMeQuedoEnCasa Festival (Instagram Live)' for almost a half million viewers.²⁷

Each additional hashtag branches into hundreds of other shared pandemic musical moments, most of which were not thematically connected to the virus itself. Yet all these music videos initiate sonic and virtual connections with people who kept busy making music as solace and escape during the pandemic.[28] These hundreds of videos are songs posted by individuals and the marketing hashtags all act as virtual and sonic substitutions for the direct social connections real-life music making would otherwise have brought. The emotional plainness of the music videos, and the situatedness of the amateur musicians and dancers in their tiny frames, is enhanced by the core message that they all shared with the professional entertainers Los Mendez: stay at home, make music, share your emotional life.

Other Peruvian professional musicians adopted a commercial and humorous approach. Josue Ñavincopa, Deiby Ñavincopa, and Xiomara Brillitd's 'EL CORONAHUAYNO' was released early in the pandemic, on 27 March 2020, and even came with a unique logo for what was clearly intended to be a resonant and popular (or possibly viral) song. 'EL CORONAHUAYNO' forefronts the sadness of shutdowns and the arrival of the virus, but with an upbeat groove played on harp, electric bass, and electronic percussion. The need for obligatory isolation in lockdown is delivered in a peppy call and response. With a forced laugh, bassist Deiby Ñavincopa acts as the personified coronavirus and shouts for the listener to die. The video reflects the upbeat nature of the song, with a smiling band dressed alike and dancing in choregraphed moves, all calling for dancing, drinking, and simply living life to the fullest, while still recognizing the implicit threat of life during pandemic times.[29]

The Peruvian singer Wilma Contreras's 'Vete pandemia' ('Go away pandemic') is a double-timed song played on an electronic requinto by Emilio Goicochea and sung endearingly by their collaborator Alma Solary. The young Solary and Contreras both appear dressed in stage costumes which explicitly evoke the colors and design of the Peruvian flag, making them seem wrapped in the national image. In 'Vete pandemia' Solary exudes confidence as she confidently confronts the pandemic. She has no doubt that the virus will depart from her young life and fly away into the sky on the wings of an eagle. The requinto reinforces every beat of her singing and also her demands, as if to underscore the power of her desire for liberation from the virus.[30]

Armando Chamorro's 'Huayno Coronavirus (Hit 2020)' is a similarly upbeat song confronting sad themes with an unusual range of affective cues. His video incongruously includes a laughter track and images of coffins, skits, and dancers in colorful costumes, while his lyrics suggest the usual range of solutions for confronting the virus, such as staying home and washing one's hands. The song begins and is framed throughout with existential cries, stern warnings about staying at home, and ponderous explorations asking why all of this is happening. Yet the composition also relies on absurdly vulgar humor accompanied by increasingly deranged cackles of laughter. 'Stay home on your mother's coochie [...] if you don't understand this you're going to die', the description of the song warns (*Quédate en casa oe conch4 de tu m4dre [...]si no entiendes así vas a morir*' [sic]).[31]

Some huayno songs about the coronavirus emphasize communitarianism and prayer. Others are earnestly sad or even tragic, focusing on lost loved ones, desolation, and shaken faith. Mickey Vergara sings of the common viral enemy of humankind and the dangers to individual destiny in his 'Maldito Coronavirus', released on 26 March 2020. This composition shares a title with a great many other pandemic-era songs from the Andean region which variously express themes of resistance, woe, fear, and communal solidarity.[32] Vergara's song in collaboration with DJ Roll Perú is presented as a lively huayno ancashino, a synthesized and upbeat central and eastern style. He encourages listeners to stay home and remain healthy until the virus is defeated and everybody can get back together.[33]

Revelación 5:40's up-tempo, saxophone cumbia (saxocumbia) 'MALDITO CORONAVIRUS' recounts how the virus took the singer's entire family and friends, one member at a time.[34] Nataly Salazar similarly bemoans losses to COVID across the country, framing her song in the lyrics as a cry from the depths of her heart. Her 'MALDITO CORONAVIRUS' starts with a traditional, percussive harp and violin arrangement. However, when she begins singing, a saxophone takes over the main repetitive figure and follows her lead. The song is recorded as a tinny, faint track which sounds like perhaps it is playing in the background to the video images. The video shows scenes of food distribution, COVID test tents, hospitals, ambulances, and other tragic scenes of the pandemic.[35]

Edith Mayta's 'Pandemia Covid19', originally released in late April 2020, uses the backing of a traditional Peruvian saxophone band in a composition about the sadness brought not just to Peru but to the entire world. She calls for divine intervention to help families broken by COVID, and performatively sobs halfway through the song before beginning the verses a second time. Mayta then utters a falsetto cry to signal an internalization of the emotional focus, and possibly to center the song back onto a more regional grounding. Her attention in the lyrics also shifts at this point, now blaming outside, selfish countries for making Peruvians pay for their own mistakes. She concludes by turning to recognition of the sufferings of Peruvian families.[36]

Mayta released several versions of 'Pandemia Covid19', each of which stressed different settings and feelings. The original featured a video with an ambulance siren, a spoken introduction and a collection of news footage. The lyrics were superimposed over the video, giving it the appearance of a news program set to music. In August 2020 she played a live version which tracked very closely to the original in tempo and timbre. This time, however, the song was introduced as an international hit for people ready to move around but dancing at home. Mayta sings backed by a large band of seven saxophones, three clarinets, a violin, a harp, and two drums. The live video on YouTube, unexpectedly, had gained only 489 views by February 2022.[37]

On 13 May 2021, more than a year after the original recording had appeared, Mayta released yet another version. Now called simply 'Pandemia', the song is here accompanied by a walking electric bass line, flute, and electronic effects. The tempo is similar to other versions but feels livelier with the added instruments. 'Pandemia' is presented as a professional glossy video, filmed in the famous Uyuni train cemetery and other places in Bolivia, along with other reenacted pandemic scenes in her bedroom, in hospitals, and at other locales. The singer, dressed as a medical worker, witnesses a death from COVID-19 and then kneels with other personnel in prayer. A year into the pandemic, the changes to the song and the video signal that while the themes and ideas presented had remained consistent, the mode of delivering the sentiment required a more performative and professional setting to be relevant and popular. Indeed, in half a year, this new version gained ten thousand more views than the original had garnered in more than twice that time (roughly 35,000 views compared to 22,700 by the end of 2021).[38]

Other songs also mined emotional veins. Deleites Andinos, from Huancabamba, Piura, Peru, released their 'MALDITA PANDEMIA' on 14 October 2020. Set to a brisk 136 bpm, the group sings of having to go through suffering, tears, and torment that stretches around the world. The song is presented, incongruously, along with a video of an evidently happy party of people drinking and dancing, which goes on for almost five minutes. The lyrics, which are sung in a higher pitch in each chorus, exhort people to get through the 'damned pandemic' and its suffering so that they can get back to life itself. The word 'maldita' is rushed in the chorus, underscoring the need to look forward to the pandemic being over; this is in contrast to other música del coronavirus, which so often dwell on all or some part of the word 'coronavirus' or 'COVID'. One commenter on the YouTube video calls it a 'a hymn to remember this tragedy', and that 'although dancing my eyes sprout tears' ('*Esta canción será un himno para recordar esta tragedia, tiene rítmo y letra, aunque al bailar de mis ojos broten lágrimas*').[39]

Juan Pena's 'Los dolores De Coronavirus' ('The Pains of Coronavirus'), uploaded to YouTube on 16 April 2020, tolls like a harbinger of events to come. The accompaniment, a warbly guitar plunking a simple waltz, sounds as if it was recorded on a computer microphone. Singing at a fraught point early in the pandemic, Pena's composition speaks of the heartbreak of losing a loved one to COVID-19.[40] The low-resolution video accompanying the song presents a montage of Google News screenshots, pictures of hospital beds and people in scrubs, and Juan Pena himself singing into the camera.

Another striking example of somber music bearing witness to the grief of the pandemic moment is a song once again titled 'Maldito Coronavirus', this time written by Walter Sanchez and performed by Sol de Pachaconas. It begins with an ethereal, twinkling harp introduction that encircles the song's defining chords. The composition features a harmonic bimodality common among huayno music, centering on two relative major and minor chords. As the song continues, a vocal line sung alternatively in Spanish and Quechua confronts the fear and anxiety of the pandemic moment, noting lives lost and pondering the imposed solitude of sheltering in place.[41] The accompanying video presents scenes of military personnel and equipment, reflecting the linkages of memory between the present public health crisis and previous crises of civil unrest and political instability from which Peru only has only recently begun to emerge.

In another huayno example, Andahuaylas-based vocalist Noemi Mallma sings an attention-grabbing introduction announcing the arrival of the coronavirus in Peru and the destruction it has left in its wake.[42] Mallma's singing on 'A QUE VENISTE CORONAVIRUS' is typical of the style, delivered with an abandon that tests the upper limits of her vocal register. She is seen clutching her heart as the video cuts between her and images of field hospitals, military checkpoints, and a funeral. Deborah Poole and Isaías Rojas Pérez write about similar images in other contexts that 'the act of seeing images of violence and suffering from the past contributes to the formation of a shared, collective, and agreed-upon memory regarding the origins and causes of that violence.'[43]

Huayno songs are not as decisive in their gloom as they might sound to the uninitiated or to non-Peruvians – huayno is a dynamic and diverse popular style that has often been misunderstood. 'In the most regional context', write Félix Julca Guerrero and Laura Nivin Vargas, 'the huayno is conceived as the most common and popular [form of] poetic-literary and musical composition in the Andean region.'[44] To a cultural outsider listening in, many huaynos about the coronavirus might sound soul-crushingly tragic. Joshua Tucker argues that 'the tendency of Western ears to associate the minor mode with gloom [...] explains the many accounts that describe huayno music as poignant, nostalgic, and haunting – or deride it as depressing.' Discussing common lyrical themes in huayno, Tucker writes that 'many huayno texts [...] explore sadness, uncertainty, loss, abandonment, grief, separation, and yearning – a trait that is hardly universal across space and time, though it is widely held to be so by outsiders to the [huayno] tradition.'[45] Movement between relative major and minor chords is used widely in Western art and popular musics to evoke melancholy, but in huayno it is a standard harmonic form that carries an entirely distinct emotional significance. Many examples of coronavirus huayno music could be easily mischaracterized as affective expressions of anguish, but these sounds actually reflect common aesthetic choices and the emotional range listeners seek and desire, especially during the pandemic moment. Romy Sotelo presents her 2022 retrospective huayno 'MALDITA PANDEMIA', which considers the overall pandemic moment, in this mode 'with pure feeling' ('*con puro sentimiento*').[46]

Reflective of both the tone of the song and the expected audience for emotive music, numerous pieces of música del coronavirus from other traditions are filled with sadness, and are even titled with the very word 'sad' (*triste*). Some take the form of unexpectedly pensive rap tracks, including Edgar Garcia's 'RAP TRISTE REFLEXIÓN COVID',[47] GD el Catracho's '(COVID-19)

(Coronavirus) Rap Triste ☹ – (La Vie Ne Ment Past)', and Daniel Rap's 'RAP TRISTE ☹ – (COVID-19)', featuring Enyel el Leon and Meyko el Frio.[48] Ruben condori ayque (sic) claims the title of 'saddest coronavirus song' for his whistle-forward power ballad 'La Canción Más Triste Del Covid-19 (coronavirus) 2020'[49] – a superlative that the Peruvian artist Jordan Riveros contests with his música criolla-influenced number of the same name.[50] Interestingly, many of these compositions balance their emphasis on sadness, melancholy, and grief with calls for hope and unity. A YouTube channel called 'Piano click 2' uploaded 'La Cancion Del Coronavirus / Cancion Triste' early in the pandemic moment. The video takes the well-established format of a YouTube piano tutorial, with musical note figures falling from above to collide with an image of a keyboard at the bottom of the screen. The lyrics of the song speak of how the virus does not discriminate based on race, class, or even moral standing, and encourage listeners to unite in the face of such a totalizing crisis. The song itself is a formulaic pop ballad; nonetheless, many comments offer a reflexive awareness of the relationship between the pandemic and its musical responses. Alex_crack commented that 'the good thing about coronavirus is that it makes you compose very good songs' (*'Lo bueno del coronavirus es que te hace componer canciones muy buenas'*), while Leslie Arce Perez proclaimed it 'the best song in times of COVID-19' (*'La mejor xancion* [sic] *en tiempos de COVID-19'*).[51]

Many commenters on música del coronavirus uploads also link to their own recordings of coronavirus songs. In one comment, Genesis Ruiz interjected 'Heyyy, wait, look! Watch my brother's video about the coronavirus', followed by a link and a postscript that 'he recorded it in the house' (*'Heyyy esperen miren !!! Miren este video de mi hermano sobre el coronavirus link ... Lo Grabo en casa* 😊😊😊*'*).[52] The song in question, an enthusiastic reggaetón recorded in Venezuela by Bery Kilers, was arguably more inspired than the video being commented upon. Writing from the United States, Omar Bautista Jr. also promoted his own coronavirus song, commenting 'here another tune about coronavirus as well, stay home' (*'Aqui otro tema igual del corona virus quedate en casa'*). This song, 'Quédate En Casa', itself sounds like an amateur attempt at a dreamy dance song, with Bautista singing off-time, out-of-tune verses about the pandemic atop synth pads and a looped drum machine.[53] While the original piece may have been labeled as a 'sad song', many of the posted comments do not reflect this sadness, instead taking an opportunity to applaud the artist and encourage a positive attitude in the face of difficulty. Others promote their own compositions that similarly capitalize on the pandemic moment.

The Ever-Present Virus: Life in Pandemic Time

In a song uploaded by the Bolivian duo Takiytinku, Oscar Beltrán Cuba acknowledges that he was losing track of time. The monotony of daily life during the onset of the pandemic, a state of psychological limbo experienced by many at this time, rendered the days of the week indistinguishable. A Plena Samba's 'El Viru Viru' muses about the blurred loss of days, the inability to exercise, and the sudden changes wrought by the virus to life and behavior.[54] Beltrán Cuba sings of this predicament alongside a renowned charango player, Betty Veigaza, in 'Bicho Chiquito' ('Little Germ'), an original composition released in May 2020. In the song, Beltrán Cuba's problems do not stop at failing to remember what day it is. He laments his inability to fit into his old pants – the result of a sedentary quarantine lifestyle – and the fact that he is no longer able to get drunk in his local bar due to shutdowns. Scenes in the music video show the musical duo alternately playing charango and guitar together, dancing alone outside, cooking and eating indoors, and demonstrating how to wash hands and put on a mask properly. In spite of the frustrated tone of the first few verses, the duo encourages the audience to shelter in place and observe the quarantine law in place at the time. Noting the deaths caused by the virus throughout the region, the performers shift from a comical tone poking fun at the daily irritations of quarantine boredom to a sobering acknowledgement of the gravity and pain of the pandemic moment and the need for collective action.[55]

Similar conflicting feelings course through many other songs, such as Gustavo Pacheco Castro's música tropical 'Canción la Pandemia', released in November 2020.[56] In this song, the danceable beat remains irresistibly fun even as Pacheco Castro wrestles lyrically with the bleak realities of the pandemic and its disruptions. Over the beat, he muses that he might be more dead than alive in this pandemic, stuck inside and terrified by the virus. In the video for the song uploaded on YouTube, Pacheco Castro walks through the streets of Barranquilla accompanied by an outrageous and fairly hilarious green foam COVID-19 mascot. Some scenes depict the solitude of quarantine and a desire for social interaction in spite of the ubiquitous, looming presence of the embodied coronavirus in all social settings. Girls dancing with poles in hand to enforce social distancing are interrupted by the virus doing the limbo under their poles. Pacheco Castro balefully peers into his empty refrigerator and ponders his empty pockets. The virus even disrupts a home robbery, shimmying eerily as the crooks flee. As Castro continues to sing of the inescapability of the pandemic, we see scenes of crowded streets, public spaces being cleaned with detergent, and queues of masked-up individuals waiting in socially distant lines. The virus ruins a game of dominos by dangling a mask in the middle of the table – a sudden and destructive intrusion. The players flee. The virus mascot, hilariously gyrating and appearing everywhere, is a plushy, approachable version of the virus. Yet the creeping fear never goes away. Pacheco Castro continues to sing, indicating that despite the fear there is nothing he can do to stop dancing. By the end, he is singing and dancing with the virus alone inside his own home studio, isolated but creative and defiant.[57]

Pacheco Castro was one of many artists across genres who produced songs featuring a costumed or cartoon coronavirus to punctuate their socially themed dance songs with humor and visual excitement. Simon El Mono's 'CANCION Covid 19 Corona virus' is sung by the virus itself.[58] Marcy Avila's profane 'PUTO COVID (OMICRON SPECIAL EDITION)' is a grinding, repetitive song with a solitary view of a crowned, grinning, toothy coronavirus.[59] In one of the most poignant examples, Miguel Duran, Jr., builds the video for his 'La Pandemia Covid – 19,' around an animated coronavirus escaping from a mad scientist's lab. Duran tragically later died of COVID himself.[60] Locomoving's 'La Canción Del Fin Del Mundo' makes extremely humorous use of a cartoon coronavirus in a song that sonically mimics the cartoon world while piling on a fearsome list of plagues and threats that the virus has joined.[61] Potro Salvaje Torreón built his 'Cumbia del Corona Virus' around his body-painted enactment of the virus.[62]

One of the most arresting uses of a comical embodied virus to underscore an earnest and emotional point comes in Cristano Vargas's Christmas-themed coronavirus cancion 'Anton Virus Virus,Virus' [sic]. Christmas is a season of good times and happiness, the song tells us, and Vargas inserts familiar refrains of 'Feliz Navidad' as well as melodies from gaitas, traditional Christmas songs from northwestern Venezuela. Throughout the video, Vargas and other musicians take the opportunity to beat a man wearing an enormous red coronavirus mask and a striped outfit marked 'COVID-19.' They beat the one who represents the virus with a wooden stick, a metal rod, and other objects. In captioning his video on his YouTube channel, Vargas wrote that it was 'a song to change crying and sadness for joy and partying' ('*Una cancion para cambiar el llanto y la tristeza por alegrias y parranda*').[63] This perfectly characterizes the approach of so much musical del coronavirus: engaging the full emotional spectrum, from earnest despair to comical abuse of the embodied virus itself.

In 'CORONAVIRUS EL LOCO DEL DESAFIO,' a song from Colombia released on 3 June 2020, Oscar Muñoz (known as El Loco del Desafío) utilizes a virus mascot to inject humor into his otherwise largely serious appraisal of the many challenges of the pandemic. Muñoz sings that he never imagined life could be so disrupted or that he would be forced to make such major adjustments, but he has been left with no choice. Everybody needs to unite and change their patterns of life, he says. Muñoz's coronavirus mascot, oddly, looks like a repurposed rectangular SpongeBob SquarePants costume, with pieces of ragged foam representing the envelope proteins and topped by a large handwritten 'CORONAVIRUS' banner. The video for the song portrays scenes of daily life in an unnamed Colombian city that are continually interrupted by the dancing, costumed coronavirus. Muñoz attempts to give a group of young men a mask, but to no avail – they disperse in terror and flee when the virus approaches. His friends dance at an indoor party in which only a few wear masks. Muñoz dances with, and then carries, a bottle of liquor for the rest of the song. The foam coronavirus is ever-present; it stands behind Muñoz when he prays or when he buys sunglasses with a woman. The virus is a guest at the party, dancing alongside the revelers, taking on the mediated role of a beguiling demon.[64]

The costumed viruses haunting these songs, and many others, signify demonic others with deep roots in a variety of regional musical cultures. In highlighting the mediator role of a morally ambiguous devil in music of the Colombian coastal region, Juan Moreno Blanco argues that 'folklore, integrated into the historical sense of society, begins to question, as a means of collective communication [...] the existing contradictions.'[65] Like the devil, the costumed coronavirus embodies both a basic representation of an evil invader and also the liminality of the pandemic and its contradictions. A longing to go out and share space with others contrasts uncomfortably with an understanding that such gatherings pose mortal danger. The carnivalesque is one way in which such a contradiction might be understood. In the words of Shulamith Lev-Aladgem, this is 'the performative means by which cultural components [are] re-decoded to transmit both a polysemic meaning as well as non-meaning at the same time.'[66] These contradictory tensions are at the forefront of such examples of música del coronavirus. While the pandemic is framed as threatening, omnipresent, and a force to be reckoned with, the carnivalesque atmosphere affords an uncanny carefree valence to the otherwise disturbing setting. Absurd coronavirus mascots make their cameos in homes, public spaces, and the corners of daily life. They are portrayed as both threatening and hilarious, appearing in vignettes of urban life during COVID that alternate between scenes of caution and disregard. Such tension between the necessity of self-restraint and the impulse simply to let loose permeates música del coronavirus. As described in the following section, the latter often prevails.

'Me Gusta Lo Bueno': Dancing, Drinking, and Living the Wild Life in the face of Coronavirus

Early at the start of the pandemic, on 21 March 2020, the popular Mexican banda singer Marco Flores released what rapidly come to be an indelible party song of the pandemic moment. In so doing, Flores channeled a defiant stance against pandemic strictures for others to inhabit as much as he described his own approach. Marco Flores y La Jerez's 'El Coronavirus' is a lively, festive cumbia arranged for an 11-piece Mexican banda (brass band). The song counsels partying and good times without fear or worry, and its accompanying video shows how this can be done. The video features Flores, decked out in a sparkly jacket, tight ripped jeans, and a black hat, dancing with his uniformed band and variously with two or three women. Flores struts and sings of his disregard for the severity of the pandemic. Forget it, he suggests; people should drink tequila and beer, throw parties in the face of lockdowns, and not allow the sadness of the moment to weigh down their spirits. As so many popular banda anthems celebrate, the party continues. There is no social distancing or anxiety-laden quarantining for Marco Flores or his band. Viewed more than three million times on YouTube by October 2021, and also streamed on all major platforms, this music video was one of the most far-reaching and popular examples of party-centric música del coronavirus.[67]

In the comments section on YouTube, Flores' defiant and celebratory approach to the pandemic situation was met with both support and critique. Top commenter 'calix Calix' noted that 'in China they build ten hospitals in ten days because of the coronaviro [sic], in Mexico they write twenty songs about coronavirus in 10 days, we're a mess' (*en China construyen 10 hospitales en diez días para el coronaviro, en México componen 20 canciones del coronaviro en 10 días somos un desmadre*). One much-liked comment showed emojis for the national flags of Argentina, Spain, the United States, Russia, and Japan, all accompanied with the caption 'be careful with the Coronavirus' (*'cuidado con el coronavirus'*), contrasted with a following emoji of the Mexican flag and the comment 'I don't give a damn about the coronavirus' ('a mi me vale el coronavirus'), drawing from Flores' irreverent chorus. Many comments referenced the irony of a video promoting partying at a time when large gatherings were discouraged by governments and media alike. Bogart Montiel announced that 'I am having a party in my house on Saturday and I'm going to play this song for my 200 invited guests hahahahaha,' (*'el sábado tengo pachanga en mi casa y pondré está rolita,a mis 200 invitados jajaja jajaja'*), while Lil David remarked that '[n]ow this is what I call dying with style' (*'A esto le llamo morir con estilo'*). Several comments also note the Mexican penchant for making light of a bad situation. 'The Mexican always looks for the positive side in whatever adversity', wrote Samuel Cholula (*'El mexicano siempre le busca el lado positivo a las adversidades* 😂😂👍👍🇲🇽😂😂😂 *México100%'*), while Maria Gabón commented that 'it is a tragedy but here in Mexico we keep dancing, as we should, there's no other way about it' (*'si es una tragedia pero aqui.en Mexico seguimos bailando, como deveser, no ay deotra'*). In spite of the overwhelmingly supportive nature of most of the comments, the video still received over four thousand 'dislikes', indicating that not all listeners were supportive of the brash attitude promoted in the video.[68]

Música del coronavirus is replete with examples of songs that are unapologetically ecstatic or devil-may-care in their messaging. There might be a global health crisis, but for some musicians this does not call for restraint. It is a time to dance and party in the abrupt absence of work or other routine responsibilities. Unsurprisingly, most of these party songs are in popular, highly danceable styles, and they often feature choreographed music videos. While it is possible for a dance rhythm to be combined with positive social messaging, a mood of carefree (or possibly care-less) festivity generally won out in such compositions. There is a market sensibility to this music as well – why would a dance band not peddle partying as the appropriate reaction to a global crisis?

One such advocate of the good life is dembow and música urbana star Chimbala, best known for his risqué songs celebrating sex, partying, dancing, and related pursuits. He released 'Cuarentena' on 4 May 2020, a few months into the pandemic and at a moment when the lockdown experience was well established among the listening audience. The song covers the frustrations of a playboy protagonist in being trapped indoors with *only* one woman during quarantine. Like most contemporary dembow musicians, a humorous and vibrant video forms a key component aspect of the song. YouTube was the song's initial release platform.[69]

In the video, Chimbala attempts to leave his apartment, desperately trying to text others (presumedly other women) to make connections and escape to the outside world. Despite living in a luxurious environment complete with a rooftop pool, and having time to play video games with his son, Chimbala exudes frustration. Unlike many of the humorous songs set up as parodies of pandemic-era tropes, with toilet paper shortages, cleaning supplies, and exaggerated expressions of fear, Chimbala presents a simple message: quarantine was boring and got in the way of his fun. While Chimbala's case of cabin fever might be extreme in its sexed-up messaging, the core impulse expressed is one of frustration. The coronavirus stymied his core need to be out in the street, just like so many who wanted to go out but were prevented from doing so. With 24.5 million views on YouTube, 'Cuarentena' was among the most watched music videos on Chimbala's heavily subscribed channel, where most of his videos achieve views in the low millions. His paean to remembrances of lost partying was surpassed only by his massively popular party songs filled with twerking women and sports cars, a handful of which received more than fifty million views; one of these, 'El Boom', had gained an impressive 84 million by the end of 2021.[70]

Most other party music purveyors do not even trouble themselves with the domestic situation covered by Chimbala. For example, on 6 August 2020 his fellow dembow stars Jowell y Randy and Kiko El Crazy co-released 'Se Acabó la Cuarentena' ('Quarantine is Over'), as another track fully embracing partying as the appropriate response to a pandemic. The chorus of the song claims that quarantine is over, while in reality the singers are simply over quarantine.[71] With its catchy dembow beat and exuberant lyrics celebrating the end of lockdowns, this dance track quickly became a hit. The song celebrates streets finally full after weeks of sheltering in place, and speaks of the wild parties resulting from all the pent-up energy after several months of lockdown. However, heard in retrospect, and especially after successive waves of variant outbreaks, the song's messaging comes off as decidedly premature. The Dominican Republic's first wave of COVID reached its original peak at the end of July 2020, with over 2012 new cases reported on 26 July alone.[72] One top YouTube commenter noted that 'This song sung victory before the fact' ('*Esta canción cantó victoria antes de tiempo*'), while another warned that 'the boys have returned to their party life, but they don't take note that this situation is getting worse, ugh, please, not like this' ('*ya los muchachos regresaron asu bida pachanga y no hacen caso queeste situacion se empeora ufff porfa asi k no*' [sic]).[73] In spite of such critiques of the song's messaging, 'Se Acabó la Cuarentena' is one of the most successful pandemic-era hits in Latin America, particularly amplified via its extraordinarily popular related TikTok dance challenges, discussed in Chapter One. Not only did the original video accrue more than 29 million views by November 2021, but a video featuring the lyrics uploaded by Steal Lyrics on 28 September 2020 was viewed an additional 16 million times in the year after its upload.[74]

To some listeners, the humorous or party-oriented *música del coronavirus* at the pandemic's outset seemed to contradict the mood of the moment. Some critics argued that only positive messaging or serious songs were appropriate. Agustín Gurza, writing online for the Strachwitz Frontera Collection of Mexican and Mexican American Recordings blog, gave Marco Flores's song a 'dishonorable mention' in his analysis of the early wave of coronavirus songs. 'These guys are having way too much fun, with their brassy banda and flashy red suits, to be bothered with social distancing', Gurza scolded. Noting that Flores dances with the women in the video, Gurza quipped that 'he proceeds to take his sexy dancers for a spin, hand-in-hand. You could say the song is catchy, in more ways than one.' He also pilloried Jose Torres' catchy and amusing 'La Cumbia del Corona Virus', a song which Gurza found to be 'conspiratorial'.[75]

Yet it seems unfair to condemn a well-executed and good-natured song like 'El Coronavirus' as dishonorable when, at its core, it is advocating the joy of life even in the face of tragedy. It does not, as with many other songs and viral social media products, push fear, xenophobia, or misinformation. Many YouTube commenters on *música del coronavirus* uploads express their dismay at the supposed downplaying of the pandemic's severity in comical and pro-partying performances, but a great many others show enthusiasm for these compositions as sources of energy, diversion, and entertainment during a dark and isolating period. It is important to consider the reception of the music as an enhancer of mood or a disappointment alongside the intent of the artists.

Escapism, and even hedonism, is undoubtedly popular, and it can be powerful as well. As Tuan Yi-Fu writes that:

> in redemption of such human foibles are the virtue of self-forgetfulness and the regard of total engagement with a type of music that

be literally meaningless but that to devoted listeners is meaning incarnate – sweatily passionate, coolly intellectual, cozily familiar, galactically remote [...] bound to place and time, yet somehow timeless and universal.[76]

The party-oriented música del coronavirus had a space, and songs and artists created new spaces on their own, 'sweatily passionate, coolly intellectual, cozily familiar, galactically remote' in the enforced timelessness of the pandemic.

A great many examples of música del coronavirus inspired listeners to dance and celebrate despite the challenges of the moment and to ignore the pandemic. Alfredo Sosa's 'El Cobycoby' refuses to accept that everything should be centered on COVID. He would rather party with a large group of women and musicians in a club, or with a scantily clad nurse.[77] Patricio Servin y Su Flamazo Tropical humorously frames the crisis as 'Coronavirus de Amor'.[78] Yorch y Su Carisma urges caution in a brisk cumbia called 'El Corona Virus'.[79] Organización Luz Azul's 'Cumbia del Coronavirus', from the Costa Chica of Oaxaca, Mexico, combines accordion-based upbeat dance rhythms with scenes of a woman dancing alone on a beach.[80] In his 'EL CORONA VIRUS CUMBIA', Fortino Reyna similarly pushes a relentless dance beat while jocularly observing the global spread of the virus and taunting it to pass by Culiacán, the capital of the Mexican state of Sinaloa.[81] These songs, and many others, pushed an outlook that denied the pandemic's power or, at least, resisted it and the notion of the realm of COVID-19 as wholly somber and tragic.

Several early examples of música del coronavirus make reference to the pandemic in the context of carnival celebrations. In many parts of Latin America, especially in diverse settings across the Caribbean, in Andean South America, and in eastern Mexico, these celebrations involve traditional music, parades, costumes, and the inversion of roles. Carnival always takes place the days before Ash Wednesday, the point in the Roman Catholic calendar that signals the beginning of forty days of Lenten fast.[82] Carnival in 2020 was an especially meaningful moment in retrospect: the onset of the pandemic coincided with the start of Lent, and for many, carnival celebrations were the last opportunity for mass gathering and collective revelry for months to come.

Los Hermanos Carrión's 'Carnaval de Coronavirus 2020', from Cañar, Ecuador, encourages attendance at carnival, promotes dancing, and celebrates the annual event as beautiful, all while referencing the coronavirus. Released on 8 February 2020 – quite early in the pandemic and before the lockdowns began in most of the world – this song shows that early attitudes towards the pandemic were often not grave. To Los Hermanos Carrión, the coronavirus was deemed worthy of a joke but not of serious concern compared to the need to celebrate carnival properly. The video for the song shifts between cuts of the musical group – which features an accordionist, two guitarists, and a percussionist playing the Afro-Ecuadorian bombo drum– and clips of carnival celebrations. Dancers in brightly colored dresses pirouette in a public square, and carnival-goers revel in the stands of a large sports arena. Midway through the song, the vocalist proclaims that, in fact, jealousy is even deadlier than the coronavirus. Many of the viewers who commented on the song – a significant number of whom identified themselves as Peruvian – were pleased with it and its message. However, a listener from Ecuador named Roland Travel berated the band. The virus should be taken seriously, he wrote, not made a mockery of while people were dying and families were being isolated into quarantines: 'and with you all singing and dancing, I sincerely think it was stupid to sing this' ('*y ustedes cantando y bailando sinceramente creo que fue algo estupido cantar esto*').[83]

Most groups embraced humor and carnival fun, undeterred by the pandemic. Karuwayra del Perú made fun of the corrosive effects of the lockdowns with a comical song and a series of jokes, but concluded that people still had to stay home and trust that things would improve.[84] A year into the pandemic, in 2021, bands such as Los Truenos marked the carnival with songs wondering at the pandemic's multiple impacts. José Guacho called for Peruvians to celebrate carnival despite COVID-19.[85] Los Reyes Del Austro of Ecuador tried to sidestep the problems of not being to celebrate 'Carnaval Coronavirus' as usual by simply directing attention backward, with a new song presenting visuals of pre-pandemic celebrations with costumes, dancing, and silly string. 'Since this 2021 the Carnival cannot be done as usual', the band wrote in presenting the song in February of that year, explaining that 'here we present a video that we made last year before the pandemic in 2020'.[86] Hermanos Chamba and Eliza Cedeño, a requinto group from Ecuador, sang of the new days of carnival in a slowed-down version of the classic 'Los Días del Carnaval' in January 2022, a rendition which almost feels dragged down by the pandemic era.[87]

The drive to celebrate by simply escaping COVID-19 converged in other songs celebrating various forms of partying and explicitly linking sexuality, humor, and pandemic necessities as central themes. In Miguelito's reggaetón 'Coronavirus', released 20 March 2020, his elaborate plans for sexual intimacy, and that of another couple, are cancelled on account of the pandemic situation.[88] Announcing his sexual intentions while a woman's cries float atop the beat, all attempts to initiate intimacy are humorously disrupted by large, red Xs superimposed over the action. The song's premise is explicitly raunchy and comical, but it also explores the disorientations of the pandemic. Miguelito raps verses about masking up, alone from his living room, dressed as if housebound in a tie-dye long-sleeve t-shirt, and holding a lapdog. The lockdowned house meanwhile rapidly morphs into gender-bending confusion. All four people dance together, performing exaggerated twerking moves with sudden swaps of clothes and roles. Women briefly grind on men in women's clothes; sexual desires are recapitulated in the lyrics and lost in a confusion of swirling, blurred, and distorted superimposed images. Miguelito and his friends don a large rain poncho and a mask, possibly reflecting a confused impulse to protect oneself from outside contagions. By the end of the goofiness, it is the coronavirus which gets the final word.

The impulse to party is framed as a necessary diversion in the face of stress. Humor too can be both distracting and an emotional bulwark in times of collective trauma.[89] Drawing on Elisabeth Kübler-Ross's theory on the five stages of grief, Cynthia and Julia Willett present five components of comedy that redress sorrow: '(1) distracting moments of comic relief; (2) self-humiliating humor; (3) anger infused, truth telling as in satire; (4) the unmasking of defenses and baring of souls; and finally, (5) the catharsis of toxic identities and norms with an ethical plea for a more inclusive society.'[90] From this perspective, relief is only the first function of comedy, followed successively by self-critique, undoing, and the assertion of a deeper truth that perhaps only comedy can access. Musical responses to coronavirus often sought to deepen the comedy beyond merely diverting farce indirectly into these more emotionally compelling and useful functions.

Comedy also opens a more complex and multidimensional understanding of people's experience of both external challenges and internal failings. Conrad Hyers argues that 'if comedy comes from tragedy […] it comes from a reaffirmation of those aspects of the human condition which tragedy has neglected, and therefore as the larger perspective and fuller spirit.'[91] The pandemic moment, while tragic on multiple scales, produced affective impacts beyond its immediate appraisal as a time of death and isolation. It was also a time of unprecedented free time for many, leading to mass boredom. While obviously less grave than illness or death, in many societies boredom in lockdown isolation helped unveil political hypocrisies and accelerate social tensions. All these experiences were fertile ground for compositions that dared, as good comedy does, to move beyond obvious statements of doom and gloom. These songs instead reframed the coronavirus in absurd, hilarious, esoteric, or just plain silly terms that at times doubled as social critique.

Esausin Contigo's 'Canción del coronavirus covid19 teporochitos', uploaded on 23 April 2020, employs a mix of slapstick comedy, wordplay and inuendo, and observational humor in a bewilderingly entertaining example of música del coronavirus.[92] The recorded band, who performed outdoors in front of a historic-looking building in Mexico, oozes visual comedy. Backed up by instrumentation featuring, among other things, a drum kit emblazoned with images of Muppets and a shiny red tuba, the large group of vocalists jumps around and trades verses in rapid-fire succession and often charmingly amateurish delivery. Those who are not shirtless wear mismatched outfits. Beyond the slapstick appeal of the recording, much of the song's comedic value rests on a classic comedic lyrical structure in which each verse uses assumptions based on rhyme schemes and context to lead the listener to believe that it will conclude in a vulgar statement or swear word. Instead, the amusement comes as each line instead ends in a surprisingly innocuous fashion. The song, about 'los teporochitos' ('the little drunks'), takes this idea a step further by ending each line with the first syllable of a vulgar word, only to have another singer steal the microphone and repurpose the syllable to start a new verse. Here are some examples of the substitutive wordplay deployed:

End/Beginning syllable	Expected swear word	Actual word used in following verse
Cul-	Culo (ass)	Culpa (fault)
Ver-	Verga (dick)	Verdad (the truth)
Mier-	Mierda (shit)	Miercoles (Wednesday)
Pende-	Pendejo/a (idiot)	-desde (since)

Wordplay is central to a Mexican phenomenon called albur, which Helena Beristáin describes as 'a manifestation of popular culture that has permeated all stations of society' and which is a *social dialect* [...] of "mexicanismo"'. A skilled alburero can imbue innocuous statements with charged double meanings. Most frequently, these center on vulgar sexual and scatological humor, though importantly, jokes 'are only one context in which the albur is found'. The true power of the albur lies in its usage in daily life, and its ability to generate 'a rearrangement of the stage and a [...] reassignment of roles.'[93]

It is this quality that elevates the albur out of the realm of adolescent dirty jokes and renders the phenomenon linguistically interesting and socially enticing. Mexican journalist Fernando Diez deo Urdanivia celebrates albur as 'creating a real scenario that only the initiated (Mexicans) perceive, understand, enjoy, and to which [only they] are able to respond so that it may be prolonged.'[94] The pandemic moment is marked by both uncertainty and occasionally forced restraint. Through its manifestation in coronavirus music, the subversive wordplay of albur allows the performer to forge a connection with the audience that both entertains and inverts, simultaneously giving listeners a reason to chuckle and a way to look through the absurdity of their experience.

Jorge Luis Huaman Arroyo's April 2020 release of 'HUAYNO DEL COVID-19' also takes a humorous approach. This song, a huayno-influenced technocumbia, begins with a shouted introduction vulgarly affronting those who do not observe social distancing, and continues into an autotuned chorus section where the singer redirects his profane put-downs toward the virus itself. Sound effects of pitch-altered laughter tracks are spliced in at varying intervals, and the video, which mostly features the vocalist and several costumed performers dancing in front of mountain landscapes, features a banner stating 'QUEDATE EN CASA' at the top of the screen and 'CONCHATU' at the bottom, a euphemistic shorthand for a common South American insult *la concha de tu madre*, which translates literally as 'your mother's shell', or more directly and vulgarly, 'your mother's cunt'.[95] Coronavirus songs are often similarly profane, in many cases calling the virus a shit, a bastard, a fucker, a motherfucker, and other colloquial epitaphs. In this case, the profanity seems directed at both the virus and the whole range of feelings and experiences produced by the pandemic.

Several examples of humorous coronavirus songs are little more than short sketches, often performed in silly voices or with unusual pretexts. Chevillo's 'Vete ya pinche coronavirus' ('Go away fucking coronavirus'), uploaded on 23 April 2020, is a 23-second, three-line ditty sung in a deliberately weird voice by a goateed man wearing a large sombrero.[96] A month later, Roger Hauteville posted 'La canción del Coronavirus', a 12-second video of a shower curtain where the singer is heard belting out a short stanza in a hilariously exaggerated nasal voice. While the content of the verse is funny in itself – he sings about how being sick with coronavirus has afforded him license to not bathe – the slapstick delivery and random spontaneity of the video afford it a mesmerizing lunacy. This music video had a mere 25 views by January 2022, but that Hauteville took the time to write, record, and upload it speaks to the comic urgency of the pandemic moment.[97]

While political satire is not a principal theme in música del coronavirus, some songs do draw upon humor and slapstick to critique the ways governments have responded to the pandemic. 'LA CANCIÓN DEL CORONAVIRUS ft. El Chasky Pum', uploaded by channel maritobaracus on 27 May 2020, explicitly pokes fun at heads of state including Donald Trump, Xi Jinping, Emmanuel Macron, and Vladimir Putin. The video itself cuts between scenes of the leaders talking. These clips are overdubbed by a singer who performs verses from the supposed perspective of each world leader, drawing from popular tropes such as Trump's vanity and Putin's strongman persona. He also caricatures their voices by noticeably mispronouncing Spanish words when dubbing for Trump and opting for a frog-like warble for Xi. In this video, venerated heads of state are portrayed as incompetent buffoons whose personal shortcomings are manifest in their attitudes toward the pandemic. YouTube user Producciones Ola K Mira commented that '[a]t least this song takes away my anxiety about coronavirus' ('*Al menos esta canción se me quita la ansiedad del coronavirus*'), reflecting the power of comedy to act as an emotional balm. Other commenters are more explicit about making note of the song's political satire. Inés Castellano observed that, in the words of Trump, 'I'll cure this virus with a big wall' ('*a este virus lo curo con un gran muro*'), while JAW BOY ironically assured other viewers to not worry, since the virus 'only affects black people and homosexuals' ('*solo le da a los negro y homosexuales*').[98]

In spite of comedy's wide net for expressing attitudes toward the pandemic moment, it only describes some of the multitudinous emotive and sentimental responses to the coronavirus crisis. Like humor, religious music also mediated affective pandemic-era experiences and reflected the ways local artists approached questions of enclosure, anxiety, death, and final judgment.

Dios Nos Protegerá: Christian Appraisals of COVID-19 Through Song

One detail that stands out in the live video of 'El Corrido del Coronavirus' recorded by the brothers Alan and Roberto Lara Meza is their baseball caps. Both caps are embroidered with the phrase 'Y Cristo Viveee' ('And Christ Lives'), punctuating the dominant religious theme of the song that brought them quite a bit of attention on both sides of the border. The pitch for this professionally promoted song was that it 'is a call for calm, community, faith and brotherhood'.[99]

Their stage name as a family band is Alan y Roberto, and they play sierreño music, a style of regional Mexican music featuring a 12-string guitar called a requinto along with a six-string guitar and occasionally other instruments. They sing in a distinctive, dragging nasal twang, underscoring the rustic, self-described 'vieja escuela' ('old school') character of the music. Originally from a small town of approximately three thousand called El Poblado 7 (a town also called variously 'Alfonso G. Calderón' or 'La Villa Gustavo Díaz Ordaz'), in Sinaloa, Mexico, the brothers today write and perform out of Arizona. Their religious-themed topical song 'El Corrido del Coronavirus' got a great deal of attention in the press, propelled mostly by a feature from the California-based alternative media site *L.A. Taco*.[100]

Alan y Roberto emerged as popular performers with a slightly different emphasis. They are a socially conscious duo who expand some of the usual topics of sierreño (a genre which is often dominated by ballads about drug trafficking called narcocorridos) to write songs about immigrant workers to the United States, farmworkers, and other themes, including música del coronavirus. In addition to their initial corrido touching on the subject, they produced a follow-up track called 'El Piscador', written in honor of the agricultural workers who harvested food during the COVID-19 pandemic.[101]

'El Corrido del Coronavirus' stands out because of the way it weaves religious themes in with common aspects of música del coronavirus, such as shortages, fear, and methods of warding off viral infection. The brothers released the song as music videos twice in March 2020. In the first video, the brothers perform sitting in a studio, reading the lyrics from smartphones, accompanied only by a requinto. The video was clearly recorded soon after the song's composition and released with haste to capture and exploit the moment, as was done by many other performers. The brothers placed a package of toilet paper along with a can of Lysol in the frame. Alan introduces the song in the name of God before they start singing.[102] The more widely known version was released four days later, live in the studio, with a requinto, a tololoche (a Mexican variant of the upright bass) and the brothers singing. Alan wears his religious-themed cap in both videos, though it does not appear in their numerous other non-coronavirus themed videos, where he favors a sombrero tejano.

In 'El Corrido del Coronavirus' the duo encourage family togetherness and social unity. Their song promises that God will solve the problem. In the live video for the song, Alan points to his hat to underscore the message: Christ lives. The description of the song is purely religious, quoting Psalm 42:5. It shouts the message in in all-capital letters: 'DO NOT ALLOW THE ANGUISH AND WORRY/THEY STEAL YOUR PEACE. PUT YOUR TRUST IN GOD. BECAUSE/WHY WOULD I WORRY?/I WILL PUT MY HOPE IN GOD/AND I WILL STILL PRAISE HIM. HE IS WHO SAVES ME, HE IS MY GOD!'[103]

'El Corrido del Coronavirus' was, at best, a moderate success. All told, the three posted versions on YouTube had garnered approximately 18,000 views by the end of 2021, a relatively modest count for a coronavirus song written in a musical style with a large commercial and popular following. Interestingly, despite the extensive press attention given to this song and to Alan y Roberto as performers, no news story mentions the song's strong religious subtheme.[104] It is unclear why the plainly religious character of the song is not noted.

A large subset of música del coronavirus considers the pandemic moment from Christian perspectives. Like Christianity itself, these songs express an enormous range of emotions, perspectives, and outlooks on the relationship between God, humankind, and the virus. As Matthew Wade and Maria Hynes have argued, a crucial question for the 'geography of religion' concerns the process by which the spiritual comes 'to be expressed and conveyed, particularly in an area of human life where words are presumably an inadequate way of expressing feeling', and here the concept of affect offers potentially rich insights.'[105] In some examples of música cristiana del coronavirus, the messaging is didactic and straightforward, encouraging believers to follow sanitary protocols as a way to care for one's neighbor and to carry out God's will. In contrast, other songs direct focus away from the virus and toward the general theme of grappling with human sin, with some suggesting that the pandemic is a sign of the apocalypse and of Christ's impending return to Earth.

Catholicism has been a defining component in Latin America's cultural, economic, and political development for over five hundred years. The expressive cultural products of ecclesiastical devotion are inseparable from many Latin American artforms, including music.[106] Efforts such as inculturation theology have deepened religious connections to vernacular musics as well: 'The emphasis is more than stylistic – the point of inculturation theology [...] is to allow the practice of Catholicism to be informed and shaped by local cultures, not just inflected by them', observes Stephen Selka.[107] Over the past half-century, Latin America has undergone a massive religious transformation. In the early 1970s, only one out of ten Latin Americans did not identify as Catholic; by the 2010s, this proportion had grown to one in three.[108] This is largely due to the explosive growth of evangelical Protestantism in the region. As a result, as Daniel H. Levine notes, 'the public face of religion and the ways in which religion is present in the public sphere have been utterly transformed.'[109] One prime example of the intersection of a rising Latin American Protestantism, regional politics, and the music industry can be found in the success of Fabricio Alvarado Muñoz, a Pentecostal balladeer from Costa Rica who was a runner-up in his country's 2018 presidential election.[110]

This shift signaled a series of wider social and cultural transformations, many of which were expressed in música del coronavirus written from avowedly Christian perspectives. Religious musical responses tracked along with the theological, cultural, and ideological transformations and struggles occurring in often dramatic fashion across the region. Latin America is the cradle of liberation theology, a Catholic religious ideology whose emphasis on a 'preferential option for the poor' is often invoked by global public health activists within the Church, particularly in the context of famine relief and AIDS prevention.[111] In the era of COVID-19, one study of liberation theology from the Philippines highlights how 'a patchwork of efforts by different religious congregations, parishes of different dioceses, [and] nonprofit foundations of the Catholic Church [...] [arose] to combat the havoc of the pandemic'.[112]

At the same time, however, Protestant voters in Latin America have catalyzed a rightward turn in social policy in Colombia, Brazil, Mexico, and Central American countries.[113] Conservative social and bioethical policies in these areas reflect evangelical positions on stem cell research, LGBTQ rights, abortion, and the proper role of government in the administration of sexual education and healthcare services. Some Protestant groups are also skeptical of the need for or efficacy of medical treatment in general. Some evangelical thought 'asserts that God is in control and that there is a greater meaning or purpose in illness of which we may not be aware', and cautions 'against a form of idolatry that invests physicians and medical interventions with more power than they have'.[114] Likewise, in Pentecostal thought, disaster is often framed favorably as a potential sign of the return of Christ to Earth and the End Times.

These competing tendencies – engaged acts of social responsibility, education, and behavioral encouragement to prevent the spread of disease versus relinquishing authority to God in the face of pestilence – are evident in examples of música cristiana del coronavirus. These religious-oriented responses to the pandemic moment highlight the paternalistic mode of the institutional Church, assert the need for faith-based solidarity in a moment of crisis, or take a more deterministic approach in treating the virus as a repercussion of sin or as a harbinger of Armageddon.

One clear expression of Catholic música del coronavirus comes from Father Sergio Valverde, a parish priest in Alajuela, Costa Rica, who sung a modified version of 'Sopa de Caracol' ('Conch Soup'). This song is a dance tune originally sung in the Garifuna language, and was made popular in 1991 by a Honduran group called Banda Blanca. In spite of the song's origins in a minority community of one of Latin America's smallest countries, it became a hit across the continent. The video Valverde made for the song features a MIDI-generated backing track with the masked and robed priest singing lyrics about COVID protocols from behind the pulpit. Periodically throughout the clip, Valverde encourages the audience to follow the protocols more enthusiastically, and he occasionally goads parishioners for not properly demonstrating the correct way to wear a mask.[115]

Valverde, whose COVID-cautious lyrics earned him some positive media attention, is also known as the director of Las Obras del Espiritu Santo, a faith-based organization dedicated to providing social services to underserved and orphaned youth. Valverde observed that 'the issue of COVID is affecting the whole world, [...] as a priest I see so many people suffering, sick, in pain; people who do not have work and are dying of hunger, and I wanted to contribute a little something.'[116] Pilo Tejada, a founding member of Banda Blanca and the author of the Spanish-language interpretation of 'Sopa de Caracol', took note of Valverde's reimagining of the song and claimed to be collaborating with the priest on a professional recording of the COVID-oriented rendition.[117]

However, the overwhelming majority of música cristiana del coronavirus has been produced by non-Catholic artists, possibly because of the diversity of approaches to worship and musical performance within various Protestant denominations. Ideological diversity among decentralized Protestant churches also produced a wide array of affective sacred responses. One of the least controversial and most widely viewed recordings of a Coronavirus-inspired song by a Christian artist was 'Lo Que Este Virus Me Enseñó' ('What this Virus Taught Me'), by Puerto Rican pastor and songwriter Samuel Hernandez. This balada cristiana begins with a gentle piano introduction atop a warm bed of synthesized strings, as the video shows clips of people standing on their balconies, waving to each other from across the street, and performing mundane tasks in their homes. The video displays a mix of urban, rural, and suburban settings, but most of the individuals are portrayed as members of middle-class nuclear families. In his verses, Hernandez laments the harm and inconvenience that the pandemic has wrought, while acknowledging that it opened up opportunities to engage in activities that are typically sacrificed in the rush of life, such as savoring one's morning coffee, spending quality time with family, and engaging in Bible study.[118] Hernandez's appraisal of the pandemic moment is relatively neutral; he bemoans the damage caused by the virus but also paints a romantic picture of the unexpected treasures of a life slowed down, and the supposed closeness to God that such a reduction of pace might afford to a good Christian. The singer steers clear of actually discussing the disease itself, treating the pandemic from the perspective of a person who, though in quarantine, feels relatively protected. The smooth vocal style, slick production, pensive lyrics, and uplifting melody culminate in a product that is cathartic, calming, and overall non-threatening.

Many examples of the Christian coronavirus genre prominently feature stylistic elements of hip hop, such as rapped verses, street-style music videos, and backbeat-heavy grooves. Josef Sorett notes that Christian hip hop is 'a window into the intersections of religion, race, and media' and discusses how the genre can serve either to bridge or define denominational divisions, depending on the theological intentions of the rapper.[119] Hip hop as both a global youth culture and transnational musical genre is also understood to link, and to mediate, individual searches for identity and social space in ways congruent to religious seeking or other varieties of affective experience. As explained by Igor Johannsen, 'Hip Hop today accommodates all social, ethnic, religious and political affiliations [...]. The spatial dimension of Hip Hop culture draws together local and global, particular and universal.'[120]

Hip hop is communitarian-oriented music even in a secular sense, a connection long observed in rap latino.[121] The local scenes which develop also serve, in the framing of Marcyliena Morgan and Dionne Bennett, as cultural communities as well as 'communit[ies] of imagination'. Hip-hop is a global, transnational movement built upon locally contingent community coherence and connectivity: 'Its artistic practices are not merely part of its culture; rather, they are the central, driving force that defines and sustains it.'[122] Joseph Winters has observed that 'if complexity, contradiction, and ambiguity are qualities that define the topography of hip hop, it makes sense that these terms have become mantras in the emergent literature on religion and hip hop.'[123] Robert Tinajero finds a strong connection between hip-hop and religion on the basis of 'struggle and marginalization.'[124]

Contingent and communitarian affect is apparent in Christian-themed música del coronavirus. Argentinian rapper Eiem's 'Desafio COVID' ('The COVID Challenge') presents a principally unifying and community-oriented message. The verses take on an elegiac tone as he speaks to the shared experience of unexpected loss and despair triggered by the pandemic.[125] Doble B draws from a similar thematic well for his verses on 'Ten Misericordia' ('Have Mercy'), though with a more positive, dance-forward beat behind his rapping. An entire verse is dedicated to asking God to bestow mercy and relief on a long list of countries, a global community of nations: Korea, China, Japan, Spain, Italy, Ecuador, Canada, England, Australia, Syria, Switzerland, Germany, the United Arab Emirates, France, Cuba, the United States, Denmark, Slovenia, Argentina, Honduras, Venezuela, Bolivia, and El Salvador. He later adds a general plea for all the countries on Earth.[126] Honduran GD El Catracho assures listeners to his '(COVID-19)(coronavirus) rap triste' that God is in control.[127]

In July 2020, Planethelio Records of Ecuador produced a deeply communitarian song called 'Nos Levantaremos' ('We Will Rise Up'), sung by a collaborative supergroup that included Marqués, Au-D, Juan Fernando Velasco, Daniel Betancourth, Maykel, Gianpiero, Gerardo Mejia, Daniel Paez, Israel Brito, Paulina Tamayo, Do Blanco, Nikki Mackliff, Los Intrepidos, and Camila Rosero. The song was dedicated, according to its description, to the idea that the 'voice of my people is the voice of God' (*La voz de mi pueblo es la voz de Dios*). The song is designed to inspire community feeling across the regions, peoples, and landscapes of Ecuador and portrays working peoples as heroes in the face of the pandemic, all under the guidance and power of God. Together under God, the song promises, the people will rise to recovery and the pandemic will pass.[128]

Religious music serves multiple purposes, from ministering to a particular flock to evangelizing the unsaved, to capitalizing on an open market for new adherents. These aims are not mutually exclusive, and crises like the pandemic moment offer new opportunities to share religious messages. Music was a principal avenue of this effort to exploit fear over the virus and offer a facile, religious solution. Grupo Fortaleza, from Ocaña, Colombia, wrote a song detailing the multiple political, moral, and medical failings of the world, describing bloodshed, abortion, rape, and a health crisis so extensive that bodies had to be burnt in the streets. The crisis and the horror of the pandemic moment was as terrible as in the days of Noah. They also assured their listeners, though, that Jesus would lead people through the coming storm.[129] In January 2022 an enthusiastic Pentecostal chorus posted by a Christian channel called Josias Pluas Studio Productions promised, as the title stated, that the 'omnicron [variant] is leaving because Jehovah arrived' (*SE VA EL OMICRON PORQUE LLEGO JEHOVÁ*). The song provoked a lot of discussion about its message and many favorable comments, including one from a Mexican listener named Tigre Mayor who wrote, profanely, 'I'm not a Jehovah's Witness but I admit that this is a fucking hit, greetings from Nuevo León' (*no soy testigo de jehova pero admito que ese es un pinche rolon, saludos desde nuevo leon*).[130]

One of the most alternatively hilarious and terrifying songs that made the same point was originally posted in Portuguese by Caminhos da Fé (Walk of Faith), and later reposted in Spanish as Luque Luuque Iri's animated 'CORONAVIRUS //CANCION CRISTIANA'. The lyrics are drawn from 2 Chronicles 7:14 ('If my people, who are called by my name, will humble themselves and pray and seek my face and turn from their wicked ways, then I will hear from heaven, and I will forgive their sin and will heal their land') and Zechariah 2 (a vision of God's restoration of Jerusalem). The biblical verses are set to a piano, synthesizer and electronic drums selection from 'Requiem for A Tower', the reorchestrated arrangement of Clint Mansell's *Lux Aeterna*.[131] In the video the coronavirus is a disembodied, yellow-eyed, red-bodied horror with hands and feet and (one glimpses) black horns. It has a head but no body. The coronavirus walks down a suburban street while people from all walks of life submissively bow down to it. The virus forces a series of people to kneel: a nurse, a sheik, the Incredible Hulk, Superman, Batman, Super Saiyan Blue Goku, a police officer, a worker, and what appears to be a punk rocker. It finally reaches a young child, who stops the virus by kneeling in the opposite direction and praying, which forces the terrifying virus to smile a toothy grin. Jesus then appears, apparently at the boy's behest, and vanquishes the virus, which at this point clearly also becomes the devil, with visible black horns. The coronavirus descends into the ground, flaming. The music video for 'CORONAVIRUS //CANCION CRISTIANA' appeared in many social media formats set to other songs as well and remixed. It also circulated widely on Facebook and on other social media sites.[132]

Most música cristiana del coronavirus did not indulge in this type of campiness, but all maintained a focus on mediating its message for its target audiences or core adherents. Some of the most intriguing Christian appraisals of coronavirus through song sidestepped the commonplace mainstream secular narratives that prioritized sanitary measures, collective action, and hope in a public-health-oriented solution to the crisis. These songs, alternatively, evoked the terrors of the End Times.

An early contribution to the body of apocalyptic música del coronavirus was a merengue by Julio Bardonado, an Afro-Dominican Pentecostal preacher and performer.[133] In the original live video of the song, uploaded on 9 March 2020, Bardonado is seen in a revivalist setting, standing on an outdoor stadium stage before a crowd of onlookers. A banner behind him features an enormous illustration of a dove, the symbol of the Holy Spirit in Christian iconography.[134] He opens by repeatedly citing Matthew 24:7, a fiery Gospel passage promising 'there shall be famines, and pestilences, and earthquakes, in diverse places.'[135] Rather than lamenting the coronavirus or encouraging people to act to limit its impact, the singer points to its inevitability as a potential harbinger of the Second Coming. Pentecostal Christianity is deeply linked to millenarian theorizations of the imminency of the End Times, and proselytizers such as Bardonado often articulate their eagerness to reach the Kingdom of God by exhibiting enthusiasm over cataclysmic occurrences that, to non-believers, seem tragic and inexplicably unfair.[136] Bardonado's raspy shouts and exaggerated body movements can be interpreted as theatrical marks of staged showmanship, or conversely as the spiritual possession of a true believer. Or both.

Evangelical musicians followed a different path. Mexican rapper G Low's 'Estoy Infectado' ('I'm Infected') is another example of Christian rap addressing the pandemic moment, but from a very different theological perspective. Rather than direct attention at the pandemic, G Low argues in his verses that the true virus is sin, and that COVID-19 is a passing symptom of humankind's fall. In the video's description, the rapper writes that

> these days we are suffering from the coronavirus, it is a test that plagues the world, but there is a much stronger virus, it is called SIN, that makes humanity live in the worst possible condition and nobody cares. 'Estoy Infectado' tells us about this virus more dangerous than the coronavirus and in turn about the antidote that is only found in the blood of Jesus Christ.

In the video, G Low raps on the side of a highway in a checkered sweatshirt and New York Yankees cap. He bemoans how facemasks will not save humankind from our sinful nature, and how COVID is a distraction from our true predicament. The music video is simple but professionally produced. The comments are full of supportive statements which signal its emotive power. Pepe Cantarell comments that 'I'm infected, but Christ is the cure.' Jonathan Olvera notes that 'we know that sin is more deadly than the Coronavirus', and Nayelli Georgina affirms the belief echoed in the rap's second verse that 'the only cure we need is to believe in the redemption of man by Jesus' crucifixion, there is no other medicine.'[137]

This approach of fusing strident messaging with hip-hop rhythm is powerful. Christina Zanfagna calls this a religious version of 'hustling', grounded in the authenticity that performance provides. As she archly puts it, religious-oriented musicians face the 'everyday struggles to balance the need for a paycheck with winning the big payback of life everlasting'. More seriously, she observes that 'gospel hip hop exists in a multidimensional configuration of social space, where the everyday activities of art, commerce, and spirituality often interact in playful indistinction.'[138] This hustling, or what can be seen as religious product marketing during the pandemic, is related to the affective organization of cultural power. Many forms of media, particularly social media and online spaces of mediated interaction like musical upload sites, are tightly imbricated in the process of shaping and utilizing cultural power to this end. As Trammel writes in his study of media texts and Christian marketing efforts: 'If religious texts inform how audiences understand their faith, then the marketing campaigns that project values about those texts can inform how consumers understand and engage with their faith. [...] The marketing not only sells a "solution" to the consumers' problem; it also sells the "problem."'[139]

While the comments responding to G Low's self-serious rapping are generally supportive, other examples of Christianity-tinged música del coronavirus received less favorable responses from listeners. One example can be seen in the comments section of Bolivian rock band Saxoman y los Casanovas' coronavirus song, which despite its poor execution still had achieved an impressive 850,000 views two years after its 5 March 2020 upload.[140] In their video, the masked-up trio appear in white suits, playing electric guitar, drums, and electric bass, as animated coronaviruses swirl in the background. The video cuts to cityscapes overlaid with animated bats, tombstones, and topsy-turvy flying coronaviruses. Suddenly Jesus himself leads an airborne, horsebacked army through the clouds to defeat the coronavirus.[141] The lead singer and guitarist becomes empowered to zap viruses of increasing menace and size with laser hands, which he does while soloing continuously for minutes on his electric guitar. Sometimes he solos behind his back while still vanquishing viruses.

It is difficult to tell if the song is an elaborate joke or if its absurd comedy is unintentional. The music and religious lyrics are delivered with gravity, but some of the unintentional humor derives from the rather amateurish playing, with harsh and thin guitar tones, off-kilter drumming, and a vocalist who consistently struggles to hit the high notes of the melody. Yet the composer, Americo Estevez Roman, certainly intended the song to be taken seriously. He warned in a written dedication that 'the only cure to eradicate the Coronavirus is God and the Holy Spirit, we must pray and have faith since He is Almighty, King of Kings and our savior' (*'la unica cura para erradicar el Coronavirus es Dios y ekl Espirito Santo, tenermous que orar y tener Fé ya que Él es Todopoderoso, Reye de Reyes y nuestro salvador'*).[142]

Despite singing about the ways in which the Holy Spirit and belief in Christ will save the world from the coronavirus, neither the style of the video nor the comments posted below it reflect the widely embraced and seemingly earnest sincerity of G Low. 'CORONAVIRUS – SAXOMAN Y LOS CASANOVAS' listeners do not prevaricate in making fun of the video; in fact, their comments are almost as comical as the video itself. Jesse M. writes that 'this song cured me of Coronavirus, but it gave me cancer', and Lean Riccio says that 'the Coronavirus committed suicide [after hearing this song].' Other comments ironically applaud the composition as a 'true work of art' and 'the sign of the great artistic reawakening after COVID-19', or, as one commenter puts it, 'better than Mozart, better than the Beatles, this is the finest musical composition in the history of humanity.'[143] Very few comments addressed the religious overtones of the lyrics, expressed spiritual longings, or spoke of coronavirus. Instead, commentators focused on the comedy of the performance and video, and the irreverent religious message was rendered irrelevant.

Christian musicians adopted a wide affective range to reflect on the meaning and proper response to the pandemic moment. Their music, rooted in particularistic understandings of appropriate religious response to an unprecedented situation which scrambled lives as well as moral certainties, harnessed sound and rhythm to reach emotional connection, save souls, and, in some cases, unintentionally provide some welcome laughs.

'Desde mi Humilde Cuartito Hasta el Mundo Entero': Songs from the Quarantined Individual

Few songs match the emotionally open rendering of 'La canción del coronavirus', written and sung by Hermes Velasco and accompanied by his brother Julio Velasco on guitarra puntera (similar to a requinto), a person named Carlos on guitar and a man identified as 'El Negro Sabrosón' playing guacharaca. The video is introduced as a reunion of brothers and old friends jamming, with good-natured introductions from Velasco. The men sing of the coming of the virus from China, the need to get through the pandemic by changing behavior, and family connections. Velasco sends shout-outs to his family. The upload, poorly shot in a living room on a blurry video, is played with evident gusto and spirit, all four men joining in with signing for each repetitive chorus. With only 40 views after more two years on YouTube, the video stands as a highly personal musical statement of 'a small reunion', as Veslaco introduces the gathering. It is a private moment playing an original song that the viewer is possibly not even meant to see or hear. 'La canción del coronavirus' is the only video uploaded by the channel owner, Andrea Restrepo Velasquez, whose only subscriber is one of the authors of this book.[144]

This chapter has explored dozens of examples of música del coronavirus that span immense ranges of emotion, ideology, and mediated outlooks on the pandemic moment. These songs each present specific approaches to production, composition, and video accompaniment. It might be tempting to afford attention to the glossiest, most professional, and widely viewed examples, or to argue that the most popular songs are likewise the most consequential. Alternatively, however, many of the most affectively striking examples of música del coronavirus are those which feature amateur performers like the Velasco brothers and their friends, often playing alone and captured in a bedroom, living room, or workplace. Such videos, which are often unedited, short, and low in resolution, exemplify the dualistic experiences of unprecedented solitude and connectivity at the onset of the global pandemic. In these videos, lay musicians employ smartphone cameras, as well as teleconferencing headsets and webcams, to record compositions that address the peculiarity of the pandemic moment with a direct and often arresting immediacy and open emotional expression.

Cellphone recordings, tight framings, and direct connections force a listener to grapple with the purposefulness of the artists directly. The fortuity of informal recordings of música del coronavirus uploaded to YouTube lends them their powerful, affective hue. Reporting from distinct locales, recording from their homes and workplaces and united by a global crisis, solo musicians cry out into their devices verses of warning, concern, and encouragement, afterwards uploading their creations to YouTube often seemingly without any intention of finding an audience. These range from an unnamed solo vihuela player in Huautla de Jiménez, Oaxaca, to solo bajo quinto player Humberto Rodriguez, to an unnamed solo forró accordion player in Brazil. Solo guitarist Silvino Encarnación Flores delivered his original composition on the beach in Guerrrero, Mexico. Miguel Nagles played solo cuatro in Bogotá, uploading only one video on his channel to address the virus.[145] There are thousands of other examples of solo performers on almost every possible instrument imaginable. While the musical styles and poetic references differ vastly depending on the location and tastes of the performer, the modalities of self-expression via intimate uploads, and many of the music's themes, are similar.

A comparable self-contained feeling is relayed in El Puma del Huascarán's solo performance on 20 April 2020 of a song written by Zenobio Cruz called 'El Huayno del Coronavirus'. El Puma sits on a couch alone, playing a capoed guitar in a lively, two-finger up-picked style. His guitar has double-course strings on the treble strings, and a detuned bass string. He plays looking largely at his hand while singing, tightlipped, of the coronavirus having arrived in Peru and bringing sadness to everybody in the country. As in many such videos, his song comments on the origins of the coronavirus and its spread around the world as much as it opines about the sadness and fear that it produces, and it suggests ways to stay safe by staying home and washing hands. But it is his playing and singing, delivered in this powerful solo performance with a huayno driven by the relentless up-picking and alternating bass line, that underscore the message of personal resistance and psychological fortitude.[146]

Similar feelings and musical confidence are relayed in solo harp performances by Rusmell Espinoza, Michael Sedano, and Julio Peñares, all of whom interpret their pieces with verve in private, intimate settings. As in the case of El Puma del Huascarán, all emphasize the instrumental breaks to deliver their messages. Espinoza plays a sprightly song called 'Primicia @2020', released 23 March 2020, which repeatedly encourages listeners to stay at home and gives other basic health advice in between vigorously plucked sections. His is a rare performance, involving another person filming and moving the camera around his harp.[147]

Peñares released his song 'Coronavirus COVID-19 LA canción en huayno en arpa' twice, in March and April 2020, as part of his channel of harp videos. His first video was shot on a vertical phone camera, with a border of coronavirus images bracketing the image. The second recording was filmed with 'inShot' in a tight shot in a corner of a room by a door. Peñares plays and sings with a frozen grin as he describes the reality of the coronavirus and the challenges of the pandemic. He emphasizes the bass as he repetitively calls for his fellow Peruvians to be strong. His playing increases in intensity and volume, as direct and personal a call as any verse. By the end of the song he is smiling and dancing.[148]

In contrast, in April 2020 Macuri y su arpa (Macuri and his harp) delivered a far more somber song in his solo harp performance of 'huayno coronavirus con arpa'. Seated wearing a salmon-colored shirt, and with the camera tightly focused on him, Macuri plays briskly while exuding not swagger, but serious intensity. He warns Peruvians to be careful around the virus, which has brought so much sadness and death.[149] Macuri also released another coronavirus song, playing faster and with greater forcefulness in a solo session, a month later, in May 2020. In this song, 'Let's fight coronavirus' (*luchemos contra el coronavirus*') he delivers an assertive and strident message with the harp directly echoing the cadence of each sung line. The music here punctuates the song in a way missing from the earlier huayno and creates a feeling of agency and resistance that his earlier song sidestepped. This time Macuri plays longer as well, the music forcefully pushing forward as a source of sustenance.¹⁵⁰

A similar set of solo music comes in a connected series of pieces by solo Argentinian guitarists playing to décimas (ten-line poetic verses) about quarantine and the need for communal solidarity and to stay indoors, all written by Santiago Porro. Each verse is played by a different guitarist performing alone in their own spaces, with startlingly different approaches to the material. The narrow cellphone framing and tiny glimpses of personal spaces add to the feeling of isolation and of the need to take the virus seriously, which the verses declare. The video begins with a section played and sung fiercely by Catherine Vergnes, who sits squarely in front of the cellphone camera and filling the frame. The composition's energy fills the available space. Her seriousness contrasts with Porro's own contribution, which is captured in a low-resolution recording. His décima takes a light tone despite positing the same message of COVID safety. Next, Araceli Arguello slows down and softens the song, while Joaquin Barreti steps outside and plays in a doorway. Clementina Sartori sits in a living room and reintroduces stridency into the song. Ricardo Berha ends with a breathy and slightly high-pitched approach to the consistently self-serious verses. This video, unlike so many solo performances with tiny audiences below a hundred, has gained a large audience of 176,000 views since it was uploaded in April 2020.¹⁵¹

There are other isolated artists singing into their own cameras as rather overt, although not always crude, attempts at relevance and at gaining attention. An unnamed son jarocho harpist uploaded a series of videos of himself accompanying his own live improvised verses on a narrow cellphone frame on 20 March 2020 – a rather incredible effort which had received only forty views two years later.¹⁵² In mid-March 2020 a shaky cellphone caught the energetic playing of an unnamed Argentinian guitarist from Córdoba singing of the basic ways to stay safe in the pandemic.¹⁵³ Amateur guitarist and relatively popular YouTuber Angelines Navarro Ciordia posted dozens of videos of herself playing guitar and singing songs dedicated, with a broad and welcoming smile and self-effacing commentary, to the return of older times after the coronavirus.¹⁵⁴ Hard Fishing Peru released an energetic, comical solo acoustic guitar piece 'al esito Cajamarca' about the quarantine.¹⁵⁵ In another video, Argentinian Hector Figueredo sits on a bed in a small room and plays an R & B-influenced song on an amplified acoustic guitar. He blows on a harmonica held in a rack on his neck into a microphone and sings in a wavering voice about the origin of the virus in China and its arrival in Argentina, all filmed with a shaky and obviously handheld camera. The song was uploaded on 26 March 2020 as the only video on Figueredo's channel, which was started on the same day. It had been viewed barely a hundred times two years later. His piece, 'Corona Virus-Cancion Con Guitarra y Armonica', is a small but emotionally laden musical intervention which captured a singular moment in a highly personal space and shared it with an uncaring world.¹⁵⁶ On 21 March

2020, early in the pandemic, Javier Moreno Olivares sang, seemingly enjoyably, of the challenges of the pandemic and the unity of life while sitting on his couch, with his child playing next to him. This song had gained only 75 views after two years on YouTube.[157] Like Figueredo's music and that of so many others, the emotional space represented by the song's creation and delivery, and thereafter secured virtually by the upload, is arguably as important as any possible reception.

The teleconferencing headset, an object that achieved central symbolic value during the pandemic moment as people worked from home, frequently makes an appearance in personal videos. Venezuelan Gustavo Cholango offered a 48-second-long ditty about the onset of the pandemic.[158] In the short video, he plays a markedly danceable rhythm on the cuatro, a four-stringed relative of the guitar, and sings into a headset. His setup evokes a home office rather than a home studio, and the unedited video begins and ends with the performer visibly adjusting his webcam and microphone. Yet the song itself, which covers the standard lyrical themes of staying home, using facemasks, and acknowledging the collective fear of the pandemic moment, is performed with gusto and features a thoughtfully concise structure.

Many solo recordings of música del coronavirus performed in regionally specific styles were brought to the world by the easy reach of cellphones, which captured otherwise largely ephemeral moments. A Colombian-Ecuadorian singer-songwriter named Ángel Alvarado gained a good deal of social media attention with his improvised solo guitar song about the virus. In an interview, the hitherto-unknown street performer expressed happiness that the song had brought him a worldwide audience on account of the positive messaging it created.[159] There are a great many different versions of the song on various channels. Numerous news reports reveal groups of people, often dozens at a time, capturing him singing the song on their own phones. Ironically, early in the pandemic, there was no social distancing between the people filming. The market in which Alvarado sang in the video was packed. Likewise, Sonia Montalvo played harp on a street in Peru, also regaling crowds with tales of the virus.[160] Angel Cruz uploaded an unnamed individual playing a solo guitar in 'La cancion del coronavirus Jarocho', although the religious song he sings was played neither in a jarocho style or on a jarocho instrument. The musician, sitting outside a workshop in front of a battered air tank, plays an acoustic guitar barely held together by a piece of wire stretched across its lower bout. The song was posted in January 2021, and by year later had received a scant 36 views.[161] Roberto Sepúlveda's short 'Cueca del coronavirus!' shows the lone guitarist sitting in front of a stone mantle atop which rest family photos and books. The face of the performer is almost entirely obscured by a large cloth facemask, thick-framed glasses, and a trucker hat.[162] Sepúlveda's strumming is characteristic of the folkloric Chilean cueca style, while his verses speak of caring for one's neighbors and observing the necessary precautions to avoid falling ill. Argentinian performer Yan

Adrover recorded 'La Milonga de la Cuarentena' from the Spanish island of Ibiza, where he notes he 'got stuck' during the onset of the pandemic. From the song's intricate, polyrhythmic intro onwards, it is clear that Adrover is a skilled guitarist. Similarly, his verses are laden with poetic imagery and go beyond the standard references and warnings found in many other examples of música del coronavirus.[163] Nonetheless, in spite of his professional abilities, the video is recorded casually. Adrover's camera is slightly off-kilter, and the wooden cabinets behind him give the impression that the video was recorded in his kitchen. The informal intimacy of the recording may detract from the video's production quality, but arguably adds to its affective power to communicate shared pandemic feelings of isolation, solitude, and social connection exclusively by way of the internet.

Guitars are the most common choice for solo accompaniment, reflecting the ubiquity of the acoustic six-string as a household instrument throughout the region. Nonetheless, the many solo accordionists playing música del coronavirus highlight the multinational influence of the instrument across Latin America. Agripino Tavarez of Sajoma, Santo Domingo played his 'Coronavirus Acapella Con Acordeon' on a two-row Hohner box staring down into a cellphone. With a quick merengue, he describes asking God to rid the world of the virus immediately, notes that the dead no longer have any worries, and realizes he has no solutions – except to play hard and fast, which he does in this video, which lasts only one minute and three seconds.[164] On 'El covid 19 vallenato', dannyjuankvallenato sits in a red plastic chair in front of a wooden wardrobe adeptly playing a three-row button accordion, a principal instrument in the vallenato tradition from Colombia's Caribbean region considered more fully in the next chapter. The video itself is rather pixelated and poorly shot, with a persistent glare. For dannyjuankvallenato, the pandemic moment required a timely response in verse accompanied by accordion, in true genre style.[165] In vallenato, songs are part of 'a tradition in which the orality and other [narrative] manifestations prevail.'[166]

It is possible to listen to examples of solo música del coronavirus performances and feel the emotional intent of the performers directly. Some of the most spontaneous and affectively powerful examples of solo performances are sung without accompaniment – the voice of the individual is left unadorned. Free of pretext, these types of videos showcase a wide range of vocal and songwriting approaches and emotional registers. Most appear to be recorded on the fly, in unplanned settings, often outdoors or in a private home. In a video from 28 October 2020 titled 'Coronavirus. Talento de mi gente' ('Coronavirus. Talent of my people') uploaded by the Colombian channel 'caridád mas alla de los sueños', an unidentified man selling food from a shoulder basket with a facemask tucked under his chin bellows out the first lines of his composition. He stops himself three words into his verse to announce the song's name – 'el Coronavirus' – and starts anew, this time with even more vigor. The video was unplanned, catching the man at work. The channel owner observed that he sang of 'the reality of the pandemic' and that he 'must be wonderful for such a beautiful voice that God gave him.'[167]

In October 2021, over a year and half into the pandemic moment, in the rural community of El Congreso, Chiapas, on Mexico's southern Pacific coast, a fisherman took a moment out of his workday to record himself singing an original two-minute-long canción about COVID. The video's narrow vertical frame indicates that it was recorded on a cellphone camera. Dressed in blue shorts and a reflective construction vest, Gabino Alvarez Villanueva's ruffled hair and suntanned skin present a man who spends much of his time working outdoors, exposed to the elements. In the video he sits atop a pile of wooden pallets, his flipflops dusty with sand, with a wide-brimmed hat set off to his side. The song was posted as the only music video on a channel called 'Pescando con Paquita' (Fishing with Paquita), which is otherwise dedicated to fishing-related videos recorded in and around Tonalá, Chiapas.[168]

After Alvarez Villanueva announces himself as the composer of the song, he begins to sing unaccompanied. His eyes light up as he belts out his take on the pandemic moment. Beginning with a description of the virus's origins in China and initial spread to countries in Asia, Europe, and Latin America, he then names local communities in his home state where the virus had at last landed. The song's verse section features an elegiac descending melody, but its chorus concludes with an unexpected high note. This is where the fisherman's full-throated tenor really grabs the listener's attention. Staring directly into the camera with an earnest, fiery expression, Alvarez Villanueva encourages his listeners to stay home and observe sanitary measures, while also calling on God to liberate humanity from the crisis. He would rather die old than die of COVID. With conviction, he remarks that he is not ready to go to heaven quite yet.

Despite the recording's simplicity, Alvarez Villanueva's canción is moving to hear. Its emotional power lies in the feelings it invokes: solitude, anxiety, the need for good conduct and faith alike. He relays a sense of being part of history, for better or for worse. Alvarez Villanueva sat alone, singing out his personal perspective on the overwhelming immensity of the pandemic moment, just as people across the region sought understanding, hope, social connection, and emotional connections in their own ways.

Notes

1. 'EL MERENGUE CORONAVIRUS, 2020', https://www.youtube.com/watch?v=7at_5BMkhuM (accessed 2 February 2022). While it was uploaded by a channel titled Angel Vicente, it is unclear whether or not this is the name of the performer. This YouTube channel was terminated by the end of 2023 but a version of the original recording remains in a remix posted by La Presión Típica EU in May 2020 which added güira, bass, conga, and tambora to the recording. 'Coronavirus Merengue Típico', https://www.youtube.com/watch?v=9ZeEJuLPm78 (accessed 10 January 2024).

2. Stephan Palmié, *The Cooking of History: How Not to Study Afro-Cuban Religion*. (Chicago: University of Chicago Press, 2013), pp. 6, 8.
3. Ruth Leys, 'The Turn to Affect: A Critique', *Critical Inquiry* 37.3 (2011): 434–72, p. 441.
4. Marie Thompson and Ian Biddle, 'Introduction: Somewhere Between the Signifying and the Sublime', in Thompson and Biddle, eds, *Sound, Music, Affect: Theorising Sonic Experience* (New York: Bloomsbury Academic, 2013), 1–24, p. 5. Music, sound, and affect is an emergent field with numerous new interdisciplinary approaches, e.g. Judith Lochhead, Eduardo Mendieta, and Stephen D. Smith, eds, *Sound and Affect: Voice, Music, World* (Chicago: University of Chicago Press, 2021).
5. Holly Watkins, *Musical Vitalities: Ventures in a Biotic Aesthetics of Music* (Chicago: University of Chicago Press, 2018), p. 1.
6. On emotional regulation and soundscape, see Marcel Zentner, Didier Grandjean, and Klaus R. Scherer, 'Emotions Evoked by the Sound of Music: Characterization, Classification, and Measurement', *Emotion* 8.4 (2008): 494–521.
7. Pablo Vila, 'Introduction', in Pablo Vila, ed., *Music, Dance, Affect, and Emotions in Latin America* (Lanham, MD: Lexington Books, 2017), xi–xxi, p. xiii.
8. Lincoln J. Colling and William F. Thompson, 'Music, Action, and Affect', in Tom Cochrane, Bernardino Fantini, and Klaus R. Scherer, eds, *The Emotional Power of Music* (Oxford: Oxford University Press, 2013), 197–212, p. 198.
9. Varvara Pasiali, 'Resilience, Music Therapy, and Human Adaptation: Nurturing Young Children and Families', *Nordic Journal of Music Therapy* 21.1 (2012): 36–56, p. 36.
10. Lauren K. Fink, Lindsay A. Warrenburg, Claire Howlin, William M. Randall, Niels C. Hansen, and Melanie Wald-Fuhrmann, 'Viral Tunes: Changes in Musical Behaviours and Interest in Coronamusic Predict Socio-Emotional Coping during COVID-19 Lockdown', *Humanities & Social Sciences Communications* 8 (2021): Article 180; Sarah Hennessy, Mathew Sachs, Jonas Kaplan, and Assal Habibi, 'Music and Mood Regulation during the Early Stages of the COVID-19 Pandemic', *PLOS ONE* 16.10 (2021): Article e0258027.
11. Leys, 'Turn to Affect', p. 443.
12. Thompson and Biddle, 'Introduction', p. 6.
13. Patrik Juslin and John Sloboda, *Handbook of Music and Emotion: Theory, Research, Applications* (Oxford: Oxford University Press, 2009), pp. 31–2.
14. Juslin and Sloboda, *Handbook*, p. 33.
15. Pablo Vila, 'Music, Dance, Affect, and Emotions: Where We Are Now', in Pablo Vila, ed. *Music, Dance, Affect, and Emotions in Latin America* (Lanham, Lexington Books, 2017), 1–37, p. 10; see also pp. 5–7.
16. Danilyn Rutherford, 'Affect Theory and the Empirical', *Annual Review of Anthropology* 45.1 (2016): 285–300, p. 286.
17. Juan F. Anta, Luis F. Oliveira, and Danilo Ramos, 'Música y afecto: una revisión bibliográfica y el análisis de tres casos problemáticos', *Revista Argentina de Musicología* 20 (2019): 103–31, pp. 109–11; Nico H. Frijda and Batja Mesquita, 'The Analysis of Emotions: Dimensions of Variation', in *Emotions, Personality, and Psychotherapy: What Develops in Emotional Development?* (New York: Plenum Press, 1998), 273–95, pp. 274–77.
18. Palmié, *Cooking*, p. 12. He is drawing on the work of Susan Leigh Star and James R. Griesemer.
19. Marie Strand Skånland, 'Everyday Music Listening and Affect Regulation: The Role of MP3 Players', *International Journal of Qualitative Studies on Health and Well-Being* 8.1 (2013): Article 20595.
20. H. Martyn Evans, 'Music, Medicine and Embodiment', *Lancet* 375.9718 (2010): 886–7, p. 887.
21. 'El huayno del coronavirus', https://www.youtube.com/watch?v=6ODruHH_rI4 (accessed 12 February 2022).

22. The full playlist of these videos is 'Cuarentena con musica, Los Mendez', https://www.youtube.com/playlist?list=PLEH9SDlsJcj5KG4o4WAAQ7wnwwodpun4C
23. 'CUARENTENA con música (Parte 11) – A Puro Dolor y Corazón Partío', https://www.youtube.com/watch?v=2r9OVpGj628 (accessed 12 February 2022); 'CUARENTENA con Música (Parte 15) – Canciones Para Dios', https://www.youtube.com/watch?v=bf5LAGWh2qw (accessed 12 February 2022); 'CUARENTENA con música (Parte 24) – HOMENAJE al reggaetón de la VIEJA ESCUELA', https://www.youtube.com/watch?v=hrjs6RCLkKs (accessed 12 February 2022).
24. https://www.youtube.com/hashtag/yomequedoencasa (accessed 20 February 2022).
25. Like '#musicaviral #musicaencasa #yomequedoencasa', by Berni Clarinet of Valencia, Spain, https://www.youtube.com/watch?v=Zq0uixSTQXY (accessed 20 February 2022); 'Saxo cubano #YoMeQuedoEnCasa', https://www.youtube.com/watch?v=QnHj1WjcgtQ (accessed 20 February 2022); '#músicaviral #día2 #edmusical #yomequedoencasa', https://www.youtube.com/watch?v=EnXwZjL4LrM (accessed 20 February 2022).
26. 'POR UNA CABEZA' – Confinamiento con música #músicaviral', https://www.youtube.com/watch?v=-BaPSTee52E (accessed 20 February 2022).
27. 'Alvaro Soler – #YoMeQuedoEnCasa Festival (Instagram Live)', https://www.youtube.com/watch?v=fZAwgW9PvaU (accessed 20 February 2022).
28. Many have the hashtag '#músicaviral', for example https://www.youtube.com/hashtag/m%C3%BAsicaviral (accessed 20 February 2022).
29. 'EL CORONAHUAYNO – JOSELIO EL DULCE PRIMICIA 2020', https://www.youtube.com/watch?v=dLKjkhf2hkM (accessed 24 February 2022).
30. 'Alma Solary – Vete pandemia – Autor: Wilma Contreras', https://www.youtube.com/watch?v=2Pc4rbETkJs (accessed 24 February 2022).
31. 'Huayno Coronavirus (Hit 2020) ✓', https://www.youtube.com/watch?v=vDxzyAi5wZk (accessed 24 February 2022).
32. Among the others described, there were dozens of other Andean examples, e.g. Hectory Buchely's religious 'Maldita pandemia' from Altiplano Nariñense, Colombia, https://www.youtube.com/watch?v=wEXStx64wm0 (accessed 24 February 2022); Miguel Retmal C.'s 'Cancion: Maldita Pandemia', https://www.youtube.com/watch?v=-Mt16DLwjYQ (accessed 24 February 2022); 'Maldita pandemia', played on an out-of-tune guitar by Jésus Quiroga, https://www.youtube.com/watch?v=SR2V7PGe3Ew (accessed 24 February 2022); Patricio Adasme's 'Pandemia maldita' from Alhué, Chile, https://www.youtube.com/watch?v=0oSTuJJOrW8 (accessed 24 February 2022); and Porfirio Ayvar's glossy huayno 'Maldita Pandemia', 'Porfirio Ayvar / Maldita Pandemia / vídeo Oficial / Tarpuy Producciones', https://www.youtube.com/watch?v=Igg-FJ3pmlQ (accessed 24 February 2022).
33. 'Micky Vergara – Maldito Coronavirus / Huayno Ancashino / Edición Visual Dj Roll Perú', https://www.youtube.com/watch?v=AMQigUNDdQ0 (accessed 2 February 2022); Ruben Y LA ONDA LLUTEÑA's 'MALDITA PANDEMIA primicia 2021', https://www.youtube.com/watch?v=PHMbWY1xwbY (accessed 2 February 2022).
34. 'REVELACIÓN 5:40 – MALDITO CORONAVIRUS – PRIMICIA 2020', https://www.youtube.com/watch?v=iIe0kcT0rqk (accessed 6 February 2022).
35. 'MALDITO CORONAVIRUS – NATALY SALAZAR', https://www.youtube.com/watch?v=cW6DqeJC3DA (accessed 2 February 2022).
36. 'Pandemia Covid19 – Edith Mayta – Santiago 2020–2021©Producciones Galvez', https://www.youtube.com/watch?v=ZSUU0Ai6AGg (accessed 2 February 2022).
37. 'Edith Mayta en concierto 2020 – Pandemia Covid19', https://www.youtube.com/watch?v=3GZpdt3fUWE (accessed 2 February 2022).
38. 'Pandemia – Edith Mayta – [Video Clip Oficial] Santiago 2021', https://www.youtube.com/watch?v=fkEl7pf_i1A (accessed 2 February 2022).

39. 'MALDITA PANDEMIA – DELEITES ANDINOS / PRIMICIA OCTUBRE 2020 / GADIEL PRODUCCIONES – HUANCABAMBA', https://www.youtube.com/watch?v=9vcUYn7TMYw (accessed 2 February 2022).
40. 'Los Dolores De Coronavirus – Cancion, 2020', https://www.youtube.com/watch?v=0KPuVVk4ssY (accessed 2 February 2022).
41. 'Sol de Pachaconas – Maldito Coronavirus, 2020', https://www.youtube.com/watch?v=f5rlZAL-Sxw (accessed 2 February 2022).
42. '✓ NOEMI MALLMA 🎵 ► A QUE VENISTE CORONAVIRUS ◄ HUAYNO PRIMICIA 2020 Full HD ☆ (YAKU STUDIOS), 2020', https://www.youtube.com/watch?v=K3voTDcJIgU (accessed 2 February 2022).
43. Translated from Deborah Poole and Isaías Rojas Pérez, 'Memorias de la reconciliación: fotografía y memoria en el Perú de la pós-guerra', *emisferica – Revista Do Hemispheric Institute* 7.2 (2005): https://hemisphericinstitute.org/en/emisferica-72/7-2-essays/e72-essay-memories-of-reconciliation-photography-and-memory-in-postwar-peru.html (accessed 2 February 2022).
44. Translated from Félix Julca Guerrero and Laura Nivin Vargas, 'Recursos Expresivos y Literarios en el Huayno Ancashino', *Letras* 90.132 (2019): 260–84, p. 264.
45. Joshua Tucker, *Gentleman Troubadours and Andean Pop Stars: Huayno Music, Media Work, and Ethnic Imaginaries in Urban Peru* (Chicago: University of Chicago Press, 2013), pp. 38–40.
46. "ROMY SOTELO – MALDITA PANDEMIA – TAKY PERÚ TV," https://www.youtube.com/watch?v=LJQJkPX6rUw (accessed 7 February 2024).
47. 'RAP TRISTE REFLEXIÓN PANDEMIA COVID EDGAR GARCIA – (VIDEO OFICIAL)', https://www.youtube.com/watch?v=YwMeq6Sl1ys (accessed 2 February 2022).
48. '(COVID-19) (Coronavirus) Rap Triste 😔 – (La Vie Ne Ment Past) GD El Catracho', https://www.youtube.com/watch?v=ZVhdbonKrcA (accessed 2 February 2022); 'RAP TRISTE 😔 – (COVID-19) – Enyel El Leon Feat. Meyko El Frio // Daniel Rap, 2020', https://www.youtube.com/watch?v=_hTwf6UqZuQ (accessed 2 February 2022).
49. 'La Canción Más Triste Del Covid-19 (Coronavirus) 2020', https://www.youtube.com/watch?v=zMhO2GzmnJM (accessed 2 February 2022).
50. 'LA CANCIÓN MÁS TRISTE DEL CORONA VIRUS 😢 EL CHOTANO', https://www.youtube.com/watch?v=aqo7a3vuspY (accessed 2 February 2022).
51. 'La Cancion Del Coronavirus / Cancion Triste, 2020', https://www.youtube.com/watch?v=DkQpmAEYaAc (accessed 7 September 2022).
52. 'Bery Kilers – 😷 SE ME PEGO EL VIRUS (AUDIO)', https://youtu.be/ZdhZYsWmHBE (accessed 7 September 2022).
53. 'Quédate En Casa', https://www.youtube.com/watch?v=p_-L0A9M1ag (accessed 7 September 2022).
54. 'El Viru Viru', https://www.youtube.com/watch?v=n5Hhsb04Q28 (accessed 7 September 2022).
55. 'DUO TAKIYTINKU – Bicho Chiquito (Salay)^HD | Video Cuarentena 2020', https://www.youtube.com/watch?v=BPrF4TKUwE8 (accessed 7 September 2022); Betty Veizaga also released the song herself as 'Bicho Chiquito', https://www.youtube.com/watch?v=X8PFyXFyq98 (accessed 2 February 2022).
56. 'Canción La Pandemia – Autor y Compositor: Gustavo Pacheco Castro, 2020', https://www.youtube.com/watch?v=9CpKRfZOpmM (accessed 7 September 2022). On música tropical in Colombia, see Juan D. Parra Valencia, *Deconstruyendo el chucuchucu: auges, declives y resurecciones de la música tropical colombiana* (Medellín: Instituto Tecnológico Metropolitano, 2017), esp. pp. 120–30.
57. 'Canción La Pandemia – Autor y Compositor: Gustavo Pacheco Castro, 2020', https://www.youtube.com/watch?v=9CpKRfZOpmM (accessed 7 September 2022).

58. 'CANCION Covid 19 Corona virus', https://www.youtube.com/watch?v=j3cfd3lZ4ik (accessed 2 February 2022).
59. 'PUTO COVID (OMICRON SPECIAL EDITION)', https://www.youtube.com/watch?v=BqbS7Ae5Uxo (accessed 7 September 2022).
60. 'LA PANDEMIA – VIDEO – (MIGUEL DURAN JR)', https://www.youtube.com/watch?v=f3P-oGKtyAk (accessed 2 February 2022). The themes in this song are discussed in the final chapter. On his death, see *El Tiempo*, 'La última canción de Miguel Durán Jr. fue dedicada a la pandemia', 3 September 2020, https://www.eltiempo.com/cultura/musica-y-libros/la-ultima-cancion-de-miguel-duran-jr-fue-dedicada-a-la-pandemia-535800 (accessed 2 February 2022).
61. 'La Canción Del Fin Del Mundo – Locomoving', https://www.youtube.com/watch?v=4CxmWd_0OIc (accessed 2 February 2022).
62. 'CUMBIA DEL CORONA VIRUS – POTRO SALVAJE TORREON (2020) Video Oficial', https://www.youtube.com/watch?v=T4hOffOx9GE (accessed 2 February 2022).
63. 'Crisanto Vargas – Anton Virus Virus,Virus – Prod JjbProducciones', https://www.youtube.com/watch?v=0Qd65Elhnbg (accessed 7 September 2022).
64. 'CORONAVIRUS EL LOCO DEL DESAFIO, 2020', https://www.youtube.com/watch?v=UsAkZJUpQR8 (accessed 2 February 2022).
65. Juan M. Blanco, 'Una mirada a la historia de la música costeña de acordeón', *Revista Poligrama* 20.1 (2011): https://bibliotecadigital.univalle.edu.co/handle/10893/3068 (accessed 2 February 2022).
66. Whereby 'unsuitability, dissimilarity and incongruity became within the overall ideology of turning the world upside-down, logical and meaningful' – Shulamith Lev-Aladgem, 'Carnivalesque Enactment at the Children's Medical Centre of Rabin Hospital', *Research in Drama Education* 5.2 (2000): 163–74, p. 165.
67. 'Marco Flores Y La Jerez – EL CORONAVIRUS', https://www.youtube.com/watch?v=9bcuygZSScw (accessed 2 February 2022).
68. 'Marco Flores Y La Jerez'.
69. '😷 Chimbala – Cuarentena (Video Oficial)', https://www.youtube.com/watch?v=emOBGstNVgM (accessed 2 February 2022).
70. 'El Boom', https://www.youtube.com/watch?v=sl23fgJ0yQw (accessed 2 February 2022). Chimbala's channel is https://www.youtube.com/c/ChimbalaHD/videos.
71. 'Jowell y Randy, Kiko El Crazy – Se Acabó La Cuarentena | Viva El Perreo [Visualizer]', https://www.youtube.com/watch?v=YNR0mFufPsE (accessed 2 February 2022).
72. Proyecto Rodillo, 'Coronavirus Stats in Dominican Republic: Trend, Number of Cases, Deaths, Hospitalizations, Tests, Quarantine Measures and Mobility', *Regiones – El termómetro del coronavirus en Latinoamérica*, 29 October 2021, https://rodillo.org/regiones/ (accessed 2 February 2022).
73. 'Jowell y Randy, Kiko El Crazy – Se Acabó La Cuarentena | Viva El Perreo [Visualizer]', https://www.youtube.com/watch?v=YNR0mFufPsE (accessed 2 February 2022).
74. 'Jowell y Randy, Kiko El Crazy – Se Acabó La Cuarentena (Letra / Lyrics), 2020', https://www.youtube.com/watch?v=CvwzLiMe1-w (accessed 2 February 2022).
75. Agustín Gurza, 'Strachwitz Frontera Collection Coronavirus Corridos: Tales of the Pandemic', The Strachwitz Frontera Collection of Mexican and Mexican American Recordings website, 15 April 2020, https://frontera.library.ucla.edu/blog/2020/04/coronavirus-corridos-tales-pandemic (accessed 2 February 2022).
76. Tuan Yi-fu, *Escapism* (Baltimore: The Johns Hopkins University Press, 1998), p. 180.
77. 'ALFREDO SOSA-EL COBYCOBY – TODO ES COVI,TODO ES COVI', https://www.youtube.com/watch?v=DVaARXFUr3w (accessed 2 February 2022).
78. 'Coronavirus De Amor – El Capo De La Cumbia Patricio Servin Y Su Flamazo Tropical', https://www.youtube.com/watch?v=U56jcD-2CKQ (accessed 2 February 2022).

79. 'E Corona Virus', https://www.youtube.com/watch?v=E2zPgSGFgfM (accessed 2 February 2022).
80. Producciones Ramiz Oficial, 'LA CUMBIA DEL CORONAVIRUS | ORGANIZACIÓN LUZ AZUL | VIDEO OFICIAL 2021 – EL COVID, 2020', https://www.youtube.com/watch?v=xZec7v8QM_s (accessed 2 February 2022).
81. 'FORTINO REYNA – EL CORONA VIRUS CUMBIA', https://www.youtube.com/watch?v=MsndjhA8S90 (accessed 2 February 2022).
82. The literature on the resonance and impact of carnival celebration across Latin America is too vast to include here, but includes Peter Mason, *Bacchanal! The Carnival Culture of Trinidad* (Philadelphia, PA: Temple University Press, 1998); Mariano Candela, *Carnaval de Barranquilla: Paftrimonio oral e intangible de la humanidad* (Bogotá, Colombia: Amalfi Editores, 2004); Kevin A. Browne, *High Mas: Carnival and the Poetics of Caribbean Culture* (Jackson: University of Mississippi Press, 2018); and Ulisses Corrêa Duarte, 'Schools of Samba in the South Brazilian Border: Circuits and Translocal Exchanges in Carnival Cultures', in Fabiana Lopes da Cunha and Jorge Rabassa, eds, *Festivals and Heritage in Latin America: Interdisciplinary Dialogues on Culture, Identity and Tourism* (Cham, Switzerland: Springer International, 2021), 57–71.
83. Producciones Brayan Records Internacional, 'Los Hermanos Carrión – Carnaval Del Coronavirus 2020', https://www.youtube.com/watch?v=e5TaAW2Pr0E (accessed 6 February 2022).
84. 'COVID Carnaval – KARUWAYRA del Perú – Coplas Cajamarquinas', https://www.youtube.com/watch?v=PWIn6-YWOfU (accessed 6 February 2022).
85. 'LOS TRUENOS-▷CORONA VIRUS ▷CARNAVAL 2021◀Solar Discos© VIDEO OFICIAL 8K', https://www.youtube.com/watch?v=fdgPS-NNwPM (accessed 8 February 2022); 'Carnaval COVID 19 – Maestro José Guacho | Video Oficial', https://www.youtube.com/watch?v=ikozI_RCWP0 (accessed 8 February 2022).
86. 'Carnavalazo Ecuatoriano 2021 – Los Reyes Del Austro (Carnaval Coronavirus)', https://www.youtube.com/watch?v=YKq0Hr4hPbI (accessed 8 February 2022).
87. 'Los Días del Carnaval 2022 (Ecuador) – Hermanos Chamba ft Eliza Cedeño', https://www.youtube.com/watch?v=YZ7meOoz2IM (accessed 8 February 2022).
88. 'Miguelito – Coronavirus', https://www.youtube.com/watch?v=q8TKTpy2fU0 (accessed 8 February 2022).
89. Philip Scepanski, *Tragedy Plus Time: National Trauma and Television Comedy* (Austin: University of Texas Press, 2021), p. 2.
90. Cynthia Willett and Julie Willett, 'The Comic in the Midst of Tragedy's Grief with Tig Notaro, Hannah Gadsby, and Others', *Journal of Aesthetics and Art Criticism* 78.4 (2020): 535–46, p. 536.
91. Conrad Hyers, *The Spirituality of Comedy: Comic Heroism in a Tragic World* (New Brunswick, NJ: Transaction Publishers, 1996), p. 57.
92. 'Canción del coronavirus covid19 teporochitos', https://www.youtube.com/watch?v=H2ByKU-Ucu0 (accessed 2 February 2022).
93. Translated from Helena Beristáin, 'El albur', *Acta Poética* 21.1–2 (2015): 399–422, pp. 399.
94. Translated from Fernando Díez de Urdanivia, *Su majestad el albur* (Discos Luzam, México DF, 2021), p. 3.
95. 'JORGE LUIS Huaman Arroyo, HUAYNO DEL COVID-19', https://www.youtube.com/watch?v=nxY7aeR7kpA (accessed 7 November 2021).
96. 'Vete Ya Pinche Coronavirus', https://www.youtube.com/watch?v=l1HmSGIywJ4 (accessed 6 February 2022).
97. 'La Canción Del Coronavirus', https://www.youtube.com/watch?v=16PcCif1N8M (accessed 6 February 2022).

98. 'LA CANCIÓN DEL CORONAVIRUS Ft. El Chasky Pum', https://www.youtube.com/watch?v=COPxVaASPuw (accessed 2 February 2022).
99. As quoted in *Latino Rebels*, 'A "Corrido del Coronavirus" From Phoenix's Alan and Roberto', 21 March 2020, https://www.latinorebels.com/2020/03/21/corridodelcoronavirus/ (accessed 3 October 2022).
100. 'El Corrido del Coronavirus (LIVE) – Alan Y Roberto', https://www.youtube.com/watch?v=3_uEgvfH310 (accessed 3 October 2022); Javier Cabral, '"Lavense Las Manos, Plebes": Here Comes "El Corrido Del Coronavirus" to Cleanse Your Paisa Soul', *L.A. Taco* 25 March 2020, https://lataco.com/corrido-coronavirus-song (accessed 3 October 2022); This article incorrectly calls the song a 'bajosexto-dominated ballad' when it does not have that instrument. Also see Lydia Pantazes, 'Singers Aim to Inspire by Writing Song about the Coronavirus', *Spectrum News*, 30 May 2020, https://spectrumnews1.com/ca/la-west/entertainment/2020/05/30/singers-aim-to-inspire-by-writing-song-about-the-coronavirus (accessed 3 October 2022); Oscar Ramos, 'La propuesta de Alán y Roberto', *Prensa Arizona*, 4 February 2021, https://prensaarizona.com/2021/02/la-propuesta-de-alan-y-roberto/ (accessed 3 October 2022); *Excélsior*, 'ALAN Y ROBERTO: Corrido del coronavirus da instrucción y aliento a la comunidad', 14 April 2020, https://www.excelsiorcalifornia.com/2020/04/14/alan-y-roberto-corrido-del-coronavirus-da-instruccion-y-aliento-a-comunidad/ (accessed 3 October 2022).
101. 'Alan y Roberto El Piscador video Oficial', https://www.youtube.com/watch?v=4Q_iRRo96Zw (accessed 3 October 2022). They also record timely pieces like their boxing corrido 'El Corrido De Andy Ruiz Jr "El Destroyer" Alan y Roberto', https://www.youtube.com/watch?v=8hFx3GR2BQ0 (accessed 20 September 2022).
102. 'El Corrido del Coronavirus – Alan Y Roberto', https://www.youtube.com/watch?v=l8EogRFitco (accessed 3 October 2022).
103. 'El Corrido del Coronavirus (LIVE) – Alan Y Roberto', https://www.youtube.com/watch?v=3_uEgvfH310 (accessed 3 October 2022).
104. For example, Homero Guerrero Jr. Y Los KDT's De Linares' rather formulaic 'El Corrido del Covid-19' had over 2.8 million views on one channel (https://www.youtube.com/watch?v=BQpIBPAhRRc (accessed 3 October 2022) and 123,434 views on another, https://www.youtube.com/watch?v=vJMzE8vGiHA (accessed 3 October 2022); Alan y Roberto had 5542 views for their first studio version, 12,834 for the live version, and 1300 for the non-video recorded version, which featured a still of an evil-looking coronavirus.
105. Matthew Wade and Maria Hynes, 'Worshipping Bodies: Affective Labour in the Hillsong Church', *Geographical Research* 51.2 (2013): 173–9, p. 173.
106. Manuel A. Vásquez and Philip J. Williams, 'Introduction: The Power of Religious Identities in the Americas', *Latin American Perspectives* 32.1 (2005): 5–26; Claudia Carmassi, Katherine M. Shear, Martina Corsi, Carlo Antonio Bertelloni, Valerio Dell'Oste, and Liliana Dell'Osso, 'Mania Following Bereavement: State of the Art and Clinical Evidence', *Frontiers in Psychiatry* 11 (2020): Article 366.
107. Stephen Selka, 'Afro-Catholicism in Latin America', *Religion Compass* 13: 5 (2019): Article e12315, pp. 4–5.
108. José D. Rodríguez Cuadros, 'The Religious Shift in Latin America', *Herodote* 171.4 (2018): 119–34, https://www.cairn-int.info/article-E_HER_171_0119--the-religious-shift-in-latin-america.htm (accessed 3 October 2022).
109. Daniel H. Levine, 'The Future of Christianity in Latin America', *Journal of Latin American Studies* 41.1 (2009): 121–45, p. 123.
110. Nicolas Castillo, 'Political Protestantism in Latin America', *SIR Journal of International Relations Blogs*, 16 January 2021, http://www.sirjournal.org/blogs/2021/1/16/political-protestantism-in-latin-america (accessed 3 October 2022).
111. Moji Ruele, 'The Diaconal and Liberation Role of the Church in the Fight against HIV/AIDS in Botswana', *Botswana Notes and Records* 35 (2003): 141–45; Olehile Buffel,

'Preferential Option for the Poor in the Current Context of Poverty in South Africa: Doing Liberation Theology in the Footsteps', *Studia Historiae Ecclesiasticae* 36 (2010): 99–113; Daniel R. Groody and Gustavo Gutiérrez, *The Preferential Option for the Poor beyond Theology* (Euclid, OH: University of Notre Dame Press, 2014).

112. Jabin J. Deguma, Melona C. Deguma, Jemima N. Tandag, and Harlene Marie B. Acebes, 'Where Is the Church in the Time of COVID-19 Pandemic: Preferring the Poor via G. Gutierrez' "Liberation" and the Catholic Church's Social Teaching in the Philippine Setting', *Journal of Social and Political Sciences* 3.2 (2020): https://papers.ssrn.com/abstract=3581766 (accessed 7 November 2021).

113. Kevin L. O'Neill, 'Delinquent Realities: Christianity, Formality, and Security in the Americas', *American Quarterly* 63:2 (2011): 337–65.

114. Merril Pauls and Roger C. Hutchinson, 'Bioethics for Clinicians: 28. Protestant Bioethics', *Canadian Medical Association Journal* 166.3 (2002): 339–43, p. 341.

115. 'Canción Contra El COVID-19 Del Padre Sergio Se Viraliza En Redes', https://www.youtube.com/watch?v=1yKrvPHxTD0 (accessed 7 November 2021).

116. Translated from quotation in Javier Córdoba, 'Costa Rica: Sacerdote se hace viral con canción del COVID', *Associated Press*, 3 May 2021, https://apnews.com/article/noticias-bf0c51b7e9bc456d1fba902abe3f1035 (accessed 3 October 2022).

117. Córdoba, 'Costa Rica'.

118. 'Samuel Hernández-Lo Que Este Virus Me Enseñó', https://www.youtube.com/watch?v=ZBZuHrUb0aw (accessed 7 November 2021).

119. Josef Sorett, '"It's Not the Beat, but It's the Word That Sets the People Free": Race, Technology, and Theology in the Emergence of Christian Rap Music', *Pneuma* 33.2 (2011): 200–17.

120. Igor Johannsen, 'Configurations of Space and Identity in Hip Hop: Performing "Global South"', *Journal of Hip Hop Studies* 6.2 (2019): 183–205, pp. 183, 185.

121. Diana Avella, 'La Etnnia: el legendario himno del hip hop latino', *Nómadas* (Bogotá, Colombia) 54 (2021): 225–35.

122. Marcyliena Morgan and Dionne Bennett, 'Hip-Hop & the Global Imprint of a Black Cultural Form', *Daedalus* 140.2 (2011): 176–96; see also Tony Mitchell, ed., *Global Noise: Rap and Hip Hop Outside the USA* (Middletown, CT: Wesleyan University Press, 2001).

123. Joseph Winters, 'Unstrange Bedfellows: Hip Hop and Religion', *Religion Compass* 5.6 (2011): 260–70.

124. 'An interesting aspect of gangsta rap's religious rhetoric is that while it embraces the life of Jesus and aspects central to religious thought such as heaven, hell, justice, redemption, and meaning in suffering, there is a strong mistrust of organized and established religion. Gangsta rap's theology, therefore, is centered on the person of Christ, specifically on His suffering, but not religion centered. That is to say, while many gangsta rappers embrace the life and suffering of Jesus – and often display this attitude through visual and textual rhetoric – they do not embrace the entity of organized religion nor live what most would recognize as religious lives' – Robert Tinajero, 'Hip Hop and Religion: Gangsta Rap's Christian Rhetoric', *Journal of Religion and Popular Culture* 25.3 (2013): 315–32, pp. 315–16.

125. 'Eiem Oficial, Eiem – DESAFÍO COVID 19 – Rap Cristiano Argentino, 2020', https://www.youtube.com/watch?v=QfgVqUuUCFA (accessed 7 September 2021).

126. 'Doble B – Ten Misericordia – (Video Oficial)', https://www.youtube.com/watch?v=H1fXDeimd4Q (accessed 7 September 2021).

127. '(COVID-19)(coronavirus) rap triste La Vie Ne Ment Past) GD el catracho', https://www.youtube.com/watch?v=ZVhdbonKrcA (accessed 7 September 2021).

128. 'Nos Levantaremos – Varios Artistas Ecuador', https://www.youtube.com/watch?v=nqTvCtRc7ac (accessed 7 September 2021).

129. 'GRUPO FORTALEZA / s.d.j_covid 19 (Las consecuencias del pecado.)', https://www.youtube.com/watch?v=U7rZ4ujL310 (accessed 7 September 2021).
130. 'CORO DE FUEGO | SE VA EL OMICRON PORQUE LLEGO JEHOVÁ', https://www.youtube.com/watch?v=9ZzqE2iFUB0 (accessed 7 September 2021).
131. Jelisa Castrodale, 'Here's Where That Weird "Jesus Fights Coronavirus" Animation Came From', *Vice*, 20 April 2021, https://www.vice.com/en/article/bvz8dz/where-that-weird-jesus-fights-coronavirus-video-came-from (accessed 7 February 2022).
132. 'CORONAVIRUS //CANCION CRISTIANA', https://www.youtube.com/watch?v=V_6O9UbEH8U (accessed 7 February 2022).
133. 'Julio Bardonado Lo Nuevo El CoronaVirus VIDEO EN VIVO', https://www.youtube.com/watch?v=DIxE4YKUOPY (accessed 7 February 2022).
134. Matthew 3:16 / Luke 3:22 link the arrival of the Holy Spirit to the appearance of a dove.
135. Matthew 24:7.
136. Stephen Hunt and David Martin, 'Christian Millenarianism: From the Early Church to Waco', *Nova Religio: The Journal of Alternative and Emergent Religions* 9:1 (2005): 139–43.
137. Translated from 'Estoy Infectado – G Low Coronavirus Rap (Video Oficial) Rap Cristiano 2020 Raperos Cristianos 2020, 2020', https://www.youtube.com/watch?v=WiiqUKI4U0 (accessed 7 September 2021).
138. Christina Zanfagna, 'Kingdom Business: Holy Hip Hop's Evangelical Hustle', *Journal of Popular Music Studies* 24.2 (2012): 196–216, pp. 196, 198.
139. Jim Y. Trammell, '"The Grandest, most Compelling Story of all Time!": Dominant Themes of Christian Media Marketing', *Journal of Religion and Popular Culture* 26.1 (2014): 23–35, pp. 25, 32.
140. As of March 2022: 'CORONAVIRUS – SAXOMAN Y LOS CASANOVAS, 2020', https://www.youtube.com/watch?v=T9oWlOTxj20 (accessed 7 February 2022).
141. This same ghostly, horseback army led by Jesus in the clouds appears in the video for 'Vallenato cristiano corona de vida', https://www.youtube.com/watch?v=SlYemAR6Q2Y (accessed 7 February 2022) and is clearly a well-worn image.
142. 'CORONAVIRUS – SAXOMAN Y LOS CASANOVAS', https://www.youtube.com/watch?v=T9oWlOTxj20 (accessed 7 February 2022).
143. Comments under 'CORONAVIRUS – SAXOMAN'.
144. 'La canción del coronavirus intérprete Hermes Velasco', https://www.youtube.com/watch?v=WfHTdz9xUkM (accessed 15 September 2022). One of this book's authors remains the only subscriber to this channel as of 10 January 2024.
145. 'Aquí te dedico una deliciosa canción para no sufras por corona virus animo Huautla', https://www.youtube.com/watch?v=nB0ViZwI8gU (accessed 24 February 2022); 'EL COVID 19 'EL CORRIDO', https://www.youtube.com/watch?v=QG3qmoP7fXY (accessed 24 February 2022); 'Prevenção do covid-19 com o VANDECO DO FORRÓ', https://www.youtube.com/watch?v=XZosh92FLgo (accessed 24 February 2022); 'El mal del corona virus llanero...', https://www.youtube.com/watch?v=nmaNcpMTklk (accessed 24 February 2022).
146. 'El Huayno del Coronavirus – El Puma del Huascarán', https://www.youtube.com/watch?v=QMekW_hDgLI (accessed 15 September 2022).
147. 'Primicia @2020 / Rusmell Espinoza "Ruso del Arpa"', https://www.youtube.com/watch?v=rMA3etKN_Kw (accessed 15 September 2022).
148. 'Corona Virus Chayaramunña Michael Sedano HUAYNO', https://www.youtube.com/watch?v=YWlY3VIn7gg (accessed 15 September 2022); 'LA CANCIÓN DE CORONAVIRUS COVID-19 HUAYNO CON ARPA JULIO PEÑARES CHARACATO DE DE ARPA', https://www.youtube.com/watch?v=tw8x5dDG3wc (https://www.youtube.com/watch?v=YWlY3VIn7gg); 'Coronavirus COVID-19 LA canción en huayno en arpa', https://www.youtube.com/watch?v=TEMbaVymUkc (accessed 15 September 2022).

149. 'huayno coronavirus con arpa', https://www.youtube.com/watch?v=z8si7aMgjwc (accessed 15 September 2022).
150. 'luchemos contra el coronavirus', https://www.youtube.com/watch?v=epx-GeIfnjo (accessed 15 September 2022).
151. 'Contrapunto contra el Covid 19', https://www.youtube.com/watch?v=3f6QEVP338Y (accessed 15 September 2022).
152. '¡Un Jarocho Le Canta Al Coronavirus!', https://www.youtube.com/watch?v=LRVE4F6n26w (accessed 15 September 2022).
153. 'Canción por la prevención del coronavirus', https://www.youtube.com/watch?v=rzwnvs4Dr08 (accessed 15 September 2022).
154. 'Noche de ronda (guitarra) coronavirus', https://www.youtube.com/watch?v=KxDQp8orsmQ (accessed 15 September 2022); 'Porompompero (guitarra) coronavirus', https://www.youtube.com/watch?v=zcEo7-Y-j68 (accessed 15 September 2022).
155. 'COPLAS CORONAVIRUS – A ESTILO CAJAMARCA', https://www.youtube.com/watch?v=goHRobQkOFI (accessed 15 September 2022).
156. 'Corona Virus-Cancion Con Guitarra y Armonica', https://www.youtube.com/watch?v=4ilKCU7FK2c (accessed 15 September 2022).
157. 'La canción del Coronavirus – Lamar', https://www.youtube.com/watch?v=9HCxoSYI8J4 (accessed 15 September 2022).
158. 'Coronavirus Canción, 2020', https://www.youtube.com/watch?v=Nu_Ne2_thpA (accessed 22 February 2022).
159. AFP Español, 'Músico le Canta a la Ansiedad por el Nuevo Coronavirus en Ecuador | AFP', https://www.youtube.com/watch?v=XhBykTRVOaY (accessed 22 February 2022); AP Archive, 'Virus Outbreak Inspires Ecuador Street Performer', https://www.youtube.com/watch?v=sPvhhSTDP4E (accessed 22 February 2022); *Sharjah24 News*, 'A Local Artist in Ecuador Turns COVID-19 Fears into a Catchy Song', https://www.youtube.com/watch?v=SDuMJmOtXTw (accessed 22 February 2022).
160. 'Sonia Montalvo y el Gitano del Perú 3/8', https://www.youtube.com/watch?v=43CFRcZxMO8 (accessed 22 February 2022).
161. 'La cancion del coronavirus Jarocho', https://www.youtube.com/watch?v=GEGBJWMNPbY (accessed 22 February 2022).
162. 'Cueca Del Coronavirus!', https://www.youtube.com/watch?v=6E5bIXnP1FU (accessed 22 February 2022).
163. 'Milonga de La Cuarentena', https://www.youtube.com/watch?v=itmp5LaAysQ (accessed 22 February 2022).
164. 'Agripino Tavarez – Coronavirus Acapella Con Acordeon', https://www.youtube.com/watch?v=bfFxmtZ2z6U (accessed 22 February 2022).
165. 'El Covid 19 Vallenato, 2020', https://www.youtube.com/watch?v=AxazzIliCn0 (accessed 22 February 2022).
166. Juan C. Urango Ospina, 'El vallenato como texto narrativo: Análisis de "El Cantor de Fonseca", de Carlos Huertas', *VISITAS al PATIO* 1.1 (2008): 29–44, p. 29.
167. '*Canción que describe la realidad de la pandemia, interpretada por un ser humano que debe ser maravilloso por tan linda voz que Dios le regaló.*' – 'Coronavirus. Talento de mi gente', https://www.youtube.com/watch?v=H7oyd-0En4o (accessed 22 September 2021).
168. 'Coronavirus cancion-compositor – Gabino Alvarez villanueva', https://www.youtube.com/watch?v=R089Lit-yIk (accessed 18 October 2021).

6 Maldita Pandemia

Prelude: COVID-19 Comes to El Charco

The tiny community of El Charco sits on the banks of the Tapaje River, nestled deep within the tropical rainforest that cloaks Colombia's Pacific coast. Like many similar towns in the region, the only way to arrive at El Charco is by boat or seaplane, as there is no road or airstrip connecting it to the rest of Nariño province. On 25 March 2020, community documentarian Omar Quiñones uploaded a video recorded in El Charco entitled 'Coronavirus canción PACHITA' to his YouTube channel EL MAGÜIREÑO, a name that references his nearby hometown of Magüí Payán.[1] In the video, a simple yet stirring song featuring an acoustic guitar and a lone woman's voice is overlaid with video showing daily life in the small river town at the edge of the rainforest. The clips show wooden houses on stilts guarded by an attentive dog, worn hands chopping onions and forming balls of dough, and a crowd of women in headwraps and brightly colored shawls descending a precarious-looking dock to board a small dinghy. The accompanying music centers the voice of Pachita Castro, who acknowledges the arrival of the coronavirus in her remote community. Despite losing her husband to the virus, as she later told us, Pachita's outlook is not bleak; she denounces the coronavirus and calls on the resilience of her community, which continues to show strength and fortitude despite so much suffering. If the people of the Colombian Pacific can persist and thrive in the face of state neglect, narcoviolence, and racial stigmatization, she is confident they can make it through the next challenge of a global pandemic.

The Pacific region is an epicenter of Afro-Colombian culture and identity. It is also a territory notoriously underserved by infrastructure and government services. In the absence of the nation-state, the region has subsequently become hotly contested among narcomilitary groups who recognize the strategic value of the region's deep-water ports, dense rainforests, and porous borders with neighboring countries. Once characterized as a 'peaceful backwater', Pacific states are now at the forefront of the Colombian national conflict. Infrastructure developments that connect the Pacific to the rest of Colombia, rather than providing opportunity and security for its residents, have instead enabled the regional incursion of paramilitary groups and organized criminal organizations.[2] In addition, successive modernizing agendas on the part of the Colombian state have both explicitly and implicitly stigmatized, reduced, or otherwise belittled the lifeways of rural Pacific communities by characterizing them as backward and superstitious.[3] Such prejudices were manifest at the outset of the COVID-19 pandemic in the region.

The Pacific coast is also known for a profoundly diverse tradition of musical and narrative forms that are intimately tied to the region's Black heritage. The best-known styles of music from the region are the *currulao*, a metrically complex genre based around the syncopated rhythms of marimbas, drums, and shakers, and *arrullos*, melodic lullabies that often carry a religious or spiritual message.[4] Some song forms, such as *alabados*, explicitly address concerns about the fragility of human life, with the singer using music to create a bridge between the living and the dead.[5] All of these styles are distinct within Colombia, while sharing characteristics with other Afro-descended genres and forms throughout the Americas.[6] Women are typically at the forefront of performing the varied musical forms of the Pacific. As noted by Michael Birenbaum Quintero, '[t]he most indispensable [instrument] is the human voice, particularly those of women, the matronly singers called *cantadoras* who are present in all the traditional musical genres'.[7]

Francisca 'Pachita' Castro was born and raised in El Charco. She has spent the past three decades living between her home village and the inland metropolis of Cali, which has become a point of arrival for many people leaving the coast in search of new opportunities. Pachita describes herself as a 'mother, sister, community caregiver and educator, bearer of ancestral knowledge, student of the river and the forest, singer of songs, and, more than anything, a resilient woman and a survivor'. Since 2000, she has served as a co-founder of Escuela Fundación Sé Quien Soy, a 'mobile school' that, in her words, 'empowers Afro-descended women from the Pacific region, many of whom do not even know to read or write, to understand themselves through the study and valorization of ancestral knowledge, medicine and wellbeing practices, customs and beliefs, forms of social organization, storytelling through music and poetry, and the power of community rootedness'.[8]

Pachita begins her coronavirus song with an idiomatic phrase of hope – '*no hay mal que por bien no venga*' – which is best translated as 'every cloud has a silver lining'. Such positivity may be hard to conceive given the losses her community has suffered. Nonetheless, Pachita offers words of encouragement: '[look to] spiritual forces, my fellow women, and to solidarity' ('*fuerza espiritual, comadres, y la solidaridad*'). She warns how the Coronavirus 'has the capacity to listen' ('*mira que el coronavirus tiene oido para escuchar*'), affording sinister agency to the disease and underscoring its capacity for destruction. Pachita observes how 'illness has slammed down on the lands where Black people live' (*'a los territorios negros ha azotaó la enfermedad'*), enumerating not only the coronavirus, but also bubonic plague, whooping cough, and varicella. Pachita links the onset of COVID-19 to previous outbreaks of diseases that have largely been eradicated in other parts of the world but that continue to plague the towns of the Pacific, where the combined effects of a tropical climate and political neglect have created the conditions for a near-perpetual public health crisis. Ancestral knowledge is a refrain to which Pachita returns in nearly every verse – 'as my father used to say' (*'así decía mi papa'*), she sings, and 'as my grandmother used to tell me' (*'así me decía mi abuela'*), 'and my mother used to recount' (*'y contaba mi mama'*). Throughout this recording, Pachita's guitarist cycles between the same two plodding chords, but as her voice rises in power and emotion his playing becomes increasingly intense, with gentle, arpeggiated finger picking giving way to full-bodied strums. Towards the end of the song, Pachita breaks into a spoken-word section which she prefaces with 'through [the practice of] orality' (*'a traves de la oralidad'*), where she mentions the names of places and people in the communities along the Tapaje River that have contributed to the region's resilience and continued vitality.[9]

In her interview with one of the authors, Pachita candidly discussed the relationship between her musical compositions and her life experience. She noted the discord between the pandemic experience in the city versus the countryside: 'In the village [of El Charco] we are used to illness. We have lived and survived here for decades with no modern clinic and no health assistance. The closest hospital is in Tumaco, and it takes almost day to get there.' As such, she related that 'we have always relied on each other, and on the knowledge of previous generations. When we get sick, we get on therapeutic diets and seek out medicinal plants in the forest.' When asked about whether she thought these remedies would be sufficient in staving off the coronavirus, Pachita responded with an anecdote:

> As early as January of 2020, people were getting very sick, and they were taking the advice of healers, and most would get better. Some died, but most got better. Then, when the crisis was declared and the government sent their people out here to help, the situation got significantly worse. It is not that we do not trust in their medicine, it is that they certainly do not trust in ours.[10]

Indeed, as Michael Birenbaum Quintero concurs: 'Life on the Pacific coast can be rough, especially outside the major towns. […] Health coverage, aside from traditional herbalism, is minimal, with small hospitals in Tumaco and Buenaventura and a decrepit clinic in Guapi serving a large geographical area.'[11] If the onset of the coronavirus took global metropolises and their highly advanced health systems by surprise, one can only imagine the impact of such illness on areas such as the Colombian Pacific. This emergent health crisis is compounded by the acute and ongoing challenges of chronic violence against women in the region, the health implications of which include psychological trauma, unwanted pregnancy, and the spread of sexually transmitted diseases.[12]

'Coronavirus canción PACHITA' was meant to provide sustenance to the local community, and it was heard by only a handful of listeners on YouTube, most of whom, according to El Magüireño's founder Omar Quiñones, live in or have family ties to the Pacific region.[13] In other examples considered in this book, coronavirus music videos provided opportunities for mass popularity, rapid diffusion, and market dominance. This case is an example of how global and free social media platforms like YouTube have allowed some creators to find select – tiny, yet committed – communities of listeners for whom their music has deeply felt meaning. A great deal of this meaning hinges on local relevance. Pachita's composition, beautiful and haunting as it may be on its own, comes into full color only to those who know the context and circumstance of its production.

Situating Locally Contingent Responses to a Global Pandemic

Latin American coronavirus music contingently reflects a range of phenomena encompassing the worldwide scope of the virus and its impact, along with the regional, hyperlocalized, and individual responses and conditions under which the pandemic was experienced. Across distinct genres and places of origin, música del coronavirus frequently links pandemic worries and experiences to embodied, trellised, and relational concepts of place, space, and regional identities.

This chapter focuses on highly regional and local responses to the global pandemic, with some excursions into global musics which actively sought to dissolve regional differences. Coronavirus musical expression, often rooted in local or translocal scenes, might best be characterized as affirmatively (perhaps even defiantly) genre-specific, following what Jennifer C. Lena describes as a shared 'basic grammar' of the genres themselves as communitarian constructions.[14] The pandemic brought shared experiences to divergent places. Aside from commercially influenced global efforts, localized manifestations of música del coronavirus presented contingent responses woven through with distinct sonic characteristics linked to their social and cultural contexts.

In coronavirus music, creative agency and decisive voice emerge in dialogue with intracultural flow and global forces and trends.[15] As Mark Hijleh has argued, 'twenty-first century musicians can and should become experts in understanding human musical history as a history of synthesis'.[16] And yet during the pandemic moment, the local, regional, and nearby were often strongly reasserted. Sonic, lyrical, and symbolic placemaking were employed to affirm identity and celebrate shared affinity. Andrew Sayer noted some time ago that 'the phrase "local contingent factors" seems to have become so well worn in locality research that "local" and "contingent" have become virtual synonyms.' The locally contingent remains 'a realm of necessity'.[17] Sayer's observations only increased in relevance during the pandemic moment. Local contexts produced a particularly powerful sense of situatedness in música del coronavirus, grounding individual experience of global crisis in collective frames tied to a specific place and time.

Clemens Greiner and Patrick Sakdapolrak argue that translocal relations 'connect and influence different localities and people at the same time' in ways that mean 'conditions or events at one place have an immediate impact on other connected places'.[18] Translocality is distinct from mere globalization in the way it centers the locality of experience, even as the systems that influence life are increasingly abstracted on a transnational level.[19] Peter Wade argues that 'while some have seen globalization as erasing local difference, most see globalization and localization as two sides of the same coin. [...] Cultural diversity is a commodity'.[20] David Conradson and Deirdre McKay argue that translocality 'recognises that localities continue to be important as sources of meaning and identity for mobile subjects'.[21] A translocal understanding of the pandemic moment and the songs produced from within it helps to resolve any dichotomies between the forces of globalization and the anchoring of place.

References to and evocations of place – from simple celebration to nationalistic sloganeering to distinct narratives that challenge pre-existing perspectives on the pandemic moment – are indelible facets of coronavirus music. In countless pandemic-era compositions, artists define themselves and their music by place, saluting their countries, regions, towns, or neighborhoods of origin or highlighting the singularity of their context even as they acknowledge the worldwide nature of the pandemic. Topophilia, 'the affective bond between people and place, or setting',[22] became a significant aperture through which musicians and audiences engaged with and interpreted the pandemic moment. For artists belonging to regional, ethnic, or national diasporas, sonic and visual markers of place in coronavirus music videos function to tether performers to a geographical imaginary of home.

Reflecting these complex relationships with place, coronavirus songs frequently esteem the singularity of local customs and propose them as antidotes to the pandemic. The coronavirus is commonly and unsurprisingly described as both an unwelcome and a foreign force. Given the region's history of colonialism and imperial meddling, invasion from outside is a familiar theme that runs through many cultural products in Latin America. Likewise, the experience of leaving home to migrate, whether for work or for safety, is commonplace throughout the region. Under pandemic lockdown conditions, a local sense of place has been emphasized and framed in a new light. At one extreme, those in the diaspora kept far from their homes may start to long for and idealize places of origin as dreamscapes. At the other, those trapped at home by the pandemic may see the situatedness of place as a constricting limitation from which they cannot escape. In contrast to both these common polarities, some songwriters, like Pachita, instead have found strength and self-affirmation in the rooted knowledge that stems from a deep sense of being situated in geographic place.

In coronavirus music videos, performers often drape themselves in their national flag and don clothing or costumes evocative of their regional ethnic group. The videos, professional or informal, are shot in front of recognizable streetscapes or landmarks that signal their location. Language is deftly employed as a marker of both place and identity, whether through a few inserted words of regional slang or an entire song composed in an indigenous tongue. Place and regional pride are marked and referenced both lyrically and sonically. Musicians connect new pandemic stories to local and indigenous ways of seeing and speaking about the world.

The present chapter briefly contrasts these often discrete local responses with music created deliberately for global consumption. The latter were less constrained by genre conventions or concerns for scene-based authenticities, and instead sought an accessible sound that could transcend provincialism and locally rooted tastes. The pandemic moment generated a significant outpouring of such shared global musical responses, which consciously sought the exchange of localized experiences for untethered and transnational connections and experiences. These efforts sought to create a new pandemic-era musical grammar of cosmopolitan inspiration, connectivity, and commercialism.

The chapter then explores how shared humanity and a sense of global community is framed as an impetus for mass mourning and transnational cooperation expressed through often highly localized music making. Despite being consciously self-contained, place-based musical responses to the coronavirus often gained audiences in the millions, reflecting the impact of regional diasporas and the fluidity of musical diffusion. For example, vallenato music responding to COVID-19 used pre-existing narrative aspects to contextualize the distinctive circumstances of the pandemic moment. Nationalist framings of música del coronavirus appealed to values of duty, civic trust, and fraternity, and not uncommonly also darker themes such as xenophobia and racism. A particular subset of socially motivated coronavirus music was an emergent type of public service announcement, which often utilized recognized nationalistic styles, like mariachi in Mexico and cueca in Chile.[23]

Finally, the chapter considers musical responses to coronavirus produced in indigenous communities that are often at the margins of nation-state politics and that reflect unique approaches to place-meaning. Many of these examples of coronavirus music, particularly from Quechua-speaking songwriters, articulate an alternative way of thinking about the relationships between humankind, disease, agency, and death than appears in other examples. This chapter explores such musical responses to the pandemic from musicians forced in many instances by the crisis to reconceptualize their sense of place within a contested and global imaginary. Idiosyncratic genre and local responses interest us the most, but there were many others worth considering.

Música del Coronavirus and the Global Aesthetic

The emergence of a self-consciously global form of shared expression during the pandemic grew out of an effort to overcome social isolation through accessible, comforting, and globally resonant sonic palettes. This effort was coupled with a long-brewing, commercialized search for fusion approaches drawn specifically from the musical idioms of global pop. One aesthetic which emerged in the early pandemic stripped music of specific style or diluted genre markers in favor of global convergences. As Nadeem Karkabi has argued in a more politicized context, the adoption of 'cosmopolitan aesthetics to appeal stylistically to both local and foreign audiences' helps to 'forge international solidarity [...] by performing universal, borderless, and stateless humanity'.[24] The uses of these 'cosmopolitan aesthetics' during the pandemic moment were community oriented, with only a vague overlay of political sensibility. In the pandemic context, music making and global fusion were not meant to guide listeners to a specific political end. Instead, the purpose was to steer people toward social connection, and, as the endeavor matured and evolved, into newly emergent but temporary virtual social spaces. For some performers, the pandemic became the source of a distinctive style. Perhaps the pandemic moment itself became a type of scene for the isolated, with its own cosmopolitan sonic signature.

The most spontaneous manifestation of this global, cosmopolitan form of COVID-era music making was the explosion of performances from isolated individuals at the very beginning of the pandemic moment. These unplanned creative outbursts were soon copied and codified around the world via social media exposure. They sometimes took the form of folk styles, nationalist musical expressions, or else well-worn popular melodies from commercial radio, often sung by groups of neighbors. From their individual seclusion, people raised their voices to push back against the isolation produced by the pandemic-era lockdowns.

This was a distinctly urban phenomenon. In physical spaces like alleys and balconies, individuals stuck in pandemic isolation found communion through socially distanced singing and music making. These spaces facilitated musical co-creation despite physical distance, and also enabled urban residents to fill emptied-out public spaces with song. Videos of these impromptu performances were then shared on social media, serving as sources of inspiration in the midst of bleak news forecasts. Albert Fernández in Barcelona called it 'La revolución de los balcones', or 'the Balcony Revolution'.[25] Social media channels dedicated to these efforts were extensive and appeared overnight on Facebook, Twitter, YouTube, Instagram, and TikTok, as well as in legacy media around the globe.[26]

The initial wave of this form emerged from urban cores, at first in Italy and then spreading rapidly to Spain and other countries in Europe, before coming to Latin America, where a shared language opened the door to even greater transcontinental affinity. This was in contrast to the United States, where collective private-to-public noise making was largely limited to honking and cheering for emergency personnel, as seen in New York City. In Washington, DC, attempts at musical contributions were declared 'a bust'.[27] Perhaps this was due to the country's urban design, where only around one-eighth of the population lives in multi-unit apartment housing but over three-quarters live in detached homes.[28] Nonetheless, for urban residents who were able to participate, these collective outcries helped afford a sense of agency and shared experience to isolated individuals. As Simon Frith notes: 'The active practice of collective music-making is pre-eminently a sphere within which people can, and regularly do, experience a justified awareness of personal meaning and control'.[29] Individuals sang, played instruments, and made noise with household objects in conjunction but from their respective private spaces. Although they could not be next to each other, the sounds they made carried, creating aural bridges between neighbors and filling the public spaces in between.

Italy was hit early and hard by the coronavirus, and the emergency lockdowns and musical outpourings in response grabbed the world's attention. On Twitter, on 12 March 2020 a user calling herself valemercurii highlighted the effort, writing that '[p]eople of my hometown #Siena sing a popular song from their houses along an empty street to warm their hearts during the Italian #Covid_19 #lockdown'. This post was viewed more than five and half million times and had more than 150,000 reactions including retweets and likes, signaling the intense attention and connectivity these soundings produced. The video she posted came from the Siena Canta YouTube channel, which promoted and captured this singing event.[30] Similarly, on 15 March 2020 Twitter user alextdr8 posted: 'A whole neighborhood in Italy is singing "Be Alright" by @ArianaGrande while they're on lockdown and self-quarantined 👑 #COVID-19'.[31] Numerous articles, YouTube channels, and other media focused and celebrated this balcony singing as examples of 'the resilience of the human spirit' which 'just might make you remember there's something beautiful about our ability to find silver linings even in very dark times', as Emily St. James wrote in a common expression of the sentiment.[32]

This initial phenomenon was reproduced in a variety of self-consciously imitative ways in other locales, and the effort that went into the viral spread of the phenomenon is apparent in the social media campaigns that accompanied the music. There remains a strong and perhaps curmudgeonly impulse to characterize the performances as generic, pro-forma, and indicative of the erasure of local customs and individual creativity. Nonetheless, the significance of such manifestations of collective musicking is clear from the number of people who engaged with this mode of pandemic-era expression.

In Spain, Georgina Rubio of Monterrey, Mexico sang mariachi music out of her window and had it posted on YouTube, gaining a quarter of a million views.[33] Sofía Ellar created the '*Yo me quedo en casa festival*' ('I stay home festival'), which pulled together an impressive 710 videos on 275 channels of linked content, most of it pandemic music performed by solo singer-songwriters.[34] Colombian singer-songwriter Salomón Beda, who specializes in folk-influenced pop music, coordinated sixteen collaborators in April 2020 to record his new composition 'Pa'lante' ('Forward') as a form of musical response to the pandemic.[35] He wrote that the recording 'has voices from Argentina, Colombia, Peru, Mexico, Ecuador, Venezuela, Chile, Puerto Rico and the United States, a synchronized Pan-American choir to help save lives and protect the most vulnerable individuals in the Region of the Americas'. Beda thought that his song had a special power to promote global health. 'Pa'lante was always a song to heal', he wrote:

> It is a song that helped me a lot personally with mental health and a song that fans always describe as a light that helped them get through a difficult time or heal from a difficult situation. That is why it seemed perfect to me to try to use that light, this song, to contribute what I can to this crisis.[36]

'Pa'lante' simultaneously invoked the full range of these global efforts: inclusive and synthetic music making built on communitarian, transnational efforts. It also served to promote his own artistic brand, consistent with global practices.

A similar global collaborative enterprise, and possibly the best known of the syncretic global music responses to COVID that spread throughout the Spanish-speaking world, was 'Resistiré 2020'. Repurposing a cover of the original popular Dúo Dinámico song 'Resistiré' from 1988, which has both lyrical and melodic echoes of Gloria Gaynor's 'I will Survive', the cover song 'Resistiré 2020' brought together thirty artists. Perhaps unexpectedly, this relatively generic pop song stressing individual fortitude and resistance to feelings of isolation and to life's challenges gained an enormous and self-replicating market of attention and production around the world during the pandemic moment. Its official YouTube release on 1 April 2020 was viewed 69 million times within two years of its release.[37] Another release two weeks later called 'Resistiré México (Video Oficial)', featuring a different group of thirty musicians, gained another 15 million views.[38] The song is a mid-tempo, synthesizer-driven pop song punctuated by quick guitar licks and performed on various instruments. Its vocals delivered with enthusiastic defiance, 'Resistiré 2020' captured the imagination of the public and became widely imitated.[39]

Throughout spring 2020, national versions were released across Latin America as a public exhortation of resistance and resilience for local communities. Each iteration in large part replicated the original, to significant but diminishing audiences. An avowedly pan-American version was released in April 2020 with artists from seven different countries in Central and South America.[40] Twenty-five musicians released 'Resistiré Perú 2020 – Del Barrio Producciones' on 7 May 2020 to 1.5 million views, the first of several Peruvian versions incorporating a variety of national instruments and styles. In August 2020, Peru's national police force got involved and released its own version, which made note of the state of emergency ('*estado de emergencia*') within the country and encouraged residents to respect state mandates regarding the exigencies of the pandemic.[41] Colombian musicians followed suit with 'RESISTIRÉ COLOMBIA 2020 (VÍDEO OFICIAL)' in June 2020, which gained 280,000 views in two years.[42] Informal collectivities and institutions alike hopped on the bandwagon. Mexican mariachis released versions, as did the Banda De Música Policía De Entre Rios of Argentina.[43] 'Resistiré' was used as a soundtrack for pandemic lockdown-themed core and zumba fitness videos and to accompany gruesome videos of medical emergencies, COVID deaths, and burials.[44] Helen Alvarez, Nancy Alvarez, Miosiris Gil Trujillo, Cintia Bolaños, Karen Seborga, Gabriela Elias, and Shary Ergueta reworked the tune into a Bolivian cumbia.[45]

Although dozens of 'Resistiré 2020' versions have been released, they share a commonality in their sonic and presentational attributes. Despite its sameness, this body of music involved thousands of people and gained tens of millions of views. Most versions, whether performed by a few musicians or a massive group, adopted the original upload's Zoom-style use of individual windows for the performers, underscoring the global familiarity with the aesthetics of teleconferencing during the pandemic. A large number of videos show singers reading the lyrics off of phones or notebooks, underscoring the supposed spontaneity of the recordings. Overall, the uploaded covers are remarkedly uniform, utilizing a roughly 100 bpm tempo, and similar timbre, instrumentation, sound, phrasing, and delivery. Even the song's key is fairly consistent across the different versions. Only a handful of uploads changed the rhythm, such as a pan-Caribbean one adding congas and another titled 'Resistire Republica Dominicana' involving forty musicians, which sped up the song to a brisk pace.[46] There were also about a dozen rock versions, which also largely maintained the look, sound, and tempo of the original music video, but with an added rock backbeat and distorted electric guitars.[47] One of the few self-distinguishing versions featured a star-studded collaboration among Peru's salsa elite, including vocalist Daniela Darcourt, percussionist Tony Succar, and Melcochita, salsa's answer to Weird Al Yankovic, among others. This rendition included a section featuring Andean instruments such as pan pipes and tinyas, followed by a salsa break.[48]

The original lyrics to 'Resistiré 2020' deal in general terms with resistance and overcoming adversity, but do not specifically mention the pandemic. In general, performers did not improvise lyrics or use comedic substitutions. The song was a consistently replicated, global pop product. The song was not cloned, but was rather what in Papua New Guinea would be called a 'kopi-kat' (copycat).[49] Covers hewed closely to the original, even when including slightly original or distinctive elements. They were earnest and intentional expressions of community resistance through global connectiveness. Each local manifestation faithfully reproduced the original to serve the purpose of spreading a readily accessible, globally consistent, mid-tempo message of strength.

A similar project with even greater global reach and stronger musical impact reflecting a new community formation within the pandemic developed around Puerto Rican singer Residente's enormous hit song of the early pandemic, 'Antes Que el Mundo Se Acabe' ('Before the World Would End'). This song was released on 14 May 2020, and its accompanying video was viewed more than forty million times on YouTube in two years (as contrasted with the 45,000 views of Beda's song).[50] The composition, which was arranged by the Argentinian-born jazz pianist Leo Genovese, is an open-hearted love song ornamented with piano, strings, and breathy singing. Residente, whose music is typically street-oriented and bravado-laden, seems to soften up in the face of the pandemic. His lyrics insist that love will triumph even if lovers are temporarily separated by the conditions of quarantine. The video, which greatly contributed to the song's appeal, features 75 couples, first in locations across Latin America and thereafter in countries across every continent of the world, kissing each other passionately.[51] The close intimacy of these kisses stands in stark contrast to pandemic norms of face covering and social distancing. These are not cinematic staged performative kisses, but real and highly varied kissing bouts between a variety of couples in different settings, many of them captured via selfie mode on a cellphone. Some couples are on the beach, in bedrooms, in living rooms, on rooftops, on fire escapes, or in kitchens. They span a wide range of ethnicities, classes, and body types, with both opposite- and same-sex couples featured. They all appear young, with each couple in isolation from anyone but themselves. The visuals, showing dozens of couples from all walks of life openly and unabashedly expressing love, are frank, intense, and profound.

The song – swelling, sentimental, and more than seven minutes long – works in direct conjunction with the video. At four and a half minutes, as the kissing couples in the Middle East and Africa appear, the song features cameos from regional artists, including Pakistani vocalist Arooj Aftab and Moroccan gnawa performer Hassan Hakmoun. At five-and-a-half minutes, when Indian couples appear, Rajna Swaminathan's distinctive tabla rolls fleetingly into the mix, only to fall away when the country frame is changed again. Despite the use of sonic shorthands that may be considered essentializing, the video's overall ethos is one of cosmopolitan unity over parochialism. The imagery, lyrics, and musical hybridity suggest that love will unite the world despite the momentary separation we may feel from our loved ones.

Residente insists that love and passion will persist in the face of COVID. Since the song's release, he has been straightforward in stating his reasons for writing the song in a style that might be considered cloying to many. It is not typical of his style, nor is it the norm for Genovese, who is a fixture in the New York City free jazz scene. Its repetitive structure, accessible melody, and gentle dynamics are all designed to facilitate a sense of comfort and community among listeners.[52] Residente's persona as an artist, and even his stage name, are contextualized within a defiant and assertive embrace of the relationship between local and global. On the one hand, he is known for being an unabashed representative of his native Puerto Rico; but on the other, his website's landing page is in English, the global lingua franca, and is full of copy that upsells his cosmopolitan vision: 'I am Residente. [...] We are all residents in the spaces that confine us. Only, here, there are no borders.' He also makes reference to his self-titled documentary and recording project, which involved taking a DNA test, reaching out to artists in his respective ancestral regions, and releasing a collaborative album with them.[53] Through co-creation, Residente overcame the territorial impulse to isolate, and instead created a space of union for musicians across the globe. It was as if as an artist, he had always been preparing for the pandemic moment and for the need for global connections that transcend cultural difference and space. His website is as much historical and socio-political as it is musical, with relatively deep dives into issues for a pop music star, interviews, sounds, images, and footage from across the planet appearing alongside links for purchasing his albums.

The public outpouring of responses to 'Antes Que el Mundo Se Acabe' was vast: the video produced a community of more than 41,000 comments, where people from around the globe expressed their emotional reaction. The majority of the comments were written in Spanish, in which viewers expressed gratitude, love, and a deepened sense of connection to each other and to their families and friends, and described how their own sense of love had been channeled and intensified by the song. Macarena De La Paz Leiva writes that after her father contracted COVID-19 and passed away, she listened to the song on the way to his funeral in October 2020. 'This song has become very important to me', she states. 'I was listening to it while watching the sunset with tears on my cheeks, just thinking that one day I will see him again and we will never be apart, every time I listen to her the lump in my throat gets stronger, my daddy, the biggest star that shines at night' ('*Está canción se volvió muy importante para mi, ya que la iba escuchando cuando iba camino al entierro de mi papá que falleció a causa del Covid, el 16/10/20 la iba escuchando mientras miraba el atardecer con lágrimas en mis mejillas, sólo pensando que algún día lo voy a volver a ver y nunca más nos separaremos, cada vez que la escucho el nudo en la garganta se hace más fuerte, mi Papito, la estrella más grande que brilla por las noches'*). Others wrote that the song increased their loneliness because they were isolated and with nobody to kiss. Steve Suarez wrote '"F" for all of us who in this quarantine don't have by our side that special person we miss kissing' (*"F" por todos los que en esta cuarentena no tenemos a nuestro lado esa persona especial a la que extrañamos darle un beso'*).[54]

The discussion was emotionally varied, with some comments themselves triggering eddies of discussion hundreds of replies deep.[55] The song and the video created a global ecosystem around a shared expression of love in defiance of the pandemic. The song also launched dozens of covers featuring synthesizers, guitars, ukuleles, and pitch-corrected vocals, in reaction and tutorial videos, and many other presentational styles.[56] For many people around the world, it is clear 'Antes Que el Mundo Se Acabe' was a major musical manifestation of their emotional response to the early pandemic moment.

Residente continued to release music reworked for the pandemic moment, such as his 'Latinoamérica (Edición Cuarentena)', released on 31 March 2020, 'Apocalíptico (Edición Cuarentena)', released 26 March 2020, 'René (Edición Cuarentena)', released 14 April 2020, and 'Muerte en Hawaii (Edición Cuarentena)', released 29 July 2020.[57] All received millions of views and were presented in the familiar pandemic-era style of Zoom video frames. 'Apocalíptico (Edición Cuarentena)' was a decidedly global effort, as a collaboration between Residente and the Chinese singer Yun Huang. Although the song had been written before the onset of COVID-19, Residente repurposed it for the pandemic moment. He described his songwriting style in distinctly cosmopolitan terms: 'I wrote this song many years ago in Beijing, China. I think that it reflects the energy going on now, at this time. Whatever happens, happens. We are humans and we will take on whatever comes at us as brothers and sisters.'[58]

Similarly, 'Muerte en Hawaii' ('Death in Hawaii') was presented as an upbeat improvised version with 'ukulele master Abe Lagrimas, Jr.' (*'Improvisando junto al maestro del ukulele directamente desde Hawaii, Abe Lagrimas Jr.'*), underscoring the possibilities of global connections through music despite the continued need for social isolation within the boxes on the screen. The original version of this unusual love song was released by Calle 13, the hip hop duo that first propelled Residente to stardom. Calle 13's video features extremely violent and bizarre imagery, but the song's pandemic re-release is upbeat and positive; Residente and Lagrimas Jr. are both all smiles.

The complex interplay of deliberate global unity, raw emotional resonance, and regional idiosyncrasy has been interestingly reimagined by a collective dance team from Lima, Peru, called 'From My Quarantine' ('Desde Mi Cuarentena'), in collaboration with musicians Vitu Valera and Mikongo.[59] Desde Mi Cuarentena's earliest releases were videos showing individuals and couples performing dance routines at their respective homes. Released in July 2020, the initiative involved 31 participants dancing to Residente's 'Antes Que el Mundo Se Acabe'. While the dancers are seen performing solo, the videos are stitched together to produce a sense of unity and embodied togetherness in spite of physical separation.

Desde Mi Cuarentena responded to the original Residente video in its own unique way by centering the experiences of individual dancers. Each person or couple prepared solo pieces, underscoring isolation. Where the original 'Antes Que el Mundo Se Acabe' featured couples kissing, the dancers responded alone, in different spaces, separated by time, space, and quarantine. As in the original video, some individuals were in kitchens, bedrooms, alone in an outdoor park or in other emptied-out public spaces. A handful of couples danced together. One couple presented an intimate section where a man caressed the swelling belly of a pregnant woman as part of the dance. Centering on embodied movement rather than kissing, this video nonetheless achieves a degree of almost unbearable intimacy. Like the couples kissing with abandon, the dancers invite viewers to delve into their emotional world – a montage of affective snapshots from the pandemic moment. The end of the video features a spoken acknowledgement of the challenges faced by dancers left isolated by the pandemic.[60]

Despite its potential for emotional resonance, the edited video from 'Desde Mi Cuarentena' did not achieve extensive reach. It had had only 300 views by the end of 2021, quite a long time after it was released on 3 July 2020, at which time the 'Desde mi cuarentena' YouTube channel had only five subscribers. This was an internally focused project of dancers responding physically and emotionally to the song and to the pandemic itself. The video set to Residente's song contrasts interestingly with the performative self-expression of TikTok culture and with the compilation YouTube streams of other responses. Rather than seeking an audience, the video seems to be for the participants themselves: although it was posted publicly on YouTube, and engaged with a globally resonant song, the apparent intent was to foster connection and mutual support among this community of dancers.[61] The sense of individual defiance was reiterated in a second video, in which male ballet dancers reject any idea that they should conform to the masculine attitudes of the society at large. Released at the end of December 2022, the members of Desde Mi Cuarentena proclaimed that 'no matter what we wear or have on our feet, we are still men, we are still artists, we are still human and we put ourselves before a macho society that stigmatizes us for the decisions of our personal life' ('*que no importa lo que llevemos encima o tengamos en los pies, seguimos siendo hombres, seguimos siendo artistas, seguimos siendo humanos y nos anteponemos a una sociedad machista que nos estigmatiza por las desiciones de nuestra vida personal.*').[62]

More than two years into the pandemic, it is clear that members of the group adopted a new approach to express themselves. In one of the most creative expressions of new música del coronavirus-adjacent forms to emerge, they created four music and dance pieces during the pandemic, including a specifically COVID-19 evocative piece called 'MAMAKUMBA' on 22 January 2022, quite late in the pandemic moment. Its arrival signaled a new phase in the affective range of music making relating to the coronavirus. Based on an electronica reimagination of Afro-Peruvian traditional rhythms and tones, the electronic sampling of folkloric sounds becomes the impetus for abstract dance pieces expressly structured to reflect the emotions of two years of COVID-19.[63]

In 'MAMAKUMBA', the visuals and choreography are as essential as the music. In an apparently abandoned housing complex covered in faded graffiti by some long-disappeared interlopers, seven male dancers execute a routine that speaks of escape, struggle, and the search for group identity. At first they move in coordinated fashion, only to successively splinter. Two of the dancers wear skirts, challenging the perception of gender solidity. They are also dressed in deliberately mismatched and oddly fitting clothes, evoking a studied disheveledness. The dancers successively gather, hold, and lift each other, forming an aggregate in which individuality gives way to collective fluidity, only to disintegrate by pushing, chasing, and fleeing one another. Over and over, they are pulled back together for a fleeting moment, briefly encountering a way to work together, before once again disaggregating. The whole movement is set to an evocative electronic track incorporating processed cajon sounds, drum samples, and synthesized percussion and ambient harmonies. A few minutes into the piece, the visuals become blurry and disoriented, as the music slows to an ominous crawl. This interlude could be pandemic time itself, which raced forward and seemed chaotic, only to slow into a disorienting experience of confusion and terror. The dancers attempt to grapple with the blurry contours of pandemic-era consciousness. In moments of clarity, they rage against it defiantly, only to become disoriented and to return to their search for escape. Violently banging their heads on a wall, they run and seek egress from the building, but cannot seem to free themselves. In the end they find an exit and escape together, only to disappear one by one. The collective experience of entrapment, rather than generating solidarity, results in atomization and alienation. The final scene shows a lone dancer running to safety. All sound fades, reflecting the eerie silence of the pandemic lockdowns. To a chorus of an enlivened natural world of insect noises, the last dancer returns to the building, choosing safety over freedom.[64]

In Peru, dozens of singers in choruses were brought together to sing, in an initiative coordinated by the Ministry of Culture to serve as a 'voice of encouragement [...] strengthening the spirit of the entire country' through shared singing. The video, produced by the government, featured dozens of people singing together via a Zoom meeting. At the outset, the singers are grouped by age and gender, though by the end they are all featured in concurrent frames as if they were all singing together.[65] A similar endeavor was launched in Cuba in March and April 2020 with the 'Tunturuntu pa' tu casa' festival, designed 'to raise awareness about the importance of staying at home at this time when we have to control the expansion of COVID19' ('*Un festival para concienciar sobre la importancia de quedarse en casa en estos momentos en que tenemos que controlar la expansión del COVID19*'). The COVID-era videos on Tunturuntu Cuba's YouTube Channel represent a wide variety of Cuban music, performed solo and in groups, as well as dance routines. All were recorded within the context of social distancing and self-isolation.[66]

Another globally and consciously consumer-oriented song during the pandemic was Lucia Gil's 'Volveremos a Brindar' ('We'll Return to Saying Cheers'), which had garnered 6.8 million views by the start of 2022.[67] Released originally at the onset of the pandemic, on 18 March 2020, the pensive ballad bemoans not so much the loss of life as the loss of human connection. In her verses, Gil encourages her listeners to remain hopeful, assuring them that soon they will be able to spend non-screen-mediated time with loved ones again. She suggests that lockdowns might even provide us with an opportunity to reconnect with our inner selves and reevaluate what is important. Verses reference the collective cheering for first responders that was commonplace in many European cities at the pandemic's outset.[68] In the chorus, Gil sings triumphantly of one day breaking social distancing and laying aside our screens in favor of face-to-face connection. 'Volveremos a Brindar' evokes sadness, but not despair. Even the song's title implies a hopeful outlook and postulates that the virus will eventually disappear.

While Lucia Gil is based in Spain, people from across Latin American were effusive in their comments responding to the official video for her song. The YouTube comments section, as with many songs dedicated to the coronavirus, functioned as a virtual communal gathering place for people both to share and to reflect upon their emotional responses to the pandemic. The virtual space created by the YouTube platform allowed this community of commenters to cohere. The numbers of commenters were not especially significant when compared to general viewers; out of its more than 6.8 million views and 98,000 subscribers to the Lucía Gil channel, only approximately 2500 people added comments. However, this self-selected group was emotionally affected. Aldo Lascuraín Moreno wrote 'Let's go "motherland" greetings from Mexico' ('*Ánimo "Madre patria" saludos desde México*'), signaling recognition of Latin America's connections to its former colonial ruler. Another Mexican, named 'dexs Martinez', commented: 'Am I the only one who comes here every night to listen to this jewel? Greetings to everyone from Tijuana, Mexico. We will stay home, we ought to be strong to end this virus' ('*Soi el unico que viene cada noche a escuchar esta jolla. Saludos a todos desde Tijuana Mexico. Quedemonos en casa* ♥ *devemos ser fuertes para acabar con este virus*'). Sentimental emojis – particularly hearts and crying faces – as well as flags were commonly used instead of text to express affective states. Vanessa Toapanta's comment – '😭😭😭😭 Greetings from Cuenca, Ecuador' ('😭😭😭😭 *Saludos desde Cuenca Ecuador*') – is short on text but clear in its emotive meaning. From Agua Chica, César, Colombia, Didier Santana shared with sadness that his cousin had fallen ill with COVID-19 and was having to spend his birthday alone in quarantine. Yulanis Kiki commented that in her home country of Argentina 'the bug has not reached the level that it has [in Spain]' but that 'the message of solidarity is welcome and will be of help [...] as the cases surge' ('*gracias desde argentina hasta españa gracias a dios que el bicho no ha llegado al nivel como ahí pero les agredesemos x esta bonita cansion y su mensaje de solidaridad q ya esta bienvenido Seguro que nos ayudara mucho cuando nos llega el pico ya que los casos sestan subiendo*'). Similar comments from El Salvador, Paraguay, the Dominican Republic, and elsewhere echo a shared sentiment of concern and a search for connection and emotional support.[69] This type of connection and virtual communitarianism was prevalent in popular songs by major artists, but often absent in other songs with similar emotional resonance but significantly smaller audiences.

The song also inspired several cover versions, many of which reworked the decidedly global-facing recording into a performance that more explicitly referenced place. On 15 May 2020, Sunset Producciones CR released 'Volveremos a brindar / Costa Rica / Lucía Gil cover / #quedateencasa'. The video stitches together individual videos of Costa Rican musicians performing in their respective homes. A few of the comments left include Costa Rican flag emojis or shout out specific local musicians who were part of the initiative.[70] On 12 April 2020, a Mexico-based channel uploaded '🎧 VOLVEREMOS A BRINDAR Lucía Gil 🎧 CANCIÓN DE CUARENTENA cover México DennMiu', which received under 200 likes in the two years after its upload.[71] Much later, in February 2021, a group of blind women 'from distinct parts of Peru' uploaded their cover 'Volveremos a brindar, Lucía Gil, (cover) chicas invidentes de distintas partes de Perú'. While the video has had under 400 views, comments abound. One commentator, named Valeria, called it 'a very beautiful interpretation' and noted 'I am also from Peru and I'm blind, can I link up with you all? ('*muy bonita interpretación. También soy de Perú y soy invidente, podría unirme a ustedes?*'). Another user, JMC 24 7, left a similar message: 'Excellent, I am also blind and I sing, and I would like to talk to one of you to see if we could record a tune together, because in addition to singing I write my own songs' ('*Exelente, yo tambienien soy invidente y canto, quisiera conversar con alguien* [sic] *de ustedes para ver si es que podemos grabar un tema Porque además de cantar yo escribo mis propios temas*'). While the outcome of these requests has yet to be seen on the public stage, comments like these showcase the joint power of music and social technology to connect people from discrete communities and promote collaboration.[72]

Perhaps the most unusual and distinctive covers of 'Volveremos a Brindar' came out of the town of San Ignacio in Argentina's Misiones province. Like so many other covers, the cellphone recording features a man playing guitar and singing. What makes this recording distinctive, however, is that it is a translation of the original song into Guaraní, an indigenous language spoken throughout Paraguay and adjoining sections of Bolivia, Brazil, and

Argentina. The performer, Germán Acosta, is identified as the cacique of the Taba Miri community.[73] His performance is simple and humble, and the video has gained fewer than 300 views since its upload in May 2020. Nonetheless, a video like this shows how a song so international in its style, reach, and branding can be reinterpreted to reflect local linguistic contingencies. Just as the virus reaches us all, circulating to every corner of the globe, so too do the objects of massified popular culture. In the following sections, this chapter explores even more locally particular manifestations of music-making during the pandemic moment.

'*El Mocoso ya ha Aterriza'o en el Valle*': Vallenatos in the Time of COVID-19

The sound of a peppy accordion hook and a camera frame of a brilliantly blue sky open 'La Pandemia – Fabian Corrales', a video posted by YouTube channel EL SHOW VALLENATO in November 2021 and featuring Corrales singing along with accordionist Leonardo Farfán. As the video continues, a downward pan brings into focus the municipal sign for Urumita, a town of around 10,000 residents in the province of La Guajira. The sign is creatively designed to highlight the region's natural and cultural emblems, with the 'M' representing a partially extended three-row button accordion, and with various reliefs of birds and butterflies integrated into the other letters.[74] Released relatively late into the pandemic moment, this song is the product of a matured sensibility: rather than reeling in the shock of the virus's early onset, its lyrics mostly focus on the economic hardships caused by the ongoing pandemic, with the protagonist asking himself how he will make enough money to eat and to pay his bills. Intercut scenes show Corrales walking into a typical corner store, counting out relatively small denominations of Colombian pesos, and looking generally exasperated. Some scenes cut to wheelbarrows full of sugar cane and yucca roots, which are common staple crops in the region. Occasionally, the video is overlaid with animations of caution tape and a swinging cartoon sign that says 'CLOSED' in English, indicating the use of generic stock footage in an otherwise highly localized expression.[75]

While place-loving lyrics are found throughout Latin American music styles, Colombia's vallenato tradition is a particularly strong exemplar of musical topophilia. This tendency certainly manifests in compositions about COVID-19, which situate the pandemic as an emergent phenomenon within a region with deep roots. Markers of place are found both sonically and visually throughout the music videos of COVID vallenatos. In responding to the COVID-19 pandemic, vallenato artists composed songs that consider it from a distinct regional perspective. Peter Moser writes that the community-situated perspective of performers connects 'both the physical geography of where community music can occur – houses, communities, rivers, community centres – and also metaphysical space – a time in life, a moment in history, a personal feeling.'[76]

A large body of coronavirus vallenatos responding to COVID-19 sits at this convergence of geographical place and temporal moment, connected to their predecessors in their lyrical treatment of the region as beloved, magical, and worthy of claiming as one's own. Most of these compositions encourage regional cooperation out of a shared love of this collective and evocative homeland, while framing the virus as a foreign invader. Without fail, most also draw upon the region's penchant for off-color humor and tall tales, reshaping the pandemic narrative through parody and epic storytelling.

Popular vallenato compositions written long before the onset of COVID-19 are rife with similar themes. Classic numbers in the regional repertory narrate love stories, similar to stories told by Gabriel García Márquez, who once described *One Hundred Years of Solitude* as 'a four-hundred-page long vallenato'.[77] These tales are inseparable from their setting, their protagonists indelible products of their place in the world. Lyrics portraying the itinerant lifestyles of cattle ranchers and troubadours have stayed relevant in the region during a prolonged era of displacement, and linkages between this style of music and its places of origin are often emphasized, well established, and celebrated.[78] On the Colombian government's English-language tourism page, an article ambitiously titled 'Vallenato, the History of an Entire Region' describes how the city of Valledupar, the geographical heart and soul of vallenato, got its name from the indigenous cacique, Upar, who presided over the region at the time of Spanish arrival. 'That's where the city gets its name (Upar Valley)', the article notes, 'and vallenato, in turn, means "born in the valley"'.[79] The linkages between place and music are deep, and a recent educational program has sought to use vallenato lyrics as didactic tools for teaching regional geography.[80] Since being declared 'intangible culture heritage in need of urgent safeguarding' by UNESCO in 2015, linkages between the music style and its home region have received heightened interest from scholars and promoters alike, with varying impact.[81] The music and the place are considered as one: Luisa Pinzón Varilla notes how vallenato's instrumentation (European accordions, African drums, and indigenous scrapers called guacharacas) has been framed as representative of mestizaje in Caribbean Colombia.[82]

Of course, there are distinct imaginaries of the region and its archetypal musical storytellers that often find themselves at odds. One such character inseparable from the form is the romantic juglar, a prankster troubadour who, dressed in an impeccable guayabera and sombrero voltiao, sings of love, of home, and of the noble things in life from a blindingly white balcony adorned with bougainvillea. Yet vallenato's true past and present are not so unblemished: even as the music may be put forward as a symbol of cultural excellence, the themes within vallenato can also be reflective of darker social tendencies within Colombia, including perpetual violence, misogyny, and xenophobia. While these less savory elements pervade even vallenatos about

COVID-19, they are often framed in humorous contexts, creating a perplexing and self-contradictory tension common in Colombian cultural history. Vallenatos about COVID-19 are surprisingly plentiful, even though most have been released and recorded in the same handful of towns that constitute the historical cradle of the tradition. As noted by Marco A. De Leon, the lyrics of many pre-pandemic vallenato compositions grappled with themes of health and the body, particularly in the way they describe the heart and stomach as the sources of emotions such as love, rage, and longing. Even in a region where medical access historically has been limited, De Leon notes, the local music historically makes frequent reference to curative actions, even if the 'doctor' in question is a herbalist or exorcist. Numerous vallenato compositions, according to De Leon, highlight 'the medical act, even the one executed under the protection of ancestral empiricism, and the poetic and metaphorical importance of the heart as a repository of emotions and the suffering of frustrated love'.[83]

One of the most widely watched and historically significant COVID vallenatos was released by Miguel Duran Jr, who comes from a line of well-respected accordionists from Sincelejo, Colombia. On 25 June 2020, his official YouTube channel published 'LA PANDEMIA -VIDEO- (MIGUEL DURAN JR)', a video that has had over 100,000 views in the two years since its release.[84] The video's title sequence shows a computer-generated image of the coronavirus zoom across the screen, followed by the logo for ACV films, the music video's production company. As the first notes from Duran's accordion herald the start of the tune, the video opens with a bizarre moment of steampunk kitsch. In the clip, a mad scientist wearing goggles and a hardhat experiments with several electrostatic generators attached to a contraption replete with a brass wheel and ribbed tubing. In the middle of the strange device, a screen shows another computer-generated coronavirus image. Lightning flashes and the camera pans to the scientist who, like Dr Frankenstein, realizes what he has done and clasps his head in shock. From the outset, the virus is portrayed as an unfamiliar and unnatural abomination.[85]

The following scene – a couple watching the news in a nondescript room – contrasts with the freakiness of the introduction. The television screen in the scene, which recurs throughout the video, flits between showing news reports of the pandemic and video clips of Duran performing. From what appears to be a television news studio, Duran plays the accordion and sings about the pandemic moment. In the first line of the opening verse, he announces the arrival of the coronavirus in Colombia. Later, he is seen looking longingly out his window and praying in his house as he sings about the lockdowns. The scene then switches back to the news studio, where Duran encourages his viewers to follow sanitary guidelines as maps of infection rates in northeastern Colombia flash on screens in the background. An interesting cut midway through the video shows Duran watching a video on a smartphone of medical personnel dressed in scrubs and dancing in a hospital hallway. It is filmed in the first person, placing the viewer in the position of the artist. Such a clip reenacts the common pandemic experience of distracting oneself on a personal device or perhaps using modern social media devices to witness the pandemic and isolate within it simultaneously.

Slightly over two months after the song's release, it took on new significance when its performer and author lost his life due to complications associated with the very disease of which he had sung. After contracting the virus in August, Duran partially recuperated, only to fall ill to a bacterial lung infection attributed to the virus's lasting impact. *El Tiempo* reported on his passing on 3 September 2020, beginning by proclaiming that 'the plains of Sucre are mourning due to the parting of one of the youngest troubadours of sabanero folklore'.[86] In the video's comments section, many offer condolences and bemoan the loss of a young talent: 'Lamentably [this was] the downfall of this singer-songwriter', ('*Lamentablemente la perdida de este canta autor* ☹️😢☹️') wrote JAG SEGURITY, while luis rebolledo chimed in with 'And to think that this damned pandemic took him; what a great artist he was' ('*Y saber que la maldita pandemia se lo llevó Que artista tan bueno se fue* ☹️'). One of the more interesting comments was from Dalis Florian, who lamented with bitterness that 'This man died and not even a single homage [was made] because his last name wasn't Díaz' ('*Éste hombre murió y ni un solo homenaje por qué no era apellido diaz*'), referring to the rampant dynasticism in how commercial vallenato is canonized and promoted. Díaz, a common surname in the provinces of Cesar and La Guajira, is held by a handful of highly esteemed and memorialized vallenato composers and performers, including among others Leandro Díaz, one of the figures to whom the annual Vallenato Legends festival is dedicated; Diomedes Díaz, whose life-sized bronze statue graces the central plaza of Valledupar; Emiliano Zuleta Díaz, of Los Hermanos Zuleta; and Marcos Díaz, the former vocalist in the group Binomio de Oro. To Dalis Florian, Miguel Duran Jr. represented yet another improperly memorialized COVID death; the loss of a soul without due ceremony.

While the above two examples were produced music videos, many pandemic-era vallenato videos showcase minimally edited live performances. In these types of videos, rather than using animations and cut scenes as place-making techniques, the background itself serves as a marker. In 'Covid 19, Vallenato', uploaded by Anderson Rafael Romero Martinez on 3 April 2020, four men including Antonio Paniza and Juan Carlos Rodriguez execute an impromptu performance with the typical instrumentation of accordion, guacharaca (scraper), caja (drum), and standalone vocalist.[87] All are standing, except for the cajista. The video is shot outdoors, with a bougainvillea and a thatched-roof hut clearly visible in the background. It is a tropical, rural setting where exuberant plant life contrasts with stained plastic chairs. The video begins with Paniza making a personal appeal to a friend by encouraging him to stay home. After this, the band launches into a puya, a mid-tempo groove in triple meter that is one of the four core rhythms of vallenato. In the lyrics, Paniza taunts the virus, noting that its fame is over and that, with the assistance of God and government, the people of Colombia will find a way to organize themselves to counteract the pandemic threat. Paniza reads the lyrics off a sheet of paper, squinting at times in the sunlight and pacing around in front of the musicians. He rarely looks at the camera, but his voice itself affords charisma to the hopeful message of the song. The informally recorded video cuts off before the band can finalize the customary final cadence signaling the end of the song.

Los Hijos de Vallenato Talento Indigena uploaded several videos of COVID-related content at the pandemic's outset. The duo identifies as Wounaan, an indigenous ethnic group and language. Wounaan's roughly 10,000 speakers straddle the border between Colombia and Panama, serving as a reminder of the arbitrary application of national borders and the ways that they violently divide the communities that pre-date them. Vallenato's roots are in the northeastern part of the country, far from the historical homeland of the Wounaan people. Nonetheless, the largely mestizo musical tradition has found resonance among certain sectors of Wounaan youth, particularly in urban areas of Chocó province.[88]

In the case of Los Hijos de Vallenato, the young musicians communicate a clear message that their identities as Wounaan and as vallenato performers are somehow linked. Their YouTube channel's description simply proclaims 'Wounaan talent' (*'talento Wounaan'*). Furthermore, at the outset of the pandemic, they released a non-musical video in which they offer a community advisory regarding COVID-19. In this video, vocalist Alix Moña identifies himself as a member of Los Hijos de Vallenato and speaks in a mix of Wounaan and Spanish, with Spanish subtitles overlaid on the video. He encourages his viewers, whether they be indigenous, Afro-descended, mulato, or mestizo, to be careful in the face of the looming health crisis. By linking an indigenous language from the Pacific region bordering Panama to a musical style from the northeastern region bordering Venezuela, Moña marks place in a complex, multilayered way. He links two distinctive regions and sets of cultural experience within Colombia by way of commenting on the global pandemic moment and its shared expediency, speaking to fans of vallenato and Wounaan speakers alike.[89]

In a follow-up video, this time featuring a musical performance, Los Hijos del Vallenato Talento Indigena perform outdoors on the banks of a river. The video for 'Mensaje por el Covid-19 Los Hijos del Vallenato Talento Indígena' earned over 28,000 views over the two years since its release on 9 April 2020.[90] At less than two minutes long, the video begins with a short lick on the accordion, followed by a 40-second speech by the two young performers. Moña, who has already proven to be an articulate speaker in Wounaan, does most of the talking, though this time in plain Spanish. He encourages people to retain their faith, stay home, and pray to God for the pandemic to end. After the speech, the two perform a brief tune, no longer than thirty seconds. Rather than reiterate the themes discussed in the speech, the ditty is a short love song encouraging the listener, the presumed paramour of the singer, to live in the moment, to not overcomplicate the situation, and to enjoy the fruits of life as it is. While it may seem an incongruous choice after a call to vigilance, the video serves as much to soothe as it does to warn. Throughout the clip, the sound of the wind overwhelms the microphone, and at the beginning the ambient noise of an outboard motor is faintly audible.

The tropical outdoor backdrops continue in 'La Pandemia – Canta Alberto Córdoba Quejada', a video that has amassed over 400,000 views since its release in September 2020.[91] Córdoba Quejada is a successful cantautor (singer-songwriter) whose appeal extends far beyond vallenato's regional center of gravity on account of his large Christian fanbase. This is made evident in the large volume of Portuguese replies in the video's comment section. Like many other authors of música del coronavirus, Córdoba Quejada calls on Jesus Christ to intervene and assist in thwarting the pandemic threat. The video even occasionally cuts to scenes of an uncredited religious film, in which bearded, robed men representing the Apostles share a supper – possibly the Last Supper – with a scraggly-haired Jesus figure. Most of the video, however, shows Córdoba Quejada playing his accordion and singing in front of a verdant background. In other scenes he plays in front of two buildings; one a whitewashed house replete with hanging planters of purple flowers, the other a purple building with a blue-trimmed roof flanked by blooming rosebushes. Despite the gravity of the situation about which he is singing, Córdoba Quejada smiles reassuringly throughout the video. Frequent scenes cut to a crowd of townspeople dancing and grinning. Occasional awkward glances and restrained laughs give the impression that the production, although well-edited and in high-resolution video, was a rather informal affair.

Jorge Peña 'El Maestro' also talks about piety and divine salvation in his vallenato 'El Coronavirus / En Su Palabra Está – Jorge Peña 'El Maestro' (VIDEO OFICIAL)', which was uploaded to his official channel relatively early in the pandemic moment, on 25 March 2020.[92] The title of the track references both the pandemic and the Word of God, and salutary shouts of 'aleluya' and 'Dios te cuide' during the introductory section establish Peña's religious stance, although the rest of the video strays from this theme. Like Miguel Duran Jr.'s video, this one opens with the logo of the production company, DFilms. The company slogan – *'Producciónes con Smartphone'* – speaks plainly to the modality of the video's recording and editing. Like many of the others, this video is shot outdoors, and begins with a clip of Peña playing the accordion in front of a tree. He is dressed in a striped shirt and a *sombrero vueltiao*, a woven hat that is widely recognized as a symbol of coastal Colombian identity. Later, as his accordion hangs from the tree behind him, Peña begins to sing. Rather than taking a reverent or pleading tone, however, he instead launches into wry observational comedy, voicing skepticism about the government's ability to quell the outbreak due to general incompetence, and noting how sneezing in public can get one ostracized.

Indeed, the central theme of Jorge Peña's video is not so much faith as xenophobia. In reference to the virus's foreign origins, Peña sings about how he will cross the street if he sees a Chinese person. He goes on to talk about how one should not eat bat soup since, he claims, that is where the virus has its origin. When he sings this, the video cuts to an image of an Asian woman eating a whole bat with chopsticks, a racist image that appeared in videos for música del coronavirus across the hemisphere, especially in spring 2020. Peña then goes on to express a preference for eating suero de arroz, a kind of rice milk that is consumed as a traditional home remedy in coastal Colombia.[93] Peña contrasts this supposedly healthy, local, and historically consumed medicinal foodstuff with a scary foreign dish, thus linking love of place to fear of the other in a stark binary. Commenters are enthusiastic in echoing the sentiment. Eriberto Rodriguez Chaparro writes: 'I thank God for my hen soup and my rice with yucca!... god bless you my brother' ('*Yo le doy gracias a Dios por mi caldito sarco y mi arroz con yuca!... bendicion mi hermano*'). JHONNI RABALLO's comment was blunter: 'go away, Chinese' ('*vayanse chinitoo*'). Ironically, the process for making suero de arroz is remarkably similar to that of preparing congee, a porridge consumed throughout China.

Jorge Peña is far from being the only composer of COVID vallenatos who hones in on this tension between supposedly dangerous foreign foods, which propagate disease and disorder, and the wholesome local foods that a *provinciano* (country boy) ought to eat. The video 'coronavirus – LUCHO COBO Y JULIO 'EL MONO' ORDOÑEZ' was released on 3 March 2020, weeks before the pandemic had brought life to a halt everywhere in Latin America.[94] The video component is just a photo of the artists dressed in t-shirts and *sombreros voltiaos*, but the musical performance is noteworthy. These two performers are no strangers to controversial satire; they are perhaps best-known for their composition 'Osama Bin Laden', a bizarre homage to the late founder of al-Qaeda, replete with local slang and backhanded compliments. A live performance of 'OSAMA BIN LADEN' on YouTube has amassed over 2.7 million views and 1200 comments since its upload in 2006. In the recording, the aforementioned terrorist is framed as a kind of misplaced Colombian hero, with Cobo encouraging a singalong from the crowd in the live version by exclaiming that 'this thing is ours' ('*esta vaina es del pueblo*') in reference to Bin Laden's story.[95] Such a song is not totally incongruous with the history of vallenato, which has at times been appropriated by paramilitary and guerilla groups in Colombia's decades-long armed conflict.[96] In the lyrics of 'coronavirus', Cobo (sometimes stylized as 'Covo') also dives into controversy, claiming that Chinese people will eat whatever they can find that flies or crawls, and envisions an imaginary soup made with bats, tabby cats, and snakes. This commentary is followed up with a warning that, if precautions are not taken, the coronavirus could enter the region and wreak havoc. The pandemic, a threat from outside, must therefore be kept at the gates.

The sonic-culinary regionalism continues in 'La Cuarentena (El coronavirus) – Horacio Mora', a song written by Gabriel Espitia and recorded by Mora.[97] The accompanying video is simply a photograph of the singer next to the names of the song's performer and author. Mora sings about the virus's origins in China, a land where they supposedly eat bats and 'chicken wolf' ('*lobo pollero*'). He then expresses his relief that he is in his homeland, where they instead eat shrimp and crab, establishing the dichotomy between foreign mystery meat and wholesome local seafood. Paradoxically, the 'chicken wolf' he mentions is a species of reptile that is endemic to the wetlands of northeastern South America, not China. In fact, in some communities in the Magdalena delta, the reptile is hunted and consumed as wild game.[98] Its foreignness as a foodstuff is thus totally imagined, as it is far more Colombian than Chinese. Mora goes on to give his friends some advice by encouraging them to eat seafood because it contains vitamins. He then rattles off a list of emblematic regional foods that utilize place-based ingredients and that might serve as a bulwark against the foreign pandemic: catfish soup ('*caldo de moncholo*'), rabbit fricassee ('*fricache de conejo*'), hen stew ('*sancocho de gallina*'), and '*toloyo frito*', a type of fritter.

Other COVID vallenatos also address the complementary themes of topophilia and xenophobia through the lens of food. 'EL CORONAVIRUS Y LA GENTE DEL PUEBLO-Alfredo Redondo X Pedro Perez' tells an apocryphal coronavirus origin story of biblical proportions, in which a Chinese man who had been fasting for thirty days quaffed a batch of poorly prepared bat soup.[99] Likewise, LESTER TV's 'VALLENATO DEL CORONAVIRUS', a video uploaded in October 2020 with only 12 views by the start of 2022, considers local food as a potential cure. In the video, the singer goes through a list of possible scenarios for vaccine production, noting that countries like the United States, the UK, China, and Russia may end up producing their own versions. He views all these options with suspicion, and eventually suggests that Colombians should drink *aguapanela*, a ubiquitous beverage containing cane sugar and lime, as a locally befitting antidote to the coronavirus.[100] In all these examples, love of place – a value with all-round positive connotations no matter the audience – is reinforced through xenophobic comparisons that might evoke scorn, laughter, or confusion, depending on who is listening.

The cancellation of mass events in spring 2020 had a powerful impact on the vallenato scene, especially considering that the genre's largest international gathering regularly takes place in April. Many COVID vallenatos situate themselves within the context of the iconic Vallenato Legends Festival, an annual gathering founded by a cadre of intellectuals, performers, and public officials who sought to consolidate and showcase the region's musical traditions. Since 1968, this festival has served as a stage for prominent vallenato artists to perform, compete for titles, and build connections with local promoters, recording executives, and state administrators.[101] The video 'Vallenato en tiempos de pandemia – Mensaje #QuedateEnCasa (Alfredo de la fe, Wilber Mendoza)', uploaded on 6 April 2020, features several former participants from the festival, including Wilber Mendoza Zuleta, 2013's King of the Accordion ('*Rey del Acordeon*').[102] Along with Mendoza Zuleta, musicians Dany Rosales, Peke Gutiérrez, and Wilson Javier Guerra each offer short greetings from their respective homes, encouraging listeners to stay home and protect themselves. Mendoza Zuleta records from an outside patio, while the others appear to be indoors. When the song starts, the video shifts between frames of each band member playing and clips of different places in Colombia, including major cities – Medellin, Cartagena, Bogotá, Cali, Santa Marta and Barranquilla – and sites of natural, historical, or agricultural interest: Caño Cristales, Ciudad Perdida, Zona Cafetera, Las Lajas, San Andrés Island, and the rainforests of the Colombian Pacific. As images of iconic Colombian landscapes and landmarks flash by on-screen, the singers encourage the listener to respect the stay-at-home orders so that, one day soon, all might be able to return to public celebrations.

Not all references to the festival are so earnest and somber, for as noted in the previous section, this is the land of the juglar. In a video uploaded in October 2020, Omar Hernández plays a lively puyas from the first virtual iteration of the Vallenato Legends stage.[103] An announcer introduces him as he stands with his cajista and guacharaca player before a panel of three judges. There is no crowd, but Hernández plays with intensity and passion. He begins to sing verses comparing his style of accordion playing to the coronavirus, noting how it has been known to induce fevers and sweats and how it has worldwide reach by way of its contagious nature. The purpose of the performance is to showcase playing, not versecraft. Nonetheless, Hernández's poetry makes odd sense in its context. As he shows off his virtuosity with deft runs and groovy syncopations, his claim that such playing causes listeners to lose their sense of smell seems plausible, if only for a moment.

Through official efforts such as the Vallenato Legends Festival, the music has taken on a 'Denomination of Origin' status which, according to Joaquin Vilora de la Hoz, 'was created with its own universe of characters and places in its region, which are identified by its followers in Colombia and other countries'.[104] Some of these characters, places, and customs are described lovingly in Silvio Brito's 'Ausencia Sentimental' ('Sentimental Absence'), in which the narrator celebrates figures and places within the vallenato tradition and bemoans the possibility that he may not be able to go back to Valledupar for the holidays. It is a song of nostalgia and longing from the perspective of an urban migrant who, despite his best efforts, cannot return home due to factors outside his control. It is therefore unsurprising that the song was selected by a group of high-profile vallenato artists who, in April 2020, released a composite video similar to that of Mendoza Zuleta. The video cuts between scenes of ten different artists singing and playing from their homes and offices.[105] Orangel 'El Pangue' Maestre plays a Hohner Corona III accordion with a Star of David emblazoned on the bellows, a reference to his status as the twice-crowned King of Vallenato. Another performer, Beto Zabaleta, is seated in a whitewashed room with modern furniture and an enormous chandelier. Margarita Doria, the only woman in the compilation, sings in front of a painting that is larger than the camera frame. Rafa Perez wears a sombrero vueltiao but is also flanked by rose-toned Chanel pillows; he wants the world to know that he is a *provinciano*, and a rich, successful one at that. A handful of the artists are more modest in how they self-stylize. Jean Carlos Centeno sits in a messy office space replete with house plants and an enormous statue of the Virgin Mary, while a blurry Ivo Díaz sings outdoors in front of a verdant field of bushes and palms. The yearning to return, a long-standing trope in vallenato, was thus re-applied in the context of the pandemic moment, a time where migration, movement, and affective connection to home were even more pronounced than usual. The following section explores how these themes are dealt with in another deeply topophilic style of regional South American music: Andean huayno.

'I Must Return, for If I Die it Should be on My Soil'

'Expresos Molina, Libertad, Flores': these are three popular intra-regional bus carriers in Peru. Such is the opening cry of a coronavirus song uploaded on 28 June 2020 by Los Atuq del Peru (the Peruvian Foxes), a trio from Pampa Gangallo in the department of Ayacucho featuring Arsenio Hinostroza on harp, Fidelito de Huamanga on violin, and Manuel Ventura on charango.[106] The group describes their composition as a *jarana*, a word that, in Peru, originally referred to a spontaneous musical celebration in relation to a religious feast or community event, but which has now come to signify a huayno-style performance from southern Peru.[107] As the music continues, the narrator sings, in the indigenous language Quechua, of his need to return from the city to his village of origin in the face of the oncoming pandemic. He sets the scene – as the sun goes down and the moon rises, he waits hopefully under cover of night for a bus that will take him back from the city to his town. He brings his music with him, though, and sings that whatever happens, whether he returns or stays, lives or dies, he hopes that there will be a violin and a harp to accompany him. He speaks of his crying mother, who knows he is suffering, and questions whether a single individual could ever stay safe from the omnipresent virus, which is wreaking havoc across the entire globe. Referring to fellow urban Quechua migrants, the narrator encourages his brothers in Lima to join him in the return trek.

The description of the video dedicates the song 'to all the compatriot brothers of Peru and the world who left their towns in search of a better future who are now having very difficult times and are forced to return to their places of origin because of the Coronavirus.'[108] Much of the video features footage of the trio performing, but the frame switches to images of people walking along the road carrying packages, presumably heading to their homeplaces. Midway through, the screen changes to a graphic paying homage to the late Victor Tomayro Ledesma, a respected huayno violinist from the region. According to a report on *Hawansuyo*, a bilingual Spanish-Quechua webzine dedicated to Andean music and culture, 'El Cholo Victor', as he was known, was the first of a slew of revered tradition-bearers to have passed away during the pandemic's early stage.[109] Death presents a very different, although not unrelated, type of homecoming than that portrayed by Los Atuq.

Many coronavirus songs in Quechua tell fraught stories of return. The Andes and the criollo societies of urban centers in or near the coast or the altiplano like Lima and Arequipa constitute distinct, albeit interwoven and interconnected, social worlds, and rural-to-urban migration in Peru, driven by political violence and destabilizing land reforms in the last third of the twentieth century,[110] has been associated with intense psychological strain and even trauma similar to out migration.[111] Urbanization in Peru has had impacts on physical and mental health, particularly among indigenous migrants.[112] This is further complicated by the country's history of political violence and destabilizing land reforms over the last six decades. According to Luigi Guarnieri Calò Carducci, these conditions 'caused the mass migration of Peruvians, mostly indigenous and Quechua-speaking, from agricultural areas to cities.'[113] In a case study specific to Lima, Fabiola Escárzaga, Julio Abanto Llaque, and Anderson Chamorro describe a process of 'Andinization', as the arrival of migrants from other parts of the country transformed a metropolitan region known for its heavy cultural investment in European heritage and outward-facing society and economy. Migrants from the highlands came to make up over 40% of the capital district's population by 1993, resulting in a marked transformation of the culture of the country's capital and biggest city.[114]

At the outset of COVID-19, the economic and social catalysts for rural–urban migration were transformed. On 15 March 2020, the government of President Martin Vizcarra decreed a national lockdown[115] As businesses shuttered and urban centers went into lockdowns enforced by the military, indigenous migrants found themselves unable to work, gather, and move in the ways that had initially drawn them to the cities. Between March and December, a quarter million Peruvians made the journey out of the city, seven percent of them on foot.[116] Mario Rufino Trelles calculates that over 165,000 migrants from northern Peru alone attempted to return to their rural communities of origin in the weeks immediately following the lockdown.[117] What once made the city attractive proved ephemeral, and as the coronavirus took its deadly toll and the state responded with lockdowns, the logic of migration became inverted. Before the pandemic, rural communities depended on remittances from urban migrant workers; during it, those who had to remain in the cities were supported by *mandados* of food from the countryside in the absence of wage pay.[118] According to a report by Save the Children Perú, at the pandemic's outset, over 7.5 million Peruvians who already lived in conditions of poverty saw their income decrease due to unemployment.[119] In a May 2020 survey by Peru's National Institute of Statistical Informatics (INEI), researchers found that 14% of polled residents in Metropolitan Lima and the neighboring Callao municipality faced difficulty in acquiring protein-rich foods (meats, fish, or eggs), with 9% reporting similar challenges in securing staple carbohydrates including potatoes, yucca, corn, and rice. Seventy-three percent of respondents cited economic difficulty as a result of job loss due to the pandemic, and 54% indicated that they had relied on non-commercial community networks to fulfill their family's food needs at some point during the pandemic.[120]

The countryside suddenly became magnetic again, with its promise of plentiful food, lower human density, and the possibility of being buried with dignity should the virus strike. While Andean funerary rites vary in their syncretic forms and customs, the presence of the body is widely considered to be an essential part of one's sendoff to the next life. Out of those who attempted the return migration, one study indicates that roughly one in five were Quechua speakers. The same study estimates that 105,000 people left the capital region to return to their areas of origin in the highland regions of Cajamarca, Ancash, Junín, Piura, and Huánuco.[121]

The members of Los Atuq del Peru lived the experience of this mass migration firsthand. Harpist Arsenio Hinostroza recounted in an interview how the group found themselves unable to find transportation home after performing in the capital in March. 'A few days before they declared quarantine in Peru, we had a presentation in Lima for Carnaval', he recalled. 'It was on a Sunday [15 March 2020], and with plans to return the following day, but by then we were in total quarantine, and there was no way to get back. We had to advance on foot, section by section, with much difficulty.' The 350-mile, cross-mountain journey from the coastal capital to Hinostroza's highland hometown of Ayacucho took over a week. Los Atuq 'carried rations, instruments, clothing, everything, and stopped along the way in places where it was safe to rest'. The intensity of the trip was justified by its necessity: 'It was a challenging trip, but we knew we had to do it', concluded Hinostroza: 'We had no place to stay in Lima – our lives awaited us in Ayacucho.' This trek inspired their version of 'Maldita Pandemia', a coronavirus composition born of a shared experience of an arduous homecoming in the face of pandemic lockdowns.[122]

By the time that the YouTube Channel RH Producciones uploaded Michael Sedano's 'Corona Virus Chayaramunña' ('The Coronavirus has Arrived / is Upon Us) on 24 April 2020, this return migration was well underway.[123] The title is in Quechuañol, a mix of Spanish and Quechua, and so highlights lexigraphical syncretism in the Andean region. According to Quechua scholar

Jermani Ojeda-Ludena, the word *chayaramunña* signifies 'the arrival and presence of something'. The root is the verb *chaya*, to arrive; the suffix *-mu* is directional towards the speaker; the suffix *-n* is from the actor (in this case, the third person who is the virus); and finally, the suffix *-ña* means something that has already arrived, something that is already present. As such, the title signifies the overbearing presence of the coronavirus as being both above and within the subject, in terms of both time and place.[124]

The accompanying video for this harp-and-voice composition features a slideshow of striking images of migrants traversing mountainous terrain in crowded buses, on motorcycles, and on foot. The crowds are enormous. While migrants completed this epic trek from city to country, trucks full of foodstuffs made the same journey in reverse, nourishing those who, for various reasons, had stayed in the cities. These trucks also appear in the slideshow, stuffed with bags of potatoes, yucca, and corn destined for the neighborhoods of urban migrants stuck in quarantine as well as the other residents. Over the syncopated bounce of the harp's relentless accompaniment, the narrator gives voice to the pandemic, warning that the coronavirus has declared its intent to kill everyone in the world. Like Los Atuq's composition, this huayno tells of crying mothers and midnight escapes from the city to the country. The verses also speak of the anxieties of dying in the city and being cremated rather than buried.[125] As part of the 15 March shutdown orders, Peru mandated the cremation of all coronavirus victims' corpses: at the time, little was known about the virus's means of transmission, and it was believed that infected corpses could serve as disease vectors. Other countries in Latin America, including the bordering states of Chile, Ecuador, and Brazil, continued to allow burials, and by late April the Peruvian national government reversed the rule largely due to a public backlash, though burial proceedings remained capped at five mourners. Nonetheless, between March and August, at least 4686 corpses of Peruvian COVID-19 victims were incinerated.[126]

Along with plentiful food and lower human density, those in the countryside were more likely to be buried with dignity should the virus strike. In Quechua cosmovision, this and the preservation of bodily relics are of central importance.[127] According to Catherine Allen, 'body and soul in Quechua though are ultimately interdependent'; she explains that 'the colonial Quechua experienced intense psychological trauma when their ancestors' mummies were destroyed by missionary Spaniards, or they themselves were threatened with death by burning',[128] although sometimes the burned were still revered as 'burned lord' or represented by monuments.[129] The relationship between full-body burial and respect for the dead continues to be a point of contention in Peru to this day, as shown when a debate over whether or not to cremate the body of a late leader of the notoriously violent Shining Path insurgency generated national controversy.[130]

Another huayno sung in Quechua, this one from Chumbivilcas in southern Peru, expands upon this theme. In Conjunto Choque Velille's video for

'SUFRIMIENTO DURANTE LA PANDEMIA -CONJ.CHOQUE VELILLE', the musicians appear outfitted in garb associated with the Qorilazo, a southern Peruvian archetype Julio Mendívil describes as similar to the Mexican *vaquero* or the North American cowboy.[131] Conjunto Choque Velille, directed by Victoriano Noa Inca, is a long-established band originally formed by students who shared a common interest in preserving the repertoire, sounds, musical techniques, and folklore of old *música chumbivilcana* and the folkways of the countryside and its people.[132] The four musicians perform on horseback, picking bandurrias and six-string guitars, and sometimes standing together. While the song is new and addresses the pandemic by name, some of the video's footage is drawn from older videos of the group. It is performed similarly to Conjunto Choque Velille's other songs, with tight unison singing hovering over elaborate and repetitive guitar runs. Rapid flights of bandurria pickwork are layered atop one another for embellishment, affording the song a strong sense of momentum despite the swaying meter.[133]

The video features two different sets of musicians intercut with occasional scenes showing people dancing, placing loads onto mules, and traversing mountainous territory in small groups. There are scenes of struggle as well, with bulls locked at the horns and a rooster administering a death blow in a cockfight. The narrators meanwhile sing of the abundance of the countryside. The lack of want is in sharp contrast with the pre-pandemic characterizations of the region as impoverished in comparison to the city. In the video's description, the poster wrote that 'this huaynito is dedicated to all brothers who have embarked on their long journey to return to their little homelands', making note of 'long thirsty walks without food, lots of suffering, burned by the sun, cold and fatigue'. Nodding to the song's standard refrain of 'maldita pandemia' ('damn pandemic'), the channel's description of the song concludes that 'you punish our brothers without mercy'.[134]

Gender roles are clearly delineated in the video, with scenes of women in traditional clothing milking cows and making cheese in buckets adding to the sense of nostalgic self-sufficiency suggested by the lyrics. In the countryside, the song promises, traditional lifeways go on regardless of lockdowns; the loss of a wage job in the pandemic does not immediately translate into a lack of food. Scenes like this imply the distinctly gendered experience of pandemic-era return migrations. According to a United Nations survey of over 38 countries, women and men both saw pandemic-era increases in their unpaid workloads, but women took the brunt of new domestic responsibilities. Women also carried a greater intensity of tasks at home than men, in some cases adding upwards of five hours a day of unpaid caregiving labor, and daughters were more likely to be pressed into familial service than sons.[135] In pre-pandemic Peru, eight out of ten women in the workforce held jobs in the informal economy. At the onset of COVID, as mandated lockdowns and social distancing squashed demand for paid domestic labor, street vending, and other mainstays of a women-driven informal economy, millions of women found themselves unable to continue earning a living, while demands at home increased.[136]

At this time, women in Latin America and the Caribbean were 44% more likely to lose their jobs than men, often due to the new burdens of increased household duties associated with the pandemic.[137] After a decade of remarkable advancement in women's participation in Latin America's labor market, experts at the Economic Commission for Latin America and the Caribbean now fear that COVID will bring the region back to 2008 levels of workforce involvement. The need to cultivate a 'care economy', in which women are compensated for currently unpaid domestic labor, they argue, is essential to achieving the region's gender equality goals.[138] While the images in Conjunto Choque Velille's video may have been meant to evoke an idyll, the viewer must consider the differences in gendered experience that produced the conditions being portrayed.

Noemi Lagos is one of the few women represented within the corpus of Quechua-language coronavirus songs. She narrates her huayno 'Coronavirus en quechua – Noemí Lagos' from the perspective of a young mother who is afraid the virus will kill her and leave her child orphaned.[139] In her verses, she questions why one must face the threat of death at such a young age, and how the coronavirus can be so cruel as to target the most vulnerable members of the community. This maternal narrative is largely absent from the wider body of coronavirus music. Indeed, much of the Quechua-language coronavirus music surveyed is performed by men, with women appearing as secondary figures in some of the videos, such as that by Conjunto Choque Velille.

Departing from the rural imagery of so many of the Quechua-language songs about COVID-19, this video shows a slice of urban Andean life in both its visual and thematic aspects. Unfortunately, like many of the videos surveyed in this book, it has since been removed from YouTube. In the original upload, Lagos performs from a concrete balcony overlooking the city of Ayacucho, backed up by a seated, minimally proficient guitarist. The performers are dressed in contemporary, cosmopolitan attire, with Lagos sporting jeggings, a stylish handbag, and a felt hat. The accompanist plays not a bandurria but a six-string guitar with an engraved pickguard. Both performers wear masks, standing on a rooftop deck. Despite the video's informal setting, the powerful singing drives the performance forward. Although it is performed in a regional style and language, the themes in this huayno find sympathetic resonance in the experiences of millions of caregivers and parental figures for whom the pandemic presented an unexpected and unprecedented threat to their way of life. It also provides a counterbalance to nostalgic portrayals of country life found in other examples of Quechua-language coronavirus music.

Whether performed by a man or a woman, in a rural or an urban setting, and in full Quechua or a Quechua-Spanish hybrid, these compositions all draw explicitly from an experience rooted in a shared culture. In the case of

Quechua speakers in Peru, the politics of language remain at the forefront of the internal migrant experience during the pandemic moment. In moving from the countryside to the city, some indigenous migrants had bought into the promise of integrating into Spanish-speaking society. Tim Marr notes that at times 'Quechua is felt to be somehow incompatible with modernity and the desired self-image of the ambitious migrant.'[140] However, this is not always the case. Ulises Juan Zavallos Aguilar, for instance, has noted how Peruvian indigenist writer and public figure José María Arguedas 'upheld the existence of a modern Quechua individual who did not have to renounce his culture to be cosmopolitan', and how this legacy has been manifested in indigenous (and indigenist) musical production. Urbanized Quechua articulated their identity in Peruvian society in syncretic, emergent forms of storytelling and music making.[141]

Quechua is by far the most widely represented non-European language among the Latin American coronavirus songs surveyed in this book. This is unsurprising, as it is the most widely spoken indigenous language in the Western Hemisphere. Quechua's over eight million estimated speakers are found across the Andes, in Latin American cities, and throughout the diaspora. In Peru and Bolivia, it is recognized as an official language by the state: 13% and 21% of each country's respective populations speak Quechua at home, and it is increasingly being valorized in cultural, educational, and political discourses across the Andes.[142] The Quechuan family, which shares a linguistic substrate with Aymara, the second-most spoken indigenous language in the Andes, is bifurcated into two main branches, one of which is spoken in central Peru and the other of which is distributed widely across the rest of the Andes.[143] While there is mutual intelligibility between these two branches, they are distinct. Most of the coronavirus music is sung in the more widely distributed 'peripheral' or 'Wanp'una' branch, which is found across most of the Andes, but some is sung in Central Quechua, which is spoken in central Peru. However, language discrimination and anti-indigenous stigma continues to threaten the language's continued use. Quechua-speakers constitute around 60% of Peruvians who do not have adequate access to healthcare, reflecting an immense disparity when compared to mestizos or criollos.[144] In Peru, Quechua speakers are, in general, poorer, less educated, and more supportive of populist left-wing political movements. Indeed, Peru's prime minister Guido Bellido stirred controversy when he initiated an August 2021 speech before the national congress in Quechua, in which he addressed, among other topics, the strains placed on Peru by the pandemic.[145]

This tension between linguistic vitality and marginalization is reflected in the sheer volume of music in Quechua responding to the coronavirus. On the one hand, the creative outpouring reflects a lively culture of linguistic resilience; but on the other, it reflects that Quechua-speaking people felt the brunt of the pandemic's burden. In this way, music was not only a form of expression but also a means of community sustenance and cultural survival.

On 23 April, Epifanio Acero released 'CompartirSentimiento del chimaychi# CORONA VIRUS# QUÉDATE EN CASÁ', a solo composition for voice accompanied by huayno violin.[146] In the spoken introduction, Acero dedicates the song 'to all those who are following the rules of lockdown and quarantine', and says that he is going to sing 'in Quechua, for all those who don't understand Castilian [Spanish]'. He then begins playing a punctuated melody full of double-stops and quick triplet turnarounds. Acero's violin is well worn, with a heavy coating of rosin dust below the bridge. Among the body of coronavirus music collected for this book there are very few examples of solo violin pieces, regardless of style. However, this composition is in a huayno subgenre known as chimaychi, a melodic style closely associated with the north-central province of Ancash. Unlike other styles, chimaychi tunes are frequently unaccompanied by a harp or guitar.[147] At about 45 seconds into the video, he begins to sing verses in Central Quechua, warning his listeners that if they wish to stay out of the hospital, they best not go outside.

Sol de Pachaconas's song 'Maldita Pandemia' offers a hauntingly solemn take on the pandemic moment.[148] The huayno begins with a characteristically pentatonic theme played on the harp which interweaves with a countermelody from an acoustic guitar. The singing style, layered with effects, is subdued yet emotive as it interacts with the harp's and the guitar's plucked motifs. Verses alternate between Spanish and Quechua, dealing with slightly different themes. While the Spanish verses ask that the virus go away and sing of the suffering of the people in abstract terms, the Quechua verses begin with the narrator speaking directly to the coronavirus itself, asking that should he be taken, that others might be spared. In Quechua, Sol de Pachaconas describes the virus as a child of the devil. Drawing on the trope of orphanhood found throughout the huayno repertory, the narrator speaks of having no mother or father to visit him in the hospital or cemetery, should the virus strike him. Félix Julca Guerrero and Laura Nivin Vargas note that, in bilingual huaynos, Spanish and Quechua are often used to convey distinctive ideas or moods; rarely are verses direct translations of one another. In choosing to write the most emotionally potent verses of their huayno in Quechua, Sol de Pachaconas affirms the 'language of the heart' and the emotions that using Quechua invokes.[149]

Sol de Pachaconas released his song in two videos on YouTube, the first on 17 April 2020 and the second one nine days later. The original video was set entirely to scenes from the pandemic, with images of emergency workers, police, and healthcare facilities, as well as street scenes of people cheering these workers from the balconies. The second video shows the singer in the studio wearing a scarf in Peruvian national colors that appears to say 'All for Peru'. The video features many different scenes of the pandemic moment, but the greatest number show Peruvians walking down highways carrying bags, apparently fleeing the cities. People wave Peruvian flags, put on masks in the national colors, and wave for the camera. As Son de Pachaconas exhorts over and over that defeating the damn pandemic can be done, we see nationalist scenes of politicians, medical personnel, and others. The videos, together with the song, promise a unity and triumph that clearly requires all to pull together as fellow citizens.[150]

Another performance of coronavirus music in Quechua was uploaded by Gustavo Adolfo Tocto Rojas on 20 June 2020. In this short video, entitled 'CANCION EN QUECHUA SOBRE COVID19', a child sings a brief, pleading verse, asking for the doctors and nurses to bring lifesaving medications to his town, and declaring that there is no reason to go outside if the coronavirus is around. It is an acapella performance, and the low-resolution video is shot in what seems to be a home setting. The child performer sings with some reservation, but never breaks eye contact with the camera. The motivation for the video is unclear; only the performer can be seen, singing into a smudged, low-resolution camera, asking for support in the face of the pandemic.[151] Like the chimaychi example from Epifanio Acero, this coronavirus performance, a child's plea, is delivered in Central Quechua. This indicates how linguistic variation musically grounds the appeal and contributes to a sense of place identity. These videos also demonstrate the active use of Quechua among youth – a hopeful trend after centuries of linguistic discrimination.

Indeed, children are common as presenters in Quechua-language coronavirus songs. In recent years, the language has been increasingly integrated into experimental educational reforms throughout Peru.[152] At the onset of COVID-19, Rosa Cañari, Juan Pablo Aguilar, and Miguel Ángel Pinto, all public-school educators from the International Bilingual Educators Association of Acomayo and Urubamba, wrote new words to an old local tune that directly addressed the pandemic moment. The song is based on the melody of 'La Puka Polleracha/Pulliracha', a ditty sung in various iterations at carnival celebrations throughout the region that has become widely taught in provincial primary schools in southern Peru.[153]

In the video, which is presumably targeted at bilingual Peruvian pupils, animated lyrics provide a didactic guide for the viewer. Quechua, like German and Japanese, is a language of long, composite words. In this video, word sections are color-coded to distinguish stems, prefixes, suffixes, and modifiers. Alongside the text appear cartoon images of an angry-looking coronavirus and various human figures dancing, singing, and dressed in traditional Andean festival attire. The original tune, the title of which translates as 'The Girl in the Red Skirt', is traditionally sung as a taunt among schoolchildren. The lyrics are sung from the perspective of a tattle-tale child who observes a peer's misbehavior and threatens to tell their parents.[154] In the reworked version, 'Yau Yau Kuruna Viruscha', the virus itself becomes the subject of the teasing. Children are encouraged to taunt the coronavirus with the threat of soap and water should it decide to cross over to their corner of the world. Many comments on the video highlight the effectiveness of the song and its purpose. Yhandy Quintana porras commented, 'cool, I love it --- And even better that I understand Quechua, hahaha' ('*bacan me encanta --- Menos mal k yo si entiendo quechua jajaja*'). Many asked for a translation, and while the original uploader did not reply, one commenter, ARIHMAN Cerquis, took a stab at the request and noted that they are still learning the language.[155]

The video also inspired an outpouring of covers. On 24 June 2020, YouTube channel Nicola945 released 'Canción coronavirus', a video of a girl in a dress standing outside introducing and performing her version of 'Yau Yau Kuruna Viruscha'. She begins the video by introducing herself by name. She explains that she is in the sixth grade at a provincial school, although at present she is learning by way of virtual classes. The video features subtitles in Spanish for the song. While almost identical to the original rearrangement, her version makes some slight changes to the lyrics, specifically to address the experience of online schooling. As she sings unaccompanied, she twirls and dances.[156] Lida Bendezu also uploaded a version to her eponymous YouTube channel, this one featuring a pre-recorded backing track.[157] The even younger girl in Bendezu's upload also dresses in regional festival attire. She sings some lines to the backing track, but overall seems more interested in dancing and waving around a string of pom-poms.

Another striking music video with a child narrator, 'Sayuri Cruz Huamani CORONAVIRUS Canción De La Cuarentena', features a young girl in a pollera dress dancing around a well. Accompanied by an older man playing bandurria cusqueña, she sings in a raspy voice while moving around, terrifyingly, at the well's rocky edge. Cruz Huamani calls out the coronavirus, begging it to not come for her as she is a wakcha, a label of poverty that signifies not only lack of financial resources but also landlessness, orphanhood, or estrangement. The wind blows hard against the microphone throughout.[158] According to Quechua scholars Jorge Alejandro Santos and Mario Mejía Huamán, this complex and multifaceted word is integral to the worldview 'that goods, technologies and media are useless without the social, family and kinship relationships that make them work.'[159] In the midst of a global pandemic that wreaked havoc even upon the nations at the supposed top of the economic and technological development ladder, such an understanding of sociality and its primacy becomes even more poignant. Without mutual aid, cooperation, and systems of egalitarian social welfare, the coronavirus turns each of us into a wakcha.

As discussed in the previous chapter, mourning and grief are consistent themes in the wider body of huaynos about the coronavirus. Bilingual Spanish-Quechua music seems particularly well-suited for describing the pandemic moment – a time of loss of life and livelihood. Indeed, expressive sorrow is a core aspect of ritual performance among Andean musicians. In Quechua musician-scholar Maximo Damián Huamani's account of his role in a funerary performance for a beloved late violin teacher, he writes that 'for six months I'll wear mourning, as we do in my village, but that won't be the end of my sorrow. I've been suffering and crying, and why not, when he was one of us.'[160]

This customary mourning is reflected in much of the coronavirus music repertory from the region. In a solo harp performance from the Cuzco department uploaded on 7 May 2020, Jhonson Ichpas voices the anxieties of living in constant uncertainty during the pandemic moment in 'QUÉDATE EN CASA // canción en quechua // Jhonson Ichpas'.[161] In one verse, he sings about how one day he might simply die unexpectedly, and that the culprit most certainly would be the coronavirus. The song, a contrafactum of a pre-existing huayno titled 'Esposa Mia', begins with a spoken intro in Spanish, but the verses are in Quechua. Ichpas performs on his harp in the middle of a forest, alone. The camera zooms in on his fingers and the vibrating strings of the harp. The visual effect of wobbling strings, combined with a cyclical bass motif played with the left hand, induces a hypnotic effect. Ichpas's haunting vocal melodies are consistently undergirded by his ethereal, sometimes syncopated harp accompaniment. At some points in the video, the scene zooms out and cuts to scenes of small towns in the Peruvian countryside, evoking nostalgia and a sense of place. Inexplicably, at about four-and-a-half minutes into the five-minute piece there is a loud overlay of ice cubes in a glass and a carbonated beverage being poured, which quickly disappears. Ichpas also addresses his fear of cremation, and encourages his Quechua brothers to follow the advice of the authorities and stay home.

Fellow Cusqueño Ebert Suni also uploaded a solo performance of a coronavirus huayno directed at the Quechua-speaking community early in the pandemic moment. Suni, who is a member of Los Hijos de Tinta, a highly sought-after group of traditional musicians from the Cuzco region, performed in a video titled 'Ebert Suni – Huayno Carnaval cusqueño / coronavirus cusco', uploaded on 20 March 2020.[162] The video is filmed indoors; Suni plays an 18-string bandurria cusqueña and sings a wailing melody in Quechua. According to Suni, the song form is borrowed from a popular carnival melody that is frequently performed in Tinta. Spanish subtitles are included in the frame, and address many of the themes already discussed: orphanhood, estrangement, fear of undignified death and cremation, crying mothers, and the sense of being made a wakcha by the virus. The force of his strumming, combined with his full-throated and quaking vocal delivery, results in audio distortion, which contributes to the video's affective intensity. Suni makes it clear that he will not leave the house until the threat of the coronavirus has passed.

Not all Quechua-language responses encourage staying at home and cursing the pandemic, however. Some accept the threat of death as a part of life, and encourage people instead to celebrate what they have in the face of tragedy. These are the themes in 'Carnaval COVID 19 – Maestro José Guacho | Video Oficial', a video uploaded on 14 February 2021, nearly one year into the pandemic moment.[163] This salutary number from the highlands of Ecuador is sung in Kichwa, a dialect of Quechua spoken in the northern Andes. This music video, shot with high production values and including wide-angle drone shots in 4K, straddles the divide between traditional and contemporary. Dozens of dancers wear *llikllas*, traditional embroidered shawls from the region, and other traditional clothing. Many others hold celebratory totems and dance with decorative masks and flags. The entire recording is undergirded by a thumping electronic percussion groove and accordion riffs. In the lyrics, vocalist Jose Guacho acknowledges to a gathered, forlorn crowd that the world has been turned upside down by the pandemic and that his community has lost many to the virus. However, rather than encouraging people to stay home and observe sanitary measures, he proposes carnaval celebrations as a cathartic way to shake off the sorrow of the moment. The group erupts into happiness and song. The crowd in the video get progressively wilder, dancing with abandon. Soon, people push each other into an enormous muddy puddle. The carnaval party song honors those who have lost their lives, while possibly propagating the very disease to which they fell. Guacho contends with this directly, acknowledging in the final verse that death is afoot at the celebrations, and that nobody is safe from the coronavirus and its omnipresent reach.[164]

On 24 March 2020, YouTube channel GADIEL PRODUCCIONES – HUANCABAMBA uploaded a music video by a popular local four-piece band called Los Caminantes de Peru. The song, 'EL CORONAVIRUS (LA PANDEMIA)', at once rallies Peruvians in unified defiance of the pandemic while warning that it was coming and that everyone should stay at home. The song warns of the arrival of the coronavirus from China to Peru and shames those who have not taken public health seriously, labeling them ungrateful citizens. The rest of the world was already being affected when it arrived in Peru. The song urges the police, armed forces, and the president to take a stand or else the coronavirus will kill more people.[165]

Los Caminantes de Peru plays huayno music on electronic and acoustic instruments, including acoustic-electric guitar and requinto, electronic drums, and synthesized panpipes. The band's name (the Walkers of Peru) evokes the lasting significance of the Inca road that once connected Quito in Ecuador and Cajamarca in Peru through the valley of Huancabamba, passing through a town of the same name. Known in Quechua as Qhapaq Ñan, this road continues to be a site of both ongoing archaeological discovery and contemporary social relevance. Travelers still use many of its old routes.[166]

In 'EL CORONAVIRUS (LA PANDEMIA)', the band does not appear performing in the over five-minute long video for the song, which instead focuses on a group of men and women dancing in a field. Three couples surrounded by horses move and wave a Peruvian flag and Cajamarca-style hats. A large crowd of at least a hundred other revelers stands on the edge of the field, a few dancing and the others observing. The scene is not of the pandemic but of a festival, possibly carnaval, the holiday celebrated in Latin America before the Catholic season of fasting known as Lent begins. Some people ride on horseback, while others sit in front of plates of food. An ever-present mountain backdrop makes it clear that this celebration is in the heart of the valley. The huyano propels along pushed by electronic requinto and drum fills. Los Caminantes de Peru's singing becomes almost a chant about ways for listeners to stay safe. In the visuals, the festival celebration continues.

Viewer comments on the song are varied, but many express a shared attachment to the region and sense of unity in the face of the virus. CARMEN ROSA CHOQUEHUANCA VELARDE wrote of the festival that 'this function is pretty in Ayacucho and Cajamarca' ('*esta fucion esta lindoen Ayacucho y Cajamarca*'). Jose Yanes noted, maybe a bit archly, that he did not see anyone wearing masks ('*No veo a nadie usando mascarilla*'), whereas Luis Aguilar jara mused that it was a 'pretty song for reflecting' ('*Hermosa camcion para reflexcionar*'). Eloy Lopez Saavedra took up the spirit of the song with a message of encouragement: 'Friends let's become aware, stay at home and avoid getting infected ('*Amigos tomemos conciencia qedemonos en casa y evitemos de contagiarnos*'). Jeffri Mendes wrote a comment that likely summed up the sentiments of many who watched the video: 'I miss that valley and I want to go back' ('*echo d menos eseballe y mekiero rebolver*'). The song, which had more than 42,000 views in two years, had the exact impact intended, by framing the experience of the pandemic in decidedly local and evocative terms. Luis Chuquitarco called it a '[g]ood record [that] sings the straight truth of what is happening to us the world over' ('*Buen disco canta solo la verdad de lo que nos esta pasando en el mundo entero exitos a los caminantes de peru*'). Jorge fernandez agreed, calling the song a 'good little huayno from Peru for the whole world' ('*buen huaynito del Perú para el mundo entero*').[167]

Throughout Latin America, musical production has empowered individuals and groups to contest, question, and reframe the experiences of the global pandemic moment in idiosyncratic ways. This chapter has drawn from a wide range of examples that reflect the diverse geographies, sociospatial positions, and identities of artists from throughout the region. It is hard to imagine better epigraphs for local musical responses to the pandemic moment than exactly this: 'a good little huyano' delivering 'straight truth of what is happening the world over'.

Notes

1. 'Coronavirus Canción PACHITA – YouTube', https://www.youtube.com/watch?v=Mp4ZDQQ-WE4 (accessed 19 April 2022).
2. Carlos E. Agudelo, 'El Pacífico colombiano: de "remanso de paz" a escenarioestratégico del conflicto armado: las transformaciones de la regióny algunas respuestas de sus poblaciones frente a la violencia', *Cuadernos de Desarrollo Rural* 46 (2001): 7–37.
3. Arturo Escobar, 'Displacement, Development, and Modernity in the Colombian Pacific', *International Social Science Journal* 55.175 (2003): 157–67.

4. Leonor Convers, Juan Sebastián Ochoa, and Oscar Hernández, *Arrullos y Currulaos: Material para abordar el estudio de la música tradicional del pacífico sur Colombiano tomos I y II* (Cali, Colomnis: Pontificia Universiedad Javeriana, 2014).
5. Julián F. González Sánchez, '"Yo he venido a buscar, los pasos que me han faltado": un acercamiento a la noción de muerto a partir del alabado en las comunidades afrodescendientes de Cértegui y Winandó', PhD thesis, Universidad del Rosario, 2021.
6. Luz A. Maya Restrepo, 'África: Legados Espirituales en la Nueva Granada, Siglo XVII', *Historia Crítica* 12 (1996): 29–42, p. 35.
7. Michael Birenbaum Quintero, *Rites, Rights and Rhythms: A Genealogy of Musical Meaning in Colombia's Black Pacific* (Oxford: Oxford University Press, 2018), p. 38.
8. Interview with Francisca 'Pachita' Castro, by J. A. Strub and Dan Margolies, 7 October 2021.
9. 'Coronavirus Canción PACHITA – YouTube', https://www.youtube.com/watch?v=Mp4ZDQQ-WE4 (accessed 19 April 2022).
10. Castro interview.
11. Quintero, *Rites, Rights and Rhythms*, p. 21.
12. Isabel Goyes Moreno and Sandra Montezuma M., 'Justicia y *Género en Nariño* en Casos de Violencia contra las Mujeres', *La manzana de la discordia* 7.2 (2012): 15–22.
13. Interview with Omar Quiñones, by J. A. Strub, 22 April 2022.
14. Jennifer C. Lena, *Banding Together: How Communities Create Genres in Popular Music* (Princeton, NJ: Princeton University Press, 2021), p. 170; On scenes and authenticity see Kathryn M. Nowotny, Jennifer L. Fackler, Gianncarlo Muschi, Carol Vargas, Lindsey Wilson, and Joseph A. Kotarba, 'Established Latino Music Scenes: Sense of Place and the Challenge of Authenticity', *Studies in Symbolic Interaction* 35 (2010): 29–50; Michael Gibson, '"That's Hip-Hop to Me!": Race, Space, and Temporal Logics of Authenticity in Independent Cultural Production', *Poetics* 46 (2014): 38–55.
15. On place making and imaginaries in Latin American cities, see Jeremy Smith, 'Southern Lights: Metropolitan Imaginaries in Latin America', *Thesis Eleven* 166.1 (2021): 118–35.
16. Mark Hijleh, *Towards a Global Music History: Intercultural Convergence, Fusion, and Transformation in the Human Musical Story* (New York: Routledge, 2019), p. 3.
17. Andrew Sayer, 'Behind the Locality Debate: Deconstructing Geography's Dualisms', *Environment and Planning A: Economy and Space* 23.2 (1991): 283–308, p. 293.
18. Clemens Greiner and Patrick Sakdapolrak, 'Translocality: Concepts, Applications and Emerging Research Perspectives', *Geography Compass* 7.5 (2013): 373–84, p. 374.
19. In assessing the novelty of translocal frames of understanding, Katherine Brickell and Ayona Datta argue that it 'takes on an "agency-oriented" approach to transnational […] experiences' in contrast to earlier understandings of globalized relations which focused 'largely on social networks and economic exchange' – Katherine Brickell and Ayona Datta, *Translocal Geographies* (Farnham, UK: Ashgate, 2011), p. 3.
20. Peter Wade, *Music, Race, and Nation: Música Tropical in* Colombia (Chicago: University of Chicago, 2000), p. 226.
21. David Conradson and Deirdre McKay, 'Translocal Subjectivities: Mobility, Connection, Emotion', *Mobilities* 2.2 (2007): 167–74, p. 168.
22. Tuan Yi-fu, *Topophilia: A Study of Environmental Perception, Attitudes, and Values* (New York: Columbia University Press, 1990), p. 4.
23. For example, Vinicio Aleman's mariachi song 'Canción a nuestros hermanos muertos por COVID' ('Song for our brothers dead of COVID') speaks plainly of the pain caused by death and loss due to the pandemic, alongside footage of masked La Cruz Roja Mexicana workers in split-screen with the faces of the dead, maps of places of infection, funerals, and other death scenes relating to the pandemic – 'Canción a nuestros hermanos muertos por COVID', 2020, https://www.youtube.com/watch?v=-vQx0G49jXk (accessed 3 February 2022). El Mariachi Loco of the Quintana Roo police department similarly put out a song in March 2020 which gained a large audience

(18,000 views on their original upload and another 125,000 on other repostings) to burnish police service credentials while also calming the public with information and song. 'Policías mexicanos informan del coronavirus con mariachi,' https://www.youtube.com/watch?v=PQ_V2iN1kYk (accessed 3 February 2022); 'Coronavirus en México. Con 'El Mariachi Loco' policía de Quintana Roo frente a la pandemia,' https://www.youtube.com/watch?v=qcZ_M4kQjPI (accessed 3 February 2022). The pandemic hit mariachis especially hard: 'How Coronavirus Threatens Mexico's Mariachi Industry,' https://www.youtube.com/watch?v=Z1vAUpOpAGI (accessed 3 February 2022); José R. Torres-Ramos, comments in 'Social Distancing, Musical Togetherness: The Nexus of Community Music, Health, and Technology during the COVID-19 Pandemic,' roundtable, 66th Annual Meeting of the Society for Ethnomusicology, 29 October 2021.
24. Nadeem Karkabi, 'Electro-Dabke: Performing Cosmopolitan Nationalism and Borderless Humanity,' *Public Culture* 30.1 (2018): 173–96, p. 174.
25. Albert Fernández, 'La revolución de los balcones.' *On Barcelona*, 18 March 2020, https://www.elperiodico.com/es/onbarcelona/a-la-ultima/20200318/balcones-coronavirus-actividades-vecinos-7895699 (accessed 8 April 2021).
26. UN Department of Global Communications, 'La Música no cura una pandemia, pero alegra el alma,' *Naciones Unidas Respuesta a la COVID-19*, https://www.un.org/es/coronavirus/articles/el-poder-de-la-musica-durante-coronavirus (accessed 1 March 2022). The general situation in Italy in multiple cities and modes was described in media reports: Vanessa Thorpe, 'Balcony Singing in Solidarity Spreads across Italy during Lockdown,' *The Guardian*, 14 March 2020, https://www.theguardian.com/world/2020/mar/14/solidarity-balcony-singing-spreads-across-italy-during-lockdown (accessed 1 July 2022); Melissa Locker and Ashley Hoffman, 'People Quarantined in Italy Join Together In Song From Balconies During Coronavirus Lockdown,' *Time*, 13 March 2020, https://time.com/5802700/lockdown-song/ (accessed 9 April 2021).
27. William Booth, Karla Adam, and Pamela Rolfe, 'In Fight against Coronavirus, the World Gives Medical Heroes a Standing Ovation,' *Washington Post*, 26 March 2020, https://www.washingtonpost.com/world/europe/clap-for-carers/2020/03/26/3d05eb9c-6f66-11ea-a156-0048b62cdb51_story.html (accessed 3 February 2022); Alan Taylor, 'Music and Encouragement From Balconies Around the World,' *The Atlantic*, 24 March 2020, https://www.theatlantic.com/photo/2020/03/music-and-encouragement-from-balconies-around-world/608668/ (accessed 18 April 2022); Esha Sarai, 'COVID-19 Diaries: Balcony Ballads a Bust in Washington, DC,' *VOA News*, 28 April 2020, https://www.voanews.com/a/covid-19-pandemic_covid-19-diaries_covid-19-diaries-balcony-ballads-bust-washington-dc/6188338.html (accessed 3 February 2022).
28. Gary V. Engelhardt, Michael D. Eriksen, and Nadia Greenhalgh-Stanley, *A Profile of Housing and Health Among Older Americans*. Research Institute for Housing America Research Paper 13.03 (MacArthur Foundation, 2013), https://papers.ssrn.com/abstract=2359676.
29. Simon Frith, *Popular Music: Critical Concepts in Media and Cultural Studies, Volume IV: Music and Identity* (London: Routledge, 2004), p. 55.
30. https://twitter.com/valemercurii/status/1238234518508777473 (accessed 4 April 2022); https://www.youtube.com/watch?v=fnbqUBBpCTs (accessed 4 April 2022).
31. https://twitter.com/alextdr8/status/1239050121461075968 (accessed 4 April 2022).
32. Emily St. James, 'Watch: Quarantined Italians are Singing their Hearts Out. It's Beautiful,' *Vox*, 13 March 2020, https://www.vox.com/culture/2020/3/13/21179293/coronavirus-italy-covid19-music-balconies-sing (accessed 3 February 2022).
33. 'Canta mexicana mariachi desde su balcón en Barcelona,' https://www.youtube.com/watch?v=bCrEd24a-jA (accessed 3 February 2022).
34. '#YoMeQuedoEnCasaFestival,' https://www.youtube.com/hashtag/yomequedoencasafestival.

35. The artists were Santiago Cruz, Sie7e, Telebit, Simon Grossman, Luz Pinos, Vicente Cifuentes, Marissa Mur, Mareh, Pilar Cabrera, Kanaku y el Tigre, Sebastián Romero, Alejandro y Maria Laura, Duina del Mar, Números Primos, Lorena Blume, and Alejandro Roca Rey, 'Salomón Beda-Pa'lante feat. 16 artistas Latinoamericanos (Video Oficial)', https://www.youtube.com/watch?v=Y5jwkDM-AQc (accessed 3 February 2022).
36. Translation from the Spanish original description.
37. 'Resistiré 2020 – Video Oficial', https://www.youtube.com/watch?v=hl3B4Ql8RtQ (accessed 3 February 2022). The musicians involved included Alex Ubago, Andrés Suárez, Álvaro Soler, Blas Cantó, Carlos Baute, Conchita, David Bisbal, David Otero, David Summers, Despistaos, Diana Navarro, Dvicio, Efecto Mariposa, Efecto Pasillo, Ele, Georgina, India, Jose Mercé, Josemi Carmona, Manuel Carrasco, Melendi, Mikel Erentxun, Nil Moliner, Pastora Soler, Pedro Guerra, Pitingo, Rosana, Rozalén, Rulo, Sofía Ellar, and Vanesa Martín.
38. 'Resistiré México (Video Oficial)', https://www.youtube.com/watch?v=uBGlv05JUJI (accessed 3 February 2022).
39. The name was similarly used by other transnational projects, such as the 30-month 'Resistiré' European Science Foundation research project dedicated to 'reducing gendered inequalities caused by the COVID-19 pandemic', https://resistire-project.eu/ (accessed 1 August 2022).
40. 'Resistiré 2020 América – Video Oficial', https://www.youtube.com/watch?v=a0qoh-vk2MI (accessed 3 February 2022).
41. The artists were Emanuel Soriano, Daniela Feijoó, Erick Elera, André Silva, Miguel Alvarez, Stephanie Orúe, Maria Grazia Gamarra, Sebastián Monteghirfo, Aldo Miyashiro, Érika Villalobos, Ximena Palomino, Cielo Torres, Melissa Paredes, Mariagracia Mora, Mayella Lloclla, Haydeé Cáceres, Arianna Fernández, Andrés Vílchez, Juan Carlos Rey de Castro, Brando Gallesi, Martín Velásquez, Ismael Contreras, Pascal, Koki Bonilla, Henry Campos, Cucho Galarza, and Juancarlos Fernández, 'Resistiré Perú 2020 – Del Barrio Producciones', https://www.youtube.com/watch?v=pbShySSHRac; 'RESISTIRÉ VERSIÓN PNP TINGO MARÍA', https://www.youtube.com/watch?v=ykOs0gtm2pM (accessed 15 April 2022).
42. 'RESISTIRÉ COLOMBIA 2020 (VÍDEO OFICIAL)', https://www.youtube.com/watch?v=TJiqyAJEqFc (accessed 15 April 2022).
43. 'RESISTIRE Mariachi IMPERIAL Elegancia Mexicana', https://www.youtube.com/watch?v=RsVyN2PnK3A (accessed 3 February 2022); 'RESISTIRE – (Montoro – Calva) BANDA DE MUSICA P.E.R.', https://www.youtube.com/watch?v=crjP4h5AECM (accessed 3 February 2022).
44. 'Resistiré 2020' CoreoFitness (MundoGuyi)', https://www.youtube.com/watch?v=-NcfjiCzlM8 (accessed 3 February 2022); 'Resistiré 2020 😷 CORONAVIRUS 😷', https://www.youtube.com/watch?v=VQsPf4XZ-Kg (accessed 3 February 2022).
45. 'RESISTIRE (Version Cumbia Boliviana)', https://www.youtube.com/watch?v=ZqYiKryCmzk (accessed 3 February 2022).
46. 'Resistiré 2020 – Caribeños 'Juntos Por La Música' (Video Oficial)', https://www.youtube.com/watch?v=5OvXZQqE1x4 (accessed 3 February 2022); 'Resistire Republica Dominicana [Official Video]'. https://www.youtube.com/watch?v=QZWQkWJdUQE (accessed 3 February 2022). The musicians included Alex Bueno, Alex Matos, Amarfis (La Banda de Atakke), Alexandra (Monchy & Alexandra), Andre Veloz, Covi Quintana, Charytin Goico, Daniel SantaCruz, Eddy Herrera, Fefita La Grande, Hector 'El Torito' Acosta, Javier Grullon, Jandy Ventura, Johnny Ventura, Jose Alberto 'El Canario', Juliana, Julio Zabala, Kiko Rodriguez, Kinito Mendez, Krisspy, Manny Cruz, Maridalia Hernandez, MerenGlass, Miriam Cruz, Milly Quezada, Natti Natasha, Nathalie Hazim, Nelson Zapata (Proyecto Uno), Pavel Nuñez, Pochy Familia, Rafa Rosario,

Riccie Oriach, Rubby Perez, Sergio Vargas, Sexappeal, Techy Fatule, Tueska, Wason Brazoban, and Wilfrido Vargas .
47. For example, 'Resistire rock', https://www.youtube.com/watch?v=cZj_qChr60c (accessed 3 February 2022); 'RESISTIRÉ 2020 (VERSIÓN ROCK) HEARTBREAKER Rob Wolf & Marco May', https://www.youtube.com/watch?v=PXqlSuOliQY (accessed 3 February 2022).
48. 'RESISTIRÉ PERÚ 2020 ♪ Daniela Darcourt, Tony Succar, Mayra Goñi, Bartola, Roberto Blades, Melcochita', https://www.youtube.com/watch?v=eTFtWYX_u5E (accessed 3 February 2022).
49. Denis Crowdy, 'Tribute Without Attribution: Kopikat, Covers and Copyright in Papua New Guinea', in Shane Homan, ed., *Access All Eras: Tribute Bands and Global Pop Culture* (New York: Open University Press, 2006), 229–40, p. 238.
50. 'Residente – Antes Que el Mundo Se Acabe (Official Video)', https://www.youtube.com/watch?v=FJi3EgUMb4k (accessed 2 February 2022).
51. A YouTube user named Juando Navarrete accounted for all the places with timestamps in a comment on the video (see previous note).
52. 'Residente – Antes que el mundo se acabe (Reacción)', https://www.youtube.com/watch?v=9qewjC2-iQk (accessed 3 February 2022).
53. http://residente.com/en/ (accessed 3 February 2022).
54. In internet parlance, 'F' refers to a 'fail' – a loss or generally undesirable situation to be in.
55. 'Residente – Antes Que el Mundo Se Acabe (Official Video)', https://www.youtube.com/watch?v=FJi3EgUMb4k (accessed 2 February 2022).
56. For example, 'Residente – Antes Que el Mundo Se Acabe (version acústico)', from Palma de Mallorca; 'Residente – Antes que el mundo se acabe (Ukulele Cover)', https://www.youtube.com/watch?v=5USemN9wXVo (accessed 2 February 2022); 'Residente – Antes Que el Mundo Se Acabe (Versión Acustica)', https://www.youtube.com/watch?v=sH_ApvsakaY (accessed 11 April 2022).
57. 'Residente – Latinoamérica (Edición Cuarentena)', https://www.youtube.com/watch?v=crXjkY1QBck (accessed 11 April 2022); 'Residente – Apocalíptico (Edición Cuarentena)', https://www.youtube.com/watch?v=3fJGAuHhlsw (accessed 11 April 2022); 'Residente – René (Edición Cuarentena)', https://www.youtube.com/watch?v=h6MV_dUZWn8 (accessed 11 April 2022); 'Residente – Muerte en Hawaii (Edición Cuarentena)', https://www.youtube.com/watch?v=HspkLi4iLxU (accessed 11 April 2022).
58. 'Residente – Apocalíptico (Edición Cuarentena)', https://www.youtube.com/watch?v=3fJGAuHhlsw (accessed 11 April 2022).
59. 'Vitu Valera & Mikongo – MAMAKUMBA (Video Clip)', https://www.youtube.com/watch?v=K57yhp1DaLA (accessed 15 April 2022).
60. 'Desde mi cuarentena – 1era Edición', https://www.youtube.com/watch?v=MFFgTDR_6Gc (accessed 2 February 2020).
61. 'Desde mi cuarentena – 1era Edición', https://www.youtube.com/watch?v=MFFgTDR_6Gc (accessed 2 February 2020).
62. 'Desde mi cuarentena – 2da Edición', https://www.youtube.com/watch?v=rcw6A2JzUMI (accessed 2 February 2020).
63. 'Vitu Valera & Mikongo – MAMAKUMBA (Video Clip)', https://www.youtube.com/watch?v=K57yhp1DaLA (accessed 2 February 2020).
64. 'Vitu Valera & Mikongo'.
65. 'Contigo Perú interpretado por integrantes del Coro Nacional y del Coro Nacional de Niños', https://www.youtube.com/watch?v=PsSZcAj_NrQ (accessed 7 March 2022).
66. For example 'Tunturuntu Pa' Tu Casa: Jueves 19 de Marzo 2020', https://www.youtube.com/watch?v=0h2z0tsM13U (accessed 7 March 2022).

67. 'Volveremos a Brindar. Lucia Gil', https://www.youtube.com/watch?v=An4T0wUerRs (accessed 7 March 2022).
68. Jessica Snouwaert, 'Watch People in Cities around the World Cheer from Their Windows and Rooftops at the Same Time to Thank Healthcare Workers and First Responders', *Business Insider*, 6 May 2020, https://www.businessinsider.com/videos-people-cities-cheering-healthcare-workers-windows-rooftops-same-time-2020-4 (accessed 7 March 2022).
69. Comments under 'Volveremos a Brindar. Lucia Gil'.
70. 'Volveremos a Brindar / Costa Rica / Lucía Gil Cover / #quedateencasa', https://www.youtube.com/watch?v=3MXXbcroydk (accessed 7 March 2022).
71. '🎧 VOLVEREMOS A BRINDAR Lucía Gil 🎧 CANCIÓN DE CUARENTENA Cover México DennMiu', https://www.youtube.com/watch?v=TeekFtnFScc (accessed 7 March 2022).
72. 'Volveremos a Brindar, Lucía Gil, (Cover) Chicas Invidentes de Distintas Partes de Perú', https://www.youtube.com/watch?v=gnDS1luf1ik (accessed 7 March 2022).
73. 'Canción de Cuarentena Traducida al Guaraní – YouTube', https://www.youtube.com/watch?v=IjFyecYZVIw (accessed 7 March 2022).
74. According to Urumita's mayoral webpage, the town's name comes from the name of a sixteenth-century cacique, Uruma, similar to the naming history of Valledupar. Alcaldía de Urumita, 'Nuestro municipio', Pueblo Municipal de Urumita – Pagina Oficial, 2017', http://www.urumita-guajira.gov.co/municipio/nuestro-municipio (accessed 7 March 2022).
75. 'La Pandemia – Fabian Corrales', https://www.youtube.com/watch?v=cUsSqLZnlJY (accessed 2 February 2022).
76. Peter Moser, 'Growing Community Music Through a Sense of Place', Brydie-Leigh Bartleet and Lee Higgins, eds, *The Oxford Handbook of Community Music* (Oxford: Oxford University Press, 2018), 213–28, p. 214.
77. Quoted in Betto Arcos, 'In Colombia, Preserving Songs That Tell Stories', *NPR*, 7 July 2016, https://www.npr.org/2016/07/07/484944084/in-colombia-preserving-songs-that-tell-stories (accessed 7 March 2022).
78. Dario B. Arboleda, 'Transculturalism and Identification Processes. Colombian-Caribbean Music in Monterrey, a Transnational Phenomenon', *Alteridades* 15.30 (2005): 19–41.
79. *Tourism Colombia*, 'Vallenato, the History of an Entire Region', 8 December 2018, https://www.colombia.co/en/colombia-culture/music/story-valledupar-home-vallenato/ (accessed 7 March 2022)
80. Jeimy Estefany Baraceta Sánchez and Ricardo Ruiz Angulo, 'La enseñanza de la geografía a partir de la música vallenata tradicional: una propuesta didáctica', *Anekumene* 19 (2020): 21–9.
81. Gretty Viviana Acosta Arregocés, *La Guajira: Espacio de Creación de Los Juglares*, 10 December 2020 (Bogata: Pontificia Universidad Javeriana, 2020); Martín Andrade Pérez, '¿A quién y qué representa la lista representativa del patrimonio cultural inmaterial de la nación en Colombia?' *Boletín De Antropología* 28.46 (2013): 53–78.
82. Luisa Pinzón Varilla, 'Lírica Popular e identidad en el vallenato', *Oralidad-es* 1.2 (2015): 156–64.
83. Marco A. de León, 'Medicina, corazón y música de acordeón', *Revista Colombiana de Cardiología* 21.3 (2014): 195–8.
84. 'LA PANDEMIA -VIDEO- (MIGUEL DURAN JR', https://www.youtube.com/watch?v=f3P-oGKtyAk (accessed 7 March 2022).
85. 'LA PANDEMIA -VIDEO- (MIGUEL DURAN JR'.
86. Luz Victoria Martinez, 'Luto en en el vallenato: falleció el cantante Miguel Durán Junior', *El Tiempo*, 3 September 2020, https://www.eltiempo.com/colombia/otras-ciudades/

ultimas-noticias-murio-el-cantante-vallenato-miguel-duran-junior-535738 (accessed 7 September 2022).
87. 'Covid 19, Vallenato', https://www.youtube.com/watch?v=ejngR4o47cM (accessed 7 September 2022).
88. John F. Beltrán Rodríguez, 'Música en la comunidad Wounaan urbana. Proyecto para la resignificación de la comunidad indígena desplazada', PhD thesis, Universidad Pedagógica Nacional, Tlalpan, Mexico, 2017.
89. 'Mensaje Por El Covid-19 Los Hijos Del Vallenato Talento Indígena', https://www.youtube.com/watch?v=73tVvQow7eU (accessed 7 September 2022).
90. 'Mensaje Por El Covid-19'.
91. 'La Pandemia – Canta Alberto Córdoba Quejada', https://www.youtube.com/watch?v=e7bD2gacZzk (accessed 7 September 2022).
92. 'El Coronavirus / En Su Palabra Está – Jorge Peña 'El Maestro' (VIDEO OFICIAL)', https://www.youtube.com/watch?v=knyAR0MMIuU (accessed 7 September 2022).
93. Diego C. Franco, 'Suero costeño, sinónimo de herencia y tradición', *CONtexto ganadero*, 3 December 2018, https://www.contextoganadero.com/cronica/suero-costeno-sinonimo-de-herencia-y-tradicion (accessed 7 September 2022).
94. 'Coronavirus – LUCHO COBO Y JULIO 'EL MONO' ORDOÑEZ', https://www.youtube.com/watch?v=2XiR7DcmZVE (accessed 7 September 2022).
95. 'OSAMA BIN LADEN', https://www.youtube.com/watch?v=X0IUwawFNKk (accessed 7 September 2022).
96. Ingrid Bolívar and Sergio Lizarazo, 'Entre sueños, montañas y vallenatos. Aprendizajes sobre la expansión regional de las FARC-EP en el Caribe', *Colombia Internacional* 107 (July 2021): 139–62.
97. 'La Cuarentena (El Coronavirus) – Horacio Mora', https://www.youtube.com/watch?v=lWrBvePSN9c (accessed 7 September 2022).
98. Jaime De La Ossa and Alejandro De La Ossa-Lacayo, 'Cacería de subsistencia en San Marcos, Sucre, colombia', *Revista Colombiana de Ciencia Animal – RECIA* 2 (2011): 213–24.
99. 'EL CORONAVIRUS Y LA GENTE DEL PUEBLO-Alfredo Redondo X Pedro Perez', https://www.youtube.com/watch?v=pHe6IvNlNEY (accessed 7 September 2022).
100. 'VALLENATO DEL CORONAVIRUS', https://www.youtube.com/watch?v=e1W8xS7ZpS4 (accessed 7 September 2022).
101. Nini G. Leal, 'Estrategias para la construcción de la identidad del festival de La Leyenda Vallenata', Professional in Information Systems, Library Science and Archival Science thesis, Bogota, Universidad de la Salle.
102. 'Vallenato En Tiempos de Pandemia – Mensaje #QuedateEnCasa (Alfredo de La Fe, Wilber Mendoza)', https://www.youtube.com/watch?v=mgObEIUbvhI (accessed 7 September 2022).
103. 'Omar Hernández – El Virus (PUYA) – Festival Vallenato 2020 Virtual', https://www.youtube.com/watch?v=djVQCTjxiBs (accessed 7 September 2022).
104. Joaquín Viloria De la Hoz, 'Un paseo a lomo de acordeón: Aproximación al vallenato, la música del Magdalena Grande, 1870 – 1960', *Memorias: Revista Digital de Historia y Arqueología desde el Caribe* 33: 7–34, p. 22.
105. 'Ausencia Sentimental | Homenaje Festival Vallenato 2020 Covid-19 Peter Ivan Villazon Otros Artistas', https://www.youtube.com/watch?v=_jTF3AqNqaA (accessed 7 September 2022).
106. 'LOS ATUQS DEL PERÚ – MALDITA PANDEMIA (UNQUY) 2020', https://www.youtube.com/watch?v=TeysSU4ZxI0 (accessed 7 June 2022).
107. Not to be confused with the use of jarana in Mexico to describe various regional guitarlike instruments. Jaime Vargas, 'Jaranas, coliseos y matinales: cuarenta años de música popular en Lima', *Crítica Latinoamericana* (2013): https://www.

academia.edu/30542596/Jaranas_coliseos_y_matinales_Cuarenta_a%C3%B1os_de_m%C3%BAsica_popular_en_Lima_pdf (accessed 7 September 2022).
108. 'LOS ATUQS DEL PERÚ – MALDITA PANDEMIA (UNQUY) 2020', (accessed 7 September 2022).
109. Fredy Amílcar Roncalla Fernández, 'Encuentros y despedidas musicales en tiempos de Covid', *Hawansuyo*, 12 September 2020, https://hawansuyo.com/2020/09/12/encuentros-y-despedidas-musicales-en-tiempos-de-covid-fredy-roncalla/ (accessed 7 September 2022).
110. Luigi G. Calò Carducci, 'Violencia y migraciónes internas en Perú (1980–2000): Los "Despazados" y la Cuestión Indígena', in Stefano Tedeschi and Alessio Surian, eds, *Pensamiento Social Italiano Sobre América Latina* (Buenos Aires: CLACSO, 2017), 121–40.
111. Domenico Branca, 'The Urban and the Rural in Puno, Highland Peru', *Anthropology Today* 35.6 (2019): 18–20.
112. J. Jaime Miranda, Robert H. Gilman, Héctor H. García, and Liam Smeeth, 'The Effect on Cardiovascular Risk Factors of Migration from Rural to Urban Areas in Peru: PERU MIGRANT Study', *BMC Cardiovascular Disorders* 9 (2009): Article 23, p. 1.
113. Luigi G. Calò Carducci, 'Violencia y migraciónes internas en Perú (1980–2000): los despazados y la cuestión indígena', in Stefano Tedeschi and Alessio Surian, eds, *Pensamiento Social Italiano Sobre América Latina* (Buenos Aires: CLACSO, 2017), 121–40.
114. Fabiola Escárzaga, Julio Abanto Llaque, and Anderson Chamorro. 'Migración, guerra interna e identidad andina en Perú'. *Política y Cultura* 18 (2008): 277–98, pp. 279–80.
115. Ciara Nugent, 'How Peru's Coronavirus Outbreak Got So Bad: What to Know', *Time*, 29 May 2020, https://time.com/5844768/peru-coronavirus/ (accessed 12 September 2021).
116. Rosa Chávez Yacila, 'Migrar para sobrevivir: en pandemia 250.000 Peruanos retornaron a zonas rurales de origen', *Ojo Público*, 12 December 2021, https://ojo-publico.com/3199/casi-250000-peruanos-retornaron-en-pandemia-zonas-rurales (accessed 7 September 2022).
117. Mario A. Rufino Trelles, 'Regresando a mis raíces: COVID19 y la migración de retorno en el norte de Peru', *CAS: Centre for Amerindian, Latin American and Caribbean Studies*, 10 June 2021, https://calacs.wp.st-andrews.ac.uk/regresando-a-mis-raices-covid19-y-la-migracion-de-retorno-en-el-norte-de-peru/ (accessed 7 September 2022).
118. 'Corona Virus Chayaramunña Michael Sedano HUAYNO'.
119. Save The Children, 'Respuesta humanitaria ante la crisis por el COVID-19 en Perú', Save the Children Perú', https://www.savethechildren.org.pe/respuesta-humanitaria-ante-la-crisis-por-el-covid-19-en-peru/ (accessed 7 September 2022).
120. Eduardo Zegarra, 'De la pandemia a la crisis de alimentos en Perú', *Ojo Público*, 25 May 2020, https://ojo-publico.com/1830/de-la-pandemia-la-crisis-de-alimentos-en-peru (accessed 7 September 2022).
121. Paloma Marcos Morezuelas, Martha Denisse Pierola, Ana Iju, Javier Puig, and Jaime Fernandez-Baca, 'Migrations Due to COVID-19: Opportunities and Challenges for a Sustainable Recovery in Peru', *Sostenibilidad*, 24 May 2021, https://blogs.iadb.org/sostenibilidad/en/migrations-due-to-covid-19-opportunities-and-challenges-for-a-sustainable-recovery-in-peru/ (accessed 7 September 2022).
122. Interview with Arsenio Hinostroza, by J. A. Strub, 11 April 2022.
123. 'Corona Virus Chayaramunña Michael Sedano HUAYNO', https://www.youtube.com/watch?v=YWlY3VIn7gg (accessed 7 September 2022).
124. Interview with Jermani Ojeda-Ludena, by J. A. Strub, 27 March 2022.
125. 'Corona Virus Chayaramunña Michael Sedano HUAYNO'.

126. Franklin Briceño, 'In Peru, Virus Erodes Centuries-Old Burial Traditions', *AP NEWS*, 2 September 2020, https://apnews.com/article/virus-outbreak-lifestyle-ap-top-news-international-news-latin-america-b75a5aded7caa12ff5a79f5d53bffc21 (accessed 7 September 2022).
127. Valerie Robin, 'Caminos a la otra vida: Ritos funerarios en Los Andes Peruanos Meridionales', in Antoinette Molinié (ed.), *Etnografías Del Cuzco* (Cuzco: Centro de Estudios Regionales Andinos Bartolomé de Las Casas-CBC, Laboratoire d'Ethnologie et de Sociologie Comparative-Labethno, 2005), 47–68.
128. Catherine J. Allen, 'Body and Soul in Quechua Thought', *Journal of Latin American Lore* 8.2 (1982): 179–196, p. 193.
129. Peter Gose, *Invaders as Ancestors: On the Intercultural Making and Unmaking of Spanish Colonialism in the Andes* (Toronto: University of Toronto Press, 2008), p. 226.
130. Marcelo Rochabrun, 'Peru to Cremate Body of Shining Path Founder and Dispose of his Ashes', Reuters, 23 September 2021, https://www.reuters.com/world/americas/peru-cremate-body-shining-path-founder-dispose-his-ashes-2021-09-23/ (accessed 7 September 2022).
131. 'SUFRIMIENTO DURANTE LA PANDEMIA – CONJ.CHOQUE VELILLE', https://www.youtube.com/watch?v=1EyPAWb0sJ0 (accessed 7 September 2022); Julio Mendívil, 'Yo soy el huayno: el huayno peruano como confluencia de lo indígena con lo hispano y lo moderno, in Albert Recasens and Christian Spencer, eds, *A tres bandas: Mestizaje, sincretismo e hibridación en el espacio sonoro iberoamericano*, (Madrid: Seacex, 2010), 37–46.
132. For descriptions of the group see YouTube video 'choque velille', https://www.youtube.com/watch?v=N_8W6wNt0Sk (accessed 25 September 2022) and their Facebook page, https://m.facebook.com/Conjunto-Choque-Velille-114992263669280/ (accessed 25 September 2022).
133. 'SUFRIMIENTO DURANTE LA PANDEMIA – CONJ.CHOQUE VELILLE', https://www.youtube.com/watch?v=1EyPAWb0sJ0 (accessed 25 September 2022).
134. Translated from '*Este huaynito está dedicado a todos hermanos que han emprendido su viaje largo para retornar a su patria chica, largas caminatas sediento sin alimentos y mucho sufrimiento, quemados por el sol, el frio y el cansancio. Maldita pandemia castigas a nuestros hermanos sin piedad*' – 'SUFRIMIENTO DURANTE LA PANDEMIA – CONJ.CHOQUE VELILLE', https://www.youtube.com/watch?v=1EyPAWb0sJ0 (accessed 25 September 2022).
135. UN Women, 'Whose Time to Care: Unpaid Care and Domestic Work during COVID-19', UN Women website, 25 November 2020, https://data.unwomen.org/publications/whose-time-care-unpaid-care-and-domestic-work-during-covid-19 (accessed 25 September 2022).
136. Anastasia Moloney, 'Women's Jobs at Risk in Latin America in Coronavirus Crisis', Reuters, 20 May 2020, https://www.reuters.com/article/us-health-coronavirus-women-trfn-idUSKBN22W05A (accessed 25 September 2022).
137. Emilia Cucagna and Javier Romero, *The Gendered Impacts of COVID-19 on Labor Markets in Latin America and the Caribbean* (Washington, DC: World Bank, 2021), https://openknowledge.worldbank.org/handle/10986/35191 (accessed 25 September 2022).
138. Economic Commission for Latin America and the Caribbean, *Moving Towards a Care Society in Latin America and the Caribbean Is Urgent for Achieving a Transformative and Sustainable Recovery with Gender Equality* (Santiago de Chile: ECLAC, 2021), https://www.cepal.org/en/pressreleases/moving-towards-care-society-latin-america-and-caribbean-urgent-achieving (accessed 25 September 2022).
139. 'Coronavirus En Quechua – Noemí Lagos', https://www.youtube.com/watch?v=oDmCkAXBEFU (accessed 7 November 2021).
140. Cucagna and Romero, *Gendered Impacts of COVID-19*.

141. While not Quechua himself, Arguedas was one of the first influential social theorists to consider Peru's distinctive pluricultural character and to celebrate Quechua society as dynamic and contemporary as opposed to timeless or backward. Ulises J. Zevallos-Aguilar, 'José María Arguedas y la música novoandina. Su legado cultural en el siglo XXI', *Cuadernos de Literatura* 20.39 (2016): 254–69, https://dialnet.unirioja.es/servlet/articulo?codigo=5271700 (accessed 1 July 2022); Stewart I. M. Adams, 'Los Urbanizadores de Arequipa: A Study of the Effects of Urbanization on Quechua Folklore, Language and Traditions in a Southern Peruvian City', PhD thesis, University of St Andrews, UK, 1980.
142. *Worlddata.info*, 'Quechua – Worldwide Distribution', https://www.worlddata.info/languages/quechua.php (accessed 10 April 2022).
143. Adrian J. Pearce and Paul Heggarty, '"Mining the Data" on the Huancayo-Huancavelica Quechua Frontier', in Adrian J. Pearce and Paul Heggarty, eds, *History and Language in the Andes* (New York: Palgrave MacMillan, 2011), 87–109; Alan Durston and Bruce Mannheim, *Indigenous Languages, Politics, and Authority in Latin America: Historical and Ethnographic Perspectives* (Notre Dame, IN: University of Notre Dame Press, 2018); Willem F. H. Adelaar, 'Modeling Convergence: Towards a Reconstruction of the History of Quechuan–Aymaran Interaction', *Lingua, Language Contact and Universal Grammar in the Andes* 122:5 (1 April 2012): 461–9.
144. Julio C. Casma, 'Discriminated against for Speaking Their Own Language', *World Bank Weblog*, 16 April 2014, https://www.worldbank.org/en/news/feature/2014/04/16/discriminados-por-hablar-su-idioma-natal-peru-quechua (accessed 25 September 2022).
145. Monica Martinez, 'Quechua Given Increased Visibility by Peru's New Leftist Gov't', *La Prensa*, 24 September 2021, https://www.laprensalatina.com/quechua-given-increased-visibility-by-perus-new-leftist-govt/ (accessed 25 September 2022).
146. 'CompartirSentimiento del chimaychi# CORONA VIRUS# QUÉDATE EN CASÁ', https://www.youtube.com/watch?v=IIMtpgyaOBs (accessed 23 September 2022).
147. Fortunato Diestra Salinas, 'Apreciación folclórica del género musical en la provincia de Sihuas Ancash, 2016', *Infinitum* 7.1 (2017): 49–54.
148. 'Sol de Pachaconas / Maldita Pandemia /COVID19 /QUEDATE EN CASA', https://www.youtube.com/watch?v=VLV5hnEO0b8 (accessed 7 June 2022).
149. Martin Lienhard, 'La cosmología poética en los huaynos Quechuas tradicionales', *Acta Poética* 26.1–2 (2005): 485–513; Félix Julca Guerrero and Laura Nivin Vargas, 'Recursos Expresivos y Literarios En El Huayno Ancashino', *Letras (Lima)* 90.132 (2019): 260–84.
150. 'Sol De Pachaconas – Maldita Pandemia', https://www.youtube.com/watch?v=EG0CUBjIprk (accessed 7 June 2022); 'Sol de Pachaconas / Maldita Pandemia / COVID19 /QUEDATE EN CASA', https://www.youtube.com/watch?v=VLV5hnEO0b8 (accessed 7 June 2022).
151. 'CANCION EN QUECHUA SOBRE COVID19', https://www.youtube.com/watch?v=Z3x16kTrkT0 (accessed 7 June 2022).
152. Laura A. Valdiviezo and Luis M. Valdiviezo Arista, 'Política y práctica de la interculturalidad en la educación Peruana: Análisis y propuesta', Ministerio de Educación Perú, 25 January 2008, https://repositorio.minedu.gob.pe/handle/20.500.12799/901 (accessed 7 June 2022).
153. Diana F. Illanes Córdova, 'Repertorio de canciones del Anexo Maramara, Apurímac para la apreciación de la música andina en los niños de 5 años, IEI 7.8, Amiguitos de San Martín, Callao', education thesis, Escuela Nacional Superior de Folklore 'José María Arguedas', Lima, 2017.
154. World Music with Daria, 'Yaw, Yaw Puka Polleracha – Free Lyric Sheet (Song In Quechua)', *Teachers Pay Teachers*, https://www.teacherspayteachers.com/Product/Yaw-Yaw-Puka-Polleracha-Free-Lyric-Sheet-Song-In-Quechua-3340027 (accessed 1 May 2022).

155. 'Coronavirus Quechua', https://www.youtube.com/watch?v=R8UeJcxDt4s (accessed 7 June 2022).
156. 'Canción Coronavirus', https://www.youtube.com/watch?v=9JvbMRpMcjA (accessed 7 June 2022).
157. 'Yau Yau Corona Viruscha', https://www.youtube.com/watch?v=qIVZVa-hS4Q (accessed 7 June 2022).
158. 'Sayuri Cruz Huamani CORONAVIRUS Canción De La Cuarentena', https://www.youtube.com/watch?v=pI3LOEg20n8 (accessed 7 June 2022).
159. Jorge A. Santos, Mario Mejía Huamán, and Santiago Gariel Durante, 'Dos conceptos andinos para pensar la sociedad contemporánea: wakcha/qhapaq, o ¿por qué no existe la palabra "pobre" en quechua?', *Papeles de Trabajo-Centro de Estudios Interdisciplinarios En Etnolingüística y Antropología Socio-Cultural* 40 (2020): 35–51.
160. Maximo Damián Huamani, 'With Tears, Not Words', *Review: Literature and Arts of the Americas* 14.25–26 (1980): 49–50.
161. 'QUÉDATE EN CASA // Canción En Quechua // Jhonson Ichpas', https://www.youtube.com/watch?v=U9YoCc4bw2I (accessed 20 September 2022).
162. 'Ebert Suni – Huayno Carnaval Cusqueño / Coronavirus Cusco', https://www.youtube.com/watch?v=qN0OSskcIG0 (accessed 20 September 2022).
163. 'Carnaval COVID 19 – Maestro José Guacho | Video Oficial', https://www.youtube.com/watch?v=ikozI_RCWP0 (accessed 20 September 2022).
164. 'Carnaval COVID 19 – Maestro José Guacho'.
165. 'EL CORONAVIRUS (LA PANDEMIA) – CAMINANTES DEL PERU / ESTRENO MARZO 2020 / GADIEL PRODUCCIONES', https://www.youtube.com/watch?v=CUmQ9DniE2U (accessed 21 September 2022).
166. This road system comprised over 25,000 miles and connected communities spanning what are now six countries: Guadalupe M. Martínez, 'Qhapaq Ñan: El Camino Inca y las transformaciones territoriales en los Andes peruanos', *Ería* 78–79 (2009): 21–38; Giancarlo M. Flores, 'Superando las dicotomías: el qhapaq ñan como ejemplo del patrimonio como proceso social', *Chungará* 51.3 (2019): https://scielo.conicyt.cl/scielo.php?pid=S0717-73562019000300457&script=sci_arttext (accessed 21 September 2022).
167. 'EL CORONAVIRUS (LA PANDEMIA) – CAMINANTES DEL PERU / ESTRENO MARZO 2020 / GADIEL PRODUCCIONES', https://www.youtube.com/watch?v=CUmQ9DniE2U (accessed 21 September 2022).

References

Note: YouTube music URLs cited in the footnotes are not replicated in this bibliography. All of the links to the musical examples and other online digital resources cited in this book which are still available online will be linked at the companion website for this book at MalditoCoronavirus.com.

Interviews

Camarera Torres, Maria del Carmen. Interview by J. A. Strub, 29 August, 2021.
Castro, Cesar. Interview by J. A. Strub and Dan Margolies, 29 August 2021.
Castro, Francisca 'Pachita'. Interview by J. A. Strub and Dan Margolies, 7 October 2021.
Hinostroza, Arsenio. Interview by J. A. Strub, 11 April 2022.
Montemayor, Iván. Interview by J. A. Strub and Dan Margolies, 7 September 2021.
Ojeda-Ludena, Jermani. Interview by J. A. Strub, 27 March 2022.
Perez Baeza, Gilberto Salvador. Interview by J. A. Strub, 25 August, 2021.
Quiñones, Omar. Interview by J. A. Strub, 22 April 2022.
S., Juanito. Interview by Dan Margolies, 19 June 2020.
Vera, Gabino, Interview Interview by J. A. Strub, 18 June 2020.
Vera, Gabino, Interview Interview by J. A. Strub, 2 July 2020.
Vera, Gabino. Interview by J. A. Strub, 19 June, 2020.

Publications

Acosta Arregocés, Gretty V. *La Guajira: Espacio de Creación de Los Juglares*, 10 December 2020 (Bogata: Pontificia Universidad Javeriana, 2020).
Acosta Morales, Rafael, *Drug Lords, Cowboys, and Desperadoes: Violent Myths of the U.S.-Mexico Frontier* (Notre Dame, IN: University of Notre Dame Press, 2021).
Adams, Stewart I. M., 'Los Urbanizadores de Arequipa: A Study of the Effects of Urbanization on Quechua Folklore, Language and Traditions in a Southern Peruvian City', PhD thesis, University of St Andrews, UK, 1980.
Adelaar, Willem F. H., 'Modeling Convergence: Towards a Reconstruction of the History of Quechuan–Aymaran Interaction', *Lingua, Language Contact and Universal Grammar in the Andes* 122:5 (1 April 2012): 461–9. https://doi.org/10.1016/j.lingua.2011.10.001

Adorno, Theodor, *Aesthetic Theory* (trans. Robert Hullot-Kentor, London: Continuum, 2002).
AFP, 'TikTok Videos Get Longer in Challenge to YouTube', *TechXplore*, 28 February 2022, https://techxplore.com/news/2022-02-tiktok-videos-longer-youtube.html (accessed 31 March 2022).
AFP Español, 'Músico le Canta a la Ansiedad por el Nuevo Coronavirus en Ecuador | AFP', https://www.youtube.com/watch?v=XhBykTRVOaY (accessed 22 February 2022).
Agudelo, Carlos E., 'El Pacífico colombiano: de "remanso de paz" a escenarioestratégico del conflicto armado: las transformaciones de la regióny algunas respuestas de sus poblaciones frente a la violencia', *Cuadernos de Desarrollo Rural* 46 (2001): 7–37.
Airoldi, Massimo, 'The Techno-Social Reproduction of Taste Boundaries on Digital Platforms: The Case of Music on YouTube', *Poetics* 89 (2021): Article 101563. https://doi.org/10.1016/j.poetic.2021.101563
Airoldi, Massimo, Davide Beraldo, and Alessandro Gandini, 'Follow the Algorithm: An Exploratory Investigation of Music on YouTube', *Poetics* 57 (2016): 1–13. https://doi.org/10.1016/j.poetic.2016.05.001
AJMC, 'COVID-19 Roundup: Coronavirus Now a National Emergency, With Plans to Increase Testing', 13 March 2020, https://www.ajmc.com/view/covid19-roundup2 (accessed 6 February 2022).
Ali, S. Harris, 'Stigmatized Ethnicity, Public Health, and Globalization', *Canadian Ethnic Studies* 40 (2008): 43–64. https://doi.org/10.1353/ces.2008.0002
Alinejad, Donya, 'Mapping Homelands through Virtual Spaces: Transnational Embodiment and Iranian Diaspora Bloggers', *Global Networks* 11.1 (2011): 43–62. https://doi.org/10.1111/j.1471-0374.2010.00306.x
Allen, Catherine J., 'Body and Soul in Quechua Thought', *Journal of Latin American Lore* 8.2 (1982): 179–196.
Alviso, Ric, 'What is a Corrido? Musical Analysis and Narrative Function', *Studies in Latin American Popular Culture* 29.1 (2011): 58–79. https://doi.org/10.1353/sla.2011.0017
Anderberg, Sune, 'Lyden af 2020', *Seismograf*, April 2020, https://seismograf.org/fokus/lyden-af-2020 (accessed 6 February 2022).
Andrade Pérez, Martín, '¿A quién y qué representa la lista representativa del patrimonio cultural inmaterial de la nación en Colombia?' *Boletín De Antropología* 28.46 (2013): 53–78. https://doi.org/10.17533/udea.boan.19520
Ansdell, Gary, *How Music Helps in Music Therapy and Everyday Life* (Farnham, UK: Ashgate, 2014).
Anta, Juan F., Luis F. Oliveira, and Danilo Ramos, 'Música y afecto: una revisión bibliográfica y el análisis de tres casos problemáticos', *Revista Argentina de Musicología* 20 (2019): 103–31.
AP Archive, 'Virus Outbreak Inspires Ecuador Street Performer', https://www.youtube.com/watch?v=sPvhhSTDP4E (accessed 22 February 2022).
Arboleda, Dario B. 'Transculturalism and Identification Processes. Colombian-Caribbean Music in Monterrey, a Transnational Phenomenon', *Alteridades* 15.30 (2005): 19–41.
Arcos, Betto, 'In Colombia, Preserving Songs That Tell Stories', *NPR*, 7 July 2016, https://www.npr.org/2016/07/07/484944084/in-colombia-preserving-songs-that-tell-stories (accessed 7 March 2022).
Arcos, Betto, *Music Stories from the Cosmic* Barrio (No location or publisher, 2020).
Arés-Muzio, Paricia, 'The Mysteries of "Pandemic Time"', *MEDICC Review* 23.2 (2021): 80. https://doi.org/10.37757/MR2021.V23.N2.6
Arjona-Martín, José-Borja, Alfonso Méndiz-Noguero, and Juan-Salvador Victoria-Mas, 'Virality as a Paradigm of Digital Communication. Review of the Concept and Update of the Theoretical Framework', *El Profesional De La Información* 29.6 (2020): 1–18. https://doi.org/10.3145/epi.2020.nov.07

Armitage, John and Mark Featherstone, 'Viral Culture', *Cultural Politics* 17.1 (2021): 1–10. https://doi.org/10.1215/17432197-8797445

Arvidsson, Adam, 'Value and Virtue in the Sharing Economy', *Sociological Review* 66.2 (2018): 289–301. https://doi.org/10.1177/0038026118758531

Aslam, Salman, 'TikTok by the Numbers: Stats, Demographics & Fun Facts', *Omnicore*, 12 February 2020, https://www.omnicoreagency.com/tiktok-statistics/ (accessed 2 November 2021).

Augoyard, Jean-François and Henry Torgue, *Sonic Experience: A Guide to Everyday Sounds* (Montreal: McGill-Queens University Press, 2005).

Avella, Diana, 'La Etnnia: el legendario himno del hip hop latino', *Nómadas* (Bogotá, Colombia) 54 (2021): 225–35. https://doi.org/10.30578/nomadas.n54a13

Avenburg, Karen, 'Interpellation and Performance: The Construction of Identities through Musical Experience in the Virgen Del Rosario Fiesta in Iruya, Argentina', *Latin American Perspectives* 39.2 (2012): 134–49. https://doi.org/10.1177/0094582X11427882

Baker, Geoffrey, '"Digital Indigestion": Cumbia, Class and a Post-Digital Ethos in Buenos Aires', *Popular Music* 34.2 (2015): 175–96. https://doi.org/10.1017/S026114301500001X

Baker, Sarah and Jez Collins, 'Popular Music Heritage, Community Archives and the Challenge of Sustainability', *International Journal of Cultural Studies* 20.5 (2017): 476–91. https://doi.org/10.1177/1367877916637150

Baraceta Sánchez, Jeimy Estefany and Ricardo Ruiz Angulo, 'La enseñanza de la geografía a partir de la música vallenata tradicional: una propuesta didáctica', *Anekumene* 19 (2020): 21–9. https://doi.org/10.17227/Anekumene.2020.num19.13595

Barrón, Elideth, '"Maldito Coronavirus!" Grita Anuel AA en su balcón', *Estación 40* (blog), 18 March 2020, https://estacion40.com.py/maldito-coronavirus-grita-anuel-aa-en-su-balcon/ (accessed 12 October 2021).

Bartalucci, Chiara, Raffaella Bellomini, Sergio Luzzi, Paola Pulella, and Giulia Torelli, 'A Survey on the Soundscape Perception Before and During the COVID-19 Pandemic in Italy', *Noise Mapping*, 8.1 (2021): 65–88. https://doi.org/10.1515/noise-2021-0005

Bartra, Bruno, 'Digital Cumbia and the Latin American Technological Utopia', *Review* 48.1 (2015): 95–9. https://doi.org/10.1080/08905762.2015.1020676

BBC News, 'Coronavirus: The World in Lockdown in Maps and Charts', 7 April 2020, https://www.bbc.com/news/world-52103747, *BBC News* (accessed 29 December 2020).

Beckett, Anne G., Loune Viaud, Michele Heisler, and Joia Mukherjee, 'Misusing Public Health as a Pretext to End Asylum – Title 42', *New England Journal of Medicine* 386.16 (2022): https://www.nejm.org/doi/full/10.1056/NEJMp2200274 (accessed 1 July 2022). https://doi.org/10.1056/NEJMp2200274

Belk, Russell, 'Sharing', *Journal of Consumer Research* 36.5 (2010): 715–34. https://doi.org/10.1086/612649

Beltrán Rodríguez, John F., 'Música en la comunidad Wounaan urbana. Proyecto para la resignificación de la comunidad indígena desplazada', PhD thesis, Universidad Pedagógica Nacional, Tlalpan, Mexico, 2017.

Bengtsson, Stefan and Katrien Van Poeck, 'What Can We Learn from COVID-19 as a Form of Public Pedagogy?' *European Journal for Research on the Education and Learning of Adults*, 12.3 (2021): 281–93. https://doi.org/10.3384/rela.2000-7426.3386

Benito, Carlo, 'La pandemia musical: cuatro horas escuchando canciones sobre el coronavirus', *El Comercio*, 28 April 2020, https://www.elcomercio.es/vivir/artes/pandemia-musical-20200428100322-ntrc.html (accessed 16 September 2022).

Benton-Cohen, Katherine, *Borderline Americans: Racial Division and Labor War in the Arizona Borderlands* (Cambridge, MA, Harvard University Press, 2009).

Beristáin, Helena, 'El albur', *Acta Poética* 21.1–2 (2015): 399–422. https://doi.org/10.19130/iifl.ap.2000.1-2.61

Berry, David M., *The Philosophy of Software: Code and Mediation in the Digital Age* (Basingstoke, UK: Palgrave Macmillan, 2011).

Bethell, Leslie, 'Brazil and "Latin America"', *Journal of Latin American Studies* 47 (2010): 457–85. https://doi.org/10.1017/S0022216X1000088X

Bhandari, Aparajita and Sara Bimo, 'Why's Everyone on TikTok Now? the Algorithmized Self and the Future of Self-Making on Social Media', *Social Media + Society* 8.1 (2022), p. 2. https://doi.org/10.1177/20563051221086241

Bialasiewicz, Luiza and Christina Eckes, '"Individual Sovereignty" in Pandemic Times – A Contradiction in Terms?', *Political Geography* 85 (2021): Article 102277. https://doi.org/10.1016/j.polgeo.2020.102277

Bigenho, Michelle, *Sounding Indigenous: Authenticity in Bolivian Music Performance* (New York: Palgrave Macmillan, 2002).

Birenbaum Quintero, Michael, *Rites, Rights and Rhythms: A Genealogy of Musical Meaning in Colombia's Black Pacific* (Oxford: Oxford University Press, 2018).

Bishop, Sophie, 'Managing Visibility on YouTube through Algorithmic Gossip', *New Media & Society* 21.11–12 (2019): 2589–606. https://doi.org/10.1177/1461444819854731

Blake, Sam, 'Livestream Concerts Boomed During Lockdown: Are They Music's Future or Just a Pandemic Fad?', *Dot.LA*, 14 October 2020, https://dot.la/livestream-concerts-boomed-during-lockdown-is-it-musics-future-or-just-a-pandemic-fad-2648201267.html (accessed 14 December 2020).

Blanco, Juan M. 'Una mirada a la historia de la música costeña de acordeón', *Revista Poligrama* 20.1 (2011): https://bibliotecadigital.univalle.edu.co/handle/10893/3068 (accessed 2 February 2022).

Boffone, Trevor, *Renegades: Digital Dance Cultures from Dubsmash to TikTok* (Oxford: Oxford University Press, 2021).

Bolaños, Marina A., 'Sin música no hay fiesta, no hay nada': aproximaciones a las expresiones musicales indígenas en Chiapas', *Música oral del Sur: revista internacional* 9 (2012): 241–51.

Bolívar, Ingrid and Sergio Lizarazo, 'Entre sueños, montañas y vallenatos. Aprendizajes sobre la expansión regional de las FARC-EP en el Caribe', *Colombia Internacional* 107 (July 2021): 139–62. https://doi.org/10.7440/colombiaint107.2021.06

Bolter, Jay D. *The Digital Plenitude: The Decline of Elite Culture and the Rise of New Media* (Cambridge, MA: MIT Press, 2019).

Bonamore Graves, Alessandra and Henry Cohen, 'Corridos from Costa Rica', in Misheal M. Caspi, ed., *Oral Tradition and Hispanic Literature: Essays in Honor of Samuel G. Armistead* (New York: Garland Publishing, 1995): 291–322.

Bonilla Burgos, Rosa M. and Juan C. Gómez Rojas, 'Son huasteco e identidad regional', *Investigaciones geográficas* 80 (2013): 86–97. https://doi.org/10.14350/rig.36646

Boon, Marcus, *In Praise of Copying* (Cambridge, MA: Harvard University Press, 2010).

Booth, William, Karla Adam, and Pamela Rolfe, 'In Fight against Coronavirus, the World Gives Medical Heroes a Standing Ovation', *Washington Post*, 26 March 2020, https://www.washingtonpost.com/world/europe/clap-for-carers/2020/03/26/3d05eb9c-6f66-11ea-a156-0048b62cdb51_story.html (accessed 3 February 2022).

Borschke, Margie, 'Rethinking the Rhetoric of Remix', *Media International Australia* 141.1 (2011): 17–25. https://doi.org/10.1177/1329878X1114100104

Botella, Caridad, 'The Mobile Aesthetics of Cell Phone Made Films: From the Pixel to The Everyday', *Revista Kepes* 9.8 (2012): 73–87.

Botstein, Leon, 'The Future of Music in America: The Challenge of the COVID-19 Pandemic', *Musical Quarterly* 102.4 (2020): 351–60. https://doi.org/10.1093/musqtl/gdaa007

Bowman, Paul, *The Invention of Martial Arts: Popular Culture Between Asia and America* (Oxford: Oxford University, 2021).

Boyce-Tillman, June, 'Heart's Ease: Eudaimonia, Musicking in the Pandemic, and its Implications for Music Education', *Frontiers in Psychology* 12 (2021): Article 698941. https://doi.org/10.3389/fpsyg.2021.698941

Branca, Domenico, 'The Urban and the Rural in Puno, Highland Peru', *Anthropology Today* 35.6 (2019): 18–20. https://doi.org/10.1111/1467-8322.12542

Briceño, Franklin, 'In Peru, Virus Erodes Centuries-Old Burial Traditions', *AP NEWS*, 2 September 2020, https://apnews.com/article/virus-outbreak-lifestyle-ap-top-news-international-news-latin-america-b75a5aded7caa12ff5a79f5d53bffc21 (accessed 7 September 2022).

Brickell, Katherine and Ayona Datta, *Translocal Geographies* (Farnham, UK: Ashgate, 2011).

Brinkerhoff, Jennifer M., *Digital Diasporas: Identity and Transnational Engagement* (Cambridge: Cambridge University Press, 2009).

Bronfman, Alejandra and Andrew Grant Wood, 'Introduction: Media, Sound, and Culture', in Alejandra Bronfman and Andrew Grant Wood, eds, *Media, Sound, and Culture in Latin America and the Caribbean* (Pittsburgh, PA: University of Pittsburgh Press, 2012): ix–xviii.

Brown, Evan N. 'Cardi B Interviews Biden: "I Just Want Trump Out"', *New York Times*, 17 August 2020 https://www.nytimes.com/2020/08/17/us/elections/cardi-b-interviews-biden-i-just-want-trump-out.html (accessed 11 January 2022).

Brown, Steven C. and Amanda E. Krause, 'Freedom of Choice: Examining Music Listening as a Function of Favorite Music Format', *Psychomusicology: Music, Mind, and Brain* 30.2 (2020): 88–102. https://doi.org/10.1037/pmu0000254

Browne, Kevin A. *High Mas: Carnival and the Poetics of Caribbean Culture* (Jackson: University of Mississippi Press, 2018).

Broyles-González, Yolanda, 'Norteño Borderlands Cumbia Circuitry: Selena Quintanilla and Celso Piña', in Gaetano Prampolini and Annamaria Pinazzi, eds, *The Shade of the Saguaro / La sombra del saguaro. Essays on the Literary Cultures of the American Southwest / Ensayos sobre las culturas literarias del suroeste norteamericano* (Florence: Firenze University Press, 2013), 173–93.

Bryce, Derek, Samantha Murdy, and Matthew Alexander, 'Diaspora, Authenticity and the Imagined Past', *Annals of Tourism Research* 66 (2017): 49–60. https://doi.org/10.1016/j.annals.2017.05.010

Bucher, Taina, 'The Algorithmic Imaginary: Exploring the Ordinary Affects of Facebook Algorithms', *Information, Communication & Society* 20.1 (2017): 30–44. https://doi.org/10.1080/1369118X.2016.1154086

Buchholz, Beth A., Jason DeHart, and Gary Moorman, 'Digital Citizenship during a Global Pandemic: Moving Beyond Digital Literacy', *Journal of Adolescent & Adult Literacy* 64.1 (2020): 11–17. https://doi.org/10.1002/jaal.1076

Buffel, Olehile, 'Preferential Option for the Poor in the Current Context of Poverty in South Africa: Doing Liberation Theology in the Footsteps', *Studia Historiae Ecclesiasticae* 36 (2010): 99–113.

Burges, Jean and Joshua Green, *YouTube: Online Video and Participatory Culture*, 2nd edition (Cambridge: Polity, 2018).

Burgos, Jenzia, 'Pablo Piddy: "Si Tu Quiere Dembow" (2011)', *Pitchfork*, 9 March 2020, https://pitchfork.com/features/lists-and-guides/guide-to-urbano-music/ (accessed 11 November 2021).

Burgos Dávila, César and Helena Simonett, 'Soy gallo de Sinaloa jugado en varios palenques: Production and Consumption of Narco-Music in a Transnational World', in Jesús A. Ramos-Kittrell, ed., *Decentering the Nation: Music, Mexicanidad, and Globalization* (Lanham, MD: Lexington Books, 2020), 99–125.

Burke, Siobhan, 'What Makes a TikTok Dance Go Viral?', *Dance Magazine*, 28 December 2020, https://www.dancemagazine.com/popular-tiktok-dances-2649519038.html (accessed 2 November 2021).

Butler, Bethonie, 'Songs about Coronavirus Pandemic Going Viral', *Columbus Dispatch*, 24 March 2020, https://eu.dispatch.com/story/lifestyle/health-fitness/2020/03/24/songs-about-coronavirus-pandemic-going/1472817007/ (accessed 5 September 2023) [also published as 'Millions are now Streaming Songs about Coronavirus. Are They Good? It Doesn't Matter', *Washington Post*, 19 March. https://www.washingtonpost.com/arts-entertainment/2020/03/19/cardi-b-jojo-coronavirus-songs/ (accessed 5 September 2023)].

Cabral, Javier, '"Lavense Las Manos, Plebes": Here Comes "El Corrido Del Coronavirus" to Cleanse Your Paisa Soul', *L.A. Taco* 25 March 2020, https://lataco.com/corrido-coronavirus-song (accessed 3 October 2022).

Calò Carducci, Luigi G., 'Violencia y migraciónes internas en Perú (1980–2000): Los "Despazados" y la Cuestión Indígena', in Stefano Tedeschi and Alessio Surian, eds, *Pensamiento social italiano sobre América Latina* (Buenos Aires: CLACSO, 2017), 121–40.

Campion Canelas, Minerva and Javier A. Rodríguez-Camacho, 'Efectos del coronavirus en el circuito punk de chapinero a partir de la cartografía de la territorialidad nómada: producción, consumo y participación', *Análisis Político* 33: 100 (2020): 27–54. https://doi.org/10.15446/anpol.v33n100.93359

Campos-Vazquez, Raymundo M. and Gerardo Esquivel, 'Consumption and Geographic Mobility in Pandemic Times. Evidence from Mexico', *Review of Economics of the Household* 19: 2 (2021): 353–71. https://doi.org/10.1007/s11150-020-09539-2

Candela, Mariano, *Carnaval de Barranquilla: Paftrimonio oral e intangible de la humanidad* (Bogotá, Colombia: Amalfi Editores, 2004).

Cannon, Alexander M., 'From Nameless to Nomenclature: Creating Music Genre in Southern Vietnam', *Asian Music* 47.2 (2016): 138–71. https://doi.org/10.1353/amu.2016.0009

Cardi B, 'Cardi B Instagram Live Talking Corona Virus and Harvey Weinstein', https://www.youtube.com/watch?v=3_D-MbIcOEQ (accessed 11 November 2021).

Cardi B Official Website, 'Cardi B Bio', https://www.cardibofficial.com/bio (accessed 9 October 2021).

Carmassi, Claudia, Katherine M. Shear, Martina Corsi, Carlo Antonio Bertelloni, Valerio Dell'Oste, and Liliana Dell'Osso, 'Mania Following Bereavement: State of the Art and Clinical Evidence', *Frontiers in Psychiatry* 11 (2020): Article 366. https://doi.org/10.3389/fpsyt.2020.00366

Casma, Julio C. 'Discriminated against for Speaking Their Own Language', *World Bank Weblog*, 16 April 2014, https://www.worldbank.org/en/news/feature/2014/04/16/discriminados-por-hablar-su-idioma-natal-peru-quechua (accessed 25 September 2022).

Castillo, Nicolas, 'Political Protestantism in Latin America', *SIR Journal of International Relations Blogs*, 16 January 2021, http://www.sirjournal.org/blogs/2021/1/16/political-protestantism-in-latin-america (accessed 3 October 2022).

Castillo-Garsow, Melissa and Jason Nichols, eds, *La Verdad: An International Dialogue on Hip Hop Latinidades* (Columbus: Ohio State University Press, 2016).

Castrodale, Jelisa, 'Here's Where That Weird "Jesus Fights Coronavirus" Animation Came From', *Vice*, 20 April 2021, https://www.vice.com/en/article/bvz8dz/where-that-weird-jesus-fights-coronavirus-video-came-from (accessed 7 February 2022).

Cator, Lauren J., Ben J. Arthur, Laura C. Harrington, and Ronald R. Hoy, 'Harmonic Convergence in the Love Songs of the Dengue Vector Mosquito', *Science* 323.5917 (2009): 1077–9. https://doi.org/10.1126/science.1166541

Cepeda, Eduardo, 'Cardi B & DJ iMarkkeyz to Donate "Coronavirus" Remix Proceeds to Those Affected by the Pandemic', *Remezcla*, 20 March 2020, https://remezcla.com/music/cardi-b-dj-imarkkeyz-donate-coronavirus-remix-proceeds-affected-pandemic/ (accessed 12 October 2021).

Chamberlain, Daniel F., 'The Mexican *Corrido* and Identity in Regional, National, and International Contexts', *Neohelicon* 30.1 (2003): 77–87. https://doi.org/10.1023/A:1024110307006

Chang, Jason O., *Chino: Anti-Chinese Racism in Mexico, 1880–1940* (Urbana: University of Illinois Press, 2017).

Chang, Vanessa, 'Records That Play: The Present Past in Sampling Practice', *Popular Music* 28.2 (2009): 143–59. https://doi.org/10.1017/S0261143009001755

Chávez, Alex, *Sounds of Crossing: Music, Migration, and the Aural Poetics of Huapango Arribeño* (Durham, NC: Duke University Press, 2017).

Chávez Yacila, Rosa, 'Migrar para sobrevivir: en pandemia 250.000 Peruanos retornaron a zonas rurales de origen', *Ojo Público*, 12 December 2021, https://ojo-publico.com/3199/casi-250000-peruanos-retornaron-en-pandemia-zonas-rurales (accessed 7 September 2022).

Chew Sánchez, Martha I. *Corridos in Migrant Memory* (Albuquerque: University of New Mexico Press, 2006).

Chiu, Remi, 'Functions of Music Making Under Lockdown: A Trans-Historical Perspective Across Two Pandemics', *Frontiers in Psychology* 11 (2020): Article 616499. https://doi.org/10.3389/fpsyg.2020.616499

Cho Eun and Beatriz Senoi Ilari, 'Mothers as Home DJs: Recorded Music and Young Children's Well-being during the COVID-19 Pandemic', *Frontiers in Psychology* 12 (2021): Article 637569. https://doi.org/10.3389/fpsyg.2021.637569

Chu, Jean Ho and Ali Mazalek, 'Embodied Engagement with Narrative: A Design Framework for Presenting Cultural Heritage Artifacts', *Multimodal Technologies and Interaction* 3.1 (2019): 1–23. https://doi.org/10.3390/mti3010001

Cities and Memory, 'Sounds from the Global Covid-19 Lockdown', https://citiesandmemory.com/covid19-sounds/ (accessed 6 February 2022).

Clarke, Eric F., *An Ecological Approach to the Perception of Musical Meaning* (Oxford: Oxford University Press, 2005).

Cobo, Leila, 'Rise Interrupted: Latin Trap Star Anuel AA was on the Cusp of Stardom when He Began a 30-Month Prison Sentence. in His First Post-Release Interview, He Describes How He Held On', *Billboard* 130.18 (2018): 33.

Cobo, Leila, 'Super Smash Bros: Anuel AA and Ozun Revitalized Reggaetón and Forged New Paths for Independent-Minded Artists with Major-Label Visions. With a New Collaborative Album, They're Aiming Even Higher', *Billboard* 133.1 (2021): 46.

Colburn, Steven, 'Filming Concerts for YouTube: Seeking Recognition in the Pursuit of Cultural Capital', *Popular Music and Society* 38 (2015): 59–72. https://doi.org/10.1080/03007766.2014.974373

Colling, Lincoln J. and William F. Thompson, 'Music, Action, and Affect', in Tom Cochrane, Bernardino Fantini, and Klaus R. Scherer, eds, *The Emotional Power of Music* (Oxford: Oxford University Press, 2013), 197–212.

Conradson, David and Deirdre McKay, 'Translocal Subjectivities: Mobility, Connection, Emotion', *Mobilities* 2.2 (2007): 167–74. https://doi.org/10.1080/17450100701381524

Convers, Leonor, Juan Sebastián Ochoa, and Oscar Hernández, *Arrullos y Currulaos: Material para abordar el estudio de la música tradicional del pacífico sur Colombiano tomos I y II* (Cali, Colomnis: Pontificia Universidad Javeriana, 2014).

Cooper, Carolyn, *Sound Clash: Jamaican Dancehall Culture at Large* (New York: Palgrave Macmillan, 2004).

Cordes, Ashley L. *Rave Identity and Self-Reflexive Compartmentalization: An Exploration of Rituals and Beliefs of Contemporary Rave Culture* (O'ahu: Hawaii Pacific University, 2012).

Córdoba, Javier, 'Costa Rica: Sacerdote se hace viral con canción del COVID', *Associated Press*, 3 May 2021, https://apnews.com/article/noticias-bf0c51b7e9bc456d1fba902abe3f1035 (accessed 3 October 2022).

Corona Concréte website, https://corona-concrete.lasse-marc-riek.de/index.php (accessed 6 February 2022).

Corrêa Duarte, Ulisses, 'Schools of Samba in the South Brazilian Border: Circuits and Translocal Exchanges in Carnival Cultures', in Fabiana Lopes da Cunha and Jorge Rabassa, eds, *Festivals and Heritage in Latin America: Interdisciplinary Dialogues on Culture, Identity and Tourism* (Cham, Switzerland: Springer International, 2021), 57–71.

Crippa, Giulia, 'Informação pandémica e capitalismo viral: a mídia, a Covid-19 e a construção dos medos', *Liinc Em Revista* 16.2 (2020): Article e5332. https://doi.org/10.18617/liinc.v16i2.5332

Crist, Eileen, 'On the Poverty of Nomenclature', in Jason W. Moore, ed., *Anthropocene or Capitalocene?: Nature, History, and the Crisis of Capitalism* (Oakland, CA: PM Press, 2016), 14–33.

Crowdy, Denis, 'Tribute Without Attribution: Kopikat, Covers and Copyright in Papua New Guinea', in Shane Homan, ed., *Access All Eras: Tribute Bands and Global Pop Culture* (New York: Open University Press, 2006), 229–40.

Cucagna, Emilia and Javier Romero, *The Gendered Impacts of COVID-19 on Labor Markets in Latin America and the Caribbean* (Washington, DC: World Bank, 2021), https://openknowledge.worldbank.org/handle/10986/35191 (accessed 25 September 2022).

Cvijanovic, Irina, 'Performing Sound of the Past: Remix in Electronic Dance Music Culture', *Muzikologija* 17 (2014): 87–104. https://doi.org/10.2298/MUZ1417087C

de Giménez, Catherine H., 'Corrido, identité, idéologie: chant populaire de tradition orale au Mexique, *Cahiers Du Monde Hispanique et Luso-Brésilien* 48 (1987): 49–58 (our translation). https://doi.org/10.3406/carav.1987.2300

de Guzman, Allan B., John Christopher B. Mesana, Maxeen E. Manuel, Kyle Christian A. Arcega, Rupert Lance T. Yumang, and Kylie Niechols V. Miranda, 'Examining Intergenerational Family Members' Creative Activities during COVID-19 Lockdown Via Manifest Content Analysis of YouTube and TikTok Videos', *Educational Gerontology* 48.10 (2022): 458–71. https://doi.org/10.1080/03601277.2022.2046372

De Jesús Chávez-Martínez, José, 'La romantización del narcocorrido en México', *Comhumanitas* 10.3 (2019): 43–53. https://doi.org/10.31207/rch.v10i3.215

De Jesús Diego Pineda, José, *Política y poder en el narcocorrido: fronteras difusas entre gobierno y 'narco'* (Mauritius: Editorial Académica Española, 2019).

De Kosnik, Abigail, 'Why it Matters that Black Men and Queer Women Invented Digital Remix Culture', *JCMS: Journal of Cinema and Media Studies* 59.1 (2019): 156–63. https://doi.org/10.1353/cj.2019.0069

De La Ossa, Jaime and Alejandro De La Ossa-Lacayo, 'Cacería de subsistencia en San Marcos, Sucre, colombia', *Revista Colombiana de Ciencia Animal – RECIA* 2 (2011): 213–24. https://doi.org/10.24188/recia.v3.n2.2011.367

de León, Marco A., 'Medicina, corazón y música de acordeón', *Revista Colombiana de Cardiología* 21.3 (2014): 195–8. https://doi.org/10.1016/S0120-5633(14)70279-7

Deguma, Jabin J., Melona C. Deguma, Jemima N. Tandag, and Harlene Marie B. Acebes, 'Where Is the Church in the Time of COVID-19 Pandemic: Preferring the Poor via G. Gutierrez' "Liberation" and the Catholic Church's Social Teaching in the Philippine Setting', *Journal of Social and Political Sciences* 3.2 (2020), https://papers.ssrn.com/abstract=3581766 (access date). https://doi.org/10.31014/aior.1991.03.02.175

Del Real, Jose A., 'Five Days, 100 Vaccine Doses and a Wildfire of Conspiracy Theories', *Washington Post*, 28 May 2021, https://www.washingtonpost.com/nation/interactive/2021/covid-vaccine-hesitancy-california-farmworkers/ (accessed 1 July 2022).

Deleuze, Gilles, *Difference and Repetition* (trans. Paul Patton, New York: Columbia University Press, 1994).

Delgado, Daniel J. and Joe R. Feagin, 'Latinos in the United States: Understanding the Historical and Systemic Foundations of Racial Oppression', in Martin Guevera Urbina and Sofía Espinoza Álvarez, eds, *Ethnicity and Criminal Justice in the Era of Mass Incarceration: A Critical Reader on the Latino Experience* (Springfield, IL: Charles C. Thomas, 2017), 61–81.

Delgado, Grace, *Making the Chinese Mexican: Global Migration, Localism, and Exclusion in the U.S.-Mexico Borderlands* (Stanford, CA: Stanford University Press, 2013).

Denisova, Anastasia, 'How to Define "Viral" for Media Studies?', *Westminster Papers in Communication and Culture* 15.1 (2020): 1–4. https://doi.org/10.16997/wpcc.375

DeNora, Tia, *Music Asylums: Wellbeing through Music in Everyday Life* (Farnham, UK: Ashgate, 2013).

Depoux, Anneliese, Sam Martin, Emilie Karafillakis, Raman Preet, Annelies Wilder-Smith, and Heidi Larson, 'The Pandemic of Social Media Panic Travels Faster than the COVID-19 Outbreak', *Journal of Travel Medicine* 27.3 (2020): Article taaa031. https://doi.org/10.1093/jtm/taaa031

Derryberry, Elizabeth P., Jennifer N. Phillips, Graham E. Derryberry, Michael J. Blum, and David Luther, 'Singing in a Silent Spring: Birds Respond to a Half-Century Soundscape Reversion during the COVID-19 Shutdown', *Science* 370.6516 (2020): 575–9. https://doi.org/10.1126/science.abd5777

Díaz-Santana Garza, Luis, *Historia de la música norteña mexicana: desde los grupos precursores al auge del narcocorrido* (México: Plaza y Valdés S.L., 2015).

Diaz-Zambrana, Rosana, 'Gastronomia, humor y nacion: estrategias retoricas en las letras de Calle 13', *Centro Journal* 22.2 (2010): 129–49.

Dickey, Dan W., *The Kennedy Corridos: A Study of the Ballads of a Mexican American Hero* (Austin: University of Texas at Austin, 1978).

Dieng, Hamady, Ching Chuin The, Tomomitsu Satho, Fumio Miake, Erida Wydiamala, Nur Faeza A. Kassim, Nur Aida Hashim, *et al.* 'The Electronic Song "Scary Monsters and Nice Sprites" Reduces Host Attack and Mating Success in the Dengue Vector *Aedes Aegypti*', *Acta Tropica* 194 (2019): 93–9. https://doi.org/10.1016/j.actatropica.2019.03.027

Diestra Salinas, Fortunato, 'Apreciación folclórica del género musical en la provincia de Sihuas Ancash, 2016', *Infinitum* 7.1 (2017): 49–54. https://doi.org/10.51431/infinitum.v7i1.62

Díez de Urdanivia, Fernando, *Su majestad el albur* (Discos Luzam, México DF, 2021).

Diminescu, Dana, 'The Connected Migrant: An Epistemological Manifesto', *Social Science Information* 47.4 (2008): 565–79. https://doi.org/10.1177/0539018408096447

Domínguez, Marlen M. and Angélica Gómez, 'Usos del internet por jóvenes estudiantes durante la pandemia de la covid-19 en México', *PAAKAT: Revista De Tecnología y Sociedad* 12.22 (2022), https://doi.org/10.32870/Pk.a12n22.724

Duinker, Ben, 'Good Things Come in Threes: Triplet Flow in Recent Hip-Hop Music', *Popular Music* 38.3 (2019): 423–56. https://doi.org/10.1017/S026114301900028X

Duinker, Ben, 'Segmentation, Phrasing, and Meter in Hip-Hop Music', *Music Theory Spectrum* 43.2 (2021): 221–45. https://doi.org/10.1093/mts/mtab003

Duque Franco, Isabel, Catalina Ortiz, Jota Samper, and Gynna Millan, 'Mapping Repertoires of Collective Action Facing the COVID-19 Pandemic in Informal Settlements in Latin American Cities', *Environment and Urbanization* 32.2 (2020): 523–46. https://doi.org/10.1177/0956247820944823

Durston, Alan and Bruce Mannheim, *Indigenous Languages, Politics, and Authority in Latin America: Historical and Ethnographic Perspectives* (Notre Dame, IN: University of Notre Dame Press, 2018).

Economic Commission for Latin America and the Caribbean, *Moving Towards a Care Society in Latin America and the Caribbean Is Urgent for Achieving a Transformative and Sustainable Recovery with Gender Equality* (Santiago de Chile: ECLAC, 2021), https://www.cepal.org/en/pressreleases/moving-towards-care-society-latin-america-and-caribbean-urgent-achieving (accessed 25 September 2022).

Edberg, Mark C., *El Narcotraficante: Narcocorridos and the Construction of a Cultural Persona on the U.S.–Mexico Border* (Austin: University of Texas Press, 2009).

El Maarouf, Moulay D., Taieb Belghazi, and Farouk El Maarouf, 'COVID – 19: A Critical Ontology of the Present', *Educational Philosophy and Theory* 53.1 (2021): 71–89. https://doi.org/10.1080/00131857.2020.1757426

El Tiempo, 'La última canción de Miguel Durán Jr. fue dedicada a la pandemia', 3 September 2020, https://www.eltiempo.com/cultura/musica-y-libros/la-ultima-cancion-de-miguel-duran-jr-fue-dedicada-a-la-pandemia-535800 (accessed 2 February 2022).

Engelhardt, Gary V., Michael D. Eriksen, and Nadia Greenhalgh-Stanley, *A Profile of Housing and Health Among Older Americans*. Research Institute for Housing America Research Paper 13.03 (MacArthur Foundation, 2013). https://papers.ssrn.com/abstract=2359676

Entertainment Tonight, 'Watch Cardi B FREAK OUT Over Health and Safety', https://www.youtube.com/watch?v=7M9_0pjW1GE (accessed 12 October 2021).

Erazno y La Chokolata, 'Viernes de Nacadas, las 10 de Erazno, el Chokolatazo, la final de la casa de las parodias, y mucho mas', El Podcast Mas Chido E1432, https://elerazno.com/?v=f24485ae434a (accessed 16 September 2022).

Escárzaga, Fabiola, Julio Abanto Llaque, and Anderson Chamorro. 'Migración, guerra interna e identidad andina en Perú', *Política y Cultura* 18 (2008): 277–98.

Escobar, Arturo, 'Displacement, Development, and Modernity in the Colombian Pacific', *International Social Science Journal* 55.175 (2003): 157–67. https://doi.org/10.1111/1468-2451.5501015

Evans, H. Martyn, 'Music, Medicine and Embodiment', *Lancet* 375.9718 (2010): 886–7. https://doi.org/10.1016/S0140-6736(10)60376-5

Excélsior, 'ALAN Y ROBERTO: corrido del coronavirus da instrucción y aliento a la comunidad', 14 April 2020, https://www.excelsiorcalifornia.com/2020/04/14/alan-y-roberto-corrido-del-coronavirus-da-instruccion-y-aliento-a-comunidad/ (accessed 3 October 2022).

Exposito, Suzy, 'Fat Joe, Cardi B, Anuel AA Team Up on Scorching New Song "Yes"', *Rolling Stone*, 6 September 2019, https://www.rollingstone.com/music/music-latin/cardi-b-anuel-aa-fat-joe-new-song-yes-listen-880624/ (accessed 5 January 2022).

Fagerjord, Anders, 'After Convergence: YouTube and Remix Culture', in Jeremy Hunsinger, Lisbeth Klastrup, and Matthew Allen, eds, *International Handbook of Internet Research* (Dordrecht: Springer Netherlands, 2010), 187–200.

Felbab-Brown, Vanda, 'AMLO's Feeble Response to COVID-19 in Mexico', Brookings Institute website, 30 March 2020, https://www.brookings.edu/blog/order-from-chaos/2020/03/30/amlos-feeble-response-to-covid-19-in-mexico (accessed 29 December 2020).

Feld, Steven, 'Pygmy POP. A Genealogy of Schizophonic Mimesis', *Yearbook for Traditional Music* 28 (1996): 1–35. https://doi.org/10.2307/767805

Feng, Jiayun, '"I Want No Smoke with the Chinese": Cardi B Wins Fans in China with Coronavirus Rants', *SupChina*, 26 March 2020, https://supchina.com/2020/03/26/i-want-no-smoke-with-the-chinese-cardi-b-wins-fans-in-china-with-coronavirus-rants/ (accessed 11 November 2021).

Fernández, Albert, 'La revolución de los balcones'. *On Barcelona*, 18 March 2020, https://www.elperiodico.com/es/onbarcelona/a-la-ultima/20200318/balcones-coronavirus-actividades-vecinos-7895699 (accessed 8 April 2021).

Fernández L'Hoeste, Héctor, 'On Music and Colombianness: Toward a Critique of the History of Cumbia', in Héctor Fernández L'Hoeste and Pablo Vila, eds, *Cumbia! Scenes of a Migrant Latin American Music Genre* (Durham, NC: Duke University Press 2013), 248–68.

Fernández L'Hoeste, Héctor and Pablo Vila, 'Introduction', in Héctor Fernández L'Hoeste and Pablo Vila, eds, *Cumbia! Scenes of a Migrant Latin American Music Genre* (Durham, NC: Duke University Press 2013), 1–27.

Fink, Lauren K., Lindsay A. Warrenburg, Claire Howlin, William M. Randall, Niels C. Hansen, and Melanie Wald-Fuhrmann, 'Viral Tunes: Changes in Musical Behaviours and Interest in Coronamusic Predict Socio-Emotional Coping during COVID-19 Lockdown', *Humanities and Social Science Communications* 8 (2021): Article 180. https://doi.org/10.1057/s41599-021-00858-y

Flores, Giancarlo M. 'Superando las dicotomías: el qhapaq ñan como ejemplo del patrimonio como proceso social', *Chungará* 51.3 (2019), https://scielo.conicyt.cl/scielo.php?pid=S0717-73562019000300457&script=sci_arttext (accessed 21 September 2022).

Fosler-Lussier, D., *Music on the Move* (Ann Arbor: University of Michigan Press, 2020).
Franco, Diego C., 'Suero costeño, sinónimo de herencia y tradición', *CONtexto ganadero*, 3 December 2018, https://www.contextoganadero.com/cronica/suero-costeno-sinonimo-de-herencia-y-tradicion (accessed 7 September 2022).
Frijda, Nico H. and Batja Mesquita, 'The Analysis of Emotions: Dimensions of Variation', in *Emotions, Personality, and Psychotherapy: What Develops in Emotional Development?* (New York: Plenum Press, 1998), 273–95.
Frith, Simon, *Popular Music: Critical Concepts in Media and Cultural Studies, Volume IV: Music and Identity* (London: Routledge, 2004).
Fundación Sierra & Foclor, https://sierrayfolclor.org/ (accessed 16 September 2022).
Gadea, Carlos A. and Rafael Bayce, 'Coronavirus: una pandemia hiperreal', *Estudios Sociológicos* 39.115 (2021): 209–36. https://doi.org/10.24201/es.2021v39n115.2074
Gallagher, Owen, *Reclaiming Critical Remix Video: The Role of Sampling in Transformative Works* (New York: Routledge, 2018).
Gardner, Robert O., 'Introduction: Spaces of Musical Interaction: Scenes, Subcultures, and Communities', *Studies in Symbolic Interaction* 35 (2010): 71–7. https://doi.org/10.1108/S0163-2396(2010)0000035008
Garnizé, Alexandre, 'Music, Pandemic, and Creative Idleness!' *Streetnotes* 28 (2022): 104–8. https://doi.org/10.5070/S528154980
Garza, Díaz-Santana, *Between Norteño and Tejano Conjunto: Music, Tradition, and Culture at the U.S.-Mexico Border* (Lanham, MD: Lexington Books, 2021).
Gehl, Robert, 'YouTube as Archive: Who Will Curate this Digital Wunderkammer?', *International Journal of Cultural Studies*, 12.1 (2009): 43–60. https://doi.org/10.1177/1367877908098854
Gemmill, Allie, 'Cardi B's Coronavirus Speech Remix Just Became a Billboard Hit Song', *Teen Vogue*, 26 March 2020, https://www.teenvogue.com/story/cardi-b-coronavirus-speech-remix-billboard-hit-song (accessed 12 October 2021).
Gibson, Michael, '"That's Hip-Hop to Me!": Race, Space, and Temporal Logics of Authenticity in Independent Cultural Production', *Poetics* 46 (2014): 38–55. https://doi.org/10.1016/j.poetic.2014.09.002
Gitirana Hikiji, Rose S. 'Música para matar o tempo intervalo, suspensão e imersão', *Mana* 12.1 (2006): 151–78. https://doi.org/10.1590/S0104-93132006000100006
Goh, Irving, 'Virus is Other People', *Cultural Politics*, 17:1 (2021): 145–9. https://doi.org/10.1215/17432197-8797641
Goldman, Dara E. 'Walk Like a Woman, Talk Like a Man: Ivy Queen's Troubling of Gender', *Latino Studies* 15:4 (2017): 439–57. https://doi.org/10.1057/s41276-017-0088-5
Gómez, Patricio, 'Cumbia y fuera', *Clarín*, 7 July 2009, http://edant.clarin.com/ (accessed 19 September 2022).
Gonzalez, Aurelio, 'El corrido: expresión popular y tradicional de la balada hispánica', *Olivar (La Plata)* 12.15 (2011): 11–36.
Gonzales, Erica, 'Cardi B Shares Her Own #MeToo Story and Stands Up for Women in Hip-Hop', *Harper's Bazaar*, 20 March 2018, https://www.harpersbazaar.com/celebrity/latest/a19486392/cardi-b-metoo-story-women-hiphop/ (accessed 11 January 2022).
González de Castilla Gómez, María, 'Fandango jarocho y ciudad: juventud y construcción de sentidos. El caso del colectivo Altepee', master's thesis, Universidad de Guadalajara, Guadalajara, Jalisco, Mexico, 2017.
González Paraíso, Raquel, 'Re-Contextualizing Traditions: The Performance of Identity in Festivals of Huasteco, Jarocho, and Terracalenteño Sones in Mexico', PhD thesis, University of Wisconsin-Madison, 2014.
González Sánchez, Julián F. '"Yo he venido a buscar, los pasos que me han faltado": un acercamiento a la noción de muerto a partir del alabado en las comunidades afrodescendientes de Cértegui y Winandó', PhD thesis, Universidad del Rosario, 2021.

Goodwin, Michele and Erwin Chemerinsky, 'The Trump Administration: Immigration, Racism, and COVID-19', *University of Pennsylvania Law Review* 169 (2021): 313–82.

Goralska, Magdalena, 'Anthropology from Home: Advice on Digital Ethnography for the Pandemic Times', *Anthropology in Action* 27.1 (2020): 46–52. https://doi.org/10.3167/aia.2020.270105

Gose, Peter, *Invaders as Ancestors: On the Intercultural Making and Unmaking of Spanish Colonialism in the Andes* (Toronto: University of Toronto Press, 2008).

Goyes Moreno, Isabel and Sandra Montezuma M., 'Justicia y *género en nariño* en casos de violencia contra las mujeres', *La manzana de la discordia* 7.2 (2012): 15–22. https://doi.org/10.25100/lmd.v7i2.1559

Gray, Chris H. 'Virus is a Language: COVID-19 and the New Abnormal', *Cultural Politics* 17.1 (2021): 92–101. https://doi.org/10.1215/17432197-8797571

Greiner, Clemens and Patrick Sakdapolrak, 'Translocality: Concepts, Applications and Emerging Research Perspectives', *Geography Compass* 7.5 (2013): 373–84. https://doi.org/10.1111/gec3.12048

Groody, Daniel R. and Gustavo Gutiérrez, *The Preferential Option for the Poor beyond Theology* (Euclid, OH: University of Notre Dame Press, 2014).

Guerrero, Jean, 'Op-Ed: How Conspiracy Theories about COVID-19 Prey on Latinos', *Los Angeles Times*, 2 May 2021, https://www.latimes.com/opinion/story/2021-05-02/latinos-covid-vaccines-resistance-skepticism (accessed 1 July 2022).

Gupta, Nisha, 'Singing Away the Social Distancing Blues: Art Therapy in a Time of Coronavirus', *Journal of Humanistic Psychology* 60.5 (2020): 593–603. https://doi.org/10.1177/0022167820927807

Gurza, Agustín, 'Coronavirus Corridos: Tales of the Pandemic', The Strachwitz Frontera Collection of Mexican and Mexican American Recordings website, https://frontera.library.ucla.edu/blog/2020/04/coronavirus-corridos-tales-pandemic (accessed 1 July 2022).

Gurza, Agustín, 'Strachwitz Frontera Collection Coronavirus Corridos: Tales of the Pandemic', The Strachwitz Frontera Collection of Mexican and Mexican American Recordings website, 15 April 2020, https://frontera.library.ucla.edu/blog/2020/04/coronavirus-corridos-tales-pandemic (accessed 2 February 2022).

Haigney, Sophie, 'TikTok is the Perfect Medium for the Splintered Attention Spans of Lockdown', *The Guardian*, 16 May 2020, https://www.theguardian.com/commentisfree/2020/may/16/tiktok-perfect-medium-splintered-attention-spans-coronavirus-lockdown (accessed 2 November 2021).

Hale, James, 'YouTube Users Watch 450 Million Hours Of Content On TV Screens Each Day', *tubefilter* 25 June 2020, https://www.tubefilter.com/2020/06/25/youtube-brandcast-tvviewership-stats/ (accessed 16 January 2021).

Hallam, Susan, Andrea Creech, Maria Varvarigou, and Hilary McQueen, 'Perceived Benefits of Active Engagement with Making Music in Community Settings', *International Journal of Community Music* 5 (2012): 155–74. https://doi.org/10.1386/ijcm.5.2.155_1

Hammond Cisneros, Melanie S. and Laura R. León Kanashiro, '#FamiliasDeCuarentena, radiografía de una comunicación en contexto de pandemia. Caso: San Fernando', *Repositorio Institucional – Ulima* (2021), https://repositorio.ulima.edu.pe/bitstream/handle/20.500.12724/12675/Hammond-Leon_Caso-estudio.pdf (accessed 9 March 2022).

Hansen, Niels C., John M. G. Treider, Dana Swarbrick, Joshua S. Bamford, Johanna Wilson, and Jonna Katariina Vuoskoski, 'A Crowd-Sourced Database of Coronamusic: Documenting Online Making and Sharing of Music during the COVID-19 Pandemic', *Frontiers in Psychology* 12 (2021): Article 684083. https://doi.org/10.3389/fpsyg.2021.684083

Hasse, Javier, 'Cumbia 420: The Super Viral, Weed-Infused Musical Phenomenon Bringing Ghetto Back To The Mainstream', *Forbes*, 27 May 2021, https://www.forbes.com/

sites/javierhasse/2021/05/27/cumbia-420-the-super-viral-weed-infused-musical-phenomenon-bringing-ghetto-back-to-the-mainstream/ (accessed 5 September 2023).

Heaven, Will D., 'Why the Coronavirus Lockdown is Making the Internet Even Stronger', *MIT Technology Review* 7 April 2020, https://www.technologyreview.com/2020/04/07/998552/why-the-coronavirus-lockdown-is-making-the-internet-better-than-ever/ (accessed 2 November 2021).

Hennessy, Sarah, Mathew Sachs, Jonas Kaplan, and Assal Habibi, 'Music and Mood Regulation during the Early Stages of the COVID-19 Pandemic', *PLOS ONE* 16.10 (2021): Article e0258027. https://doi.org/10.1371/journal.pone.0258027

Hermida, Luis, Ignacio Pavón, Antonio C. Lobo Soares, and J. Luis Bento-Coelho, 'On the Person-Place Interaction and its Relationship with the Responses/Outcomes of Listeners of Urban Soundscape (Compared Cases of Lisbon and Bogotá): Contextual and Semiotic Aspects', *International Journal of Environmental Research and Public Health* 16.4 (2019): 551–72. https://doi.org/10.3390/ijerph16040551

Hernandez, Deborah P., *Oye Como Va! Hybridity and Identity in Latino Popular Music* (Philadelphia: Temple University Press, 2010).

Hernández Vaca, Víctor, 'Son huasteco, son de costumbre. Etnolaudería del son a lo humano ya lo divino en Texquitote, San Luis Potosí', *Revista de Literaturas Populares* 10.1–2 (2000): 3–17.

Herrera-Sobek, María, *The Mexican Corrido: A Feminist Analysis* (Bloomington: Indiana University Press, 1990).

Hesmondhalgh, David, Ellis Jones, and Andreas Rauh, 'SoundCloud and Bandcamp as Alternative Music Platforms', *Social Media + Society* 5.4 (2019). https://doi.org/10.1177/2056305119883429

Heuguet, Guillaume, 'Towards a Micropolitics of Formats', *Revue d'Anthropologie Des Connaissances* 13.3 (2019), https://doi.org/10.4000/rac.3263

Heyd, Theresa, 'Narratives of Belonging in the Digital Diaspora: Corpus Approaches to a Cultural Concept', *Open Linguistics* 2 (2016): 287–99. https://doi.org/10.1515/opli-2016-0013

Heyes, Cressida J., 'The Short and the Long of it: A Political Phenomenology of Pandemic Time', *Philosophy Today* 64.4 (2020): 859–63. https://doi.org/10.5840/philtoday20201110367

Hijleh, Mark, *Towards a Global Music History: Intercultural Convergence, Fusion, and Transformation in the Human Musical Story* (New York: Routledge, 2019).

Hispanically Yours, 'Anuel AA's 'Emmanuel' Debuts at No. 1 on Billboard's Top Latin Albums & Latin Rhythm Albums Charts', 9 June 2020, https://www.hispanicallyyours.com/anuel-aas-emmanuel-debuts-at-no-1-on-billboards-top-latin-albums-latin-rhythm-albums-charts/ (accessed 5 January 2022).

Hissong, Samantha, 'A Coronavirus Song Featuring Cardi B's Voice is Going Viral – and May Violate Copyright Law', *Rolling Stone*, 17 March 2020, https://www.rollingstone.com/pro/news/coronavirus-viral-song-cardi-b-copyright-968695/ (accessed 12 November 2021).

Horden, Peregrine, ed., *Music As Medicine: The History of Music Therapy Since Antiquity* (New York: Routledge, 2016).

Huamani, Maximo Damián, 'With Tears, Not Words', *Review: Literature and Arts of the Americas* 14.25–26 (1980): 49–50. https://doi.org/10.1080/08905768008594033

Hunt, Stephen and David Martin, 'Christian Millenarianism: From the Early Church to Waco', *Nova Religio: The Journal of Alternative and Emergent Religions* 9:1 (2005): 139–43. https://doi.org/10.1525/nr.2005.9.1.139

Hutchinson, Andrew, 'YouTube Underlines Its Value for Musicians as TikTok Continues to Rise', *SocialMediaToday*, 2 June 2021, https://www.socialmediatoday.com/news/youtube-underlines-its-value-for-musicians-as-tiktok-continues-to-rise/601179/ (accessed 3 June 2021). https://doi.org/10.1017/S0261143011000055

Hutchinson, Sydney, '*Típico, Folklórico* or *Popular*? Musical Categories, Place, and Identity in a Transnational Listening Community', *Popular Music* 30.2 (2011): 245–62.
Hutchinson, Sydney, *Tigers of a Different Stripe: Performing Gender in Dominican Music* (Chicago: University of Chicago Press, 2016), 168–9.
Hyers, Conrad, *The Spirituality of Comedy: Comic Heroism in a Tragic World* (New Brunswick, NJ: Transaction Publishers, 1996).
Illanes Córdova, Diana F., 'Repertorio de canciones del Anexo Maramara, Apurímac para la apreciación de la música andina en los niños de 5 años, IEI 7.8, Amiguitos de San Martín, Callao', education thesis, Escuela Nacional Superior de Folklore 'José María Arguedas', Lima, 2017.
Ingham, Tim, 'The Three Biggest Myths Deluding the Modern Music Business', *Rolling Stone*, 26 January 2021, https://www.rollingstone.com/pro/features/the-three-biggest-myths-deluding-the-modern-music-business-tim-1119106/ (accessed 7 January 2022).
Ishtar, Cardona and Christian Rinaudo, 'Son jarocho entre méxico y estados unidos: definición "afro" de una práctica transnacional', *Desacatos* 53 (2017): 20–37.
Iten, Moses, 'Mexican Sonidero Sound System Culture Online: From Dancing on the Streets to Social Media in Times of Covid-19', *Dancecult* 13.1 (2021). https://dx.doi.org/10.12801/1947-5403.2021.13.01.12
Jameson, Fredric, 'Globalization and Hybridization', in Nataša Durovicová and Kathleen E. Newman, eds, *World Cinemas, Transnational Perspectives* (New York: Routledge, 2009), 315–19.
Jedwab, Remi, Amjad M. Khan, Jason Russ, and Esha D. Zaveri, 'Epidemics, Pandemics, and Social Conflict: Lessons from the Past and Possible Scenarios for COVID-19', *World Development* 147 (2021): Article 105629. https://doi.org/10.1016/j.worlddev.2021.105629
Johannsen, Igor, 'Configurations of Space and Identity in Hip Hop: Performing "Global South"', *Journal of Hip Hop Studies* 6.2 (2019): 183–205.
Johansson, Sofia, Ann Werner, Patrik Åker, and Greg Goldenzwaig, *Streaming Music: Practices, Media, Cultures* (New York: Routledge, 2017).
John, Nichoas A., *The Age of Sharing* (Cambridge: Polity, 2017).
Jones, Ellis, 'The Role of Mashup Music in Creating Web 2.0's Democratic Promise', *Convergence* 27.4 (2021): 1112–8. https://doi.org/10.1177/1354856520983758
Jordan, Pamela and André Fiebig, 'COVID-19 Impacts on Historic Soundscape Perception and Site Usage', *Acoustics* 3.3 (2021): 594–610. https://doi.org/10.3390/acoustics3030038
Jost, Christofer, 'Professionalism as Style: Music Amateurs on YouTube and the Transformation of Production Techniques', *Lied und Populäre Kultur* 62 (2017): 55–70.
Ju, Shirley, 'Meet the DJ Who Created the Viral Cardi B Coronavirus Rant Remix', *Variety*, 26 March 2020, https://variety.com/2020/music/news/cardi-b-coronavirus-rant-remix-dj-imarkkeyz-interview-1203545575/ (accessed 12 October 2021).
Julca Guerrero, Félix and Laura Nivin Vargas, 'Recursos expresivos y literarios en el huayno Ancashino', *Letras (Lima)* 90.132 (2019): 260–84. https://doi.org/10.30920/letras.90.132.12
Juslin, Patrik and John Sloboda, *Handbook of Music and Emotion: Theory, Research, Applications* (Oxford: Oxford University Press, 2009).
Kaiser, Jonas and Adrian Rauchfleisch, 'Birds of a Feather Get Recommended Together: Algorithmic Homophily in YouTube's Channel Recommendations in the United States and Germany', *Social Media + Society* 6.4 (2020). https://doi.org/10.1177/2056305120969914
Kaiser, Jonas, Adrian Rauchfleisch, and Yasodara Cordova, 'Fighting Zika with Honey: An Analysis of YouTube's Video Recommendations on Brazilian YouTube', *International Journal of Communication* 15 (2021): 1244–62.
Kale, Sirin, 'How Coronavirus Helped TikTok Find its Voice', *The Guardian*, 26 April 2020, https://www.theguardian.com/technology/2020/apr/26/how-coronavirus-helped-tiktok-find-its-voice (accessed 2 November 2021).

Kanai, Akane, 'DIY Culture', in Eduardo Navas, Owen Gallagher, and xtine burrough, *Keywords in Remix Studies* (New York: Routledge, 2018), 125–34.
Karkabi, Nadeem, 'Electro-Dabke: Performing Cosmopolitan Nationalism and Borderless Humanity', *Public Culture* 30.1 (2018): 173–96. https://doi.org/10.1215/08992363-4189215
Kartsaki, Elrini, *On Repetition: Writing, Performance and Art* (Chicago: Intellect, 2016).
Katz, Mark, *Capturing Sound: How Technology Has Changed Music* (Berkeley: University of California Press, 2010).
Kendal, Evie, 'Public Health Crises in Popular Media: How Viral Outbreak Films Affect the Public's Health Literacy', *Medical Humanities* 47.1 (2021): 11–19. https://doi.org/10.1136/medhum-2018-011446
Kennedy, Jenny, 'Conceptual Boundaries of Sharing', *Information, Communication & Society* 19.4 (2016): 461–74. https://doi.org/10.1080/1369118X.2015.1046894
Kennedy, Melanie, '"If the Rise of the TikTok Dance and e-Girl Aesthetic has Taught Us Anything, it's that Teenage Girls Rule the Internet Right Now": TikTok Celebrity, Girls and the Coronavirus Crisis', *European Journal of Cultural Studies* 23.6 (2020): 1069–76. https://doi.org/10.1177/1367549420945341
Ketelaar, Eric, 'Archives as Spaces of Memory', *Journal of the Society of Archivists* 29.1 (2008): 9–27. https://doi.org/10.1080/00379810802499678
Kile, Meredith B., 'The Best TikTok Songs and Dance Challenges that Got Us Through 2020', *ET*, 22 December 2020, https://www.etonline.com/the-best-tiktok-songs-and-dance-challenges-that-got-us-through-2020-157969 (accessed 2 November 2021).
Kirchhoff, Drew, 'More Tok on the Clock: Introducing Longer Videos on TikTok', TikTok, 1 July 2021, https://newsroom.tiktok.com/en-us/longer-videos (accessed 7 September 2022).
Kivy, Peter, *New Essays on Musical Understanding* (Oxford: Clarendon Press, 2001).
Knobel, Michele and Colin Lankshear, 'Remix: The Art and Craft of Endless Hybridization', *Journal of Adolescent & Adult Literacy* 52.1 (2008): 22–33. https://doi.org/10.1598/JAAL.52.1.3
Koch, Sabine, Teresa Kunz, Sissy Lykou, and Robyn Cruz, 'Effects of Dance Movement Therapy and Dance on Health-Related Psychological Outcomes: A Meta-Analysis', *The Arts in Psychotherapy* 41.1 (2014): 46–64. https://doi.org/10.1016/j.aip.2013.10.004
Krause, Amanda E,. Adrian C. North, and Brody Heritage, 'The Uses and Gratifications of Using Facebook Music Listening Applications', *Computers in Human Behavior* 39 (2014): 71–7. https://doi.org/10.1016/j.chb.2014.07.001
Kreutz, Gunter, 'Does Singing Facilitate Social Bonding?' *Music and Medicine* 6.2 (2014): 51–60. https://doi.org/10.47513/mmd.v6i2.180
Kukla, Rebecca, 'Slurs, Interpellation, and Ideology', *Southern Journal of Philosophy* 56 (2018): 7–32. https://doi.org/10.1111/sjp.12298
Kunisch, Sven, Blagoy Blagoev, and Jean M. Bartunek, 'Complex Times, Complex Time: The Pandemic, Time-Based Theorizing and Temporal Research in Management and Organization Studies', *Journal of Management Studies* 58.5 (2021): 1411–14. https://doi.org/10.1111/joms.12703
Lai, Gina and Ka Yi Fung, 'From Online Strangers to Offline Friends: A Qualitative Study of Video Game Players in Hong Kong', *Media, Culture & Society* 42.4 (2020): 483–501. https://doi.org/10.1177/0163443719853505
Lai, John and Nicole O. Widmar, 'Revisiting the Digital Divide in the COVID-19 Era', *Applied Economic Perspectives and Policy* 43.1 (2021): 458–64. https://doi.org/10.1002/aepp.13104
Lambert, Alex, 'Intimacy and Social Capital on Facebook: Beyond the Psychological Perspective', *New Media & Society* 18.11 (2016): 2559–75. https://doi.org/10.1177/1461444815588902

Latino Rebels, 'A "Corrido del Coronavirus" From Phoenix's Alan and Roberto', 21 March 2020, https://www.latinorebels.com/2020/03/21/corridodelcoronavirus/ (accessed 3 October 2022).

Leal, Nini G., 'Estrategias para la construcción de la identidad del festival de La Leyenda Vallenata', Professional in Information Systems, Library Science and Archival Science thesis, Bogota, Universidad de la Salle.

Lecocq, Thomas, Stephen P. Hicks, Koen Van Noten, Kasper Van Wijk, Paula Koelemeijer, Raphael S. M. De Plaen, Frédérick Massi et al., 'Global Quieting of High-Frequency Seismic Noise due to COVID-19 Pandemic Lockdown Measures', *Science* 369.6509 (2020): 1338–43.

Lehman, Eric T., '"Washing Hands, Reaching Out" – Popular Music, Digital Leisure and Touch during the COVID-19 Pandemic', *Leisure Sciences* 43.1–2 (2021): 273–9. https://doi.org/10.1080/01490400.2020.1774013

Lena, Jennifer C., *Banding Together: How Communities Create Genres in Popular Music* (Princeton, NJ: Princeton University Press, 2021).

Lenzi, Sara, 'The Sound Outside – Listening to the world at Covid-19 Time', *Soundesign*, 28 March 2020, https://www.soundesign.info/2020/03/28/the-sound-outside/ (accessed 2 November 2021).

Lessig, Lawrence, *Remix: Making Art and Commerce Thrive in the Hybrid Economy* (New York: Penguin, 2008).

Leurs, Koen, *Digital Passages: Migrant Youth 2.0. Diaspora, Gender & Youth Cultural Intersections* (Amsterdam: Amsterdam University Press, 2015).

Lev-Aladgem, Shulamith, 'Carnivalesque Enactment at the Children's Medical Centre of Rabin Hospital', *Research in Drama Education* 5.2 (2000): 163–74. https://doi.org/10.1080/713692882

Levine, Daniel H., 'The Future of Christianity in Latin America', *Journal of Latin American Studies* 41.1 (2009): 121–45. https://doi.org/10.1017/S0022216X08005130

Levinson, Jerrold, *Music in the Moment* (Ithaca, NY: Cornell University Press, 1997).

Levstek, Maruša Rubie Mai Barnby, Katherine L. Pocock, and Robin Banerjee, '"It All Makes Us Feel Together": Young People's Experiences of Virtual Group Music-Making during the COVID-19 Pandemic', *Frontiers in Psychology* 12 (2021): Article 703892. https://doi.org/10.3389/fpsyg.2021.703892

Lewis, Jon, 'Cardi B's Coronavirus Rant Lands On Pop Charts', *NPR*, 29 March 2020, https://www.npr.org/sections/coronavirus-live-updates/2020/03/19/818524291/cardi-bs-coronavirus-rant-lands-on-pop-charts (accessed 12 November 2021).

Leys, Ruth, 'The Turn to Affect: A Critique', *Critical Inquiry* 37.3 (2011): 434–72. https://doi.org/10.1086/659353

Li Yachao, Guan Mengfei, Paige Hammond, and Lane E. Berrey, 'Communicating COVID-19 Information on TikTok: A Content Analysis of TikTok Videos from Official Accounts Featured in the COVID-19 Information Hub', *Health Education Research* 36.3 (2021): Article PMC7989330. https://doi.org/10.1093/her/cyab010

Lienhard, Martin, 'La cosmología poética en los huaynos Quechuas tradicionales', *Acta Poética* 26.1–2 (2005): 485–513. https://doi.org/10.19130/iifl.ap.2005.1-2.180

Lindahl, Chris, 'TikTok Is Making YouTube Change Its Game – and It's Costing Alphabet a Fortune', *IndieWire*, 18 June 2022, https://www.indiewire.com/2022/06/youtube-competes-tiktok-1234734526/ (accessed 16 September 2022).

Lingel, Jessa and Mor Naaman, 'You Should Have Been There, Man: Live Music, DIY Content and Online Communities', *New Media & Society* 14.2 (2011): 332–349. https://doi.org/10.1177/1461444811417284

Lippman, Alexandra, 'Listening Across Borders: Migration, Dedications, and Voice in Cumbia Sonidera', *Latin American Science, Technology and Society* 1:1 (2018): 201–15. https://doi.org/10.1080/25729861.2018.1497273

Litchfield, Ian, David Shukla, and Sheila Greenfield, 'Impact of COVID-19 on the Digital Divide: A Rapid Review', *BMJ Open* 11.10 (2021): Article e053440. https://doi.org/10.1136/bmjopen-2021-053440

Liu Jinxuan, Xu Jian, Wu Zhicai, Cheng Yuru, Gou Yuxin, and Ridolfo Jesse, 'Soundscape Preference of Urban Residents in China in the Post-pandemic Era', *Frontiers in Psychology* 12 (2021): Article 750421. https://doi.org/10.3389/fpsyg.2021.750421

Llamoca, Janice, 'Meet Anuel AA, the Viral Boricua MC Building a Hip-Hop Empire From Prison', *Remezcla*, 9 August 2016, https://remezcla.com/features/music/anuel-aa-profile/ (accessed 5 January 2022).

Lochhead, Judith, Eduardo Mendieta, and Stephen D. Smith, eds, *Sound and Affect: Voice, Music, World* (Chicago: University of Chicago Press, 2021).

Locker, Melissa and Ashley Hoffman, 'People Quarantined in Italy Join Together In Song From Balconies During Coronavirus Lockdown', *Time*, 13 March 2020, https://time.com/5802700/lockdown-song/ (accessed 9 April 2021).

López-Cevallos, Daniel F., S. Marie Harvey, and Jocelyn T. Warren, 'Medical Mistrust, Perceived Discrimination, and Satisfaction with Health Care among Young-Adult Rural Latinos', *Journal of Rural Health* 30.4 (2014): 344–51. https://doi.org/10.1111/jrh.12063

Lozano-Blasco, Raquel, Alberto Quilez-Robres, Diego Delgado-Bujedo, and M. Pilar Latorre-Martínez, 'YouTube's Growth in use among Children 0–5 during COVID19: The Occidental European Case', *Technology in Society* 66 (2021): Article 101648. https://doi.org/10.1016/j.techsoc.2021.101648

MacDonald, Michael B., *Remix and Life Hack in Hip Hop: Towards a Critical Pedagogy of Music* (Rotterdam: Sense Publishers, 2016).

MacDonald, Raymond, Gunter Kreutz, and Laura Mitchell, eds, *Music, Health, and Wellbeing* (Oxford: Oxford University Press, 2012).

Madianou, Mirca and Daniel Miller, 'Polymedia: Towards a New Theory of Digital Media in Interpersonal Communication', *International Journal of Cultural Studies* 16.2 (2012): 169–87. https://doi.org/10.1177/1367877912452486

Madrid, Alejandro L., 'Rigo Tovar, Cumbia, and the Transnational *Grupero* Boom', in Héctor Fernández L'Hoeste and Pablo Vila, eds, *Cumbia! Scenes of a Migrant Latin American Music Genre* (Durham, NC: Duke University Press 2013), 105–18.

Maggi, Ana L., Jimena Muratore, Sara Gaetán, Mauricio F. Zalazar-Jaime, Diego Evin, Jorge Pérez Villalobo, and María Hinalaf, 'Perception of the Acoustic Environment during COVID-19 Lockdown in Argentina', *Journal of the Acoustical Society of America* 149.6 (2021): 3902–9. https://doi.org/10.1121/10.0005131

Maier, Carla J., *Transcultural Sound Practices: British Asian Dance Music as Cultural Transformation* (New York: Bloomsbury Academic, 2020).

Mamo, Heran, 'We Found 5 Very Good TikTok Videos That Use Cardi B's Coronavirus Rant', *Billboard*, 23 March 2020, https://www.billboard.com/music/rb-hip-hop/cardi-b-coronavirus-tiktoks-9340674/ (accessed 12 November 2021).

Mann, Larisa. Kingston, *Rude Citizenship: Jamaican Popular Music, Copyright, and the Reverberations of Colonial Power* (Chapel Hill: University of North Carolina Press, 2022).

Marcos Morezuelas, Paloma, Martha Denisse Pierola, Ana Iju, Javier Puig, and Jaime Fernandez-Baca, 'Migrations Due to COVID-19: Opportunities and Challenges for a Sustainable Recovery in Peru', *Sostenibilidad*, 24 May 2021, https://blogs.iadb.org/sostenibilidad/en/migrations-due-to-covid-19-opportunities-and-challenges-for-a-sustainable-recovery-in-peru/ (accessed 7 September 2022).

Marengo, Davide, Matteo Angelo Fabris, Claudio Longobardi, and Michele Settanni, 'Smartphone and Social Media use Contributed to Individual Tendencies Towards Social Media Addiction in Italian Adolescents during the COVID-19 Pandemic', *Addictive Behaviors* 126 (2022): Article 107204. https://doi.org/10.1016/j.addbeh.2021.107204

Margolies, Daniel and J. A. Strub, 'Community Music Making, Improvisation and Social Technologies in Música Huasteca', *Frontiers in Psychology* 12 (2021): Article 648010. https://doi.org/10.3389/fpsyg.2021.648010

Margolies, Daniel and J. A. Strub, '*#QuédateEnCasa y Huapango!* Diasporic Community and Musical Wellbeing in Streamed Live Performances of Son Huasteco music', in J. Williams, E. Ruddock, A. Mohseni, S. J. Gibson, N. Fleshner, P. Yeoh, A. Cusworth, J. Leong, S. Cohen, and D. Stringham, eds, *Musicking through COVID-19: Challenges, Adaptations, and New Practices*, special issue of *Journal of Music, Health and Wellbeing* (2021), https://www.musichealthandwellbeing.co.uk/musickingthroughcovid19 (accessed 14 February 2024).

Margulis, Elizabeth Hellmuth, *On Repeat: How Music Plays the Mind* (Oxford: Oxford University Press, 2021).

Marino, Sara, 'Making Space, Making Place: Digital Togetherness and the Redefinition of Migrant Identities Online', *Social Media + Society*, 1.2 (2015). https://doi.org/10.1177/2056305115622479

Marino, Sara, 'Cook It, Eat It, Skype It: Mobile Media Use in Re-Staging Intimate Culinary Practices Among Transnational Families', *International Journal of Cultural Studies* 22.6 (2019): 788–803. https://doi.org/10.1177/1367877919850829

Márquez, Israel, 'Bailando con Zizek: orígenes y evolución de la cumbia digital en Buenos Aires', *América Latina, Hoy* 78 (2018): 87–104. https://doi.org/10.14201/alh20187887104

Marshall, Wayne, 'Dem Bow, Dembow, Dembo: Translation and Transnation in Reggaetón', *Lied Und Populäre Kultur* 53 (2008): 131–51.

Marshall, Wayne, 'From Música Negra to Reggeatón Latino: The Cultural Politics of Nation, Migration, and Commercialization', in Raquel Z. Rivera, Wayne Marshall, and Deborah Pacini Hernández, eds, *Reggaetón* (Durham, NC: Duke University Press, 2008), 19–78.

Marshall, Wayne, 'Dembow: A Loop History', *Red Bull Music Academy Daily*, 2 July 2013, https://daily.redbullmusicacademy.com/2013/07/dembow-a-loop-history (accessed 11 November 2021).

Marshall, Wayne, 'Representing Dembow Dominicano', *Wayne & Wax*, 13 February 2019, https://wayneandwax.com/?p=9262 (accessed 11 November 2021).

Martens, Cheryl, Cristina Venegas, and Etsa F. S. Sharupi Tapuy, eds, *Digital Activism, Community Media, and Sustainable Communication in Latin America* (Cham, Switzerland: Palgrave Macmillan, 2020).

Martínez, Guadalupe M. 'Qhapaq Ñan: El Camino Inca y las transformaciones territoriales en los Andes peruanos', *Ería* 78–79 (2009): 21–38.

Martinez, Kiko, 'Cardi B Becomes First Female Rapper With Multiple Diamond Tracks', *Remezcla*, 1 December 2021 (accessed 2 December 2021).

Martinez, Monica, 'Quechua Given Increased Visibility by Peru's New Leftist Gov't', *La Prensa*, 24 September 2021, https://www.laprensalatina.com/quechua-given-increased-visibility-by-perus-new-leftist-govt/ (accessed 25 September 2022).

Martínez de la Rosa, Alejandro, 'Investigación de campo para la regionalización del patrimonio cultural inmaterial', *Diálogos de Campo* 2.4 (2017): 2–24. https://doi.org/10.22201/enesmorelia.26832763e.2017.4.36

Masciantonio, Alexandra, David Bourguignon, Pierre Bouchat, Manon Balty, and Bernard Rimé, 'Don't Put all Social Network Sites in One Basket: Facebook, Instagram, Twitter, TikTok, and their Relations with Well-Being during the COVID-19 Pandemic', *PloS One* 16.3 (2021): Article e0248384. https://doi.org/10.1371/journal.pone.0248384

Mason, Peter, *Bacchanal! The Carnival Culture of Trinidad* (Philadelphia, PA: Temple University Press, 1998).

Maya Restrepo, Luz A. 'África: Legados Espirituales en la Nueva Granada, Siglo XVII', *Historia Crítica* 12 (1996): 29–42. https://doi.org/10.7440/histcrit12.1996.03

McConnell, Bonnie B. and Buba Darboe, 'Music and the Ecology of Fear: Kanyeleng Women Performers and Ebola Prevention in The Gambia', *Africa Today* 63.3 (2017): 29–42. https://doi.org/10.2979/africatoday.63.3.03

McDowell, John H., 'Coaxing the Corrido: Centering Song in Performance', *Journal of American Folklore* 123.488 (2010): 127–49. https://doi.org/10.1353/jaf.0.0130

McDowell, John H., '"Surfing the Tube" for Latin American Song: The Blessings (and Curses) of YouTube', *Journal of American Folklore* 128.509 (2015): 260–72. https://doi.org/10.5406/jamerfolk.128.509.0260

Meis, Morgan, 'Timothy Morton's Hyper-Pandemic', *New Yorker*, 8 June 2021, https://www.newyorker.com/culture/persons-of-interest/timothy-mortons-hyper-pandemic (accessed 12 September 2021).

Mejia, Daniel F., 'Anuel AA y su ira contra el coronavirus', 18 March 2020, http://www.lafm.com.co/entretenimiento/anuel-aa-y-su-ira-contra-el-coronavirus (accessed 12 October 2021).

Melina, Natasha, 'Kiko El Crazy Talks Viral "Se Acabó La Cuarentena" Collab Alongside Jowell y Randy, Maffio Collab "Como Eh," and Upcoming Album "Llego El Domi"', *Urban Latino*, 8 October 2021, http://urbanlatino.com/kiko-el-crazy-talks-viral-se-acabo-la-cuarentena-collab-alongside-jowell-y-randy-maffio-collab-como-eh-and-upcoming-album-llego-el-domi/ (accessed 20 October 2021).

Mendívil, Julio, 'Yo soy el huayno: el huayno peruano como confluencia de lo indígena con lo hispano y lo moderno', in Albert Recasens and Christian Spencer, eds, *A tres bandas: Mestizaje, sincretismo e hibridación en el espacio sonoro iberoamericano* (Madrid: Seacex, 2010), 37–46.

Mikkelsen, Matt, 'Hear the Soundscapes of Cities Transformed', *AtlasObscura*, 17 April 2020, https://www.atlasobscura.com/articles/changing-sound-of-cities (accessed 12 September 2021).

Millar, Oscar and Ian Warwick, 'Music and Refugees' Wellbeing in Contexts of Protracted Displacement', *Health Education Journal* 78.1 (2019): 67–80. https://doi.org/10.1177/0017896918785991

Miller, Joanne M. 'Psychological, Political, and Situational Factors Combine to Boost COVID-19 Conspiracy Theory Beliefs', *Canadian Journal of Political Science/Revue Canadienne de Science Politique* 53.2 (2020): 327–34. https://doi.org/10.1017/S000842392000058X

Min Wonjung, Dal Yong Jin, and Benjamin Han, 'Transcultural Fandom of the Korean Wave in Latin America: Through the Lens of Cultural Intimacy and Affinity Space', *Media, Culture & Society* 41.5 (2019): 604–19. https://doi.org/10.1177/0163443718799403

Miranda Nieto, Alejandro, *Musical Mobilities: Son Jarocho and the Circulation of Tradition Across Mexico and the United States* (London: Routledge, 2017).

Miranda, J. Jaime, Robert H. Gilman, Héctor H. García, and Liam Smeeth, 'The Effect on Cardiovascular Risk Factors of Migration from Rural to Urban Areas in Peru: PERU MIGRANT Study', *BMC Cardiovascular Disorders* 9 (2009): Article 23. https://doi.org/10.1186/1471-2261-9-23

Mitchell, Andrew, Tin Obermanc, Francesco Alettad, Magdalena Kachlickae, Matteo Lionellof, Mercede Erfaniang, and Jian Kangh, 'Investigating Urban Soundscapes of the COVID-19 Lockdown: A Predictive Soundscape Modeling Approach', *Journal of the Acoustical Society of America* 150 (2021): Article 4474. https://doi.org/10.1121/10.0008928

Mitchell, Tony, ed., *Global Noise: Rap and Hip Hop Outside the USA* (Middletown, CT: Wesleyan University Press, 2001).

Mitlin, Diana C. 'Dealing with COVID-19 in the Towns and Cities of the Global South', *International Institute for Environment and Development Blog*, 27 March 2020, https://www.iied.org/dealingcovid-19-towns-cities-global-south (accessed 12 September 2021).

Molanphy, Chris, 'Feat. Don't Fail Me Now: The Rise of the Featured Rapper in Pop Music', *Slate*, 31 July 2015, https://slate.com/culture/2015/07/the-history-of-featured-rappers-and-other-featured-artists-in-pop-songs.html (17 January 2022).
Moloney, Anastasia, 'Women's Jobs at Risk in Latin America in Coronavirus Crisis', Reuters, 20 May 2020, https://www.reuters.com/article/us-health-coronavirus-women-trfn-idUSKBN22W05A (accessed 25 September 2022).
Morgan, Glennisha, 'Cardi B Becomes RIAA's Most Certified Woman Rapper, Surpassing Nicki Minaj', *V101.9*, https://v1019.com/2019/09/06/cardi-b-becomes-riaa-most-certified-woman-rapper-surpassing-nicki-minaj/ (accessed 14 March 2021).
Morgan, Marcyliena and Dionne Bennett, 'Hip-Hop & the Global Imprint of a Black Cultural Form', *Daedalus* 140.2 (2011): 176–96. https://doi.org/10.1162/DAED_a_00086
Morgan-Ellis, Esther, 'Non-Participation in Online Sacred Harp Singing during the COVID-19 Pandemic', *International Journal of Community Music* 14.2–3 (2021): 223–44. https://doi.org/10.1386/ijcm_00046_1
Morinville, Amélie, Dave Miranda, and Patrick Gaudreau, 'Music Listening Motivation is Associated with Global Happiness in Canadian Late Adolescents', *Psychology of Aesthetics, Creativity, and the Arts* 7.4 (2013): 384–90. https://doi.org/10.1037/a0034495
Morrison, Amanda M., 'Musical Trafficking: Urban Youth and the Narcocorrido-Hardcore Rap Nexus', *Western Folklore* 67.4 (2008): 379–96.
Morton, Timothy, *Hyperobjects: Philosophy and Ecology After the End of the World* (Minneapolis: University of Minnesota Press, 2013).
Moser, Peter, 'Growing Community Music Through a Sense of Place', Brydie-Leigh Bartleet and Lee Higgins, eds, *The Oxford Handbook of Community Music* (Oxford: Oxford University Press, 2018), 213–28.
Mowitt, John, *Percussion: Drumming, Beating, Striking* (Durham, NC: Duke University Press, 2002).
Mulemi, Benson A., 'Lyrics and Artistic Improvisations in Health Promotion for the COVID-19 Pandemic Control in East Africa', *Global Health Promotion* 28.1 (2021): 23–32. https://doi.org/10.1177/1757975920973671
Muñoz, Kim A. Carter, 'Huapangueros Reclaiming Son Huasteco in Trans-local Festivals: Youth, Women and Nahua Musicians', PhD thesis, University of Washington, 2013.
Nahai, Nathalie, *Webs of Influence: The Psychology of Online Persuasion* (Harlow, UK: Pearson, 2012).
Nahon, Karine and Jeff Hemsley, *Going Viral* (Cambridge: Polity, 2013).
Nappo, Daniel J., 'Looking Back to the End of Time: Millennial Imagery in Selected Novels and Corridos of the Mexican Revolution, 1890–1947', PhD thesis, Michigan State University.
Navas, Eduardo, 'Regressive and Reflexive Mashups in Sampling Culture', in Stefan Sonvilla-Weiss, ed., *Mashup Cultures* (New York: Springer 2010), 157–77.
Navas, Eduardo, *Remix Theory: The Aesthetics of Sampling* (Vienna: Springer 2012).
Navas, Eduardo, 'The Originality of Copies: Cover Versions and Versioning in Remix Practice', *Journal of Asia-Pacific Pop Culture* 3.2 (2018): 168–87. https://doi.org/10.5325/jasiapacipopcult.3.2.0168
Navas, Eduardo, 'Remix', in Eduardo Navas, Owen Gallagher, and xtine burrough, *Keywords in Remix Studies* (New York: Routledge, 2018), 246–58.
Nedelcu, Mihaela, 'Migrants' New Transnational Habitus: Rethinking Migration Through a Cosmopolitan Lens in the Digital Age', *Journal of Ethnic and Migration Studies* 38.9 (2012): 1339–56. https://doi.org/10.1080/1369183X.2012.698203
Negrón-Muntaner, Frances and Raquel Z. Rivera, 'Reggaeton Nation', *NACLA Report on the Americas* 40.6 (2007): 35–9. https://doi.org/10.1080/10714839.2007.11725387
Neustadt, Robert, 'Bone Flutes and Quechua Love Songs: Excavating Traces of Colonial Trauma in Néstor Taboada Terán's *Manchay Puytu*', *Confluencia* 23.1 (2007): 29–42.

New York Times, 'Mexico Coronavirus Map and Case Count', 2020–, https://www.nytimes.com/interactive/2020/world/americas/mexico-coronavirus-cases.html (accessed 29 December 2020).

Nieves Moreno, Alfredo, 'A Man Lives Here: Reggaetón's Hypermasculine Resident', in Raquel Z. Rivera, Wayne Marshall, and Deborah Pacini Hernandez, eds, *Reggaetón* (Durham, NC: Duke University Press 2009), 252–79.

Noe, Mark, 'The *Corrido*: A Border Rhetoric', *College English* 71.6 (2009): 596–605.

Nowak, Raphaël, 'Understanding Everyday Uses of Music Technologies in the Digital Age', in Andy Bennett and Brady Robards eds, *Mediated Youth Cultures: The Internet, Belonging and New Cultural Configurations* (Basingstoke, UK: Palgrave Macmillan, 2014), 146–61.

Nowak, Raphaël, 'The Intricate Relationship Between Music and the Sharing Economy', in Thomas Siglar and Jonathan Corcoran, eds, *A Modern Guide to the Urban Sharing Economy* (Northampton, UK: Edward Elgar, 2021), 267–80.

Nowotny, Kathryn M., Jennifer L. Fackler, Gianncarlo Muschi, Carol Vargas, Lindsey Wilson, and Joseph A. Kotarba, 'Established Latino Music Scenes: Sense of Place and the Challenge of Authenticity', *Studies in Symbolic Interaction* 35 (2010): 29–50. https://doi.org/10.1108/S0163-2396(2010)0000035006

Nugent, Ciara, 'How Peru's Coronavirus Outbreak Got So Bad: What to Know', *Time*, 29 May 2020, https://time.com/5844768/peru-coronavirus/ (accessed 12 September 2021).

Nunes, Joseph C., Andrea Ordanini, and Francesca Valsesia, 'The Power of Repetition: Repetitive Lyrics in a Song Increase Processing Fluency and Drive Market Success', *Journal of Consumer Psychology* 25.2 (2015): 187–99. https://doi.org/10.1016/j.jcps.2014.12.004

Nylund Hagen, Anja, 'The Playlist Experience: Personal Playlists in Music Streaming Services', *Popular Music and Society* 38.5 (2015): 625–45. https://doi.org/10.1080/03007766.2015.1021174

Nylund Hagen, Anja and Marika Lüders, 'Social Streaming? Navigating Music as Personal and Social', *Convergence: The International Journal of Research into New Media Technologies*, 23.6 (2017): 643–59. https://doi.org/10.1177/1354856516673298

Ó Briain, Lonán, 'Beyond the Digital Diaspora: YouTube Methodologies, Online Networking and the Hmong Music Festival', *Journal of World Popular Music* 2.2 (2015): 289–306. https://doi.org/10.1558/jwpm.v2i2.26561

O'Neill, Kevin L. 'Delinquent Realities: Christianity, Formality, and Security in the Americas', *American Quarterly* 63:2 (2011): 337–65. https://doi.org/10.1353/aq.2011.0014

Onuki, Janina, Fernando Mouron, and Francisco Urdinez, 'Latin American Perceptions of Regional Identity and Leadership in Comparative Perspective', *Contexto Internacional* 38 (2016): 433–65. https://doi.org/10.1590/S0102-8529.2016380100012

Ortiz, Catalina and María Mercedes Di Virgilio, 'Laboratorios de Vivienda (LAVs): Asentamientos precarios y vivienda social: impactos del covid-19 y respuestas', Urban Housing Practioners Hub working paper (2020), https://www.uhph.org/sites/default/files/2020-11/lav_covid-10_y_asentamientos_sisca.pdf (accessed 17 March 2021).

Osmundson, Joseph, *Virology: Essays for the Living, the Dead, and the Small Things in Between* (New York: Norton, 2022).

Packer, Jan and Julie Ballantyne, 'The Impact of Music Festival Attendance on Young People's Psychological and Social Well-Being', *Psychology of Music* 39.2 (2011): 164–81. https://doi.org/10.1177/0305735610372611

Palmié, Stephan, *The Cooking of History: How Not to Study Afro-Cuban Religion* (Chicago: University of Chicago Press, 2013).

Pantazes, Lydia, 'Singers Aim to Inspire by Writing Song About the Coronavirus', *Spectrum News*, 30 May 2020, https://spectrumnews1.com/ca/la-west/entertainment/2020/05/30/singers-aim-to-inspire-by-writing-song-about-the-coronavirus (accessed 3 October 2022).

Paredes, Américo, *'With His Pistol in His Hand': A Border Ballad and Its Hero* (Austin: University of Texas Press, 1958).

Paredes, Americo, 'The Ancestry of Mexico's *Corridos*: A Matter of Definitions', *Journal of American Folklore* 76.301 (1963): 231–5. https://doi.org/10.2307/538524

Paredes, Américo and María Herrera-Sobek, 'The *Corrido*: An Invited Lecture at the "Music in Culture" Public Lecture Series', *Journal of American Folklore* 125.495 (2012): 23–44. https://doi.org/10.5406/jamerfolk.125.495.0023

Parikka, Jussi, *Digital Contagions: A Media Archaeology of Computer Viruses* (Oxford: Peter Lang, 2007).

Parra Valencia, Juan D., *Deconstruyendo el chucu-chucu: auges, declives y resurecciones de la música tropical colombiana* (Medellín: Instituto Tecnológico Metropolitano, 2017).

Pasiali, Varvara, 'Resilience, Music Therapy, and Human Adaptation: Nurturing Young Children and Families', *Nordic Journal of Music Therapy* 21.1 (2012): 36–56. https://doi.org/10.1080/08098131.2011.571276

Patraca Rueda, María C. 'Prácticas educativas en la enseñanza-aprendizaje del zapateado en el son jarocho', master's thesis, Universidad Veracruzana, Xalapa, Veracruz, Mexico, 2019.

Patterson, Ashley N., 'YouTube Generated Video Clips as Qualitative Research Data: One Researcher's Reflections on the Process', *Qualitative Inquiry* 24.10 (2018): 759–67. https://doi.org/10.1177/1077800418788107

Pauls, Merril and Roger C. Hutchinson, 'Bioethics for Clinicians: 28. Protestant Bioethics', *Canadian Medical Association Journal* 166.3 (2002): 339–43.

Payne, Robert, 'VIRALITY 2.0: Networked Promiscuity and the Sharing Subject', *Cultural Studies* 27.4 (2013): 540–60. https://doi.org/10.1080/09502386.2012.707219

Pearce, Adrian J. and Paul Heggarty, '"Mining the Data" on the Huancayo-Huancavelica Quechua Frontier', in Adrian J. Pearce and Paul Heggarty, eds, *History and Language in the Andes* (New York: Palgrave MacMillan, 2011), 87–109.

Pecherska, Izabela, '"Maldito coronavirus": Anuel AA se desahoga gritando desde el balcón', *CiberCuba*, 18 March 2020, https://www.cibercuba.com/noticias/2020-03-18-u198484-e198484-s27065-maldito-coronavirus-anuel-aa-estalla-desahoga-gritando (accessed 12 October 2021).

Perez, Sarah, 'Kids Now Spend Nearly as Much Time Watching TikTok as YouTube in US, UK and Spain', *TechCrunch*, 4 June 2020, https://techcrunch.com/2020/06/04/kids-nowspend-nearly-as-much-time-watching-tiktok-as-youtube-in-u-s-u-k-and-spain/ (accessed 2 November 2021).

Perez, Sarah, 'YouTube's Latest Experiment is a TikTok Rival Focused on 15-Second Videos', *TechCrunch*, 25 June 2020, https://techcrunch.com/2020/06/25/youtubes-latest-experiment-is-a-tiktok-rival-focused-on-15-second-videos/ (accessed 2 November 2021).

Pietrobruno, Sheenagh, 'YouTube and the Social Archiving of Intangible Heritage', *New Media & Society* 15.8 (2018): 1259–76. https://doi.org/10.1177/1461444812469598

Pietrobruno, Sheenagh, 'YouTube Flow and the Transmission of Heritage: The Interplay of Users, Content, and Algorithms', *Convergence* 24.6 (2018): 523–37. https://doi.org/10.1177/1354856516680339

Pinos Calderón, Doris Elena and Cristina Venegas, 'Sounds of the Neighborhood: Innovation, Hybrid Urban Space, and Sound Trajectories', in Cheryl Martens, Cristina Venegas, and Etsa F. S. Sharupi Tapuy, eds, *Digital Activism*, 53–79. https://doi.org/10.1007/978-3-030-45394-7_3

Pinyodoonyachet, Jutharat, 'Arturo O'Farrill's "Fandango at the Wall"', *New Yorker*, 1 July 2022, https://www.newyorker.com/magazine/2022/07/11/arturo-ofarrills-fandango-at-the-wall (accessed 20 August 2022).

Pinzón Varilla, Luisa, 'Lírica Popular e identidad en el vallenato', *Oralidades* 1.2 (2015): 156–64.

Plaut, Ethan R., 'Enlightenment, the Remix: Transparency as a DJ's Trick of Seeing Everyone from Nowhere'. *Communication, Culture & Critique* 9.2 (2016): 303–21. https://doi.org/10.1111/cccr.12107

Poole, Deborah and Isaías Rojas Pérez, 'Memorias de la reconciliación: fotografía y memoria en el Perú de la pós-guerra', *emisferica – Revista Do Hemispheric Institute* 7.2 (2005), https://hemisphericinstitute.org/en/emisferica-72/7-2-essays/e72-essay-memories-of-reconciliation-photography-and-memory-in-postwar-peru.html (accessed 2 February 2022).

Powers, Ann, 'A Playlist Tracking the Many New Tracks Being Written about the Coronavirus', NPR, 23 March 2020, https://www.npr.org/sections/coronavirus-live-updates/2020/03/23/820305127/a-playlist-tracking-the-many-new-tracks-being-written-about-the-coronavirus (accessed 1 July 2022).

Putter, Kaila C., Amanda E. Krause, and Adrian C. North, 'Popular Music Lyrics and the COVID-19 Pandemic', *Psychology of Music* 50.4 (2021): 1280–95. https://doi.org/10.1177/03057356211045114

radio aporee, 'Cl. 44 #50, Bogotá, Colombia, Covid sunrise', https://aporee.org/maps/work/projects.php?project=corona (accessed 1 July 2022).

radio aporee, 'Panelaço (Pot-banging protest) – Fora Bolsonaro! – 20h30', https://aporee.org/maps/work/projects.php?project=corona (accessed 1 July 2022).

Radio UdeG Ocotlán, 'Corridos Tumbados, una evolución del corrido mexicano', *UDG TV* (blog), 11 December 2020, https://udgtv.com/noticias/ocotlan-noticias/corridos-tumbados-una-evolucion-del-corrido-mexicano/ (accessed 1 July 2022).

Ragland, Cathy, *Música Norteña: Mexican Americans Creating a Nation Between Nations* (Philadelphia: Temple University Press, 2009).

Ramírez-Pimienta, Juan C. 'El Narcocorrido En La Frontera y La Frontera En El Narcocorrido', *Revista Iberoamericana* 265 (2018): 1101–16. https://doi.org/10.5195/reviberoamer.2018.7679

Ramos, Oscar, 'La propuesta de Alán y Roberto', *Prensa Arizona*, 4 February 2021, https://prensaarizona.com/2021/02/la-propuesta-de-alan-y-roberto/ (accessed 3 October 2022).

Ramos-Kittrell, Jesús A., ed., *Decentering the Nation: Music, Mexicanidad, and Globalization* (Lanham, MD: Lexington Books, 2019).

Rautiainen-Keskustalo, Tarja and Sanna Raudaskoski, 'Inclusion by Live Streaming? Contested Meanings of Well-Being: Movement and Non-Movement of Space, Place and Body', *Mobilities* 14:4 (2019): 469–483. https://doi.org/10.1080/17450101.2019.1612611

Redel-Macías, Maria D., Pilar Aparicio-Martinez, Sara Pinzi, Pedro Arezes, and Antonio J. Cubero-Atienza, 'Monitoring Sound and Its Perception during the Lockdown and De-Escalation of COVID-19 Pandemic: A Spanish Study', *International Journal of Environmental Research and Public Health* 18.7 (2021): Article 3392. https://doi.org/10.3390/ijerph18073392

Redinha, Maria R., Maria R. Guimarães, and F. L. Fernandes, eds, *The Sharing Economy: Legal Problems of a Permutations and Combinations Society* (Newcastle-upon-Tyne: Cambridge Scholars Publishing, 2019).

Rendell, James, 'Staying in, Rocking Out: Online Live Music Portal shows during the Coronavirus Pandemic', *Convergence* 27.4 (2021): 1092–111. https://doi.org/10.1177/1354856520976451

Rieder, Bernhard, Ariadna Matamoros-Fernández, and Òscar Coromina, 'From Ranking Algorithms to "Ranking Cultures": Investigating the Modulation of Visibility in YouTube Search Results', *Convergence* 24.1 (2018): 50–68. https://doi.org/10.1177/1354856517736982

Rivera, Michael, 'Music, Media, and the Ethnopoetics of Two Ebola Songs in Liberia', *Africa Today* 63.3 (2017): 63–76. https://doi.org/10.2979/africatoday.63.3.05

Rivera-Rideau, Petra R., *Remixing Reggaetón: The Cultural Politics of Race in Puerto Rico* (Durham, NC: Duke University Press, 2015).
Robb, John D. *Cancionero: Songs of Laughter and Faith in New Mexico* (Albuquerque: University of New Mexico Press, 2015).
Robin, Valerie, 'Caminos a la otra vida: Ritos funerarios en Los Andes Peruanos Meridionales', in Antoinette Molinié (ed.), *Etnografías Del Cuzco* (Cuzco: Centro de Estudios Regionales Andinos Bartolomé de Las Casas-CBC, Laboratoire d'Ethnologie et de Sociologie Comparative-Labethno, 2005), 47–68.
Rochabrun, Marcelo, 'Peru to Cremate Body of Shining Path Founder and Dispose of his Ashes', Reuters, 23 September 2021, https://www.reuters.com/world/americas/peru-cremate-body-shining-path-founder-dispose-his-ashes-2021-09-23/ (accessed 7 September 2022).
Rodillo, Proyecto, 'Coronavirus Stats in Dominican Republic: Trend, Number of Cases, Deaths, Hospitalizations, Tests, Quarantine Measures and Mobility', *Regiones – El termómetro del coronavirus en Latinoamérica*, 29 October 2021, https://rodillo.org/regiones/ (accessed 2 February 2022).
Rodríguez, Zalvide, Carmen and Luis Fernando Ramos Simón, 'Piratas y creadores: Autoría, creatividad y automatización en Youtube', *Cuadernos De Documentación Multimedia* 31 (2020): 1–8. https://doi.org/10.5209/cdmu.68441
Rodríguez Cuadros, José D., 'The Religious Shift in Latin America', *Herodote* 171.4 (2018): 119–34, https://www.cairn-int.info/article-E_HER_171_0119--the-religious-shift-in-latin-america.htm (accessed 3 October 2022).
Roiz, Jessica, 'Karol G & Anuel AA Are Loving Cardi B's "Coronavirus Remix" & The Rapper Loves Them Right Back', *Billboard*, 20 March 2020, https://www.billboard.com/music/latin/karol-g-anuel-aa-cardi-b-coronavirus-remix-video-9339292/ (accessed 12 October 2021).
Roiz, Jessica, 'Latin Songs Born During Coronavirus Quarantine (Updating)', *Billboard*, 2 January 2021, https://www.billboard.com/music/latin/latin-songs-quarantine-coronavirus-9355057/ (accessed 1 July 2022).
Romero, Dennis, 'YouTube Thrives as a Window for Those Isolated by Coronavirus', *NBC News*, 1 April 2020, https://www.nbcnews.com/tech/social-media/youtube-thrives-window-thoseisolated-coronavirus-n1173651 (accessed 1 July 2022).
Roncalla Fernández, Fredy Amílcar, 'Encuentros y despedidas musicales en tiempos de Covid', *Hawansuyo*, 12 September 2020, https://hawansuyo.com/2020/09/12/encuentros-y-despedidas-musicales-en-tiempos-de-covid-fredy-roncalla/ (accessed 7 September 2022).
Roozenbeek, Jon, Claudia R. Schneider, Sarah Dryhurst, John Kerr, Alexandra L. J. Freeman, Gabriel Recchia, Anne Marthe van der Bles, and Sander van der Linden, 'Susceptibility to Misinformation about COVID-19 around the World', *Royal Society Open Science* 7.10 (2020). https://doi.org/10.1098/rsos.201199
Rose, Gillian, 'Rethinking the Geographies of Cultural "Objects" through Digital Technologies: Interface, Network and Friction', *Progress in Human Geography* 40.3 (2016): 334–51. https://doi.org/10.1177/0309132515580493
Ruele, Moji, 'The Diaconal and Liberation Role of the Church in the Fight against HIV/AIDS in Botswana', *Botswana Notes and Records* 35 (2003): 141–45.
Rufino Trelles, Mario A., 'Regresando a mis raíces: COVID19 y la migración de retorno en el norte de Peru', *CAS: Centre for Amerindian, Latin American and Caribbean Studies*, 10 June 2021, https://calacs.wp.st-andrews.ac.uk/regresando-a-mis-raices-covid19-y-la-migracion-de-retorno-en-el-norte-de-peru/ (accessed 7 September 2022).
Rutherford, D. 'Affect Theory and the Empirical', *Annual Review of Anthropology* 45.1 (2016): 285–300. https://doi.org/10.1146/annurev-anthro-102215-095843

Ruud, Even, 'Can Music Serve as a "Cultural Immunogen"? An Explorative Study', *International Journal of Qualitative Studies on Health and Well-being* 8.1 (2013): 20597–609. https://doi.org/10.3402/qhw.v8i0.20597

Saarikallio, Suvi, 'Music as Emotional Self-Regulation throughout Adulthood', *Psychology of Music* 39.3 (2010): 307–327. https://doi.org/10.1177/0305735610374894

Samuel Challéat, Amandine Gasc, Nicolas Farrugia and Jérémy Froidevaux, 'Silent·Cities: A Participatory Monitoring Programme of an Exceptional Modification of Urban Soundscapes', https://renoir.hypotheses.org/files/2020/03/Silent%C2%B7Cities-Project.pdf (accessed 1 July 2022).

Sánchez García, Rose V., 'Los principles géneros liricos en la música tradicional de México', in Aurelio Tello, ed., *La música en México panorama del siglo XX* (México: FCE-CONACULTA, 2010), 106–79.

Sandoval-Reyes, Juan, Sandra Idrovo-Carlier, and Edison J. Duque-Oliva, 'Remote Work, Work Stress, and Work–Life during Pandemic Times: A Latin America Situation', *International Journal of Environmental Research and Public Health* 18.13 (2021): Article 7069. https://doi.org/10.3390/ijerph18137069

Santos, Jorge A. Mario Mejía Huamán, and Santiago Gariel Durante, 'Dos conceptos andinos para pensar la sociedad contemporánea: wakcha/qhapaq, o ¿por qué no existe la palabra "pobre" en quechua?', *Papeles de Trabajo-Centro de Estudios Interdisciplinarios En Etnolingüística y Antropología Socio-Cultural* 40 (2020): 35–51. https://doi.org/10.35305/revista.v0i40.177

Sara, Lenzi, Sádaba Juan, and Lindborg PerMagnus, 'Soundscape in Times of Change: Case Study of a City Neighbourhood During the COVID-19 Lockdown', *Frontiers in Psychology* 12 (2021): Article 570741. https://doi.org/10.3389/fpsyg.2021.570741

Sarai, Esha, 'COVID-19 Diaries: Balcony Ballads a Bust in Washington, DC', *VOA News*, 28 April 2020, https://www.voanews.com/a/covid-19-pandemic_covid-19-diaries_covid-19-diaries-balcony-ballads-bust-washington-dc/6188338.html (accessed 3 February 2022).

Save The Children, 'Respuesta humanitaria ante la crisis por el COVID-19 en Perú', Save the Children Perú, https://www.savethechildren.org.pe/respuesta-humanitaria-ante-la-crisis-por-el-covid-19-en-peru/ (accessed 7 September 2022).

Sayer, Andrew, 'Behind the Locality Debate: Deconstructing Geography's Dualisms', *Environment and Planning A: Economy and Space* 23.2 (1991): 283–308. https://doi.org/10.1068/a230283

Scepanski, Philip, *Tragedy Plus Time: National Trauma and Television Comedy* (Austin: University of Texas Press, 2021).

Schultze, Ulrike, 'Performing Embodied Identity in Virtual Worlds', *European Journal of Information Systems* 23.1 (2012): 84–95. https://doi.org/10.1057/ejis.2012.52

Schulze, Holger, 'Scientific Sonification – The Sound of Corona', *Passive/Aggressive*, 1 May 2020, http://passiveaggressive.dk/scientific-sonification-the-sound-of-corona/ (accessed 1 July 2022).

Schwantes, Melody, Tony Wigram, Cathy McKinney, Allison Lipscomb, and Cathy Richards, 'The Mexican *Corrido* and its Use in a Music Therapy Bereavement Group', *Australian Journal of Music Therapy* 22 (2011): 2–23. https://doi.org/10.1093/mtp/28.1.22

Sciullo, Nick J., *Communicating Hip-Hop: How Hip-Hop Culture Shapes Popular Culture* (Santa Barbara, CA: Praeger, 2019).

Scully, Marc, 'BIFFOs, Jackeens and Dagenham Yanks: County Identity, "Authenticity" and the Irish Diaspora', *Irish Studies Review* 21.2 (2013): 143–63. https://doi.org/10.1080/09670882.2013.808874

Searle, Adam, Jonathon Turnbull, and Jamie Lorimer, 'After the Anthropause: Lockdown Lessons for More-Than-Human Geographies', *Geographical Journal* 187.1 (2021): 69–77. https://doi.org/10.1111/geoj.12373

Selka, Stephen, 'Afro-Catholicism in Latin America', *Religion Compass* 13: 5 (2019): Article e12315. https://doi.org/10.1111/rec3.12315

Seneviratne, Oshani and Andres Monroy-Hernandez, 'Remix Culture on the Web: A Survey of Content Reuse on Different User-Generated Content Websites', in *Proceedings of the WebSci10: Extending the Frontiers of Society On-Line*, http://dig.csail.mit.edu/2010/Papers/WebScience/paper.pdf (accessed 11 January 2022).

Shafer, Murray R., *The Tuning of the World* (New York: Knopf, 1977).

Sharjah24 News, 'A Local Artist in Ecuador Turns COVID-19 Fears into a Catchy Song', https://www.youtube.com/watch?v=SDuMJmOtXTw (accessed 22 February 2022).

Sheehy, Daniel, 'The "Son Jarocho": The History, Style, and Repertory of a Changing Mexican Musical Tradition', PhD thesis, University of California Los Angeles, 1979.

Shields Dobson, Amy, Brady Robards, and Nicholas Carah, eds, *Digital Intimate Publics and Social Media* (Cham, Switzerland: Springer, 2018).

Shields Dobson, Amy, Nicholas Carah, and Brady Robards, 'Digital Intimate Publics and Social Media: Towards Theorising Public Lives on Private Platforms', in Amy Shields Dobson, Brady Robards, and Nicholas Carah, eds, *Digital Intimate Publics and Social Media* (Cham, Switzerland: Springer, 2018), 3–27.

Shields Dobson, Amy, Brady Robards, and Nicholas Carah, 'Introduction', in Amy Shields Dobson, Brady Robards, and Nicholas Carah eds, *Digital Intimate Publics and Social Media* (Cham, Switzerland: Springer, 2018), xix–xxviii.

Shifman, Limor, *Memes in Digital Culture* (Cambridge: MIT Press, 2014).

Shiga, John, 'Copy-and-Persist: The Logic of Mash-Up Culture', *Critical Studies in Media Communication* 24.2 (2007): 93–111. https://doi.org/10.1080/07393180701262685

Sierra y Folclor, https://www.culturarecreacionydeporte.gov.co/en/node/80955 (accessed 16 September 2022).

Silba, Malvina, '"Argentina is Cumbia": Sociocultural Trajectories of Young "Cumbieros" in Urban Peripheries', *Journal of World Popular Music* 4.2 (2017): 171–90. https://doi.org/10.1558/jwpm.33203

Simonett, Helena, *Banda: Mexican Musical Life Across Borders* (Middleton, CT: Wesleyan University Press, 2001).

Simonett, Helena, ed., *The Accordion in the Americas: Klezmer, Polka, Tango, Zydeco, and More!* (Champaign: University of Illinois Press, 2021).

Simpson, Paul, 'Anuel AA Biography, Songs, & Albums', *AllMusic*, https://www.allmusic.com/artist/anuel-aa-mn0003551236/biography (accessed 9 October 2021).

Sinnreich, Aram, Mark Latonero, and Marissa Gluck, 'Ethics Reconfigured: How Today's Media Consumers Evaluate the Role of Creative Reappropriation', *Information, Communication & Society* 12.8 (2009): 1242–60. https://doi.org/10.1080/13691180902890117

Skovgaard-Smith, Irene, 'Transnational Life and Cross-Border Immobility in Pandemic Times', *Global Networks* 23.1 (2023): 59–74. https://doi.org/10.1111/glob.12350

Smith, Jeremy, 'Southern Lights: Metropolitan Imaginaries in Latin America', *Thesis Eleven* 166.1 (2021): 118–35. https://doi.org/10.1177/07255136211043923

Snouwaert, Jessica, 'Watch People in Cities around the World Cheer from Their Windows and Rooftops at the Same Time to Thank Healthcare Workers and First Responders', *Business Insider*, 6 May 2020, https://www.businessinsider.com/videos-people-cities-cheering-healthcare-workers-windows-rooftops-same-time-2020-4 (accessed 7 March 2022).

Solomon, Thomas, 'Theorizing Diaspora and Music', *Lidé města* 2 (2015): 201–19.

Sorett, Josef, '"It's Not the Beat, but It's the Word That Sets the People Free": Race, Technology, and Theology in the Emergence of Christian Rap Music', *Pneuma* 33.2 (2011): 200–17. https://doi.org/10.1163/027209611X575014

Sorlin, Sandrine, *The Stylistics of 'You': Second-Person Pronoun and its Pragmatic Effects* (Cambridge: Cambridge University Press, 2022).

Soundscapes of Pandemia website, https://soundscapesofpandemia.info/ (accessed 1 July 2022).

St. James, Emily, 'Watch: Quarantined Italians are Singing their Hearts Out. It's Beautiful', *Vox*, 13 March 2020, https://www.vox.com/culture/2020/3/13/21179293/coronavirus-italy-covid19-music-balconies-sing (accessed 3 February 2022).

Stige, Brynjulf, 'Health Musicking: A Perspective on Music and Health as Action and Performance', in Raymond MacDonald, Gunter Kreutz, and Laura Mitchell, eds, *Music, Health, and Wellbeing* (Oxford: Oxford University Press, 2012), 183–95.

Stollery, Pete, 'COVID-19 Sound Map', Google Earth, https://tinyurl.com/covid19soundmap (accessed 1 July 2022).

Stollery, Pete, 'This is What lockdown Sounds Like', *The Conversation*, 29 January 2021, https://theconversation.com/this-iswhat-lockdown-sounds-like-153590 (accessed 1 July 2022).

Strand Skånland, Marie, 'Everyday Music Listening and Affect Regulation: The Role of MP3 Players', *International Journal of Qualitative Studies on Health and Well-Being* 8.1 (2013): Article 20595. https://doi.org/10.3402/qhw.v8i0.20595

Sturman, Janet, *The Course of Mexican Music*, 2nd edition (London: Routledge, 2015).

Taylor, Alan, 'Music and Encouragement From Balconies Around the World', *The Atlantic*, 24 March 2020, https://www.theatlantic.com/photo/2020/03/music-and-encouragement-from-balconies-around-world/608668/ (accessed 18 April 2022).

Taylor, Luke, 'Covid-19 Misinformation Sparks Threats and Violence against Doctors in Latin America', *BMJ* 370 (11 August 2020): Article m3088. https://doi.org/10.1136/bmj.m3088

Tellis, Gerard J., Deborah J. MacInnis, Seshadri Tirunillai, and Zhang Yanwei, 'What Drives Virality (Sharing) of Online Digital Content? The Critical Role of Information, Emotion, and Brand Prominence', *Journal of Marketing* 83.4 (2019): 1–20. https://doi.org/10.1177/0022242919841034

Temple, Mark D., 'Real-Time Audio and Visual Display of the Coronavirus Genome', *BMC Bioinformatics* 21 (2020): Article 431. https://doi.org/10.1186/s12859-020-03760-7

Tenorio-Trillo, Mauricio, *Latin America: The Allure and Power of an Idea* (Chicago: University of Chicago Press, 2020).

Terasawa, Hiroko, Masaki Matsubara, Visda Goudarzi, and Makiko Sadakata, 'Music in Quarantine: Connections Between Changes in Lifestyle, Psychological States, and Musical Behaviors during COVID-19 Pandemic', *Frontiers in Psychology* 12 (2021): Article 689505. https://doi.org/10.3389/fpsyg.2021.689505

Thelwall, Mike, Pardeep Sud, and Farida Vis, 'Commenting on YouTube Videos: From Guatemalan Rock to El Big Bang', *Journal of the American Society for Information Science and Technology* 63.3 (2012): 616–29. https://doi.org/10.1002/asi.21679

Thompson, Marie and Ian Biddle, 'Introduction: Somewhere Between the Signifying and the Sublime', in Thompson and Biddle, eds, *Sound, Music, Affect: Theorising Sonic Experience* (New York : Bloomsbury Academic, 2013), 1–24.

Thornton, Leslie-Jean, 'The Photo is Live at Applifam: An Instagram Community Grapples with How Images Should be Used', *Visual Communication Quarterly* 21.2 (2014): 72–82. https://doi.org/10.1080/15551393.2014.928147

Thornton, Sarah, *Club Cultures: Music, Media and Subcultural Capital* (Cambridge: Polity, 2013).

Thorpe, Holly, Allison Jeffery, Simone Fullager, and Nida Ahmad, '"We Seek Those Moments of Togetherness": Digital Intimacies, Virtual Touch and Becoming Community in Pandemic Times', *Feminist Media Studies* 23.7 (2023): 3419–36. https://doi.org/10.1080/14680777.2022.2112738

Thorpe, Vanessa, 'Balcony Singing in Solidarity Spreads across Italy during Lockdown', *The Guardian*, 14 March 2020, https://www.theguardian.com/world/2020/mar/14/solidarity-balcony-singing-spreads-across-italy-during-lockdown (accessed 1 July 2022).

Thurnell-Read, Thomas, '"A Couple of these Videos is all You really Needed to Get Pumped to Skate": Subcultural Media, Nostalgia and Re-Viewing 1990s Skate Media on YouTube', *Young* 30.2 (2022): 165–82. https://doi.org/10.1177/11033088211057365

Tiffany, Kaitlyn, 'How Quickly Can a Girl Go Viral on TikTok?', *The Atlantic*, 16 September 2020, https://www.theatlantic.com/technology/archive/2020/09/tiktok-teens-fandom-mooptopia/616371/ (accessed 14 January 2021).

Tinajero, Robert, 'Hip Hop and Religion: Gangsta Rap's Christian Rhetoric', *Journal of Religion and Popular Culture* 25.3 (2013): 315–32. https://doi.org/10.3138/jrpc.25.3.315

Tirado, Monica, 'Anuel AA se hace viral gracias a su remix contra el coronavirus', *HOLA!*, 19 March 2020, https://www.hola.com/us-es/celebrities/20200319flpnqkah27/anuel-aa-remix-coronavirus-viral/ (accessed 15 November 2021).

Torres-Ramos, José R., comments in 'Social Distancing, Musical Togetherness: The Nexus of Community Music, Health, and Technology during the COVID-19 Pandemic', roundtable, 66th Annual Meeting of the Society for Ethnomusicology, 29 October 2021.

Tourism Colombia, 'Vallenato, the History of an Entire Region', 8 December 2018, https://www.colombia.co/en/colombia-culture/music/story-valledupar-home-vallenato/ (accessed 7 March 2022).

Trammell, Jim Y., '"The Grandest, most Compelling Story of all Time!": Dominant Themes of Christian Media Marketing', *Journal of Religion and Popular Culture* 26.1 (2014): 23–35. https://doi.org/10.3138/jrpc.26.1.23

Tuan Yi-fu, *Escapism* (Baltimore: The Johns Hopkins University Press, 1998).

Tuan Yi-fu, *Topophilia: A Study of Environmental Perception, Attitudes, and Values* (New York: Columbia University Press, 1990).

Tucker, Joshua, 'From The World of the Poor to the Beaches of Eisha: Chicha, Cumbia, and the Search for a Popular Subject in Peru', in Héctor Fernández L'Hoeste and Pablo Vila, eds, *Cumbia! Scenes of a Migrant Latin American Music Genre* (Durham, NC: Duke University Press 2013), 138–67.

Tucker, Joshua, *Gentleman Troubadours and Andean Pop Stars: Huayno Music, Media Work, and Ethnic Imaginaries in Urban Peru* (Chicago: University of Chicago Press, 2013).

Tucker, Joshua, 'Peruvian Cumbia at the Theoretical Limits of Techno-Utopian Hybridity', in Alejandro L. Madrid, Ana R. Alonso-Minutti, and Eduardo Herrera, eds, *Experimentalisms in Practice: Music Perspectives from Latin America* (Oxford: Oxford University Press, 2018), 85–106.

Twine, France W. and Charles A. Gallagher, 'Introduction: The Future of Whiteness: A Map of the "Third Wave"', in Charles A. Gallagher and France W. Twine, eds, *Retheorizing Race and Whiteness in the 21st Century: Changes and Challenges* (New York: Routledge, 2012), 1–20.

UN Department of Global Communications, 'La Música no cura una pandemia, pero alegra el alma', *Naciones Unidas Respuesta a la COVID-19*, https://www.un.org/es/coronavirus/articles/el-poder-de-la-musica-durante-coronavirus (accessed 1 March 2022).

UN Women, 'Whose Time to Care: Unpaid Care and Domestic Work during COVID-19', UN Women website, 25 November 2020, https://data.unwomen.org/publications/whose-time-care-unpaid-care-and-domestic-work-during-covid-19 (accessed 25 September 2022).

Unni, Zoya and Emily Weinstein, 'Shelter in Place, Connect Online: Trending TikTok Content during the Early Days of the U.S. COVID-19 Pandemic', *Journal of Adolescent Health* 68.5 (2021): 863–8. https://doi.org/10.1016/j.jadohealth.2021.02.012

Urango Ospina, Juan C., 'El vallenato como texto narrativo: Análisis de "El Cantor de Fonseca", de Carlos Huertas', *VISITAS al PATIO* 1.1 (2008): 29–44. https://doi.org/10.32997/2027-0585-vol.1-num.1-2008-1570

Valcarce, David P. and Charo O. Mallero, 'El uso del podcast para la difusión del patrimonio cultural en el entorno hispanoparlante: análisis de las plataformas iVoox y SoundCloud', *Naveg@mérica* 24 (2020).

Valdiviezo, Laura A. and Luis M. Valdiviezo Arista, 'Política y práctica de la interculturalidad en la educación Peruana: Análisis y propuesta', Ministerio de Educación Perú, 25 January 2008, https://repositorio.minedu.gob.pe/handle/20.500.12799/901 (accessed 7 June 2022).
Váradi, Judit, 'New Possibilities in Cultural Consumption: The Effect of the Global Pandemic on Listening to Music', *Central European Journal of Educational Research* 3.1 (2021): 1–15. https://doi.org/10.37441/cejer/2021/3/1/9345
Vargas, Jaime, 'Jaranas, coliseos y matinales: cuarenta años de música popular en Lima', *Crítica Latinoamericana* (2013), https://www.academia.edu/30542596/Jaranas_coliseos_y_matinales_Cuarenta_a%C3%B1os_de_m%C3%BAsica_popular_en_Lima_.pdf (accessed 7 September 2022).
Vásquez, Manuel A. and Philip J. Williams, 'Introduction: The Power of Religious Identities in the Americas', *Latin American Perspectives* 32.1 (2005): 5–26. https://doi.org/10.1177/0094582X04271847
Västfjäll, Daniel. Patrik N. Juslin, and Terry Hartig, 'Music, Subjective Well-Being, and Health: The Role of Everyday Emotions', in Raymond MacDonald, Gunter Kreutz, and Laura Mitchell, eds, *Music, Health, and Well-Being* (Oxford: Oxford University Press, 2012), 405–23.
Vibe, 'Watch Fat Joe's 'Yes' Video Feat. Cardi B And Anuel AA', 7 October 2019, https://www.vibe.com/music/videos/fat-joes-yes-cardi-b-anuel-aa-665966/ (accessed 1 July 2022).
Victoria Martinez, Luz, 'Luto en en el vallenato: falleció el cantante Miguel Durán Junior', *El Tiempo*, 3 September 2020, https://www.eltiempo.com/colombia/otras-ciudades/ultimas-noticias-murio-el-cantante-vallenato-miguel-duran-junior-535738 (accessed 7 September 2022).
Victorino, Daniella B., Carla A. Scorza, Ana C. Fiorini, Josef Finsterer, and Fulvio A. Scorza, '"Mozart Effect" for Parkinson's Disease: Music as Medicine', *Neurological Sciences* 42.1 (2021): 319–20. https://doi.org/10.1007/s10072-020-04537-9
Vila, Pablo, 'Introduction', in Pablo Vila, ed., *Music, Dance, Affect, and Emotions in Latin America* (Lanham, MD: Lexington Books, 2017), xi–xxi.
Vila, Pablo, 'Music, Dance, Affect, and Emotions: Where We Are Now', in Pablo Vila, ed. *Music, Dance, Affect, and Emotions in Latin America* (Lanham, Lexington Books, 2017), 1–37.
Villalobos, Jose P. and Juan Carlos Ramirez-Pimienta, '*Corridos* and *La Pura Verdad*: Myths and Realities of the Mexican Ballad', *South Central Review* 21.3 (2004): 129–49. https://doi.org/10.1353/scr.2004.0050
Viloria De la Hoz, Joaquín, 'Un paseo a lomo de acordeón: Aproximación al vallenato, la música del Magdalena Grande, 1870 – 1960', *Memorias: Revista Digital de Historia y Arqueología desde el Caribe* 33: 7–34. https://doi.org/10.14482/memor.33.10872
Wade, Matthew and Maria Hynes, 'Worshipping Bodies: Affective Labour in the Hillsong Church', *Geographical Research* 51.2 (2013): 173–9. https://doi.org/10.1111/1745-5871.12010
Wade, Peter, *Music, Race, and Nation: Música Tropical in Colombia* (Chicago: University of Chicago, 2000).
Wald, Elijah, *Narcocorrido: A Journey Into the Music of Drugs, Guns, and Guerrillas* (New York: HarperCollins, 2012).
Waldron, Janice L., 'YouTube, Fanvids, Forums, Vlogs and Blogs: Informal Music Learning in a Convergent On- and Offline Music Community', *International Journal of Music Education* 31.1 (2013): 91–105. https://doi.org/10.1177/0255761411434861
Waldron, Janice L. and Kari K. Veblen, 'The Medium is the Message: Cyberspace, Community, and Music Learning in the Irish Traditional Music Virtual Community', *Journal of Music, Technology and Education* 1.2 (2008): 99–111. https://doi.org/10.1386/jmte.1.2and3.99_1
Wallach, Jeremy, Harris M. Berger, and Paul D. Greene, *Metal Rules the Globe: Heavy Metal Music Around the World* (Durham, NC: Duke University Press, 2011).

Wallin, Jason J. and Jennifer A. Sandlin, 'Capital Immunodeficiency and the Viral Contagion of Capitalism', *Knowledge Cultures* 8.3 (2020): 20–7. https://doi.org/10.22381/KC8320203

Watkins, Holly, *Musical Vitalities: Ventures in a Biotic Aesthetics of Music* (Chicago: University of Chicago Press, 2018).

Waugh, Michael, '"My Laptop is an Extension of my Memory and Self": Post-Internet Identity, Virtual Intimacy and Digital Queering in Online Popular Music', *Popular Music* 36.2 (2017): 233–251. https://doi.org/10.1017/S0261143017000083

Wedderburn, Alister, 'Pandemic Time', *Soundings* 75 (2020): 31–5.

Weheliye, Alexander G., 'Rhythms of Relation: Black Popular Music and Mobile Technologies', in Sumanth Gopinath and Jason Stanyek, eds, *The Oxford Handbook of Mobile Music Studies*, vol. 2 (Oxford: Oxford University Press, 2014): 361–80.

Weinberg, Melissa K. and Dawn Joseph, 'If You're Happy and You Know It: Music Engagement and Subjective Wellbeing', *Psychology of Music* 45.2 (2017), 257–67. https://doi.org/10.1177/0305735616659552

Wiggins, Bradley E., *The Discursive Power of Memes in Digital Culture: Ideology, Semiotics, and Intertextuality* (New York: Routledge, 2019).

Willett, Cynthia and Julie Willett, 'The Comic in the Midst of Tragedy's Grief with Tig Notaro, Hannah Gadsby, and Others', *Journal of Aesthetics and Art Criticism* 78.4 (2020): 535–46. https://doi.org/10.1111/jaac.12765

Williams, J., E. Ruddock, A. Mohseni, S. J. Gibson, N. Fleshner, P. Yeoh, A. Cusworth, J. Leong, S. Cohen, and D. Stringham, eds, *Musicking through COVID-19: Challenges, Adaptations, and New Practices*, special issue of *Journal of Music, Health and Wellbeing* (2021).

Winters, Joseph, 'Unstrange Bedfellows: Hip Hop and Religion', *Religion Compass* 5.6 (2011): 260–70. https://doi.org/10.1111/j.1749-8171.2011.00279.x

World Music with DARIA, 'Yaw, Yaw Puka Polleracha – Free Lyric Sheet (Song In Quechua)', *Teachers Pay Teachers*, https://www.teacherspayteachers.com/Product/Yaw-Yaw-Puka-Polleracha-Free-Lyric-Sheet-Song-In-Quechua-3340027 (accessed 1 May 2022).

Woodruff Smith, David, 'Intersubjectivity: In Virtue of Noema, Horizon, and Life-World', in Frode Kjosavik, Christian Beyer, and Christel Fricke, eds, *Husserl's Phenomenology of Intersubjectivity: Historical Interpretations and Contemporary Applications* (New York: Routledge, 2019), 114–41.

World Forum for Acoustic Ecology, 'COVID-19 Soundscape Resources', https://www.wfae.net/covid-19-soundscapes.html (accessed 1 July 2022).

Worlddata.info, 'Quechua – Worldwide Distribution', https://www.worlddata.info/languages/quechua.php (accessed 10 April 2022).

Yaşin, Burcu, 'The Soundscape of Covid-19 In Istanbul', *terrabayt*, 17 Nisan [=11 April] 2020, https://terrabayt.com/dusunce/english/the-soundscape-of-covid-19-in-istanbul/ (accessed 1 July 2022).

Yeh, Emily T., 'Exile Meets Homeland: Politics, Performance, and Authenticity in the Tibetan Diaspora', *Environment and Planning D: Society & Space* 25.4 (2016): 648–67. https://doi.org/10.1068/d2805

Yu Hui and Sary Schroeder, 'Distribution and Popularity Patterns of Chinese Music on YouTube: A Case Study of Local Music's Representation on a Global Internet Platform', *Journal of New Music Research* 47.1 (2018): 68–77. https://doi.org/10.1080/09298215.2017.1369129

Zamudio Serrano, Cecilia del Mar, 'Dos tarimas, un fandango. Dinámicas y relaciones transfronterizas entre los jaraneros de Tijuana, México-San Diego, EUA: un análisis desde el lado sur de la frontera', master's thesis, Universidad Veracruzana, Xalapa, Veracruz, Mexico, 2014.

Zanfagna, Christina, 'Kingdom Business: Holy Hip Hop's Evangelical Hustle', *Journal of Popular Music Studies* 24.2 (2012): 196–216. https://doi.org/10.1111/j.1533-1598.2012.01325.x

Zegarra, Eduardo, 'De la pandemia a la crisis de alimentos en Perú', *Ojo Público*, 25 May 2020, https://ojo-publico.com/1830/de-la-pandemia-la-crisis-de-alimentos-en-peru (accessed 7 September 2022).

Zeng Jing and Crystal Abidin, '"#OkBoomer, Time to Meet the Zoomers": Studying the Memefication of Intergenerational Politics on TikTok', *Information, Communication & Society* 24.16 (2021): 2459–81. https://doi.org/10.1080/1369118X.2021.1961007

Zentner, Marcel, Didier Grandjean, and Klaus R. Scherer, 'Emotions Evoked by the Sound of Music: Characterization, Classification, and Measurement', *Emotion* 8.4 (2008): 494–521. https://doi.org/10.1037/1528-3542.8.4.494

Zevallos-Aguilar, Ulises J., 'José María Arguedas y la música novoandina. Su legado cultural en el siglo XXI', *Cuadernos de Literatura* 20.39 (2016): 254–69, https://dialnet.unirioja.es/servlet/articulo?codigo=5271700 (accessed 1 July 2022). https://doi.org/10.11144/Javeriana.cl20-39.jmam

Zhang Jin, Chen Ye, Zhao Yuehua, Dietmar Wolfram, and Feicheng Ma, 'Public Health and Social Media: A Study of Zika virus-related Posts on Yahoo! Answers', *Journal of the Association for Information Science and Technology* 71.3 (2020): 282–99. https://doi.org/10.1002/asi.24245

Zoladz, Lindsay, 'How Cardi B's Off-the-Cuff Video Became a Coronavirus Anthem', *New York Times*, 17 March 2020, https://www.nytimes.com/2020/03/17/arts/music/coronavirus-cardi-b.html (accessed 12 October 2021).

Index

acapella 3, 153, 155, 159, 161, 163, 208, 253
accordions 82, 93, 98, 143, 151, 153–5, 158–60, 162, 164, 190, 204, 208, 236, 238–41, 244–5, 256
affect 8, 26, 45, 165, 174–6, 178, 196, 199
afro 21, 43, 136, 191, 201, 219–20, 233, 240
albur 193
alcohol 144, 153
algorithms 4, 16, 30
Alvarez Villanueva, Gabino 209
amateurs 1, 3, 22, 37, 47, 54, 58, 91, 99–100, 109–10, 152–3, 163, 165, 173, 179, 183, 204, 206
American Music Awards 34
Andes 2, 246, 251, 256
'Antes que el mundo se acabe' 229–32
anthropause 13
anthropocene 13, 28
anti-Chinese expression 6, 61, 98, 151
Anuel AA 3, 6, 34–6, 41–6, 56, 61
archives 14–15, 19, 31, 156
Argentina 2, 14–15, 29, 82, 87, 92, 99, 187, 199, 227–8, 235–6
assemblages 175
Atuq del Peru, Los 245, 247
'Ausencia Sentimental' 244
avian flu 7, 201
Aymara 251, 157

bachata 2, 34, 178
bajo sexto 143, 151, 158, 162, 164

balconies 34, 42, 225–6, 237, 250
ballad 22, 83, 162, 183, 234
banda 2, 93, 96, 98, 101, 160–2, 186–7, 189, 197–8, 228
bandurria 249–50, 254–5
bats, eating of. 94, 97, 144, 151, 159, 202, 242–3
beer 92, 94–5, 97, 108, 155, 161–2, 187
Bin Laden, Osama 242, 263
Bogotá 14–15, 28–9, 100, 204, 244
bolero 108, 145–7
Bolivia 101, 181, 199, 235, 251
Bolsonaro, Jair 14, 29
borders 27, 79, 87, 94, 97, 136–7, 149, 152, 163, 195, 205, 240
borderlands 2, 22, 83, 87, 96, 143, 145, 148–9, 151–5, 160
boredom 1, 46, 96, 100, 166, 184, 192
Brazil 23, 40, 101, 197, 204, 235, 248
burials 248

Cadetes de Linares, Los 143, 146
Camarera Torres, Maria del Carmen *see* QuerrequeFilms
Cardi B 3, 33–6, 39–46, 50, 56, 60
Caribbean 2, 21, 34, 41, 43, 84, 190, 208, 228, 237, 250
carnival 190–1, 253, 255
see also festivals
Castro, Cesar –3, 133, 159
Catholicism 190, 196–8
see also Christianity

celebrity 40, 43, 45–6, 58
cell phones 28, 119
Centers for Disease Control and Prevention 41
chikungunya 7, 24, 92
children 2, 25, 30, 58, 84, 127, 162, 247, 253
Chile 2, 152, 154, 224, 227, 248
Chimbala 3, 188
China 6, 29, 30, 33, 61, 81, 128, 92, 94–5, 97–8, 144, 151–2, 156, 158–9, 163 164, 187, 199, 203, 206, 209, 231, 242–3, 256
Christianity 3, 29, 59, 155, 174, 195–203, 241
Cities and Memory 14, 29
class 28, 45, 85, 87–8, 94, 121, 132, 183
clothing 144, 207
Colombia 2, 5, 29, 61, 87, 185, 197, 200, 208, 220, 227–8, 234, 236–8, 240, 242, 244
Colombian Pacific 219, 222, 244
comedy 96, 192, 194, 203, 241
communitarianism 1, 21, 52, 133, 180, 235
conspiracy theories 156–60
Content ID 18, 120
Corona beer 92, 95, 97
coronavirus, personified 95–6, 179
corrido 22, 24, 83–4, 143–56, 158–72, 195–6
  corrido tumbado 159–60
cosmopolitanism 24, 84, 224–5, 230–1, 250–1
Costa Chica 2, 101, 190
Costa Rica 108, 197, 235
coughing 40, 46, 60, 221
crying 42, 185, 234, 245, 248, 255
Cuba 184, 199, 233–4
cueca 23, 207, 224
cumbia 3, 21–2, 24, 26, 50, 53–5, 65, 78–102, 161, 164, 180, 185–6, 189–90, 228
  diaspora and 86
Cumbia 420 89
currulaos 220

dance 1–2, 6, 15, 34, 36, 39, 50, 53, 55–61, 82, 84–5, 87, 90, 108, 111–13, 125, 133, 136, 178, 183, 185–91, 197, 199, 231–4, 256

death 6, 21–2, 55, 62, 111–12, 152, 155–7, 159, 174, 181, 192, 194, 205, 224, 231, 239, 246, 248–50, 255–6
Delgado Flores, Hector Manuel *see* QuerrequeFilms
Delta variant 87, 243
dembow 2, 6, 21, 34, 36, 41–3, 54–66, 188
dengue 7, 25
dialects 193, 256
diasporas 28, 43, 86, 109–10, 113–18, 122–3, 126, 149, 163, 223, 251
digital divide 6, 24
DIY 7, 16–17, 19–20, 36, 47, 54, 92, 99–101, 108–9, 111, 115, 117, 125
DJ iMarkKeyz, 39–41, 43–4, 60
DJ Jamz Turn Me Up 41, 44, 66
Dominican Republic 2, 65, 189, 235
drugs 62, 89, 94, 156, 195
drums 65, 92, 100, 180, 200, 202, 220, 237, 256
Duo Guayabamba 3, 23
Duran Jr., Miguel 238–9, 241

earth 13, 29, 155, 196–7, 199
ebola 7, 24
Ecuador 24, 190–1, 199–200, 227, 234, 248, 255–6
education 25, 27, 30–1, 197
El Alfa 42
El Capi 91–2
El Salvador 145, 199, 235
El Violento PM 42
emoji 32, 108, 120, 123, 187, 234–5
Encuentro Virtual de Tríos Huastecos 110, 117, 121–2
End Times 156, 174, 197, 201
ethnomusicology 19, 45
Europe 14, 83, 120, 132, 209, 226
evangelicalism 196–7, 201
  see also Christianity

Facebook 11, 15, 18, 29, 31, 34, 54, 109, 118, 121, 125–6, 129, 131, 133–4, 201, 226
Facebook Live 18, 118, 129
fandango 111–13, 133, 135–7, 142
Fandango Fronterizo 136–7, 142
Fat Joe 34, 67

festivals 27, 84, 108, 123, 128–9, 178, 227, 233–4, 239, 243–4, 253–4, 256–7
   see also carnivals
flags 64, 95, 179, 187, 224, 235, 256
Flor Amargo 96
food 66, 94, 112, 161–2, 177, 180, 195, 208, 243, 247–9, 257
forró 3, 204

GavBroadcast 117–23, 130
gender 28, 44, 76, 85, 101, 120, 145, 191, 233, 249–50, 265
global phenomena 1–2, 4–7, 9, 12–17, 19–22, 24–5, 27–30, 33–7, 39–43, 45, 47–53, 56–7, 61, 63, 66, 81, 83–6, 90–1, 97, 112, 115–17, 119–20, 132, 135, 145, 147–8, 151, 154–5, 157–9, 165, 173–5, 187–8, 190, 197, 199, 204, 219, 221–5, 227–31, 235, 240, 254, 257
Google 13, 29, 181
government 17, 33, 40, 117, 158–60, 197, 219, 221, 233, 237, 240, 242, 246, 248
grupera 2, 84, 101
Grupo Laberinto 162–3
Guaraní 3, 235–6
guitars 5, 92, 98, 100, 151–2, 155, 157, 159, 161–3, 165, 181, 184, 195, 202–3, 205–7, 219, 227, 235, 249–50, 252, 256

harps 5, 25, 179–81, 205, 207, 245, 248, 252, 255
Hinojosa, José 5, 23
Hinostroza, Arsenio 10, 27, 245, 247, 264
hip hop 24, 39–40, 67, 199, 202
   see also rap
HIV/AIDS 7, 176, 197
Honduras 199
huapango 25, 85, 108–9, 111–15, 117, 119–21, 123–32
Huasteca 25, 111–15, 117–20, 122–5, 128–30
huayno 5, 10, 23, 177, 179–82, 193, 205, 245–6, 248, 250, 252, 255–7
hyperobjects 10

improvisation 25, 111, 127
Indigenous groups 2–3, 22, 111–12, 224, 235, 237, 240, 245–6, 251

informality 20, 22, 31, 44, 129, 161, 163, 204, 208, 224, 228, 241, 249–50
Instagram 15, 33–5, 39–41, 56, 58, 62, 178, 226
Internacionales Conejos, Los 84
interpellation 45–7, 57, 65
isolation 1, 8, 10–11, 13, 18, 45–6, 61, 100, 109, 113, 116–17, 130, 153–4, 166, 176, 178–9, 192, 206, 208, 225, 227, 229, 231–2, 234
Italy 29, 144, 158–9, 199, 226

jarana 112, 118, 128, 134, 136, 142, 245
Jiménez, José Alfredo 151–2
Jowell y Randy and Kiko El Crazy 55, 188

Karol G 41
KDTs 144
Kumbia Klan 92

labor 124, 249–50, 265
landscapes 16, 113, 121, 130
Lapizin Bunny 62, 76
laughter 42, 177, 179, 193, 243
López Obrador, Andrés Manuel 81, 116, 144
loss of life 234, 254
   see also death
Lucho Cobo 242

mad scientist 185, 238
mariachi 2, 151, 160–1, 224, 227
masks 92, 98, 145, 156, 186, 250, 252, 256–7
media studies 19, 86
memes 35, 40, 44, 46, 48, 54, 56, 58–59, 80–1, 89, 94, 97, 151, 165–6
merengue 2, 63, 173, 201, 208
metaphors 35, 48, 155
Mexico 2, 14, 21–2, 27, 79–84, 87, 91–3, 96, 101, 108–9, 111, 116–18, 120–2, 125–8, 132–3, 136, 143, 145, 148–9, 151–5, 158–9, 164, 178, 187, 190, 192, 195, 197, 204, 209, 224, 227, 234–5
migration 76, 136, 153, 245–7, 264
Mister Cumbia 50, 65, 78, 80–5, 88, 90–2, 95–6, 98, 101–3
Montemayor, Ivan *see* Mister Cumbia

música del coronavirus, concept of 1–9, 13, 15–19, 21–4, 26, 36–7, 42–3, 46–9, 51–5, 59, 61–2, 79, 84–5, 91, 98, 144, 147, 151, 174, 177–8, 181–3, 186–7, 189–90, 192, 194–7, 199, 201–2, 4, 207–8, 222–5, 232, 241–2
música norteña 2, 23, 85, 87, 93, 98, 143, 144–8, 151–4, 158, 160–4
música urbana 21, 34, 48, 188

Nahuatl 3, 111
narco 166
nationalism 24, 224–5
natural world 14, 233
Negra Flow 65
news 8, 30, 40–1, 44, 79–82, 94, 96, 147, 149, 154, 163, 180–1, 196, 207, 225, 238
nostalgia 31, 113, 116, 128, 244, 255

Omicron variant 55, 185, 200
Organización Luz Azul 101, 190

Pachita 3, 219–22, 224
Panama 159, 240
pandemic moment 1–13, 15–18, 20–2, 33–8, 40, 43–5, 47, 49, 52–4, 56–7, 59–63, 65–6, 78–9, 85, 88–93, 96, 98, 100, 109–11, 113–16, 123–4, 126, 128–9, 131–3, 144–5, 152, 155–6, 159–60, 162, 174–7, 181–4, 186, 192–4, 196–8, 200–1, 203–4, 207–9, 222–5, 227, 230–3, 236, 238, 240–1, 245, 251–5, 257
pandemic time 5, 9–11, 27, 174, 184, 233
Paraguay 235
parody 92–3, 95, 98, 152, 174, 237
participatory culture 13–14, 16, 19–20, 28, 31, 36–7, 53, 56, 58, 61, 109, 111, 113–17, 121, 123–4, 130, 135
partying 6, 62, 89, 95, 174, 185–9, 191
Pentecostalism 197, 200–1
    see also Christianity
Perez, Felipe 3–4
Peru 3, 55, 87, 178, 180–2, 205–7, 227–8, 231, 233, 235, 245–9, 251–3, 256–7
    Lima 14, 55, 231, 245–7

place 1–2, 6, 12, 15, 20–3, 29, 81–2, 96, 108, 113–14, 116, 120, 125, 128, 130, 132, 136, 148–9, 151, 159, 164, 176, 182, 184, 188, 190, 222–5, 234–7, 240, 242–3, 247–8, 253, 255
platformization 17, 52
playlists 8–9, 23, 26–7
police 9, 14, 177, 200, 228, 252, 256
prayer 173, 180–1
professionals 1, 3, 12, 22, 37, 43, 54, 63, 91–2, 98, 101, 117, 127, 132, 134, 145, 164–5, 179, 181, 198, 204, 208, 224
public health 25, 27, 29, 35, 78, 84, 90, 157, 182, 197, 221, 256
public service announcements 82, 224
    see also warnings
public transportation 245
Puerto Rico 35, 127, 227, 230

quarantine 9, 26, 184, 188, 23
Quechua 2, 3, 24, 181, 224, 245–8, 250–6
#QuedateEnCasa 122, 244, 263
QuerrequeFilms 118, 122–3

racism 97–8, 149, 151, 156–7, 224, 242
radio 79
rap 40, 83, 87, 182–3, 199, 201–2
    see also hip hop
Recording Industry Association of America 35
reggaetón 2, 21, 34, 36, 41, 53, 55, 57, 63, 83, 89, 178, 183, 191
remixes 21, 35–44, 46–7, 49–56, 59–61, 65–76, 83, 85, 90–1
removed videos 4, 34, 43, 250
repetition 21, 36, 41–2, 46, 53, 57, 59–62, 64–6
requinto 159–60, 179, 191, 195, 203, 256–7
Residente 3, 229–32, 261
resistance 87, 90, 116, 145, 149, 160, 180, 205, 227–9
'Resistire' 228
return migration 247
riddim 55, 57, 62–3
rock 3, 39, 178, 202, 228, 261, 294
rural 13, 79, 132, 198, 220, 239, 246, 250

salsa 93, 177–8, 228
salvation 155, 164, 174, 241
samba 3, 184
sampling 21, 36–7, 44, 49–50, 57, 59, 62, 165, 233
Santa Fe Klan 87
saxophone 180
'Se acabó la cuarentena' 55–9, 188–9
sex 62, 65, 89, 92, 94, 188, 229
Sierra y Folclor 100–1
sierreño 2, 96, 147, 159, 161, 195
Simonelmono 62
singing 3, 22, 25, 62–3, 65, 84, 96, 98, 112, 133, 148–9, 151, 153–4, 156, 159, 161, 163, 165, 177, 179–83, 185, 191, 195, 198, 203, 205–7, 209, 225–6, 229, 233, 235–6, 241, 244, 249–50, 252–3
smartphone 12, 30, 204, 238, 241
Sol de Pachaconas 181, 252
solo performance 204–5, 255
son huasteco 21, 25, 109, 111–13, 117, 120, 122, 128–30
son jarocho 21, 109–11, 113, 132–8, 206
sonidero 2, 25, 93
Sonora Dinamita, La 98
'Sopa de Caracól' 197–8
sorrow 192, 254, 256
sotavento 113
SoundCloud 17, 30, 39
Soundesign 14, 29
soundscapes 1–2, 12–15, 22, 28–9, 37, 101
Spain 82, 84, 108, 144, 154, 159, 187, 199, 226–7, 234–5
Spinditty 9, 26
Spotify 4, 9–10, 26, 40–1, 82
suffering 156, 164, 181–2, 198, 201, 219, 238, 245, 249, 252
Suni, Ebert 255, 267
synthesizers 200, 227

Tamaulipas 79, 123–4, 126–7, 157
Tehran 14
Tenek 118
Texas 27, 118, 125, 127–8, 145
theory, social 77, 157, 192
Tierra Caliente 2, 153
Tigres del Norte, Los 23, 162–3

TikTok 15–16, 29–30, 34, 40–1, 43, 55–9, 178, 189, 226, 232
topophilia 223, 236, 243
Totó la Momposina 92, 100
towns 79–80, 84, 98, 136, 154, 195, 219, 235–6, 245, 253, 256
translocalism 135, 222–3
tropical (style) 92, 184, 190, 221, 239, 241
Trump, Donald 144, 157, 194

ukuleles 231, 261
unemployment 99, 247
UNESCO 237
United States 31, 40, 43–4, 80, 82–3, 96, 108, 118, 120, 123, 127–8, 132, 143, 145, 149, 153, 156–8, 160, 164, 183, 187, 195, 199, 226–7, 243
  Los Angeles 95, 132, 157, 165
urban environments 2, 13–14, 21, 28–9, 31, 39, 87, 96, 132, 186, 198, 225–6, 240, 244–6, 248, 250

vaccination 64, 157, 160
vaccines 62, 64, 160, 243
Vallenato 208, 224, 236–45
Vallenato Legends Festival 239, 243–4
Venezuela 5, 101, 136, 183, 185, 199, 227, 240
Vera Benito, Gabino 117–23
Veracruz 14, 111, 122–4, 126, 132–3, 135–7, 159
verses 81, 98, 111–12, 153, 155, 160–1, 164, 192–4, 199, 202, 205–6, 208–9, 221, 238, 253, 255–6
Vin, Kevin 65
violence 83, 100, 156, 182, 222, 237, 246
violins 5, 108, 112, 154, 180, 245, 252, 254
viral culture 47–9, 85, 88–90
virtual space 20, 38, 120, 135, 234
'Volveremos a brindar' 234–5, 262
vulgar language 33–4, 39, 41–2, 46, 96–7, 147, 158, 193–4, 200

walking 200
warnings 5, 83, 93, 111, 155, 163, 204, 242, 248, 252, 256
  see also public service announcements

washing 9, 25, 92–3, 108, 145, 179, 205
webcams 4, 207
weddings 113, 222
wellbeing 6–9, 20–1, 25–6, 59, 109–11, 113–15, 122, 125, 130, 174, 220
WhatsApp 34, 94
WindowSwap 13
women 24, 42–3, 50, 56, 58, 62, 93, 119–20, 129, 131, 157, 165, 177, 187–91, 219–20, 222, 235, 249–50, 256
World Health Organization 34, 78
Wounaan 240, 263

Xalapa 14
xenophobia 151, 189, 224, 237, 242–3

Yofrangel 2, 23, 62–6
youth 30, 39, 116, 133, 165, 198–9, 240, 253
YouTube 3–5, 7, 9, 11, 15–21, 23–7, 29–32, 34–5, 39–41, 43, 49, 56, 58, 60, 62, 65, 78, 81–5, 90–1, 93, 95–6, 99–101, 109–11, 114–24, 126, 128, 132–4, 143, 146–7, 151, 153–5, 158, 160–1, 163, 173, 178, 180–1, 183–5, 187–9, 194, 196, 204, 207, 219, 222, 226–7, 229, 232, 234, 236, 238, 240, 242, 247, 250, 252, 254, 256

zika 7, 24–5
Zoom meetings 94, 136, 178, 228, 231, 233, 238